AP* EUROPEAN HISTORY:
AN ESSENTIAL COURSEBOOK,
2nd Edition

By Ethel Wood

WoodYard Publications

AP* European History: An Essential Coursebook, 2nd edition

Published by WoodYard Publications
285 Main Street
Germantown, NY 12526

Ph. 610-207-1366
Fax 610-372-8401
ejw@woodyardpublications.com
http//:woodyardpublications.com

ISBN 978-0-9895395-3-1

TABLE OF CONTENTS

ACKNOWLEDGEMENT:

Many thanks go to my friends and former colleagues at Princeton High School, Princeton, New Jersey – Greg Hand and Carol Joyce – who read the manuscript and provided many helpful comments. Their scholarship, thoughtfulness, and diligence contributed greatly to this book, just as those qualities have made them two of the finest teachers I have every known.

CHAPTER 1:
INTRODUCTION

"History teaches everything including the future."
Alphonse de Lamartine

The quote above captures two important principles for studying the history of Western civilization: the broad nature of history as well as its ongoing process. The first principle – the broad nature of history – is evidenced by its many sub-fields. The political, military, and diplomatic history of the West has been well documented by countless historians, but history in its broadest sense also includes important social, cultural, intellectual, and economic events and trends. We may only begin to do justice to "everything" that has happened in the past by examining it through many lenses that help us to understand that particular aspects of history, such as political or economic, do not stand alone. Secondly, the past is not only connected to the present but to the future as well. It is a mistake to assume that all of history leads to a fixed point we call the present because events of the present inevitably influence the future in an ongoing story with no end in sight. These two underlying principles shape the AP European History curriculum with its focus on the time period from 1450 to the present.

Modern European history covers a lot of ground, both in terms of geography and time. How can one learn all of the history of Europe since 1450 in one school year? Clearly that is an impossible task. However, it is possible to learn the broad "story" of Europe by using some tools that help to connect the parts of the story from its beginning to the present day. Once you know the plot, you are in a good position to learn the sub-plots that in turn help make sense of all the facts that support the overall story. This kind of thoughtful learning enables a life-long expansion of knowledge that gives history meaning that enriches the present and shapes the future.

TOOLS FOR LEARNING HISTORY

What are these magical tools that transform the study of history? We will begin with these:

1) Think About the Big Picture – Although the history of the universe obviously dwarfs that of the modern European era, the 'story' of Europe since 1450 is nevertheless very big. To understand that story, it is important to identify **"marker events"** that make a difference in the course of history, and to distinguish them from the myriad of details that can make us feel that history is just a bunch of unrelated facts.

2) Think About Themes – An important tool in organizing and understanding history is thinking about themes, or unifying threads, that may be analyzed separately, even though they often intertwine. The themes in the AP European History curriculum that may be followed throughout are these five: the interaction of Europe and the world, poverty and prosperity, objective knowledge and subjective visions, states and other institutions of power, and the individual and society.

 3) Think About Chunks – The study of modern European history becomes more manageable if you "chunk it" into different time periods, a process called **periodization**. History textbooks often chunk content into regions, but periodization is much more than that. It requires a student to think cross-culturally about a time period and analyze interactions among different European societies, as well as changes in political, economic, or social arrangements within societies. Even though history is broken up into periods, you still see the big picture because you are concerned with broad patterns and **"marker events"** that have changed and still change the course of modern European history. Big picture events and trends that make one period distinct from another are generally cross-cultural in that they impact several areas of Europe and often other areas of the world, and they also often create change with respect to more than one theme. For example, an international war (such as World War II in the 20th century) that not only challenges government structures and officials, but also brings about major economic and social class changes is likely to be a marker event.

4) Think comparatively – Another way to think effectively about history is to analyze it by making use of the big picture, themes, and chunks. For example, you may be interested in comparing political developments (a theme) in England and France during the 17th century (a chunk). If you think about how political developments in the two societies were different as well as similar, you gain a better understanding of both than you would if you just learned about them separately. You may compare many categories in history: societies or regions, belief systems (such as Catholicism and Protestantism), economic systems (such as capitalism and communism), revolutions (such as the English and French revolutions), or demographic patterns (such as different migrations of people from one area to another).

AP EUROPEAN HISTORY THEMES

The AP European History course is organized around five major themes, or topics:

Interaction of Europe and the world – This theme explores the reasons that Europeans have sought interactions and contacts with others, as well as the technological, intellectual, and political developments that have allowed those interactions and contacts to occur. This theme also examines the impact of global contacts on Europe and, in turn, European influence on other parts of the world.

Poverty and prosperity – This theme focuses on the development of capitalism as an economic system and the important role that Europe played in shaping its development. Poverty and prosperity also examines the social and cultural impacts of capitalism in Europe and explores the causes and consequences of economic inequality in various European societies as well as individual, political, and group reactions to economic inequality.

Objective knowledge and subjective visions – This theme follows the evolution of European intellectual thought from 1450 to the present. First, it analyzes the roles of traditional sources of authority – such as the church and classical civilizations – in the creation and transmission of knowledge. This theme also explores the changes brought by reliance on the scientific method and reason as shaped by Enlightenment thought. A third focus is the questioning of the value of objective thought and analysis beginning in the 19th century with an emphasis on subjective interpretations of reality.

States and other institutions of power – This theme analyzes the changing forms of governments in Europe since 1450, including the development of and reactions to democratic structures and practices. It also explores the development of civil institutions over time as they relate to the evolution of political institutions. An important focus is the development of nation-states, shaped by war and diplomacy, and the role that the concept of balance of power has played in inter-European relations.

Individual and society – This theme focuses on changes and continuities over time in European families, class, and social groups. It examines tensions that have arisen as changes have occurred, as well as the impact of change on the fortunes of specific groups within European society.

HISTORICAL TIME PERIODS

The curriculum framework for the AP European History course investigates course themes and concepts in four chronological time periods. Each period is weighted equally on the AP Exam.

Period 1: c.1450 to c. 1648

Period 2: c.1648 to c. 1815

Period 3: c.1815 to c. 1914

Period 4: c.1914 to the present.

5) Think about continuity and change over time – To approach history as a story necessarily means that you must think about continuity and change over time. What happens in the beginning of the story? What events occur that makes the story change? What happens in the middle of the story that is caused by something that occurred earlier? How do all the events and characters that interact throughout the story influence the ending? Every time you tell a story, you are make chronological connections as the plot unfolds. In the same way, history is much more meaningful if you make connections across time periods. What happened in Russia during the 18th century that shaped the events in that country of the 19th century? What happened in the 19th century that shaped the 20th century? How have events and people during all three time periods interacted to help explain modern day news stories from Russia? Just as importantly, you must think about continuity over time: despite the changes, what threads remain the same?

6) Think about perspective – We will never know all the events that have occurred in the past because knowledge of many of them has not been passed on to later generations. No one thought to tell their children about these occurrences, and so remembrance of them ceased when individuals died. However, some people, places, and events are remembered, sometimes through stories told around the fireside at night, or often through written records. Historians look at all kinds of evidence in order to reconstruct the past, including physical evidence left behind, such as remnants of buildings, pottery, and clothing. In order to find out what really happened, a historian (or history student) needs many skills, including the ability to analyze **perspective**, or point of view. The slave's view is usually different from the slaveholder's, and the conqueror usually doesn't see things the same way as the conquered. If a historian finds a letter from a 16th-century European nobleman that praises his king, the historian must take into account the nobleman's point of view. To a historian, history is not a collection of static facts, but is an exciting, dynamic puzzle that must be interpreted and analyzed.

7) Think about Causation – Historical events always have effects on later happenings, and so it is important to analyze and evaluate the interaction of multiple causes and/or effects. A good historian understands which events are related and which are not, and so distinguishing among coincidence, causation, and correlation is an important skill to apply. A **correlation** exists when a change in one event or pattern coincides with a change in the other. Correlations are an indication that causality *may* be present; they do not necessarily indicate causation. Historical researchers seek to identify the causal link among events and patterns by collecting and analyzing many kinds of data. Historians are interested in both short term and long term effects of events. For example, a short term effect of the French Revolution was the beheading of King Louis XVI. A long-term effect was to upset the balance of power in Europe and pave the way for new forms of government that transformed the continent.

8) Think about Contextualization – Historical thinking requires the connection of historical events and processes both to specific circumstances of time and place and also to broader processes. Whereas the broad context for world history is the world, the broad context for European history is Europe. However, these contexts often intertwine. For example, Europe's involvement in the two 20th century world wars cannot be understood without considering the wars within the context of world history. Likewise, regional movements within Europe must always be considered within the context of the continent as a whole.

A WORD ABOUT GEOGRAPHY AND THE PHYSICAL ENVIRONMENT

Have you ever looked through an historical atlas of Europe to study changes in kingdoms, principalities, and countries? If you have, you know that change is the rule rather than the exception. Europe in 300 B.C.E. looked very similar physically to the continent today. If you pick out the familiar land and water shapes you realize that geological history moves at a much slower pace than political history. On the other hand, try to trace any European nation in existence today, and while some are older than others, you don't have to go very far back in history to find its origins. Yet no matter what time period you choose over the past 2000 years or so, the political imprint of human beings is there, and political change occurs much more rapidly than geological change.

Study the map below by concentrating on the physical features of Europe that it shows. Notice the bodies of land and their topography, as well as the lakes, seas, and oceans. Larger scale maps of different regions would of course show many more physical features that are very similar to those that Europeans in much earlier times were familiar with. Before people began transforming the landscape with their cultural imprints, physical geography shaped and limited their activities. These alterations became apparent first as people settled into agricultural communities, and grew more profound with the growth of cities and eventually industry. In even the earliest civilizations, people devised and used maps that not only represented physical geography but their cultural transformations (such as cities and roads) as well. Today geography still shapes European countries, setting limitations and channeling the direction of their growth.

Physical Map of Europe

THE AP EUROPEAN HISTORY EXAM

The College Board administers AP exams each May during a two-week period. The AP European History Exam is offered during this time. Total testing time is 3 hours and 15 minutes. Starting in May 2016, significant changes have been made to the exam, not only in periodization and thematic emphases, but also in question styles. The questions are based on the themes identified on page 7 of this book, and will require you to make use of the tools listed on pp. 6-9. The exam consists of four parts, organized into two sections.

Section 1:

  Part A: Multiple-choice questions (55 questions, 55 minutes); 40%

  Part B: Short answer questions (4 questions, 50 minutes); 20%

Section 2:

  Part A: Document-based question (1 question, 55 minutes); 25%

  Part B: Long-essay question (1 question chosen from a pair, 35 minutes); 15%

The questions cover all four of the periods listed on page 8 in approximately the percentages indicated on the chart: 25% for the period from 1450 to 1648; 25% for the period from 1648 to 1815; 25% for the period from 1815 to 1914; and 25% for the period since 1914. One of the essays – either the document-based or long-essay question – will address long-term developments that cross time periods. No document-based question or long essay will focus exclusively on the period before 1450.

Section I: Part A: Multiple-Choice Questions

The 55 multiple-choice questions test student knowledge of European history from 1450 to the present. Starting in May 2016, the questions will have only four answer-choices, as compared to five choices in previous years. A number of questions may be cross-chronological or may combine themes, and only a few questions cover the period since 1980. All of the following areas of history are included: political, social, cultural, intellectual, economic, and diplomatic. The questions are challenging. Some points to keep in mind about the multiple-choice section are:

- On the exam, the College Board no longer subtracts one-fourth of the number of questions answered incorrectly from the number of questions answered correctly. Since there is no penalty for guessing, it is advisable to answer all questions the best that you can.

- The questions are organized into sets of two to five questions that ask students to respond to a primary or secondary source. These sources may be quotations, cartoons, or charts. While a set may focus on a particular time period, the questions may ask students to make connections to other time periods.

The multiple-choice questions require you to draw upon knowledge within the bounds of the curriculum framework, and each question will address one of the five "AP European History Themes" described on p. 7. Most questions focus on one particular period of European history, but some ask you to make connections to the same thematic topic from another period. The questions assess your ability to interpret the stimulus material, but they also require outside knowledge of the historical issue at hand. This book provides many multiple-choice questions throughout that will help prepare you for Section I of the exam.

Section I, Part B: Short-answer questions

Part B consists of four short-answer questions that ALL must be answered in 50 minutes. Short-answer questions are based on the thematic learning objectives for the course, but they do not require a thesis statement. Some questions have internal choices, but others do not. Many short-answer questions ask you to respond to a primary source, a historian's argument, or secondary sources such as data or maps. Often you must provide and analyze examples of historical evidence relevant to the question.

Section II: Free-Response Questions

Section II consists of 2 free-response questions that must be answered in 90 minutes. Since you can allocate your time in any way you wish during this part of the exam, it is important to not get bogged down too long in either one of the questions. Otherwise, you will not have enough time to properly answer both questions. Part A is a document-based question (DBQ) that includes a period for reading and studying the documents and planning your essay, and a period for writing the essay (a total of 55 minutes). In Part B, you will answer your choice of ONE of TWO thematic questions in 35 minutes. The questions ask you to use historical thinking skills to explain and analyze significant issues in European history. Both the DBQ and the thematic question require the development of a thesis or argument supported by relevant, specific historical evidence.

Part A: The Document-based Question (DBQ)

The DBQ is designed to test your content knowledge and also to measure your skills as an historian. The question is presented first, and is followed by a set of primary documents that must be read before the question can be answered. Depending on the topic and focus, the question may or may not require you to discuss change over time. For example, look ahead to page 171 to see the DBQ for Unit One. The question reads, "Analyze the motivations for the European voyages of discovery during the time period between the mid-15th and the mid-17th centuries." Since you haven't read Unit One yet, don't worry if you can't answer the question yet, but look at how it is worded. The question is followed by 8 documents, each written by an individual from the time period. Some DBQs may include photographs, paintings, charts, maps, or graphs about the particular topic. Your task is to come up with a thesis that answers the question, and then back it with your existing knowledge about the topic and with specific evidence from the documents. Imagine that you are a historian deeply involved in seeking the truth. Documents shed light on the truth, but each is only a small piece of the answer. How can you put them all together to come up with a solid thesis that provides insightful answers to the mysteries of the past? The DBQ exercise is meant to simulate the historian's methods for interpreting the past.

Your response will be assessed according to a rubric with these basic guidelines:

1) **Thesis** – Answer the question, don't just repeat it. A good thesis requires some judgment and interpretation of the evidence, and it must be squarely focused on the question. For example, in Unit One's question, your thesis should not just read, "European voyages of discovery had many motivations behind them." A strong thesis should describe several different motivations for voyages of discovery to the Americas, and supporting paragraphs should provide the details that support the thesis.

2) **Substantial and relevant outside information** – You must include a substantial amount of outside factual information that supports your thesis, so you need to organize your existing knowledge of the topic before you start writing and using the documents. You must demonstrate specific outside knowledge – information not included in the documents – in order to score well on the DBQ.

3) **Use of a substantial number of the documents** – You must make use (not just mention) most of the documents. For full credit you must make use of all or all but one of the documents. You may refer to each document in any way you like, but it must be clear to the reader which one you are citing. For example, you may refer to documents by number (such as "Document 1"), by author, or by a brief description.

4) **Understanding of the documents** – You must demonstrate understanding of the documents, and you must use them effectively to support your thesis. Pay attention to the document's content, the identity and point of view of the author, and the date, and try to determine the document's pur-

pose. All documents are designed to promote understanding of the topic, and no documents are deliberately misleading.

5) **Supporting evidence** – The documents must be used to support the thesis. You may use a particular quote from the document, or simply describe which part of the document you are using to support your thesis. Do not quote extensively from the documents because it is too time consuming; just make sure that your references are clear.

DBQ SCORING RUBRIC

Maximum Possible Points: 7

A. Thesis 0-1 point
States a thesis that directly addresses all parts of the question. The thesis must do more than restate the question.

B. Analysis of historical evidence and support of argument: 0-4 points

1 point – offers analysis of a majority of the documents and explicitly uses them to support the thesis.

2 points – offers analysis of a majority of the documents and explicitly uses them to support the thesis. Also analyzes at least one of the following in the documents: intended audience, purpose, historical context, and/or the author's point of view

3 points – offers analysis of all or all but one of the documents and explicitly uses them to support the thesis. Also analyzes at least one of the following in the documents: intended audience, purpose, historical context, and/or the author's point of view.
AND/OR

1 point – offers plausible analysis of historical examples beyond/outside the documents to support the thesis.

C. Contextualization: 0-1 point
Accurately and explicitly connects argument to broader historical events and/or processes.

D. Synthesis: 0-1 point
Synthesizes the argument, evidence, analysis of documents, and context into a coherent and persuasive essay.

6) **Contextualization** – In your essay, you must also connect your argument to broader historical events and/or processes. For example, for the DBQ for Unit One, the reactions to European exploration and settlement in the Americas should be put broadly into the context of a world in which the hemispheres had recently been united – reshaping interactions of the Americas with other parts of the world.

7) **Synthesis** – You must synthesize the argument, evidence, analysis of documents, and context into a coherent and persuasive essay. This synthesis may occur by elaborating on the thesis or arguments, by accounting for sometimes contradictory evidence in the documents, by connecting the topic of the question to other historical periods, geographical areas, or circumstances, or by drawing ideas from other fields or disciplines, such as world or European history.

Part B: Long Essay Question (35 Minutes)

For the long essay question, you will choose ONE of TWO questions that explain and analyze significant issues in European history in terms of one of the thematic learning objectives. The questions will focus on topics that allow you to include any number of examples that you may use as evidence for your thesis. Each question will target one of the following historical thinking skills:

- Continuity and Change Over Time

- Comparison

- Causation

- Periodization

Make your choice carefully based on the topics you feel most comfortable writing about, and be sure that each essay meets the following criteria:

- **A relevant thesis** – It doesn't have to be complex, but the thesis must answer the question directly, and must not simply repeat the question.

- **Thorough answer** – Don't neglect to answer any part of the question. This means that it is important to read the question thoroughly, and in your planning outline, be sure to have a section for each part of the question.

- **Specific evidence** – You may choose to use any evidence that comes to mind, but it must directly substantiate your thesis and make your arguments more convincing. Clear, specific examples are usually helpful in coming up with successful arguments.

- **Clear, consistent, supportive organization** – A well-organized essay states a thesis clearly, and organizes supporting evidence so that the reader can easily follow the main arguments. This criterion is best met if you outline your essay carefully before you actually begin to write.

LONG ESSAY SCORING RUBRIC

Maximum Possible Points: 6

A. Thesis: 0-1 point
States a thesis that directly addresses all parts of the question. The thesis must do more than restate the questions.

B. Support for argument: 0-2 points
1 point: Supports the thesis using specific evidence.
2 points: Supports the thesis using specific evidence, clearly explaining how the evidence supports the thesis and establishing clear links between the thesis and the evidence.

C. Application of historical thinking skill: 0-2 points
Continuity and Change Over Time:
1 point: Describes historical continuity AND change over time.
2 points: Describes historical continuity AND change over time, AND analyzes specific examples to illustrate.
Comparison:
1 point: Describes similarities AND differences among historical developments.
2 points: Describes similarities AND differences AND analyzes reasons for similarities and/or differences OR evaluates the relative significance of the historical developments.
Causation:
1 point: Describes causes and/or effects of a historical development.
2 points: Describes causes and/or effects AND analyzes specific examples to illustrate.
Periodization:
1 point: Describes the ways in which the historical developemtn was different or similar to developments from other time periods.
2 points: Analyzes the extent to which the historical development was different and similar to developments from other time periods.

D. Synthesis: 0-1 point
1 point: Synthesizes the argument, evidence and context into a coherent and persuasive essay.

For both the free-response questions, it is important to plan your answers carefully and to be sure that you answer ALL parts of the question. Once you know what to expect on the exam, the best preparation for the exam is to know your stuff. The questions do require reading and writing skills, but the surer you are of the material, the more likely you are to answer the questions correctly. This book provides the concepts and information, as well as plenty of practice questions that will prepare you for the exam.

THE ORGANIZATION OF THE BOOK

This book is organized to help you to learn historical thinking skills and to understand important themes that run throughout modern European history. It begins with a chapter on medieval European History, which won't be tested on the College Board Exam, but it gives a background to the important changes that began to happen about 1450. The rest of the book is organized by these four time periods:

- c.1450 - c.1648
- c.1648 - c.1815
- c.1815 - c.1914
- c.1914 to the Present

Throughout the book, the historical thinking skills are identified by these images:

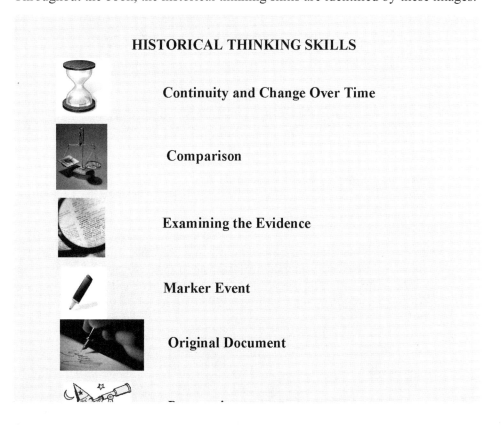

HISTORICAL THINKING SKILLS

Continuity and Change Over Time

Comparison

Examining the Evidence

Marker Event

Original Document

In addition, periodization is addressed with "Big Picture" features that highlight major concepts that distinguish one time period from another.

Throughout the book, the thematic learning objectives are identified by these symbols:

THEMATIC LEARNING OBJECTIVES

Interaction of Europe and the World

Poverty and Prosperity

Objective Knowledge and Subjective Visions

States and Other Institutions of Power

Politics

Individual and Society

These themes and tools for learning will help you to understand the broad "story" of Europe as well as the sub-plots that in turn help make sense of the facts that support the overall story. Hopefully, your study of the past will prove Alphonse de Lamartine to be right when he said, "History teaches everything including the future."

Modern Europe emerged after medieval Europe left; shift to civilization

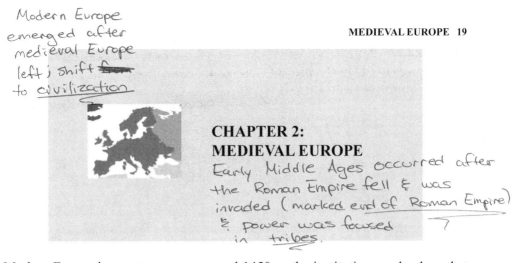

CHAPTER 2:
MEDIEVAL EUROPE

Early Middle Ages occurred after the Roman Empire fell & was invaded (marked end of Roman Empire) & power was focused in tribes.

Modern Europe began to emerge around 1450 as the institutions and values that shaped Medieval Europe were fading. Whereas large empires existed in many other parts of the world, no such political unification occurred on the European continent. Instead, a patchwork of tribal kingdoms took shape in western Europe. Even though the Byzantine Empire rose in the lands around the eastern Mediterranean Sea, political organization throughout Europe was generally weak after the 6th century. However, in this age when societies were unified by belief systems, Christianity, like Islam, provided order and organization that the political leaders did not provide. By 1450, the Byzantine Empire was on the verge of collapse under pressure from Turkish invasions, and western Europe, though still politically divided, had laid the foundation for the central place it would occupy on the world stage for the next five hundred years.

WESTERN EUROPE: AFTER THE FALL OF ROME

Historians refer to the period of western European history from 500 to 1500 C. E. as the "Middle Ages", or medieval times. The term "middle" means that the period falls in between two others, preceded by the Roman Empire and followed by the European Renaissance. Another way of referring to the time is the "Dark Ages," which implies that the periods on either end are "light." Although controversial, the metaphor is not inappropriate if you take the view that civilization (see insert on p. 20) is superior to simpler forms of life, such as hunting and gathering, pastoral nomadism, or simple subsistence farming. During the early Middle Ages civilization was clearly suspended. However, the period is more complex than that. It is helpful to divide the era in two:

1) **The Early Middle Ages** (500-1000 C. E.) – During this era the Germanic tribes that had invaded the Roman Empire settled into various parts of Europe. Most of the inhabitants of their kingdoms were pastoral nomads or subsistence farmers, and their political leaders were tribal chieftains. Very few people could read and write, little long distance trade took place, and settlements were mainly villages and small towns.

CIVILIZATION: excess, division of
labor, social classes, bigger
cities, gov't, trade, writing

View civilization
as more organized
+ more educated
organization = further divisions

PERSPECTIVES:
THE MEANING OF
CIVILIZATION

When you refer to Medieval European times as the "Dark Ages," the
implication is that "light" existed before and after the era in the form of
"civilizations" – Ancient Greece and Rome before and Renaissance Europe
after. What developments must occur in order for a society to be called a
civilization?   Some important characteristics of civilizations are:

1) **Generation of reliable surpluses** – Agricultural technology allows
   farmers to produce more than their families need.
2) **Highly specialized occupations** – Whereas village and town life are
   characterized by division of labor, occupational specializations in
   civilizations are far more complex, including jobs in government,
   trade, merchandise, and religion.
3) **Clear social class distinctions** – With the growing complexity of
   occupations, civilizations set status distinctions among them, so that
   big differences appear in prestige levels and wealth.
4) **Growth of cities** – As economic, political, social, and cultural life grow
   more interrelated, towns grow into cities.
5) **Complex, formal governments** – Early needs for government to
   coordinate agricultural activities become even greater as more economic
   activities develop and cities grow larger.
6) **Long distance trade** – Civilizations have large internal trade networks,
   as well as long distance trade networks among different civilizations.
   This trade stimulates economic development, encourages cultural
   development, and accentuates social class distinctions.
7) **Organized writing systems** – Most civilizations have highly developed
   forms of writing that enable traders, religious leaders, and political
   leaders to communicate.

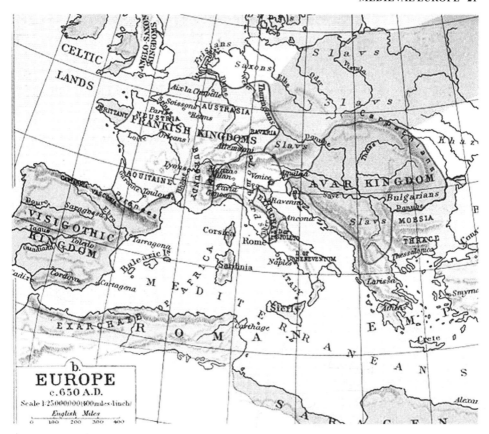

Early Medieval Europe. After the fall of the Western Roman Empire, the Germanic tribes that had invaded the empire settled into different parts of Western Europe and formed their own kingdoms. The map above shows the major kingdoms that were in place by the beginning of this period (650 C. E.) The borders of the kingdoms changed frequently as the groups invaded one another's territory, and many other smaller groups were involved in the fighting.

Source: Muir's Historical Atlas--Mediaeval and Modern (London, 1911)

2) **The High Middle Ages** (1000-1500 C. E.) – About midway through the Middle Ages, signs of recovery began, accelerating especially after about 1200. Towns grew, small cities emerged, trade with other areas of the Eastern Hemisphere was established, and the social class system grew more complex with the emergence of a small middle class. By the end of the era, the European Renaissance was well entrenched in Italy and was spreading into northern Europe.   *Age of new ideas + new forms of expression*

The Early Middle Ages   *Roman Empire acted as Europe's form of organization + civilization; large impact on the natural state of*

When the Western Roman Empire fell, western Europe was left in the chaos that *order* resulted from the collapse of the political, social, and military order formerly imposed by Rome. Continuing invasions and conflicts among the invaders left the successor states in jeopardy, and in this uncertain environment they sought and

RELIGION created cultural unity (explains the struggle between church + state)

gradually built new political and economic orders. New infrastructures were built within the framework of the Christian Church based in Rome, which provided cultural unity throughout Western Europe despite the lack of political centralization. Although Christianity came too late to provide the necessary cultural glue to hold the Roman Empire together, it served that purpose during the Early Middle Ages in Europe, enabling the area to regain economic, political, social, and military organization that had been lost when Rome fell.

Fall of Roman Empire = regression into tribal ways

Political Development

In the last years of the Western Roman Empire, the Roman provinces were dismantled by the Germanic tribes, and the borders of their kingdoms changed constantly with the fortunes of war. The Roman governors were replaced by tribal chieftains, but more importantly, the Roman concept of rule by law was replaced by informal governments based on family ties and personal loyalty. The Germanic people did not identify with a state, or even a kingdom, but with an extended family that followed a particular leader. Warrior groups were bound to their chief through oaths of loyalty, and in return the chief gave them food, shelter, and weapons. The Germanic kingdoms were loose configurations of many such loyalty patterns that allowed little opportunity for centralized government to form. Economically, people settled on manors, or large estates operated by leaders who provided protection for others, in exchange for free labor. Eventually, the lords acquired title to whatever land claims the peasants may have had. Thus, the groundwork was laid for the development of **feudalism**, a complex system of political and military loyalties that linked landholding lords together, and **manorialism**, an economic system in which peasants were tied to the land to supply labor to their lords.

feudalism – lords
manorialism – peasants to lords

For a brief time in the late 8th and early 9th centuries, it looked as if one group – the **Franks** – would unite all of Western Europe under one king. Even though they eventually failed, their imprint for political and economic organization was left on the entire area. Starting with Clovis, who was their ruler from 481 until 511, the Franks managed to organize a series of Germanic kingdoms mainly through military conquest. Clovis and his supporters first destroyed the last vestiges of Roman power, then imposed control over other Franks, and finally organized campaigns against neighboring Germanic peoples. By the time of his death, the Franks clearly had formed the most powerful kingdom in western Europe. Significantly, Clovis converted to Christianity, which won support for him from other Christians as well as the pope in Rome.

Clovis's descendants lost control of the Frankish realm to Charles Martel ("Charles the Hammer") of the **Carolingian family**, whose grandson, **Charlemagne**, conquered most of mainland western Europe, temporarily unifying it. He ruled for half a century, and as long as he was alive, his growing kingdom paid him allegiance. One important factor in explaining the rising power of the Carolingians

CHARLEMAGNE — protect from Vikings
counties
royal agents

was the need for protection from the wave of attacks on Europe by the Vikings, raiders from Scandinavia, that began in 793 and continued for the next two centuries. Charlemagne kept control through military prowess, but he also insured the loyalty of those conquered by setting up an administrative system divided into counties. Each county was governed in the king's name by a powerful landholder called a count. The counts administered justice and raised armies, and Charlemagne wisely placed checks on their power by sending out royal agents called *missi dominici* (the sovereign's envoys) as the "eyes and ears" of the king to report back on any abuses of power. Charlemagne himself constantly moved around his kingdom in order to make his presence felt. In 800, the pope crowned Charlemagne "emperor," implying that he was heir to the Roman throne. Of equal importance is that the act symbolized the superior authority of the church over political leaders, even though in reality Charlemagne needed no such endorsement

Charlemagne = the people's leader

PERSPECTIVES:
WILLIAM MANCHESTER ON
THE DARK AGES

Many explanations have been given for why historians have dubbed the era from about 500 to 1500 in Europe as the "Dark Ages." Most of them center on the notion of lost civilization that was eventually regained before the end of the period. One controversial interpretation may be found in *A World Lit Only by Fire,* by historian William Manchester, who describes a time that was indeed dark:

"The Dark Ages were stark in every dimension. Famines and plague, culminating in the Black Death and its recurring pandemics, repeatedly thinned the population...It says much about the Middle Ages that in the year 1500, after a thousand years of neglect, the roads built by the Romans were still the best on the continent...Among the lost arts was bricklaying; in all of Germany, England, Holland, and Scandinavia, virtually no stone buildings, except cathedrals, were raised for ten centuries...
Surrounding them was the vast, menacing, and at places, impassable Hercynian Forest, infested by boars; by bears; by the hulking medieval wolves who lurk so fearsomely in fairy tales handed down from that time; by imaginary demons; and by very real outlaws, who flourished because they were seldom pursued..Although homicides were twice as frequent as deaths by accident...only one of every hundred murderers was ever brought to justice..."

Reference: William Manchester, *A World Lit Only by Fire.* Boston: Little, Brown & Company, 1992, pp. 5-6.\\

controversy over State + church

to maintain his empire. This controversy over the relationship between religious and political leaders would lead to clashes between popes and kings throughout the Middle Ages in Europe.

After Charlemagne's death, his empire fell apart under his less talented heirs. His son, Louis the Pious, divided the empire among his three sons, who fought among themselves for supremacy. Their disputes were settled by the Treaty of Verdun, which divided Western Europe along general linguistic and cultural borders which still exist today. Had Charlemagne's successors kept his empire together, the course of European history would almost certainly be quite different. Instead, . Europe fragmented into smaller political units that would compete and quarrel with one another for centuries. *Louis Led to Linguistic Borders (division of Europe)*

Politics

THEMATIC LEARNING OBJECTIVE: STATES AND OTHER INSTITUTIONS OF POWER:
CAPITULARY ON THE MISSI

One way that Charlemagne kept order in his kingdom was by sending *missi dominici* (the sovereign's officials) to oversee the work done by the counts, or the regional administrators. In 802 Charlemagne issued the *Capitulary on the Missi,* a document that established regulations for the *missi* to enforce. The *Capitulary* was written by Charlemagne's secretaries in his name, since he was unable to read or write. The following excerpts reflect some of Charlemagne's concerns about his empire as well as an attempt to reestablish the rule of law:

"5. That no one shall presume to rob…the churches of God, or widows, or orphans, or pilgrims, for the lord emperor himself…has constituted himself their protector and defender…

7. That no one shall presume to neglect a summons to war from the lord emperor; and that no one of the Counts shall be so presumptuous as to dare to excuse any one of those who owe military service…

8. …no one shall dare to neglect to pay his dues or tax.

28. …That the Counts…shall provide most carefully, as they desire the good-will of the emperor, for the *missi* who are sent out…

32. Murders, by which a multitude of the Christian people perish, we command in every way to be shunned and to be forbidden…"

Source: D.C.Munro, trans., *University of Pennsylvania Translations and Reprints.* Philadelphia: University of Pennsylvania, 1900, vol. 6 no.5, pp. 16-27.

The model for political organization set in place by the Franks was a version of **feudalism** based on loyalties among the elite: lords, vassals, and overlords. Partly because the origins of the system were local and informal, the web of connections was incredibly complex. For example, a lord may have controlled his vassals (i.e., those who owed loyalty to him), but he in turn was a vassal to an overlord, who in turn was a vassal to a king. The authority of the king was based on these ties, which could come to cross-purposes with loyalties owed to a rival. These often contradictory loyalty ties led to conflict characterized by heavily armed knights who fought to fulfill their loyalty obligations. The European version of feudalism allowed knights (vassals) to hold land usually granted to them by their lords, so they were not just a fighting force, but were also a part of the overlapping hierarchies among elites. *Feudalism developed a well-defined "social class" Based on LOYALTY*

Economic Development
serfs ≠ slaves
Manorialism developed an economic exchange between boss + serf
The economic system that evolved in Western Europe during early medieval times was **manorialism,** which defined both economic and political obligations between lords and peasant laborers.   Most people were **serfs** who lived on and were tied to self-sufficient agricultural estates (manors). Serfs received protection, administrative justice, and the right to graze their animals from the lord of the manor, and in return they were obliged to give a portion of their produce to the lord and to stay on the land. The manorial system originated in the later Roman Empire, but it strengthened during early medieval days once trade declined and Roman political protection disappeared. As a result of these developments, the manors became self-sufficient. In the early Middle Ages, trade was based on **barter,** or the exchange of goods directly. Because manors were self-sustaining, trade with outsiders was limited, and money wasn't necessary. At first, the serfs' labor was difficult as they tried to use wooden plows for the heavy soils of France and Germany, but during the 9th century a better plow with an iron plate, the moldboard, made the work a little easier. Another 9th-century development was a new three-field system, which improved productivity through a rotation of crops that involved leaving one third of the fields unplanted each year, allowing the soil to be replenished before it was replanted. Serfs were not slaves. They were not bought and sold, and they had ownership rights to their houses and lands as long as they honored their obligations to the lord. *+trade ↓   manorialism ↑   Self-Sufficient*

The Political and Religious Power of the Roman Catholic Church

A split in political authority between eastern and western parts of the Roman Empire began during the late 3rd century C.E., mainly because the empire was so large that it was difficult to administer from Rome. This division was reinforced in the early 4th century when the Roman emperor Constantine moved his capital from Rome to Constantinople, far to the east on the Bosporus between the Black Sea and the Mediterranean Sea. After his conversion to Christianity, church of-

DIVIDED EAST + WEST

ficials were recognized all over the empire, with the most important settling in Rome and Constantinople. The split in political authority between the two cities also led to a split in religious authority, with the bishops in Rome eventually called "popes" who headed the Roman Catholic Church. "Patriarchs" in Constantinople were associated with the Eastern Orthodox Church that allowed the emperor a good bit of authority in religious matters. Over the years the two branches of Christianity developed different practices, and even though the formal split did not come until the 11th century, in reality they operated independently from one another long before that. The Frankish king Clovis converted to Roman Catholicism, an event that hastened the emergence of the church as an important political and religious power in Western Europe.

Beginning in the 300s and 400s, many Roman Catholic missionaries traveled across Western Europe, converting the Germanic and Celtic people to the religion. One of the most famous was St. Patrick, who established Christian churches throughout Ireland. The conversion of Clovis was particularly important because many Germanic groups had chosen a branch of Christianity called Arianism. Catholic Christians considered the Arians heretics, so Clovis's conversion marked a partnership between Frankish kings and the Catholic Church. The Church developed a hierarchical organization that gave structure to politically fragmented groups across Western Europe, and church officials soon gained political as well as religious power.

Bishops generally directed churches in urban areas, but because Roman cities were dwindling in size, the Church supported monasteries in rural areas. Here Christian men and women gave up their private possessions to live simply and devote their lives to the Church. Like the local priests, monks and nuns were expected to be poor, chaste, and obedient. Rules for their behavior were written by a monk named Benedict around 540; they included daily rituals of prayer, manual labor, and simple eating. **The Benedictine Rule** came to be followed by almost all Italian, English, and Frankish monks and nuns. The monasteries played an important role in providing stability during the Dark Ages. They protected refugees, operated schools, maintained libraries, and copied books. Many books had been destroyed when Rome was attacked by the Germanic tribes, but some of those that survived did so because monk-scholars carefully copied the manuscripts, saving at least a portion of the intellectual heritage of the ancient Greek and Roman civilizations.

The Revival of Civilization: The High Middle Ages

By 1000 C. E., western Europe was showing some signs of waking from its years of self-sufficiency and isolation. Gradually, agricultural techniques and technologies from eastern Europe and Asia were making some differences, particularly the moldboard plow, the three-field system, and a new horse collar that allowed horses

ORGANIZATION OF THE CATHOLIC CHURCH IN MEDIEVAL TIMES

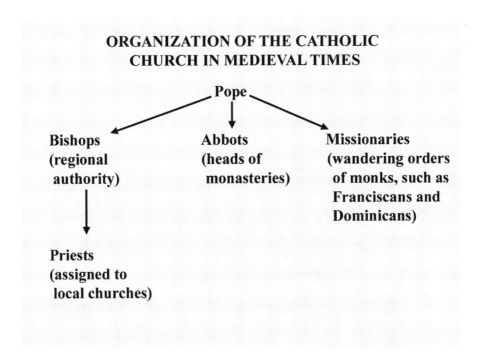

The Catholic Church provided organizational "glue" for western Europe during medieval times by ensuring that its presence was felt in many ways. The pope gained authority as the head of a hierarchy that included regional and local churches, monasteries, and missionary orders. Other high officials included archbishops and cardinals, who appointed popes from their ranks.

to pull plows without choking. The use of the stirrup in warfare spread from Central Asia, and better agricultural methods were promoted by the monasteries. During the 10th century, Viking raids became less serious as regional governments grew stronger and Vikings settled in European communities to intermarry with the natives. As agricultural production increased, it supported a larger population, creating a demand for more trade, which in turn caused towns to grow. As local economies grew, political and cultural changes occurred as well.

Political Developments

Two factors discouraged the growth of strong central government. Feudalism did so by its very nature and the Catholic Church did so by countering the power of the kings. The Church established moral boundaries for its members, partly by setting **canon law,** or rules for behavior that first filled the void of political authority in the early days, but eventually canon law inhibited the development of a separate political authority. For example, the church had the power to **excommunicate** its members, or separate them from the church and its sacraments. Even more powerful was the Church's authority to impose the **interdict,** which could deny religious rites to all people within a ruler's realm. In this Age of Faith, that meant that all babies born could not be baptized, no marriages would be valid in the eyes of the church, and no last rites could be read to those on their deathbeds. If a ruler misbehaved, the church could put his region under an interdict in order to pressure the ruler to submit to the will of the church. As political leaders grew stronger, friction increased between kings and popes – a dynamic that worked against the development of centralized political power. Another limitation to the growth of strong central government was resistance by the nobility, who enjoyed the independence that feudalism and manorialism afforded them.

Because of these limitations, many areas of Europe remained feudalistic long past 1450, including the **Holy Roman Empire**, established in spirit with Charlemagne's crowning in 800, but not officially until 962, when a loose confederation of German princes named one of their own as the Holy Roman emperor. The emperor was crowned by the pope, implying that power rested in the hands of the pope, but the princes always asserted their independence and often paid little attention to the emperor. In most areas of eastern Europe, feudalism also remained in place for many years, partly because trade and commerce grew more rapidly in the west.

In contrast with the pattern in eastern Europe, the power of monarch in England, France, Spain, and other kingdoms in the west, grew into centralized governments by 1450, although not without many challenges along the way. For example, our

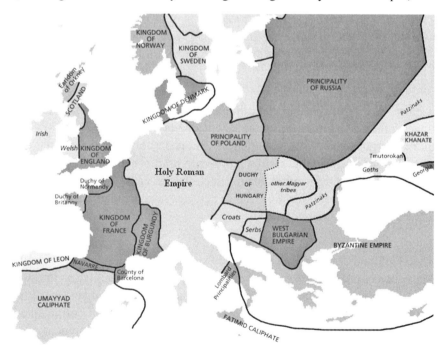

Europe about 1000 C. E. By 1000 the map of Europe shows kingdoms, principalities, duchies, and empires that form the basis for modern European countries. However, feudalism decentralized power, so that local aristocrats and church leaders also had a great deal of political power.

modern concept of **limited government** (limits on the power of the ruler) is based partly on the **Magna Carta**, a document that nobles forced King John of England to sign that guaranteed rights to the nobility. Late in the 13th century, **parliaments** were created to give nobility and the clergy a voice in policymaking. Although competition for political control remained a contest among the elite (church officials, nobles, and political leaders), these struggles created the cradle that fostered the eventual growth of modern democracies.

Stronger monarchs were able to gather larger armies, so one result was some large-scale warfare during the late Middle Ages. For example, William of Normandy (the "Conqueror") was able to command a large army to invade and conquer England in 1066, when English forces clashed with Normans at the Battle of Hastings. The **Hundred Years' War** during the 14th and 15th centuries between the kings of France and England was fought over territories the English king controlled in France – a great clash between the old governing rules under feudalism and the newly emerging claims of national states.

The Impact of the Crusades

By the 11th century, western European states were expanding in many directions: south into Spain to push back the Muslims, eastward into sparsely populated areas of Poland; and at the end of the century, into the Middle Eastern lands controlled by Muslims. Population increases fueled the expansion, as did the missionary zeal of Christians. The most dramatic moves were those made into the Middle East in a series of attacks called the **Crusades**, prompted by a request from the Byzantine emperor, Alexius I, for help in raising troops to resist Turkish incursions into the empire. In 1095 Pope Urban II called upon Christian knights to save the holy city of Jerusalem from "an accursed race" [the Turks] by undertaking a journey "for the remission of your sins" and assuring them of "the reward of imperishable glory in the Kingdom of Heaven." The response was immediately overwhelming, with the crowds responding, "God wills it! God wills it!" In 1096 between 50,000 and 60,000 knights from western Europe joined the Crusades, beginning a series of attacks that lasted for two centuries.

The First Crusade managed to win Jerusalem from the Turkish armies and establish a number of forts in the area around it. Although the Crusaders held Jerusalem for close to a century, the Turks reorganized under the great Muslim general, **Saladin**, who took it back during the 12th century. The Crusaders never succeeded in recapturing Jerusalem, and the Venetian city-state turned the Fourth Crusade during the early 13th century into an attack on its commercial rivals in Constantinople. Ultimately, the Crusaders failed to accomplish their goals. The failure of the Crusades did not alter their importance in shaping the course of European history during the era from 600 to 1450. More than any other single

PERSPECTIVES: MOTIVATIONS FOR THE CRUSADES

The Christian Crusades were phenomenal events in which thousands of European knights left their homes – with full knowledge that they probably would never return – in order to fight for a cause. This mass movement of people from one area to another is unusual enough that a good historian should ask, "How did it happen?" and "Why did they go?"

From the pope's perspective: By the late 11th century, Byzantine and Roman Christians had gone their separate ways for some time, with the pope claiming to be the supreme head of the Church, and the Byzantine emperor denying the claim. Pope Urban II almost certainly hoped that a successful Crusade would convince the Byzantine emperor to change his mind. Besides, from the pope's point of view, it was better to have the knights fighting the Turks than one another.

From the knights' perspectives: The First Crusade was undoubtedly fueled by religious fervor, especially since the pope promised forgiveness of sins for any man that died in the Crusades. For other knights, the Crusades were a chance to win glory in battle. Especially in the later Crusades, plunder was a motivation, because the lands of the Middle East were far richer than those in western Europe.

factor, the Crusades laid the foundation for the emergence of European countries in the next era as powerful forces on their way to eventually controlling most other areas of the world. Why? Most importantly, it put the Crusaders in direct contact with the oldest areas of world civilizations and made them aware of worlds they never knew existed. Those that returned brought back with them material evidence of civilization: fine silks, beautiful porcelains, exquisite carpets, perfumes, spices, and preservatives. No longer would Europeans be content to remain in their isolated, drafty castles; they had tasted the pleasures of civilization, and change was inevitable.

Economic Developments

Two cities that directly benefitted from the Crusades were Venice and Genoa in Italy. Because they were so close to the heart of the old Roman Empire, the cities of Italy never quite succumbed to the feudalistic patterns in the rest of Europe.

Instead each city maintained control over the countryside around it and continued to serve as a center of trade. When the Crusades began, Venice and Genoa promoted sea routes for the knights to travel to the Holy Lands, disembarking from one of the cities and arriving on the eastern shore of the Mediterranean Sea. Since most European knights had little money, in exchange for their passage, they often offered their services to protect the ships from pirates and internal disputes. The ships carried goods both ways across the sea, bringing woolen and cotton textiles and French wines from Europe, and delivering luxury goods from the Middle East to Europe. By the time of the Fourth Crusade in the early 13th century, both cities were wealthy enough to rival older trading cities such as Constantinople.

With the growth of Genoa and Venice, Italian business people introduced banking to the West to facilitate the long-distance exchange of money and goods. Towns in France, the Holy Roman Empire, and England grew in response to the trade, and the use of money spread steadily. Wealthy merchants invested in trading ships and the goods they carried, hoping to make a profit. Trade within Europe grew as well, with towns exchanging timber and grain from the north for cloth and metal products in the south. Cities in northern Germany and southern Scandinavia formed the **Hanseatic League** to facilitate trade throughout the regions bordering the Baltic and North Seas. As more towns purchased charters from kings and severed their feudal ties to lords on the rural manors, they became a strong source of revenue for kings, who were able to use the money to build armies and gain power over the aristocrats. The craftsmen in the towns formed merchant **guilds**, associations of people who worked in the same occupation. These groups grew powerful enough to control trade, and they also were responsible for training apprentices and setting standards for membership that encouraged the quality of their products to increase.

The growing towns and cities were home to a rising merchant class, who often allied with kings as a counterbalance to the landed aristocracy. Although the manorial system still existed in rural areas, more people were living in towns, and the social class structure grew more complex as former serfs became craftsmen, traders, and merchants. The new urban classes often clashed with the landed nobility, sometimes in open warfare, and by the early 1300s, traders had achieved an independent political status, protected by their own warriors as well as their wealth.

The growth of trade and banking in the late Middle Ages formed the basic building blocks of western capitalism, especially as merchants invested in trading ventures, hoping to make a profit but taking the risk of losing everything if the ship sank or was looted by pirates. Because the Catholic Church took an official stand against **usury** (lending money for profit), bankers were often Jews, the descendants of those who had fled Israel during the diaspora, or scattering of their people by conquerors, during the 6th century B.C.E. and 2nd century C. E. The Church eventually eased its policies and allowed Christians to participate more fully in the new

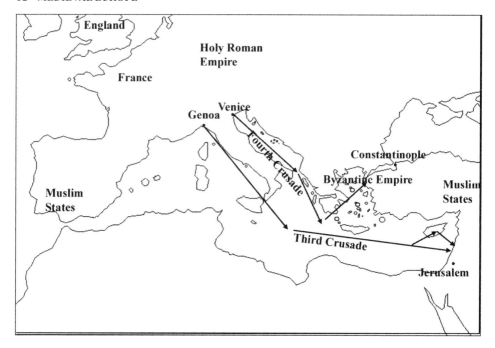

Venice and Genoa. Two Italian trading cities became wealthy through new contacts established by the Crusades. During the Third Crusade, knights disembarked from Genoa and headed toward Jerusalem. By the time of the Fourth Crusade, Venice influenced Crusaders to attack Constantinople, even though the Crusades originally began as an effort to help Constantinople. With the sacking of the city, Venice profited by securing trade routes to the Middle East.

capitalism. The Catholic Church had promoted the commercial and naval growth of Venice, and church officials began to seek the patronage of the rising merchant classes. By the 13th century, the church itself had become a great property holder, as well as a lender of money.

European Christians demonstrated their religious fervor not just by attempting to drive back the "infidels" (Muslims) from Jerusalem, but also through their treatment of Jews, who were often legally and forcibly segregated from the Christian majority in small urban areas called **ghettos**. Other forms of discrimination against Jews included restrictions on owning land or entering craft guilds, so banking and trading were some of the only occupations open to them. Before the 13th century, Jews were seldom attacked, but in that century, English and French kings denounced and expelled them and seized their property. About the same time, **pogroms**, or anti-Semitic mob actions drove Jews from western to eastern Europe, where they experienced less discrimination.

As medieval social and economic life grew more complex, a longstanding pattern became apparent: more restrictions on the lives of women. Germanic customs in early medieval times allowed women considerable freedom, and women were thought to have the gift of prophecy and a special holiness. As in most other agricultural societies, in some cases they carried out household duties with the help of slaves, and their advice was often sought and respected. Strong matrilineal ties existed, and the relationship between a man and his sisters' sons was particularly strong. The Christian emphasis on the equality of all souls, as well as the reverence for Mary, the mother of Jesus, almost certainly gained women more respect than they had in many other societies. They were not as segregated in religious services as were Muslim women, although they could not lead them. Women also had an alternative to married domestic life; monastic life was open to them as well as to men. However, with the growth of cities, women were often excluded from guilds, and their roles in local commerce seem to have decreased during the High Middle Ages. The literature of the day stressed women's roles as subservient to men and praised docile and obedient women as the ideal.

Culture and Arts

Once trade and new businesses created some wealth in western Europe, more specialized occupations grew, allowing cultural developments to follow, including the founding of institutions of higher education. As early as the 700s Charlemagne had brought learned men to his court to teach and train others. He opened a school for clergy and government officials headed by Alcuin, an Anglo-Saxon monk of

ORIGINAL DOCUMENTS: THOMAS AQUINAS ON BUSINESS AND TRADE

By the 13th century, the Catholic Church was modifying its earlier denunciations of business practices, particularly of usury, or the charging of interest. The change in policy is reflected in these passages from *Summa Theologica*, written between 1265 and 1274 by **Thomas Aquinas,** the great medieval theologian:

"Buying and selling seem to be established for the common advantage of both parties...The just price of things is not fixed with mathematical precision, but depends on a kind of estimate, so that a slight addition or subtraction would not seem to destroy the equality of justice...Nothing prevents gain from being directed to some necessary or even virtuous end, and thus trading becomes lawful."

great ability and skills. Although the era is sometimes referred to as the "Carolingian Renaissance," it did not last, and the court collapsed after Charlemagne's death. Shortly after the Crusades began, the first universities were established in Italy, not surprisingly, since Italy was the first area of Europe to directly benefit from the trade sparked by the Crusades. Other universities were founded later in France, England, and Germany. Most of them were created for the clergy, but as early as the 1200s they were combining Christian learning with books of the Greek and Roman Classical age. Since the Muslims in the Middle East had preserved and copied many of these books, once western Europeans came in contact with these areas during the Crusades, Greek and Roman learning made its way back into Europe. Christian teachers, such as Thomas Aquinas, Albertus Magnus, and Peter Abelard used Aristotelian arguments and Socratic methods to teach the truths of Christian faith. A notable intellectual development was **scholasticism,** or the attempt to reconcile the beliefs and values of Christianity with the logical reasoning of Greek philosophy. For example, St. Thomas Aquinas believed that it was possible to prove rationally that God exists by seizing on Aristotle's argument that a conscious agent had set the world in motion.

An important development in medieval literature was the use of **vernacular languages**, beginning in the 13th century. Before that, all serious literature was generally written in Latin, but starting with Dante Alighieri's *Divine Comedy*, written in Italian, the common people's oral languages (the vernacular) began to replace the old Roman language. Somewhat later came the first important work in English: Geoffrey Chaucer's *Canterbury Tales*, which reflected a great deal of insight into medieval life in England. Other works followed in German, French, and Spanish vernaculars, so that by the end of the 14th century, Latin was no longer the only written language in Europe.

Gothic cathedrals are the most impressive of late medieval forms, combining architecture, painting, sculpture, inlay, carving, stained glass, music, and literature. A cathedral took many years to construct, and was almost always the most impressive building in town. Particularly after the 13th century, European painting became more sophisticated, with experimentation with perspective (making a painting look three-dimensional) and portrayal of individual faces. Most formal art was produced for the church as an institution or for wealthy clergymen. By the 1300s art and culture were beginning to take shape in Italy as the **Renaissance**, or rebirth, which would spread over Europe and come to full flower during the 15th and 16th centuries.

THE BYZANTINE EMPIRE

After the Western Roman Empire fell, the Eastern Empire lived on for almost a thousand years, known during most of that time as the **Byzantine Empire**, after "Byzantium," the town that Constantine renamed "Constantinople" as the capital

Romanesque and Gothic Architecture. Before the end of the 11th century, Europeans had recovered enough from the fall of Rome to begin to build some impressive churches. The photo on the left is the interior of a Romanesque church in Comps, France. Its simple design and small windows reflect the architectural style of early medieval Europe, borrowed from Roman designs. In contrast, the photo on the right shows the towering Gothic style of the Salisbury Cathedral in England – a later design with large stained glass windows, very high ceilings, and complex vaulting.

city. The empire controlled the eastern Mediterranean until the 12th century, the only classical civilization to survive into this era. The Byzantines inherited the Roman line of authority, complete with Roman roads, communications, and functioning imperial institutions. The Empire also became an economic powerhouse, and its manufactured goods were highly desirable, especially their silks, which matched the quality of Chinese products. Its cultural impact was also significant; the Slavic peoples of eastern Europe and Russia were very much influenced by the Byzantines, and many adopted the Eastern Orthodox religion. By the 12th century, the Empire had weakened, with the Islamic states crowding it to the east, Slavic people dominating the lands to the north, and western Europeans gaining strength to the west. However, the empire survived until 1453 when Constantinople fell to the Ottoman Turks who renamed the city Istanbul.

Political Developments

Although Germanic invasions threatened the Eastern Empire as well as the Western Empire, the east was better fortified because it was wealthier than the west. The major political threat to the early Byzantine Empire was the **Sassanid Empire**

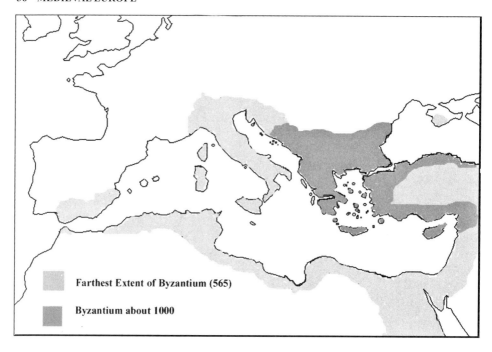

The Byzantine Empire. At its largest, the Byzantine Empire spread from Italy to Anatolia (modern day Turkey), and included the southern Mediterranean coastline and the southern coast of Spain. Much land was later lost, however, and by 1000 the empire only controlled lands in Greece and Anatolia.

to the east. The Sassanids had sought to rebuild the old Persian Empire, but their hopes were dashed when they were attacked and defeated by the Arab Muslims in the 7th century. The precedent for Byzantine leadership style was set by Constantine, who claimed divine favor and sanction for his rule. In contrast to the separate political and religious powers developing in the west, the emperor often intervened in theological disputes, and used his political position to define "orthodox" (accepted, true) beliefs and condemn others as **heretical** (false, often considered to be dangerous). This policy of political and religious power concentrated in the emperor's hands was called **caesaropapism** (caesar and pope). Emperors stood above the law, and their power was enhanced by a bureaucracy so large and complex that today we use the adjective "byzantine" to describe unnecessarily complicated or outdated structures.

The most important of the early Byzantine emperors was **Justinian**, who ruled from 527 to 565 C. E. Like Constantine, Justinian put a great deal of time, money, and effort into public buildings in Constantinople, most notably the **Hagia Sophia**, or Church of Holy Wisdom, that still stands today as one of the most important examples of Christian architecture in the world. Justinian also embarked on a major military campaign to win back the lost lands of the Roman Empire, and he made significant progress toward that goal, reclaiming lands in northern Africa and Spain. His efforts were ultimately a failure, since within two generations almost all of the reconquered areas fell to new invaders. Justinian's most important contribution was his codification of Roman law. Over the centuries, Roman law had been revised and systemized, first under the republic and then during imperial times, but Justinian's work is usually seen as the definitive codification of Roman law. It is preserved in his *corpus juris civilis (Body of the Civil Law),* and it served as the basis for civil law codes that developed throughout much of western Europe.

From the early 600s, the empire was under almost constant attack for two centuries. The Muslims almost took Constantinople in 717, when the Byzantines famously used "Greek fire" (a combustible liquid) to drive them back to sea. The Arab threat continued, and the Turks seriously pressured the empire during the 11th century, resulting in the emperor's call for help to the Catholic pope in the west in 1095. Meanwhile, Slavic kingdoms, especially Bulgaria to the north, also had to be held back from their incursions into Byzantine territory. In the 10th century a Bulgarian king took the title of *tsar,* Slavic for *Caesar,* reflecting his ambitions. The Bulgarian army was defeated soundly in 1014, and Bulgaria became part of the empire. All in all, the Byzantines showed a remarkable ability to survive despite continuing threats to their power.

Economic Development and Social Distinctions

The Byzantine economy was centrally controlled by the bureaucracy in Constantinople, with a large peasant class that supplied food to people in the cities. The bureaucracy kept food prices artificially low to placate the urban lower classes, but this policy put great hardship on the peasants. Constantinople was by far the largest city, not just because it was the capital, but also because of its geographic position at the Bosporus that connects the Black Sea to the Mediterranean Sea. This location not only was ideal for defending the city, but also for controlling long-distance trade routes that connected East Asia, India, and Russia to the growing market in western Europe. Once the Byzantines learned the Chinese secrets for silk production, they developed a brisk silk production business, and also began manufacturing cloth, carpets, and other luxury products. Like the Chinese, the Byzantines did not grant merchants political power, primarily because the government bureaucrats did not want to share their power. In contrast to both China and Byzantium, merchants in western Europe gained a greater political voice.

The situation for women deteriorated from the earlier freedom that Roman women had to venture outside their homes. Of course, the *paterfamilias* (oldest male authority) had controlled family and public life, but during Byzantine times, women increasingly found themselves confined to the home. Some sources say that when they left their homes, they concealed their faces with veils. The only men they socialized with were members of their families. Despite these restrictions, it is interesting to note that from 1028 to 1056 women ruled the Byzantine Empire jointly with their husbands. Much earlier, Empress **Theodora** had exerted a great deal of influence over her husband, **Justinian**, who listened to and often followed her advice.

Cultural Achievements

In the early days of the Byzantine Empire, the official language was Latin, but most of the inhabitants spoke Greek. Eventually, Greek replaced Latin in government documents. The philosophy and literature of classical Greece had a much deeper influence in Byzantium than in western Europe. This was especially notable in Byzantine education. Byzantine aristocrats often hired tutors to provide private instruction for their children, girls as well as boys. Additionally a state-organized school system offered a primary education in basic reading, writing, and grammar, and those that entered the bureaucracy additionally studied classical Greek literature, philosophy, and science. Most peasants and many urban workers had no formal education, but basic literacy was widespread. The most ambitious and accomplished citizens attended a school of higher learning in Constantinople to study law, medicine, and philosophy. Byzantine scholars studied and wrote about the works of Homer, Plato, and Aristotle, and between the 10th and 12th centuries, they copied many classical Greek works, preserving and transmitting the classical legacy.

One of the biggest accomplishments of the Eastern Orthodox Church was the conversion of many eastern Europeans to its branch of Christianity. Beginning in the 9th century, a competition emerged between the Eastern Orthodox and the Roman Catholics for the allegiance of the Slavs. Both religions gained converts, with the Eastern Orthodox being most successful in Russia, Romania, Serbia, Bulgaria, and Greece. In those areas, Constantinople served not only as a religious model, but also as a legal, literary, and artistic influence as well. In contrast, the Poles, Czechs, and Croats turned more toward the Roman Catholic Church, as demonstrated by their adoption of the Roman alphabet for their languages. The **Cyrillic** writing system was adopted in the Eastern Orthodox countries, as invented by two Byzantine missionaries in order to communicate with their followers in their native languages. The expansion of both religions into eastern Europe deepened the rift between them that had been developing since the 4th century. After many years of friction and uneasy truces, the division came out into the open in 1054 when the Roman Catholic pope clashed with the Eastern Orthodox patriarch over a number of issues, with each attacking the other's practices. It ended with the two leaders excommunicating each other, resulting in a divide that still exists to this day.

The chart on the opposite page identifies some differences between Roman Catholicism and Eastern Orthodoxy:

COMPARISON: ROMAN CATHOLICISM AND EASTERN ORTHODOXY

The two major branches of Christianity split gradually over time, partly because they had very different geographic centers. They shared many common beliefs, but the chart below defines some of their differences.

ROMAN CATHOLICISM	EASTERN ORTHODOXY
Separation between political and religious leaders; competition between popes and kings for political power	Union between political and religious leaders (caesaro-papism)
Religious art conveyed Jesus as suffering for the sins of mankind.	Religious art conveyed Jesus as majestic and divine.
Priests could not marry.	Priests could marry.
Gothic architecture was used for churches.	Church architecture was inspired by ancient Rome (arches, domes).
Theology was less influenced by Greek philosophy.	Theology was more influenced by Greek philosophy.

Byzantium and Russia

To the north of Byzantium, a Slavic people known as the Russians began to organize a large state from several principalities. The origins of the Russians are not entirely clear; however, Vikings invaded the area inhabited by Slavic tribes early in the 9th century, and their descendents certainly shaped the development of Russia. The most important early city was Kiev, a thriving trading center on the Dnieper River, along the main trade route between Scandinavia and Byzantium. Kiev came to dominate many of the other principalities, and their princes sought alliances with Byzantine rulers. Many Russian merchants visited Constantinople, became acquainted with Byzantine culture, and sparked the interest of their rulers in Orthodox Christianity. After the conversion of Prince Vladimir of Kiev in about 989, Byzantine influences flowed rapidly into Russia, including art, the Cyrillic alphabet, architecture, law codes, and missions. By the early 12th century Kiev's population approached 30,000, and the city controlled trade all over the

Constantinople's Geographic Advantage. Constantinople became one of the great cities of the world during the period from 600 to 1450 C.E. partly because of its geographic location on the Bosporus, a narrow connection between the Black Sea and the Aegean Sea. From that position the city was central to long distance trade that connected east Asia, India, and Russia to western Europe. The position was also easily defensible since three sides of the city were surrounded by water, and ships could easily be seen from a long distance. On the one vulnerable side of the city to the west, strong walls were built, just as the Romans had done for centuries.

region, with eight thriving marketplaces within its borders. Long after Constantinople fell to the Turks in 1453, Byzantine influences lived on in Russia, with the Orthodox faith and Byzantine customs spreading rapidly as the Kievan principality transformed over time into the great Russian Empire that stretched from the Baltic Sea to Alaska.

As the mid-point of the 15th century approached, western Europe was very much on the rise, and Byzantium was headed for its final fall in 1453 when a Turkish sultan captured Constantinople with a powerful army equipped with artillery purchased from western Europe. Despite its demise, the Byzantine Empire left a lasting imprint on the world's history through its law codes, distinctive architecture, religion, and organizational structure long after the other classical civilizations had crumbled.

MARKER EVENT IN RUSSIA: ACCEPTANCE OF BYZANTINE CULTURE

As Russia began to develop from the early Kievan state, Vladimir I made some important decisions that oriented Russia toward Byzantium and away from western Europe. When he first came to power, he built a temple to the six gods his Slavic subjects worshipped, but soon became interested in the monotheistic religions developing in regions around him. The earliest Russian chronicle reports that Vladimir decided against Islam because of its ban on alcohol, and rejected Judaism because he could not understand how a powerful god would allow his people's temple to be destroyed. Although the chronicle does not clearly say why he did not choose Roman Catholicism, he almost certainly was swayed by the magnificent wealth of 10th century Constantinople and the beauty of Orthodox churches. Once Orthodox Christianity was accepted, the Cyrillic alphabet began to be used and trade was oriented toward Byzantium. After the Byzantine Empire fell, Russia became the incubator for Byzantine ways, and despite later attempts by Russian tsars to "westernize" and form alliances with western European nations, a different path was set for Russia. The cultural divide that arose during the High Middle Ages set the stage for many tensions between eastern and western Europe that developed in later times, including the "Cold War" of the 20th century.

CONCEPTS AND IDENTIFICATIONS

Benedictine Rule
Byzantine Empire
caesaropapism
canon law
Carolingian family
Charlemagne
Clovis
Crusades
excommunication, interdict
feudalism
Franks
ghettos
guilds

Hagia Sophia

Hanseatic League

heresy

Holy Roman Empire

Hundred Years War

Justinian, Justinian Code

limited government, parliaments

Magna Carta

manorialism

"Middle Ages"

missi dominici

pogroms

Renaissance

Saladin

Sassanid Empire

scholasticism

serfs

Theodora

usury

vernacular languages

Vikings

UNIT ONE:
THE TRANSFORMATION
OF EUROPE (1450-1648)

In 1450, Europe was connected by trade, communication, and travel to other parts of the Eastern Hemisphere, but the region was still on the periphery of interactions among regions. The old centers of civilization in the Middle East, South Asia, and East Asia still were the most important axes of commerce and culture, while Europe had only recently recovered from the Dark Ages that followed the fall of the Western Roman Empire. By 1648, Europe had moved to front and center stage, although the older centers continued to be important players in world interactions. How did this transformation occur? Three interrelated changes help to explain the rise of Europe:

1) **Important cultural and intellectual changes** – including the Renaissance, the Reformation, and the Scientific Revolution – oriented European minds toward invention and allowed them to escape the social and intellectual boundaries of the Middle Ages.

2) **Political consolidation of strong centralized states** meant that kings had enough power and money to control regional lands and people and to sponsor trade expeditions and diplomatic envoys to other civilizations.

3) **Technological advances and the development of capitalism** allowed European states to increase their riches through trade and territorial claims in the Western Hemisphere. Although they often built on inventions from previous eras by other people, Europeans made good use of their innovations.

In the period between 1450 and 1648 these three changes evolved together, and change in one area brought about reactions in the others, which in turn brought further alterations in the first area. By 1648, these changes interacted to bring about the transformation of the continent, so that the Europe of 1648 was significantly different – politically, culturally, socially, and economically – from the Europe of 1450.

THE BIG PICTURE:
THE TRANSFORMATION OF EUROPE
1450-1648

Important themes that interacted throughout this period of history include:

1) The reliance on religious authority shifted to the belief that human beings often control their own destinies. This shift is evidenced by the Renaissance, religious reformation, the voyages of discovery, the rise of capitalism, and the Scientific Revolution. All of these developments reflect the importance of individual effort and innovation.

2) Political states in western Europe – including England, France, and Spain – centralized government in the hands of a monarch at the expense of the old nobility. Other areas of Europe – such as the Holy Roman Empire and Italy – did not centralize power, and as a result, their political and economic development was hampered.

3) Economic innovations, including capitalism and mercantilism, supported a growth in trade and business that eventually led to European explorations and foreign land claims. As a result, Europe became central to the development of the first truly global economy in world history.

4) Religious pluralism replaced the dominance of the Catholic Church in Europe and served as a permanent end to the hope of a unified Christendom. Religious strife characterized the era from 1517 to 1648.

5) The old social order based on landowning nobles and serfs tied to the land broke up in western Europe and was rapidly changing by 1648. New social classes emerged – including the bourgeoisie or gentry – and the old nobility lost economic and political power. Towns and cities grew, populated by a larger number of artisans and merchants, and peasants were likely to move from rural areas to towns. In eastern Europe, however, serfdom remained in place, and the landed nobility retained their control.

CHAPTER 3:
RENAISSANCE
EUROPE

"The whole glory of man lies in activity."

Leonardo Bruni
Chancellor and Historian
Florence, 1433

The sentiment in the simple statement above reflects some important changes in European attitudes that began to take place during the 15th century. Although important economic changes had taken place during the late Middle Ages, most people of that era still saw themselves as humble servants of God who were in need of salvation from a painful and sinful world. To refer to the "whole glory" of frail humans was virtually unthinkable, and the contemplative life focused on thoughtful prayer and passive acceptance of God's will was considered to be the best of all possible approaches to life. In contrast, Bruni's statement above suggests that human activity, not meditative withdrawal, was to be treasured, and so cultural and social values were clearly changing by the early 15th century.

These cultural and social changes in Europe continued throughout the era from 1450 to 1648, and they were sparked almost certainly by economic changes late in the previous era. The Crusades of the 12th and 13th centuries started a movement of European knights to the Middle East, which stimulated trade and contact between the Middle East and Europe. Two Italian city states – Genoa and Venice – grew wealthy from the new interactions, so it is not surprising that cultural changes began in Italy and worked their way to the north.

THE ITALIAN RENAISSANCE

The word "renaissance," which is French for "rebirth," was first used in the 16th century to refer to a revival of interest in the poetry, prose, and art of classical Greece and Rome. The first reference to this movement was actually the Italian word *rinascita*, used by Italian painter and architect **Giorgio Vasari** in his *Lives of the Most Excellent Italian Architects, Painters, and Sculptors* in 1550. Vasari explained that much classical art and literature was lost after the fall of the Western

Roman Empire in the 5th century, and interest in it did not revive until the 14th century, when the "most excellent" Italian artists began the rediscovery. Gradually, the term "renaissance" came to define a broader consciousness that caused 14th century northern Italians to think of themselves as living in an age distinct from the Middle Ages, with values influenced by, but different from, those of Ancient Greece and Rome.

Perhaps the most obvious reason that the Renaissance began in Italy was that the Roman Empire was centered there, and the ruins of Ancient Rome were all over the peninsula. Two significant legacies from the Roman Empire were Roman law and roads. Roman law provided a framework for order and the development of political life within the Italian city-states. Roman roads linked cities and towns, particularly those in the northern part of the peninsula. In the 1300s scholars studied ancient Latin manuscripts that had been preserved in monasteries. Then when Constantinople (the capital of the Byzantine Empire) fell to the Ottoman Turks in 1453, Byzantine scholars fled to Rome with ancient Greek manuscripts, which Italian scholars had assumed were lost forever. Despite this important event, it alone would not have sparked the Renaissance without the influence of the new patterns of long distance trade that had enriched northern Italy by the 15th century.

Economic Changes

When the Christian Crusades began in the late 11th century, the Italian city-states of Venice and Genoa promoted a sea route for the knights to travel to the Holy Lands, disembarking from one of these cities and arriving on the eastern shore of the Mediterranean Sea. The ships carried goods both ways across the sea, bringing woolen and cotton textiles and French wines from Europe, and delivering luxury goods from the Middle East to Europe. By the time of the Fourth Crusade in the early 13th century, both Italian cities were wealthy enough to rival older trading cities such as Constantinople. Their economic success was bolstered by important strides in shipbuilding that for the first time allowed their ships to carry more cargo and to sail all year long. Other northern Italian cities that prospered from trade were Milan and Florence, with both possessing enormous wealth despite their less than ideal geographic location.

In contrast to Venice and Genoa, which were both seaports, Florence was an inland city without easy access to sea transportation. The city's big breakthrough came when Florentine merchants and bankers gained the right to collect taxes for the pope. This power allowed these merchants and bankers to establish offices all over Europe that set up loans, investments, and money exchanges that greatly enriched the city. The wool industry was particularly profitable, with fine-quality wool purchased from England and Spain and then manufactured into cloth by Florentine weavers. This superb-quality cloth brought the highest prices all over Europe, Asia, and Africa. Florence's gold florin became a standard currency in

MARKER EVENT:
THE RENAISSANCE

Most scholars agree that the Renaissance was an important "marker event" in European history, but they don't always agree on the reasons. Historian Jakob Burckhardt argued in *The Civilization of the Renaissance in Italy* (1860) that the Renaissance ushered in the modern era of European history because individuals were freed from the domination of society and the repression of the Roman Catholic Church. As a result, the Renaissance represented the beginning of a secular society with an appreciation for creative individual geniuses.

Burkhardt's ideas were revised significantly by later scholars who have argued that the Renaissance was not a strictly secular age, but was still profoundly influenced by religion. Others have emphasized continuities between the late Middle Ages and the Renaissance, especially in terms of economic growth. However, despite their differences, most scholars agree that the Renaissance represents a distinct cultural period lasting from the 14th to the 16th century, centered on the revival of Greek and Roman culture, that began in northern Italy and spread to northern Europe.

European trading centers, and the bankers of Florence became central to European commerce. The economic foundation built by the early 14th century was so sound that even the ravages of the Black Death did not destabilize Florence, even though it lost at least half of its population to the disease.

Social Structure

As the Italian city-states grew in wealth and size, the social structure changed to reflect the central importance of trade, manufacturing, and banking. The old rural-based nobility were attracted by the growing wealth of the cities, and so often married into prominent merchant families to form alliances as a new urban elite, who were tied by blood, economic interests, and social connections. This gradually helped them to expand their rights. This urban nobility, composed of wealthy merchants and manufacturers, were called the ***popolo grasso***, or "fat people." The *mediocri* were a middle group of smaller merchants and master artisans, and the *popolo minuto*, or "little people," made up the largest group composed of laborers and artisans. At the very bottom of the hierarchy were slaves and servants, usually women from the hinterlands employed in domestic service. Urban elites owned much of the farmland outside the cities, where tenant farmers, sharecroppers, and agricultural laborers worked their land. In northern Italy, most peasants were poor but free, whereas in the south they still owed obligations to their lords.

The "fat people" of the city-states made up no more than 5 percent of the population, but the most influential ones were princes of their cities, including dukes and cardinals, or in the Papal States, the pope himself. Whereas social class distinctions were important, social mobility was possible through commercial wealth, and newly rich families often rose to political power. However, this social mobility declined significantly by the end of the 15th century as urban **patriarchs** (male heads of powerful families) came to dominate their cities through **patronage**, granting titles, privileges, and money in exchange for political support. They often flouted their wealth and power by supporting architects and artists to build and decorate their homes and public places.

Wealth and class determined family life, with the poor generally unable to support large families. The wealthy had more children, and they valued social and political ties among extended family members. Marriages represented alliances of money, political status, and family standing, so they were usually arranged by the male heads of household. Like most other societies of the day, the urban-city states were **patriarchies** (domination of social, political and economic life by men) that traced descent through the male line. Inheritances went to male children, and a daughter could claim inheritance only through her **dowry**, or sums of money offered by a woman's father to a prospective bridegroom's family to seal a marriage.

Political Organization: the City-States

During the 13th and 14th centuries trade-rich cities of Italy expanded to become powerful **city-states** that dominated the political and economic life of the surrounding countryside. Unlike in northern Europe, where cities were usually subject to the rule of kings or princes, the great Italian cities lacked central control and became independent states. By the 15th century, five states – Milan, Florence, Venice, the Papal States, and the Kingdom of Naples – overshadowed other smaller city-states, and were in fierce competition with one another for economic and political power.

The Italian states may be divided into two broad categories: **republics** based on the old medieval *communes*, or associations of free men who sought complete political and economic independence from local nobles; and **principalities**, which were ruled by hereditary despots called *signori* who had absolute power. The most powerful republics were Venice and Florence, and the strongest

COMPARISONS:
THE STATUS OF RENAISSANCE WOMEN IN ITALY AND NORTHERN EUROPE

The Italian city-states were patriarchies dominated by men of the most prominent families, and wealth was inherited by male family members only. In contrast to these privileged sons, a daughter's name often disappeared from family records after her marriage. Women's subordination in marriage was reflected in significant age differences between spouses, with young women often marrying much older men. The different ages of husbands and wives reinforced the gender divisions in Renaissance families, especially in upper-class families.

In contrast, marriage partners in northern Europe were much closer in age. In England, the Low Countries, and Germany, women often participated actively in the economy, not just in peasant households, but also in cities, where they worked as peddlers, weavers, shopkeepers, brewers, and seamstresses. In towns, women often acted informally as their husbands' business partners. Women also shared inheritances with their brothers, represented themselves in legal transactions, testified in court, belonged to guilds, and controlled their own dowries.

principalities were Milan and Naples. The Papal States, ruled by the pope, formed another important power. None of the city-states were democratic; even though Venice and Florence called themselves "republics," they generally were **oligarchies,** or governments ruled by a few merchant aristocrats from prominent families. Despite their similarities, the five most powerful city-states had contrasting governing styles and economic characteristics:

- **Venice** – More than any other city, Venice built its fortunes on profits made during the Christian Crusades. The city was ideally located to control trade stimulated by new contacts between Europe and the much wealthier Middle East, and Venetian ships sailed the Mediterranean, the Atlantic coast, and the Black Sea. Venice maintained a republican form of government based on a constitution that offered a balance of political power. The **doge** was the chief executive elected for life by the Senate, a body which represented the nobility. Senators in turn were selected by the Great Council, which consisted of about 2,500 patricians. Despite these seemingly representative bodies, they only gave power to the aristocracy, and the poor had no voice in political decisions. However, the Venetian city-state was relatively calm and cohesive, probably because its citizens had to band together to protect themselves from the Ottoman Turks who challenged Venice for control of trade on the eastern Mediterranean Sea.

- **Florence** – In contrast to the relatively peaceful Venice, the republic of Florence was almost always in turmoil, with families, social classes, and political factions embroiled in seemingly endless conflict. For example, in 1378 a revolt known as the Ciompi, or "the wooden shoes," broke out because many laborers could only afford wooden shoes. The cloth workers joined with members of the lower guilds to start a bloody insurrection that left the *popolo grasso* in fear of further violence. In 1434 the **Medici family** seized control of Florentine political life, building their power on great wealth from banking and the manufacture and commerce of textiles.

The Italian City-States in 1494. By the end of the 15th century, the Italian Peninsula was divided into a number of independent city-states. The major city-states – Milan, Florence, Venice, the Papal States, and the Kingdom of Naples – dominated the others.

- **Cosimo de' Medici,** the head of the family, was supported by a few patrician families who helped him to banish prominent members of the most powerful rival clans. From 1434 to 1494 the Medici controlled the offices of government, with Florentine nobles generally accepting Medici rule because it brought the necessary stability to maintain the growing prosperity of the city-state. Cosimo's grandson **Lorenzo** ("the Magnificent") promoted his family's power with an extravagant patronage of the arts. Despite the immense power and wealth of the Medici family, the turmoil continued, with Lorenzo narrowly escaping an assassination attempt in 1479. Only two years after Lorenzo's death in 1492, Medici enemies took advantage of the family's weakened control and drove them from Florence. The Medici returned to power in 1512, were driven out again in 1527, only to return in 1530 to declare Florence a "duchy," naming themselves as its dukes.

EXAMINING THE EVIDENCE: THE INFLUENCE OF LORENZO DE' MEDICI

The Medici family rose to prominence as bankers in the early 15th century, a time when Florence was becoming increasingly wealthy from trade and banking. The first member of the family to control the city was Cosimo, who skillfully manipulated the constitution and influenced elections. By the time his grandson Lorenzo (the Magnificent) came to power in 1469, he ruled in almost totalitarian fashion, despite the fact that Florence remained a republic in name.

Beyond his wealth and political power, Lorenzo was known as a lavish patron of the arts. Not only did he arrange commissions for many works of art, he also brought talented artists into his household, including the young Michelangelo Buonarotti. Michelangelo lived with Lorenzo and his family for several years, dining at the family table and participating in many family events. Although Lorenzo could be quite brutal in exercising political power, in many ways he represented the ideal Renaissance prince who truly loved the art, literature, and music that he supported with his money and influence. Lorenzo was an accomplished poet himself, writing mainly in his native Tuscan language.

- **Milan** – This northern city grew prosperous from armaments and textile manufacturing. It was ruled until 1447 by the Visconti family, who struggled but failed to control all of northern and central Italy when faced with resistance from Venice and Florence. When the last Visconti duke died without a male heir, the nobility proclaimed Milan to be a republic. In 1450 the despotic Sforza family overthrew the republican government with the support of Milanese nobles and ruled Milan until 1494, when France invaded Italy. The duke tolerated a council of 900 men drawn from the patrician class, but he generally ruled as he pleased. Milan was primarily a military state, and many of its leaders had little interest in supporting the arts.

- **The Papal States** – Just as rulers in the other city-states, the pope ruled the Papal States with great political authority. Of course, the pope was also a spiritual leader, elected for life by the cardinals, the highest bishops of the Church, who in turn were appointed by the pope. The pope's concern with politics was based on the efforts to restore papal authority, greatly undermined by the Great Schism of 1378-1417, when church members' loyalties were split between two popes – one in Rome and one in Avignon, France. For example, Pope Julius II came to be known as the "warrior pope" because he brought the Renaissance papacy to its peak of military and political strength. He gained enough support to drive the Venetians out of papal territory, and he later was instrumental in driving French invaders out of Italy. Popes enhanced their political power by increasing taxation, enlarging the papal army and navy, and extending papal diplomacy. They also sponsored church renovations, and were often great patrons of the arts.

- **Naples** – South of the Papal States was the kingdom of Naples, which controlled almost all of southern Italy and, at times, Sicily. The kingdom of Naples had long been sought by Aragon (later part of Spain) and France, with Aragon gaining control in 1435. Like rulers in other city-states, the most prominent ruler of Naples in the 15th century – Alfonso I – was a generous patron of the arts. However, in contrast to the northern states, Naples was dominated by powerful feudal lords – not merchants – who challenged the ruler's power. This infighting threatened royal power, leaving Naples vulnerable to attack from the Ottoman Turks, and eventually to French invasion. During the 16th century, Spain exercised its power to seize control of southern Italy from the French.

The major Italian city-states controlled the smaller ones, such as Siena, Mantua, and Ferrara, and competed among themselves for territory. They often formed shifting alliances that tended to control the rise in relative power of any one state. Even though they were fierce rivals, all the states realized they needed a fair amount of peace in order to conduct successful trade, so they negotiated with one another using techniques that became the forerunners of modern diplomacy. They had permanent embassies headed by resident ambassadors assigned with monitoring political and commercial ties.

New Intellectual Developments

By 1450 the economic, social, and political changes were spawning the cultural and intellectual developments that made the Renaissance so transformative. The intellectual and artistic creativity of northern Italy was more than a "rebirth," although it was characterized by a renewed interest in the ancient classical civilizations of the Mediterranean – Greece and Rome. **Humanism**, or the interest in the capabilities and accomplishments of individuals, grew from Greek culture, but during the Italian Renaissance, its emphasis extended also to challenging the authority of the Catholic Church, a change that was reflected through portrait painting, autobiography, and philosophies. Writers such as Petrarch and Boccaccio had revived interest in classical writing and secular subjects (such as love and pride) in opposition to the emphasis on theology and spiritual topics of the Middle Ages. Many new works were written in the vernacular (Italian) rather than the Latin that medieval monks and scholars had used for their works. Although religion remained important, it began to lose its role as the central focus of interest in many areas of life.

The roots of humanism may be traced to the late 13th century, when medieval scholars began to argue that education should be reformed to give more attention to the Latin classics and to help people lead more moral lives. One piece of the medieval educational curriculum, **rhetoric**, was concerned with the art of good speaking and writing. The Latin classics provided models for good writing, and they were readily available in Italy. Their study was promoted by the close relationship between the Italian language and Latin and by their frequent reference to the people and places of Italy. The Florentine **Leonardo Bruni** first gave the name *humanitas* ("humanity") to the learning of grammar, rhetoric, poetry, history, politics, and moral philosophy based on the Greek and Latin classics. The early humanists held by the rules of medieval **scholasticism**, or the attempt to reconcile the beliefs and values of Christianity with the logical reasoning of Greek philosophy, but by the 14th century, humanist writings had become far more secular, and reflected much broader interests. Unlike scholastics, humanists were less bound to church doctrine, and they were more inclined to go directly to original sources and draw their own conclusions, even if they contradicted church authorities. Even though they focused on the classics, humanists were more likely than medieval scholars to question the ancients, and they were fully aware that classical authors often disagreed with one another. Despite their breaks with the Catholic Church, humanists were still deeply religious, and so judged Greek and Roman paganism through Christian eyes. Italian humanists used Greek and Latin sources

THEMATIC LEARNING OBJECTIVE: OBJECTIVE KNOWLEDGE AND SUBJECTIVE VISIONS: RENAISSANCE SECULARISM

One important change that shaped the Renaissance as a new era distinct from the Middle Ages is the emphasis on secularism, or an interest in matters of the material world rather than the spiritual world. The secular writer was more interested in day-to-day activities and thoughts of human beings, and the secular sculptor was more likely to glorify the beauty of the human body. Renaissance secularism did not entirely desert its interest in religion, but often blended secular and religious themes. For example, Michelangelo carved his masterpiece "David" as a symbol of civic independence and resistance to oligarchical tyranny, two very secular topics. However, he chose the Biblical figure of David – the slayer of Goliath – to celebrate youthful physical perfection and to convey his civic message. In doing so, he blended the religious with the secular to create the piece of art that, more than almost any other, has come to embody the very spirit of the Renaissance.

extensively, so a mastery of the ancient languages was important for their study. Most believed Ancient Roman Latin writings to be much purer than medieval Latin writings, and some came to value the form of writing more than the content.

The "Father of Humanism"

The 14th century writer, Francesco Petrarca, better known as **Petrarch**, is often called the "Father of Humanism." He was a lawyer and cleric who turned from those professions to devote his life to writing poetry, letters, treatises, and other scholarly works. He wrote both in Latin and in Italian, and was instrumental in standardizing the Florentine **vernacular** (spoken tongue) as the modern Italian language. Two writers that he most admired – Cicero and St. Augustine – reflected a blending of secular and religious topics that shaped the later development of Renaissance thought. Petrarch admired the ancient writer Cicero for his common sense and love of political liberty, but he found in Cicero's writings a deep religious concern. He valued St. Augustine for his great religious vision, but he also saw in St. Augustine an active man, heavily engaged in the secular controversies of his time.

Petrarch was famous for his Italian verse, short sonnets well suited to the vernacular. He also wrote an epic poem in Latin that inspired his designation as "poet laureate," a revival of an ancient title that celebrated great poetry writing. In his famous dialogue with St. Augustine called *My Secret,* Petrarch discussed his search for a worthy moral life. He rejected the leaders of the Church as models because they were worldly and materialistic, and he concluded that he had to turn to the earliest Christians – the Church fathers – and the ancient Romans for good examples.

The Spread of Humanism

Humanism soon became very influential in Florence, aided by Petrarch's contemporary Giovanni Boccaccio, famous for a collection of short stories known as *The Decameron,* the first prose masterpiece written in Italian. Led by the chancellor of Florence, Coluccio Salutati, a group of humanists began to collect ancient manuscripts and form libraries where their collections of classical writings could be housed and accessed. The Florentines enhanced their knowledge of the Greek language by inviting Byzantine scholars to the west, starting in the late 14th century. As the movement spread to other city-states and other areas of Europe, western scholars translated more and more Greek works into Latin and Italian, including histories, tragedies, lyric poetry, mathematical treatises, and the dialogues of Plato.

The influence of humanists was enhanced after 1450 with the printing advances made by a German goldsmith and printer, **Johann Gutenberg** of Mainz. The Gutenberg Bible was first printed in 1454, and the craftsmanship that created it was widely admired and imitated across Europe. Although movable type had been invented earlier in China and Korea, Gutenberg's printing press made it practical for European humanists to work closely with printers to make their writings available to wider audiences. By 1500, at least 10 million printed copies of books were circulating around Europe, greatly increasing the number of people that had access not only to Bibles, but also to Renaissance ideas.

Humanism and Education

Humanism had a very important impact on education that soon took hold throughout Italy and eventually spread to other areas of Europe. Its impact was manifested in many ways. Medieval universities remained primarily places for professional training in theology, medicine, and law, but the preparation of young men for the universities or for life in general was changed profoundly by the Renaissance. The organized education of women did not come till much later, so Renaissance schools were attended almost exclusively by young males, who for the first time were separated by age groups or levels of accomplishment into separate classes. Latin and Greek were studied, with an emphasis on rhetoric, including the use of the Italian language. Once proficient in Latin and Greek, students read the ancient writings, including epics, lyrics, orations, histories, dialogues, and philosophy. This program of studies shaped education for generations to come, and these subjects are still referred to as "the humanities" in Western schools. Following Petrarch's example, young men were encouraged to take moral lessons from ancient writings that provided models of ideal human behavior and values. Children also learned that social duties are important, and that they should be mindful of their personal influence on others.

In keeping with these educational goals, polite habits came to be valued, and books of etiquette began to appear. The most famous was **Baldassare Castiglione's *The Courtier***, written in 1528. Castiglione explained that the educated man of the upper class should not only have a broad background in many academic subjects, but should also have spiritual and physical training. The courtly, ideal gentleman (the "courtier") should be familiar with dance, music, and the arts, and, above all, be an eloquent speaker and writer. *The Courtier* was widely read in the 16th and 17th centuries, and shaped the model of the European gentleman.

The Prince

Perhaps the most influential of all Renaissance humanist writings was a short political treatise called ***The Prince***, published by **Niccolò Machiavelli** in 1513. The subject is the use of political power by leaders, or "princes." As a humanist, he was quite interested in human nature, and his assumption that human beings are selfish and generally evil led him to conclude that a prince must manipulate people in order to reach his goals for the state. Though he was a republican at heart, Machiavelli saw that the strongest rulers were not in Italy, but instead in Aragon, France, and England. He admired these leaders because they knew how to exercise power and how to build strong states. He took the approach of analyzing what rulers actually did, not what they should do from a religious or moral point of view. What really happens, he said, is that effective rulers and governments act in their own political interest, and although such behavior might be bad, the self-interested ruler is more likely to be successful. This approach has often been seen as unduly cynical, but his famous treatise provided the first treatment of politics as a science, and it foreshadowed the coming of an age when politics was breaking from religion. Machiavelli's important assumption is that the building of states and political authority are goals in themselves that do not have to be justified by religion. He exhorted princes to adopt the ways of both the fox and the lion "because the lion cannot defend himself against snares and the fox cannot defend himself against wolves. Therefore, it is necessary to be a fox to discover the snares and a lion to terrify the wolves."

Politics

THEMATIC LEARNING OBJECTIVE: STATES AND OTHER INSTITUTIONS OF POWER:
THE PRINCE BY NICCOLO MACHIAVELLI

During the early 16th century, a time when Leonardo, Raphael, and Michelangelo were at their peak of creativity, the Italian city-states were attacked repeatedly by the French, Spanish, and Habsburg armies, and their very existence as independent states was threatened. In response to these threats, **Niccolo Machiavelli** wrote *The Prince,* a famous philosophical view of the ideal political leader, based on his view of ancient Roman rulers:

"Here the question arises; whether it is better to be loved than feared or feared than loved. The answer is that it would be desirable to be both but, since that is difficult, it is much safer to be feared than to be loved, if one must choose. For on men in general this observation may be made: they are ungrateful, fickle, and deceitful, eager to avoid dangers, and avid for gain, and while you are useful to them they are all with you, offering you their blood, their property, their lives, and their sons so long as danger is remote...but when it approaches they turn on you. Any prince, trusting only in their words and having no other preparations made, will fall to his ruin... Men have less hesitation in offending a man who is loved than one who is feared, for love is held by a bond of obligation which, as men are wicked, is broken whenever personal advantage suggests it, but fear is accompanied by the dread of punishment which never relaxes."

Reference: The Prince (1513) Niccolo Machiavelli, trans. and ed. by Thomas G. Bergin (New York: Appleton-Century-Crofts, 1947), p. 48.

Achievements in Art and Architecture

By the 14th century, northern Italy had many urban areas, while the rest of Europe was still mostly rural. Urbanization was a function of the region's growing trade and the resulting wealth of merchants, who came to dominate politics and society as well as business. The powerful, independent city-states ran their own affairs, each collecting taxes and supporting an army. Wealthy merchants competed with one another for economic and political power, and by the 15th century, they also were **patrons,** or supporters of the arts. Patrons found talented artists, often when they were young, and bankrolled their work, allowing them the time to spend on artistic endeavors. Three famous examples of patron-supported artists were **Leonardo da Vinci**, **Michelangelo**, and **Raphael**, all born in the mid-to-late 1400s. They, and countless other artists and writers, were sponsored by rich merchant families, including the powerful **Medici** family of Florence. The Catholic Church also sponsored Renaissance endeavors, and some of the most famous patrons were the popes in Rome. Many artists were interested in science, philosophy, and politics, giving rise to the concept of the **"Renaissance Man,"** or the person – often genius – who knows a great deal about many things. For example, Leonardo painted and sculpted, but he also made numerous drawings of inventions that demonstrate an extensive knowledge of mathematics and science, as well as a vivid imagination.

Renaissance art and architecture reflected the growing influence of humanism, especially in its preoccupation with all things human. The center of Renaissance art was first in Florence, partly because of the patronage of the Medici and other wealthy families, but also because the greatest painters of the late 1200s and 1300s – Cimabue and Giotto – were identified with Florence. The city also had a tradition of excellence in artisan designs of silk and gold objects, and many artists began their careers as apprentices to goldsmiths, in whose workshops they learned creative techniques that they applied to their painting, sculpture, and architecture.

From Artisan to Artist

The artist was a new social type in the Renaissance. Artisans, or craftsmen, populated medieval towns and cities, and they made their living by skillfully creating useful objects for customers. Many were concerned with creating beautiful objects. In contrast, artists were seen as people with innate talents who produced works of art according to their imagination rather than following the instructions of customers. In truth, most of the major Renaissance artists were supported by wealthy patrons, and they often had to follow restrictions imposed by those that commissioned their work. However, famous artists developed followings, and they headed workshops where they trained apprentices and negotiated contracts with clients. Of course, many of their works have lived through the ages, and their magnificent accomplishments made them the most famous men of the era. Artists worked as painters, sculptors, and architects, with the most talented often being masters in more than one area.

- **Sculpture** – Artists of the Middle Ages did produce sculpture for cathedrals, but sculpture emerged as an independent art during the Italian Renaissance. Like the humanist writers, sculptors drew their inspiration from the Greek and Roman tradition, and they produced realistic statues of human beings, often with beautiful nude bodies that clearly broke from the work and style of medieval artists. Like the ancients, Renaissance sculptors produced portrait busts of great leaders and eminent contemporaries, and they also created characters from Greco-Roman history and mythology.

- **Painting** – Painting was less influenced by Greco-Roman times than sculpture was, since few paintings had survived through time. The invention of painting in oils redefined the Renaissance era, and meant that the paintings have been better preserved over time. Renaissance art was distinguished from that of earlier eras by its use of visual **perspective**, or the ability to create an illusory three-dimensional space on a two dimensional surface. Its humanist concern with reality contrasts with art from medieval times, as well as with Persian, Chinese, and Byzantine art. All those traditions were much more concerned with conveying symbolism than reality, but Renaissance art ordered the arrangement of painted objects from one viewpoint. This control of space was an assertion of human control over space, and the new technique shaped the later development of western art. Renaissance painters showed people with distinctive attitudes and individual personalities reflected in their postures and faces, often with a background of landscape or scenery. A part of the distinctive Renaissance style was that the real world was caught and put in a painting.

- **Architecture** – Renaissance architects embodied the humanist ideals of uniting artistic creativity and scientific knowledge, and they made wide use of classical styles, such as Greek columns and Roman arches. One of the most accomplished architects was **Filippo Brunelleschi**, whose most famous creation was the dome (Duomo) of the central Florentine cathedral, Santa Maria del Fiore. The dome was inspired by the ancient Pantheon in Rome, but it was larger than its model, and it was visible for miles around – a symbol of Renaissance man's ingenuity and scientific

Renaissance Architecture in Florence. In this view of modern-day Florence, Italy, Renaissance architecture still dominates the skyline. The large dome near the center is the Duomo, or the Dome of the Cathedral, Santa Maria del Fiore, that was completed in the mid-15th century.

knowledge. Technically Brunelleschi employed a system that suspended an interior shell from the exterior structure that originated in Roman technology. He invented all kinds of machines and devices to erect the dome, and the building process intrigued the city fathers and ordinary citizens alike. **Leon Battista Alberti** wrote a theory of architecture that summed up the Renaissance ideal of perfection: the emulation of perfect forms – the square and the circle – and the application of the rules of harmony that govern music. According to Alberti, architectural beauty is the result of the correct observation and application of rules of proportion that create harmony and order.

Three famous "Renaissance Men"

These three famous artists lived and worked during the years of the high Renaissance from the mid-15th to mid-16th century:

- **Leonardo da Vinci** – More than any other person in the period, Leonardo exemplified the multi-talented "Renaissance Man." He was one of the greatest artists of all time, and he was also a military engineer in Milan and France. Leonardo was an avid scientist who studied botany and dissected corpses to learn anatomy. His drawings reflect the imagination to foresee airplanes and submarines. He constantly moved from one activity to another, but managed to focus on one project long enough to create the

Santa Maria Novella in Florence. This church was first constructed in the mid-13th century in the medieval Gothic style, but the façade shown in the photograph is the work of Leon Battista Alberti in the 15th century. It reflects Alberti's emphasis on the "perfect forms" of circles and squares – the Renaissance ideal for architecture.

Mona Lisa. This famous work reflects the humanist interest in individual facial expressions and in realistic landscapes as backgrounds.

- **Michelangelo** – Like Leonardo, Michelangelo excelled in a variety of arts. His eighteen-foot sculpture *David* stood for many years in the great square of Florence, and it has been one of the most popular sculptures in the world. Four different popes commissioned works by Michelangelo, the most famous of which are the frescoes for the Sistine Chapel. His work there is a stunningly complex example of the humanist tradition, which combines religious themes with classical figures, a masterpiece that took four years for him to complete.

- **Raphael** – Unlike Leonardo and Michelangelo, Raphael lived only a short while, but he, like them, was much loved by his contemporaries. He is famous for his madonnas, but his best known work is *The School of Athens*, a grand fresco that portrays a vast array of great philosophers and scientists from antiquity. At the center are Plato and Aristotle, and included in the surrounding figures are Raphael's famous contemporaries Leonardo and Michelangelo. The painting is one of the most perfect examples of Renaissance technique.

The cultural achievements of these men and many others were made possible by the wealth created by commerce, but they in turn changed the nature of business and politics because humanistic values that emphasized individual capabilities and accomplishments supported an entrepreneurial spirit. Partly because of the emphasis on individual endeavors, Renaissance merchants improved their banking techniques and became more openly competitive and profit-seeking. City-state leaders, who were also the patrons of the arts, experimented with new ways to govern. Since their political positions were not hereditary or determined by claims to divinity, political power came to be based on individual efforts to promote the city's well-being and cultural accomplishments. Despite the increasing emphasis on the secular, they also competed to see who could build the most glorious churches. The construction of religious buildings inspired experimentation with architecture that strayed from the medieval Gothic model to focus on grand and architecturally challenging domes. The churches were filled with sculpture and paintings of the best artists, further stimulating cultural creativity. The original interest in classical models remained, but the innovations of the Renaissance era resonated in culture, religion, politics, science, literature, and the economy.

THE NORTHERN RENAISSANCE

Wealth through trade eventually reached other parts of Europe, but its growth was much slower than it was among the Italian city-states. During the 14th and 15th century, northern Europe had few large cities, with most people living either in towns or rural areas. The feudal system was still in place, and Roman traditions and physical remnants were not as numerous as they were in Italy. However, as trade trickled north and west, humanism also came to influence literature, art, and philosophy in the north. In Italy, cultural life centered on vibrant trade cities; in northern Europe, it was dominated by the courts of kings and princes. By the 16th century, northern universities became centers of humanistic study, gradually taking over the role royal and noble households had played earlier in educating the young. Meanwhile, Spain, Portugal, and the Netherlands were busy creating new world trade patterns across the Atlantic Ocean and by the end of the century, Britain and France had joined them. Just as in Italy, the confluence of economic, technological, social, political, and cultural change transformed life all over the continent by 1650.

Northern Humanism

In the late 15th century, Italian Renaissance thought and ideals were spreading to the Low Countries, France, the Holy Roman Empire, and England, as students from those areas traveled to Italy to experience the "new learning." The invention of a printing press with movable type also meant that books were more readily accessible in many areas of the continent. By 1500, humanism was very influential in northern Europe. In general, northern humanists differed from the Italian variety by their focus on the ancient texts of the Christian religion rather than on the writings of Roman and Greek antiquity. Like the Italian humanists, they studied Latin and Greek, but they applied their knowledge to editing the Bible and reading the writings of the Church Fathers. As a result, they directed the attention of learned men to the early history of Christianity rather than to ancient Greek and Roman history. Whereas secular and pagan themes received more attention in Italy, the northern Renaissance had a distinctly religious character.

Two of the best known northern humanists were Dutch scholar **Desiderius Erasmus** and Englishman **Thomas More**. Both men did most of their writing during the early 16th century.

Erasmus began his writing career with dialogues that he prepared for his students. These dialogues were intended to teach them how to speak and live well, and to exhibit good manners worthy of the gentlemen he wanted them to become. He published a collection of dialogues under the title *Colloquies*, which also included satires on popular religious superstitions. He also collected ancient and contemporary proverbs in a work he called *Adages,* and many of his sayings became quite famous. For example, he urged his readers to "leave no stone unturned," and warned them "where there is smoke, there is fire." More than any other northern humanist, he united the classical ideals of humanity and civic virtue with the Christian virtues of love and piety. He edited the works of the Church Fathers and made a Greek edition of the New Testament, and in doing so, he got into some trouble with church authorities. He was criticized for changing the Vulgate, the

THEMATIC LEARNING OBJECTIVE: OBJECTIVE KNOWLEDGE AND SUBJECTIVE VISIONS: NORTHERN HUMANISTS

Christian humanists did not entirely reject the ancient classical civilizations, but they believed that the best elements of classical and Christian cultures should be combined. As such, they stressed the use of reason, and they too were impatient with scholasticism, which refused to question the dogma of the Church. Yet they also emphasized the Christian virtues of love, faith, and hope, and they were profoundly interested in the development of an ethical way of life.

Bible that the Church had accepted for over a thousand years, and many bishops and priests were unhappy with his anticlerical satires. At one point, most of his works were placed on the *Index of Forbidden Books*.

Thomas More and Erasmus were good friends, and Erasmus dedicated *The Praise of Folly* – one of his most famous works – to More. In his early life, More lived in a monastery, but eventually married and practiced law. He entered government service under Henry VIII, but he was deeply interested in combining the classics with Christian values. His most famous work was *Utopia,* which described an ideal community located somewhere off the mainland of the New World. His vision contradicted the norms of contemporary society, and it rivaled the plays of Shakespeare as a most-read 16th century work. In More's utopia (a pun on "nowhere"), profits from business and property were held by all members of the community, and there was absolute equality. He based his society on a view of human nature that was strikingly different from others of his day. Instead of seeing humans as evil or self-interested by nature (as Machiavelli did), he believed that society's institutions (such as private property) were responsible for war and corruption. According to More, reform of social institutions that mold human values and actions is the key to a better society.

ORIGINAL DOCUMENTS:
UTOPIA BY THOMAS MORE

The excerpt below from Thomas More's *Utopia* reflects his view of a perfect society that treats its citizens as equals and encourages humanist values.

"The chief, and almost the only business of the [political leaders], is to take care that no man may live idle, but that every one may follow his trade diligently: yet they do not wear themselves out with perpetual toil, from morning to night, as if they were beasts of burden, which, as it is indeed a heavy slavery…but they dividing the day and night into twenty-four hours, appoint six of these for work; three of which are before dinner, and three after. They then sup, and at eight o'clock, counting from noon, go to bed and sleep eight hours. The rest of their time besides that taken up in work, eating and sleeping, is left to every man's discretion; yet they are not to abuse that interval to luxury and idleness, but must employ it in some proper exercise according to their various inclinations, which is for the most part reading. It is ordinary to have public lectures every morning before daybreak; at which none are obliged to appear but those who are marked out for literature; yet a great many, both men and women of all ranks, go to hear lectures of one sort of other, according to their inclinations. But if others, that are not made for contemplation, choose rather to employ themselves at that time in their trades, as many of them do, they are not hindered, but are rather commended, as men that take care to serve their country."

Reference: Thomas More, *Utopia* (New York: Penguin Classics), 1965.

Northern Artists

Most leading Renaissance artists were Italian, but northern artists also made significant contributions. **Jan Van Eyck**, a 15th century Dutchman, was one of the early proponents of oil painting on wood or canvas. His most famous painting, *The Arnolfini Wedding,* combined earthiness with piety in its portrayal of a bride whose dress was folded to imply pregnancy, but the painter carefully surrounded the couple with many religious symbols important to their marriage. Another leading northern artist was **Albrecht Dürer**, a German who blended the northern and southern styles. He made two trips to Venice, where he studied the southern styles, but his work clearly reflected that attention to small details and religious emotion characteristic of the northern style. Dürer returned to Germany to live simply in his home city of Nuremberg, where he produced both copper engravings and woodcuts. One of his most famous works was a book of illustrations of the biblical *Apocalypse* (the revelation of God's will), with the text of the Bible on one side and full-page woodcuts on the other.

Unlike the visual arts, which clearly centered in Italy, Renaissance music developed largely from innovations in the Low Countries. The choirmasters of many great cathedrals employed professional singers who developed complex vocal harmonies that needed no instrumental accompaniment. Instruments too were developed in new ways, with experimentation both in secular and religious music. Many modern instruments – including the violin, lute, and keyboard instruments – evolved to allow composers and musicians to explore new musical ideas. Modern woodwind and brass instruments like the bassoon and the trombone also appeared. These new music styles spread from the northern Europe to the south, instead of the other way around.

RENAISSANCE EUROPE AND NATION-BUILDING

While the Italian city-states flourished economically but remained politically divided, states in other parts of Europe enlarged under centralizing political power during the late 15th and early 16th centuries. The rulers of England, France, and Spain were especially successful in establishing centralized royal power, and are sometimes called the "**new monarchs**". They emphasized royal majesty and authority over their subjects, and they suppressed opposition and rebellion, especially from nobility that might challenge their authority. The boundaries that they set became the forerunners of later European nations that based their strength on a common identity as a people. However, in this transitional time period, these "new monarchs" continued the practices of strong rulers during the Middle Ages, such as reliance on middle-class civil servants, the building of large armies, and protection of townspeople in return for tax payments.

France

In France **Louis XI** of the Valois family did a great deal to centralize the king's power during his reign from 1461 to 1483. The first French king had been crowned five centuries before, but the early monarchs only had control of the lands around Paris. The royal domain steadily expanded through a combination of inheritance, marriage, war, conquest, and diplomacy. France had won the Hundred Years' War with England (see page 29) in the early 15th century, but it emerged commercially and agriculturally weak and very much under the shadow of the powerful Burgundian dynasty. The **Burgundians** were part of the French royal house, but they acted as heads of an independent kingdom by rapidly acquiring land, primarily in the Netherlands, building their own armies, and commanding a great deal of loyalty from their subjects. When the Burgundian duke Charles the Bold died without an heir in 1477, Louis XI took advantage of the temporary weakness by seizing large pieces of Burgundian territory. France also gained land when Louis inherited Anjou lands in the south, and by the end of the 15th century, France had doubled its territory to the size and shape that were close to its modern-day boundaries.

Louis XI accomplished the centralization of French power by building a royal army, and by acquiring great power to raise taxation without parliamentary consent. The French monarchy also enlarged its powers over the clergy after Francis I reached an agreement with Pope Leo X in 1516 that seriously limited the ability of the Church to manage its own administrative affairs within French borders. Thereafter, the French king appointed French bishops and abbots, even though the pope continued to receive money income from the French clergy.

Spain

In the mid-15th century, the Iberian Peninsula was divided into many distinct kingdoms, with the kingdoms of Castile and Aragon dominating the weaker Navarre, Portugal, and Granada. All were Christian, with the important exception of Granada, which had been a Muslim stronghold for many years. During the early Middle Ages, Christians, Jews, and Muslims had generally lived side by side in relative peace, but as Muslim strength began to weaken by the 11th century, the Christian kingdoms launched offensives against the Muslims that carried on intermittently in a movement called the *Reconquista*, or the "Reconquest." It was in this atmosphere that **Isabella**, future queen of Castile, in 1469 married **Ferdinand**, future king of Sicily and heir to the throne of Aragon. The nobles of Castile opposed the marriage because it would strengthen royal power at their expense, but Isabella and Ferdinand emerged victorious after a ten-year civil war. When they assumed the thrones of Castile and Aragon in 1474 they created a new political state: the Kingdom of Spain.

To reinforce their authority over the fragmented peninsula, Ferdinand and Isabella sharply reduced the power of the great nobles by filling the political bureaucracy – including the royal council – with *hidalgos,* lesser aristocrats who owed their positions to the throne. They managed to take over the nobles' military orders and to create centralized control over their armies. As the two monarchs' power increased, their ability to collect taxes improved, and Spain grew into a prosperous kingdom by the end of the 16th century.

The most important actions that Ferdinand and Isabella took to unify Spain were to gain control over the Catholic Church and then to extend Christian influence over the entire peninsula. After the civil wars in Castile ended in 1479, the king and queen took up the cause of the *Reconquista* to drive the Muslims from southern Castile. This effort not only kept the nobility busy with war, but it also stimulated the country's religious fervor, which in turn inspired loyalty and enthusiasm for the monarchs. With their growing power, the king and queen gained from the pope the right to appoint bishops and abbots, as well as the right to establish their own **Inquisition**, a tribunal originally set up to monitor the sincerity of former

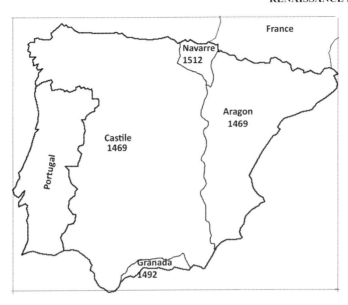

The Iberian Peninsula during the Late 15th Century. Before 1469, the Iberian Peninsula was fragmented into many kingdoms, with the strongest ones illustrated on the map above. Castile and Aragon were united when Isabella of Castile married Ferdinand of Aragon, even though the two remained separate at first. Their union was cemented by the defeat of Muslim-dominated Granada in 1492 and of Navarre in 1512.

Muslims and Jews who had converted, often by force, to Christianity. Even after the last Muslim stronghold in Granada fell in 1492, the campaign for Christian uniformity did not stop. Later that year, all Jews were expelled from Spain, with about 150,000 people given four months to leave. In 1502, all Muslims who had not accepted Christianity were also expelled from the country, and the persecution of all non-Christians as well as those judged to be **heretics** (false believers), fostered a religious unity that enhanced the political centralization that Ferdinand and Isabella had achieved.

England

After England's defeat by France in the Hundred Years' War, turmoil continued as families of the nobility fought the **Wars of the Roses** from 1455 to 1485. Under Henry VI, a weak king of the Lancastrian wing of the royal family, the great lords fought among themselves, and when Richard of York rebelled, his son crowned himself as King Edward IV in 1461. The House of Lancaster and the House of York feuded over the throne for more than twenty years, until finally a compromise was reached when a new royal house – the **Tudors** – emerged in 1485 by intermarriage between the two warring families. Henry Tudor ruled as Henry VII, the first of the new Tudor dynasty that would dominate England throughout the 16th century. He succeeded in taming the English nobility through the creation of the Court of Star Chamber, a court that allowed Henry to use English law to further his own ends. He confiscated noble lands and fortunes so successfully that he had enough resources to rule England without calling on Parliament for financial support. As a result, power centralized in the monarchy and passed to his famous descendents, Henry VIII and Elizabeth I.

The Decentralized States

While France, Spain, and England centralized their power during the 15th and 16th centuries, the Italian city-states and the Holy Roman Empire remained highly decentralized. In Germany, princes of territories and independent cities resisted every effort to consolidate under one rule, and by the late 15th century Germany was divided into about 300 autonomous political entities. The Holy Roman Empire continued to exist in name, with the emperor elected by a seven-member electoral college of princes and bishops, and the emperor's powers were often renegotiated with the seven electors. The emperor's demands were balanced against the needs of the princes, and so the empire developed little central control. A national assembly called the **Reichstag** composed of the electors, other princes, and representatives of the free cities was created to control feuding. The Reichstag managed to launch a court of justice to enforce internal peace and a council to coordinate executive policy. However, no true national unity emerged, and by the 17th century, the territorial princes were virtually sovereign rulers of their lands.

As we have seen, Italy was a land of autonomous city-states during the 15th and 16th centuries. Even though their political fragmentation did not prevent them from gaining economic wealth and cultural sophistication, it did compromise their safety in the face of foreign invasion. During the last half of the 15th century, the city-states protected themselves through a strong political alliance constructed by the **Treaty of Lodi.** The terms of the treaty brought Milan, Naples, and Florence into an alliance that stood for decades against Venice and the Papal States. However, at the end of the century, Milan and Naples began to feud, and the resulting instability left them vulnerable to their newly centralizing neighbor to the north – France. Charles VIII, the son of Louis XI, crossed the Alps and marched his armies from Milan in the north to Naples in the south. Florence, Rome, and Naples bowed to his ambitions, but Pope Leo X called on Spain and the Holy Roman Empire to expel the French from Italy. As a result, Italy became a battleground among the various powers, with the conflict between the French Valois family and the Habsburgs of the Holy Roman Empire being particularly fierce. The Italian city-states paid dearly for their lack of unity, and outside invaders disrupted the peninsula for centuries. Italy would not be unified until 1870.

Despite the political turmoil that the Italian city-states fell into by the 16th century, their many achievements had already made a lasting impact on Europe. The Renaissance that they sponsored began a transformation of Europe that continued long after the economic and cultural heydays of Florence, Venice, and Milan had passed. One of the most important aspects of that transformation was religious, as the all-encompassing influence of the Catholic Church was seriously challenged by the Protestant Reformation.

CONCEPTS AND IDENTIFICATIONS

Alberti, Leon Battista
Brunelleschi, Filippo
Bruni, Leonardo
Burgundians
Castiglione, Baldassare
city-states
The Courtier
David
doge
Dürer, Albrecht
Erasmus, Desiderius
Ferdinand and Isabella
Gutenberg, Johann
heretics
humanism
Inquisition
Italian Renaissance
Louis XI
Machiavelli, Niccolò
Medici, Cosimo de'
Medici family
Medici, Lorenzo de'
Mona Lisa
More, Thomas
"new monarchs"
oligarchies
Papal States
patriarchs, patriarchies
perspective
Petrarch
popolo grasso
The Prince
principalities
Raphael
Reconquista
Reichstag
Renaissance
"Renaissance Man"
republics

rhetoric
The School of Athens
scholasticism
secularism
Treaty of Lodi
Tudors
Utopia
Van Eyck, Jan
Vasari, Giorgio
vernacular
Vinci, Leonardo da
War of the Roses

CHAPTER 4:
RELIGIOUS REFORMATION

The changes in European attitudes that inspired the Renaissance also influenced a powerful 16th century religious movement that contributed greatly to the transformation of Europe in early modern times. During the Middle Ages the Catholic Church had been one of the most important organizing institutions of society, so the revolt against the church impacted far more than the religious lives of Europeans. Because the church had so much political, economic, and social power, the voices that led the protests resonated throughout the continent and stimulated changes that eventually spread to many other areas of the world. In turn, the Catholic Church reacted to the Protestant ("protester") threat with reforms that stabilized its influence in Europe, and allowed it to continue to grow by converting many people in faraway Asia and America to its religion.

The Protestant reformers embraced many Renaissance values, including humanism and individualism. Their movement never would have started without independent actions of individuals who were confident in the ability of human beings to shape their own destinies. Like the Italian humanists, the Protestant reformers studied ancient languages and went directly to original sources instead of relying on established church dogma. However, Protestantism was directly inspired by the northern humanists – like Erasmus – who were more interested in studying Hebrew and Greek Scriptures than the secular works of the ancient civilizations. Whereas classical Greeks and Romans often glorified human nature, Protestants were more impressed by the human potential to do evil. Indeed the new religion splintered into many different denominations partly because leading spokesmen disagreed about just how sinfully inclined people really are by nature. As a result, the followers of the German priest Martin Luther became Lutherans, while those of John Calvin called themselves Calvinists, and King Henry VIII established the Anglican Church in England. Even though their movement is known as the **"Protestant Reformation"**, it did far more than "reform" the Catholic Church; it marked a major division in Christendom, just as profound as the earlier split between Roman Catholicism and Eastern Orthodoxy (pp. 25-26).

SEEDS OF REVOLT

During the late Middle Ages, the power and prestige of the Catholic Church were still intact, but church officials were beginning to run into some problems that eventually developed into full-fledged revolt. Challenges to the authority of the church came from many people, including kings and princes, as well as those who believed that the church had strayed from the original principles of Christianity.

One problem had to do with the growing power of kings and princes. The political power of the Catholic Church was considerable, and as long as feudalistic obliga-tions kept the political power of kings and princes in check, church officials could govern through canon law, including excommunication and the interdict. Howev-er, as the monarchies of France, England, and Spain centralized their powers, they often came into conflict with church officials, including the pope. In the Italian city-states and the Holy Roman Empire, the very complexity of political authority often limited the direct authority of the pope, and the princes relied on their own bureaucracies and armies to allow them the freedom to rule their domains as they pleased. In Germany, where the Protestant Reformation began, the pope was a long way away, and slow transportation and communications made it difficult for the pope to discipline errant princes.

The Great Schism

Papal clashes with kings and princes were increasingly common during the late Middle Ages, but one conflict that particularly weakened the authority of the church began between King Philip IV of France and Pope Boniface VIII in 1296. When Philip demanded that the French clergy pay taxes to help finance his war against England, Boniface responded with a papal bull (proclamation) that pro-hibited taxation of the clergy without the pope's approval. The conflict intensified when Boniface issued another bull – *Unam Sanctam* – in 1302 that stated that resistance to the will of the pope was resistance to the will of God. Enraged, Philip sent agents to Italy to take the pope prisoner, although he soon set him free. After the death of the pope in 1303, Philip used his political clout to arrange for the ap-pointment of a more compliant pope, Clement V, who agreed to live in Avignon, France, in a new papal enclave that the French king could keep under his watchful eye.

During the **"Avignon Papacy"** from 1303 to 1378, the pope remained under the influence of the king of France. However, in 1377 Pope Gregory XI decided to move back to Rome, partly to exert papal authority in Rome, where years with-out a pope in residence had led to chaos. When Gregory died the next year, the cardinals elected an Italian pope, Urban VI, in hopes of quelling the Roman mob. Offended that the new pope was not French, the French cardinals refused to accept Urban's election, but instead elected a Frenchman as pope, who became Clement VII. Clement took up residence in Avignon, beginning the **Great Schism,** which

ORIGINAL DOCUMENTS:
UNAM SANCTAM

The papal bull *Unam Sanctam,* issued by Pope Boniface VIII in 1302 so angered Philip IV of France that he sent agents to Rome to imprison the pope. Below is a quote from the bull that heightened the growing tension between secular and religious power.

"We are taught by the words of the Gospel that in this church and in power there are two swords, a spiritual one and a temporal one...Certainly anyone who denies that the temporal sword is in the power of Peter [the disciple of Jesus] has not paid heed to the words of the Lord when he said, 'Put up thy sword into its sheath' (Matthew 26:52). Both then are in the power of the church, the material sword and the spiritual. But the one is exercised for the church, the one by the hand of the priest, the other by the hand of kings and soldiers, though at the will and suffrance of the priest. One sword ought to be under the other and the temporal authority subject to the spiritual power. For, while the apostle says, 'There is no power but from God and those that are ordained of God' (Romans 13:1), they would not be ordained unless one sword was under the other and, being inferior, was led by the other to the highest things."

Reference: Brian Tierney, *The Crisis of Church and State 1050-1300* (Toronto: The University of Toronto), 1980, pp. 188-189.

lasted from 1378 to 1417 – a time when two men claimed the papacy – one in Rome and one in Avignon. Each pope sought to win the allegiance of rulers in order to outdo the other one, with France, Castile, Navarre, and Scotland supporting the Avignon pope, and most of the Italian states, Portugal, the Holy Roman Empire, and England supporting the Roman pope. To add to the competition, church officials gathered at the Council of Pisa in 1409, and in order to resolve the conflict, elected yet a third pope. Neither the Avignon pope nor the Roman pope bowed to the pressure, but instead intensified their efforts to gain political supporters. By the time the situation was finally resolved in 1417 – with the pope taking up residence in Rome – secular rulers had forced the popes to make agreements that steadily eroded the authority of the church. For many devout Catholics, the Great Schism cast serious doubt on the authority of the pope, and opened the way for criticisms of the church in other areas as well.

Church Practices

By the late Middle Ages, the church had grown quite wealthy and controlled vast amounts of property across Europe. Many critics believed that the pope and other church officials had become much too concerned with promoting their financial welfare and no longer adhered to original Christian values that emphasized spiritual well-being. By the early 16th century, one of the church's most controversial practices was the sale of **indulgences**, or remission of punishment for sins after the sinner confessed and received absolution. Under Catholic teaching, every sin must be purified either here on earth or after death in a state called purgatory. The practice of selling indulgences began during the Crusades as a way to raise money for churches and hospitals. Originally, the belief was not that God's forgiveness could be purchased, but just that a soul's suffering in purgatory could be reduced. Eventually, though, many people came to believe that purchasing indulgences rather than real repentance assured immediate entry to heaven for oneself or one's relatives.

Another clerical practice that came under criticism was the sale of church offices. By the late 15th century, popes were literally putting high posts up for purchase, and those that benefitted were usually Italian clerics and nobility. Some prominent families bought income-generating positions for their children, making them wealthy while doing very little work for the church. Many **cardinal**s – the highest Catholic officials other than the pope – accumulated great wealth from lands they oversaw (called sees) but rarely visited. Many priests were resented for charging exorbitant fees for burial of the dead, and for paying no taxes. Other priests awarded posts to relatives or friends, who shared the financial benefits of being part of the clergy.

Besides financial abuses, many people criticized the clergy for moral laxity. Since the 4th century, church law had required that priests be absolutely celibate. That requirement had always been difficult to enforce, but by the 15th century, many priests were blatantly ignoring it. For example, in some areas, many priests kept mistresses, and some popes of the late 15th and early 16th century fathered children. Other criticisms included clerical drunkenness, gambling, and extravagant clothing. It is impossible to know how widespread these abuses were, but all were in direct conflict with the church's rules and moral standards.

The call for church reform came from many people. Europeans in the early 16th century were deeply loyal to the Roman Catholic Church. Villagers celebrated saints, and those that could afford it made pilgrimages to the great shrines. The wealthy often bequeathed large parts of their fortunes to the church. Some popes and bishops expressed support for reform. For example, Pope Julius II summoned a council of church officials to meet in Rome from 1512 to 1517. Even though they recommended elimination of corruption and significant doctrinal reforms, many abuses remained widespread. Little progress had been made toward these goals by 1517, when a young priest from Wittenberg, Germany, began to cause trouble for the Catholic Church.

MARTIN LUTHER AND THE BEGINNINGS OF PROTESTANTISM

According to his own words, **Martin Luther** – one of the first of the Protestant reformers – was called to religious work by a frightening thunderstorm that he survived as a young man. Amidst the thunder and lightning, he called on St. Anne, the mother of the Virgin Mary, to protect him, and in return for his safety, he promised to enter God's work as a monk. He kept his promise, even though it was his father's strong wish that he become a lawyer. In the monastery Luther found himself confused by his own sinfulness, and he did everything he could to discipline himself so as to earn worthiness in the sight of God. In 1508, he was assigned to the faculty of a new university in Wittenberg, the capital of Saxony in the northern part of the Holy Roman Empire. There he spent his days pursuing his scholarly interests, especially applying them to the study of the Bible. While preparing his university lectures, he had the "**experience in the tower**", which helped him to understand how he, a mortal and sinful man, could become righteous in God's eyes. Luther's insight became the basis of his new faith: God bestows righteousness through a gift of grace to those who have religious faith.

Luther's understanding of Christianity led him to question many practices of the Roman Catholic Church, even though he was a part of the clergy himself. Most famously, he became outraged by the behavior of **Johann Tetzel**, a Dominican friar who came to Saxony to sell indulgences at the request of Albrecht of Brandenburg, the archbishop of Mainz. The proceeds were to go toward the cost of constructing St. Peter's Basilica in Rome and to cover the fees that the archbishop had paid to obtain his high position. In 1517, Luther composed his *95 Theses* that questioned the sale of indulgences and the purchase of Church offices. He posted this collection of bold challenges to the church door – the usual place where people went to get the latest news – where they quickly became a catalyst for unleashing pent-up resentments and frustrations among the townspeople.

Luther's first followers were young Christian humanists and clerics, many from middle-class backgrounds with university educations. None were influential church officials, but they spread enthusiasm for Luther's protests among merchants, artisans, and literate urban lay people in northern Germany. At first Luther saw himself as a loyal clergyman, but in 1520, he broke with church teachings even further when he questioned the many rules concerning "good works" for Christians. In keeping with his earlier beliefs, he wrote in *Freedom of a Christian,* that salvation does not come from good works but from personal faith in a

THEMATIC LEARNING OBJECTIVE:
OBJECTIVE KNOWLEDGE AND SUBJECTIVE VISIONS:
JUSTIFICATION BY FAITH ALONE

Martin Luther was a prolific, influential writer who later in life described his transformational "experience in the tower" that helped him to understand the righteousness of a merciful God:

"At last, by the mercy of God, meditating day and night, I gave heed to the context of the words, namely, 'In [the gospel] the righteousness of God is revealed, as it is written, He who through faith is righteous shall live' [Romans 1:17]. There I began to understand that the righteousness of God is that by which the righteous lives by a gift of God, namely by faith. And this is the meaning: the righteousness of God is revealed by the gospel, namely the passive righteousness with which merciful God justifies us by faith, as it is written, 'He who through faith is righteous shall live.' Here I felt that I was altogether born again and had entered paradise itself through open gates. There a totally other face of the entire Scripture showed itself to me...I also found in other terms an analogy, as, the work of God, that is, what God does in us, the power of God, with which he makes us strong, the wisdom of God, with which he makes us wise, the strength of God, the salvation of God, the glory of God."

Reference: Preface to the Complete Edition of Luther's Latin Writings (1545), in *Luther's Works,* Vol.3\\4, ed. by Lewis W. Spitz (Philadelphia: Muhlenberg Press, 1960) pp. 336, 337.

merciful God. He urged believers to study true gospel teachings – found primarily in the Bible – and to distinguish those teachings from later church doctrines. He suggested that each person with faith has a personal relationship with God that should not be intercepted by a professional caste of clerics. Although Luther wrote in Latin, *Freedom of a Christian* was translated into German, and with the help of the newly invented printing press, was widely circulated throughout the region. The principles he supported became famous phrases that inspired dissent: "by faith alone," "by Scripture alone," and "**the priesthood of all believers**". Luther continued writing treatises that criticized church practices, and he called on German princes to assert the right to control their own lands without constraints by the church.

Even as Luther's writings became more radical, the church first reacted to what Pope Leo X called the "Luther Affair" as a matter of clerical discipline. Luther was asked to keep quiet, but his words had already spread throughout the Holy Roman Empire, where they not only inspired religious rebellion, but political resistance as well. In one angry reaction to church criticism, Luther suggested that the pope be driven from his position by force. In reply, the pope issued a decree threatening Luther with excommunication unless he took back his words. Instead, Luther publicly threw the pope's decree into a bonfire. In 1521, Luther went before the newly elected Holy Roman Emperor **Charles V**, a devout Catholic who questioned him at the **Diet of Worms**, the formal assembly that Charles presided over. There Luther stood trial, with many German princes and bishops crowded into the hall to witness the testimony. When told to recant, Luther said instead, "I am bound by the Scriptures…and my conscience is captive to the Word of God. I cannot and I will not retract anything, since it is neither safe nor right to go against conscience."

A month after the trial, Charles V issued an imperial order, the **Edict of Worms**, which declared Luther an outlaw and a heretic. The edict ordered that no one in the empire should give Luther food or shelter, and that all his books were to be burned. However, the independent princes paid little heed to their emperor, and Prince **Frederick the Wise of Saxony** sheltered Luther in one of his castles for

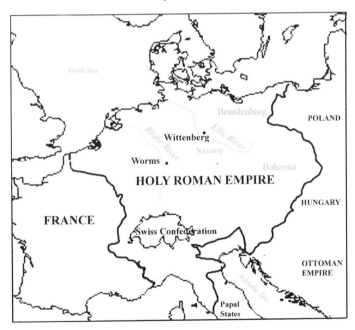

The Beginnings of Protestantism. In reaction to a commission by the Archbishop of Mainz to sell indulgences in the region, Martin Luther posted his *95 Theses* to the church door in Wittenberg, the capital city of Saxony, one of the many small states that made up the Holy Roman Empire. His famous trial was held at Worms, where he refused to recant his criticisms of the church.

almost a year. There he lived in safety, spending his time translating the New Testament into German. By the time Luther returned to Wittenberg in 1522, his ideas were already being put into practice, with priests dressing in ordinary clothes and calling themselves "ministers." Services were led in German instead of in Latin, and some ministers had married, since Luther had criticized the church's rules for clerical celibacy as creating a rift between church leaders and lay people. Eventually, Luther himself married, had children, and settled in as the founder of a separate religious group, called **Lutherans.**

THE REFORMATION IN SWITZERLAND AND FRANCE

As Lutheranism spread throughout the Holy Roman Empire, the movement to break from the Roman Catholic Church took other forms, notably in the sparsely populated cantons (small states) of Switzerland. These thirteen cantons were loosely joined under a federal Diet (assembly), but, like many other parts of the Holy Roman Empire, they were fiercely independent. No powerful princes – like Frederick of Saxony – held sway over territories in Switzerland, so the reformers were free to spread their influence to urban areas, and so their movements grew from towns that were not controlled by any central powers. These new urban-based versions of Protestantism soon spread to parts of France, although the French monarchy succeeded in keeping the kingdom primarily Catholic.

The Beginning of the Swiss Reformation: Zwinglianism and Anabaptism

The first of the Swiss reformers was **Ulrich Zwingli** of Zurich, a priest who much admired the humanist philosophy of Erasmus (pp. 62-63). While Luther was gaining influence in the northern part of the Holy Roman Empire, Zwingli was criticizing many of the same church practices from his position in the south. Like Luther, Zwingli based his ideas entirely on the Bible and emphasized salvation by faith alone. He also rejected the celibacy of the clergy, encouraged the clergy to marry, supported broad-based education, and emphasized simplicity in worship. However, his reform of the church was more drastic than Luther's, since he emphasized the independence of the individual believer and de-emphasized the importance of the clergy, especially in terms of the relevance of church rituals. He established a tribunal of clergy and secular officials to enforce discipline among the faithful, so his confidence in the individual believer's ability to monitor his or her own personal morality was limited. This tribunal had the power to excommunicate those who strayed from community beliefs, and they operated through a network of informers to keep the faithful godly. Unlike Luther, he insisted on long church services, and the churches themselves were stripped bare of virtually all ornamentation.

COMPARISONS: LUTHER AND ZWINGLI AT MARBURG

Disagreements among Protestants began very soon after Luther's posting of his *95 Theses* in Wittenberg in 1517. In 1529, Philip of Hesse sought to unite German and Swiss Protestants when he brought Martin Luther and Ulrich Zwingli together for a discussion at his castle in Marburg. There the two leaders discussed their differences, but Philip's efforts failed mainly because of disagreement over the topic of **transubstantiation**.

Luther and Zwingli's disagreement centered on their understanding of the Eucharist, a sacrament in which Christians remember the death of Jesus by partaking of bread and wine. The church held to the doctrine of transubstantiation, the belief that the bread and wine actually become the body and blood of Christ during the ceremony, so that Jesus is physically present, as he was the night before his death when he shared bread and wine with his disciples. Luther did not completely reject the church's interpretation of the Eucharist; he supported "consubstantiation," or the belief that God was somehow present in the service, even if the bread and wine were not literally a part of Jesus. Zwingli went further, maintaining a symbolic interpretation of Jesus's words, "This is my body," and that Jesus was only symbolically represented by the bread and wine of the Eucharist.

Luther left Marburg believing Zwingli to be a dangerous fanatic, and Zwingli accused Luther of still having one foot in Rome. The disagreement set the precedent for further splintering of Protestantism over other specific beliefs and practices, a characteristic that is still in place today.

Zwingli's ideas spread rapidly through the Swiss cantons, and a civil war eventually broke out between reformers and Catholics. Zwingli himself was killed in this conflict in 1531, and even though Zwinglianism never became a major religion, Zwingli's ideas greatly influenced later forms of Protestantism.

Although Zwingli was considered by many to be a radical reformer, he and Luther both agreed that some church practices – including infant baptism – should be retained. Infant baptism has no specific scriptural sanction, but according to church doctrines, infant baptism was the moment a human being entered the church. The rejection of this practice became the central belief of another group of Protestants called **Anabaptists** ("rebaptizers") by their enemies. The Anabaptists followed the model of adult baptism provided in the New Testament of the Bible.

They argued that only mature adults could make a conscious choice to receive the grace of God, and that infants could not understand what was happening. Roman Catholics and Lutherans alike condemned Anabaptists for their belief in complete separation of church and state. The formation of the Anabaptists demonstrates the tendency for Protestantism in these early days to splinter over specific religious issues. Some other groups established little utopian communities with common ownership of property. Others rejected all worldly goods and focused on the idea that true believers could literally make direct contact with God himself. Others prepared themselves for the end of the world and the belief that God would separate believers from non-believers in a great Day of Judgment.

CALVINISM

Within a few years after Zwingli's death, another leader of the Swiss Protestants rose. Born in France in 1509 as "Jean Cauvin," **John Calvin** based his name on its translation from the Latin as "Calvinus." Calvin studied law and theology, and was strongly influenced by the ideas of Martin Luther, but he developed his own views of Protestantism that became the basis of another major denomination called **Calvinism**. Since France remained a strongly Catholic country, Calvin fled to nearby Switzerland, where Zwingli's church was already established. He eventually settled in Geneva in 1536, where he created his own following.

The Principles of Calvinism

Calvin drew his religious principles from both Luther and Zwingli, and he agreed with them on justification by faith and not by works. Calvin took a middle ground between Zwingli's view of the symbolic nature of the Eucharist and Luther's view that God was somehow present in the bread and wine used in the service. Zwingli's view of the necessity of monitoring the behavior of the faithful influenced Calvin, who set up a church-centered government in Geneva that strictly supervised its citizens. Although Calvin agreed with Luther in believing that human beings could never earn salvation by their own actions and that any grace came from the free action of God alone, he put much more emphasis on the idea of **predestination**.

Predestination drew heavily on the assumption that humans are weak and sinful by nature, an idea that Luther did not reject. The doctrine was based on the belief that God, being almighty, knew and willed in advance all things that happened, including those who would be saved and those who would not. Calvin felt that those who had grace were relatively few, and though their salvation was through no actions of their own, this "elect" group of people could feel in their own minds that they were saved. This status was reflected in their ability to pursue a saintly life, and since Calvinism put such strong restrictions on moral behavior, the "saved" of the world were surely the Calvinists. Those whose behavior did not come up to the community's expectations were cast out, since they were not imbued with this spiritual purity. This emphasis on uncompromising perfection became one characteristic that distinguished Calvinism from other Protestant movements.

Calvinism also differed from Lutheranism in its belief that religious leaders should also be political leaders, so that Calvinist Geneva became a **theocracy**, or a society with no separation of secular and religious power. Calvinists did not recognize the subordination of church to state, or the right of political leaders or parliaments to set laws that restricted religious beliefs and practices. Whereas Luther retained the institution of church bishops, Calvin provided that the church should be governed by "presbyteries," elected bodies made up of ministers and devout laymen. This view of the relationship between church and state was reflected in the community that Calvin created in Geneva. A body of ministers ruled the church, and a council of ministers and pious laymen (called "elders") ruled the town. The rules were strict, and all frivolous activities – such as dancing, use of instrumental music, card playing, consumption of alcohol, and swearing – were banned or severely limited. Constant self-examination and sober study of the Bible were encouraged, and like Zwingli, Calvin required public confession of sins. Church services were starkly simple and concentrated on long sermons meant to inspire godly behavior. Ministers dressed in black, rejecting the colorful garb of the Catholic clergy, and images representing the saints, Mary, or Jesus were prohibited. In all ways, Calvin sought to regulate his church by the Bible, and religious dissenters were persecuted. The most famous case of persecution involved Michael Servetus, a Spaniard who had been declared a heretic by the Catholic Inquisition. He fled to Geneva to escape his death sentence in Spain, but he found no respite there, where he was seized by the Calvinist authorities and burned at the stake.

The Spread of Calvinism

Reformers from many parts of Europe traveled to Geneva to study Calvin's *Institutes of the Christian Religion* that explained his basic beliefs, and to spend time in this "model community" of Christians. As a result, Geneva became an international center of Protestant doctrine. When visitors returned to their home countries, they brought the religion with them, and Calvinist beliefs spread from Switzerland to France, the Netherlands, Scotland, England, and some parts of eastern Europe. Lutheranism remained the most prevalent form of Protestantism in the Holy Roman Empire and in Scandinavia.

In France, Calvinists were called **Huguenots**, and they received some support from members of the nobility who opposed the growing power of the French monarchy, but they remained a minority among a Catholic majority. **John Knox**, who became a disciple of Calvin after he visited Geneva, brought the new faith to Scotland, where his followers came to be called **Presbyterians**, after the governing bodies that Calvin set up for his theocracy. In 1560, Scotland's parliament

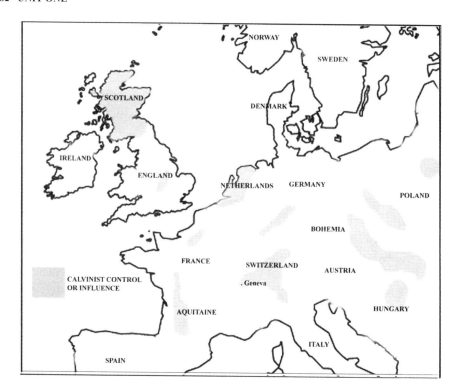

Calvinist Control or Influence by 1560. Calvinism spread from its origins in Geneva as reformers came to the city to study and carried the religion back to their countries of origins. The Anglican Church dominated England, Lutheranism was prevalent in Germany and Scandinavia, and Roman Catholicism remained the dominant religion in France, Spain, Italy, and much of eastern Europe.

adopted Presbyterianism as the country's official religion. In Hungary and Bohemia large numbers turned Calvinist, partly as a way of opposing the Habsburg rule, and in Poland Calvinists coexisted with other Protestant groups, such as Anabaptists and Unitarians. In England, Calvinists came to be called "Puritans" who later reached British America, giving birth to the Presbyterian and Congregationalist churches there.

THE ENGLISH REFORMATION

In contrast to the Protestant movements in Switzerland and Germany, the English Reformation began with a conflict between the king and the pope, not with theologians – like Luther and Calvin – who broke from the Catholic Church. However, this dispute would not have led to England's separation from the Catholic Church without the discontent created by Protestant doctrines from the continent that influenced people in England from many walks of life. Intellectuals such as William Tyndale, who published the first English translation of the New Testament, were among Luther's followers, but none had been successful in establishing a solid Protestant movement in England. King **Henry VIII**, who ruled from 1509 to

1547, was for many years an important impediment to the growth of Protestantism because he was a staunch supporter of the Catholic faith. In 1521 he published a book defending the Catholic view of the sacraments and condemning Martin Luther, and the pope reacted by granting him the title of "Defender of the Faith." Henry already enjoyed quite a bit of independence from the pope, since English kings had been granted the authority to appoint bishops since the 14th century.

Henry VIII and the Creation of the Anglican Church

England's break with the Catholic Church began when Henry asked Pope Clement VII to annul his marriage to Catherine of Aragon, who had been unable to give him a son. The brutal Wars of the Roses had been fought during the late 15th century between two families over who was the rightful heir to the throne, and Henry did not want the pattern to repeat itself. An annulment would mean that the marriage had never taken place, and the pope would not accept it, since Henry had obtained a special papal dispensation to marry Catherine, who was his brother's widow. Henry justified his request by invoking a quote from the Bible that placed a curse of childlessness on any man who married his brother's widow, even though he and Catherine had a surviving daughter, Mary Tudor. The pope's conscience was supported by the fact that he had been taken prisoner by **Charles V**, the Holy Roman emperor, whose armies occupied Rome. Charles was a devout Catholic who also happened to be Catherine of Aragon's nephew. When the pope opposed the annulment, Henry tried to have the case heard in London by the archbishop of Canterbury, **Cardinal Thomas Wolsey**, but the pope ordered the case transferred to Rome.

Henry reacted furiously by blaming Wolsey, who died on his way to his trial for treason, and by secretly marrying his pregnant mistress, **Anne Boleyn**. In 1533 he pressed Parliament to pass a series of acts that cut the ties between the English church and Rome, including the Act in Restraint of Appeals, which denied the pope's authority. Thomas Cranmer, who succeeded Wolsey as archbishop of Canterbury, declared Henry's marriage to Catherine annulled. In 1534 the Act of Succession required all of the king's subjects to recognize the king as the head of the Church of England by taking an oath of loyalty. Almost all took the oath, with the notable exception of **Thomas More**, the humanist writer who was serving as the king's lord chancellor. More, a vigorous opponent of the reform movement, refused and paid for his loyalty to the church with his life. As a result of his execution as a traitor to the king, he became a martyr and saint to the Catholic Church. **The Act of Supremacy of 1534**, which proclaimed the king "supreme head of the Church of England," represented the final separation of the English Church (or **Anglican Church**) from the Roman Catholic Church. The outcome of this famous struggle between king and pope reflected not only the growing problems of the pope in retaining loyalty to Catholicism, but also a consolidation of power in the English monarchy.

The Aftermath of the Anglican Split

Since Henry's motivation for breaking with Rome was not doctrinal, the Anglican Church at first kept most of the practices and beliefs of the Catholic Church. The Anglican Church did affirm several tenets of Lutheranism, including salvation by faith alone and the rejection of the concept of Purgatory, but it retained the doctrine of transubstantiation and clerical celibacy according to traditional Catholic doctrines. However, the king was determined to assert his authority, and he ordered the dissolution of England's 600 monasteries. Most of the monasteries were sold, and the proceeds enriched the royal coffers, allowing Henry to build up his army and navy, and in turn to enhance royal power. However, his marital life did not succeed quite as well. Anne Boleyn disappointed Henry by producing a female child, **Elizabeth**, and no sons, and Anne was eventually executed after being tried on charges of adultery. In all, Henry had six wives and produced only one male heir, Edward, who did succeed to the throne when his father died. However, Edward was sickly and only lived a short while, leaving the throne first to his half-sister, Mary Tudor, and then to his half-sister, Elizabeth Tudor. Mary – Catherine of Aragon's daughter – was a staunch Catholic whose efforts to undo her father's heresy were foiled by her death, and Elizabeth (Anne Boleyn's daughter) inherited a kingdom beset with religious divisions.

THE CATHOLIC (OR COUNTER) REFORMATION

Even before the rise of Protestantism, the Catholic Church had acted to reform many of the practices that its critics had attacked. The church called this movement the **Catholic Reformation**, although Protestants preferred to call it the **Counter Reformation**, implying a reform reacting to the Protestant schisms. The Catholic reform movement strengthened during the 1530s and 1540s primarily among the elite, who stressed biblical ethics and moral discipline. Under Paul III (who became pope in 1534) and his successors, the papacy began to take the lead in church reform. The backbone of the movement was in Italy and Spain, and it had two important consequences: the calling of a general church council and the founding of new religious orders.

The Council of Trent

In 1545 Pope Paul III and Charles V, the Holy Roman Emperor, called a general church council to meet at Trent, a town on the border between Italy and the Holy Roman Empire. The **Council of Trent** met several times between 1545 and 1563, and its work charted the essential course for Catholicism until the 20th century. Although its meetings were characterized by stormy battles between many political and religious factions, most of its conclusions reinforced the dominance of the pope. One result was that doctrines of the medieval theologian **Thomas Aquinas** became central in defining practices and beliefs for the church. At the same time, the Council's decrees were designed to affirm teachings that had been rejected by

CHANGE OVER TIME:
THE ANGLICAN CHURCH
UNDER ELIZABETH I

Even though the English church did not split with Rome for ideological reasons, over time its practices became distinctly Protestant, especially during the reign of Elizabeth I from 1558 till 1603. Elizabeth became queen when her half-sister Mary, a devout Catholic, died. Elizabeth does not appear to have had deep religious convictions, but since the Catholic Church did not recognize her as Henry's legitimate child, she had little choice but to be Protestant.

Under Elizabeth the Anglican Church took on a form of its own, with its organization resembling the Lutheran Church. It was a state church, and its doctrines were determined by the monarch acting through Parliament. English replaced Latin as the language of its liturgy, there were no recognized saints, and the clergy were allowed to marry. Elizabeth saw that the stated doctrines were broad and ambiguous so as to accommodate a wide variety of believers. The Thirty-nine Articles that were composed in 1563 by a committee of bishops to define the creed of the Anglican Church reflected this philosophy. Elizabeth's tolerance was limited, however, because religious conflict between Catholics and Protestants continued to threaten her authority during her entire reign. For example, even though Protestantism was imposed on Ireland with the creation of the official Church of Ireland, many Irish remained solidly Catholic, and Catholic priests, often in hiding, became national leaders of a discontented people.

Protestants. For example, the clergy's authority over the laity was supported, and transubstantiation – the belief that the bread used in the sacrament of the Eucharist actually becomes Christ's body – was reaffirmed. Trent also specified that all marriages should take place in churches and be registered by the parish clergy, and it rejected the willingness among Protestants to allow divorce. The Council also declared that the Bible is not the exclusive authority for the believer, but that church tradition holds an equal place in establishing religious truth.

A significant result of the Council of Trent was that the break between Protestantism and Catholicism became permanent, and all hope of reconciliation faded. However, it also revitalized the church as its leaders vowed to cleanse it of moral laxity and correct its focus on material wealth. Popes became the leaders of an enormous counterattack on Protestantism, causing many Catholics to rededicate themselves to the religion and to join the effort to spread their beliefs to other parts of the world.

The Jesuits

An important way that Catholicism expressed the definition and renewal of its faith was the founding of new religious orders. The most important of these, the **Society of Jesus,** or the **Jesuits,** was founded by Ignatius of Loyola, a Spanish nobleman who served as its charismatic leader from 1540 till 1556. The Jesuits became the most vigorous defenders of papal authority, and their numbers swelled, even after Ignatius's death. Jesuits established hundreds of colleges throughout Europe, which adopted the modern humanist curricula and methods. Even though they first concentrated on the children of the poor, they soon educated the sons of the nobility. As confessors and spiritual directors to kings, Jesuits exerted great political influence.

Jesuits were joined by other religious orders, including the Franciscans and Dominicans, in the effort to convert Native Americans in the New World. True to the goal of converting as many natives to Christianity as possible, most ships that arrived in the New World from the Iberian Peninsula carried Catholic priests. Priests went out into the countryside in order to contact the natives, and individually or in pairs they often set up residences and churches in areas far from other Europeans in the cities. Their willingness to spread out throughout the countryside and live among the Amerindians was primarily responsible for the tremendous number of conversions they had. This pattern almost certainly made many priests quite sympathetic to the Amerindians, with some speaking up and eventually protesting Spanish exploitation.

Efforts to convert the Chinese to Roman Catholicism were revived in the 16th century by the Jesuits. The most famous of these Jesuit missionaries was **Matteo Ricci**, an ambitious Italian who impressed the Chinese with his scientific and technological knowledge. Jesuits also travelled to Japan, where they were less welcome than in China. Even though Asians did not convert in large numbers to Catholicism, the Jesuits were successful enough that their religion took hold in Asia, and its converts increased over the years.

POLITICAL IMPACTS OF THE REFORMATION

Religious divisions between Catholics and Protestants created special problems for European rulers. As we have seen, England's political stability was threatened as Henry VIII's daughters were faced with the double challenge of controlling a country that not only was divided religiously but also had problems accepting female rulers. Under Mary Tudor, a devout Catholic, prominent Protestants went into exile but continued to plot the queen's demise. When Elizabeth took over after Mary's death, Protestants returned and Catholics went into hiding, only to devise plans to remove Protestants from power. The challenges to Elizabeth were great, and her ability not only to keep her throne, but also to advance England's power, helped to make her one of the most remarkable sovereigns in British

PERSPECTIVES:
BARTHOLOMÈ DE LAS CASAS
ON THE SPANISH IN THE
NEW WORLD

The Catholic priests that travelled with Spanish and Portuguese explorers to the New World usually spread out from the cities to live among the Amerindians. As a result, they often sympathized with their converts who were dominated by European masters. One of the most famous was Bartolomè de Las Casas, a conquistador turned Dominican priest who dedicated himself to protecting Amerindian rights. Below is a passage from *A Short Account of the Destruction of the Indies* that he sent to the Spanish king Philip II.

"They [the Spanish] forced their way into native settlements, slaughtering everyone they found there, including small children, old men, pregnant women, and even women who had just given birth. They hacked them to pieces, slicing open their bellies with their swords as though they were so many sheep herded into a pen. They even laid wagers on whether they could manage to slice a man in two at a stroke, or cut an individual's head from his body, or disembowel him with a single blow of their axes...They spared no one, erecting especially wide gibbets [gallows] on which they could string their victims up with their feet just off the ground and then burn them alive thirteen at a time, in honor of our Savior and the twelve Apostles..."

Reference: A Short Account of the Destruction of the Indies by Bartholomè de Las Casas, translated by Nigel Griffin (Penguin Classics, 1992), pp. 14, 15.

history. Elsewhere in Europe, religious reform movements instigated political unrest throughout much of the 16th and 17th centuries.

- **France** – The most serious conflict in France during the early days of the Reformation occurred in 1534, with an incident called the Affair of the Placards. Broadsheets that denounced the Catholic Mass were posted on church doors in Paris, unleashing a wave of royal repression across France. Hundreds of Protestants were arrested, some were executed, and others – including John Calvin – fled the country. After that, persecution of Huguenots – French Protestants – was only sporadic, and the Reformed Church grew steadily. During the 1540s and 1550s church meetings were held openly under the protection of converted nobles, especially in southern and western France. Francis I and his successor, Henry II, maintained a balance of power between Catholic and Huguenot factions, and the hostility was kept in check until after 1560, when the country became intensely involved in religious wars that engulfed most of Europe.

- **Scotland** – Protestantism came to Scotland when John Knox returned from a stay in Calvin's Geneva, but his efforts to find new converts were fiercely opposed by the royal family, particularly Mary of Guise, the queen regent. After her husband, James V, died in 1542, Mary gained support from her native France to protect her daughter and heir to the throne, **Mary Stuart**, from Protestant efforts to seize power. Many Scottish noblemen were alienated by the attachment of both mother and daughter to France, especially since Mary Stuart was married to the heir to the French throne. The Protestants joined with Knox to dethrone Mary of Guise and take over Parliament in 1560, and later forced her daughter Mary, Queen of Scots, to flee to England. They allowed the throne to pass to Mary's infant son James, reflecting the fact that some of their hostility was directed toward female rulers, not just Catholicism. Ironically, Mary, Queen of Scot's fate was decided by Elizabeth I, England's female ruler, who first imprisoned her, and eventually ordered her execution.

- **The German States** – Martin Luther survived his defiance of the Catholic Church largely because he was supported by many German princes, such as Frederick III of Saxony who protected Luther after his famous declaration at the Diet of Worms. Although many princes undoubtedly were moved by religious beliefs, others were concerned more with material interests. In 1517 – the year that Luther first spoke out against the sale of indulgences – the Catholic Church was the largest landowner in the Holy Roman Empire. Since there was no strong central government, no one could stop the princes who rejected Roman Catholicism and adopted Protestantism from legally confiscating church property, including farmlands, rich monasteries, and wealthy shrines. Even though these princes risked the possibility of being stripped of their titles by the Emperor, many of them banded together to resist Charles V, and in 1529 they signed a declaration protesting an imperial decree that no religious innovations were to be introduced in the empire. This action caused these princes to be called "Protestants," a name that eventually came to be applied to all the reformers. Charles tried to resolve the growing political divisions between his supporters and the Protestant princes, but war eventually broke out, and Charles's armies defeated the Protestant armies in 1547. However, his enemies regrouped to declare war against him in 1552, leaving Charles virtually bankrupt and exhausted from the struggle. Finally Charles V agreed to the **Peace of Augsburg** in 1555, the settlement that officially recognized the Lutheran church in the empire and accepted the secularization of church lands. Most importantly the Peace of Augsburg established the principle that all princes, whether Catholic or Lutheran, had the right to determine the religion of their lands and subjects. As for Charles, he gave up his political power in 1556, giving some of his lands to his son and some to his brother, retiring to a monastery in southern Spain for the rest of his life.

SOCIAL IMPACTS OF THE REFORMATION

By 1560, religious issues were still very much unsettled, even in Protestant lands such as England and the Holy Roman Empire. The Catholic Church had not accepted the situation and still hoped to regain its authority. However, the unity of Latin Christendom had been shattered, and a world of separate churches, states, and nations was taking its place. These changes had many consequences for people at all levels of society, and everyday lives of people were often profoundly impacted, especially in areas where Protestantism was the strongest. No matter what their denomination, Protestants all rejected papal authority, and their clergy were called ministers, not priests. Although Protestant clergy still had a special status in their communities, no special Protestant religious orders were created, and unlike Catholic nuns and priests, the clergy were allowed to marry and have children.

Marriage and the Family

One of the most important social changes brought on by the new religious movements was a different attitude toward marriage and the family. During medieval times, priests and nuns were regarded as morally superior to ordinary people, partly because they dedicated their lives to the church and were not distracted by family obligations. Sexual abstinence was seen as ideal, and those that could not practice it were seen as weaker versions of humanity than the clergy. Protestantism strongly promoted marriage as not just acceptable but preferable, and parenthood became honorable for even the most pious religious leader. Because they no longer considered marriage a sacrament, Protestants also reluctantly accepted divorce in limited cases. Luther believed that adultery, impotence, and abandonment were all grounds for divorce, but the practice remained quite rare.

For a woman, the model was that of a devoted mother who guided the spiritual well-being of her family. Ironically, even though religious reform promoted more equality between the clergy and the laity, it did close the door on the limited opportunities for leadership that some medieval women had found in convents and religious communities. As a result, nuns in Protestant territories were often among the last people to accept the new religious beliefs. Reformers did encourage women to take a more active role in religious activities, including services. Protestant women, like men, were encouraged to read the Bible themselves, and

THEMATIC LEARNING OBJECTIVE:
THE INDIVIDUAL AND SOCIETY:
WITCHES AND RELIGION

Belief in witchcraft was prevalent in early modern Europe among Catholics and Protestants alike. Witch hunts became common during the late 16th and early 17th centuries, and in the southwestern states of the Holy Roman Empire alone, more than 300 witch trials took place between 1570 and 1630. Almost all of the 2,500 executed as a result of these trials were women. Why? One probable root was the common belief that the female body was a source of sin, and therefore had to be controlled. "Evil" came to be associated with women.

Theologians and judges sought to demonstate that witches were evil creatures from the kingdom of the devil who should be removed from society. Although they appeared to be ordinary women, they could be recognized in many ways. For example, they might speak Latin prayers backward, or they might be responsible for misfortunes, such as fires or unexplained deaths and illnesses. Most of those accused of being witches were rural, poor, and single women who somehow angered town officials or wealthy peasants. By punishing these women as defiant deviants, authorities affirmed their power and reminded ordinary people of the importance of conformity to accepted beliefs and practices.

Luther especially advocated that women should receive basic educations. Anabaptists apparently allowed women to make decisions about not baptizing their children, and most Anabaptist martyrs were women. In Calvinist services, men and women sang psalms together, and a few women published religious pamphlets in the early 1520s. However, Protestant reformers still believed that women should be subordinate to men. Women could not be ministers, nor could they hold positions as church elders or deacons. Calvin believed that women's obedience to their husbands was necessary for moral order. These attitudes often led to suspicion of female rulers and regents, as John Knox – the Calvinist leader of Scotland – reflected in *The First Blast of the Trumpet against the Monstrous Regiment of Women* in 1558. He declared that

> "to promote a woman to bear rule, superiority, dominion, or empire above any realm, nation, or city is repugnant to nature, contumely to God, a thing most contrary to his revealed will and ap-

proved ordinance and, finally, it is the subversion of good order, of all equality and justice."

His words were directed at both Mary Tudor of England and Mary of Guise, the regent of Scotland.

Social Class

By the time that Martin Luther died in 1546 people of all social classes had become Lutheran. Educated people and humanists were much affected by Luther's teachings. He advocated a simpler, personal religion based on faith and a return to Christianity as it was in its early days, just as northern humanists had supported. The newly invented printing press made access to Luther's writings relatively easy, and his dialect of German became the standard version of the language. His insistence that everyone should read and personally interpret the Scriptures validated the middle-class urbanite's sense of self worth. Luther's criticisms of the church's wealth echoed their own thoughts, particularly since the business classes had to work hard to make their money. Lutheranism appealed to their sense of fairness by criticizing the fact that their tax burden was heavy, whereas the church was largely exempt from taxation. The new religion not only raised the religious status of the commercial classes, it also protected their pocketbooks.

Peasants too were drawn to the teachings of Protestantism. They admired Luther's defiance of church authority, and they resented paying taxes to both their secular lords and to the church. In the early 16th century, economic woes were deep, and crop failures in 1523 and 1524 aggravated an already difficult situation. Peasant discontent was stirred by many wandering preachers who put voice to their complaints, including the seizure of village common lands, new services required of peasants by lords, and unjust death duties. In 1525, many peasants in southern and central Germany rebelled, and some urban workers and artisans joined them in plundering monasteries, refusing to pay church taxes, demanding village autonomy and the abolition of serfdom, and insisting on the right to appoint their own pastors. This **Peasants' War of 1525** was directly inspired by Luther's writings, with slogans such as "God's righteousness" and the "Word of God" invoked to justify their rebellion. Luther first thought the peasants' demands were reasonable, but as the unrest spread, he withdrew his support. Freedom for Luther meant independence from the authority of the Roman church, not from legally established secular powers. He argued that rebellion meant the end of civilized society, and he supported the nobility as the revolt was savagely crushed, with over 75,000 peasants killed in 1525. In taking this position, Luther championed the power of the state and subordinated religion to secular governments, just as Henry VIII did in England a few years later. Even though the peasants lost the war, some economic conditions did improve for them, and some of the enclosed fields, meadows, and forests were returned to common use.

By the middle of the 16th century the Protestant Reformation had become a major force behind the changes that moved Europe from its relative isolation in medieval times to its front-and-center position in the world that was to follow. The Reformation broke the sway that the Catholic Church held over cultural, social, economic, and political lives of all Europeans, and emphasized the importance of secular interests and power. At the same time it continued to focus on religious salvation, a topic that had been central to medieval society as well. This volatile mixture of religious divisiveness and political and economic secularization was not to rest easy, but instead touched off a series of conflicts that would ravage the continent for the next century.

CONCEPTS AND IDENTIFICATIONS

95 Theses
Act of Supremacy of 1534
Anabaptists
Anglican Church
Aquinas, Thomas
Avignon Papacy
Boleyn, Anne
Calvin, John
Calvinism
cardinals
Catholic (Counter) Reformation
Charles V
Council of Trent
Diet of Worms
Edict of Worms
Elizabeth I
English Reformation
"experience in the tower"
Frederick the Wise of Saxony
Great Schism
Henry VIII
Huguenots
indulgences
Knox, John
Las Casas, Bartolomè
Luther, Martin
Lutherans
Mary Stuart
More, Thomas
Peace of Augsburg
Peasants' War of 1525

predestination
Presbyterians
"priesthood of all believers"
Protestant Reformation
Ricci, Matteo
Society of Jesus (Jesuits)
Swiss Reformation
Tetzel, Johann
theocracy
transubstantiation
Unam Sanctam
Wolsey, Cardinal Thomas
Zwingli, Ulrich

CHAPTER 5:
A CENTURY OF CONFLICT
AND CRISIS: 1555-1648

The religious turmoil that exploded across Europe after Martin Luther began the Protestant Reformation in 1517 was not settled by the Peace of Augsburg in 1555. Although this agreement brought temporary calm to the Holy Roman Empire by granting each ruler the right to determine the religion of his territory, the late 16th century was a period of intense religious warfare in other areas of Europe, including France, Spain, the Netherlands, and England. By the early 17th century, tensions between Protestants and Catholics led to the Thirty Years' War in the Holy Roman Empire, a series of military conflicts that devastated central Europe and produced permanent changes in European politics and culture. These battles began as religious struggles, but political power was also at stake, and by the time peace finally returned in the mid 17th century, the balance of power among European countries had shifted significantly, and religious divisions were permanently entrenched among the people.

POLITICS, RELIGION, AND WARFARE

The Peace of Augsburg addressed the conflicts between Lutheranism and Catholicism in the Holy Roman Empire, but did not extend recognition to Calvinism, an omission that fueled the wrath of a growing number of Calvinist believers. They challenged Catholic rulers in France, the Spanish-ruled Netherlands, Scotland, and Poland-Lithuania. In England, Calvinists confronted the Anglican Church and, in turn, the authority of the monarchy. Another religious/political conflict of the day was between Muslims of the Ottoman Empire and Spanish Christians who clashed over control of the Mediterranean Sea. In eastern Europe, the Russian tsar, Michael Romanov, promoted Orthodox Christianity as he competed with Lutheran Sweden and Poland-Lithuania, which was divided by conflicts among Catholics, Lutherans, and Calvinists.

The almost constant wars of the late 16th and early 17th century were a complex, varied mix of politics and religion. The warfare itself was considerably different from that waged during medieval times, with much larger, more expensive armies. With some forces numbering as many as 50,000 men, governments had to strengthen and centralize their financial control, often by building larger, more efficient bureaucracies to collect taxes and distribute revenues. The use of gunpowder changed the nature of warfare dramatically, making castles defenseless and knightly armor ineffective, and giving an almost insurmountable advantage over those without the technology. Gunpowder also weakened the medieval notion that warfare is a noble conflict that rewards the bravest and most skilled warriors since guns and cannons killed and wounded indiscriminately from a distance. These wars left Europe exhausted by the mid 17th century, but they played an important role in the crucial, transformation from medieval to early modern times.

FRENCH WARS OF RELIGION, 1562-1598

For almost 40 years, France was torn apart by civil war that was both political and religious in nature. The wars began in 1562 when Huguenot armies organized by the Bourbon family first met Catholic armies led by the Guise family to fight over control of the French throne. However, this event was preceded by years of increasing tensions among powerful political factions that intensified as some identified with the Huguenots and others defended the Catholic majority.

The Origins of the French Religious Wars

In the first half of the 16th century, French kings continued to extend their control over a very large, populous area. At a time when a traveler could move no more than 30 miles a day, it took about three weeks to cross the kingdom, which was about three times as large as England. The traditional power of the nobility gradually weakened as trade and commerce strengthened towns, a trend that encouraged peasants to leave their lords' lands to settle in as urban craftsmen and merchants. Two strong Valois kings – Francis I and Henry II – consolidated royal power by placing all of France under the jurisdiction of the royal law courts and made French the language of those courts. The **taille,** a tax on land, provided the funds to finance a strong royal army that further enhanced the power of the monarchy. However, by the mid-16th century, the French king ruled over provinces – such as Brittany, Burgundy, Provence, and Languedoc – that still had their own identities, autonomy, laws, courts, taxes, and assemblies. To all this was added the diversity of religion as Calvinism rapidly spread through France.

The growth of Calvinism led to persecution by the French king, which did little to stop its spread. The first wave of Protestant persecution in France began in 1525 when Francis I was captured by Catholic Habsburg forces under Charles V at the Battle of Pavia. The Valois and Habsburg families had fought for years over far-flung lands as far away as southern Italy, and when the French king was captured, his supporters tried to find ways to secure his release. Since Charles V was a devout Catholic, the French government sought to win his favor by cracking down on French Protestants. A second wave of persecution began a few years

Politics

THEMATIC LEARNING OBJECTIVE: STATES AND OTHER INSTITUTIONS OF POWER: RIVALRY AMONG FRENCH FAMILIES

One of the disadvantages of a government based on hereditary monarchy was the instability that could occur when the king died before an acceptable heir was in place. For example, in 1559, Henry II, a strong and capable king of France, was accidentally killed during a tournament held to celebrate the marriage of his daughter. This unforeseen event brought Henry's sickly 15-year-old son, Francis II, to the throne, followed in succession by his weak, incapable brothers, Charles IX and Henry III. Although their mother, Catherine de' Medici, tried to control them through her position as regent, three powerful families competed to gain control of the throne, and sent France into a long, destructive civil war. Those that would be king were:

The Guise Family – A strongly Catholic faction arose under the Duke of Guise and the Cardinal of Lorraine. They had large land holdings in the east, and they also sought to control Scotland.
The Montmorency-Chatillons – Admiral Gaspard de Coligny led this family as a political leader of the French Protestant resistance. Their land holdings were mainly in central France.
The Bourbons – This powerful family with extensive lands in the south and west had strong Huguenot sympathies, and eventually won the throne in 1589.

later after Protestants plastered French cities with anti-Catholic placards. The government arrested masses of suspected Protestants, sending many into exile, including John Calvin, who fled to Switzerland. In 1540, the Edict of Fontainebleau subjected French Protestants to the Inquisition, and another edict established legal procedures against Protestants in 1551. The Valois monarchy remained staunchly Catholic, partly because the church allowed French kings to appoint bishops and abbots and control church policy, according to the Concordat of Bologna signed in 1516.

Despite these persecutions, Calvinism grew steadily, drawing converts from all layers of society: artisans and shopkeepers hurt by rising prices and a rigid guild system, merchants and lawyers who wanted local privileges, and members of the nobility. Possibly 40 to 50% of the French nobility became Huguenots, including the house of Bourbon, which also had claims to the royal line of succession. The conversion of so many nobles made the Huguenots a potentially dangerous political threat to monarchical power. Though only about 7% of the French people were Calvinists, they were a strong-willed and well-organized minority.

Religious Riots and Civil War

The powerful families – Guise, Montmorency-Chatillons, and Bourbon – that challenged the throne after the death of King Henry II in 1559 based their opposition partly on their religious beliefs. The Guise were devout Catholics who believed that the monarchy allowed too much Calvinist dissent, and the Monmorency-Chatillons and Bourbon families wished to enhance the rights of French Protestants. However, all three families were politically ambitious, and their actions during this 40-year civil war reflect their desire to capture political power by weakening or seizing the monarchy. For example, the regent **Catherine de' Medici**, wife of Henry II and mother of the three kings that followed him, was Catholic, and yet the Guise (also Catholics) struggled to restrict her influence over her sons. Although the Bourbons and Monmorency-Chatillons were both Protestant, each family saw the other as a competitor for political power. As a result, the political and religious intrigues that surrounded the war were complex, and alliances constantly shifted as religious emotion and political ambition combined to shape the progress of the war.

Although the elite families competed for power at the highest level, many ordinary people were drawn into the war by their religious concerns. Both Calvinists and Catholics believed that the others' books, services, and clergy polluted the community. The clergy incited violence, with Protestant pastors encouraging their followers to destroy statues and attack Catholic religious rituals, and Catholic priests urging their followers to seek vengeance against Calvinist heretics. Dozens of Protestant attacks on Catholic churches resulted in the destruction of sacred vestments, vessels, and statues. In 1561, a Catholic crowd captured a group of just-released Protestant prisoners, killed them, and burned their bodies in the street. Hundreds of Huguenots were tortured, maimed, or murdered. City officials often criticized crowds' actions, but the participation of pastors and priests in these riots lent them some legitimacy.

The most savage event of all occurred on August 24, 1572, and came to be known as the **Saint Bartholomew's Day massacre**, named after the Catholic holiday on which the massacre occurred. Four days earlier, King Charles IX's sister – Margaret of Valois – had married Protestant **Henry of Navarre**, a wedding meant to help reconcile Catholics and Huguenots. Among the many Calvinist wedding guests was **Admiral Gaspard de Coligny** from the Monmorency-Chatillons family, who had come to have a great deal of influence over young King Charles IX. The night before Saint Bartholomew's Day, agents of **Henry of Guise** entered Coligny's bedchamber, where they hacked him to death with their swords. The assassination of Coligny may have been engineered by Henry of Guise, but the plan was endorsed by Catherine de' Medici, the mother of the king and regent. Catherine was Catholic, but she generally tried to balance the ambitions of the Guise family with those of the Protestants. However, in this case she feared that Coligny would lead an invasion of the Netherlands, an action that would almost certainly trigger a war between France and Spain. When the assassination was carried out, rioting and slaughter followed, spread throughout France, and did not abate for more than a month. First the Huguenot gentry in Paris were massacred, and then religious violence spread to the provinces. Between August 25 and October 3, perhaps 12,000 Huguenots were killed, with many deaths occurring in Meaux, Lyons, Orléans, and Paris.

The Saint Bartholomew's Day massacre led to the larger **War of the Three Henrys** fought among factions led by Henry of Guise, Henry of Navarre, and **King Henry III**, who succeeded his sickly brother, Charles IX. The War continued for

ORIGINAL DOCUMENT: EYEWITNESS TO COLIGNY'S DEATH ON SAINT BARTHOLOMEW'S DAY, 1572

The following description of Coligny's murder by agents of the Duke of Guise was written by an eyewitness to the event, the statesman and historian, Jacques-Auguste de Thou.

" Coligny awoke and recognized from the noise that a riot was taking place... He arose from his bed and having put on his dressing gown said his prayers... [Then] he said: 'I see clearly that which they seek, and I am ready steadfastly to suffer that death which I have never feared...'

Meanwhile the conspirators, having burst through the door of the chamber, entered, and [one named] Besme, sword in hand, demanded of Coligny, who stood near the door, 'Are you Coligny?' Coligny replied, 'Yes, I am he.' As he spoke, Besme gave him a sword thrust through the body, and having withdrawn his sword, another thrust in the mouth, by which the face was disfigured. So Coligny fell, killed with many thrusts. Others have written that Coligny in dying pronounced...these words: 'Would that I might at least die at the hands of a soldier and not [at those] of a valet.' "

Reference: James Harvey Robinson (Ed.), *Readings in European History,* Vol. 2 (Boston: Ginn and Co., 1906), pp. 180-182.

fifteen years, and destroyed agriculture and commercial activity in many areas, resulting in starvation and death beyond the rioting itself.

The Triumph of the *Politiques*

The religious wars were eventually quelled by a small group of moderates of both faiths called ***politiques*** who took a very pragmatic approach to the situation: no doctrine was important enough to justify everlasting war. They concluded that France had room for two churches, and that what the country needed above all else was civil order. The secular approach of the *politiques* emphasized the importance of obedience to the king, putting politics above religion.

Henry of Navarre, the Huguenot bridegroom on Saint Bartholemew's Day of 1572, was at heart a *politique* who inherited the throne in 1589 when both the reigning king (Henry III) and Henry of Guise (the Catholic leader who was trying to depose him) were assassinated, leaving only one Henry (of Navarre) alive. He ruled as **Henry IV**, the first of the Bourbon dynasty, which was to last until the late 18th century. His *politique*-inspired actions solidified the country behind him and helped to restore internal peace in France. First, he converted to Catholicism, the dominant religion in France, quite famously explaining that "Paris is worth a Mass." Henry's willingness to sacrifice religious principles to political necessity also inspired him to publish in 1598 the **Edict of Nantes**, a document that granted religious rights to Huguenots, including the freedom of public worship, the right of assembly, admission to public offices and universities, and permission to maintain fortified towns. Concession of the right to fortify Protestant towns reflected the fact that there were still ongoing hostilities between Protestants and Catholics. Indeed, Henry IV was assassinated in 1610 by a Catholic fanatic, and the Edict was eventually revoked in 1685 by Louis XIV. However, Henry IV laid the foundations for royal power, and his actions contributed to the transformation of France into an absolute monarchy, one of the most powerful kingdoms of the world by the early 18th century.

PHILIP II AND THE CAUSE OF MILITANT CATHOLICISM

For a time – the early 16th century – it looked as if Europe would fall under the control of one family, the path to empire that so many regions of the world had followed before. The powerful **Habsburg Family**, whose ancestral home was Austria, claimed territory all over Europe from Spain to Italy to the Netherlands to Hungary. All Holy Roman emperors had been Habsburgs since 1273, and Emperor Charles V dreamed of unifying all of these areas under his centralized control. Holy Roman emperors had struggled to maintain political power before, and Charles's efforts were doomed to failure, partly because of religious conflict between Protestants and Catholics. The Habsburgs were Catholic, and Protestants did not want to see them gain political power. Additionally, Charles experienced strong opposition from the French king and the Ottoman sultan. In the end,

Charles abdicated his throne to join a monastery in Spain, and his land holdings fragmented, with his son **Philip II** inheriting the Habsburg lands in Spain, Italy, and the Netherlands.

After Charles V's unsuccessful attempt to unify Europe, Philip II ruled Spain at the height of its power. The kingdom had only been unified in the late 15th century by the marriage of Ferdinand and Isabella, which combined the two smaller kingdoms of Castile and Aragon. This powerful couple not only sponsored the voyages of Christopher Columbus, but they drove the last of the Muslim rulers from southern Spain with the conquest of Granada in 1492. Spanish rulers remained devoutly Catholic, and they presided over a state that grew rich from New World wealth. It was under Philip II's reign (1556-1598) that Spain reached its greatest height of cultural and political power. Philip was also a great advocate of militant Catholicism.

Philip II's first goal was to consolidate and secure the lands he had inherited. These included Spain, the Netherlands, and possessions in Italy and the New World. Philip, however, was also a devout Catholic, and he believed that strict conformity to Catholicism within his lands would help to establish strong monarchical authority. To pursue these twin goals – centralization of political power and uniformity in religion – he aggressively backed the Spanish Inquisition and he also sought to make the monarchy less dependent on the traditional landed aristocracy. Philip, often called the "Most Catholic King," became the champion of Catholicism throughout Europe, a role that led him to form a "holy league" against the Ottomans to drive them from the Mediterranean.

At the time of Philip's rule, the Ottoman Empire was one of the most formidable powers in the world. In 1453, they had captured Constantinople with a successful siege, and had renamed it Istanbul. The city that had been the most important center of Orthodox Christianity became an important Muslim center, and its great church, the Hagia Sophia, constructed by Justinian in the 6th century, became an important mosque, a center for Islamic worship. The Ottomans continued to expand their empire, which reached its height of power under **Suleiman the Magnificent**, who ruled from 1520 to 1566. Suleiman commanded the greatest Ottoman assault against Europe, conquering Belgrade in 1521, laying siege to Vienna in 1529, and retreating only when the onset of winter made it impractical to stay. Had Vienna fallen, some historians speculate that the Ottomans might well have overrun the weakened Holy Roman Empire and threatened the budding western states, just as those states were beginning their voyages of discovery across the Atlantic. As it was, Suleiman was stopped, but the Ottoman Empire remained an important world power that controlled much of the water traffic between the Black and Mediterranean Seas. The Ottomans reduced Venice to a tributary state, and their huge army continued to expand or defend their frontiers.

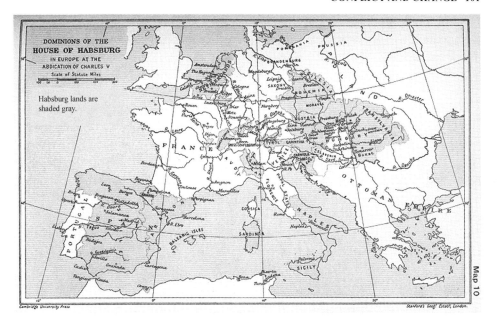

Habsburg Land Claims in 1556. The above map from *The Cambridge Modern History Atlas* (1912) shows the widespread holding of the Habsburg Family at the time of Charles V's abdication of the Holy Roman Empire's throne. The Habsburg lands included Spain, the Netherlands, much of the Holy Roman Empire, and southern Italy. The attempt to consolidate Europe into one empire was resisted by Protestants, the French royal house, and the Ottoman sultan.

Philip's efforts to contain the Ottomans led to a stunning victory over the Turkish fleet in the **Battle of Lepanto** in 1571, and he forced 50,000 **Moriscos** (Spanish Muslim converts to Christianity who remained secretly faithful to Islam) to leave their villages and settle in other regions, many in North Africa. However, his efforts to snuff out Protestantism in the Netherlands were far less successful, as were his encounters with England's Queen Elizabeth.

The Revolt of the Netherlands

Calvinists in the Netherlands were far from Spain and accustomed to being left alone. The seventeen Netherlands provinces operated with traditional local autonomy, and were much more inclined toward variety and toleration than conformity to a ruler's orders. The southern provinces were predominantly Catholic, and the provinces in the north were largely Protestant. When Philip attempted to impose his will within the Netherlands, the Protestants strongly resisted, especially those in merchant towns where Calvinism was the strongest. One of the most prominent dissenters was **William of Orange**, known as "the Silent" because his circle of confidants was very small. William was a *politique* who valued the Netherlands' political autonomy more than his religious creed, which originally was Catholic, then Lutheran, and then Calvinist. His conversion to Calvinism was a reaction to the Saint Bartholomew's Day massacre, but his resistance to Spanish rule began before that.

In 1566, Philip sent an army to stop Calvinist attacks on Catholic churches in the Netherlands, and more than 1,100 people were executed by the Spanish during the next six years. Philip appointed the **Duke of Alba** to control the situation, and he levied new taxes on the Netherlands to pay for the suppression of its own revolt. One of these taxes, the "tenth penny," a 10% tax, met such resistance from merchants and artisans that many refused to pay. Combined persecution and taxation sent tens of thousands into exile, including William of Orange, who emerged as the leader of an independence movement for the Netherlands. William encouraged adventurers and pirates known as "Sea Beggars" to invade northern ports, and in response, Philip's mercenary armies sacked Antwerp, then Europe's wealthiest commercial city. In eleven days in November 1576 the Spanish soldiers killed 7,000 people, and the provinces formally allied – both Catholic and Protestant areas – to expel the Spaniards. For the next two years the Spanish faced a unified and determined Netherlands.

**ORIGINAL DOCUMENT:
THE *APOLOGY* OF
WILLIAM OF ORANGE**

William the Silent, Prince of Orange, became the leader of the northern Protestant provinces of the Netherlands in their revolt against Spain that began in 1565. As a result, he was branded as disloyal to his sovereign, Philip II of Spain, and in reply he defended himself in his famous *Apology,* issued in 1581. The following excerpt reveals an important motive for his rebellion.

" They [the Spanish] intend above all [to exterminate] the true religion...I tell you frankly that the condition of your country is such that if the practice of the reformed religion is no longer allowed the country cannot survive for even three days. You see how miraculously the numbers of its adherents have increased and that hatred of the pope has taken deep root in the hearts of all the inhabitants of the country because his evil practices against this whole state have been so clearly exposed. Who can pride himself on loving this country and still recommend that so many people should be driven out of it, people who will leave the country desolate, poor and waste and will populate and enrich foreign countries? But if they refuse to go away, who can force them to do so? Let us look at our neighbours and at what happened in our own country; unless we are raving mad we will never follow such evil advice, advice which will completely upset this country."

Reference: "The Apology of William of Orange," *Texts Concerning the Revolt of the Netherlands,* edited by E.H. Kossman and A.F. Mellink. Cambridge University Press, 1974.

Despite this unified Spanish defeat, the southern, largely Catholic provinces remained fearful of Calvinist extremism, and so they returned to the Spanish fold in 1579 by forming their own union under Spanish supervision. In an effort to quell the rebellion in the north, Philip II declared William of Orange an outlaw and placed a large bounty on his head. In 1581, in a famous defiant speech known as the *Apology* (see excerpt), William publicly denounced Philip as a heathen tyrant whom the Netherlands need no longer obey. Spanish efforts to reconquer the Netherlands continued for several years, but even though William was assassinated in 1584, Dutch resistance continued, and eventually succeeded, with help from England and France. The situation in the Netherlands heightened the already strong competition between England, France, and Spain, and eventually resulted in a permanent weakening of Spanish power.

The northern provinces came to be called the Dutch Republic, even though Spain did not formally recognize its independence until 1648. Throughout the late 16th and early 17th centuries the Dutch Republic developed a thriving economy based

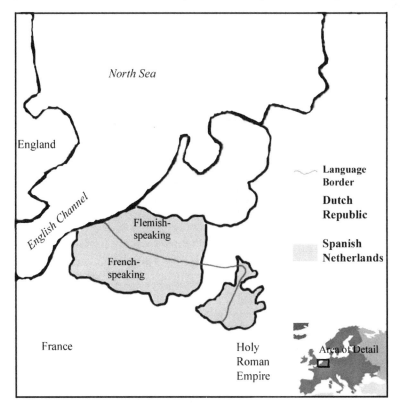

The Netherlands during the Revolt, 1580. When Charles V left the throne of the Holy Roman Empire in 1556, the provinces of the Netherlands were all Habsburg possessions that passed to Philip II, King of Spain, and son of Charles V. The provinces were divided between French and Flemish-speaking peoples and also between Catholics and Protestants. When Philip tried to impose political and religious control, the provinces rebelled, but the predominantly Catholic southern provinces returned to Spain in 1579. The northern provinces, primarily Protestant, remained independent, and came to be known as the Dutch Republic.

on shipping and shipbuilding, and Amsterdam became the main European money market for the next two centuries. Dutch entrepreneurs produced goods at low prices and marketed them efficiently, controlling many overseas markets. By 1670, the Dutch commercial fleet was larger than the English, French, Spanish, Portuguese, and Austrian fleets combined. One-third of the Dutch population remained Catholic, and the political authorities allowed them to worship as they chose in private. The Dutch Republic also had a relatively large Jewish population because many Jews had settled there after being driven out of Spain and Portugal, and they too were allowed to worship openly. By the mid-17th century, the Dutch Republic was one of the most prosperous, tolerant, and secular societies in all of Europe.

The Defeat of the Spanish Armada

As the Dutch revolt became a major concern for Philip II, he tried to solidify his relationship with England. Philip had been married to Mary Tudor, Queen of England, and together they had hoped that England would return to Catholicism. However, Mary died in 1558, leaving the throne to her half-sister Elizabeth, to whom Philip promptly proposed marriage. Elizabeth rejected his proposal, and instead charted an independent course based on Protestantism and her ability to resist the tangling alliances of matrimony. She enraged Philip further when she sent aid to the Dutch rebels, but he withheld any negative reaction since Elizabeth remained unmarried and her Catholic cousin Mary Stuart (Queen of Scots) stood next in line to inherit the English throne. Then, in a complicated international intrigue, Scottish Calvinists forced Mary to abdicate the Scottish throne to her baby son James, who was then raised as a Protestant. Mary fled to England where she sought protection from Elizabeth, and there she conspired for twenty years with other Catholics to recover England for her faith. When Elizabeth discovered a letter from Mary offering her succession rights to Philip, Elizabeth's patience ended, and she ordered Mary's execution.

In response, Pope Sixtus V launched a Catholic crusade against the English queen, and Philip II sent his famous ("invincible") **Spanish Armada** to challenge the English fleet. In May 1588, 130 ships sailed from Lisbon to the English Channel, where the English scattered the Armada by sending blazing fire ships into their waters. Then, nature intervened, and a great gale forced the Spanish to flee northward across the North Sea and around the furthest tip of Scotland, west around Ireland, and finally home to Spain. By the time the great Spanish fleet arrived back home in September, half of its ships had been lost and thousands of sailors had died. The defeat of the Spanish Armada was not only a military disaster; it was also a terrible psychological blow to Philip and all of Catholic Spain. Although Spain remained a significant power for years afterward, the Spanish Empire was experiencing decline even by the time that Philip II died in 1598. The costs of fighting the Dutch, the English, and the French were astronomical, and taxes

MARKER EVENT:
TECHNOLOGICAL TRIUMPH OF
THE ENGLISH FLEET IN 1588

The "invincible" Spanish Armada was considered to be the finest navy in the world in 1588. With crosses on the sails and banners bearing the images of Mary, the mother of Jesus, the Armada impressively defeated the Ottoman fleet at the Battle of Lepanto in 1571. This victory wrested control of the Mediterranean Sea (previously called the "Ottoman Lake") from the Turks, and helped to establish the Armada's growing reputation as the most powerful assemblage of naval power that the world had ever seen. By 1588 the Spanish Armada consisted of 130 ships weighing 58,000 tons, carrying 30,000 men, and 2,400 pieces of artillery.

When the Armada headed toward England in 1588, the ships were intercepted by some 200 English vessels, which encircled the Spanish fleet in the English Channel. The English ships were lighter, smaller, and faster, and were well equipped with guns, but the Spanish hardly imagined that they were a serious threat. The little ships harrassed the lumbering Armada vessels, broke up their formations, and attacked their vessels one by one. Then the English fireships drove them out to sea, where a great storm – which the English dubbed "the Protestant wind" – blew the Armada northward, where many ships broke up in the uncharted waters around the tip of Scotland, the Orkneys, and northern Ireland. The defeat of the Spanish Armada, then, not only symbolizes the reversal of political power in Europe, but also the technological triumph of the small, fast English ships that bested the outwardly more impressive Spanish vessels.

overburdened Philip's subjects. On the other hand, victory over the Spanish Armada accelerated England's rise to international dominance, enormously boosting English self-confidence. Even though the war between England and Spain dragged on until 1604, the English victory over the Armada in 1588 symbolized a shift in power from southern to northern Europe, with Spain on a slow path downward and England on a steady path upward.

THE THIRTY YEARS' WAR (1618-1648)

By the early 17th century, the Holy Roman Empire extended across a huge expanse of Europe, from France on the west to Poland and Hungary on the east. It included diverse people, such as those who spoke Czech and French, but most who lived within its boundaries were German. Language, however, was much less divisive than was religion, and the Empire was split almost evenly between Catholics and Protestants. In contrast, Roman Catholics made up only about 3% of the population in England, and only about 5% of all people in France were Huguenots. The Peace of Augsburg had determined in 1555 that each state's religion would be that of its prince, but many Protestants lived in Catholic states, and many Catholics lived in Protestant states. To complicate religious divisions, Calvinism continued to spread to many areas, and the Peace of Augsburg did not provide for Calvinist princes, only for those that were Lutherans. The Austrian Habsburgs made no attempt to impose Catholic uniformity in the late 16th century, and they granted Protestants limited rights to worship within the Habsburgs' ancestral lands. However, during the early 17th century, a Catholic resurgence began, with members of the Jesuit order establishing Catholic schools and advising Catholic elites. In 1609 a league of Catholic German states was organized by Bavaria with support from Spain. Meanwhile, Lutheran princes had established the Protestant Union in 1608, and the two alliances narrowly averted war. Religious tensions continued to mount, and contributed to the outbreak of the **Thirty Years' War** that eventually involved many kingdoms within the Holy Roman Empire, as well as many outside powers.

The Four Phases of the War

1) Historians usually divide the war into four phases, with **the first phase** (1618-1625) centered on civil war in Bohemia in the eastern part of the Holy Roman Empire. The event that sparked the war was the **"defenestration of Prague"** (from the French word for "window" – *fenêtre*) in which Protestants threw two Catholic emissaries from a window of the royal castle in Prague. Even though both men survived the fall, **Ferdinand** – king of Bohemia – sent troops to restore order, and in reaction the Czechs (the largest ethnic group in Bohemia) established a Protestant assembly to spearhead resistance. A year later, when Ferdinand was elected emperor (as **Ferdinand II**), the rebellious Bohemians refused to recognize him and chose in his place the young Calvinist Frederick V of the Palatinate. A few months later Frederick lost his crown when Protestant forces were defeated by the emperor's army at the Battle of the White Mountain. Ferdinand followed up his victory by forcing conversions to Catholicism and by calling on the Jesuits to help him to wipe out Protestantism in Bohemia. Within ten years, Bohemia was completely Catholic.

2) **The second, or Danish, phase** of the war began in 1625 and lasted until 1629. It was led by **King Christian IV** of Denmark, a Protestant who also had large land holdings within the boundaries of the Holy Roman Empire. He had help from other Protestant states – such as England and the Dutch Republic – but also from the French minister Cardinal Richelieu, who although Catholic, was wary of any expansion of Habsburg power. Emperor Ferdinand commissioned **Albert of Wallerstein** to raise an army of professional soldiers against the king of Denmark, and Waller-

stein conducted the war according to his own principles. His army swept through the northern parts of the empire and into Denmark, and won victory after victory against the Protestants. Wallerstein was an opportunist who encouraged his men to pillage as they conquered, and his ambitious grabbing for land for himself caused a major split in the Catholic forces. Despite this dissent, the emperor issued the **Edict of Restitution** in 1629, ordering all Catholic properties lost to Protestantism since 1152 to be restored to the church. The Edict also forbade all Protestants except the Lutherans to practice their faiths, and it seemed for a time that the whole Protestant Reformation, now a century old, might be undone.

3) **The third, or Swedish, phase** of the war (1630-1635) was promoted by the Swedish king **Gustavus Adolphus**, a devout Lutheran and able political leader. His motivations were to assist oppressed Protestants within the empire, and to help his relatives, the exiled dukes of Mecklenburg (an area in the northern Holy Roman Empire). **Cardinal Richelieu** of France came to his aid, again prioritizing French political goals over religious beliefs. The Swedish king won impressive victories in 1631 and 1632, although he was fatally wounded in battle in 1632. His victories, however, were enough to turn the tide of the war and give the Protestants some hope. By the time of his death, Gustavus Adolphus had gained control of Denmark, Poland, Finland, the smaller Baltic states, and had effectively ended the Habsburg hope of uniting all the German states under the emperor. Even though the Swedish army was defeated in 1634, their actions prompted the French to enter the war on the side of the Protestants.

4) **The fourth, or French, phase** of the war (1635-1648) was international in nature. The Swedish defeat in 1634 had led to the Peace of Prague (1635), a general peace treaty favorable to Catholics. The treaty brought only a temporary peace since Emperor Ferdinand II died shortly after it was signed, encouraging the French to support the Protestant forces against the Habsburgs. France tried to seize Habsburg territories along the French border and generously funded Protestant princes and mercenary soldiers in those areas. France declared war on Spain, which was also controlled by the Habsburgs, greatly expanding the war and causing it to drag on for several years. French, Dutch, and Swedish soldiers burned, looted, and destroyed German agriculture and commerce, and French troops streamed over the Pyrenees into Spain, spreading devastation. When Portugal and Catalonia rebelled against the Spanish king Philip IV, France immediately recognized the independence of Portugal. England, the Dutch Republic, and Sweden also recognized Portuguese independence in the hope that this loss of control would weaken Spain. In Germany the last phase of the war was not so much a civil war among Germans as an international

struggle on German soil because few German states now sided with the French and Swedes.

Physically the Holy Roman Empire was wrecked by the Thirty Years' War, with many of its cities sacked and plundered. Whole areas were looted to maintain the armies, and some cities were besieged several times. Populations dwindled as townspeople and peasants alike were murdered or fled from encroaching armies. Agriculture was ruined, and starvation and disease followed. In many areas of the Holy Roman Empire as much as a third of the population died, with some succumbing to the war itself, but others perishing from the effects of fire, disease, homelessness, and exposure.

The Peace of Westphalia (1648)

By 1648, all sides in the war were completely exhausted and realized that a quick, decisive victory was impossible. Finally, the war ended with the **Peace of Westphalia**, treaties signed in October 1648. The treaties represented a "marker event" in European history for many reasons:

1) The treaties recognized the sovereign, independent authority of the German princes. Each ruler's authority was enhanced to include the powers to declare war and make peace. This action effectively destroyed the Holy Roman Empire as a real state, since the emperor was left with no central government that could control the princes.

2) The independence of the United Provinces of the Netherlands (the Dutch Republic) was recognized, and Swiss cantons were acknowledged as sovereign and independent. From the disintegrating western frontier of the Holy Roman Empire, the French seized pieces of land in Lorraine and Alsace. The king of Sweden received territories in northern Germany. The treaties also allowed France to intervene at will in German affairs, since central authority in the Holy Roman Empire was seriously compromised.

3) Regarding religion, the treaties made the Augsburg agreement of 1555 permanent, but they modified it to include Calvinism as a legally permissible creed. In practice, the northern German states remained Protestant; the southern German states, Catholic. After thirty years of war, religious affiliations remained almost unchanged.

The Peace of Westphalia blocked the Counter Reformation and seriously restricted the power of the Habsburg family. It also reinforced the fragmentation of the German states, effectively suspending German unification for more than two

ORIGINAL DOCUMENT:
SIMPLICISSIMUS (1669)

Simplicissimus was written by Hans von Grimmelshausen, a storyteller and soldier during the Thirty Years' War. The title is translated as "The Simplest of the Simple." In the novel, he takes the point of view of a naive peasant who does not understand what is happening around him as a group of cavalrymen ransack his village. No other work of the period so vividly describes the horror of the war.

"Some [soldiers] stabbed their swords through hay and straw as if they had not enough pigs to stab...Others smashed the ovens and windows as if to announce an eternal summer. They beat copper and pewter vessels into lumps and packed the mangled pieces away...Our maid had been treated in the stable in such a way that she could not leave it any more – a shameful thing to tell! They bound the farm-hand and laid him on the earth, put a clamp of wood in his mouth, and emptied a milking churn full of horrid dung water into his belly. This they called the Swedish drink...The soldiers now started to take the flints out of their pistols and in their stead screwed the thumbs of the peasants, and they tortured the poor wretches as if they were burning witches. They put one of the captive peasants into the baking-oven and put fire on him, although he had confessed nothing."

Reference: Hans von Grimmelshausen, *The Adventures of Simplicius Simplicissimus,* 2nd ed. Translated by George Schulz-Behrend (Columbia, S.C.: Camden House, 1993), pp. 6, 7.

centuries. Politically Germany ceased to play any significant part in European affairs, since it was not only fragmented but also physically ravaged by the war. France, England, and the Netherlands began to take the lead in European politics, trade, and culture. Europe overall remained fragmented – in contrast to much larger empires in other parts of the world – and developed its essential character of unconnected sovereign states which acted according to their own laws yet often remained in conflict with one another. The cycle was set in place of forming and dissolving alliances, exchanging envoys and delegations, and shifting balances in power, all patterns that continued to characterize Europe for the centuries that followed.

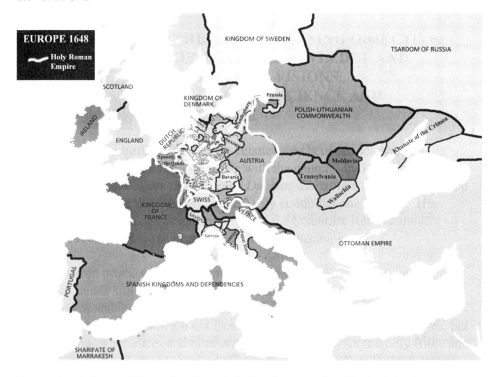

Europe after the Peace of Westphalia. Although the Holy Roman Empire still existed after the treaties were signed in 1648, many of its lands were lost, including the Swiss cantons and many areas along the western border of the empire. The many states within the borders of the Empire were given complete autonomy, so the emperor's power was virtually eliminated.

PURITANS V. ANGLICANS IN ENGLAND

After the defeat of the Spanish Armada in 1588, the Spanish threat to England receded, and for a time England became less involved with kingdoms on the continent. The English played no significant part in the Thirty Years' War, and they had no representatives at the Congress of Westphalia in 1648. Instead, the country was embroiled in its own civil war that was a milder version of the Wars of Religion in France, Germany, and the Netherlands. It was not fought between Catholics and Protestants since Catholicism had few adherents in England by the 1640s, but between Calvinists and Anglicans.

Although the conflicts in England between Protestants and Catholics were intense during the reign of Elizabeth I (1558-1603), the greater threat to royal authority eventually came from **Puritanism**, an English version of Calvinism. The Puritans were strict Calvinists who opposed the extensive rituals and lavish church ornamentations of Catholics and believed that the Anglican Church had not "purified" enough. Puritan ministers denounced the Anglican "popish attire", tithing, and holy days, and they tried to decentralize Anglican control of religious practices. Puritans supported the "Presbyterianism" (control by the local minister and the elders) advocated by John Knox (see p. 81), the founder of Scottish Calvinism. The most extreme Puritans wanted every congregation to be autonomous, so they came to be called **Congregationalists**, a movement that Elizabeth did not tolerate. Despite Elizabeth's rejection of their arguments, Puritans continued to grow in numbers and influence during her reign. John Calvin's ideas of predestination influenced their attempts to close England's theaters and Sunday fairs, and they believed themselves to be God's elect meant to save England from false doctrines.

Conflicts in Stuart England

With the death of Queen Elizabeth in 1603, the Tudor dynasty ended and the Stuart line began with the accession to the throne of Elizabeth's cousin, King James VI of Scotland, who became **James I** of England. James had been raised as a Protestant, but his mother was Mary, Queen of Scots, who had been an important advocate for Catholicism in Elizabethan England. He was well-educated and politically shrewd, and had thirty-five years of experience as king of Scotland. However, he did not live up to the majesty and mystique that Elizabeth had built around the monarchy, and his Scottish accent brought to the surface the English tendency to distrust all things Scottish. Perhaps most problematic of all was his well-developed philosophy of the **divine right of kings**. According to James I, a monarch has a divine (or God-given) right to his authority and is responsible only to God. He believed that monarchs should be free from control by Parliament, churchmen, or laws and customs from the past. He viewed the king as a father to his people, who looked after their welfare and stood above all others. The fact that the king's authority was based on God's will meant that no one had the right to question his motives or actions.

The Growing Power of Parliament

Probably any ruler succeeding Elizabeth would have had trouble with Parliament. Even though the monarch still had a great deal of power, Parliament's demand to be heard was getting stronger. About three-fourths of the House of Commons consisted of **gentry**, a social group just below the nobles. They ranged from local leaders to courtiers who were known at a national level. Most of the gentry were well-to-do economically, profiting from land holdings and royal offices. They were well-educated, and nearly half of them had legal training. They also had to approve all taxation that the monarch levied. Many members of Parliament were Puritans, whose Calvinist beliefs made them dissatisfied with the Church of England. Whereas Elizabeth tried to assuage religious troubles, James I promised to "harry the Puritans out of the land," and his doctrine of divine right of kings made many members of Parliament fear that common law (the traditional rule of law) was threatened. A particular concern was that James would no longer honor Parliament's right to approve taxes, especially since most members of the House of Commons were landowners.

Despite the prosperity that England experienced under Elizabeth, money had often been an issue, mainly because of the war with Spain and an economic depression. James added to the economic woes with his own extravagant habits, and a serious inflation he could not control made it necessary for him to be constantly in search of additional revenues. He levied – independently from Parliament – new custom duties known as *impositions* that Parliament viewed as an affront to its authority. As the economic dispute grew, the religious problems also worsened. To the dismay of the Puritans the king declared his intention to maintain the elaborate religious ceremonies of the Anglican Church. When James said, "No bishop, no king," he meant that the bishops were among the chief supporters of the throne. The Anglican Church also questioned James's loyalty to Protestantism when he hesitated in 1618 to rush English troops to the aid of Protestants in Germany at the outbreak of the Thirty Years' War. By the time that James I died in 1625, England was not only in a great deal of debt; religious tensions were increasing, and a power struggle between the king and Parliament was beginning to brew.

Charles I and the "Long Parliament"

Tensions between Crown and Parliament increased under James's son, **Charles I**, who ruled from 1625 to 1649. From the beginning of his reign Charles I had to face serious opposition that drew its strength from political, legal, economic, and religious quarrels. The opposition found voice and focus in the House of Commons. Debts mounted as Charles declared war on Spain and supported the Huguenot rebellion in France, and Charles found it almost impossible to govern without the cooperation of Parliament. The royal income was inadequate to keep the administration going without grants of taxes from Parliament. However, the Parliaments which Charles summoned were unwilling to agree to taxes unless he acknowledged their right to a say in how taxes were to be spent. Charles also challenged some of the gentry's land ownership rights, alienating them further. In 1628, Parliament presented the king with the **Petition of Right**, which protested his financial policies as well as arbitrary imprisonment for those who had refused to loan money to the crown. Overall, the petition claimed that expanded parliamentary participation in government was an English tradition that Charles was ignoring. In response, Charles dissolved Parliament in March 1629 and ruled England for eleven years without reconvening the assembly.

Discontent in England became intense and widespread, yet if Charles had not attempted to impose the English Prayer Book upon the Scots, the crisis might have been averted or at least postponed. In 1637, the king ordered the Scottish Church – which was Calvinist – to conform to the ritual of the Anglican Church. This action precipitated revolt in Scotland, and the king could not find funds to raise an army to suppress the rebels. Charles, then, had no alternative but to summon Parliament again in 1640. Puritans, however, had little sympathy for Charles's desire

PERSPECTIVES:
JAMES I'S VIEW OF THE DIVINE
RIGHT OF KINGS

One of the most vocal defenders of the divine right of monarchy was James I of England, also known as James VI of Scotland. Before he became the English king in 1603, he anonymously published a book called *True Law of Free Monarchies*. By "free" he meant that monarchs should have no outside controls on their powers. The excerpt below is from a speech James gave to the British Parliament in 1610.

"...The state of monarchy is the supremest thing upon earth: for kings are not only God's lieutenants upon earth and sit upon God's throne, but even by God himself they are called gods...In the Scriptures kings are called gods, and so their power after a certain relation compared to the Divine power. Kings are also compared to fathers of families: for a king is truly [parent of the country], the political father of his people. And lastly, kings are compared to the head of this microcosm of the body of man...
...I would not have you [Parliament] meddle with such ancient rights of mine as I have received from my predecessors, possessing them [as ancestral customs]: such things I would be sorry should be accounted for grievances."

Reference: Select Statutes and Other Constitutional Documents Illustrative of the Reigns of Elizabeth and James I, 3rd ed., ed. G.W. Prothero (Oxford: Clarendon Press, 1960), pp. 400-401.

to quell the Scottish rebels, whose religion so much resembled their own. Charles dismissed Parliament when they refused to cooperate with him, only to be forced to recall the assembly when the Scots marched into northern England. The new Parliament that he summoned in November 1640 was called the **Long Parliament** because in contrast to the "Short Parliament" (which convened earlier in 1640), it sat from 1640 till 1653. Charles was forced to agree not to dissolve or adjourn Parliament without the members' consent, and in spite of the Scottish invasion, the members of the Long Parliament refused to grant taxes to the king without many concessions to them. Parliament abolished many of the king's sources of revenue, and they impeached and removed from office his leading ministers. Charles' leading minster, the Earl of Strafford, was tried and executed, and the special courts which the king had used to enforce his will upon his subjects were abolished. Finally, Parliament voted a special poll tax to pay off the Scottish army, which then returned home.

After a rebellion erupted in Ireland in 1641, members of Parliament argued over whether or not Charles could be trusted to command an invading army, since many feared that he would use the army not only to overthrow the Irish Catholics but to impose absolute rule on England as well. In November 1641, the House of Commons passed by a majority of only eleven votes the **Grand Remonstrance**, which listed all the demands for change which the Puritans supported. Had it stood, it would have established something close to parliamentary sovereignty. However, Charles refused, and when Parliament deprived him of command of the army, he declared the act illegal and Parliament traitorous. The English Civil War had begun.

The English Civil War (1642-1649)

In general the religious conservatives supported the king, although some distrusted his belief in the divine right of kings. His supporters, called **Cavaliers** or royalists, were strong in northern and western England, the parts of the country with the fewest number of gentry. The nobility, identifying their power with preserving the monarch and the church, were generally supporters of the king. Parliament found support mainly in towns and in southeastern England. The members of the parliamentary opposition, known as **Roundheads** because of their close-cropped hair, were mostly Puritans, although they varied in terms of religious moderation or extremism.

At the opening of the war in 1642 the Cavaliers generally had the upper hand, but Parliament reorganized its forces under the effective leadership of **Oliver Cromwell**, a stern Puritan of the gentry class, and with the help of Scottish Presbyterians, his **New Model Army** defeated the royalist forces utterly by 1646. Cromwell based his organization of the army on Puritan discipline that provided soldiers with the will to fight, and Cromwell – who was also a member of Parliament – became both a political and military leader. From 1646 to 1648 Parliament and the Army faced the problem of what to do with their newly-won power. Debates raged regarding both religion and politics. Most members of the House of Commons wanted a Presbyterian system modeled after the one in Scotland in which local congregations were controlled by a central authority, but others – including Cromwell – wanted each congregation to manage its owns affairs independently. Many radical religious ideas had taken root among the soldiers of the New Model Army, including a group called "**Levelers**" because they wanted to equalize the political rights of all Englishmen.

By 1647, the internal quarrels between Presbyterians and independents renewed civil warfare, with Cromwell's army facing both the king and the Presbyterians. However, when the king invaded in alliance with the Scots and the Presbyterians, Cromwell was able to defeat them, and his victorious army brought the king to trial. Most members of the House of Commons did not support the proceedings,

CHANGE OVER TIME:
THE ENGLISH HOUSE OF COMMONS
FROM HENRY VIII TO CHARLES I

The English House of Commons during the early 17th century reigns of James I and his son Charles I was very different from the assembly that had allowed Henry VIII to form the Anglican Church in 1534. A social revolution had brought about the change by enlarging and enriching the gentry class. When Henry ordered the monasteries dissolved, the sale of Church lands benefited many people and created new landowners. In the 17th century, old common lands from the days of medieval manors were enclosed and became areas where the well-to-do experimented with new agricultural techniques that made the land more productive. Other people invested in commercial ventures, especially since the crown – particularly Elizabeth I – supported overseas exploration and investment.

These social changes were reflected in the English Parliament, so that many of the gentry who populated the House of Commons were wealthier than the nobility who made up the House of Lords. Many Commoners acquired at least some legal knowledge and became more aware of rights that had been established under English common law. Members of the House of Commons were willing to tax themselves provided they had some say in state expenditures and policymaking. The Stuarts, however, considered the gentry's ambitions to be a threat to the divine right of kings, and so England was brought to crisis as the kings refused to empower the rising gentry.

but Cromwell's army expelled the reluctant members, leaving only about 60 of Cromwell's supporters to form what came to be known as the "**Rump Parliament**". This body decided that their king was untrustworthy and a troublemaker, and after a trial of questionable legality, King Charles I was executed by his subjects in January 1649. The execution of a king was shocking to most people in England, Scotland, and Ireland, but Cromwell's army was strong enough to crush all possible resistance. At mid-century, then, England was controlled by radical Protestants and appeared to have discarded monarchical rule forever. This path would be significantly modified during the late 17th century, although the English Parliament would not lose power and would forge a new government model that eventually influenced many other countries.

By the mid-17th century, religious quarrels still divided Europeans in most areas of the continent, but patterns of dominance had generally settled in. France, Spain, and Poland-Latvia remained predominantly Catholic, but the Peace of Westphalia

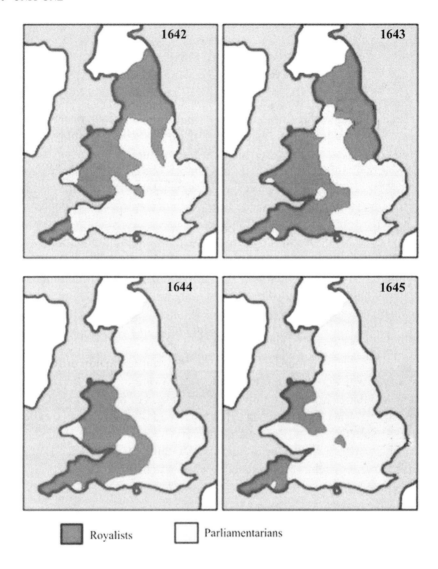

The Progress of the English Civil War. In the early years of the war, the Cavalier forces of King Charles I secured much English land, especially in the north and west where the nobility was still powerful. The southern and eastern lands, dominated by cities and towns, had more supporters of Parliament. By 1644, Cromwell's New Model Army forced the king to give up many of his gains, and by 1645, the king had lost control of most areas of the country.

assured that Protestantism would remain a viable religion throughout the Holy Roman Empire. Calvinists had temporarily gained control of England, and Protestants were entrenched in Scotland. Ireland, however, remained strongly Catholic. In virtually all places, religion was linked closely to politics, so that religious and political motives and consequences were difficult to separate, and the religious wars of the era helped to shape the Europe that would emerge in the early modern period.

CONCEPTS AND IDENTIFICATIONS

Albert of Wallerstein
Apology
Bourbon Family
Cardinal Richelieu
Catherine d'Medici
Cavaliers
Charles I
Christian IV
Coligny, Gaspard de
Congregationalists
Cromwell, Oliver
defenestration of Prague
divine right of kings
Duke of Alba
Edict of Nantes
Edict of Restitution
English Civil War
Ferdinand II (Frederick of Bohemia)
four phases of the Thirty Years' War
gentry
Grand Remonstrance
Guise Family
Gustavus Adolphus
Habsburg Family
Henry III
Henry IV (Henry of Navarre)
Henry of Guise
James I
Lepanto, Battle of
Levelers
Long Parliament
Montmorency-Chatillons Family
Moriscos
New Model Army
Peace of Westphalia
Petition of Right
Philip II
politiques
Puritans
Roundheads
Rump Parliament

Saint Bartholomew's Day massacre
Simplicissimus
Spanish Armada
taille
Thirty Years' War
War of the Three Henrys
William of Orange

CHAPTER 6:
ECONOMIC AND SOCIAL
CHANGES
1450-1648

The period from 1450 to 1648 is often called "The Age of Discovery," a reference to the era's advances in geographical travel, knowledge, and technology. Just as the Renaissance and the religious reformations broke with past beliefs and customs to forge new ones, the emphasis on individualism and humanism underlay the quest to discover and explore new lands. In 1350, it took as long to sail from the eastern end of the Mediterranean to the western end as it had taken a thousand years earlier. Even in the 15th century, Europeans knew little more about the earth's surface than the Romans had. By 1648, however, Europeans had sponsored voyages to many parts of the earth's surface, and had drawn roughly accurate maps of the whole earth. These accomplishments were shaped by economic developments on the European continent, and they resulted in broad changes that created the first truly global economy and transformed the social order as well.

ECONOMIC EXPANSION AND INNOVATION

The cultural and political changes of early modern Europe were accompanied by equally important economic expansion and innovation that supported the growing emphasis on individual abilities and accomplishments.

Population Increase, Food Prices, and Urban Growth

An important basis for the economic growth that began during the mid-15th century was population growth. Exact measurements are not possible, but the loss of population that began with the Black Death in the 1340s had run its course by the 1460s. Plagues, though recurrent, took fewer lives, and bad harvests became less frequent, probably due to favorable climate conditions that began during the late 15th century. Families grew in size as more children survived into adulthood. As a result, Europe's population rose by about 50% between 1470 and 1620. Cities expanded rapidly, with London growing from 50,000 inhabitants in the early 15th century to about 200,000 in the early 16th century.

The rise in population was followed by a dramatic jump in food prices, since food production did not keep up with population increases. By the early 1600s, wheat cost about five times more than in the late 1400s, an increase far greater than the movement of prices for other commodities. In response to the growing demand for food, a great wave of **enclosures** began in Britain, with major landowners putting up fences around common tilling and grazing land, traditionally open to all. Since this movement reserved land for crops and animals of major landowners only, many peasants sought to make a living by moving to towns and cities.

As markets began to grow in response to increasing demand by the growing population, the volume of trade also increased so that commercial profits kept pace with those of agriculture. Although Italian city states – such as Venice and Florence – were the most vibrant centers of trade during the 16th century, trade expanded to western and northern Europe as well, with ships crossing the Baltic Sea, and a booming shipbuilding business taking root in southern England and the Netherlands. The English cloth trade was brisk, and wool from sheep raised in many areas from Spain to England was in great demand. The German linen industry and the northern Italian silk industry were growing, and printing and glass-making became widespread occupations.

Capitalism and Mercantilism

As the volume of trade rose, new mechanisms for organizing large-scale economic activity were put in place, a process called the **commercial revolution**. New systems of bookkeeping, banking, merchandising, and investing characterized these changes, with the development of capitalism and mercantilism being most influential.

A unique European development was **capitalism**, an economic system based on private ownership of property and businesses that produce goods to be bought and sold in a free market. In a capitalist system, private individuals pursue their own economic interests, hire their own workers, and decide which goods to produce. Capitalism was later explained by Adam Smith in his *Wealth of Nations* as an economic system controlled by an "invisible hand" – the natural law that defines the relationship between supply and demand. In theory, fair prices are set because supply and demand naturally vary together, and no government intervention is necessary. In many ways, capitalism was an outgrowth of **mercantilism**, which emphasized the responsibility of government to promote the state's economy to improve tax revenues and limit imports to prevent profits from going to outsiders. Whereas mercantilism implied more government control than capitalism, both emphasized the advantages of allowing individuals to develop their own business initiatives. Capitalism did require merchants and businessmen to take risks with their money, and so some support from government and other organizations could minimize the damage if enterprises went awry.

Early capitalism in Europe came to be supported by institutions organized to promote the accumulation of wealth and the ease of buying and selling products.

Some of these institutions – such as banks, investment organizations, and insurance underwriters – had been in existence for many years in older civilizations that had experimented with various credit and trade mechanisms, some more successfully than others. Banks began appearing in all major European cities, in which businessmen and merchants could keep their money and secure loans for their business ventures. Insurance companies formed to share the risk of these ventures, as did **joint-stock companies**, which organized commercial ventures on a large scale by allowing investors to buy and sell shares. Companies such as the English East India Company put together the largest businesses in history to that point, and often made a great deal of money for stockholders. If the business failed, all were damaged, but it was less likely that any one investor would be completely ruined. Most joint-stock companies formed in Britain and the Netherlands, states that were supportive of rule by law and the use of contracts, whereas in Spain, where absolutism held sway, the government was more likely to control business ventures directly. In Britain and the Netherlands, governments chartered joint-stock companies, enforced contracts, and settled disputes among businessmen and merchants.

The new capitalist system largely replaced the old guild system of the Middle Ages. The craft guilds had monopolized the production of goods by fixing prices and wages and regulating standards of quality. Because guilds represented collective – not individual – efforts and did not emphasize profit-making, entrepreneurs sought to find ways to operate without them. One tactic was to produce goods in the countryside outside the guilds' control through the "**putting-out system**," in which entrepreneurs delivered raw materials to workers in their homes, where they transformed them into finished products to be picked up later by the entrepreneur or his representative. For example, a rural family would receive raw wool that they would spin into yarn, and then weave the yarn into cloth to be sold in town by the entrepreneur for a profit. Only later would factories organize, where workers came to a central place to produce goods. By 1750, most workers were still operating under the putting-out system.

Technological Advances

Technological advances also greatly contributed to the transformation of Europe between 1450 and 1648. Mostly, Europeans altered inventions made elsewhere to suit their needs. For example, hulls of sailing ships in the Indian Ocean trade were designed to navigate relatively peaceful waters. Europeans designed the hulls of their sailing ships to sail the deep, often turbulent, waters of the Atlantic and to carry heavy arms. They used an earlier invention of the Chinese – the compass – for navigation, but Europeans improved it by making it less likely to inaccurately respond to the magnetic pull of iron in the ship's structure. A new mapmaking technique produced the **Mercator projection**, which was particularly well suited for travel on the Atlantic. The Chinese had invented gunpowder many centuries before, but Europeans made advances in metalwork that allowed them to make cannons – and eventually guns – that were more accurate and less dangerous to use than those used in earlier times.   This last innovation was particularly important in the buildup of European military might.   Their ships, now mounted with cannons and carrying soldiers armed with guns, had a tremendous advantage over much larger armies without them, including those of the Aztecs and Incas half a world away.

EXPANSION OVERSEAS

Long before Europe's demographic and economic recovery began in the late 1400s, explorers had taken the first steps toward creating huge empires overseas. For example, Marco Polo's travels to China sparked interest in faraway lands during the 13th century, and sailors had begun exploring the northwestern coast of Africa, looking for a route to Asia.   The first Europeans to take long voyages away from home during this era were the Portuguese and Spanish.   Both had just

MARKER EVENT: THE MERCATOR MAP PROJECTION

Mapmaking is a field that became well-developed during much earlier times, but the Mercator projection was a new approach, developed during the 16th century by Gerhard Kremer, known as "Mercator" (the merchant) because his maps were tailored to aid European ocean traders. Although the interiors of North and South America and Africa were still unexplored,  he still was able to outline their coastlines, even though his methods exaggerated the size of any land that was a long distance from the equator. In order to represent the globe on a flat surface, Mercator drew the lines of longitude – which actually meet at the poles – as parallel lines, a process that made areas like Greenland and Antarctica look much larger than they really are. The advantage for sailors on the Atlantic was that they could draw a straight line between their point of departure and their destination, making their travel more reliable. As a result, Atlantic trade was stimulated, and the Mercator projection is still a common one. Europeans also may have liked it, though, because in proportion to other landmasses, it made Europe look bigger than it really is!

consolidated their governments and built strong militaries, and they were well situated on the Atlantic Ocean, close to the Strait of Gibraltar that led to the Mediterranean Sea. However, the two kingdoms had little hope of competing for trade on the Mediterranean because it was dominated by Venice and Genoa. These two city-states had forged trade alliances with Muslim states to continue the lucrative trade with the East that had begun during the era of the Crusades, and they had little interest in exploring possible trade routes across the Atlantic. Spain and Portugal were inspired by the new cultural and economic forces that were transforming Europe, and they also were interested in finding new converts to Christianity. In 1492, Spain – newly united under Ferdinand and Isabella – finally defeated Granada, the last Muslim kingdom on the Iberian Peninsula, and all Jews were expelled only three months later. Their religious devotion, coupled with newly centralized political power, provided incentive to spread Christianity to new regions.

Portuguese Explorations

The Portuguese began their explorations in the early 15th century after they attacked the rich Muslim Moroccan city of Ceuta, which was only across the Strait of Gibraltar from the newly conquered Muslim state of Granada. There the Portuguese observed the caravans that brought gold and slaves across the Sahara from the African states to the south, and they were encouraged to sail down the African coast in hopes of establishing some trade contacts. These first ventures were led by the third son of the Portuguese king, Prince Henry, who devoted his life to navigation, and is known in history as **"Henry the Navigator"**. His most important contribution was the creation of a navigation school, which became a magnet for the Genoese, many of whom were Jewish cartographers who were familiar with Arab maps, and a number of young Portuguese men, some of whom became far more famous than he. Henry and his staff studied and improved navigation technology, including the magnetic compass and the astrolabe, which helped mariners determine their locations on the oceans. The Portuguese also made some important advances in the design for ships, since the square-sailed vessels propelled by oarsmen in the Mediterranean would not work in the more turbulent Atlantic Ocean. The new ship developed by the Portuguese was called the **caravel**, which was much smaller than a Chinese junk. Its size allowed the exploration of shallow coastal areas and rivers, yet it was strong enough to withstand storms on the ocean. The caravel had two sets of sails: one set were square to catch ocean breezes for speed, and the other set were the triangular lateen sails that had been used for maneuverability for many years on the Indian Ocean. The newly perfected European cannons made the caravel a fighting ship as well.

Henry had to convince explorers to strike out along the coast of Africa because of common concepts that southern waters were boiling hot and full of monsters, and so it took the Portuguese many years to venture beyond southern Morocco. They were further discouraged by the long stretch of desert that extended for hundreds of miles south of Morocco. Although it was not originally Henry's goal, some of the students from his school, most notably **Bartholomew Dias** and **Vasco da Gama**, set out to find the tip of Africa and connect beyond it to the Indian Ocean. These feats were accomplished by the end of the 15th century, after years of experimenting with wind and ocean currents and discovering the fastest and safest ways to return home to Portugal. These experiments also encouraged both the Portuguese and the Spanish to venture away from the coast and take to the high seas. In 1500, **Pedro Cabral** sailed too far west and reached the South American coast by mistake, but it allowed him to claim Brazil for Portugal, its one possession in the New World.

Spanish Explorations

Spanish exploration developed gradually, with the rulers only becoming interested in overseas explorations during the last decade of the 15th century. A Genoese mariner named **Christopher Columbus** convinced Ferdinand and Isabella to sponsor a voyage across the Atlantic after he was turned down by the Genoese and Portuguese governments. Columbus believed that he could reach East Asia by sailing west, and in estimating the distance, he used the calculations of the Ancient Greek geographer Ptolemy. Ptolemy had believed that the circumference of the earth was about 16,000 miles, which was 9,000 miles short of reality. As a result, it is not surprising that Columbus believed he had reached the East Indies when he arrived in the Americas in 1492. He made three voyages between 1492 and 1498,

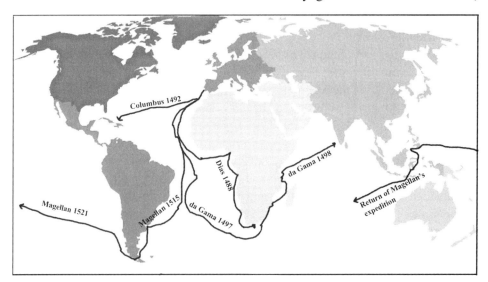

Early European Discoveries. The first European explorers of the early modern era were Spanish and Portuguese, with the Spanish arriving in the New World in 1492, and the Portuguese exploring a sea route around the tip of Africa by the end of the century. Ferdinand Magellan's expedition was sponsored by the Spanish and was the first circumnavigation of the globe.

and continued to insist that he had reached Asia even after he sighted the coast of South America on the third voyage. Of course, he had encountered the New World instead, which would be named "America" after Amerigo Vespucci, a later explorer sponsored by Spain and Portugal.

Columbus's voyages inspired Spain to sponsor other New World adventures. Since the last Muslim kingdom in southern Spain was conquered by the Castilians in 1492, many experienced soldiers were available for hire. The prospect of un-limited land and military adventure appealed to men of all social classes, and **con-quistadors,** or conquerors, led Spanish troops into the Caribbean, Mesoamerica, and South America.

The Treaty of Tordesillas

Despite the fact that the two kingdoms of Portugal and Spain sent explorers in dif-ferent directions, they began to argue shortly after Columbus's first voyage about who controlled the newly discovered lands. Both looked to the Catholic Church

COMPARISONS: ETHNOCENTRISM IN EARLY EUROPE AND CHINA

Ethnocentrism is a term that describes the tendency of human beings to view other cultures through the eyes of their own, and usually conclude that their own culture is superior. Ethnocentrism is not necessarily malicious, but it almost always involves the belief that one's culture is the "center" of the world, and all others revolve around it.

Very early, ethnocentrism was reflected in China, where people referred to their land as the "Middle Kingdom," or the culture at the center of all others. During the early part of the era 1450-1648, the Ming Dynasty ruled China, and one of their greatest fears was the threat that outside influence would harm Chinese purity. During the same time period, the Spanish and Portuguese were quarreling over land claims, generally oblivious to the presence of other powers on the earth. For example, Portugal hoped to capture India, a feat that was virtually impossible since a strong, established civilization was already in place there. Like most other societies in history, the Spanish and Portuguese saw land as theirs to conquer, with one another as the only real threat, an attitude that spurred great accomplishments, but also reflected a great deal of ethnocentrism.

for guidance. First, in 1493, the Spanish-born Pope Alexander VI endorsed an imaginary line drawn through the Atlantic from the North to South Pole as the boundary for Spanish land claims, allowing Spain all land west of the line. Portuguese King John II protested the line that ran 100 leagues (about 350 miles) west of the Cape Verde islands and the Azores, so both countries agreed in the **Treaty of Tordesillas** in 1494 on a line moved to 370 leagues west of the islands. As Portugal pushed its explorations to India and beyond, and the Spanish began to explore the Pacific Ocean, they eventually began to argue about lands on the opposite side of the earth, eventually resulting in a treaty in 1529 that set the line in the Pacific. A Spanish adventured named Vasco Nunez de Balboa crossed the Isthmus of Panama from the east and "discovered" the Pacific Ocean on the other side in 1513, and **Ferdinand Magellan** was commissioned by Spain in 1519 to sail westward from Spain, cross the Atlantic, find a way through the Americas, cross the Pacific, and come back home to Spain. Though Magellan himself died in the Philippines, one of his ships made it all the way back to Spain, a significant accomplishment because it was the first to circumnavigate the globe.

The Treaty of Tordesillas was a fateful agreement for both Spain and Portugal, since it oriented Spain toward the Americas (except for Brazil) and Portugal toward Africa and the Indian Ocean. As the Portuguese entered the Indian Ocean Basin, they encountered well-established trade routes and ports frequented, shared, or controlled by many different people. With their sea-worthy caravels equipped with very effectively cannons, the Portuguese were able to dominate trade from Africa to China during the 16th century. As their ships rounded the Cape of Good Hope at the tip of Africa, they first turned their attention to the Swahili city-states on the eastern shore of Africa, many of which they burned to the ground. However, because different ports along the basin were pieces of an Indian Ocean community that was only loosely connected, the "enemy" could not be defeated clearly through a blow to a non-existent head of state. The Portuguese, then, had to be content with quick profits from trade, and they seldom settled in ports they controlled. Muslims, Buddhists, and Hindus had very little interest in converting to the Christianity that the Portuguese tried to impose, and despite the violence that the Portuguese dealt, in many ways life along the Indian Ocean trade circuit went on as it always had. On the other hand, the Spanish turned toward the New World, a place where they discovered that after the conquest of two clear enemies – the Aztecs and the Inca – all would be theirs. Thus began the transformation of the Americas.

The Spanish Empire in the Americas

The Spanish set about their conquest of the Americas in the same manner that Ferdinand and Isabella drove the Muslims out of the Iberian Peninsula. Through a combination of religious fervor to spread their faith and a desire for riches, individual conquistadors ventured out from Hispaniola (a large island which

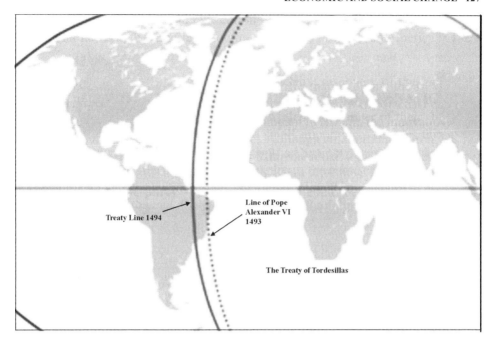

The Treaty of Tordesillas. The first line drawn by Pope Alexander VI gave Spain all the land west of the dotted line. Portugal protested, resulting in the treaty line of 1494, the Treaty of Tordesillas, which moved the line west, allowing Portugal to claim lands east. Notice that the move allowed Portugal to claim Brazil, an area given mostly to Spain by the first line.

Columbus claimed in the Caribbean), to search for gold and convert the natives to Christianity. **Hernan Cortés** left Cuba in 1519 with 600 soldiers to march toward the interior of Mexico, where they sought to find the Aztec capital, **Tenochtitlán**. They were aided in their search by Amerindians who were controlled by but not loyal to their Aztec conquerors. Particularly important was Malintzin (Malinche), a native woman who became a translator and guide for Cortés after she had been given to him as a mistress. Meanwhile, the Aztec emperor, **Moctezuma**, decided to welcome the Spaniards to Tenochtitlán, an action that, at least according to legend, may have been inspired by the belief that Cortés was Quetzalcoatl (an Aztec god) returning home at last. The natives had never seen men with beards before, and descriptions of Spanish faces that were relayed to Moctezuma may have sounded like a description of the "feathered serpent." Whatever his real reason, it was clearly a mistake, and the Spanish took over the city and imprisoned Moctezuma, who was soon killed during a counterattack. How did 600 men take over the great city, protected by thousands of Aztec warriors? One reason was the disloyalty of other Amerindian groups that sided with the Spanish against the Aztecs. Another was the outbreak of illness that hit Tenochtitlán after the Spanish arrived. The natives had never been exposed to the diseases that Europeans carried, while most of the Spanish themselves were immune to it. It has been said that more Aztecs died from disease than from battle wounds. However, the battle

THEMATIC LEARNING OBJECTIVE: INTERACTION OF EUROPE AND THE WORLD: MESOAMERICAN LEGENDS

Mesoamerican cultures were rich in legends passed down from one group to the next, most stories told orally, but many written down in the Aztec pictographic records, or *codices*. The Spanish preserved some of these records, and a Franciscan monk, Bernardino de Sahagun, compiled many others from years of individual interviews with Aztecs. Since these stories were recorded exclusively by the Spanish, some modern scholars question the accuracy of the accounts. However, one of the most famous legends is that of Topiltzin, a Toltec priest affiliated with the god Quetzalcoatl ("feathered serpent") who lost a struggle for power with another faction and was forced into exile. When he left, he promised to return, an event so much anticipated that the Aztecs, who followed the Toltecs to power in central Mexico, at first were hospitable to the Spaniards because they thought that the Spanish leader might be the exiled hero. The following is one account of Topiltzin's departure:

"Thereupon he [Topiltzin] looked toward Tula, and then wept...And when he had done these things...he went to reach the seacoast. Then he fashioned a raft of serpents. When he had arranged the raft, he placed himself as if it were his boat. Then he set off across the sea."

wounds were also important because the Spanish had weapons that the Aztecs did not have: guns and swords: the fine results of years of technological diffusion and perfection all across the Eastern Hemisphere.

A few years after Cortés conquered the Aztecs, another conquistador, **Francisco Pizarro**, led a group of soldiers to the Andes to find the great Inca Empire that he had heard about while living in Panama. The Inca had just been through a bitter civil war between two rival brothers for the throne, and though one – **Atahualpa** – had won, the empire was much weakened. Pizarro met Atahualpa near the city of Cajamarca in 1532, where his small group of soldiers seized Atahualpa from a litter carried by Inca nobles. Forty thousand Inca soldiers surrounded them, but the Spaniards' guns and swords carried the day. Atahualpa was imprisoned and agreed to fill rooms with gold in exchange for his release. Atahualpa kept his promise, but the Spaniards did not. Atahualpa was first baptized as a Christian and then strangled. A massive native rebellion followed that made the conquest of the Inca take longer than the Aztec conquest, but by 1540, the Spanish had the former Inca Empire under control.

ORIGINAL DOCUMENT: THE BATTLE FOR TENOCHTITLÁN

The following selection is based on oral accounts of Aztecs who survived the Spanish capture of Technoctitlán between 1519 and 1521. The author is Bernardino de Sahagún, a Franciscan priest who tried to preserve Amerindian culture by recording their stories.

"When the festivity [annual celebration of the sun god] was being observed and there was dancing and singing...They [the Spaniards] came and closed off each of the places where people went in and out...they stationed themselves in each, and no one could come out any more...Then they surrounded those that were dancing, going among the cylindrical drums. They struck a drummer's arms; both of his hands were severed. Then they struck his neck; his head landed far away. Then they stabbed everyone with iron lances and struck them with iron swords...And when it became known what was happening, everyone cried out, 'Mexica warriors, come running, get outfitted with devices, shields, and arrows, hurry, come running, the warriors are dying..O Mexica warriors!
Before the Spanish [returned] first an epidemic broke out...Large bumps spread on people; some were entirely covered. They spread everywhere, on the face, the head, the chest. The disease brought great desolation; a great many died of it...And when things were in this state, the Spaniards came, moving toward us from Tetzcoco..."

Reference: James Lockhart, ed. and trans., *We People Here: Nahuatl Accounts of the Conquest of Mexico* (Berkeley: University of California press, 1993), pp. 96-112.

Following these two conquests, the Spanish conquistadors marched into other parts of Mesoamerica, South America, and the southern part of North America, claiming land as they went, converting natives to Christianity, and searching for gold. By the end of the 16th century, they had built a massive colonial empire in the New World.

The Colonial Economy in Latin America

The epidemic diseases that the immune Europeans carried with them to the New World may have helped the Spanish to defeat the Aztecs in Tenochtitlán, but the large number of natives that died from smallpox, measles, diphtheria, whooping cough and influenza certainly inhibited the economic development of the colonies.

The Spanish set up silver mines in Peru and Mexico, where huge silver deposits were found, as well as agricultural plantations in the Caribbean. The Portuguese organized sugar plantations in Brazil, since there were few precious metals there. Both mines and plantations required large work forces that the Europeans planned to fill with native workers. Even before the colonial administrative systems developed, individual conquistadors had forced natives to work for them under the **encomienda** system, which gave Spanish settlers – known as **encomenderos** – the right to force natives to work in their mines or fields. In return, they were responsible for their workers' well-being, including their conversion to Christianity. The Spanish system of forced labor in Peru was modeled after the old Inca mit'a system; they required one-seventh of adult male Amerindians to work at any given time for two to four months each year for their Spanish masters. In both arrangements, work was greatly hampered by the death of so many Amerindians. Often the plantations and mines had too few workers to function, and the mit'a system broke down as the Spanish first increased the time commitments, but eventually could not make it work as it had under the Inca rulers. As a result, the Spanish and Portuguese turned more and more to importing slaves from Africa.

The Portuguese sugar plantations had always relied on slave labor, and even after disease killed so many natives, slave raiders forged inland to find new workers in more remote areas of the New World. Importing slaves was more expensive, but the enslaved Africans proved to be more resistant to disease, so in the long run, were better investments. In Mexican and Peruvian mines, the mit'a eventually gave way to a system of wage workers, who were paid good wages to take on the dangerous work. The amount of silver produced rose dramatically in the late 16th century as the population stabilized, and for several decades, silver from Spanish mines dramatically affected the world economy, and made Spain one of the richest states in the world. Mining stimulated the Spanish American economy, and rural estates (called haciendas) produced abundant food for the workers, and small textile shops made their clothing.

The silver mines were a mixed blessing for the Spanish. Since Spanish galleons crossing through the Caribbean and the Atlantic toward Spain were almost always carrying silver, pirates often attacked them, as did crews on ships from rival European countries. Silver that did arrive in Spain flowed out of the country to pay for its many wars with England, France, and the Ottoman Empire, and to buy manufactured goods through the long-distance trade networks. So much silver went into circulation that prices rose sharply, setting off an inflation that greatly wounded the Spanish economy.

Society in Colonial Latin America

The political and economic structures put in place by Spain and Portugal greatly impacted social classes and practices. Since Amerindians were seen by the Iberians as their subjects, the greatest societal division was between European and

THEMATIC LEARNING OBJECTIVE: THE INDIVIDUAL AND SOCIETY: NEW WORLD PATRIARCHIES

The Spanish and Portuguese carried their traditional patriarchal societies across the ocean, and fathers had a great deal of authority over their children. Women were subordinate to men, and could not hold political positions or run plantations or mines. However, a woman with a dowry (payments made to her husband at marriage) maintained control of it throughout the marriage. Widows often carried on family businesses after husbands died, and women also had full rights to inheritance.

Amerindian. The political administrators, military leaders, soldiers, and plantation and mine owners were European; the workers were Amerindian. The old Aztec and Inca class distinctions were wiped away, and all were treated the same by Europeans. Once Spanish and Portuguese children were born in the New World, a distinction arose between those born in the Old World **(peninsulares)** and those born in the new **(creoles***)***. Over time, the peninsulares faded, and creoles came to dominate politics and the economy. However, few women came over from Spain and Portugal, so Spanish soldiers and officials took native wives and mistresses, and their children – half European and half Amerindian – were called **mestizos**. Once African slaves arrived in the New World, another dimension for social distinctions was added. People who were part African and part European were called **mulattoes,** and together with the mestizos they composed the **castas**, a middle-level status between Europeans at the top, and Amerindians and Africans at the bottom.

DUTCH, ENGLISH, AND FRENCH COLONIZATION

Three other European powers set their sights on land in the Americas: the Netherlands, Britain, and France. The Netherlands developed as a center of trade during the High Middle Ages, and unlike the Iberian Catholics, the Dutch Protestants were not particularly interested in spreading their religion to new lands. Instead, their religious zeal was channeled by the **Protestant Work Ethic** that encouraged individual endeavors toward gaining wealth. Newly empowered by independence of the Netherlands from Spain in the late 16th century, shrewd Dutch businessmen noticed that Portugal was losing control of the Indian Ocean trade by the early 17th century. Dutch ships headed toward eastern destinations, where they bought luxury goods from East and Southeast Asia and sold them for a profit in Europe. They prospered partly because many Muslims preferred to trade with them, since the Dutch did not try to convert them to Christianity as the Portuguese Catholics attempted to do. However, the Dutch, like the Portuguese, were not averse to using their cannons to back up their business deals. The Dutch, like the British and French, organized **joint-stock companies** to share the risk of their business ventures, with the largest and most famous one being the **Dutch East India Company** that specialized in the spice and luxury trade with the East Indies. While the company quickly gained control of Dutch trading in the Pacific during the early 17th century, it also became a dominant force in the trans-Atlantic slave trade. Additionally, in 1624 the Dutch West India Company established the colony of New Netherland with its capital located on Manhattan Island in North America.

European Colonization of the Americas by 1640. By 1640, most European land claims were in coastal areas that were more accessible to ships. Much land in the Americas was still unexplored by Europeans, but the largest amount of territory was claimed by Spain.

Explorations in North America

The British got a rather late start in their colonization efforts, partly as a result of an internal power struggle – the Wars of the Roses – that took their attention and drained their resources during the 15th century. Struggles between Catholics and Anglicans resulted from Henry VIII's establishment of the Anglican Church in the early 16th century, but by the reign of his daughter, Elizabeth I, England demonstrated its superior naval power when its fleet defeated the Spanish Armada in 1588. Their first venture to North America was a disappointment – Sir Walter Raleigh's "Lost Colony" on the Carolina coast failed – but by the early 1600s, they had founded several joint-stock companies to begin English settlement of the eastern coast of North America. Beginning with **Jamestown** (Virginia) in 1607, the British established diverse colonies up and down the coast. Puritans, who had broken with Anglican England, settled in Massachusetts; Quakers under the guidance of William Penn sought refuge in New Jersey and Pennsylvania; Anglicans settled in the south; and Catholics found respite in Maryland. The joint-stock companies intended to make profits, and many that came to North America under their sponsorship had economic rather than religious goals. In 1664, the English solidified their control of the Atlantic coast from Massachusetts south when they seized New Netherland from the Dutch to rename it "New York." This victory came on the heels of two successful wars against the Dutch that secured England's status as the world's leading naval power by the late 17th century.

Like England, France entered the race for colonies in the Americas rather late – more than a century after Columbus. They explored the waterways of the Gulf of St. Lawrence and the St. Lawrence River to establish colonies at Port Royal (Nova Scotia) in 1604 and Quebec in 1608. French explorers eventually set up forts along the Ohio and Mississippi Rivers, and French colonies were founded in the Caribbean as well. As in all other European colonies in the New World, control of the French colonies ultimately rested with the king. However, the French, like the Spanish and Portuguese, were also interested in converting natives to Catholicism, so some of the early inhabitants were Jesuit priests. The French were particularly interested in the strong European fur market. French fur traders set up traps along the waterways and involved natives in the trade as well. They exchanged guns, textiles, and alcohol for furs, a practice that not only led to overhunting, but also put firearms into the hands of Amerindians. Since both sides had the use of modern weaponry, confrontations between Amerindians and Europeans became more deadly. Even though the fur trade flourished, the population in French colonies grew more slowly than in English colonies. The cold Canadian colonies held little appeal for French settlers, and France did not allow Protestant Huguenots to settle in their North American colonies. Also, the lifestyle of fur traders, constantly on the move to follow traps and trade deals with natives, was not conducive to family life. In contrast, the English colonies were often settled by families, who came to farm and to provide work for the joint-stock companies.

THEMATIC LEARNING OBJECTIVE: POVERTY AND PROSPERITY: MERCANTILISM

In all colonies in the Americas, European governments tried to control the economies through mercantilism, a system in which they intervened in the market constantly, with the understanding that the goal of economic gain was to benefit the mother country. For most, the official policy was that goods and services that originated in the home country could be exported to colonies only and all colonial exports had to go to the home country. Whether the government controlled the economy directly, as it did in France, Spain, and Portugal, or through government-endorsed joint-stock companies, as happened in England and the Netherlands, mercantilism expanded the mother country's economy far beyond its borders, helping to tilt the balance of power in the world toward Europe.

Relations with Amerindians

In contrast to the densely populated Aztec and Inca Empires, the Indian populations in North America were generally small in the areas that the Dutch, British, and French explored and settled. Most practiced slash-and-burn agriculture or other semi-nomadic life styles, so European colonists could displace them rather easily, usually forcing them further inland. North American Indians were just as susceptible to the diseases brought by Europeans, so their populations were reduced as more settlers arrived. As natives were pushed westward, some adapted to their new environments by abandoning settled agriculture and practicing hunting, a lifestyle made possible by the earlier introduction of horses by the Spanish in Mexico during the 16th century. As some Amerindian groups migrated away from the Europeans, they intruded into lands claimed by other natives, setting off numerous territorial wars. Although Europeans interacted with North American natives, sometimes cooperating with them and sometimes mistreating them, they did not have to conquer as powerful, unified empires as the Spanish had to do in order to control Latin America.

Social classes in the English colonies were less rigidly based on ethnicity than in the Spanish colonies (where a mestizo class became established), partly because the European and Amerindian groups led separate lives in the early days. With

COMPARATIVE COLONIES IN THE AMERICAS

LATIN AMERICA	NORTH AMERICA
Encomienda, mit'a, and slave labor systems developed.	Labor systems that developed were slavery and indentured servitude.
Many single men came as soldiers from Europe and married native women.	More families came, and so less intermarriage took place until English settlers began moving west.
Governments were authoritarian viceroyalties with no assemblies and elaborate bureaucracies.	Governments operated more independently from the kings, with assemblies and less elaborate bureaucracies.
Amerindians were forced into labor by Europeans.	Amerindians were usually pushed aside and not used as a labor force.
Social structures were hierarchical, with several classes strictly based on ethnicity.	Social classes were hierarchical in the southern colonies (based on black vs. white), but generally less hierarchical and rigid than in Latin America.

Amerindians out of the way, the colonies were composed of all English people, and so there were fewer differences among them to form the basis for social class distinctions. Intermingling of blood did take place, but was more common as settlers pressed westward. The southern English colonies developed strict social classes between blacks and whites, and anyone of mixed race was considered to be black, even though the term "mulatto" was used as it was in Latin America. The English believed that blacks and native people were inferior people, but because they maintained strict geographical boundaries between natives and Europeans, the social classes that developed within the middle and northern colonies were mainly among Europeans (except in the south), and were more fluid than in Latin America, where the races were in closer everyday proximity. French trappers, on the other hand, often took native wives, and the French relationship with natives was generally more cooperative, especially since they shared fur-trapping responsibilities and rights.

Regardless of whether they came to North America as a result of religious perse-cution or a desire to make economic gains, most of the English colonists farmed or went into trade. As a result, their forced labor systems developed differently than those in Latin America, where encomienda and mit'a systems predominated. Slaves were brought to North America, just as they were to the Caribbean and to Brazil, but were not practical in areas with small farms, such as New England. In the English middle colonies, another type of compulsory labor appeared: **indentured servitude**. An indentured servant was usually ethnically the same as free settlers, but he or she was bound by an "indenture" (contract) to work for a person for four to seven years in exchange for payment of the voyage to the New World. At the end of the contract, the indentured servant would often get a small piece of land, tools, and clothes, although many of them died during the period of their indenture.

PERSPECTIVES: HOW NATIVES AND NEWCOMERS SAW ONE ANOTHER

As Europeans came to the Americas during the period 1450-1750, conflicts arose between natives and the newcomers, with Amerindian rebellions continuing through the 19th century. From the beginning, each side saw the other through the lens of their respective cultures, as reflected in the quotes below.

"We consider ourselves...much happier than thou, in this that we are very content with the little that we have...[We] find all our riches and all our conveniences among ourselves, without trouble, without exposing our lives to the dangers in which you find yourselves constantly through your long voyages."

An anonymous Quebec Indian leader to French settlers

"In respect to us, they are a people poor, and for want of skill and judgement in the knowledge and use of our things, do esteem our trifles before things of great value...[It] may be hoped, if means of good government be used, that they may in short time be brought to civility, and the embracing of true religion."

Captain Arthur Barlowe, describing natives in Virginia

References: *New Relation of Gaspésie,* Father C. Leclercq, trans. and ed. by William F. Ganong. (Toronto: The Champlain Society, 1910.) *Voyages and Travels by John Pikerton,* Arthur Barlowe (London: Longman, 1812, Vol. 12) p. 604.

GLOBAL EXCHANGES

Once European ships were regularly crossing the Atlantic and venturing into the Pacific Ocean as well, the sustained contact between hemispheres had profound implications for almost all areas of the world, not just for Europe and the Americas. Some of the new exchanges were biological – plants, food, animals, human beings, and disease – and others were commercial, involving manufactured goods, non-biological raw materials, and money. Both types of exchanges combined to establish global networks of trade and communications on a much larger scale than had been seen before in world history.

The Columbian Exchange

The **Columbian Exchange** was the global diffusion of crops, other plants, human beings, animals, and disease that took place after the exploratory voyages to the New World of the late 15th and 16th centuries. More than previous diffusions, the Columbian Exchange put people of the world in touch with biological species that were radically different from what they had known before. In previous times, species had developed in isolation, resulting in an almost completely different set of flora and fauna in the Western and Eastern Hemisphere, as well as in Oceania. When these worlds were brought together, people had access to all three areas, bringing about vast changes in natural environment, health, and demographic patterns.

A dramatic demographic change occurred in the New World as astoundingly high death rates occurred among Amerindians as a result of contact with Europeans. Because of their long isolation, Amerindians had no immunities to smallpox, influenza, typhus, measles, and diphtheria, and once a disease was communicated, it spread rapidly, killing the majority of the people. Smallpox was the deadliest of the early epidemics, but often it combined with other diseases to increase mortality rates even more. Death rates were highest in densely populated areas, such as the Aztec and Inca empires, but they spread to other areas as well. Persistent accusations were made that Europeans spread their diseases on purpose, but no conclusive historical proof has been found to support them. However, the exchange of diseases worked both ways, and by the mid-17th century, European immigrants to the Caribbean were dying of malaria, a disease found in the tropical country along the Gulf of Mexico. As Europeans made their way into Oceania, contagious diseases spread to many previously unexposed people, resulting in high death tolls, although on a smaller scale than in the Americas.

As devastating as the disease pathogens were, the Columbian Exchange also had some very positive consequences, and over time, it probably increased rather than decreased world population overall. Supplies of food increased so that people were less likely to go hungry in times of drought or local food shortages. The variety of available food increased with the exchange, giving people wider access

NEW EXCHANGES IN THE COLUMBIAN EXCHANGE

From the Americas	From the Eastern Hemisphere
beans, squash, tomatoes, sweet potatoes, peanuts, chilis, chocolate, maize (corn), potatoes, avocados, pineapple, manioc	wheat, rice, olives, grapes, bananas, rice, citrus fruits, melons, figs, sugar, coconuts, okra horses, cattle, pigs, sheep, goats, chickens, rabbits, rats

to an assortment of nutrients necessary for good health. Even though it took some time to adjust to new types of food, caloric intake increased in many areas, a trend especially important for growing children.

The European conquests in the Americas were important "marker events" in the development of western civilization because they established European values, religion, economic goals, and languages in the New World and set the boundaries for a new world trade system that would become increasingly dominated by European countries. In turn, Indian religion, language, and values were suppressed so that "South America" and "Central America" were transformed into "Latin America."

ECONOMIC CRISIS AND REALIGNMENT IN THE EARLY 17TH CENTURY

During the 16th century, large amounts of silver and gold from the Spanish Empire made their way into the new world trade circuits and contributed to a steady rise in prices that created an inflation rate estimated at about 2% a year. Improvements in mining techniques raised the output of silver and copper mines in central Europe as well. These new supplies of precious metals from the Americas led to an increase in prices of many goods that further fed inflation. Although the price increases were gradual, prices doubled in Spain by the mid-16th century and quadrupled by 1600. Generally, wages remained well behind the rise in prices, causing a financial crisis for many households, and tight food budgets led to smaller families and contributed to a decline in population. Furthermore, governments overspent revenues by backing explorations and military competitions and wars, leaving most of Europe's rulers facing deep deficits. The devastation caused by the wars of religion contributed to the deepening crisis. In the early 1600s prices began to level off and even to drop, and in most places population growth slowed.

THEMATIC LEARNING OBJECTIVE: POVERTY AND PROSPERITY: CLIMATE CHANGE AND THE RECESSION OF THE EARLY 17TH CENTURY

Historians disagree about what actually caused the deep recession in Europe during the early 17th century, but in recent years many have come to believe that climate change had something to do with it. The period between 1600 and 1850 is sometimes called **"The Little Ice Age"** because glaciers advanced, temperatures dropped, and winters were often quite severe. Colder weather meant lower crop yields, which in turn led to increased famine and greater susceptibility to disease.

Since reliable records of European temperatures were not kept until the 1700s, historians have had to rely on newly discovered primary documents of the era. As a result of these findings, new perspectives on the recession have been explored. For example, one source from a village in the French Alps wrote, "We are terrified of the glaciers...which are moving forward all the time and have just buried two of our villages." Late harvests, particularly of wine grapes, also provide evidence that crops were not as plentiful as they had been before. Today scientists also study ice cores from Greenland to better understand fluctuations in temperature, and they have found that temperatures during the 1600s appear to have been quite cool. Another bit of evidence comes from tree rings studies, since in cold summers trees have thinner growth rings. Tree rings tell us that four out of five of the coldest summers in the past 400 years were during the 17th century.

Reference: The Making of the West. Lynn Hunt, et. al. (Boston: Bedford/St. Martin's) 2005, p. 600.

Warning signs for recession were clear by the third decade of the 17th century, with foreign trade slumping as war and an uncertain money supply made business riskier. After 1625, silver imports to Spain declined, in part because so many of the Amerindians who worked for Spanish mines died from disease. Textile production fell in many countries, and even the relatively small African trade stagnated until the latter part of the 17th century. Population growth came to a standstill, and overall population of Europe probably declined slightly, from about 85 million in 1550 to about 80 million in 1650. The Thirty Years' War led to dramatic population decline in the Holy Roman Empire, with about one-fourth of the Empire's inhabitants dying in the 1630s and 1640s. Slight population increases occurred only in England, Wales, the Dutch Republic, the Spanish Netherlands, and Scandinavia. This reversal in population trends caused agricultural prices to decline, since food demands dropped, and farmers who produced for the market suffered.

In some places farmers deserted their lands and left land to waste, as had happed during the 13th century plague epidemic. The exception was farming in the Dutch Republic, where agricultural innovation – such as field drainage, crop rotation, and animal breeding – kept production high, and their foreign trade and textile industry continued to grow as well.

SOCIAL CHANGES – 1550-1648

Religious conflict disrupted the everyday lives of people all across Europe during the late 16th and early 17th centuries. Wars devastated many areas and contributed to severe economic decline in the Spanish Netherlands, France, and the Holy Roman Empire. Inflation also impacted most people, including wealthy elites and common people alike.

Effects of Economics and Religious Wars on Social Class

During the 16th century, the established nobility lost power to monarchs, and to urban dwellers, who were growing wealthier with trade. The economic and political **gentry** – a class of wealthy, educated, and socially-ambitious families in urban and rural areas of western Europe – grew tremendously during the 16th century. Their capital came from profits from expanded production and trade, and from a rise in the value of land as population and prices rose. The gentry were especially prominent in England, where many of the men came to be royal officeholders. In France the gentry came to be called the "**bourgeoisie**", a term that – like the English "burgher" – originally meant a person living in a chartered town or borough. Many bought titles of nobility outright, and others received them as benefits of their offices. They often lent money to the government, and as we saw in Chapter Five, they played an important role in the rise of the House of Commons as it clashed with the king during the English Civil War. City governments also changed, with town councils dominated by small numbers of privileged families, not by the trade associations (guilds) as in medieval times.

The lives of artisans and laborers were affected by the development of overseas trade. For example, production of cloth on a large scale for export now required a great deal of capital – far more than a typical guild craftsman could amass. As a result, new investor-producers bought up large amounts of wool and hired it out to go through each of the stages of production – cleaning, spinning, weaving, and piece-working. As workers began to be treated as hired hands, fewer and fewer positions were available for master artisans and their apprentices. As competition for jobs increased, restrictions tightened particularly for women, who had often combined assisting their artisan husbands with housework. New laws forbade widows from continuing to practice their husband's enterprises, and many town governments tried to restrict women's rights to sell in marketplaces.

Even before the recession of the early 17th century, peasants were feeling economic strain, as population growth caused many farms to be subdivided among numerous children. Countless peasants lost their land to newly wealthy gentry, and others were unable to rent land as rents rose. With shrinking opportunities for farming, many found their way to cities, where they often took odd jobs or remained unemployed.

Common people were often at odds with one another over religious matters and sometimes took the initiative in attacking members of other faiths to rid their communities of them. Heretics – whether they erred from the Catholic or Protestant faiths – were considered to be dangerous provokers of God's wrath, and many believed that it was their responsibility to act against them. Ordinary people fought in wars not only from religious conviction but also from the need for self-defense or economic betterment. They filled the armies under the command of their military leaders (who came mostly from the nobility), and they built walls around their towns and dug siege works. Since the religious wars often left towns and the countryside decimated, peasant rebellions and urban uprisings were a constant threat. Most people, however, did not respond to their circumstances by rebelling. Instead they took to the road in search of food or work. Many were reduced to eating roots, bark, and grass.

Social Roles of Education

Education in the late 16th century took on a new importance for the social system for several reasons. One result of the religious reformations was the attempt to revitalize the clergy with well-educated men. The growth of commerce meant that literate clerks and agents were needed, and the growing government bureaucracies increased the demand for workers who understood finance, could keep records, and draft proposals. The need for lawyers became more important as governments expanded their authority and laws became more numerous and complex. New universities were founded in France, the Dutch Republic, Germany, Spain, and the Swiss cantons, and in England, new colleges were established at Oxford and Cambridge.

Changes in Family Life and the Status of Women

Even in the best of times, families of the late 16th and early 17th century often lost children at a young age. One-fifth to one-fourth of all children died in their first year, and only half the population lived beyond the age of 20. Childbirth was still the leading cause of death for women, with about 10% of the female population lost during the process. Midwives delivered most babies; physicians were few and far between, and even if they were in attendance, their methods were often less than helpful. A common practice for many maladies of the day was blood-letting, often by the application of leeches. Blood-letting was believed to prevent miscarriages, but women and their babies were not helped by the treatment.

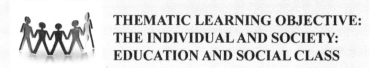

THEMATIC LEARNING OBJECTIVE: THE INDIVIDUAL AND SOCIETY: EDUCATION AND SOCIAL CLASS

The schools and colleges drew students from a wide range of social classes. Most schools remained open only to boys, although many new Catholic convents were established with the express purpose of educating girls. Surprisingly, intelligent boys appeared to have more opportunity for advancement through education than they did in the 18th and 19th centuries in most countries across Europe. Such opportunity could be seen at Oxford in England, where the status of students was recorded when they first enrolled, classifying them as "esquires," "gentlemen," "clergy," and "plebeians" (a term for commoners from the Ancient Romans). From 1560 to 1660, about half of the Oxford students were "plebeians."

Starting in the early 17th century, with the economic recession and religious wars raging, families in all classes of society limited the number of children they had, a trend that continued until the end of the 18th century. Because contraception was not widely used, the number of births was usually controlled by later marriage; the average age of marriage rose from the early twenties in 1600 to the late twenties by the end of the century. The average family had about four children, but wealthier families had more than poorer families did. Despite later marriages, the number of births out of wedlock was relatively small at about 2-5% of all births, partly because both the Reformation and the Counter-Reformation stressed sexual abstinence before marriage.

Theological and popular literature on marriage emphasized the ideal qualities of both husbands and wives. A husband was obliged to provide for the material comforts of his wife and children, protecting his family in a steady and self-controlled manner. The husband was the head of the household, but he was to rule firmly and justly, and not as a tyrant. A wife should be a mature manager of her household and a respectful and obedient spouse. Each partner was expected to be sexually faithful to the other, contrary to the customary "double standard," which through history has generally allowed men more sexual freedom than women. For women, their households had first priority, although they often assisted their husbands in business or other work, and they frequently engaged in charitable work. Religious beliefs backed these gender roles, with the submission of women justified as the punishment they had inherited from Eve. According to Biblical teachings, a man

EXAMINING THE EVIDENCE:
THE DEBATE ABOUT WOMEN
(1620)

The *Quarrells des Femmes,* or Debate About Women, continued in Europe during the entire early modern era. It sometimes centered on *"Hic Mulier,"* or the "Mannish Woman," and *"Haec Vir,"* or the "Womanish Man." The excerpts below were written in England during the late 16th and early 17th centuries.

"Come then you masculine women, for you are my subject, you that are stranger than strangeness itself, whom wise men wonder at, boys shout at, and goblins themselves start at...keep those parts concealed from the eyes that may not be touched with the hands. Let not a wandering and lascivious thought read in an enticing index the contents of an unchaste volume...But for those things which belong to this wanton and lascivious delight and pleasure, as eyes wandering, lips billing, tongue enticing, bared breast seducing, and naked arms embracing, O hide them..."

Hic Mulier responded to *Haec Vir* by admonishing him to "cast then from you our ornaments and put on your own armors. Be men in shape, men in show, men in words, men in actions, men in counsel, men in example: then will we love and serve you; then will we hear and obey you; then will we, like rich jewels, hang at your ears to take our instructions, and like true friends follow you through all dangers."

Reference: Anonymous, *The Debate About Women;* Hic Mulier *and* Haec Vir.

earned the family's bread "by the sweat of his brow." Catholics viewed marriage as a religious union that could not be dissolved, but Protestants saw marriage as a contract of mutual promises to support, share, and provide companionship. Protestants recognized a mutual right to divorce and remarry for reasons of adultery or irreparable breakdown. Some single women of the middle and working classes worked as butchers, shopkeepers, laborers, nurses, goldsmiths, and midwives.

Despite these strict religious standards for "ideal" men and women, sensuality was characteristic of the era. Artists' drawings show that plump, voluptuous women were prized as beauties, and muscular men were preferable to thin ones. Homosexuality was noted in literary works, and prostitutes were plentiful. In 1566, Pope Pius IV expelled all the prostitutes from Rome, an action that left the city with such a loss of revenue that he had to rescind his order in less than a month. Since the late Middle Ages, licensed houses of prostitution had been common in towns and cities, and especially during the era of recession in the early 17th century, poverty almost certainly forced both men and women into the "world's oldest profession."

The Hunt for Witches

Certain types of witchcraft had long existed in Europe. For example, "black magic" – such as one peasant casting a spell on another's cow – had been common since the Middle Ages. However, between 1550 and 1648, Europe saw a dramatic increase in the persecution of women and men for witchcraft. Approximately 100,000 people were tried and about 60,000 executed as witches. The surge in witch-hunting was closely linked to religious concerns about heretics and to the social tensions that resulted from economic difficulties. The vast majority of those convicted were women, and the idea developed that they made pacts with the devil in return for the power to work mischief on their enemies. Since pacts with the devil meant the rejection of God, witchcraft was considered heresy.

Most individual accusations of witchcraft came from within a witch's community, usually from ordinary people. Often the accused person had been known for practicing black magic, but the villagers did not take action until some type of crisis occurred, such as an epidemic or a famine. Women's work often made them vulnerable to charges of witchcraft because they usually handled food supplies and medicines, and the deaths of young children and/or domestic animals (such as cows) could trigger the accusations. Isolated cases often led to more suspects being identified, so that localized frenzies of active witch-hunting would occur before the anxiety subsided. Torture or threat of torture led to most of the confessions, which often identified other "witches" in the community.

Widespread witch-hunting ended by the late 17th century, in part because the intellectual energies of literate Europeans shifted from religious to scientific thought. The practice of witchcraft continued for some time, although it never reached the same frenzy again.

Regional Economic and Social Variations

Between 1550 and 1648, the economic **balance of power** changed, with the economies of southern Europe declining and those of the northwest emerging stronger. The economic crisis of the 17th century ended the dominance of Mediterranean economies – such as the Italian city-states – and increased the power of those that based their prosperity on the Atlantic trade, such as England and the Dutch Republic. Amsterdam replaced the Italian cities as the center of European trade and commerce.

Western Europe also became quite distinct from eastern Europe, where serfdom remained entrenched throughout the 16th and 17th centuries. As the west moved away from the medieval manorial system, and commoners became either independent peasants or moved to town, the old system did not change in eastern Europe. In the west, the changes brought by the commercial revolution were advantageous to the middle class and to many peasants. In eastern Europe, it was the lords who benefited from rising prices and the growing market for grain and forest products. The price rise of the 16th century caused Polish and eastern German nobles to increase their holdings and step up their production of grain, which they sold to western Europeans. To raise production, they forced peasants to pay more rent and dues, and those who could not come up with the money were forced into becoming serfs completely tied to the land. All over eastern Europe, the old relationship between landlords and serfs checked economic development and kept most of the population illiterate and desperately poor. In contrast, in western Europe there were peasants who were already on the way to becoming small proprietors, and they were free people under the law. They could migrate, marry, and learn trades as opportunity offered. In contrast, the Code of Laws in Muscovy recognized serfdom in 1649, and the rural masses lost personal freedom and lived in deep poverty no longer experienced by the majority of peasants in the west..

By 1648, economic and social developments had played as big a role in the transformation of early modern Europe as did the cultural changes of the Renaissance and the religious changes of the two Reformations. As power shifted from areas around the Mediterranean to the north, new literary contributions from the north and west reflected and influenced the new economic and social systems, and scientific thought began to lessen the powerful influence of religion, especially in the lives of the elites and the middle class.

CONCEPTS AND IDENTIFICATIONS

Atahualpa
balance of power
bourgeoisie
Cabral, Pedro
capitalism
caravel
castas
Columbian Exchange
Columbus, Christopher
commercial revolution
conquistadors
Cortés, Hernan
creoles
Dias, Bartholomew

Dutch East India Company
enclosures
encomenderos
encomienda
gentry
Henry the Navigator
indentured servitude
Jamestown
joint stock companies
"The Little Ice Age"
Magellan, Ferdinand
mercantilism
Mercator projection
mestizos
mit'a system
Moctezuma
mulattoes
peninsulares
Pizarro, Francisco
Protestant Work Ethic
putting out system
Tenochtitlán
Treaty of Tordesillas

CHAPTER 7:
NEW CULTURAL AND
SCIENTIFIC DEVELOPMENTS
1550-1648

As we have seen in previous chapters, the transformation of Europe between 1450 and 1648 came from a wide variety of cultural, economic, social, political, technological, and intellectual sources. Changes evolved together, and change in one area brought about reactions in the others, which in turn brought further alterations in the first area. By 1550, the intellectual innovations of the Renaissance interested many Europeans, and the discovery of the New World provided them with a different set of intellectual challenges as well as new material opportunities. The Protestant Reformation encouraged them to challenge traditional authority, and new economic patterns broke up the old social class structure, at least in western and northern Europe. Between 1550 and 1648, these changes interacted to create new developments in literature and the arts, and to shape an important marker event in European history – the Scientific Revolution.

ART AND LITERATURE

The Renaissance shaped art and literature during the early modern era, but both also experienced changes that were closely linked to the emerging religious, political, and intellectual developments of the period. Artists experimented with new styles – **mannerism** and the **baroque** – and literature found a new form, as drama became popular, and professional theater companies appeared for the first time in Europe. In both areas, secular values remained important, but religion played a significant role as artists and writers reflected the religious turbulence of the era.

Art: Mannerism and the Baroque

By the 1520s and 1530s the principles of the artistic Renaissance – balance, harmony, and moderation – were breaking down as religious and political turbulence increased. Before the end of the 16th century, the artistic style known as **mannerism** emerged in the Italian states and spread across Europe. Mannerism deliberately distorted Renaissance principles (such as perspective) in order to convey a message or emphasize a theme. As anxiety and suffering resulted from war and economic upheavals, mannerist painters deliberately portrayed people in scenes that reflected anxiety and the desire to escape reality. Artists often tried to create an atmosphere in their paintings that conveyed strong emotions, and a common technique was to deliberately elongate human figures to portray how out of sorts they felt. The most famous mannerist painter was **El Greco** ("the Greek"), so called because he was of Greek origin, but he trained in Venice and Rome and spent much of his life in Spain. El Greco's paintings are full of people and objects that created new and often odd visual effects. He sometimes filled the heavens with religious figures above humans on earth, and his works of art are still open to various interpretations because of their mysterious allusions. El Greco used color to convey emotion, with his elongated figures often portrayed in unusual shades of yellow and green, and his skies were often full of turbulent gray clouds.

Mannerism was eventually replaced by the **baroque** style that became popular by the turn of the 17th century and dominated the artistic world for another century and a half. Like mannerism, the baroque originated in the Italian states, where artists first experimented with it in church design. The term "baroque" was not used by people living at the time, but came about in the 18th century, perhaps from the Portuguese *barroco,* used to describe irregularly shaped pearls. The term as applied to the arts was originally derogatory, implying that the works were bizarre, confused, and extravagant. Although the baroque style did not convey the same uneasiness that mannerism did, it too evoked passion and mystery in contrast to the Renaissance emphasis on harmonious design, unity, and clarity. The baroque was closely associated with the Counter-Reformation in its attempt to glorify both the Catholic Church and the monarchy. The Catholic Habsburg territories, including Spain and the Spanish Netherlands, embraced the style. The Spanish built baroque churches in their American colonies as they successfully converted Amerindians to the Catholic faith. However,, the Protestant countries of Europe largely rejected baroque art and architecture. For example, Dutch painters of the next generation (such as Rembrandt van Rijn) preferred realistic portraits and everyday, simple scenes. However, nearly a century later Protestants embraced the baroque style of music – such as that of the endlessly inventive Johann Sebastian Bach – in the early 18th century.

Baroque painting was distinguished by the dramatic use of color and shading and by dynamic, energetic figures. Baroque artists based their work on Renaissance achievements in representing the human form in three-dimensional space. However, they used light, movement, and more robust human figures to enhance the drama and emotional impact of their paintings. The first great baroque painter was the Italian-trained **Peter Paul Rubens**, who lived in the Spanish Netherlands. Rubens was a devout Catholic who concentrated on themes that glorified great rulers or that emphasized the grandeur and mystery of Catholic ceremony. His paintings often were intended to stimulate the viewer's piety by stressing the power of the faith. A less well known painter was **Artemisia Gentileschi**, one of the few female painters of the age. Her fame today rests on a series of pictures of heroines from the Old Testament, including Judith, Esther, and Bathsheba. Especially well known is her *Judith Beheading Holofernes,* a dramatic, gory scene in which Judith slays the Assyrian general Holofernes in order to save her besieged town. In the painting, Judith struggles to saw off the general's head, a perfect illustration of the action-packed, emotional baroque style.

Like baroque painters, baroque architects modified the precision, symmetry, and orderliness of Renaissance architecture to produce a sense of grandeur and emotion. Façades and interiors were both massive and suggestive of movement, and churches were filled with sculpture that reflected the baroque spirit. Perhaps the most famous baroque architect and sculptor of all was **Gian Lorenzo Bernini,** who completed Saint Peter's basilica in Rome and designed the colonnade enclosing the piazza in front of the church. One of the most famous sculptures of all times is his *Throne of Saint Peter* that virtually hovers in midair inside Saint Peter's, and is held by the hands of four great doctors (or teachers) of the Catholic Church. Above the chair, rays of light drive clouds and angels toward the viewer, enhancing the sculptor's intent to convey the majesty and grandeur of the pope.

Throne of Saint Peter. In the center of Saint Peter's basilica is the light-bedazzled *Throne of Saint Peter,* perfectly situated for maximum effect of grandeur and awe. Bernini designed the famous sculpture, completed the basilica that had been started much earlier, and created a vast colonnade for the piazza in front of the church.

La Compaña de Jesús. This church built in Cuzco, Peru, during the mid-17th century is a good example of the baroque style as it appeared in the Spanish colonies. It was built on the site of an important Inca palace destroyed by the invaders, symbolizing Spanish dominance over the old regime. The elaborate fountain in front of the church and the many dynamic figures and symbols tucked into the heavy façade are typical of the baroque style. Inside are a stunning gilded altar and several important works of art. Compare this baroque-style church with the 15th Renaissance church in Florence designed by Leon Battista Alberti on page 60.

Art: The Dutch Style

In the Dutch Republic a strong style of painting developed that was quite different from the baroque. One influence was Protestantism, and since the Reformed Church frowned on religious art, artists tended to create works that expressed personal faith. Another factor was the lack of a royal court, which meant that the chief patrons of art were merchants, who were interested in dignified portraits, not in ornate baroque displays. The most famous painter of the Dutch School was **Rembrandt van Rijn**, whose subjects were presented in a calm, restrained way that reflected inner personality, human character, and subtle self-revelation. His portraits were of many types of people – young and old, rich and poor – and they all reflected his interest in light, especially as it illuminated the faces he painted. His most famous paintings were a series of sixty self-portraits that began in his youth and continued through till his later years. His work presaged a change in art styles; after his death in 1669, the next generation of painters adopted the serenity, calm, and elegance of his distinctive style.

LITERATURE

As often occurs during times of political and economic uncertainty, intellectuals of the era between 1550 and 1648 pondered and wrote about their troubled environment. As a result, some extraordinary literary contributions were made, including those of Michel de Montaigne, Miguel de Cervantes, and William Shakespeare. The spread of education and literacy in the late 16th century had a dramatic impact on attitudes toward literature and on literature itself. The value of education – especially the humanist attempt to recover ancient wisdom – was reflected in much of the literature of the period. Writers captured a vision of what it meant to be an educated and disciplined intellectual instead of a warrior focused on war and conquest.

Michel de Montaigne

Michel de Montaigne was a member of the French nobility who received a classical education before studying law and securing a judicial appointment in 1554. Despite his strong identification as a noble, he highly disapproved of nobles who were more concerned with war and sports than with the cultivation of the intellect. At the age of 38, Montaigne resigned his judicial post and devoted the rest of his life to the life of the mind. As a humanist, he was particularly concerned with understanding himself, since he believed that self-knowledge teaches people how to live in accordance with nature and God. In his writings, Montaigne developed a new literary genre, the **essay** (from the French *essayer,* meaning "to test or try") to express his thoughts and ideas.

Montaigne's writings reflect an early form of **skepticism**, a school of thought founded on doubt that total certainty or definitive knowledge is ever attainable. His philosophy was captured by a statement he painted on the beams of his study: "All that is certain is that nothing is certain." Some of his essays directly rejected cruelty and violence, and others asserted his belief in the natural nobility of human beings. His philosophy anticipated that of many 18th-century thinkers, and his work represented a sharp break with the past. Faith and religious certainty had characterized western society for a millennium; in contrast, Montaigne demonstrated secularism and skepticism.

ORIGINAL DOCUMENT:
MONTAIGNE "ON CRUELTY"

Michel de Montaigne lived during the time of the French civil wars between Catholics and Protestants, and his essays demonstrate how troubled he was by the turbulence and violence of 16th century France. His gentle and sensitive nature are apparent in this excerpt from his famous essay "On Cruelty":

" Among other vices I cruelly hate cruelty, both by nature and by judgment, as the extreme of all vices...

I live in a time when we abound in incredible examples of this vice, through the license of our civil wars; and we see in the ancient histories nothing more extreme than what we experience of this every day. But that has not reconciled me to it at all."

Reference: D.M. Frame, trans., *The Complete Works of Montaigne* (Stanford, Calif.: Stanford University Press, 1958), pp. 175-176.

Miguel de Cervantes

In Spain, **Miguel de Cervantes** reacted to the brutality and disregard for human values that he saw in Spain, as the country declined politically and economically during the late 16th century. During his lifetime he saw King Philip II fight many destructive and bloody wars to secure Spanish lands in the name of Catholicism, only to have Philip's power gradually slip away by the time of his death in 1598. Cervantes's great novel **Don Quixote** is a blistering social satire that ridiculed the Spanish nobility and revealed the wide gap between the ideals and realities of his day. The two main characters of his book illustrated this divide, with the knight Don Quixote de La Mancha as the visionary who saw only the ideal and not the real. For example, he thought that windmills were four-armed giants and a shaving basin was a golden helmet. In contrast, his squire, Sancho Panza, was the realist who tried to get his master to see the true conditions around them. Through their many lively adventures, the two characters eventually came to see the value of the other's perspective. Cervantes avoided politics and commented mostly on ordinary people and their hypocrisies and intolerances, and his sharpest criticisms were directed at the violent disregard for human values that was characteristic of his times.

PERSPECTIVES:
HISTORICAL "GOLDEN AGES"

The era of Queen Elizabeth I (the Elizabethan era) is often seen as a "golden age" in English history. What is a golden age? Historians use the term to describe important eras of many civilizations. During a golden age, a civilization is usually quite prosperous, and it also tends to be innovative in arts, science, and literature. These characteristics are based on the principles of civilization (see p. 20). For example, surpluses and specialized occupations often lead to prosperity because economic activities are specialized and efficient with food supplies to support them. Innovations in arts, science, and literature require the time to focus on these endeavors, so prosperous societies with surpluses can generally afford to support scholars, artists, and technologists. Commonly mentioned golden ages include Ancient Greece during the 5th century B.C.E., the Italian city-states (such as Florence and Venice) during the Renaissance, the Abbasid Dynasty (an Islamic civilization that stretched from about 800 to 1200 C.E.), and Qing China under Emperor Kangxi during the early 18th century. During Elizabethan times, England was full of political, technological, and economic exuberance and pride that spilled over into its literature, producing the great dramatist **William Shakespeare**, who presided over a "golden age of theater."

William Shakespeare and Drama

During the reign of Queen Elizabeth I (1558-1603), English literature experienced a **Golden Age**, or a time of great accomplishment. Writers expressed themselves most famously in terms of poetry and drama, and one of the most celebrated writers of all times emerged – **William Shakespeare**. Shakespeare was the son of a prosperous glove-maker from Stratford-upon-Avon, and when he arrived in London in 1592 as a young man, theater was already very popular. By 1576, two professional theaters run by actors' companies existed, and Shakespeare contributed greatly to their rising success. Audiences varied greatly, and people from almost all walks of life were attracted to the theater. The lower classes could find entertainment for a penny or two, and the nobility and well-to-do gentry paid higher prices for better seats in more expensive theaters.

Shakespeare, of course, was the most influential playwright of the era, and arguably of all times. He wrote three dozen plays – both dramas and comedies – and acted in one of the chief troupes. None of his plays were set in his day, but they reflected Elizabethan concerns: the nature of power and the crisis of authority. He was a master of the English language, but perhaps his most enduring talent was an incredible insight into human psychology. One of his favorite themes was the legitimacy of rulers, as evidenced in *Hamlet* and *Macbeth,* both set in medieval times, and *Julius Caesar,* set in the days of the late Roman Republic. However, his concerns were very contemporary, especially as Queen Elizabeth aged and eventually died in 1603, bringing about uncertainty as the throne passed to her nephew, James of Scotland, who indeed proved to be a troublesome monarch. His plays also reflected a growing sense of English nationalism, as evidenced in this famous excerpt from *Richard II:*

> *This royal throne of kings, this scept'red isle,*
> *This earth of majesty, this seat of Mars,*
> *This other Eden, demi-paradise,*
> *This fortress built by Nature for herself*
> *Against infection and the hand of war,*
> *This happy breed of men, this little world,*
> *This precious stone set in the silver sea...*
> *This blessed plot, this earth, this realm, this*
>   *England...*

(*Richard II,* act 2, sc. 1, lines 40-50)

During the period, professional theater was also popular in Spain, where the best-known dramatist was Lope de Vega, who wrote more than fifteen hundred works on a wide range of topics. Although religious themes remained popular in Spanish theater, many plays treated secular subjects and some were disguised political commentary. Touring companies brought Spanish plays to all parts of the Spanish Empire.

THE SCIENTIFIC REVOLUTION

Just as it impacted art, literature, and religion, the growing humanistic emphasis of the era 1450-1648 shaped attitudes toward scientific thought. Scientists loosened their research from the theories devised during the classical era, and based their knowledge of the natural world on direct observation and mathematics. The new vision of science that developed during this time is known as the **Scientific Revolution**, and its reliance on human reason to understand scientific phenomena reinforced changes brought about by the Renaissance and the Protestant Reformation, including a further weakening of the influence of the Roman Catholic Church.

Astronomy

The origins of the Scientific Revolution lie, for the most part, in developments in astronomy. Because of astronomy's role in the explanation of the natural world

MARKER EVENT:
THE DEVELOPMENT OF SCIENCE

During the 16th and 17th centuries, European intellectuals devised new ways of thinking that released them from blind acceptance of church teachings and principles developed by ancient Greeks and Romans. To be sure, they borrowed heavily from other civilizations, particularly the Islamic caliphate of the 13th century. However, men like Copernicus, Kepler, Galileo, Bacon, and Descartes deserve credit for new achievements based on empirical evidence and mathematical formulas that shaped not only views of the natural universe, but also of society, state, the arts, and religion as well.

Why is the development of science in early modern Europe a marker event? Not only has it represented new frontiers for the human mind, but science has also increasingly affected practical affairs and has influenced the way many non-scientists think. For example, today the ideas of Charles Darwin about evolution and natural selection have spread far and wide. Perhaps most importantly, scientific thought has shaped basic human perceptions of the world, including the belief that the physical universe is orderly and harmonious for the most part. Science also affirms the importance of human reason as a way of understanding and dealing with the world, and it encourages the idea that human affairs can be conducted through peaceful exchange of ideas and rational discussion. In short, science is basic to many beliefs that people in the modern world hold today.

that had been devised by ancient and medieval scientists and philosophers, any questioning of the old views was bound to have widespread intellectual repercussions. By the early 1600s, many beliefs that had stood for hundreds or thousands of years were proved to be inaccurate, or were at least changed significantly.

The methods devised by scientists of these early modern times form the basis for science today: mathematical formulation, **empirical evidence** (information verifiable by observations), and freedom of inquiry. The new science contrasted to the scholasticism of the Middle Ages that held that principles established by the church should direct the inquiries of scholars. This new emphasis on the freedom of inquiry sometimes resulted in clashes between scientists and religious and political authorities, and so the researchers didn't always make their findings public. One of the first European scientists to experience this conflict was **Nicholas Copernicus**, a Polish monk and mathematician who based his early mathematical tables and models on those developed by **Nasir al-Din**, an Islamic scholar of the

13th century. Copernicus was commissioned by Pope Paul III to revise the Julian calendar – devised during the time of Julius Caesar – to correct for slight inaccuracies that caused the calendar year to continuously lose time. Copernicus analyzed the astronomy underlying the calendar, which the Romans had based on the work of the Greek astronomer Ptolemy. Ptolemy believed that the earth was at the center of the universe, and that all heavenly bodies revolved around it, including the sun and the moon. Ptolemy's theory had been adopted by the church as official doctrine, so to question Ptolemy was also to question the church. Based on his own empirical observations, Copernicus discovered that the earth was revolving around the sun. His formulations also revealed that the earth turned on its axis every 24 hours, so that differences in night and day were not caused by the universe revolving around the earth. Since his free inquiry led him in a direction contrary to church doctrine, he tested his developing theory over and over again, and only revealed his outcomes just before his death. Even then, the findings were released only to a handful of scientists and mathematicians.

Two astronomers that followed – **Tycho Brahe** and **Johannes Kepler** – used the Copernicus model to develop a more comprehensive theory of the structure of our solar system. Kepler's observations led him to conclude that planets had elliptical, not circular, orbits around the sun. Unlike Copernicus, Kepler published his results as a relatively young man, fueling a controversy between religious officials and scientists. Protestant leaders criticized the new scientific models, too, with Martin Luther attacking the Copernican model as early as 1539. The Catholic Church was slower to condemn it, but in 1610, it declared Copernicus's work a heresy, and by 1616 all writings that claimed that the earth moved on its axis were forbidden to be taught or read. This course of events entangled an Italian astronomer, **Galileo Galilei**, as he turned his newly invented telescope toward the sky in 1609. The telescope had been created for optical purposes in the Netherlands, but Galileo was the first to use it to study the heavens, where he discovered that the Milky Way was a huge collection of stars, the moon's light is reflected from the sun, and the earth is not the only planet with moons.

These discoveries and many more were disconcerting to people of early modern Europe because they indicated that the earth is nothing special, and is only one of many heavenly bodies in the universe. For the religious, the new science implied that the earth was not central to God's creation, and they called into question the belief that God's throne is in a fixed place in heaven. Galileo – like Copernicus, Brahe, and Kepler – stressed his own empirical observations, but more than the earlier scientists, he wrote for a general audience, not for just scientists. His writings were in the vernacular (Italian) as well, so the impact of his bold questioning of church doctrine was greater. In 1633, Galileo was tried by the Catholic Church and found guilty of teaching his theories against the orders of the church. He was forced to recant his beliefs and spent the rest of his life under house arrest. His book, *The Starry Messenger*, was put on the "Index of Forbidden Books," and he was prohibited from publishing anything else on the subject of heavenly bodies and their movements.

Chemistry, Biology, and Medicine

The world view that supported innovations in astronomy also influenced developments in chemistry, biology, and medicine. The understanding that all matter is composed of atoms did not come until later, so scientists of the 16th and early 17th century had a very limited knowledge of the properties and behaviors of the combination of elements. However, some chemical discoveries and developments were made. For example, even though the nature of gases was unknown, gunpowder (a chemical explosive) continued to improve. Experimentation continued and data slowly accumulated, building the base for later concepts and principles of chemistry.

Some major breakthroughs occurred in biology during the 16th and 17th centuries. Because biological knowledge resulted mostly from the practice of medicine, biological studies were often based on medical experiments. One important work – *The Structure of the Human Body* published in 1543 by **Andreas Vesalius** – renewed and modernized the study of anatomy. Formerly scientists had relied almost exclusively on the 2nd century writings of the ancient physician, Galen, who wrote an authoritative description of all human muscles and tissues. Those who dissected cadavers had dismissed those not conforming to Galen's description as abnormal or atypical. Vesalius, however, demonstrated a number of errors in Galen's knowledge by dissecting human cadavers, and so improved the understanding of anatomy. Just as Copernicus did not completely reject Aristotle's theories of physics, Vesalius did not question Galen's overall theory about the functioning of the human body, but he corrected Galen's inaccuracies.

Further revelations about the human body were produced by **William Harvey** in his book, *On the Movement of the Heart and Blood,* published in 1628. Harvey was the first to suggest that the blood continually circulated through arteries and veins. The technology of the day did not allow him to observe the tiny capillaries where arterial blood moves into the veins, but through his experiments on animals that revealed the actual functioning of the heart and lungs, he reasoned that circulation must occur. After the microscope was invented in the late 17th century, scientists confirmed Harvey's postulations.

Despite these achievements, 16th and 17th century developments in chemistry and biology were overshadowed by those in astronomy and physics. In the latter two fields, mathematics could be most fully applied, and mathematics developed rapidly during the 17th century. Decimals came into use to express fractions, the symbols used in algebra (an earlier Arab invention called "al-jabr") were improved and standardized, and in 1614 logarithms were invented by John Napier, a Scotsman.

THEMATIC LEARNING OBJECTIVE: OBJECTIVE KNOWLEDGE AND SUBJECTIVE VISIONS: GALILEO ON SCIENCE AND THE BIBLE

Galileo's boldness in discussing the relationship between science and the Bible eventually got him into trouble with the church. In the following excerpts from his *Letter to the Grand Duchess Christiana* in 1615, he argued that the Bible and science don't necessarily contradict one another. His words also illustrate two basic precepts of the Scientific Revolution: empirical observation and reliance on human reasoning.

"The reason produced for condemning the opinion that the earth moves and the sun stands still is that in many places in the Bible one may read that the sun moves and the earth stands still...I think that in discussions of physical problems we ought to begin not from the authority of scriptural passages, but from sense-experiences and necessary demonstrations; for the holy Bible and the phenomena of nature proceed alike from the divine World, the former as the dictate of the Holy Ghost and the latter as the observant executrix of God's commands...I do not mean to infer that we need not have an extra-ordinary esteem for the passages of holy Scripture...but I do not feel obliged to believe that the same god who has endowed us with senses, reason, and intellect has intended to forgo their use and by some other means to give us knowledge which we can attain by them."

Reference: Discoveries and Opinions of Galileo by Galileo Galilei. Trans. and ed. by Stxillman Drake (Garden City, N.Y.: Doubleday Anchor Books, 1957), pp. 181-183.

Perhaps the greatest mathematician of the day was **René Descartes**, whose broad understanding of the world reconstructed by science influenced generations of scientists and philosophers who followed.

Bacon and Descartes

Two men stood out as prophets of the new worldview offered by science: **Frances Bacon** (1561-1626) and **René Descartes** (1596-1650). Both were philosophical in their approach to science, asking abstract questions about the nature of being or the essence of reality. They questioned earlier methods of seeking knowledge, including medieval scholasticism, as well as the **deductive thinking** of Ancient Greek philosophers, particularly Aristotle. Deductive thinking starts with accepted definitions and general propositions and then discovers what further knowledge could be logically deduced from the accepted truths. According to Bacon, deductive thinking does not easily produce new knowledge of nature, and so another type of reasoning, **inductive thinking**, should be employed. This method does not start with an accepted truth, but finds truth at the end, after a process of investigation, experiment, and intermediate thought. As a proponent of inductive reasoning, Bacon began to fashion the basis of the scientific method that could be used to understand the real workings of nature.

Frances Bacon was not a practicing scientist, and he did not conduct his own experiments. Instead, he was a visionary who planned a multi-volume work on new methods of acquiring knowledge. He encouraged his contemporaries "to commence a total reconstruction of sciences, arts, and all human knowledge, raised upon the proper foundations." His *Instauratio Magna,* or "Great Restoration"

ORIGINAL DOCUMENT:
FRANCIS BACON'S
NEW ORGANON

Francis Bacon's *New Organon* was designed to replace Aristotle's logical works collectively called the *Organon.* In this work, Bacon called for a new approach to the study of nature that called for scientists to cast aside old beliefs. In the excerpt below, he identified four "idols" or false notions that hamper human understanding.

"XXXIX. There are four classes of Idols which beset men's minds...
  XLI. The Idols of the Tribe have their foundations...in the tribe or race of men. For it is a false assertion that the sense of man is the measure of things. On the contrary, all perceptions...are according to the measure of the individual.
  XLII. The Idols of the Cave are the idols of the individual man. For everyone has a cave or den of his own which refracts and discolors the light of nature.
  XLIII. There are also Idols formed by the...association of men with each other, which I call Idols of the Market Place, on account of the commerce and consort of men there.
  XLIV. Lastly, there are Idols which have immigrated into men's minds from the various dogmas of philosophies, and also from wrong laws of demonstration. These I call Idols of the Theater, because in my judgment all the received systems are but so many stage plays, representing worlds of their own creation after an unreal and scenic fashion."

Reference: Frances Bacon, *Essays, Advancement of Learning, New Atlantis, and Other Pieces,* ed. by Richard Foster Jones (New York: Odyssey, 1937), pp. 278-280.

was only partially complete when he died in 1626, but his new foundation built on inductive principles that shaped the development of the Scientific Revolution. Bacon advised his readers to put aside all traditional ideas, and to look at the world with new eyes to observe and study with the senses the many natural phenomena in their surroundings. Some thinkers before Bacon had used inductive reasoning, but he formalized it as the **empirical method**, which relies on observation and experimentation. His stated goal for science was "that human life be endowed with new discoveries and power" by creating devices that would benefit industry, agriculture, and trade. His writings reflected a confidence that science would allow people to "conquer nature."

Bacon enthusiastically directed European intellectuals toward the new world view offered by science, but he never had much influence on the development of science as a field of study. He did his writing on the side, and his "day job" as Lord Chancellor of England kept his mind more focused on government duties rather than the latest scientific methods and concepts. Bacon's greatest weakness was his failure to understand the role of mathematics in scientific developments. In contrast, René Descartes was a great mathematician in his own right.

Like Bacon, Descartes was critical of the ancient and medieval methods of deductive thinking, but he did not dismiss the role of these methods in science. He began by questioning the old methods by doubting everything that could reasonably be doubted, thus sweeping away past ideas and clearing the ground for his own discoveries. Descartes called this process "systematic doubt," and he famously concluded that his own existence was the surest thing that he could not doubt. From his essential truth – "I think, therefore I am," – deductive reason could proceed from this essential truth to other truths, such as the existence of God. He also deduced the principle of the separation of mind and matter, since "the mind cannot be doubted but the body and material world can, [so] the two must be radically different." This separation of mind and matter, which came to be known as "**Cartesian dualism**". encouraged scientists to investigate matter objectively as something that was totally separate from their minds which they used to understand the matter. It allowed the human mind to be detached from the world and yet at the same time objectively analyze the world. This deductive approach presumed that inherent in the mind are mathematical principles, logical relationships, the principle of cause and effect – ideas that exist independently of human experience with the external world. Descartes's reliance on human reason irritated religious and political leaders because in their view, he reduced God to the role of guarantor of knowledge. Many fellow scientists and interested laypeople feared that Descartes's system encouraged atheism. As a result, his books were placed on the papal Index of Forbidden books and condemned by many Protestant theologians, and Descartes left France to live in the more tolerant Netherlands.

MARKER EVENT:
RENÉ DESCARTES AND THE
BIRTH OF PHILOSOPHY

In the *Discourse on Method* (1637), Descartes brought to his narrative a complete confidence in the power of his own judgment and a deep discontent with the learning of his times. In the excerpt below, he explained how he arrived at his famous dictum "I think therefore I am," marking the beginning of modern philosophy.

"As I desired to devote myself wholly to the search for truth, I thought that I should...reject as absolutely false anything of which I could have the least doubt, in order to see whether anything would be left after this procedure which could be called wholly certain. Thus, as our senses deceive us at times, I was ready to suppose that nothing was at all the way our senses represented them to be...Finally, as the same precepts which we have when awake may come to us when asleep without their being true, I decided to supposed that nothing that had ever entered my mind was more real than the illusions of my dreams. But I soon noticed that while I thus wished to think everything false, it was necessarily true that I who thought so was something. Since this truth, *I think, therefore I am,* was so firm and assured that all the most extravagant suppositions of the sceptics* were unable to shake it, I judged that I could safely accept it as the first principle of the philosophy I was seeking."

* The skeptics were Ancient Greek philosophers who held true knowledge to be beyond human grasp and treated all knowledge as doubtful.

Reference: René Descartes, *Discourse on Method,* trans. by Laurence J. Lafleur, Macmillan Ltd., 1960, pp. 20-21.

Science and Religion

Science and religion had close ties during the 16th century, and the Catholic Church had long been involved with scientific advancements. Most research in the sciences to this point had occurred within universities sponsored and staffed by members of religious orders, who had the education, time, and resources necessary for scientific investigation. Copernicus was a cleric, as were many philosophers and scientists after him, and some of Descartes's closest collaborators were clerics, as were some of Galileo's patrons and protégés. Of course, science and religion have always been concerned about big questions basic to the human experience, such as "Where did we come from?" and "What is man's place in the universe?" For example, the entire Cartesian process of reasoning about the world was grounded in Descartes's certainty about God. Most other scientists perceived God's purpose in the patterns of nature.

THEMATIC LEARNING OBJECTIVE: OBJECTIVE KNOWLEDGE AND SUBJECTIVE VISIONS: JOHN DONNE ON RELIGION V. SCIENCE

The English poet John Donne commented on the confusion caused by new scientific theories that questioned the old beliefs that had been commonly accepted during ancient and medieval days:

"[The] new Philosophy calls all in doubt,
The Element of fire is quite put out;
The Sun is lost, and th'earth, and no man's wit
Can well direct him where to look for it.
. . . .
Tis all in pieces, all coherence gone;
All just supply, and all Relation;
Prince, Subject, Father, Son, are things forgot,
For every man alone thinks he hath got
To be a Phoenix, and that then can be
None of that kinde, of which he is, but he."

Reference: Complete Poetry and Selected Prose of John Donne, ed. John Hayward (Bloomsbury, England: Nonesuch Press, 1929), p. 365.

The perception in this era that religion was the opponent of science began with Galileo's trial in 1633. The Catholic Church was clearly invested in the old view, and their resistance to new views was evidenced by their rigid response to Galileo's teachings. Part of the explanation for the church's harsh reactions to early scientists is based on the lesson that churchmen derived from the Protestant Reformation: any challenges to the church's authority should be dealt with firmly and directly. Galileo was perceived as a particular threat, since he was well known and read by a popular audience. Galileo, like the Protestants, presumed to interpret the Scriptures, a privilege previously reserved to the church hierarchy. As a result of the condemnation of Galileo, scientific investigation in most Catholic regions of Europe either stopped or took place quietly. Additionally, Protestants did not readily adopt the new scientific thought, since they too resisted the scientists' boldness in interpreting the scriptures. For Protestants and Catholics alike, some scientific principles – such as the notion that the earth is actually moving – defied both scripture and common sense.

Scientific Societies

By 1648, the new science had caught the interest of many Europeans, and scientific societies began to form to encourage and facilitate discussion and cooperation among scientists. The first major scientific society of the era was founded in Rome in 1603. Shortly afterward, a French monk, Marin Mersenne, organized an international network of correspondents interested in scientific work. With his encouragement, scientists were brought together for discussions and experiments, and these meetings eventually led to more permanent organizations for scientific activity.

England provided a unique environment for the development of science during the mid 17th century. As the civil war raged, different views of science became matters for debate among Puritans, Anglicans, and royalists. During the 1640s, Puritan philosophers argued that science could bring life on earth closer to perfection and even accelerate the end of the earth prophesied in the New Testament – the reign of the saints followed by the return of Jesus. When the Roundheads captured the city of Oxford, they replaced those at the university with Puritan-leaning scholars, and a few of these newcomers formed what they called the Invisible College. The group included the chemist **Robert Boyle**, who formed – along with eleven others – the **Royal Society of London for Improving Natural Knowledge** in 1660. The Royal Society's purposes were based on the writings of Frances Bacon, and it hoped to gather all knowledge about nature, particularly if it had practical uses. In 1666, King Louis XIV gave his blessing to the founding of a **French Royal Academy of Sciences**, and similar organizations were established in Naples and Berlin by 1700.

By 1648, the Scientific Revolution was well established, and would continue to develop and influence many other areas of life over the centuries that followed. The year 1642 saw both the death of Galileo and the birth of Sir Isaac Newton, one of the most influential scientists of all time, demonstrating the fact that the new scientific worldview was just getting started by the middle of the 17th century. During the second half of the century, the principles of science and the newly founded field of philosophy would grow in influence and fuel revolutionary changes during the 18th century.

CONCEPTS AND IDENTIFICATIONS

Bacon, Francis
baroque
Bernini, Gian Lorenzo
Boyle, Robert
Brahe, Tycho
Cartesian dualism
Cervantes, Miguel de

Copernicus, Nicholas
deductive reasoning, inductive reasoning
Descartes, René
Don Quixote
El Greco
empirical evidence
essay
French Royal Academy of Sciences
Galileo Galilei
Gentileschi, Artemisia
Golden Age
Harvey, William
Kepler, Johannes
mannerism
Montaigne, Michel de
Nasir al-Din
Rembrandt van Rijn
Royal Society of London
Rubens, Peter Paul
Scientific Revolution
Shakespeare, William
skepticism
Vesalius, Andreas

UNIT ONE QUESTIONS

MULTIPLE-CHOICE QUESTIONS:

Questions 1-3 are based on the following quote:

"Here the question arises; whether it is better to be loved than feared or feared than loved. The answer is that it would be desirable to be both but, since that is difficult, it is much safer to be feared than to be loved, if one must choose. For on men in general this observation may be made: they are ungrateful, fickle, and deceitful, eager to avoid dangers, and avid for gain, and while you are useful to them they are all with you, offering you their blood, their property, their lives, and their sons so long as danger is remote...but when it approaches they turn on you. Any prince, trusting only in their words and having no other preparations made, will fall to his ruin...Men have less hesitation in offending a man who is loved than one who is feared, for love is held by a bond of obligation which, as men are wicked, is broken whenever personal advantage suggests it, but fear is accompanied by the dread of punishment which never relaxes."

> Niccolo Machiavelli
> 1513

1. The author of the passage, Niccolo Machiavelli, is one of the most famous 16th century writers most directly influenced by

   (A) scholasticism
   (B) skepticism
   (C) Renaissance humanism
   (D) dualism

2. In the passage above, the main subject that the author is addressing is

   (A) relationships within the family
   (B) political leadership
   (C) sea-based power vs. land-based power
   (D) political vs. religious power

3. Which of the following is the most important assumption that Machiavelli based his observations on?

(A) The building of states and political authority are goals in themselves, separate from religion.
(B) Religion and family shape the nature of political institutions.
(C) Only states with both powerful navies and armies can be successful.
(D) Political leaders must always be subject to religious leaders, and moral principles should shape political decisions.

(Questions 4-6 are based on the following quote):

"At last, by the mercy of God, meditating day and night, I gave heed to the context of the words, namely, 'In [the gospel] the righteousness of God is revealed, as it is written, He who through faith is righteous shall live' [Romans 1:17]. There I began to understand that the righteousness of God is that by which the righteous lives by a gift of God, namely by faith. And this is the meaning: the righteousness of God is revealed by the gospel, namely the passive righteousness with which merciful God justifies us by faith, as it is written, 'He who through faith is righteous shall live.' Here I felt that I was altogether born again and had entered paradise itself through open gates. There a totally other face of the entire Scripture showed itself to me...I also found in other terms an analogy, as, the work of God, that is, what God does in us, the power of God, with which he makes us strong, the wisdom of God, with which he makes us wise, the strength of God, the salvation of God, the glory of God."

Martin Luther
Description of his
"experience in the tower"

4. Which of the following was a common practice of the Catholic Church that Luther believed to be directly opposed to his understanding of Christianity reflected in the excerpt above?

(A) posting the names of sinners on church doors
(B) allowing church leaders to marry
(C) selling indulgences
(D) praying to God directly

5. Which of the following principles most directly supports Luther's understanding of Christianity as reflected in the excerpt above?

   (A) the priesthood of all believers
   (B) predestination
   (C) transubstantiation
   (D) theocratic government

6. Which of the following is a common practice of Protestantism that most directly resulted from Luther's beliefs as expressed in the excerpt above?

   (A) baptism for adults only
   (B) church leaders dressing in ordinary clothes
   (C) ornamentation in church buildings
   (D) limitation of frivolous activities among church members

(Questions 7-9 are based on the following quote):

   "...The state of monarchy is the supremest thing upon earth: for kings are not only God's lieutenants upon earth and sit upon God's throne, but even by God himself they are called gods...In the Scriptures kings are called gods, and so their power after a certain relation compared to the Divine power. Kings are also compared to fathers of families: for a king is truly [parent of the country], the political father of his people. And lastly, kings are compared to the head of this microcosm of the body of man...

   ...I would not have you [Parliament] meddle with such ancient rights of mine as I have received from my predecessors, possessing them [as ancestral customs]: such things I would be sorry should be accounted for grievances."

                                                                    King James I
                                                                    1610

7. In the excerpt above, King James defended

   (A) joint rule by the king and Parliament
   (B) separation of church and state
   (C) the rights of nobles to seize land from peasants
   (D) the divine right of monarchy

8. Which of the following major events directly resulted from disagreement with King James's beliefs expressed in the excerpt?

   (A) the Battle of Lepanto
   (B) the Edict of Nantes
   (C) the English Civil War
   (D) the settlement of Puritans in the New World

9. Which of the following most openly disagreed with King James's beliefs expressed in the excerpt?

   (A) Catherine d'Medici
   (B) Oliver Cromwell
   (C) Henry of Guise
   (D) Cardinal Richelieu

(Questions 10 and 11 are based on the following chart):

NEW EXCHANGES IN THE COLUMBIAN EXCHANGE

From the Americas	From the Eastern Hemisphere
beans, squash, tomatoes, sweet potatoes, peanuts, chilis, chocolate, maize (corn), potatoes, avocados, pineapple, manioc	wheat, rice, olives, grapes, bananas, rice, citrus fruits, melons, figs, sugar, coconuts, okra horses, cattle, pigs, sheep, goats, chickens, rabbits, rats

10. An important demographic change that occurred as a direct result of the exchange illustrated above was that

   (A) death rates among Amerindians rapidly increased, killing much of the population
   (B) the Americas were overcrowded by the end of the 16th century
   (C) much more intermarriage between Amerindians and Europeans occurred in North America than in Latin America
   (D) labor systems in the Americas were highly dependent on slavery

11. Which of the following was a positive consequence of the Columbian Exchange, apparent by the late 17th century?

    (A) Many diseases became much less commonplace than they had been before.
    (B) Many domesticated animals native to North America were brought to Europe, Africa, and Asia.
    (C) The variety of available food increased, giving people wider access to an assortment of nutrients.
    (D) Antagonisms among European countries decreased, since all had access to new wealth.

(Questions 12 and 13 are based on the following quote):

"The reason produced for condemning the opinion that the earth moves and the sun stands still is that in many places in the Bible one may read that the sun moves and the earth stands still...I think that in discussions of physical problems we ought to begin not from the authority of scriptural passages, but from sense-experiences and necessary demonstrations; for the holy Bible and the phenomena of nature proceed alike from the divine World, the former as the dictate of the Holy Ghost and the latter as the observant executrix of God's commands...I do not mean to infer that we need not have an extraordinary esteem for the passages of holy Scripture... but I do not feel obliged to believe that the same god who has endowed us with senses, reason, and intellect has intended to forgo their use and by some other means to give us knowledge which we can attain by them."

                         Galileo Galilei
                         Letter to the Grand Duchess Christiana, 1615

12. The quote reflects basic precepts that shaped the

    (A) Protestant Reformation
    (B) Scientific Revolution
    (C) Catholic Reformation
    (D) philosophy of mercantilism

13. The quote directly refutes the philosophy of

    (A) scholasticism
    (B) humanism
    (C) deism
    (D) divine right

(Questions 14-16 are based on the following photo):

14. *The Throne of Saint Peter* in Saint Peter's Basilica, illustrated above, is a famous example of

(A) mannerism
(B) baroque style
(C) scholasticism
(D) northern Renaissance style

15. The style of *The Throne of Saint Peter*, created in the mid-17th century, contrasts directly with the Renaissance emphasis on

(A) strong emotions
(B) mysterious illusions
(C) human character, inner personality, and self-revelation
(D) harmonious design, unity, and clarity

16. The artistic style of *The Throne of Saint Peter* was embraced nearly a century later by European Protestants in the music of

(A) Johann Sebastian Bach
(B) Ludwig Beethoven
(C) Frederic Chopin
(D) Wolfgang Mozart

SHORT-ANSWER QUESTION: (12 minutes)

Answer parts A, B, and C.

A) Briefly explain ONE important similarity between European colonies in Latin America and North America.

B) Briefly explain ONE important difference between European colonies in Latin America and North America.

C) Briefly analyze ONE factor that accounts for the difference you identified in part B.

FREE-RESPONSE DOCUMENT-BASED QUESTION (Suggested reading time – 15 minutes; suggested writing time – 40 minutes)

Write an essay that:

- Provides an appropriate, explicitly stated thesis that directly addresses all parts of the question.

- Supports the thesis with evidence from all or all but one of the documents and your outside knowledge of European history

- Analyzes a majority of the documents in terms of intended audience, point of view, purpose, argument strength, and/or social context

- Places the argument in broader regional, national, or global contexts.

Analyze the motivations for the European voyages of discovery during the time period between the mid-15th and the mid-17th centuries.

Document 1

And you should note well that the noble spirit of this Prince [Henry], by a sort of natural constraint, was ever urging him both to begin and to carry out very great deeds. For which reason, after the taking of Ceuta [in Morocco] he always kept ships well armed against the Infidel, both for war, and because he had also a wish to know the land that lay beyond the isles of Canary and that Cape called Bojador, for that up to his time, neither by writings, nor by the memory of man, was known with any certainty the nature of the land beyond that Cape.

> Gomes Eannes de Azurara,
> Description of Prince Henry
> "the Navigator"
> *The Chronicle of Guinea*
> 1453

Document 2

I promise, that with a little assistance afforded me by our most invincible sovereigns, I will procure them as much gold as they need, as great a quantity of spices, of cotton, and of mastic (which is only found in Chios), and as many men for the service of the navy as their Majesties may require. I promise also rhubarb and other sorts of drugs, which I am persuaded the men whom I have left in the aforesaid fortress have found already and will continue to find…

But these great and marvelous results are not to be attributed to any merit of mine, but to the holy Christian faith…Let Christ rejoice on earth, as he rejoices in heaven in the prospect of the salvation of the souls of so many nations hitherto lost.

> Christopher Columbus
> Letter from the First Voyage
> March 14, 1493

Document 3

Every generous mind is the most readily delighted and incited to great deeds by novel events. Wherefore, in order to satisfy many of this disposition, I will add concisely the custom which is observed in their sacrifices [of Muslims in observing the rites of pilgrimage in Mecca]. Every man and woman kills at least two or three, and some four and some six sheep; so that I really believe that on the first day more than 30,000 sheep are killed by cutting their throats, facing the east. Each person gives them to the poor for the love of God, for there were about 30,000 poor people there, who made a very large hole in the earth, and then put in it camels' dung, and thus they made a little fire, and warmed the flesh a little and then ate it.

> Ludovico di Varthema
> an Italian adventurer
> *Travels, ca. 1508*

Document 4

Your Imperial Majesty doubtless knows how I and my kinsmen have ever hitherto been disposed to serve the House of Austria in all loyalty to the furtherance of its well-being and prosperity...We have...advanced to Your Majesty's Agents...a Great Sum of Money, of which we ourselves have had to raise a large part from our Friends. It is well known that Your Imperial Majesty could not have gained the roman Crown save with mine aid, and I can prove the same by the writings of Your Majesty's Agents given by their own hands....For had I left the House of Austria and had been minded to further France, I had obtained much money and property, such as was then offered to me.

> Jacob Fugger
> House of Fugger, a great international
> financial house
> Letter to Charles V (Holy Roman
> Emperor)
> 1523

Document 5

Our captain [Cortés] said to Montezuma, half laughingly, "Lord Montezuma, I do not understand how such a great prince and wise man as yourself can have failed to come to the conclusion that these idols of yours are not gods, but evil things – devils is the term for them. So that you and your priests may see it clearly, do me a favor: Let us put a cross on top of this tower, and in one part of these oratories, where you Uichilobos and Tezcatepuca are, we will set up an image of Our Lady [an image that Montezuma had already seen], and you will see how afraid of it these idols that have deceived you are."

> Bernal Díaz
> Soldier who accompanied Cortés
> on the conquest of the Aztecs
> *The True History of the Conquest of New Spain*
> Mid-16th century

Document 6

Yea, if we would behold with the eye of pity how all our prisons are pestered and filled with able men to serve their country, which for small robberies are daily hanged up in great numbers,…we would hasten…the deducting [conveying] of some colonies of our superfluous people into those temperate and fertile parts of America, which, being within six weeks' sailing of England, are yet unpossessed by any Christians, and seem to offer themselves unto us, stretching nearer unto Her Majesty's dominions than to any other part of Europe….

> Richard Hakluyt
> Preface to his published collection
> of documentts relating to early English
> explorations
> `1582

Document 7

The kings of Spain and Portugal, since the first discovery of the Indies, have not only mightily enlarged their territory, greatly enriched themselves and their subjects, but have also tripled the number of their ships, masters, and mariners, a matter of no small importance. Besides this, it will prove a general benefit to our country. Not only a great number of men which do now live idly at home on charity shall be set to work...And moreover, our idle women shall also be employed in such work as the gathering of cotton and diverse things needed for dyeing.

> Sir George Peckham
> New World land owner
> Letter to Queen Elizabeth
> 1583

Document 8

In the name of God, amen. We whose names are underwritten, the loyal subjects of our dread sovereign lord, King James, by the grace of God, of Great Britain, France, and Ireland King, Defender of the Faith, etc., having undertaken, for the glory of God, and advancement of the Christian faith, and honor of our King and country, a voyage to plant the first colony in the northern parts of Virginia, do by these presents solemnly and mutually, in the presence of God and one another, covenant and combine ourselves together into a civil body politic...

> The Mayflower Compact
> Pilgrims in Massachusetts
> 1620

LONG-ESSAY QUESTION: (35 minutes)

Explain how economic developments in Europe during the period from 1450 to 1648 contributed to the creation of the first truly global economy.

UNIT TWO:
NEW HORIZONS
1648-1815

The era from 1648 to 1815 is bookended by two important marker events in European history – the Treaty of Westphalia in 1648 and the Congress of Vienna in 1814-1815. The Treaty of Westphalia formally ended the religious strife that characterized the previous period (1450-1648), and made religious pluralism an accepted pattern of life in Europe. Although religious tension continued, the new agreements allowed states, especially those that bordered the Atlantic Ocean and its expanding trade routes, to concentrate on building their political and economic prowess,. The absolute power of European monarchs peaked during the time between 1648 and 1750, only to be challenged during the late 18th century by new political forms that allowed legislatures to restrict the authority of hereditary rulers. New concepts of states emphasized national identity and shared power as the basic building blocks of political systems. As the era ended, powerful states were struggling with questions of political organization that Napoleon Bonaparte had thrust upon them, and the Congress of Vienna answered the challenge by reinforcing the rights of hereditary monarchs and the carefully orchestrated balance of power among European nations.

These political developments were complemented by the rapid regional and global growth of European economic systems, as land claims in the Americas evolved into lucrative established trade routes. Mercantilism and capitalism continued to fuel economic growth, and eventually sparked one of the most important marker events in world history, the Industrial Revolution, which began in England during the late 18th century. The era is also characterized by the deepening divide between countries that bordered the Atlantic and those in central and eastern Europe, which did not participate significantly in the expanding global economy.

Culturally, growing secularism supported the continuing influence of the Scientific Revolution that had begun during the 16th century, and scientific principles were applied to political and social realms of life. Baroque art and music continued to glorify religious feelings, but rationalism dominated the lives of many European elites for most of the period. Rationalism sparked the French Revolution in 1789, but by the end of the period, it unleashed the forces of romanticism and nationalism that encouraged people to question basic rational assumptions about life.

THE BIG PICTURE: 1648-1815

The "chunk" of European history from 1648 to 1815 is distinguished from other periods in these ways:

1) Absolutism reached its peak as a type of political system that concentrated power in the hands of hereditary monarchs. An important exception was the development of constitutionalism in England and the Dutch Republic, where legislatures contained the rulers' power. By the end of the era, Enlightenment thought had spawned an interest in democratic forms of government.

2) European economic hegemony extended regionally and globally, as nations that rimmed the Atlantic Ocean became leaders in the worldwide economic network. The Industrial Revolution transformed economic development by removing the traditional constraints of limited resources and replacing them with the possibilities of self-generating economic growth.

3) The popularization of the Scientific Revolution spread scientific knowledge to many more people, and its emphasis on rationalism influenced political philosophy and views of social structures. By the end of the era, romanticism and nationalism seriously questioned rationalism as a basic philosophical approach.

4) The population explosion of the 16th century continued to cause hardship during this era, with food shortages and disease that often resulted in high mortality rates. By the late 18th century, improvements in transportation, sanitation, and agricultural crops caused mortality rates to decline, and famine became less widespread. Environmental and demographic changes occurred as cities grew and industrial centers began. With urbanization and early industrialization, family patterns changed to create a demographic revolution that resulted in longer life spans, later marriage, and smaller families.

Overall, between 1648 and 1815 Europe continued its evolution from the relative isolation of the highly religious Middle Ages to the globally-connected modern continent that would dominate the globe by the end of the 19th century.

CHAPTER 8:
THE CONSOLIDATION OF
POLITICAL POWER
1648-1740

The many cultural, social, and economic changes in Europe between 1450 and 1648 were accompanied by political changes, most notably the consolidation of weak medieval kingdoms into strong, centralized states. These states claimed relatively small land spaces, but the constant competition among them inspired them to seek power through land exploration and trade claims in other parts of the world. European kings generally benefitted from the Reformation because the Catholic Church lost its political power as many Christians joined the ranks of the Protestant churches. Kings and popes had long clashed over political power, and the 16th-century religious crisis gave kings and princes the opportunity to assert themselves. Religion remained very important, and religious issues continued to fragment the Holy Roman Empire, but strong kings emerged in England, France, and Spain by the late 16th century. In the time period between 1648 and 1740, the consolidation of political power continued in England and France and extended to other states, including Sweden, Austria, Prussia, and Russia.

TWO MODELS: ABSOLUTISM AND CONSTITUTIONALISM

Two important models developed as countries sought order after the previous chaos caused by the religious wars: **absolutism**, which was more common, and **constitutionalism**, which though less widely practiced, served as the stimulus for the development of democracies during later time periods.

The Spanish and French kings gained enough power to become **absolute monarchs**, who held complete control over their kingdoms. The Spanish kings grew weaker after they lost control of the Netherlands and the great Armada suffered defeat, but French kings steadily built their power during the 17th century as their armies grew and nobles became less rebellious, especially with the threat of cannon fire on their castles. The monarchies of Prussia in eastern Germany and the Habsburg kings in Austria-Hungary also practiced absolutism, with the Prussian rulers particularly emphasizing a strong military. Russia emerged as an important absolutist power during the rule of Peter the Great. In Sweden and Poland, kings tried to assert absolute power, but nobles contained royal authority and formed governments controlled by the aristocracy.

Meanwhile, Britain and the Netherlands developed a different style of government, **constitutionalism**. In these states the rulers shared power with a legislature, a body of representatives selected by the nobility and leading urban citizens. Both Britain and the Netherlands were growing commercial and colonial powers, and wealthy merchants were involved in political affairs and often served as members of legislatures. The term "constitutionalism" implies not a written constitution as such, but an agreement that the ruler, like everyone else, is subject to the **rule of law,** with laws of course passed by a parliament.

THE DECLINE OF SPAIN

During most of the 16th century – under the rule of Philip II – Spain was the most powerful country in Europe. However, even during its heyday, Philip had found it difficult to hold together his many land possessions across Europe.

Economic Difficulties

Spain was a rich country during the 16th century, but most profits were monopolized by a few groups. Philip claimed absolute power based on divine right, but he

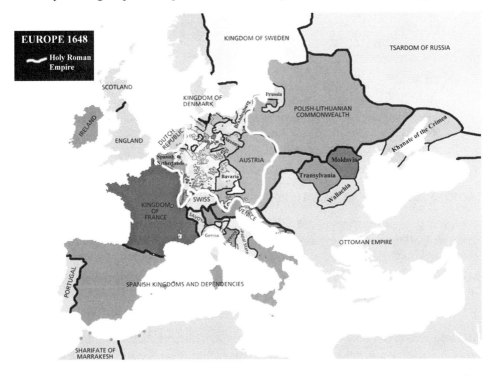

Europe in 1648. This chapter focuses on political power in several of the states shown on the map, including Spain, France, Austria, Brandenburg-Prussia, Russia, Sweden, Poland-Lithuania, the Netherlands, and England.

SOME 17TH AND EARLY 18TH-CENTURY RULERS

This chapter discusses many countries and their rulers. The chart below lists a few of the most important, along with the dates of their rule.

Austria (Holy Roman Empire)
   Leopold I (1658-1705)

Brandenburg-Prussia
   Frederick Willim of Hohenzollern, the Great Elector (1640-1688)
   Frederick II (the Great) (1740-1786)

England
   Oliver Cromwell (1653-1658)
   Charles II (1660-1685)
   James II (1685-1688)
   William and Mary (1689-1702)

France
   Louis XIV (1642-1715)

Poland
   John III Sobieski (1674-1696)

Russia
   Peter the Great (1682-1724)

Spain
   Philip IV (1621-1665)

Sweden
   Charles XII (1697-1718)

allowed Castilian nobles to run the government's bureaucracy, causing resentment from his subjects in other regions. He gave the city of Seville a monopoly over shipping routes to and from the New World, and he granted control of wool and wine production to a small number of insiders. Philip allowed the participation of large numbers of Spaniards in only one economic activity – shipping on the Mediterranean Sea – that created wealth in the trading center of Barcelona. Despite a large infusion of silver from the Americas, Spain's economy suffered because only a minority of Spaniards benefitted from it. Like many other European monarchs during the turbulent 16th century, Philip's coffers were drained by constant warfare and the expense of maintaining a large standing army.

Unfortunately, Philip's son, Philip III, was incompetent, and he allowed economic and political corruption to magnify during the early 17th century. At the same time, the flow of precious metals from the New World began to dwindle, partly because more remained in the colonies or was captured by Dutch and English pirates, but also because the mines failed as few new supplies of silver and gold were found. As a result, Spain was deprived of its most important source of income. Economic woes accelerated as tax revenues declined because of a series of plagues that drastically reduced Spain's population. When large-scale fighting began against the Dutch and French under Philip IV (r. 1621-1665), Spain could no longer bear the financial burden, and was forced to recognize Dutch independence in the Treaty of Münster, which was a part of the Westphalia settlement of 1648 that ended the Thirty Years' War.

Revolt and Secession

Since the days of its unification under Ferdinand and Isabella (late 15th century), regions in Spain had always maintained separate identities. Many resented the power of Castilian nobles and did not believe that the Spanish king operated in their interest. When Philip IV's chief minister, the count of Olivares, increased taxes and military requirements during the 1630s and 1640s, a series of revolts

IMPORTS OF PRECIOUS METALS TO SPAIN FROM THE NEW WORLD, 1591-1660

One important reason for Spain's decline during the 17th century was the decreasing value of precious metals imported from the New World. The chart below reflects this trend, as calculated in Spanish ducats.

1591-1600	85,536,000
1611-1620	65,568,000
1631-1640	40,110,000
1651-1660	12, 785,000

Adapted from J.H. Elliott, *Imperial Spain, 1469-1716.* Edward Arnold, Hodder Neadling PLC Group, 1964, p. 175.

broke out in Catalonia, Portugal, Naples, and Sicily that split the country apart. By 1641 Catalonia and Portugal had declared themselves independent republics, placed under French protection. The resistance in Portugal was successful, as Portuguese troops defended their region's autonomy and even invaded Castile in the 1640s, and Spain ultimately granted Portugal its independence in 1668. Other regions remained subject to Spain, but not without further weakening royal power. The Catalonian rebellion continued for eleven years, and failed largely because peasants and town mobs turned their grievances toward Catalonian nobility, causing the nobles to side with the king against the rebellion. The last major holdout, Barcelona, fell to a royal army in 1652, ending the revolt. Likewise, in Sicily and Naples, the poor turned against their Castilian rulers, and violently attacked any representatives of government and wealth that they could find. Although the government managed to end the revolt, the crisis contributed to Spain's decision to withdraw from its most ambitious international endeavors. By the second half of the 17th century, the country had regained stability, but it settled into a role as a second-level state, with a weakened king who allowed the nobility to run the government and control the economy.

ABSOLUTISM IN FRANCE

The legacy of centralizing governmental power in one geographical location in the hands of one man had deep roots in France. As early as the 8th century C.E. a large portion of Europe, including what is now France and Germany, was ruled by Charlemagne, king of the Franks. He maintained power by military might and was recognized by the Catholic Church as the ruler of the Holy Roman Empire in a famous ceremony in 800 C.E. French kings of the Valois family steadily built their power from the 14th through the 16th centuries, and during the 17th century the early Bourbon kings consolidated power as their armies grew and nobles became less rebellious. French kings built a strong bureaucracy that helped them collect taxes and keep their eyes on dissidents, and they cultivated a belief in the **divine right** of kings. With God's blessing of the king's authority, the legitimacy of royalty across Europe was enhanced. The apex of absolutism in France occurred under the long reign of **Louis XIV** during the late 17th and early 18th centuries.

Cardinal Richelieu

Like most other European states, France suffered through the wars and religious dissent of the period between 1550 and 1648. However, in contrast to the Spanish king, French royal power remained largely intact by the 1640s. One source of strength was the bureaucratic structure built by Louis XIII's chief minister, **Cardinal Richelieu**. As the financial burdens of the Thirty Years' War increased, Richelieu obtained the necessary revenue by increasing the power of *intendants*, the government's chief agents in local areas around France. Unlike nobles, *intendants* depended entirely on royal favor for their position. As a result, they vigorously supported the king by recruiting for the army, raising taxes, and enforcing royal decrees. Despite peasant uprisings and resistance by the nobility, Louis XIII kept control of the country during his lifetime.

The Fronde, 1648-1653

[handwritten: Louis XIV was too young, so why does Mazarin have power?! Bc of this, everyone was mad]

When Louis XIII died in 1643, the French throne passed to his five-year-old son, Louis XIV, and the country was ruled by a regent until the king came of age. Louis's mother, Anne of Austria (widow of Louis XIII), placed all the power in the hands of **Cardinal Jules Mazarin**, who used his power to amass a great personal fortune. This situation stimulated unrest among the nobility and peasants alike, leading to a crisis called **the Fronde**, named after the sling (*"fronde"*) used as a weapon by the rebels. The precipitating event occurred in 1648 when a coalition of Mazarin's opponents presented him with a charter of demands that would give the members of regional courts and legislatures (called **parlements**) the right to approve new taxes. Mazarin responded by arresting the leaders of the Paris parlement, an action that led to a series of revolts that at one time or another involved nearly every social group in France for the next five years. The royal family had to flee from the capital, and Mazarin and Anne were forced to compromise with the parlements. The nobles saw an opportunity to reassert local control, which they had lost when the religious wars ended in 1598. The middle and lower classes protested the constant tax increases, and conflicts erupted throughout France as nobles, parlements, and city councils all raised their own armies to fight either the crown or each other. Finally, amid the chaos, Mazarin used military force and threats of force to subdue Paris and most of the rebels in the countryside, and he brought the regency to an end by declaring the fourteen-year-old Louis of age in 1652. Louis remained under the tutelage of Mazarin until the latter's death in 1661, when at the age of 23, he took supreme power. Even though neither the nobles nor the judges of the parlements wanted to overthrow the king, the violence and uncertainty of his childhood impressed the young king, who asserted his absolute power in order to avoid such revolts during his reign. *[handwritten: Mazarin's struggles = need for absolute power]*

The Absolute Monarchy of Louis XIV

King Louis XIV ruled France for 72 years, first as a child under a regent, but then, until his death in 1715, as an absolute monarch. In the magnificence of his court, his absolute power, and the brilliance of the culture that he presided over, he dominated all of Europe so that the second half of the 17th century and the early 18th century is often called the "Age of Louis XIV." He called himself the "Sun King," implying that all others revolved around him, and his likeness was drawn and painted and carved into architecture with rays of sun emanating from his head. In 1651, he reputedly told the Paris high court of justice, *"L'état c'est moi"* ("I am the state") in a famous classic statement of absolute power. Louis was a devout Catholic who attended Mass daily and scrupulously performed his religious duties. He was taught from a young age that God had established kings as his rulers on earth, and granted their powers through **divine right**. Though kings were a race apart, they were still subject to God's laws and they were expected to rule for the good of the people, but their authority could not be questioned by other human beings, since kings were ordained by God. Throughout his long life, he cleverly manipulated the affections and ambitions of his courtiers, chose middle-class men as his ministers, and tolerated no religious or political opposition. Even though he personified more than any other person the absolute power of kings, Louis still ruled through carefully balancing the demands of a firmly entrenched nobility, influential clergy, an increasingly discontented middle class, and peasants and urban poor who could burst into mob action under the right conditions.

Building a Centralized Bureaucracy

Despite the efforts of Richelieu and Mazarin to centralize the French government, France was still a bewildering system of overlapping authorities when Louis XIV came to power. Provinces had their own regional courts and unique sets of law, and members of the nobility with huge estates still exercised much authority over lesser nobles and the peasantry. Both towns and provinces had their own privileges and authority that they held fast.

One important pillar of Louis's power was his ability to reconfigure the central policymaking structures of government as part of his own court and household. The royal court at **Versailles Palace** was not only the king's personal residence; it was also the place where government officials met and had their offices. In order to control the high nobility and princes, Louis invited them for extended visits to the palace, where he kept a watchful eye on them as rival aristocratic factions clashed or became consumed with court gossip. Despite this extension of hospitality to the nobles, he removed them from the royal council, the chief administrative body of the king and overseer of the central workings of the government. Instead Louis appointed ministers from relatively new aristocratic families who generally were more in awe of the king and more likely to do his bidding. Although he managed to dominate religious, economic, and foreign policy, as well as the making of war and peace, he continued to have problems containing the local and regional power of nobles, officials, and town councils. He often managed to secure their cooperation through endorsing bribes for carefully selected people who were important in seeing that the king's policies were carried out.

Finance was a serious weakness of Louis XIV's absolutism. An expanding professional bureaucracy, the court at Versailles, and the maintenance and modernization of the military all cost a great deal of money.   The king named **Jean-Baptiste Colbert**, the son of a wealthy merchant-financier, as controller general of finances. Colbert came to manage the entire royal government and proved himself a financial genius by rigorously applying the benefits of **mercantilism** to France.

Asserted power w/

Politics

THEMATIC LEARNING OBJECTIVE: STATES AND OTHER INSTITUTIONS OF POWER: THE DIVINE RIGHT OF KINGS

Bishop Jacques-Bénigne Bossuet, court preacher and tutor to Louis XIV's son, was a vocal defender of the divine right of kings, and in the following excerpt he based his arguments on quotes from the Bible.

"The royal power is absolute....The prince need render account of his acts to no one....'I counsel thee to keep the king's commandment, and that in regard of the oath of God...Where the word of a king is, there is power; and who may say unto him, What doest thou?' [Eccles. 8:2-5]. Without this absolute authority the king could neither do good nor repress evil. It is necessary that his power be such that no one can hope to escape him, and finally, the only protection of individuals against the public authority should be their innocence. This confirms the teaching of St. Paul: 'Wilt thou then not be afraid of the power? Do that which is good.' [Rom. 13:3].

God is infinite, God is all. The prince, as prince, is not regarded as a private person: he is a public personage, all the state is in him; and the will of all the people is included in his. As all perfection and all strength are united in God, so all the power of individuals is united in the person of the prince. What grandeur that a single man should embody so much!"

Reference: "Politics Drawn from the Very Words of Holy Scripture," as quoted in James Harvey Robinson, ed., *Readings in European History, Vol. 2* (Boston: Athenaeum, 1906), pp. 275-276.

Mercantilism is a collection of governmental policies that regulate economic activities – especially commercial activities – by and for the state. According to economic theory of the day, a nation's international power was thought to be based on its wealth, especially its gold supply. Since gold is a limited commodity, a country could only accumulate the precious metal by selling more goods abroad than it bought. Colbert insisted that the French sell abroad and buy nothing back in order to enhance the country's wealth. He sought to make France self-sufficient, able to produce within its borders everything the country needed. To accomplish this goal, the government subsidized various French industries, compelled craftsmen to organize into guilds, and encouraged skilled foreign craftsmen to immigrate to France. Colbert saw that roads and canals were built to transport goods and improve communications, and he enacted high tariffs to prevent foreign products from competing with French ones.   Probably his most important work was the creation of a powerful merchant marine that consisted of hundreds of frigates, galleys, and other ships of transport.   Colbert organized and regulated the entire French economy as the civil servant of the absolute monarchy.   Despite all of his efforts, France slipped deeper into debt during Louis's latter years, when court expenses and numerous wars made Colbert's goals impossible to attain.

The Court Culture at Versailles Palace

Louis set out to tame the unruly French nobles by enticing them to follow elaborate court rituals that took them away from their local domains.   He hosted grand balls, ballets, and theatricals that required all to follow rules of etiquette that he supervised.   Important nobles vied for the honor of serving the king in small ways, such as holding his shirt when he dressed in a three-hour morning ceremony called the levee.   He created an atmosphere in which others competed for his attention, a situation that Madame de Lafayette described in her novel, *The Princess of Clèves* (1678): "Nobody was tranquil or indifferent – everybody busily trying to better his or her position by pleasing, by helping, or by hindering somebody else."

Louis manipulated his subjects within the spectacular setting of the Versailles Palace and its grounds.   Louis's father built Versailles as a hunting lodge in its location about twelve miles from Paris, but under Louis XIV, it was enlarged into what was considered by most to be the grandest palace in the world.   One reason that Louis chose to build his palace outside Paris was the protection it gave him from the urban mobs, such as those that had haunted his youth during the years of the Fronde.   The transformation of the palace began in the 1660s but Louis did not move there until 1682, after he had reigned as monarch for 39 years.   Construction continued throughout his lifetime and beyond, and at times it housed as many as 15,000 people in its apartments, including all the highest military officers, the ministers of state, and the separate households of each member of the royal family.   Wings were added to the original building to make the palace U-shaped.   Enormous staterooms became display galleries for beautiful furniture, Italian marble statuary, and precious tapestries.   The largest room was the **Hall of Mirrors**, where hundreds of candles lit the domed ceiling, and their light was intensified by mirrors that reflected allegorical paintings celebrating the king's victories.   The gardens were designed by landscape architect André Le Nôtre, and their geometrical arrangements and clear lines tamed the natural landscape just as Louis controlled the inhabitants of the palace.

The reputation of the dazzling court spread throughout Europe, where French became the language of polite society and the vehicle of diplomatic exchange. French also gradually replaced Latin as the language of international scholarship and learning. Other kings, intellectuals, and artists imitated their French counterparts, and the royal courts of Sweden, Russia, Poland, and Germany all spoke French.

The Revocation of the Edict of Nantes

Louis XIV's attempts to create an orderly society led him in 1685 to revoke the Edict of Nantes, in which his grandfather Henry IV had granted religious freedoms to French Huguenots. The new law ordered the destruction of churches, the closing of schools, the Catholic baptism of Huguenots, and the exile of Huguenot ministers who refused to renounce their faith. The devoutly Catholic king took these actions despite the fact that Protestantism had weakened significantly in France during the 17th century, especially after Richelieu had deprived many French Calvinists of political rights, causing some to convert to Catholicism and others to immigrate to other countries. In Louis's view, religious toleration was never meant to be permanent, and the Edict had done its job of averting religious strife during Henry IV's reign. More than anything, however, Louis considered religious unity necessary for realizing his goal of "one king, one law, one faith." Religious unity, then, was essential to the maintenance of the absolute state. The revocation was enormously popular at the time, since many aristocrats had long petitioned Louis to limit Protestant rights, but scholars later criticized the king's action because of the impact it had on the economy and foreign affairs. Tens of thousands of Huguenots carried their skills to other countries, and shared their bitterness with Protestants abroad, confirming anti-Catholic feelings outside France. While modern historians dispute the economic impact, the revocation of the Edict of Nantes did enforce French religious uniformity, further reducing the country's religious diversity.

Louis XIV's Wars

Although Louis's finance minister, Jean-Baptiste Colbert, advised the king to be financially prudent, his military advisor, the **marquis of Louvois**, warned that France was geographically vulnerable to outside attack, especially on its flat northeast corner. Whereas Colbert believed that the government should give priority to increasing France's wealth, Louvois emphasized the army as the foundation of French power. Louis tried to balance these two goals, but military readiness often came with a high price tag, making the twin goals contradictory. Another influence on Louis's decisions to conduct frequent wars may be reflected in his alleged deathbed statement: "I have gone to war too lightly and pursued it for vanity's sake." Whether or not Louis actually said this, he clearly believed that a successful monarch must be a military conqueror.

The French army had grown significantly under Richelieu, increasing from about 25,000 men in 1635 to about 100,000 men in 1642. Louis XIV continued this military expansion, so that by 1659, the French army was composed of about 250,000 soldiers. Under the king's supervision, Louvois created a professional army in the sense that personnel were employed by the state, not by individual nobles. Louis personally appointed top military leaders, and Louvois recruited men domestically through conscription and seizure of men off the streets and from prisons. Regiments of foreign mercenaries also were formed, and uniforms and weapons were standardized, and a rational system of training and promotion was created.

EXAMINING THE EVIDENCE: THE "THEATRE STATE" OF LOUIS XIV

Many rulers throughout history have enhanced their power through the use of "theatre state," or the art of awing subjects into remaining loyal to the ruling family. Louis XIV developed this technique to its height by creating an elaborate court at the magnificent Versailles Palace. Some important court rituals were captured in the following excerpt from a letter from Madame Le Marquise de Sévigné to her daughter, written in 1676.

"...at three o'clock the magnificent royal suite is thrown open and the King and Queen....the princes and princesses, Madame de Montespan [the king's mistress] and her suite, the courtiers and their ladies, indeed the entire French Court assemble there. The apartments are sumptuously furnished...and the guests move from room to room....As you instructed me to do, I bowed to the King who bowed back as if I were young and lovely....[Madame de Montespan's] dress was of French point lace, her head adorned with hundreds of little curls, the two longest hanging down on each side of her face...She wore pearls...enriched with ...festoons of priceless diamonds.... When a courier is announced the King retires to read his letters, returns anon and is always ready to listen to any music being played...He discourses with the ladies who are specially chosen as recipients for this honour....Later on the guests are rowed in gondolas on the canal to the strains of music, return-ing about ten, when a play is staged, and at the stroke of midnight mediaroche is served; thus Saturday draws to its close..."

Reference: Letters from Madame La Marquise de Sévigné, translated by Violet Hammersley (New York: Har-court, Brace, and Co., 1956).

Wars initiated by France dominated the attention of most European states in the second half of the 17th century. Other European countries formed coalitions and alliances of common defense, designed to keep Louis's ambitions in check. From this response emerged the concept of a state system and the notion of a **balance of power** among the countries of Europe. Some of the many wars that Louis XIV fought were:

- **War of Devolution (1667-1668)** – One of Louis's early concerns was the threat of Spanish power on French frontiers. To establish French domi-nance, Louis ordered his army to invade the Spanish Netherlands (modern Belgium) and Franche-Comté to the east. He based his actions on the claim that these lands should "devolve" to him because the Spanish king had failed to pay the dowry of Louis's Spanish bride. Louis defeated the

Spanish armies but had to make peace when England, Sweden, and the Dutch Republic joined the war. The Treaty of Aix-la-Chapelle (1668) awarded France several towns along the border of the Spanish Netherlands.

- **The Dutch War (1672-1678)** – After his limited gains in the War of Devolution, Louis turned his attention to breaking the alliance of England, Sweden, and the Dutch Republic. First he convinced King Charles II of England to ally with him against England's long-standing trade rival, the Dutch Republic. His motivations were partly economic since the Dutch dominated the international trading economy, but the Dutch also blocked Louis's territorial ambitions when they allied with Spain in order to hold off the French. When Colbert was unable to offset the Dutch advantage in trade with tariff barriers against Dutch goods, Louis personally led his armies against the Dutch in 1672, initiating a war that continued until 1678. Although the French initially succeeded in their efforts against the tiny Dutch army, the Dutch cleverly opened dikes and flooded the countryside, making it virtually impossible for the French armies to move against them. Once again the balance of power principle emerged, and German and Austrian forces joined the Dutch against the French and English. The war ended with the Peace of Nijmegen in 1678-79, which allowed France to take over the Franche-Comté and several additional towns along the border of the Spanish Netherlands.

- **The Nine Years' War (1688-1697)** – Taking advantage of the Habsburgs' seeming weakness, Louis again was the aggressor as he marched his armies to the northeast, seizing the city of Strasbourg in 1681 and invading the province of Lorraine in 1684. His main motivation was to push France's frontier into territory along the Rhine River. The war was stirred up after Louis's Dutch opponent – **William of Orange** (grandson of William the Silent) – also became the king of England in 1688. In that same year, Louis attacked some of the small German cities of the Holy Roman Empire, an action that provoked William and most other European monarchs. The war is sometimes called the War of the League of Augsburg, since a grand alliance of European states formed to defeat France. The League of Augsburg – consisting of England, Spain, Sweden, the Dutch Republic, the Austrian emperor, and various German princes – managed to fight France to a stalemate. When the war ended in 1697 with the Peace of Rijswijk, Louis returned many of his conquests made since 1678, although France kept Alsace, including the city of Strasbourg.

- **The War of the Spanish Succession (1701-1714)** – The last of Louis XIV's wars, the War of the Spanish Succession, was both the longest and the hardest fought. In some ways it was a direct dynastic clash between

France and its longtime foe, the Habsburgs. Both Louis and **Leopold I** – the Holy Roman emperor – claimed their rights to the throne of Spain, left open at the death in 1700 of the last Spanish Habsburg, Charles II. Leopold was from the Austrian branch of the Habsburg family, but Charles II bequeathed the throne to Louis's grandson, Philip of Anjou, since Louis's wife, Maria Theresa, was a Spanish princess. Leopold challenged the succession, claiming the Spanish crown for his son Charles. The stakes were great, since the victor would acquire not only Spain, but all Spanish possessions in Europe and the Americas as well. Other major European powers became involved in the war after Louis renounced the condition of Charles's will that would preclude Philip from rights to the French throne should he accept the Spanish crown. The fact that Philip was third in line for the French throne reflected Louis's belligerence, signaling to other rulers that the European balance of power was again threatened by the French. Spurred on by the need to defend their colonial interests, the Dutch and English joined Leopold to form the Great Alliance in 1701. The French fought a major war on several fronts on land and at sea. Major revolts broke out inside France in response to crushing taxes meant to pay for the war. Despite these problems, the superior organization of the French forces helped them to hold their own in battle. The war ended with two treaties – the **Peace of Utrecht** in 1713 and the Treaty of Baden and Rastatt of 1714 – after a twist of fate brought about deaths in the Habsburg family that threatened the balance of power. Had the Austrian claimant to the Spanish throne lived and prevailed, he would have inherited rule of Austria and the Spanish Empire as well. The English – caught between their desire to control both French and Habsburg power – called for peace negotiations. The peace settlement recognized Philip of Anjou as King Philip V of Spain, but provided that neither he nor his successors could claim the French throne. The Austrian Habsburgs were compensated by the acquisition of the Spanish Netherlands, Naples, Sardinia, and Milan. Another important provision of the peace settlement was that the France gave to England some of its lands in Canada and the Caribbean. The Peace of Utrecht, then, marked the beginning of England's dominance of the Atlantic trade and colonization in North America.

The Peace of Utrecht and the Treaty of Baden and Rastatt ended the French expansionist policy. When Louis died in 1715, his long quest for military glory was over. To raise revenue for the wars, 40,000 additional political offices had been sold, exempting their recipients from future taxation, and the country's debt was enormous. France was on the brink of financial bankruptcy, allowing one of Louis's fiercest critics, the **Duc de Saint-Simon**, to declare that the king's death brought this reaction: "…the people, ruined, abused, despairing, now thanked God for a deliverance which answered their most ardent desires."

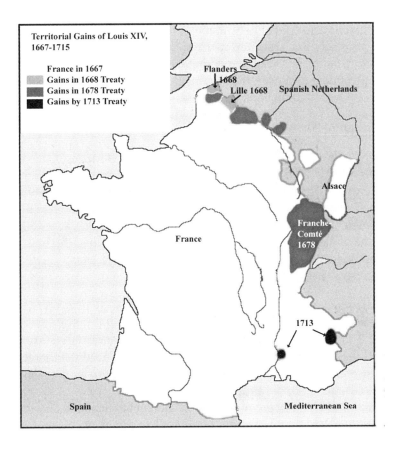

Territorial Gains of Louis XIV,
1667-1715

France in 1667
Gains in 1668 Treaty
Gains in 1678 Treaty
Gains by 1713 Treaty

Flanders
1668
Lille 1668   Spanish Netherlands

Alsace

Franche-
Comté
1678

France

1713

Spain   Mediterranean Sea

The Wars of Louis XIV. Despite the enormous expense of Louis's wars, France made only modest gains of territory along its eastern and northern frontiers.

ABSOLUTISM IN CENTRAL AND EASTERN EUROPE

During the Age of Louis XIV, three states dominated central and eastern Europe: Austria, Brandenburg-Prussia, and Russia. After the Thirty Years' War ended in 1648, the Habsburgs lost control of many parts of their empire and focused on strengthening their hold on hereditary possessions centered in what became modern Austria. The rulers of Brandenburg-Prussia had acquired lands in the Peace of Westphalia, and they built their small, scattered holdings into one of the most powerful states in Europe. Russia gained new stature in eastern Europe as its greatest rival, Poland, weakened, and an ambitious new tsar – **Peter the Great –** took control of the government.

The three states were in fierce competition for territory, and they all gained power and stability through the political model of absolutism. Although the monarchs of eastern Europe were awed by Louis XIV and his governing style, states in central and eastern Europe differed from France in some important ways. Louis built French absolutism on the foundation of a strong monarchy with an efficient and effect royal bureaucracy staffed by lesser nobility and middle-class officials. Town and regional councils also tended to be controlled by middle-class merchants, and peasants were generally free from serfdom. In contrast, eastern absolutism operated within a very different social, economic, and political reality: land-owning nobility had a great deal of power, the middle-class was almost non-existent, and peasants were still bound to the land as serfs.

The Consolidation of Austria

In contrast to France, Austria was not a national state. Germans, Hungarians, Italians, Czechs, Croats, Serbs, Romanians, and many others were united under the Habsburg crown. The Austrian state was held together almost solely by the common allegiance that various kingdoms, duchies, marks, and counties owed to the Habsburg ruler. Thus Austria was not so much a single state as a collection of states, and the authority of the Austrian emperor was less than the bulk of his territories might indicate. Nevertheless, after the Peace of Rastatt, Austria stood in power and prestige in Europe second only to France.

Louis's contemporary in Austria was **Leopold I**, his nemesis in the War of the Spanish Succession. Leopold had inherited the Holy Roman Empire shortly after the end of the Thirty Years' War, and he built his armies and state authority in order to defend the empire's international position. He replaced the mercenaries hired during the war with a permanent standing army that promoted professional discipline. Like Louis, Leopold promoted his court as the center of all political and social life, and as a result, the nobility were drawn to Vienna, a city that had previously been inhabited mainly by small-time traders. He planned a new palace, **Schönbrunn**, which was supposed to outshine Versailles, but had to be modified because of a lack of funds. In contrast to Louis's royal council, Leopold's privy council, which in effect ran the government, was filled largely with members of aristocratic families, and his chief advisers were always prominent nobles. Unlike the other courts of Europe, Schönbrunn promoted a nobility of diverse ethnic backgrounds, including Czechs, Germans, Italians, Spaniards, and Irish. Leopold extended his control over Bohemia, where many Protestant nobles had supported the 1618 revolt against Austrian authority, so that it became a virtual Austrian colony.

Leopold's personal ambition was to re-establish devout Catholicism throughout his territories, and he saw the church as an important institutional and ideological support for the imperial state. Virtually all the favored nobility were Catholic, and Leopold encouraged Jesuit activities as teachers and organizers throughout his lands. This goal of a united Catholic Austria was tested most seriously in the kingdom of Hungary. In 1682, only a narrow strip of northwest Hungary was under Austrian control; the center was occupied by Turks, and in the east, Transylvanian princes paid tribute to the Turks. Hungary had been the chief battle zone between Austria and the Ottoman Empire for almost 150 years, and while Leopold was occupied with Louis XIV's aggression in the west, Hungarian nobles, offended by

Austrian Gains from the Ottomans under Leopold I, 1683-1699. In the early 16th century Austria had not yet consolidated as a powerful state, and faced a strong Ottoman Empire to the east. By the late 17th century, the Ottoman Empire had weakened, and Austria emerged as a major European power after Austrian-led forces successfully took control of Hungary, Transylvania, and Croatia from the Ottomans.

Leopold's centralizing policies and oppression of Protestantism, began a revolt, aided by the Turks. Their aim was a reunited Hungary under Ottoman protection. In 1683, the Turks pushed all the way to Vienna, where they laid siege to the city. However, they overreached their supply lines, and the siege failed, allowing Habsburg armies to slowly press east and south. With the help of Venetians, Russians, and Poles, who also were threatened by the Turkish attack, the Austrians counterattacked and decisively defeated the Turks in 1687. Austria took control of Hungary, Transylvania, and Croatia, effectively establishing an Austrian Empire in southeastern Europe. At the end of the War of the Spanish Succession in 1713, Austria gained possession of the Spanish Netherlands, and became the dominant power in divided Italy. As a result, the house of Austria had acquired a large empire by the end of the Age of Louis XIV in 1715.

The Rise of Brandenburg-Prussia

The second state to rise to power after the Peace of Westphalia left the Holy Roman Empire a hodgepodge of autonomous and sovereign political units was Brandenburg-Prussia, composed of holdings of the **Hohenzollern dynasty**. The state began as Brandenburg, a small territory on the Elbe River with a ruler who was one of the seven German princes entitled to select the Holy Roman Emperor. Since the 16th century the ruler had also controlled the duchy of East Prussia; after 1618, the state was called Brandenburg-Prussia. These scattered lands were welded into an absolutist state by **Frederick William of Hohenzollern, the Great Elector** of Brandenburg-Prussia from 1640 to 1688. The

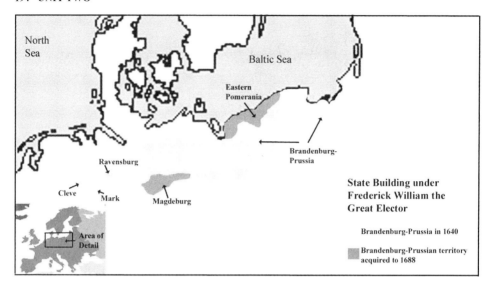

Brandenburg-Prussia by 1688. The state grew from the land possessions of the Hohen'zollern family, and began to consolidate under Frederick William the Great Elector, who ruled the area from 1640 to 1688. After the Thirty Years' War ended in 1648, Brandenburg-Prussia aggressively expanded its military and territorial base.

Peace of Westphalia granted Frederick control of east Pomerania and lands on the west bank of the Elbe. By the 17th century, then, Brandenburg-Prussia consisted of three disconnected land masses in western, central, and eastern Germany.

Frederick William never held a crown, but he collected taxes by military force, and used the money to build up an army that allowed him to enforce his will without the approval of the nobles. He maintained absolute power through tradeoffs with his **Junkers**, or German noble landlords, in which they were given almost complete control over serfs on their estates. In exchange for loyalty to the Hohenzollerns, the Junkers received the right to demand obedience from their serfs. His tax collectors were mainly nobles, and tax burdens fell most heavily on peasants and the urban middle-class and poor. Over time, sons of Junkers came to dominate the army officer corps, a practice that became even more pronounced as the 17th century passed. All government officials and army officers took an oath of loyalty directly to the Elector, so the army and the Elector provided the unity necessary to allow the state to rise to power.

The Hohenzollern family finally acquired a crown under the Great Elector's son, Frederick I in 1701, when he put his army at the disposal of the Habsburgs at the beginning of the War of the Spanish Succession. In exchange for this service, the emperor allowed Frederick to assume the title of "King in Prussia," and he passed his royal title to his son **Frederick William I** in 1713. The army grew in importance under Frederick William I, who cared very little for luxurious living and devoted virtually every penny possible to building the military. All his policies were oriented toward the military, and he was the first Prussian king to appear always in uniform.

Frederick William I's love of the army was based on a competitive, practical view of international politics that assumed that power could only be attained through force or threat of force. He devised new forms of discipline and war techniques, founded a cadet corps to train the sons of Junkers, and invented the canton system, a new recruitment method in which each regiment was assigned a particular district or canton as a source of soldiers. Frederick William I more than doubled the size of the army during his reign from 1713 to 1740, with Berlin growing to be a city of 100,000, of which 20,000 were soldiers. Only the much more populous states of France, Russia, and Austria had larger forces, and even France's army was only twice as large as Prussia's. Ironically, he fought very few wars, and he spent money very frugally, so that when he died, he left a huge war chest to his successor. With this army and war chest **Frederick II**, later called the Great, eventually moved his forces into Silesia, a part of the kingdom of Bohemia that the Hohenzollerns claimed as theirs through hereditary rights. This addition of Silesia in 1740 almost doubled the population and added valuable industries, so that Prussia at last established itself as a great power.

Russia: the Emergence of a Powerful Absolutist State

Russia's origins go back to early medieval times, when a Slavic people know as the "Rus" began to organize a large state from several principalities. The most important early city was Kiev, a thriving trading center on the Dnieper River along the main trade route between Scandinavia and Byzantium. Kiev came to dominate many of the other principalities, and its princes sought alliances with Byzantine rulers. Many Russian merchants visited Constantinople, became acquainted with Byzantine culture, and sparked the interest of their rulers in Orthodox Christianity. After the conversion of Prince Vladimir of Kiev in about 989, Byzantine influences flowed rapidly into Russia, including art, the Cyrillic alphabet, architecture, law codes, and missions. By the early 12th century, Kiev's population approached thirty thousand, and the city controlled trade all over the region, with eight thriving marketplaces within its borders. Long after Constantinople fell to the Turks in 1453, Byzantine influences lived on in Russia, with the Orthodox faith and Byzantine customs spreading rapidly as the Kievan principality transformed over time into the great Russian Empire that stretched from the Baltic Sea to Alaska.

By 1450, the Russian princes had escaped Mongol control that since the early 13th century had extended across eastern Europe, and the power of Muscovy (later Moscow) rose to eclipse Kiev. However, Russia was still a backwater area in the eyes of other organized states. Russians had aligned themselves much earlier to Byzantine culture and politics, a decision that seemed to doom them when the last of the Byzantine Empire slipped away with the Muslim capture of Constantinople in 1453. Russian lands were located far inland and to the north of most other civilizations, and logically the ascendancy of sea-based powers between 1450 and 1750 should have ensured their continuing obscurity. However, the gradual concentration of political power, supported by actions and policies of its tsars, defied the odds and propelled Russia to the ranks of the great empires by 1740.

The Expansion and Centralization of Russia Before 1650

Even before the Mongols were ousted in 1480, Moscow princes began to expand their control of nearby lands. As Mongol presence weakened, the princes continued to pay tribute, but acted virtually independently in the years leading up to 1480. The leader that ultimately refused to pay tribute to the Mongols was **Ivan III**, also known as Ivan the Great, who declared himself "tsar" – a derivative of "Caesar" – with the claim that he was establishing the "Third Rome." Ivan acquired new lands by war, marriage, and purchase, and he consolidated his hold by recruiting the **Cossacks,** a people of the southern Russian and Ukrainian plains, to settle in new territories in exchange for their freedom from serfdom. After the demise of the Byzantines, Ivan saw Russia as the carrier of Roman tradition, although with the distinct cultural characteristics of the Eastern Empire, including the Russian Orthodox Church. Like the Byzantine emperors, Ivan III ruled not only as head of the government but as head of the church as well, and as a result, the influence of the church increased as Ivan's power grew.

Centralization of power continued under Ivan's grandson, **Ivan IV**, but his nickname – Ivan the Terrible – reflects the problems that tsars faced as their power increased. Russia's economic system was based on feudalism, with the nobility, called **boyars,** holding land worked by serfs. The boyars also had military responsibilities to overlords, including the tsar, that were similar to those of western European knights and Japanese samurai. As the tsar centralized his power, the boyars resisted. Ivan responded by redistributing their lands to a new aristocracy, the *oprichniki*, and by killing the rebels, often in very cruel ways, such as cooking them and skinning them alive. Ivan insured that the time that followed his rule would be called "The Time of Trouble" when he executed his oldest son, touching off competition among boyar families for control of the throne and encouraging nearby kingdoms to invade Russian territory. Amidst the chaos, the boyars cooperated to select Mikhail Romanov from the distinguished **Romanov family,** as the heir to the throne. The Romanovs ruled Russia until the early 20th century, when the last tsar was executed by the new regime of communist leaders.

Peter the Great

Although Ivan III, Ivan IV, and the early Romanov tsars expanded the Russian Empire greatly, the tsar most responsible for transforming Russia into a great world power was **Peter the Great**, who ruled from 1682 to 1724. Peter understood, perhaps better than anyone else of his era, the ongoing changes that were occurring in the global balance of power, and he realized that Russia was far from the cutting edge of innovation. He looked to the west, saw the importance of

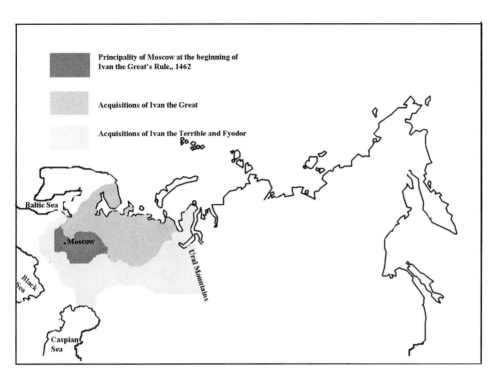

The Expansion of Russia before the Romanovs. When Ivan the Great became tsar in 1462, the principality of Moscow was a totally landlocked territory that grew from the old city of Muscovy. Ivan expanded Russia north and east, greatly increasing the size of the Empire. Russia continued to grow under Ivan the Terrible and his successor, Fyodor, so that it stretched from the Baltic Sea to the Caspian Sea and eastward to the Ural Mountains.

controlling the oceans and seas, studied European methods of shipbuilding and engineering, applied all that his brilliant mind could put together, and pulled Russia by the bootstraps into its new role as an important player in global history.

Resistance → absolutism

As a young man Peter was caught up in the intrigues of boyar competition for political influence. Although the Romanovs were clearly in control, boyar families still strove for power, a situation that was exacerbated by the fact that his father Alexis had two wives, the second one after the first one's death. When Tsar Alexis died, infighting between the two wives' families eventually led to Peter (son of Alexis's second wife) succeeding his father, but not until after he had his half-sister removed as regent and placed in a monastery. Tsars were absolute rulers, and Peter never hesitated to use his power, including the order he gave much later in his life to execute his son for conspiring against him. Despite this absolute power, the threat from boyar uprisings was always present, and many of Peter's goals for the empire were met with resistance from the nobility, making his accomplishments even more remarkable.

Peter had to seize power w/ absolutism

MARKER EVENT:
PETER THE GREAT AND
THE SEXTANT

Peter the Great grew up in a Russia that was quite isolated from the many changes going on in western Europe during the 17th century. However, when Peter was sixteen, a Russian prince brought him a present from France: a sextant . Peter was amazed by the instrument "by which distance and space could be measured without moving from the spot," and he quickly learned the arithmetic and geometry necessary to learn how to use it. With instruction from a Dutchman living in the "German suburb" outside of Moscow, Peter went on to learn about the western countries that used the sextants, and he developed an interest in shipmaking after he and his tutor came across a ruined English ship in a building filled with junk. The Dutchman explained to him that the ship would have had sails, which Peter had never seen before. The young tsar eventually went to western Europe to see these wonders for himself, and he brought back a host of ideas about how to apply the new technology in Russia. No doubt, Peter would still have been a remarkable tsar if the sextant had not been presented to him when he was a boy, but his drive to modernize Russia may well be traced to that event.

Reference: Peter the Great, Robert K. Massie (New York: Alfred A. Knopf, 1980), pp. 71, 72.

Peter did not reject his predecessors' efforts to centralize power and to expand the empire, but his appreciation for the importance of sea power led him to direct the expansion toward access to warm water ports. He was successful in gaining solid access to the Baltic Sea, and built a new capital on its shores, St. Petersburg, often called his "**Window on the West**". The city served as a port for the navy he built, and it also allowed closer access to western countries. He tried to capture lands adjacent to the Black Sea, but the Ottomans held fast to the area, and Peter's efforts in that direction were ultimately unsuccessful.

Peter's program for westernization included these reforms:

- **Military reform** – Peter increased the size of his army by drafting peasants to serve as professional soldiers and increasing pay. He encouraged the use of western technology, including the training of troops in the use of cannons and firearms. He ordered the building of roads and bridges to more easily transport troops and equipment across the countryside. He built a navy from scratch, and brought in European experts on shipbuilding, sailing, and navigation. Ports, including St. Petersburg, were built to accommodate the new ships.

- **Social reform** – Peter ordered the boyars to dress like Europeans, which meant they had to abandon their bearskin capes and beards. By tradition, boyars grew their beards without shaving, giving them a very un-western appearance, so Peter ordered them to shave. If they refused, Peter himself was known to hack their beards off with scissors, although eventually the beards could stay if their owners paid fines to the government. Until Peter's rule, Russian women followed the Byzantine custom of secluding themselves at home and wearing veils in public. Previous tsars' courts were all-male, but Peter insisted that women appear unveiled in his court, dressed as European ladies of fashion. He extended rights for women and men in less superficial ways as well, such as a decree that young people, rather than their parents, should determine for themselves who they would marry.

- **Bureaucratic reform** – In order to pay for and promote his expanded army, new navy, and improved infrastructure, Peter reorganized the bureaucracy to more efficiently gather taxes and to encourage industrial production. He replaced boyars with government officials selected according to his newly established **Table of Ranks**, which allowed officials to attain government positions based on merit, not on aristocratic status. He eliminated many titles of nobility, and he ensured that the new bureaucrats were loyal to him as the person responsible for their newly acquired positions.

At the end of his reign, Peter had brought many changes to Russia, including a basic conflict that had not existed in Russia before: the Slavic, traditional ways vs. the new impetus to westernize. Peter only selectively imitated western ways; he took little interest in Enlightenment ideas about government, although in truth those influences were far greater all over Europe in the years that followed his death in 1725. He also did not aim to build an international export-oriented economy, as was characteristic of the west, and he saw economic development mainly as a way to support his military efforts. He continued to rule autocratically as tsars always had, but he sent a very strong message to his subjects that European ways were to be emulated. A successor tsar, Catherine the Great, understood both sides of the cultural conflict that Peter had created, and she too continued the autocratic traditions of the tsars, although she was fully aware of the Enlightenment ideas of her contemporaries of the late 18th century. Russians continued to value their Slavic ways, including their Russian Orthodox religion, but after Peter, they began to turn one ear toward the west.

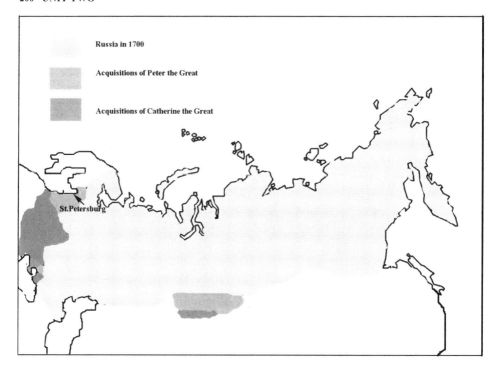

The Expansion of Russia. By 1700 Russia had grown from its origins in the east to encompass land in northern Eurasia all the way to the Pacific Ocean. Both Peter and Catherine sought access to the Baltic and Black Seas that would connect them to the world waterways that were replacing overland trade in importance.

ALTERNATIVES TO ABSOLUTISM

The absolutist regimes of France, Austria, Prussia-Brandenburg, and Russia offered one model of political and social organization, but an alternative model that sought to limit the power of the monarch emerged by the late 17th century. In some cases – such as in Sweden and Poland – the aristocracy was in control, but in England, the institution of Parliament grew in power, and served as the quite different model of **constitutionalism**, in which governments are limited by law. Constitutionalism also implies a balance between the authority and power of the government, on the one hand, and the rights and liberties of the subjects, on the other. The Netherlands, officially called the Republic of United Provinces of the Netherlands by the mid-17th century, developed as another model of the modern constitutional state.

Sweden

Swedish King Gustavus Adolphus II (r. 1611-1632) had played an important role as a Protestant leader against the Habsburgs during the Thirty Years' War. During the rest of the 17th century, Sweden had consolidated its control of the Baltic, preventing Russia from establishing a Baltic port and permitting Polish and German access to the sea only on Swedish terms. The Swedes also possessed one of the better armies in Europe. As in most other European countries, the king had long struggled with the nobles for control of Sweden. During the reign of Charles XI (1660-1697), the monarchy was able to force the great lords to return large tracts of land they had received as rewards for loyalty earlier in the century. Since Charles generally stayed out of European wars, he managed his expenses without relying on the nobility. His successor, **Charles XII** (r. 1697-1718), however, revived Sweden's military involvement. In response to Peter the Great's drive to the west through Swedish territory to gain a foothold on the Baltic, Charles XII led a vigorous and often brilliant campaign. In 1700, he defeated the Russians at the Battle of Narva, but then he turned south to invade Poland. The conflict dragged on, the Russians recovered, and Charles' army became bogged down in the brutal Russian winter. The next year, 1709, Peter decisively defeated him at the Battle of Poltava. From there, Charles had to retreat, and by the time he was killed in battle nine years later, neighboring countries had begun to overrun his lands. In treaties signed from 1719, Sweden reverted to roughly the territory it had possessed a century before.

The Swedish nobles took advantage of the situation, and reasserted their authority while Charles was away fighting his wars. By the time of his death, they ran the government, and emerged as the country's dominant political voice after they forced his successor, Queen Ulrika, to accept a constitution that gave them effective control over the government. The nobles created the **Riksdag**, a new structure modeled on England's parliament, but composed of nobility rather than gentry, as in the English House of Commons. The aristocrats sponsored a splendid, elegant court that became one of the most important social, if not political, centers in Europe.

Poland-Lithuania

By the end of the 16th century the Polish-Lithuanian Commonwealth was a large state that dominated the Baltic coast and claimed lands that had long borders with the Ottoman Empire, the Holy Roman Empire, and Russia. The duchy of Lithuania had conquered the territories known as Ruthenia (modern day Belarus and Ukraine) in the 14th century, and had joined with Poland through royal marriage in 1386. For 200 years, the Polish and Lithuanian cultures remained distinct, but in 1569, they were brought under a single set of institutions by the Treaty of Lublin. The two states that comprised the Commonwealth were formally equal, although in reality Poland was the dominant partner in the union. Despite this political unity, Poland-Lithuania's ethnic differences, including language and religion, remained strong, keeping regional nobility strong and discouraging the development of loyalty to the king. The Polish–Lithuanian Commonwealth was one of the largest and most populous countries in 16th and 17th-century Europe. As a political model, Poland by the late 17th century was a strong contrast to the French political and social model. It was a republic of the nobility, with a weak king elected by the nobles at its head. The Commonwealth's political system, often called the "noble's democracy" or "Golden Freedom," was characterized by the king's reduced power and a nobility-controlled legislature (Sejm). Its constitution protected religious minorities, and for a time, Poland was one of the most diverse, tolerant societies in Europe. However, the system was undermined by the absolute veto power granted to each of the major nobles, who often exercised their veto, resulting in a frequently deadlocked parliamentary government.

Internal strains began to weaken Poland-Lithuania by the early 17th century. The Counter-Reformation had increased religious tensions among Catholics, Protestants, and Orthodox Christians, and peasant resentment mounted as nobles grew richer from the profitable international trade of grain from their lands. As in other parts of eastern Europe, peasants remained tied to the land through serfdom, and the lesser nobility were shut out of political power by Polish aristocrats. In Ukraine, disaffected peasants and lesser nobility joined the Cossacks, the nomadic farmer-warriors who had long been tolerated because they served as a military buffer against the Ottoman Turks to the south. In 1648, the Polish crown faced a major uprising led by the Cossacks, and the Polish armies were unable to contain it. The king tried to reach a peace agreement, but the noble landlords blocked it, causing the Cossacks to side with the Russians as they invaded Poland-Lithuania in 1654. At the same time, Sweden seized central Poland in a military campaign, and the obstinate Polish nobles were unable to cooperate enough to resist the takeover. Even though the Polish royal armies eventually managed to recover much territory, the invasions and subsequent fighting were disastrous. During these wars, later called "the deluge," the population of Poland declined by as much as 40%, and vital urban centers lay in economic ruin.

When the Polish crown passed in 1674 to the military hero, King **John III Sobieski**, the commonwealth briefly revived under his capable and ambitious leadership. He gained a reputation throughout Europe when he led 25,000 Polish cavalrymen into battle at the Siege of Vienna in 1683. His cavalry helped turn the tide against the Ottomans, and John became known as "Vanquisher of the Turks." However, he was unable to keep Poland's power from declining, since the nobles cooperated only long enough to win the battles, and then refused to grant the king any real authority over them. While the nobles grew rich from serf labor on fertile lands, the crown had neither revenue nor bureaucracy to speak of, and Poland remained locked in feudalism, with power remaining in the localities. The price of the "Golden Freedom" of the nobles would eventually be the disappearance of Poland from the map of Europe during the last half of the 18th century.

The Netherlands

The 17th century is often called the "golden age of the Netherlands," a time of many Dutch scientific, artistic, and literary achievements. Dutch ideas and attitudes played an important role in shaping a new and modern world view. At the same time, in the political realm, the United Provinces provided another model of the development of the modern constitutional state.

ORIGINAL DOCUMENT:
KING JOHN III OF POLAND
AND THE SIEGE OF VIENNA

In 1683 the Ottoman Empire had laid siege to Vienna, the Habsburg center of Austria, and the Turks threatened to overrun central Europe. John III Sobieski of Poland came to the Habsburgs' aid, rescuing the city and repulsing the last great Turkish advance upon central Europe. The excerpt below reflects the Polish view of their king, the Austrians, and the Turks.

"The Victory which the King of Poland hath obtained over the Infidels, is so great and so compleat that past Ages can scarce parallel the fame; and perhaps future Ages will never see any thing like it....On the one hand we see Vienna besieged by three hundred thousand Turks; reduced to the last extremity; its Outworks taken; the Enemy fixed to the Body of the Place....We see an Emperor [the Habsburg ruler] chased from his Capital; retired to a Corner of his Dominions; all his Country at the mercy of the Tartars [allies of the Turks], who have filled the Camp with an infinite Number of unfortunate Slavs that had been forcibly carried away out of Austria. On the other hand, we see the King of Poland, who goes out of his Kingdom, with part of his Army, and hastens to succour his...Allies,...to march against the enemies of the Christian religion willing to act in Person on this Occasion, as a true Buckler of Religion."

Reference: Polish Manuscripts: or the Secret History of the Reign of John Sobieski, the III of That Name, King of Poland, trans. By M. Delerac (London: D. Rhodes, 1700), pp. 355, 364.

In 1648, the Treaty of Westphalia formally recognized Dutch independence from Spain as the Republic of United Provinces of the Netherlands. Each province held a great deal of political, economic, and social autonomy. In contrast to most European nobles, the Dutch aristocrats did not come from ancient families and bureaucratic dynasties, but most were merchants, financiers, traders, and/or mayors. An oligarchy of wealthy merchants called "regents" served as representatives from their provinces to the Estates General of the United Provinces. That body handled virtually all domestic affairs, including the naming of the provincial **stadholder**, the executive officer responsible for defense and for representing the state at all ceremonial occasions. Each province almost always chose one of the princes of the House of Orange, so that the prince of Orange resembled a president, despite the fact that, strictly speaking, there was no stadholder for the United Provinces as a whole. The Orange family had enjoyed great prestige in the republic since the days of William the Silent and the wars for independence, but the prince of Orange, apart from being stadholder, was simply one of the feudal noblemen of the country. In general, however, the commercial class had more wealth than the older noble families, and affairs were usually managed by the **burghers**, or town officials. The decentralized state encouraged and protected trade, and the Dutch dominated overseas commerce with their shipping.

During times of war or threatened invasion, the power of the stadholder increased. When all was quiet, the stadholder had little power, so the Peace of Westphalia had the effect of encouraging burghers to control their own communities, and these decentralizing tendencies were reflected in the fact that no new stadholder was elected for 22 years after the death of William II in 1650. **William III** was born a few days after his father's death, and for many years it seemed as if he would pass through life as a private nobleman on his own estates. Then, political changes in England altered the course of Dutch history.

As the Netherlands was stabilizing after the Peace of Westphalia, England was locked in its own civil war (pp. 114-116). When the war ended with the beheading of Charles I, the leader of the victorious Roundheads – **Oliver Cromwell** – took political control of the country. Among his many aggressive actions was a decision that England's trading policies should change. In 1651, the English Parliament passed a Navigation Act, which provided that goods imported into England and its dependencies must be transported on English ships or on ships belonging to the country exporting the goods. Since the Netherlands was a small country that produced very little itself but depended on revenue from carrying the goods of others, the Navigation Act seemed to be aimed directly against the Dutch carrying trade. The two countries soon entered into a series of three wars, running on and off from 1652 to 1674. Meanwhile, Louis XIV also challenged the Dutch in 1667, when he argued that the lineage of his Spanish wife gave France grounds to claim the Spanish Netherlands and Franche-Comté. Under threat of a disruption of the balance of power, the English temporarily sided with the Dutch – suspending their own war against them – in a Triple Alliance (Sweden was the third partner) to limit French aggressions.

This new set of international conflicts changed the future for William III of the House of Orange, and kept the Netherlands from being relegated to the sidelines of history. War inspired the Dutch to rally together by selecting him as the stadholder in six provinces. In 1673, these provinces voted to make the position of stadholder hereditary in the House of Orange. Despite William's attempts to centralize and consolidate his government, the United Provinces remained a decentralized republic. William, however, cleverly manipulated the balance of power by forming an alliance with Denmark, Brandenburg, Spain, and Austria to contain the ambitions of France. As a result, the Dutch preserved their territory intact. In an important turn of events that resulted from the British attempt to establish an effective constitutionalism, William was asked to be the king of England in 1689. With this new power over a country that had resisted involvement in European affairs, William presided over another important change in the European balance of power. England was a decisive addition to the balance formed against French expansion, and France never gained the control of western Europe and its overseas offshoots that Louis XIV desired.

Constitutionalism in England

Britain began its gradual path toward constitutionalism as early as the 13th century when nobles forced King John to sign the Magna Carta, a document that recognized some key rights of nobles to check the king's authority. Although King John generally ignored the nobles' demands, later kings often found it necessary to consult nobles in order to raise funds, especially for war. During the 16th century, King Henry VIII used parliamentary authority to add legitimacy to his break with the Catholic Church and the creation of an English church headed by the monarch. Queen Elizabeth I managed Parliament quite well, but she too needed support from the nobility and the growing middle class to accomplish her goals. The English Civil War of the 1640s was a conflict between the supporters of the king, Charles I, and those of Parliament (the Roundheads). Parliament won, the king was executed, and the Roundhead leader, Oliver Cromwell, took over the country.

In contrast to the decentralized Dutch Republic, in England there was only one Parliament for the whole country. However, by the time of the English Civil War, Parliament was split into two houses – the **House of Lords** for the nobility and the **House of Commons** for the gentry, merchants, and wealthy townspeople. After Parliament condemned King Charles for "treason" and sent him to death on the scaffold in 1649, England was declared a republic named the Commonwealth.

Cromwell and the Protectorate

In theory, the legislative power of the Commonwealth rested in Parliament, but in fact the army that had defeated the royal forces controlled the government, and Oliver Cromwell controlled the army. Though called **"the Protectorate"**, the rule of Cromwell from 1653 to 1658 was a military dictatorship. Cromwell was from the gentry class, and he had sat in the Long Parliament (see p. 113). He achieved fame by infusing the army with his Puritan beliefs and molding it into the highly effective "New Model Army." In 1653, the army presented a constitution that invested executive power in a "lord protector" (Cromwell) and a council of state, and Parliament was given the sole power to raise taxes. However, after numerous disputes, Cromwell tore the document up. He kept the standing army and divided England into twelve military districts, each governed by a major general. Although Cromwell protected the rights of different Protestant sects to practice their faith, he considered Irish Catholicism to be sedition. In 1649 – at the end of the Civil War – he crushed a rebellion in Ireland with such cruelty that it left a legacy of Irish hatred for England that is still alive today. True to his Calvinist roots, Cromwell censored the press, forbade sporting events, and closed theaters all over England. In short, though he was not a hereditary monarch, England under

COMPARISON: ABSOLUTISM VS. CONSTITUTIONALISM IN EARLY MODERN EUROPE

CONSTITUTIONALISM	ABSOLUTISM
Degree of centralization varied	Highly centralized state
Rule of law	Rule by divine right of kings
Rule over relatively homogeneous populations	Rule over relatively homogeneous populations
Practiced mercantilism	Practiced mercantilism
Power of king shared with parliament	No sharing of power with parliament
Recognition of some individual rights	No recognition of individual rights

Cromwell was an absolutist state. Military government ended when Cromwell died in 1658. England had long valued civilian government, common law, and social stability, and so by 1660, the country was ready to restore the monarchy. As a result, Cromwell's rule is often called the "**Interregnum**", or the time between kings.

The Restoration of the English Monarchy

In 1660 the **Restoration** of the monarchy took place as **Charles II**, the eldest son of the beheaded Charles I, was crowned king. Not only was the monarchy re-stored, but the Church of England and Parliament as well. The difference was that Charles II, ever mindful of his father's fate, was careful not to provoke Parliament to extremes. Also, many people were fed up with the Puritanism of the Cromwell era, and so welcomed the reestablishment of the Anglican Church. Like his father, Charles II still summoned and dissolved Parliament, made all appointments in the bureaucracy, and signed every law. However, he no longer had his own courts, nor could he arrest members of Parliament nor create new seats in the House of Commons. In general, the relatively good rapport between Charles II and Parlia-ment rested on the king's appointment of a council of five men who served both as his major advisers and as members of Parliament. These liaisons between the executive and the legislature called "first ministers"; they gave rise to the concept that the king was answerable through royal ministers to Parliament. However, despite substantial political harmony, deep-seated problems continued, especially the uneasy relationship among Puritans, Catholics, and Anglicans.

Tensions between Catholics and Protestants were still high in 17th century Europe, and in England the national feeling was decidedly anti-Catholic. The king was personally inclined to Catholicism, as were most other members of the Stuart family before him. He greatly admired Louis XIV, and since Parliament had given Charles an inadequate income, he entered into a secret agreement with the French king in 1670. In return for three million livres a year, Charles agreed to join Louis XIV in fighting the Dutch, relax laws against Catholics in England, and eventually convert to Catholicism himself. Although the terms of the agreement were unknown in England, it was apparent that an alliance had been struck with France when England went to war against the Dutch. The king's brother and heir, James, Duke of York, publicly converted to Catholicism, and in 1673, Charles suspended all laws against Catholics and Protestant dissenters. Fearing that the king would further promote Catholicism, Parliament passed the **Test Act**, which required all officeholders to take communion in the Anglican Church, making it impossible for Catholics to serve in the government or the military. A strong movement developed in Parliament to keep James from inheriting the throne, and these "exclusionists" came to be called the "**Whigs**", a derogatory Irish Catholic designation for a Presbyterian Scot. When Charles refused to deny his brother's right to the throne, two distinct factions developed in Parliament: the Whigs and the **Tories** (a term for Irish Catholic bandits), who supported a strong, hereditary monarchy. The Whigs also pressed for tolerance of Protestant dissenters such as Presbyterians, and the Tories supported the restored ties between the king and the Anglican Church.

The **"Glorious Revolution"** of 1688

When Charles II died in 1685, his brother became king as **James II**, and just as the Whigs feared, he pursued pro-Catholic and absolutist policies more aggressively than his brother had. He soon antagonized even the Tories when he ignored established laws, and the rift between Parliament and the king became definitive when James' newborn son was baptized into the Catholic faith in 1688. Leading men of both parties abandoned James, and they offered the throne to his grown daughter **Mary**, born and brought up a Protestant before her father's conversion to Rome. Mary also was married to William of Orange, the stadholder who was leading the Netherlands as the provinces resisted Louis XIV's attempts to gain Dutch territory and trade. William promised to use Dutch armies to invade England and take power from James; in return, Whig and Tory leaders offered the throne to **William and Mary** as co-rulers. Before they were crowned, they signed an agreement that guaranteed Parliament's full partnership in a constitutional government.

In the **Bill of Rights,** William and Mary agreed not to raise a standing army or to levy taxes without Parliament's consent. They also agreed to call Parliament to meet at least every three years, to guarantee free elections to Parliament, and to not suspend laws. The agreement provided a written, legal basis to the government, and this clear transition to constitutional government was called the **Glorious Revolution** by its supporters, once James II was finally overthrown. The Toleration Act of 1689 granted all Protestants freedom of worship, and Catholics were generally left alone to worship privately, though Parliament extended no rights to them. When Catholics in Ireland rose to defend James II, William and Mary's troops brutally suppressed them.

Despite the importance of the Glorious Revolution in establishing constitutionalism, it did not yet mark a movement toward democracy. Most representatives to

CHANGE OVER TIME: KEY FEATURES IN THE DEVELOPMENT OF CONSTITUTIONALISM IN BRITAIN

By the end of the 17th century, Britain's political system was clearly based on **rational-legal authority** – a system of well-established laws and procedures. Despite Britain's beginnings centuries before in the traditional legitimacy of an hereditary monarch, the country had gradually developed a "Constitution of the Crown" through many important documents and legal principles, including these:

- **Magna Carta** – In 1215 King John signed this document, agreeing to consult nobles before he made important political decisions, especially those regarding taxes. The Magna Carta, then, forms the basis of limited government that placed restrictions on the power of monarchs.

- **The Bill of Right** – This document lists rights retained by Parliament, not by individual citizens. William and Mary signed this document in 1688, giving important policymaking power to Parliament, including the power of the purse.

- **Common Law** – This legal system is based on local customs and precedent rather than formal legal codes. It developed gradually in Britain, and today is found in Great Britain, the United States, and other countries with a strong English influence. Common law allows the decisions that public officials and courts make to set precedents for later actions and decisions, eventually forming a comprehensive set of principles for governance.

both the House of Commons and the House of Lords were landed gentlemen or well-to-do townspeople, and the aristocratic landowning classes enjoyed many privileges and conducted the government. Not until the early 19th century would ordinary Englishmen come to have political rights. Still, England in the late 17th century was a place where political liberty had been established, even if only within strict social limits.

IDENTIFICATIONS AND CONCEPTS

absolutism, absolute monarchs
balance of power
Bill of Rights (English)
Bossuet, Bishop Jacques-Bénigne
boyers
burghers
Charles II (England)
Charles XII (Sweden)
Colbert, Jean-Baptiste
constitutionalism
Cossacks
Cromwell, Oliver
divine right
Duc de Saint-Simon
the Dutch War
Frederick II
Frederick William I
Frederick William of Hohenzollern, the Great Elector
the Fronde
Glorious Revolution
Hall of Mirrors
Hohenzollern dynasty
House of Commons (England)
House of Lords (England)
intendants
Interregnum
Ivan III
Ivan IV
James II
John III Sobieski
junkers
Leopold I
limited monarchy
Louis XIV

Marquis of Louvois
Mazarin, Cardinal
mercantilism
Nine Year's War
parlements
Peace of Utrecht
Peter the Great
the Protectorate
rational-legal authority
Restoration
revocation of the Edict of Nantes
Richelieu, Cardinal
Riksdag
Romanov family
rule of law
Schönbrunn
stadholder
Table of Ranks
"theatre-state"
Test Act
Tories
Versailles Palace
War of Devolution
War of the Spanish Succession
Whigs
William III
William and Mary
"Window on the West"

CHAPTER 9:
ECONOMIC EXPANSION
IN THE 18TH CENTURY

During the period from 1450 to 1650, Europe experienced some important economic changes, including those brought about by exploration of the Americas and the growing trade across the Atlantic Ocean. However, religious wars and the accompanying unrest had limited economic expansion until the Peace of Westphalia allowed political leaders to concentrate on building state power and increase the wealth of nations. During the last half of the 17th century, new overseas colonies provided a stimulus for European economic growth, and a brisk colonial trade in slaves, sugar, and tobacco fed port cities like London and Bristol in England and Bordeaux and Nantes in France. Still, by 1700 the great majority of Europe's people made their living through farming, and the everyday lives of most had changed very little since the Middle Ages. All of that changed by the early 19th century, with remarkable economic developments taking place during the 18th century, bringing with them new technologies and social arrangements that dramatically transformed European life. The transition began with changes in agricultural production and demographic trends, and eventually led to the early stages of industrialization, a process that removed the traditional constraints of limited resources and replaced them with the possibilities of self-generating economic growth.

AGRICULTURE AND THE LAND

At the end of the 17th century, about 80% of the people in western European countries earned their living through agriculture. In Holland, the percentage was probably smaller; in eastern Europe it was considerably higher. Even in an area with good land, such as the Po Valley in northern Italy or in many areas of France, grain yields were scarcely any better than they had been in fertile, well-watered areas during ancient times. Additionally, crops were not always reliable, since every eight or nine years, harvests completely failed, and people were forced to live on reserves and eat less. If bad conditions – such as too much or too little rain – continued, the results could be disastrous, and some people would starve to death. Those who survived often did so by gathering chestnuts, stripping bark from trees, or eating grass and dandelions. Such conditions left people weak and extremely susceptible to illness and epidemics, and some who avoided starvation might die of influenza, smallpox, or dysentery. This pattern that had been in place in Europe since the Middle Ages allowed fairly large numbers of people to survive, but could never produce material abundance.

At that time, peasants farmed the land by organizing an **open-field system**, which divided the land around each village into several large fields, which were each cut up into long, narrow strips. The fields were open, with no fences or hedges separating the strips, so peasants farmed each large field as a community, with each family tending its assigned strips of land according to the traditional regular patterns of plowing, sowing, and harvesting. Because the land had limited fertility, farmers rotated crops usually on a three-year cycle, planting wheat or rye one year and beans or oats the next, followed by a year of leaving the field fallow to regain its nutrients. In addition to rotating field crops, villages maintained open meadows for hay and natural pasture. These lands were called "commons", and were open to draft horses, oxen, cows, and pigs of the village community. After the harvest, animals were pastured on the wheat or rye stubble, and peasants were often allowed to go through the fields to pick up and keep any grain that had fallen to the ground during the harvesting process.

The Agricultural Revolution

Historians believe that the break from past agricultural patterns during the 18th century began after bread prices slowly but steadily rose, spurred largely by population growth. Since bread was the most important staple of the diet, this price increase negatively affected the poor, but it benefitted landowners and wealthier peasants who had surplus grain to sell. Encouraged by potential profits, landlords in western Europe began a series of innovations in farm production that became known as the **Agricultural Revolution**. The experimentation began in the Netherlands, where the shortage of land made the population pressures particularly strong. Dutch landlords and farmers devised better ways to build dikes and to drain lands, and they experimented with new crops, such as clover and turnips, that would help to restore the soil.

The most striking agricultural improvements occurred in England, where landlords adapted Dutch ideas or spread techniques that had originated earlier. One important innovator was **Jethro Tull**, who advocated the use of iron plows to turn earth more deeply, as well as seed drills to plant rather than cast wheat. Others experimented with new methods for using fertilizers, and a new system of crop rotation was developed that eliminated the need to leave fields fallow. Increased crop production meant that livestock had more winter fodder, so animals increased in size and number and produced more manure to provide fertilizer for the crops. Experiments also created new methods of animal breeding that produced more and better animals with more milk and meat. So a new cycle developed that provided more food for both animals and human beings.

THEMATIC LEARNING OBJECTIVE: POVERTY AND PROSPERITY: REGIONAL DIFFERENCES

In general, the peasants of eastern Europe were worse off than those in the west. They were still serfs bound to the lands, and there were few limitations on the amount of forced labor the lord could require. In Russia, the complete enserfment of the peasantry would eventually be recognized in the Code of Laws in 1649. Although enserfment produced short-term profits for landlords, in the long run it stifled economic development in eastern Europe and kept most of the population illiterate and poor.

Social conditions were better in western Europe, where peasants were generally free from serfdom. In France, western Germany, and the Netherlands, they owned land and could pass it on to their children. Yet poverty was prevalent in the west as well, and peasants often suffered hardships, especially in years of bad harvests. In most countries the nobility held vast tracts of the best land, and peasants often had to toil and till for others or take odd jobs to make a living.

These innovations eventually dismantled the open-field system and replaced it with **enclosure**, in which landlords enclosed or consolidated their lands to increase production. Common lands were fenced, previously untilled crop waste was reclaimed, and strip fields were replaced by large block fields. These changes brought protests from peasants, who were long accustomed to the old system and did not profit directly from the new one. In order to enforce their actions, English landowners called on Parliament to pass laws that enclosed specific acreage between 1727 and 1760 and eventually provided for general enclosure in 1801. The new system benefited only a small number of large landowners, while tenant farmers worked for them for wages, carrying out the tasks of fencing, fertilizing, building drains, and planting according to the landowner's specifications. As the landlords became increasingly concerned about profits, they began to leave the peasants to the mercy of the marketplace. An important change was that small, independent English peasant farmers could not compete with the entrepreneurial large landowners, and many were forced to become landless rural wage earners.

PERSPECTIVES:
WHY WAS ENCLOSURE CONTROVERSIAL?

The enclosure of common lands by English landlords was controversial when it occurred during the 18th and early 19th centuries, and it remains so among historians today.

On the one hand, enclosure permitted innovations that increased food production and broke the old cycle of poor yields and bad harvests that kept many people on the edge of starvation and sickness. Enclosure marked the beginning of commercial agriculture, which allowed more crops and animals to be raised by fewer people, providing the base for industrialization, which in turn created much more wealth than the world had ever known. On the other hand, landlords no longer honored their long-understood responsibility to look after peasants, especially in hard times. Small traditional communities were disrupted, and independent farmers were forced off the land by laws passed by a Parliament that was controlled by large landowners. Landless farmers lost their age-old access to the common pasture without any compensation at all. From this point of view, the well-to-do benefitted at the expense of the poor, who lost ownership and/or rights to the land.

The Agricultural Revolution improved farm production in the west more than in the east. Dutch farming became quite efficient, and even though France allowed only very limited enclosure of land, many French farmers improved their agricultural methods, and the food supply became larger and more reliable. In Prussia, Austria, Poland, and Russia, the Agricultural Revolution had a much more limited impact. The relationship of the serfs to their lords did not change, and the chief method of increasing production was to bring previously untilled land under the plow. No open-fields system was already in place, so serfs had no land privileges to begin with, and when new lands were tilled, the great landlords made serfs work harder than ever. The main impact of the Agricultural Revolution on eastern Europe was the introduction of maize and the potato, which created nutritional gain. However, livestock production did not increase significantly.

A NEW DEMOGRAPHIC ERA

Demography is the study of population growth and movement, especially as it impacts the earth's environment and natural resources. Historians study demography because it has impacted the course of the world's unfolding story, and the changes that occurred in 18th century European demographics are of special inter-est because they impacted so many economic, social, political, and cultural areas of life.

Traditional Patterns

Before the 18th century, the relationship between Europeans and the land had fol-lowed predictable, consistent, and longstanding patterns. Population might in-crease substantially over several generations, but eventually disease or crop fail-ures would reduce population levels significantly. If low population levels led to abandonment of land, entire villages could disappear completely. For centuries Europe's population had gone through this cycle, with poor harvests or crop fail-ures leading to inadequate food supplies that would drive up the price of grain and flour beyond what many could afford. Malnutrition also made people more vul-nerable than usual to disease, lowering population levels even further. Birthrates also tended to decrease during these down cycles, since supporting children was more difficult during times of soaring food costs.

Population Growth

No formal population censuses were taken in Europe before the early 19th century, but most scholars believe that historical population patterns were broken during the 18th century; the overall population of 100 to 120 million in 1700 rose to 180 to 190 million by 1800. Europe's population growth continued during the 19th century, a trend that provided further confirmation that the cyclical patterns of the past were no longer in place.

Although historians and demographers do not always agree about the causes, they cite several of the following factors that probably led to the population increase. Most agree that the decline in death rates accounts for more of the population growth than a rise in birthrates, although England seems to have been an exception. Advances in medical knowledge did not contribute much to the declining death rates since the most important advances were not made till later. The most important medical advance during the 18th century was in-oculation against smallpox, but this great improvement only benefited Eng-land (where it was invented) and did not spread to the continent till the end of the century. More plausible causes of the decline in the death rate include:

- **Fewer Epidemic Diseases** – Fewer epidemics contributed to the clear decline of the death rate during the 18th century. Even though the Black Death had mysteriously disappeared in the 14th century, plagues had re-mained a part of the European experience. For example, as late as 1720, a ship from Syria had brought the plague to Marseilles, France, wiping out almost half of its population within a few weeks and then sweep-ing through southern France, killing many townspeople. However, the

CHANGE OVER TIME: ESTIMATES OF POPULATION GROWTH DURING THE 18TH CENTURY

Since the first censuses were not taken until the early 19th century, all population figures are only estimates.

	Beginning of the 18th Century	End of the 18th Century
Europe Overall	100-120 million	180-190 million
Spain	7.5 million	11.5 million
England and Wales	5-6 million	9-10 million
France	19 million (1715)	26 million (1789)
Russia	19 million (1722)	29 million (1766)
Italy	11.5 million	17.5 million

epidemic passed, and after that, no more major plagues descended on western and central Europe. The final disappearance of plague was attributable partly to stricter quarantine measures in Mediterranean ports and along the Austrian border with Turkey. Another factor was the replacement of the black rat – the carriers of the fleas that carried the plague – by a larger brown rat, whose fleas did not usually carry disease. The brown rats first appeared in Asia, where they infested the ships and drove the black rats out.

- **Improved Sanitation and Hygiene** – Improvements in the water supply and sewerage promoted somewhat better public health and helped reduce such diseases as typhoid and typhus in some urban areas of western Europe. Water supply improvements and the drainage of swamps and marshes may also have reduced disease-carrying insects, such as flies and mosquitoes, which not only spread serious epidemics but more common diseases as well.

- **Better and More Stable Food Supplies** – Even though Europeans were still very vulnerable to disease, a better-nourished population could stand up to illness with better success. Improved and expanded grain production contributed to longer, healthier lives during the 18th century. Another and even more important change was the cultivation of the potato, a product that made its way via the Columbian Exchange (see pp. 137-138) from the New World to other parts of the world, particularly to Europe. Potatoes came into widespread European production during the 18th century, and they served as a nutritious alternative food for the poor, especially when the grain crops were small or had failed. On a single acre enough potatoes could be raise to feed one peasant's family for an entire year, contributing to health improvements, especially among children who in previous times might never have survived to adulthood. Another possible factor in creating a better and more stable food supply was the mild increase in average temperatures compared with those of the 17th century.

With the exception of England, birth rates in most parts of Europe probably did not increase in the 18th century. One important check on birth rates was the fact that people were marrying at older ages, with women typically well into their twenties and men in their mid-to-late twenties. Since illegitimate births were still relatively rare, late marriages usually meant fewer children per family, with women having less time over the course of their lives to have children. In England, however, greater economic opportunities and geographic mobility may have encouraged earlier marriage, so that the average age at marriage came down and birthrates increased, helping to explain why Britain's population increased more rapidly than those in other countries.

THE GROWTH OF "COTTAGE INDUSTRY"

As overall population levels grew, the number of rural workers with little or no land increased, and this in turn contributed to the development of industry in rural areas. Rural manufacturing appeared first in England, and gradually spread to continental Europe. The rural poor supplemented their earnings from agriculture with other types of work, and urban capitalists were happy to employ them, especially since they could often pay lower wages than those they paid to urban workers. The new process that developed was called the **putting-out system**, and was also known as "**cottage industry**". The two main participants in the system were the merchant capitalist and the rural worker. The merchant loaned, or "put out," raw materials to several cottage workers, who processed the raw materials in their own homes and returned the finished product to the merchant. For example, a merchant might bring raw wool, and the workers would spin and weave the wool into cloth. Workers were paid by the piece, and some were much more dependent on this income than others were. The putting-out system was an important part of the increasingly international capitalism developing in western Europe, with merchants seeking profits by selling the rural workers' piecework to buyers in markets in many parts of the world. This cottage industry was especially well suited for producing textiles, housewares, buttons, gloves, and musical instruments meant for consumption by ordinary people. Luxury goods for the rich generally needed close supervision by master craftsmen, so fine porcelain and high-quality tapestries were generally not "put out" to rural workers.

CITIES

Even before the Industrial Revolution began, cities all across Europe had been growing rapidly, especially during the 18th century. One important reason, of course, was the population explosion. Over the 300-year time span between 1500 and 1800, the percentage of the European population living in urban areas nearly doubled, rising from just over 5% to just over 9%. By 1800, 363 cities had 10,000 or more inhabitants, and 17 of them had populations larger than 100,000. An important demographic shift was that urban concentrations shifted from Mediterranean Europe to the north. Between 1500 and 1750, the major urban expansion took place within already established large cities. After 1750, the pattern changed with the birth of new cities and the rapid growth of older smaller cities.

- **Growth of Capitals and Ports** – Between 1600 and 1750, the most vigorous growth took place in capitals and ports. As monarchs consolidated their power in capital cities, their bureaucracies, armies, and courts grew as well, and service industries rose to support them. Port cities grew as European overseas trade expanded, especially those cities that were connected to the Atlantic trade routes. As these cities grew, cities with populations of fewer than 40,000 people declined. These included older landlocked trading centers, medieval industrial cities, and religious centers. Additionally, the expansion of the putting-out system transferred to the countryside much production that had once occurred in medieval cities. Rural labor was cheaper than urban labor, and cities with concentrations of labor declined as production was moved from the urban workshop into the country.

- **New Cities and Growing Small Towns** – In the mid-18th century, a new pattern of urban growth appeared. The rate of growth of existing large cities declined, while new cities began to emerge and existing smaller cities began to grow. One reason was the new prosperity of European agriculture. Improved agricultural production promoted the growth of nearby market towns and other urban centers that provided farmers with consumer goods and recreation. The putting-out system also encouraged the growth of small towns, and as the first factories began to appear, they often created new cities populated with factory workers.

This urban growth was an important demographic trend, but in 1800, as in the past, most European still lived in the countryside. Even in France and Great Brit-

EXAMINING THE EVIDENCE:
EUROPEAN CITIES IN 1800

Cities grew rapidly in many parts of Europe during the 18th century. Many cities grew to more than 100,000 inhabitants, and smaller cities of 20,000 to 50,000 increased rapidly as well. Below are some population estimates of several capital cities by 1800.

London	1,000,000
Paris	500,000
Berlin	170,000
Warsaw	120,000
Saint Petersburg	250,000

ain, probably somewhat less than 20% of the population lived in cities, and most of them inhabited small cities.

INFLATION

As population grew in 18th-century Europe, the scale of economic activity increased as well, especially after about 1730. During the first decades of the 18th century, prices generally remained stable, but with Europe's demographic growth, significant economic growth began around 1730 and lasted until the early 19th century. Prices gradually rose, with the growing population increasing demand for food, land, goods, and employment. In general, this mild, gradual inflation supported economic growth, and not all products experience price increases. The cost of grains – the diet staple of the poor – rose slightly more than the average and considerably more than other agricultural products, such as wine and meat. Rents rose significantly, suggesting a shortage of available land. As a result, some tenant farmers were driven from the soil. Real wages increased much less rapidly, since the increase in population created a large labor pool. One impact of high rents in the countryside and low wages in the city was a widening of the gap between the rich and the poor.

THE EARLY INDUSTRIAL REVOLUTION

In the period between 1650 and 1815, Europeans used many technological innovations to capture control of the world's waterways, a substantial accomplishment that tilted the balance of power among world civilizations in their favor. During the late 18th century, westerners continued to build their technological knowledge, so that they laid the foundation for a great technological revolution that brought about more economic change between 1750 and 1850 than had occurred in all of world history. The **Industrial Revolution** eventually impacted virtually every part of the globe in almost all areas of life.

Simply defined, the Industrial Revolution was a change in the source of energy for work. Before the Industrial Revolution, energy was provided primarily through human and animal effort. Civilizations had always organized around this basic principle, and had built economic, social, and political structures to support it. Agricultural societies had used many arrangements: serfs had toiled for lords; small farmers had labored in their own fields; governments had ordered workers to construct public buildings; and plantation owners had bought and sold people to work for them. The substitution of machine labor for human and animal labor changed these basic building blocks of civilization forever, and although it did not eliminate old forms of work entirely, the relationship of people to their work was fundamentally altered. Early inventions that changed the source of energy first used moving water and then steam to operate large machines in mills and factories. The experimentation began first in Britain.

Industrialization consisted of two types of changes: technological innovation and organizational changes. Technological innovations made it possible to produce goods by machines rather than by hand, and organizational changes moved the place of work from homes and farms to factories where workers were brought to run the new machinery. Instead of agricultural needs determining the division of labor, work was divided according to what was necessary to make the machinery operate the most efficiently. The potentially profitable opportunities created by the development of larger, more complex and more expensive machines encouraged the formation of large businesses by people with plenty of capital. This process began in Britain because many changes during the 1648 to 1815 era paved the way for the new systems to succeed.

Why Britain?

Why did the Industrial Revolution begin in Britain? Some reasons include:

1) **A well-developed middle class and capitalist structure** – Through years of trading and entrepreneurship, Britain's middle class, or **bourgeoisie**, was large and growing. The landowning lords were no longer the wealthiest people in the realm, and urban areas were the well-established homes for entrepreneurs who often had connections in many other lands. The English colonies were spread around the world, and even with the loss of the North American colonies in 1783, trade with them did not end. The English national bank had been in existence since the early 17th century, and the English stock markets provided a flexible way to raise capital.

Enlightenment ideals had inspired people to pursue individual goals, and widely available printed materials had increased literacy rates, making the achievement of their goals more likely.

2) **Agricultural improvements** – As the Agricultural Revolution increased the productivity of land and of farm labor, the food supply increased, while a smaller percentage of the population was needed to produce it. A greater number of the English country people became wage earners, working for farmers and landlords, or spinning or weaving in their cottages for merchants in the towns. Many English working men and women became mobile; they were no longer tied to the land since many of them no longer owned it, and they were free to go where the jobs were, or where the wages were slightly higher. They also became available for new kinds of work because fewer of them were needed on the land to produce food, and they moved to urban areas just as businessmen were looking to fill their new factories with laborers. As a result, a ready urban labor supply was at hand.

3) **Population increase** – Despite the overall tendency for industrialization to encourage smaller families, other forces led to a population increase in the early days of the Industrial Revolution. Partly because food production increased, Britain's population soared during the 18th century, probably about 15 percent per decade, creating not only a larger labor force but also a larger consumer market for goods that industry produced. More dependable food supplies and better job opportunities led people to marry at earlier ages and have more children. All the reasons for the population increase are not clear, but the death rate steadily fell in Europe after 1750, and the birth rate steadily rose in England, leading to large growth rates there.

4) **Transportation** – At a time when water transportation was far cheaper and more efficient than land travel, Great Britain had the advantages of an indented coastline, navigable rivers, and a growing network of canals. Britain's relatively flat topography and short distances between population centers made moving goods across land easier.

5) **Stable government** – Britain's government had developed into a stable constitutional monarchy by the mid-1700s, in contrast to many countries – such as France – that were experiencing revolutionary upheavals in the late 18th and early 19th centuries. Parliament had developed into two bodies, with a House of Commons in which merchants and businessmen were well-represented. The government was generally supportive of entrepreneurial efforts and allowed a great deal of private control over business matters.

6)   **Early inventiveness** – The English were the first to experiment with new energy sources, and it was an Englishman – James Watt – that built the first steam engine. This important invention became the standard form of mechanical energy during the 19th century, and it spawned other inventions that revolutionized energy production. Once the inventions began, England had a head start in their use and improvement.

7)   **Raw materials** – A key ingredient for providing the fuel for the new steam engines was coal, and England's coalfields were plentiful, and Britain's healthy supply of coal meant that much industry could develop there. As the Industrial Revolution proceeded, factories were built in areas with abundant coal and iron-ore deposits.

Early Technological Innovations

One of the earliest areas of technological experimentation in Britain was **mass production** – the making of many identical items by dividing the work into simple repetitive tasks – of pottery. China and Korea had produced fine porcelain for many years, but the high cost of transporting it to European countries meant that only the wealthy could buy it. Especially as the English developed a taste for tea and coffee sweetened with sugar from the Caribbean, the demand increased for dishes and tableware that would enhance these treats. The first person to develop a pottery business that specialized in mass-produced porcelain was **Josiah Wedgwood**, who divided the work among his employees to maximize efficiency. For example, some unloaded the clay, others mixed it, and some specialized in pressing the pieces or putting handles on cups. He also used molds for creating identical dishes, a much faster process than shaping each dish by hand. The Wedgwood factory grew to employ several hundred workers, and Wedgwood "China" became popular on the European continent as well.

Another industry that experimented with more efficient, less expensive ways to produce goods was textiles, particularly cotton. Cotton had been produced by hand in China, India, and the Middle East for many years, but like porcelain, it was expensive for Europeans to import, although wealthy people often preferred it to wool. Beginning in the 1760s a series of inventions made it possible to produce cotton cloth in Britain, although the climate was too cool to actually grow the plant. The first was the spinning jenny that twisted cotton fibers into thread. Once thread production speeded up, inventors were inspired to devise machines to weave the threads into cloth, and even more inventions for perfecting the quality of thread and cloth produced. By the 1830s, large English textile mills were performing the entire process of transforming raw cotton into printed cloth, and because of the large quantities they were able to produce, prices for the consumer were lower. **Eli Whitney's** invention in 1793 of the cotton gin (a device that separated the cotton seeds from the cotton fibers, or boll) increased the amount of cotton that farms in the American South were able to produce, so America became a major supplier to the British textile mills.

The iron industry also experienced a major transformation during the 18th century after **Abraham Darby** discovered that coke (a purified form of coal) could be used in smelting iron, and since coal was abundant in Britain, the innovation made it possible to mass-produce iron in Europe. Although coke-produced iron was not as high quality as had earlier been crafted using charcoal, it was much less expensive, and iron became an important component for buildings, machines, firearms, and **interchangeable parts** – identical parts that could be used to replace each other, should one break or wear out. The ability to repair a complex machine by replacing only the defective part with an identical part produced for that reason was critical in keeping factories running efficiently.

Probably the most important invention of all was the **steam engine**, a substitute for energy produced by humans, animals, wind, and water. In 1764, **James Watt** from Glasgow devised a way to efficiently produce steam from coal to power machines in many industries. The steam forced a piston to turn a wheel, whose motion could be used to power machines in many industries. Watt's steam engines were used in the textile industry, where they greatly increased productivity. They also drained water from mines and made possible the production of more coal to feed steam engines elsewhere. Steam also took the place of water power in flour mills, malt mills used in breweries, flint mills supplying the china industry, and in mills in the West Indies used to crush sugar cane. Steam power also promoted important breakthroughs in the English iron industry, when Henry Cort devised a system called puddling, in which the coke used in processing iron burned away impurities to produce an iron of high quality. As a result, the production of iron soared.

The Factory System and the Evolution of Big Business

The Industrial Revolution was fueled by technological innovations, but new ways of organizing work were equally important in the transformation of economies. Most of the new machinery was too large and expensive to be used at home according to the old putting out system, so it made sense to centralize it close to the areas where it was produced. The workers were brought to the machines, each doing a specialized task in a highly coordinated production process. Managers then could directly supervise work and demand discipline from workers in ways that were not possible under the earlier arrangement. The factory system created a strict division between workers and managers, as well as a small group of factory owners who bought the equipment and machinery. As the wealth of the latter group increased, the pay of workers generally did not, and the gap between the

ORIGINAL DOCUMENT: ADAM SMITH ON THE IMPORTANCE OF DIVISION OF LABOR

In his classic book, *The Wealth of Nations* (1776), **Adam Smith** explained the transformational potential of technological innovations, especially as they are allowed to exist within a free market system of capitalism. In the excerpt below, he gives an example of the power of division of labor.

"[In pin-making] one man draws out the wire, another straightens it, a third cuts it, a fourth points it, a fifth grinds it at the top for receiving the head; to make the head requires two or three distinct operations; to put it on is a peculiar business, to whiten the pins is another; it is even a trade by itself to put them into the paper; and the important business of making a pin is, in this manner, divided into about eighteen distinct operations...ten persons, therefore, could make among them upwards of forty-eight thousand pins in a day. Each person, therefore, making a tenth part of forty-eight thousand pins might be considered as making four thousand eight hundred pins in a day... But if they had wrought separately and independently, and without any of them having been educated to this peculiar business, they certainly could not each of them have made twenty, perhaps not one pin in a day...In every other art and manufacture, the effects of the division of labour are similar to what they are in this very trifling one..."

Reference: *The Wealth of Nations,* Adam Smith (London: Everyman's Library, M. Dent & Sons, Ltd., 1910), Book I, Chapter 1.

rich and poor in this new industrializing English society grew substantially. The managers often became a part of the urban middle class, although they might aspire to factory ownership if they could only raise the substantial amount of capital necessary. The new division of labor on the factory floor, where each worker performed the same task over and over, was often quite tedious, and workers who had been artisans before now had no place in the factory setting. The jobs were broken down into such small tasks that unskilled workers – or even children – with low wages could perform them. Managers were expected to pressure workers to speed up production, often at the expense of their safety. The new industries transformed England's landscape. Cities grew dramatically, especially in the Midlands of north-central England, where a belt of major coalfields extended from west to east.

TOWARD A GLOBAL ECONOMY: MERCANTILE EMPIRES AND WORLD TRADE

The Atlantic routes established during the 17th century grew to become more important links in a global trading economy during the 18th century. One factor that limited growth during the 17th century was the decline in the supply of gold and silver (see p. 138), so governments were constantly trying to overcome a chronic shortage of money. During the 18th century, this problem was met by the establishment of new public and private banks and the issuance and acceptance of paper notes. For example, the Bank of England, established in 1694, also made loans. In return for lending money to the government, the bank was allowed to issue paper "banknotes" backed by its credit. These soon became negotiable and provided a paper substitute for gold and silver currency.

Although bankers and industrialists would come to dominate the economy during the 19th century, in the 18th century merchants and traders still were in control. Most trade took place among European countries, where wheat, timber, wine, wool, fruit, and silk produced in Europe were exchanged. Whereas this continental trade increased slightly during the 18th century, overseas trade boomed. By the beginning of the century, Spain, Portugal, and the Dutch Republic – which had dominated trade during the 17th century – lost ground steadily to England and France. The rivalry between these two powers was especially strong in the Americas and the East.

The Decline of the Dutch

In the 17th century, the United Provinces, or Dutch Netherlands, was the greatest maritime power in Europe. Dutch ships carried merchandise to many parts of the globe, making large profits despite the tiny size of the country and its small population – about 2.5 million people in 1700. The physical environment was challenging, with the "Low Countries" often in danger of severe flooding and short on arable land. In many ways, the Dutch accomplishments were a reaction to their limitations; the people responded by taking advantage of their good location for sea trade. During the Age of Louis XIV (1648-1715), the Netherlands was weakened by wars with France, and although the country survived intact, it suffered demographic losses and political stagnation. In contrast to France and Britain, Dutch population did not grow very much, and the highly decentralized government had trouble providing for the common defense of the realm.

The Dutch economy suffered when French and English merchants sought to take over the Netherlands' trade. Heavy taxes and the high wages demanded by Dutch artisans forced up the price of Dutch products, making them less attractive for international trade. However, the Dutch, ever inventive, held on to a great deal of power by shifting their activity away from the actual trading ventures into the safer, profitable areas of credit and finance. The Netherlands was the first country to perfect the uses of paper currency, a stock market, and a central bank. Amsterdam's merchant-bankers loaned large amounts of money to private borrowers and foreign governments, as the Dutch became financial brokers instead of traders. as a result, the Dutch, though weakened, remained important players in the global economy.

The Rising British and French Commercial Empires

By 1700, the British and French governments had consolidated considerable political power in their capital cities, although their governing styles were quite different. Britain had met the challenge created by competition between king and Parliament by settling into a constitutional monarchy. France, on the other hand, was ruled by Louis XIV, the most famous of the absolutist rulers of the 17th century. Both countries had contributed to the weakening of Dutch power, and Spain was long past its peak. Britain and France governed their colonies in very different ways, with Britain allowing a great deal of autonomy, and France ruling through *intendants* and military governors who were stationed across the seas. However, both applied mercantilist principles to the regulation of colonial trade, and both strengthened their navies for protection.

Seaborne commerce depended on naval power. Merchant ships had to be protected, trading rivals excluded, and regulations enforced. The deployment of naval forces accentuated the competition between the two countries, and it also required the acquisition of ports as stopping places for reprovisioning and refitting. As a result, both England and France captured control of ports in strategic locations such as Africa, India, and the Caribbean. Clearly, naval power was a key element in the growth of the British and French commercial empires.

The Great Circuit and the Atlantic Economy

The voyages of discovery not only revolutionized biological exchanges, but they also allowed the economic innovations developing in Europe to expand, as capitalism, especially in the form of mercantilism, was applied to economic exchanges across the Atlantic and Pacific Oceans. The joint-stock companies began the process in North America, as did the government-sponsored expeditions to Latin America. Investors sought profits in the production and export of colonial products, some native and some introduced from the Old World. For example, Europeans learned about the uses of tobacco from natives and found that Virginia and North Carolina were good places for tobacco to grow and then ship to Europe. Sugar, on the other hand, originated in the Eastern Hemisphere, but Brazil and the Caribbean Islands became the world's principal sources of sugar by 1700. Sugar, by the nature of its production, had to be raised on large plantations because raw sugar cane could not survive the voyage from the New World to the Old. The cane had to be processed before it was shipped, so the producer had to not only maintain the growing fields but a processing plant as well. This investment was quite large, and only a few could afford it, so small sugar farmers could not survive, and only large plantations with many workers were successful. Early attempts to use indentured servants on Caribbean plantations failed, since servants, seeing few opportunities to establish their own farms on islands where the land was already claimed by plantations, would not come there. Therefore, most plantation owners settled on slave labor.

New products, new methods of transportation, and new lands – as well as experimentation with labor systems and capitalistic enterprise – combined to create a clockwise network of sea routes known as the **Atlantic Circuit**. Ships first went from Europe to Africa, to which they carried guns, cotton textiles, and other manufactured goods to sell at ports along the western coast. Some ships returned to Europe with gold, ivory, and other traditional African products, but many loaded slaves to be taken on the next leg of the circuit – known as the **Middle Passage** – across the Atlantic to the New World. Most were destined for the Caribbean and Brazil, but some came to the southern English colonies along the North American coast and other parts of Latin America. On the third part of the circuit, ships laden with goods produced in the New World were taken to Europe, where they would begin the circuit all over again. New World products included sugar, tobacco, gold, silver, and food crops. Ships also crossed the Pacific, most notably the **Manila galleons**, which crossed between Manila in the Philippines, where they picked up Asian luxury goods, and Acapulco on the west coast of Mexico, where they loaded their large cargo areas with silver.

The African Slave Trade

The slave trade of the 17th and 18th centuries was not new to Africa. Camel caravans had carried slaves across the Sahara for many years, with most destined for the Middle East where they became servants, soldiers, or concubines to wealthy men. Slave trade within Africa also was common, with slaves generally captured as prisoners of war. Africans enslaved by other Africans before 1450 were not seen as private property, but those who controlled them were able to amass wealth through their labor. These slaves sometimes obtained their freedom or became members of the controlling group's clan. However, the first contact of Africans with the Portuguese during the 15th century opened the new slave market that eventually extended across the Atlantic. According to Philip Curtin in *The Atlantic Slave Trade: A Census*, about 10 million African slaves arrived in the Americas before slavery was outlawed, making the voyages probably the largest forced migration in world history. The first African contacts with the Portuguese occurred in the early 15th century with the exploratory voyages along Africa's western coast sponsored by Prince Henry the Navigator. At first their progress was slow, but by 1487 they reached the Cape of Good Hope. Along the way they established forts and trading posts called **factories,** where local African merchants brought goods

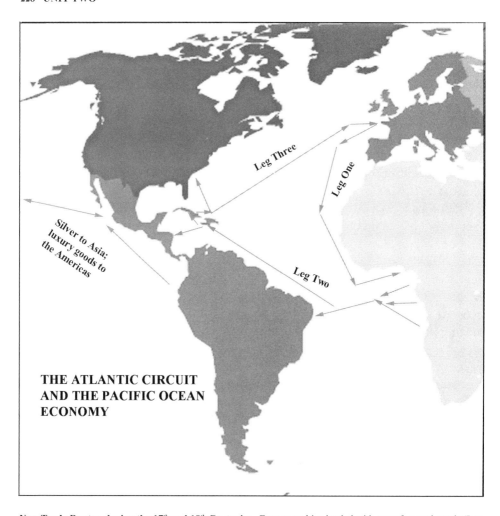

Silver to Asia:
luxury goods to
the Americas

Leg Three

Leg One

Leg Two

**THE ATLANTIC CIRCUIT
AND THE PACIFIC OCEAN
ECONOMY**

New Trade Routes during the 17th and 18th Centuries. European ships loaded with manufactured goods (Leg One) stopped first in Africa, sold goods and reloaded with slaves on the Middle Passage headed for the New World (Leg Two), and finally headed home again (Leg Three) loaded with colonial products. Spanish galleons (ships designed with large hulls to hold the silver) also headed from the New World to Manila in the Philippines, where they traded silver for Asian luxury goods.

to be traded. The Portuguese were not militarily strong enough to venture inland, and traded with African merchants on terms dictated by the Africans. At first they were more interested in gold and ivory than slaves, but some slaves were brought to Portugal as early as 1441.

Christian missionaries accompanied sailors on the voyages, and one of their earliest successes was in **Kongo**, a kingdom just south of the Congo River. There they converted members of the royal family, and the whole kingdom was brought to Christianity in the early 16th century. At first, interactions between the Portuguese and Kongo kings were relatively equal, but soon the attempt to "Europeanize"

PERSPECTIVES: SLAVE TRADE STATISTICS AND THE IMPORTANCE OF SUGAR

Historian Philip Curtin revised common conceptions about the Atlantic slave trade in his 1969 study, *The Atlantic Slave Trade: A Census*. He carefully studied how many slaves came, as well as where they arrived in the Americas. Below are some of the estimates he compiled by studying records of the slave trade between 1521 and 1773. Notice that the vast majority of slaves were destined for areas where sugar plantations dominated the economy.

DESTINATION	NUMBERS OF SLAVES
Brazil	3,646,800
British West Indies	1,665,000
French West Indies	1,600,200
Spanish America	1,552,000 (702,000 to Cuba alone)
Dutch West Indies	500,000
United States and pre-1776 North America	399,000
Danish West Indies (now the Virgin Islands)	28,000

Reference: The Atlantic Slave Trade: A Census by Philip D. Curtin (Madison: University of Wisconsin Press, 1969).

the natives reflected the general Portuguese view that Africans were inferior. Unfortunately for the people of Kongo, the growing slave trade to the Americas that began about the same time encouraged the Portuguese to look to the Kongo to supply slaves for the Atlantic Circuit trade. They sometimes went on slave raids themselves, but more often made deals with native traders and local leaders who captured and delivered slaves to coastal forts in exchange for manufactured goods, especially guns. By 1665, the kings of Kongo were so distressed by slave raiding that they went to war with the Portuguese, but superior arms (including guns) helped the Portuguese to win. Further south, the Europeans colonized Angola, which became another source of slaves for the Atlantic trade. Eventually other European nations set up competing trading posts, especially along the "Slave Coast" north of the Kongo. Once the Portuguese rounded the Cape of Good Hope at the southern tip of Africa, they captured and took over Swahili trading cities, where they intensified the slave trade already taking place across the Indian Ocean.

The Middle Passage

Slaves usually were carried from Africa to the Americas in ships with specially built holds where they were packed together, although girls, boys, and women were in separate compartments from the men. The voyage lasted from four to ten weeks, depending on the weather, and some cargoes arrived more safely than others. The traders wanted to keep as many slaves alive as possible, but they usually packed the ships to maximize their profits. Voyages before 1700 usually lost larger percentages of their slaves than later ships did, so the traders appear to have improved their ability to figure the most practical number of bodies they could keep in cargo. Male slaves were chained together to keep individuals from jumping overboard while still close to land, but the ships had special nets around their outsides to catch any that decided to jump together. Once the voyage was underway, African men were kept below the deck and were only brought up in small groups under close guard. Deaths aboard ship were caused by contagious disease, bad food, dysentery, and refusal to eat. Others died from whippings or an occasional execution. Crew members also died from diseases, and were particularly vulnerable to malaria, a disease that Africans were immune to but Europeans were not.

In the period between 1650 and 1815, Europe experienced major economic changes that interacted closely with political changes. As power in European states became consolidated in the hands of a central government, rulers gained more control over their economies. The two countries – Britain and France – that experienced both consolidation of power and economic growth were the ones that held the most power by the early 19th century.

EXAMINING THE EVIDENCE: THE ACCOUNTS OF OLAUDAH EQUIANO

Much of our knowledge about the experience of Africans captured by slave traders comes from **Olaudah Equiano**, who was born east of the Niger Delta, kidnapped as a slave in Africa, and crossed the Atlantic on the Middle Passage to be sold in the New World. Because New World slaves were not taught to read and write, very few first-person written accounts exist, and so we rely on Equiano, who learned English and later became active in the abolitionist movement. His feelings when he first boarded the slave ship are described below.

"I was immediately handled and tossed up to see if I were sound by some of the crew, and I was persuaded that I had gotten into a world of bad spirits and that they were going to kill me. Their complexions too differing so much from ours, their long hair and the language they spoke (which was very different from any I had every heard) united to confirm me in this belief... When I looked round the ship too and saw a large furnace or copper boiling and a multitude of black people of every description chained together, every one of their countenances expressing dejection and sorrow, I no longer doubted of my fate; and quite overpowered with horror and anguish, I fell motionless on the deck and fainted. When I recovered a little I found some black people about me...they talked to me in order to cheer me, but all in vain..."

Reference: Equiano's Travels. Paul Edwards, ed. and trans. (Oxford Heineman1n Educational Books, 1967) pp. 25-42.

IDENTIFICATIONS AND CONCEPTS

Agricultural Revolution
Atlantic (or Great) Circuit
bourgeoisie
"cottage industry"
Darby, Abraham
demography
enclosure
Equiano, Olaudah
factories (in Africa)
Industrial Revolution
interchangeable parts

Kongo
Manila galleons
mass production
Middle Passage
open-fields system
putting out system
Smith, Adam
steam engine
Tull, Jethro
Watt, James
The Wealth of Nations
Wedgwood, Josiah
Whitney, Eli

CHAPTER 10:
18TH CENTURY SOCIETY
AND CULTURE

As rulers consolidated power in European regimes and important economic changes occurred in western Europe, the society and culture of Europe also evolved. In the early part of the 18th century, established patterns from the past continued, but as the years passed, a clear transition occurred to beliefs and customs that are much more similar to those of modern Europeans. By the end of the century, France was embroiled in a life-altering revolution that affected the entire continent, an event that was preceded by significant changes in attitudes, customs, and beliefs. The mixture of old and new characterized the entire time period, but by the early 19th century, it was apparent that the changes were long-lasting and that many pre-revolutionary European ways of life would not return, at least in many respects.

TRADITIONAL EUROPEAN SOCIETY

During the days when absolute rulers controlled most of the countries of Europe and agriculture dominated the economy, the social structure was hierarchical and traditional. Men and women living during the period saw themselves less as individuals than as members of distinct groups that possessed certain privileges and rights and carried out duties and responsibilities closely linked to their stations in life. Society was not static, since economic change and innovation – first in agriculture and then in the early stages of the Industrial Revolution – changed the everyday life of Europeans significantly, but the basic patterns remained in place for most of the century. For most people, the past shaped beliefs and customs more than the future, and few placed much intrinsic value in change or innovation regardless of their social standing. Nowhere was this emphasis on tradition more important than in the interactions between people of different social classes.

Social Class

The social class system that had been in place for many generations by the 18th century included these four basic groups: aristocratic elites, peasants, townspeople, and the clergy.

Aristocratic elites

About 1 to 5% of the population belonged to the aristocracy. In every country, the nobility was the single wealthiest sector of the population, with the most social, political, and economic power. In most governments, the nobility was represented by their own house in the legislature, and in Hungary and Poland, no one other than nobles had any kind of political representation. Wealth was still based primarily on land ownership, but other types of aristocratic participation in the economy varied from country to country. In much of Europe, it was felt that manual labor was beneath the dignity of a noble, so even the poorer nobles had a great deal of leisure time. In general, many European aristocrats were quite sensitive to the threat to their social position and privileges posed by the expanding power of the monarchs. Some forms of autocratic resistance included making it more difficult to become a noble, and reserving appointment to the bureaucracy, ministries, officer corps of the armies, and the Church to those from aristocratic families. Nobles also challenged kings by controlling the legislatures and courts, and they often refused to pay taxes, or at least to having their taxes raised.

Peasants

Although serfdom had been abolished in western Europe well before the 18th century, many people in all areas were still peasants that tilled the soil. Peasants in Britain, northern Italy, the Netherlands, Spain, most of France, and some areas of western Germany were legally free. Most peasants in eastern Europe were still serfs, just as their ancestors had been for generations before them. Many in western Europe owned small plots of land, but others were **tenant farmers** who farmed plots of land for landowners. Tenant farmers owed portions – often as much as one-third – of their crops to the aristocratic landowners or town officials. In addition, some peasants also owed a variety of dues and fees for using flour mills, community ovens, and wine and oil presses that were owned by the aristocrats. Resentment between peasants and aristocrats often festered because of these tithes and fees, and also because nobles often claimed exclusive hunting rights for some of the best land. Peasants seldom ventured far from their villages, where local government and church officials provided public order and support for the poor, maintained roads and bridges, and established common procedures for farming. Villages were often dominated by more prosperous peasants, who usually valued adherence to tradition and resisted innovations, such as new agricultural practices.

Townspeople and Urban Dwellers

Townspeople were still a distinct minority during the 18th century, except in the Dutch Republic, Britain, and parts of Italy. Despite their relatively small numbers, townspeople had many advantages that peasants did not have, such as

COMPARISONS: ARISTOCRACY IN ENGLAND, FRANCE, AND EASTERN EUROPE

Throughout 18th century Europe, aristocrats had many common privileges, but important variations existed. In some countries, the nobility fostered economic innovation, especially commercial change that helped to protect or enhance their wealth. For example, British aristocrats invested in commerce, canals, urban real estate, mines, and even industrial ventures. Because of the practice of **primogeniture** – in which only the eldest son inherited the title and the land – younger sons moved into commerce, the army, the professions, and the Anglican Church. Parliament (even the House of Commons) was controlled by these aristocrats, and local society generally centered on life in their great country houses. In France, the aristocracy was divided between nobles of the sword (the military) and those of the robe (the bureaucracy), but they had many common privileges, including exemption from taxes (English nobility paid taxes), exclusive hunting and fishing rights, and the right to collect feudal dues from their tenants. In eastern Europe, military traditions were generally more important to the aristocracy than they were in England or France. In Austria and Hungary, nobles had broad judicial powers over the peasants through their manorial courts, and in Russia, Peter the Great linked state service to noble social status through his Table of Ranks. Although the greatest Russian nobles were later exempted from compulsory state service, in 1785, Catherine the Great legally defined noble rights and privileges in exchange for the assurance that the nobility would serve the state voluntarily.

education, cultural offerings, and material prosperity. Peasants often felt exploited by towns and cities because tithes, rents, and feudal dues forced them to support urban dwellers, and often kept them from making any profit on food sold to them.

A wide variety of people lived in the towns. Many landowners kept residences in town, where they ate fine food, wore extravagant clothing, and rode through the streets in grand coaches. Others at the top of the urban social structure were wealthy merchants, bankers, financiers, clergy, and government officials. These rich families employed many artisans, shopkeepers, and domestic servants, who made up a large bulk of the urban population. The middle classes of officials, merchants, professionals, and small landowners developed distinctive ways of life that set them apart from both the rich noble landowners and the lower classes. Their primary residences were in town, and they ate more moderately than nobles but much better than peasants or laborers. Beer was the main drink in London, and many families brewed their own. Even children drank beer because of the lack of potable water. Middle-class houses usually had about seven rooms, including four or five bedrooms and one or two living rooms. Below the middle classes came the artisans and shopkeepers, who were usually organized by professional guilds. Next were journeymen, apprentices, servants, and laborers, and at the bottom of the social scale were the unemployed poor, who survived by occasional work and charity. Every middle-class and upper-class family and some artisans and shop-keepers employed servants, and about 80% of all domestic servants were female.

Clergy

Although in France and Prussia the clergy was called the first "estate" (social class), the clergy did not really form a social group separate from others. Instead, the clergy reflected the social divisions between rich and poor that permeated European life in general. Most village priests and ministers shared the poverty and hardships of their parishioners. The members of the French clergy generally were the most literate, and Russian Orthodox priests were the least. The lower clergy usually had family roots in the lower middle class or the relatively prosperous peasantry, and they often resented the bishops and other high clergy in the same way that the lower and middle classes resented the rich landowners and merchants. In the Catholic Church, the high clergy were almost always drawn

 **THEMATIC LEARNING OBJECTIVE:
INDIVIDUAL AND SOCIETY:
CLOTHING AND HOUSING AS SIGNS
OF SOCIAL STATUS IN THE CITIES**

In 18th century European cities, social status was often quite visible. One readily recognizable social indicator was clothing. The poorest working women in Paris wore dark woolen skirts and blouses over petticoats, a bodice, and a corset. The clothing of working men was even more colorless. A man's occupation might be indicated by his dress, with lawyers dressing in dark robes, and masons and butchers wearing special, distinctive aprons. The wealthy wore a greater variety of fabrics, colors, and unusually designed clothes, and had many different outfits. Another visible sign of social status was housing. The rich lived on wide, spacious streets in houses with many rooms, and in poor districts the streets were narrow, dirty, and dark, and the houses were small, crowded, and damp. In some districts, rich and poor lived in the same building: the poor lived in crowded accommodations on the top floors and attics; the wealthy lived in more convenient, spacious apartments on the bottom floors.

from the families of the great landowners, and many were more concerned with political and economic influence than with their religious duties. For example, in the 1760s at least forty bishops lived in Paris, only one of whom was, in principle, supposed to live there.

Although many parts of Europe were becoming increasingly secularized, religion still played an important part in daily life. The clergy baptized children and registered their births, married couples, and buried almost everybody. Priests and ministers supervised charitable activities and provided certificates of good behavior for those leaving in search of work elsewhere. In general, the clergy was better educated than in previous centuries, due in part to efforts to improve clerical training. Even so, parish priests were often caught between the standards demanded by the Catholic Church and the persistence of popular superstitions shared by all social groups. Many people continued to believe in the mystical healing powers of remains of the saints, and church relics – such as clothing, jewelry, and body parts of important religious figures – were often imbued with magical powers that reflected old beliefs from the Middle Ages.

MARRIAGE AND THE FAMILY

Family structures in preindustrial Europe may be divided into two models, one characterizing northwestern Europe and the other eastern Europe.

Northwestern Europe

Despite the fact that sociologists often associate extended families with agrarian societies, three-generation families were rare in northwestern Europe by 1700, partly because of relatively high mortality rates, and partly because of late marriage. The family structure, then, was nuclear rather than extended. When young couples married, they normally established their own households and lived apart from their parents. Most people did not marry young in the 17th and early 18th centuries. The average person married many years after reaching adulthood and many more after beginning to work. In a study of one English village, both men and women married for the first time at an average age of 27 or older. A similar pattern existed in early 18th-century France. A substantial number of men and women never married at all. Except for wealthy families, households were small, usually consisting of not more than five or six members.

Children lived with their parents only until their early teens. Then they normally left home, usually to enter the work force. A child of a skilled artisan might remain with his or her parents to learn a valuable skill, but usually children's labor was better paid outside the home. These young men and women who had left home would often live several years on their own before marrying and starting their own families. Why was marriage delayed? The main reason was that couples did not marry until they could support themselves economically. The land was still the main source of income. The peasant son often had to wait until his father died to inherit the family farm, and the peasant daughter and her family needed to accumulate a small dowry to help her fiancé buy land or build a house. So important was the value of independence before marriage that couples needed to get the legal permission or tacit approval of the local lord or landowner in order to marry. In Austria and Germany, there were legal restrictions on marriage, and securing the approval of local officials was particularly difficult. Officials worried that early marriage would increase the numbers who were poverty-stricken, leading to more abandoned children and more people living on charity. This pattern of late marriage based on economic stability fostered and required self-reliance and independence, and some scholars have speculated that it was the foundation of creativity and energy that sparked Europe's growing stature in the world as the 19th century approached.

Eastern Europe

In eastern Europe, marriage and family patterns were quite different from those in northwestern Europe. There, both men and women usually married before the age of twenty, and soon after began having children. Often, especially among Russian serfs, wives were older than their husbands. Because of earlier age at marriage, families in eastern Europe were generally larger than those in the west. For example, a rural Russian household consisted of more than nine and possible as many as

COMPARISON: FAMILY TYPES

Sociologists often categorize families into two broad types: the **extended family** and the **nuclear family**. In most preindustrial societies, people take a broad view of family ties, recognizing the extended family as a family unit that includes parents and children as well as other kin. This group is also called the consanguine family, meaning that it includes everyone with "shared blood." With industrialization, however, increasing social mobility and geographic migration give rise to the nuclear family, a family unit composed of one or two parents and their children. The nuclear family is also called the conjugal family, meaning "based on marriage."

Recent research has shown that during the 18th century, most people in northwestern Europe lived in nuclear families, despite the fact that most agrarian societies throughout history have favored extended families. With urbanization and industrialization in Europe, even more emphasis began to be placed on the nuclear family.

twenty members, with three or perhaps even four generations of the same family living together. The system of serfdom accounts for at least some of these differences between household structures in western and eastern Europe. The lords of the manor who owned land wanted to ensure that it would be cultivated so they could receive their rents, and the more hands at work tilling their soil the wealthier they grew. For example, in Poland, landlords might forbid marriage between their own serfs and those from another estate, and they sometimes required widows and widowers to remarry to assure adequate labor.

Women and the Family

Most historical research on the lives and personal experiences of women in European preindustrial society has focused on women in western Europe. There, women functioned mainly within the confines of family life. Some women succeeded in becoming economically independent, but they were the exception. The first part of a woman's life after early childhood was spent maintaining her parents' household and the later part to establishing her own household. By the age of seven a girl would have begun to help with household work. Peasant girls might look after chickens, water farm animals, or carry food to workers in the field. In an urban artisan's household, she would clean or carry supplies, and perhaps sew or weave. The girl usually remained at home until her labor was more valuable elsewhere. Some became servants in other households, and often even middle-class families sent their daughters into service. These young servant girls worked hard but had little real independence. Sometimes the employer paid her wages directly to her parents. There were no laws to limit exploitation, and often the work load was overwhelming. Court records are full of complaints by servant girls of physical mistreatment by their mistresses.

Once a young woman left home, her chief goal was to accumulate enough money for a dowry. Marriage was a joint economic undertaking, and the wife was expected to make an immediate contribution of capital for establishing the household. Because it often took a long time to save the required amount of money, marriage was usually postponed until a woman was in her mid-to-late twenties. Once married, couples tried to limit the number of children, and young children were often placed with wet nurses to feed them so the mother could continue to make her economic contribution to the household.

The work of married peasant women was quite different from that of an urban wife. In the countryside, women spent much time tending to the needs of their farmer-husbands through chores such as carrying water and food to them while they labored in the fields. If the husband had to do work besides farming, such as fishing or migrant labor, the wife might actually do the plowing, planting, and harvesting on the farm. The wife of an artisan or merchant was often in charge of the household finances, and she might also participate in managing the family's

PERSPECTIVES: WOMEN OF THE THIRD ESTATE

The vast majority of 18th-century Europeans were not members of the aristocracy. Over 90% were peasants, artisans, domestic servants, and laborers – often referred to in France as members of the **"Third Estate."** The excerpt below from a "Petition of the Women of the Third Estate to the King," written in 1789, identifies some special problems of women in this social group.

"Almost all women of the Third Estate are born poor. Their education is either neglected or misconceived, for it consists in sending them to learn from teachers who do not themselves know the first word of the language they are supposed to be teaching...At the age of fifteen or sixteen, girls can earn five or six sous a day. If nature has not granted them good looks, they get married, without a dowry, to unfortunate artisans and drag out a grueling existence in the depths of the provinces, producing children whom they are unable to bring up. If, on the other hand, they are born pretty, being without culture, principles, or any notion of morality, they fall prey to the first seducer, make one slip, come to Paris to conceal it, go totally to the bad here, and end up dying as victims of debauchery. Today, when the difficulty of earning a living forces thousands of women to offer themselves to the highest bidder and men prefer buying them for a spell to winning them for good, any woman drawn to virtue, eager to educate herself, and with natural taste...is faced with the choice either of casting herself into a cloister which will accept a modest dowry or of going into domestic service..."

Reference: Not in God's Image, by Julia O'Faolain and Mauro Martines. Harper Rom, Inc: 1973.

business. When her husband died, she might take over the business or hire an artisan to replace her husband's work. Many occupations and professions were closed to women, and those that were open to them often paid lower wages to women than to men.

Attitudes toward Children

In general, in both western and eastern Europe, once women were married, they began bearing children rapidly. If a woman married before she was thirty and lived for another fifteen years, she often gave birth to six or more children. Infant mortality rates were high, with one in five likely to die during the first year of life. Even in rich families, little could be done for ailing children, since childhood illnesses were common and not well defined, and very little could be done for those who did not recover on their own. Women of the lower classes generally breast-fed their children, sometimes for several years. By nursing their babies, women limited their fertility, and children were usually born two or three years apart. Most women of the aristocracy and upper middle class did not nurse their own children, since it was widely seen as a crude and undignified practice. Instead, a wet nurse was hired to feed a new baby. The wet-nursing industry was well organized, with urban children frequently transported to wet nurses in the country, where they would remain for months or even years.

Throughout Europe, the birth of a child was not always welcome or expected. Until about 1750, very few illegitimate babies were born in western Europe, but premarital sex was clearly commonplace. These seemingly contradictory patterns were possible because pregnancy often compelled a couple to marry. Although few babies were born outside of wedlock, a significant number were conceived before marriage. Once a girl's pregnancy became known, parents, priests, village elders, and/or landlords pressured her and her partner into marriage. These controls probably meant that premarital sex was not entered into lightly and that it generally occurred between two young people contemplating marriage.

In the second half of the 18th century, the patterns of late marriage and few illegitimate births began to change. The number of births out of wedlock rose sharply between about 1750 and 1850 in western Europe. For example, in Frankfurt, Germany, illegitimate births rose from about 2% in the early 1700s to about 25% in 1850. Historians still debate the explanations for this phenomenal change, but one possibility is the increasing mobility of people once cottage industries began, and towns and cities attracted young people to plentiful jobs. Young people became more independent from their villages, and the old constraints fell away, including a young man's promise to marry his sexual partner. Even those who might sincerely want to marry their partners might not be able to, since their jobs as soldiers, day laborers, and male servants were often not secure.

Infanticide and Foundling Hospitals

Even for married couples a child might represent another economic hardship on an already overburdened household. The statistics are far from reliable, but infanticide almost certainly did occur. For example, some children died from "overlaying" that occurred when a parent rolled over and suffocated a child placed in the bed. These deaths were not all infanticides, but in Austria, suspicious authorities made it illegal for parents to take children under five into bed with them. Children were often abandoned, and the number of foundling hospitals increased during the 18th century. These hospitals cared for thousands of European children, and though most were established in cities, they served large areas, since people from the countryside often left their children at the hospitals. Many children in foundling hospitals were illegitimate, but some were left because their parents could not support them. In Paris, for example, the number of abandoned children increased as food prices rose.

Education

Schools and formal education played only a modest role in the lives of ordinary children, and many, especially girls, never learned to read. However, basic literacy rates rose during the 18th century, and the role of schools and formal education outside the home grew more important, even for the children of commoners. Unlike medieval schools, which mingled all age groups, elementary schools specialized in instructing boys and girls from age seven to twelve in basic literacy and religion. The Protestant and Catholic Reformations had earlier stimulated this push to literacy as a means of instilling religious beliefs in the minds of young children. The growth of popular education continued during the 18th century, but even so, many common people received no formal education. The idea of universal education gradually took hold, though, with Prussia leading the way by making attendance at elementary schools compulsory in 1717. Other Protestant German states followed with similar laws later in the century, and Austrian ruler Maria Theresa established a general system of elementary education throughout her realm in 1774. The Church of England and dissenting Protestant groups established "charity schools" to instruct the children of the poor, and Presbyterian Scotland established an effective network of parish schools for rich and poor alike. Even though they lagged behind men in most countries, women also became increasingly literate.

HEALTH AND HYGIENE

Health and hygiene were affected by differences in social class, since the rich had access to the services of doctors, and the poor had to rely on popular healers, who were often women whose remedies consisted of strange herbs or mysterious potions. However, rich and poor alike were subject to diseases that resulted from tainted food, polluted water, and filthy streets. Overcrowding was worst in rapidly growing cities, such as London, Paris, Amsterdam, and Naples, where the differences between wealth and poverty were both more extreme and more visible. Many areas of Europe were still susceptible to shortages of food after local crop failures or famine, which could lead to starvation and malnutrition. In some towns charitable organizations developed, often supported by upper-class women, to finance and assist religious sisters in relief of the poor. Hunger and the fear of hunger sometimes produced riots, which generally had little political impact before the late 18th century.

Some cities began campaigns to improve public sanitation, basing their programs on the findings of 18th-century scholars who focused on environmental studies. Efforts included draining low-lying areas, burying refuse, and cleaning wells, all of which eventually helped lower the death rates from epidemic diseases. During

THEMATIC LEARNING OBJECTIVE: OBJECTIVE KNOWLEDGE AND SUBJECTIVE VISIONS: LADY MARY WORTLEY MONTAGU ON SMALLPOX INOCULATIONS IN THE OTTOMAN EMPIRE

In 1716 Lady Mary Wortley Montagu traveled with her husband to Istanbul, where he served as British ambassador to the Ottoman Empire. There she witnessed firsthand the Turkish use of inoculation to prevent smallpox, a dread disease that killed many Europeans. She described the process in a letter written in 1718, as excerpted below.

"The small-pox, so fatal, and so general amongst us, is here entirely harmless, by the invention of engrafting, which is the term they give it. There is a set of old women, who make it their business to perform the operation, every autumn, in the month of September, when the great heat is abated. People send to one another to know if any of their family has a mind to have the small-pox; they make parties for this purpose, and when they are met (commonly fifteen or sixteen together) the old woman comes with a nut-shell full of the matter of the best sort of small-pox, and asks what vein you please to have opened. She immediately rips open that you offer to her, with a large needle (which gives you no more pain than a common scratch) and puts into the vein as much as can ly [lie] upon the head of her needle, and after that, binds up the little wound with a hollow bit of shell, and in this manner opens four or five veins."

Lady Mary had her own children inoculated, but when other patients died after inoculation in England, clergymen and physicians attacked the practice, which remained controversial for decades.

Reference: Letter 31, to Mrs. S.C. from Adrianople, April 1, 1718, in *Letters of the Right Honourable Lady M—y W—y M—e: Written During her Travels in Europe, Asia and Africa...*(London: A. Homer, 1764), 113-116.

the century, hospitals evolved from charities that focused on the moral worthiness of the poor to medical institutions that classified patients by their diseases. The attempt to diagnose and treat diseases became controversial when physicians conducted postmortem dissections in the hospital to gain better knowledge. Press reports of physicians who robbed graves and snatched bodies outraged the public.

Health care was limited, as it had been for centuries, by a lack of scientific knowledge and by the fact that no nationwide organizations or licensing programs existed to distinguish physicians from quacks. Bloodletters, bonesetters, amateur druggists, and potion-bearing women treated many people, and physicians often used traditional remedies for their patients because they had nothing better to offer. Antiseptics were virtually unknown, midwives delivered most babies, and trained physicians were almost nonexistent outside cities.

Until the mid-1700s, most people considered bathing dangerous. Public bath-houses had disappeared from cities in the 16th and 17th centuries because they encouraged disorderly behavior, and they exposed many to epidemic diseases. In the 18th century even bathing at home was disfavored because people feared that contact with water would make the skin susceptible to cold in winter and sun in summer. Physicians warned that bathing opened the body to disease, and even newly-built mansions were unlikely to have bathrooms. Instead of bathing, upper-class men and women powdered their hair, applied perfume, and frequently changed their linens. These actions were believed to counteract corrupt and foul air.

ELITE CULTURE

The deep divide between social classes in Europe fostered a split between **elite** (or "high") and **popular culture**. The values, beliefs, and customs of the aristocrats were quite different from those of ordinary people. The middle class sometimes participated in elite culture, but they were often barred from privileges enjoyed by the aristocracy, a situation that created resentments that helped to spark the revolutions of the late 18th and early 19th centuries. However, for most of the century, the educated and wealthy, though numerically small, created a sense that all elites across Europe belonged to a common civilization. The international language of this culture was French, allowing ideas and literature to circulate easily past language barriers. Among writers, intellectuals, and scientists, the sense of a sophisticated, common European culture came to be called the "**republic of letters**". The phrase was popularized by Pierre Bayle, who published a critical journal that he called *News of the Republic of Letters,* a title that assumed that the cultural realm did not stop at political borders. The most important requirement for joining the republic was education, and those who were talented enough might even break the barriers of class to mix with the aristocrats, who admired writers, intellectuals, and scientists for their interesting ideas.

"The Grand Tour"

Although transportation was cumbersome and slow, many elite Europeans embarked on a **"Grand Tour"** of European cities – such as London, Paris, and Rome – and the ruins of antiquity. A travel literature industry rose to support this eagerness to visit foreign places, and travelers experienced both the marvels of modern urban life and the beauty of the surviving examples of Greek and Roman architecture and sculpture. Grand plazas, public gardens, theaters, and opera houses were built in the major cities, and street lighting and public transportation appeared toward the end of the century. New attractions included the coffeehouses, where customers could talk or read, and storefront window displays meant to draw customers from the street inside the shops.

Salons, Masonic Lodges, and Learned Academies

The large drawing rooms of wealthy urban women became the settings for **salons,** regular social gatherings that brought the wealthy together with philosophers, writers, artists, scientists, and other great intellects to discuss ideas and enjoy artistic performances. The salons in Paris were the most renowned, but they also operated in Vienna, London, and Berlin. Perhaps the most influential of the salon hostesses of the mid-18th century was **Marie-Thérèse Geoffrin**, a self-educated woman from the well-to-do middle class, who was friends with both philosophers and heads of state. She placed a premium on elegant conversation and wit, and she insisted that writers and philosophers make their ideas comprehensible to those present, increasing the likelihood that their thought and writings would have some impact. The salons helped to enlarge the audience and contacts of intellectuals by introducing them to a flow of foreign visitors taking the "Grand Tour." Private newsletters kept interested members of the "republic" informed of activities when they could not attend personally. Although most that attended salons were men, the hostess generally controlled the flow of conversation, providing an opportunity for intelligent, articulate women to exert their influence.

Throughout Europe, freemasonry was another important form of cultural sharing that often crossed the lines of class. **Masonic lodges** originated as clubs or fraternities dedicated to humane values, and they operated in an aura of secretiveness and symbolism. They took form in England and soon spread to the Continent. Although they usually valued reason, progress, toleration, and humane reforms, they met secretly in lodges, in an atmosphere of mysterious ritual and occult knowledge. They attracted a wide range of educated nobles, commoners, and liberal clergy, and brought people of different social classes together to discuss mutual self-improvement. Freemasonry aroused suspicion, however, because of its secrecy, and toward the end of the century, many lodges were torn by sectarian controversies, so their influence waned.

Other organizations that promoted the spread of ideas were **learned academies**, founded first in the early 18th century. Most began as literary institutes, concerned with upholding literary style. By midcentury, many had shifted their interests from literary matters to scientific and practical questions in commerce, agriculture, and political administration. Academies existed in almost every capital city, and in France academies were established in more than thirty provincial cities. Although academies began as privileged groups for nobles, by the 1770s, membership was extended to commoners, such as civil servants, doctors, and professionals.

Journals, Newspapers, and Banned Books

Periodicals first began proliferating in England, where the number of journals and newspapers increased from 25 to 158 between 1700 and 1780. One example of a successful journal was Addison and Steel's *Spectator*, with each issue consisting of a single essay that sought to convey morality and taste in elegant but clear prose. Another type of journal published extracts and summaries of books and covered current events and entertainment, while others specialized in book reviews and serious articles on science and philosophy.

The daily newspaper originated in England. Papers like the *London Chronicle* at first provided family entertainment and then began to run classified advertisements. English newspapers had to fight for permission from the government to cover parliamentary debates, but they eventually won that right. In France, newspapers were carefully censored by the government, forcing those who wished to discuss politics to publish outside French borders. Also forbidden inside France were books that made fun of or criticized aristocrats – including the king – and pornography. Publishers of these books set up just across the border and smuggled this material into France, where the police were kept busy trying to stop the flow.

Art

In the second half of the 17th century, France replaced Italy as the cultural leader of Europe. Rejecting the baroque style as overly showy and passionate, French art instead reflected **classicism**, or a style faithful to that of the High Renaissance, with its emphasis on clarity, simplicity, balance, and harmony of design. While it rejected the high drama of the baroque, French classicism – like baroque – portrayed noble subjects, especially those from classical antiquity. Both baroque and French classicism (also called "neoclassicism") continued into the 18th century, but by the 1730s a new style known as **rococo** began to affect decoration and architecture all over Europe. The term was originally derogatory, literally meaning "shellwork" in French, but implying "frivolous decoration". Rococo abandoned the majesty, power, and movement of baroque and instead emphasized grace and gentle action. Like the baroque, the rococo emphasized irregularity, asymmetry, and curvature, but it did so on a much smaller, subtler scale. Rococo style followed the wandering lines of natural objects, such as seashells and flowers, and it focused more on personal portraits and pastoral paintings than baroque's heroic landscapes and grand, ceremonial canvases. Rococo paintings adorned homes as well as palaces and served as a form of interior decoration. Porcelain vases imported from China were decorated with rococo art, often depicting scenes that conveyed pleasure, happiness, and love.

Music

During the 18th century the heartland of Europe's music tradition shifted from Italy and France to Austria, where composers perfected the art of writing great symphonies. Early works had been bound by rigid formulas of composition that provided little more than pleasant melodies in familiar forms. However, a

PERSPECTIVES:
A JOURNAL FOR WOMEN

The audiences for most of the early journals were men, but one journal – called *The Female Spectator* – was meant for women. Its author was Eliza Haywood, who also wrote plays and novels. *The Female Spectator,* published in 1741, was the first magazine by and for women, and was extremely popular. It was a collection of essays that allegedly originated in letters from readers. The essays provided an ideal forum of discussion about how women might operate better in a society that did not place restrictions upon them. Haywood knew the difficulties of female life within a patriarchal system, but she wrote to show how not to accept such difficulties as definitive of women's possibilities. Haywood's explicit recommendations to women urged them to work within the existing system, gain an education, and develop a strong sense of personal power.

Haywood spoke through four imaginary women, created as people who the public could relate to but could also help deliver her message. First was Mira, a lady descended from a family to which "wit" was hereditary. She married a gentleman that deserved a great wife, and together they lived in perfect harmony. Next was a wise widow of quality, who was able to find innocence and honor in most situations. The third was the daughter of a wealthy merchant, who was charming, but so accomplished that to those who knew her truly, her beauty was the least distinguished part of her. The fourth was the "Female Spectator," the clearest vehicle for the voice of Haywood herself.

number of creative geniuses wrote original and enduring masterpieces that altered the symphonic form from three to four movements, achieved great harmonic virtuosity, and brought a deep, though reserved, emotionalism to this music.

The 18th century was one of the greatest in the history of European music. In the first half of the century, two of the most famous musicians of all time – **Johann Sebastian Bach** and **George Frederick Handel** – produced their great works. Bach came from a family of musicians, and was the organist and music director of a number of small German courts before coming to work at the Church of St. Thomas in Leipzig in 1723. There he composed his *Mass in B Minor* and his *St. Matthew's Passion.* He composed secular works, such as the "Coffee Cantata" for the public and a variety of private patrons. Handel was a German by birth, but he wrote operas in Italy and then moved in 1710 to Britain, where he wrote music for the court and began composing oratorios – a new form of music that combined opera and religious and ceremonial music and featured the chorus over the soloists.

The "Hallelujah Chorus" from Handel's *Messiah,* written in 1741, is perhaps the single best-known work of western classical music. These musicians – and many others – stimulated a growing taste for public music concerts. City concert halls typically seated about two hundred, but the relatively high price of tickets limited attendance to the better-off. However, music clubs provided less expensive venues in smaller towns and villages, and the number of regular public concerts grew substantially during the century.

In the late 18th century, another great musician appeared. **Wolfgang Amadeus Mozart** was a child prodigy who gave his first harpsichord concert at six and wrote his first opera at twelve. His debt-ridden life illustrated the continuing importance of patrons, but even though he failed to find a permanent patron in Vienna, he wrote prolifically, producing music for string quartets, sonatas, symphonies, concerts, and operas. *The Marriage of Figaro, The Magic Flute,* and *Don Giovanni* are three of the world's most famous operas.

Literature

The public taste for new forms of entertainment was reflected in enthusiasm for a new type of literature – the novel. This form of fiction told its story and treated the development of personality in a realistic social context that seemed to mirror its times better than other forms of fiction. Most novels focused on family life and everyday problems of love, marriage, and social relations. More than 300 French novels appeared between 1700 and 1730, and during this time the novel took on its modern form. The popularity of this literary form was closely tied to the expansion of the reading public, and novels were available in serial form in periodicals or from the many booksellers who served the new market.

A pioneer of this new genre was **Samuel Richardson**, whose best known book was *Pamela, or Virtue Rewarded* (1740), which recounted the trials and tribulations of an honest servant girl who kept her virtue, despite repeated challenges from her wealthy employer. Henry Fielding's *Tom Jones* (1749) was another popular novel – a colorful and comic panorama of English society with well-developed, appealing characters. Women writers abounded, including **Eliza Haywood**, who focused on women as models of virtue in a changing world. A popular male writer was **Daniel Defoe**, who is best known for his novels *Robinson Crusoe* (1719) and *Moll Flanders* (1722). Robinson Crusoe was a shipwrecked sailor who had to be flexible, entrepreneurial, and innovative to survive, and so he stood as a model of the new man in a changing time.

Throughout most of the century the audience for poetry was the narrowest segment of the reading public, generally only appealing to the aristocracy. By the end of the century however, the restraints of **neoclassicism**, which assumed that poetry was only meant to echo eternal standards of truth and beauty, were broken by **William Wordsworth** and other young poets. The new movement came to be known as **romanticism,** which celebrated individual feeling and inner passion. Hoping to appeal to a much broader audience, these poets changed the nature of poetic composition by emphasizing poetry as a vehicle for artistic expression.

A writer who clearly reflected the impact of the romantic movement was **Johann von Goethe.** He inspired a literary movement known as *Sturm and Drang* (Storm and Stress), which emphasized strong artistic emotions and inspired the direction of romanticism throughout the late 18th and 19th centuries. Goethe lived his life in the small city-state of Weimar, where he wrote poetry, dramas, art and literary criticism, translations, philosophic reflections, travel accounts, and scientific studies. His masterpiece, *Faust,* was about a man who made a pact with the devil in order to master all of knowledge, but in the end realized the importance of discipline in reaching one's life goals.

EXAMINING THE EVIDENCE: SOCIAL REFLECTIONS IN *ROBINSON CRUSOE*

In the following excerpt from his famous novel, **Robinson Crusoe**, Daniel Defoe placed his youthful main character in the social context of early 18th century Europe, where the classic break with parental authority occurred when a young man set out to sea.

"Being the third son of the family, and not bred to any trade, my head began to be filled very early with rambling thoughts. My father, who was very ancient, had given me a competent share of learning, as far as house-education and a country free school generally goes, and designed me for the law, but I would be satisfied with nothing but going to sea; and my inclination to this led me so strongly against the will, nay, the commands, of my father, and against all the entreaties and persuasions of my mother and other friends, that there seemed to be something fatal in that propension of nature tending directly to the life of misery which was to befall me....My father, a wise and grave man, gave me serious and excellent counsel against what he foresaw was my design. He called me one morning into his chamber, where he was confined by the gout, and expostulated very warmly with me upon this subject....
It was not till almost a year after this that I broke loose...But being one day at Hull, where I went casually, and without any purpose of making an elopement that time; but I say, being there, and one of my companions being going by sea to London, in his father's ship....I consulted neither father nor mother any more, nor so much as sent them word of it... and in an ill hour, God knows, on the first of September, 1651, I went on board a ship bound for London."

Reference: Robinson Crusoe by Daniel Defoe. Renascence Editions http://darkwing.uoregon.edu/~rbear/ren. htm

POPULAR CULTURE

For most 18th century Europeans, culture primarily meant recreation, which generally took place collectively and in public. One important type of group activity was the festival, a broad name used to describe a wide variety of public celebrations. Most festivals had a religious theme, but they were special occasions mainly for eating, drinking, and celebrating to excess. A well-known festival was **Carnival**, which was celebrated in the Mediterranean world of Spain, Italy, and France, and began around the start of the year and lasted until the first day of Lent. Since Lent was the forty-day period of fasting and purification leading up to Easter, during Carnival people indulged themselves through hearty consumption of drink and food, especially meat and other delicacies, and with plentiful sexual activities. Songs that normally would be considered lewd could be sung with abandon during Carnival, and aggressive behavior – such as pelting food and water-filled pigs' bladders – was allowed.

The importance of sociability was evident in the local taverns and cabarets. Taverns functioned as regular gathering places for neighborhood men to share gossip, play games, and conduct business, while cabarets provided some local entertainment. In some countries, heavy drinking often caused problems. For example, gin was cheap in England, and vodka was cheap in Russia; in both countries many people regularly drank themselves into oblivion. In the 1750s, drunken behavior led the English government to pass strict laws to restrict gin sales.

Although literacy rates remained low, some journeymen and peasants did read, and publishers produced small booklets for this audience, often to be read aloud by those who could read to those who could not. These booklets were written anonymously and were sold for a few pennies each by itinerant peddlers. Some were religious in nature, and focused on saints' lives or recounted Bible stories. Others were almanacs that discussed everything from what to take for illnesses, to reading the stars and foretelling the future. Another type of popular literature provided entertainment – tales and fables or mixtures of fiction and history.

A particularly important facet of popular culture was storytelling. The oral tradition has been important to many societies throughout history, and in 18th century Europe, stories and songs helped to pass the time, especially on long winter nights at the fireside. Songs and tales could be joyful and/or bawdy, or they could touch on the hardships and dangers of daily life. Some complained about parents; others expressed the desperation of beggars on the road. A favorite tale was one in which a stranger turned into a prince, or on the other hand, one in which the stranger turned into a wolf or a witch.

RELIGION AND THE CHURCHES

Despite the increasing secularization of the times, the great majority of Europeans remained at least nominal Christians, and many individuals were serious and devout in their religious practices. Catholic and Protestant churches were basically conservative institutions that upheld society's traditions and hierarchical class system. Parish churches remained the center of religious practice, keeping records of births, deaths, and marriages, and providing charity for the poor and orphaned.

Quakerism and Methodism

Some new Protestant movements grew during the 18th century, including **Quakerism** and **Methodism**. **George Fox**, the founder of the Society of Friends, popularly called Quakers, emphasized the personal inner religious experience as opposed to ceremony and formality. Church services were spontaneous, with no designated leaders, and gathering houses were almost completely unadorned. Quakers became particularly notable for their resolute and radical rejection of participation in war. Methodism's founder was **John Wesley**, an ordained Anglican minister who had a transforming experience that convinced him that any person could be saved by experiencing God and opening the doors to his grace. Wesley's impatience with the indifference and opposition of Anglican clergymen to his movement gradually led to a separation of the Methodists (as his followers were called) from the general body of Anglicans. Methodists emphasized inner conversion as the key to all religion. They found their main support among the poor of the new industrial towns of England and in the frontier communities of the United States. Although Wesley sought to keep Methodism within the Anglican Church, after his death it became a separate and independent sect. Both Methodism and Quakerism represented an important revival of Christianity that proved that the need for spiritual experience had not disappeared in the secular atmosphere of 18th century Europe.

The Suppression of the Jesuits

Within the Catholic Church, a noteworthy development was the suppression of the Jesuit Order, the devout priests who had played an important role in the 16th century Catholic Reformation. The Jesuits aroused the hostility of the rulers of France, Spain, and Portugal by their intervention in political affairs, their zeal in persecuting groups they considered to be heretical, and their extensive commercial activities that did not always conform to the laws of the countries in which the Jesuits lived. As a result of the demands of these monarchs, the pope suppressed the Order in 1773. Many Jesuits found refuge in Russia and Prussia, and the Order continued to exist in disguise in these and some other parts of Europe until the pope once more extended it official recognition in 1814.

Toleration and Religious Minorities

Out of political necessity, a certain level of tolerance of different creeds had occurred in the 17th century, but many rulers still oppressed religious minorities. At the end of the 17th century, Louis XIV had revoked the Edict of Nantes (see

THEMATIC LEARNING OBJECTIVE:
INDIVIDUAL AND SOCIETY:
THE JEWISH GHETTO

From the time that Jews were expelled from Spain at the end of the 15th century until the late 18th century, they often were required to live in separate communities known as **ghettoes.** These communities were distinct districts of cities or towns, and in the countryside, Jews usually lived in their own villages separate from those of non-Jews. Exceptions were in Poland and England, where religious toleration of Jewish minorities was higher than in other countries. Elsewhere, Jews were restricted in their movement, forbidden to own land, and forced to pay burdensome special taxes. They could not pursue their professions freely; they could not change residence easily; and they often had few legal rights. Jews were sometimes subject to outbursts of popular wrath, and the resulting **pogroms,** in which the ghettoes were looted and people were massacred, made life difficult for most.

p. 187), requiring religious uniformity and suppressing the rights of the Huguenots in Fance. Persecution of heretics continued in many Catholic countries, with the last burning of a heretic taking place in 1781. Among Protestants and Catholics alike, Jews were the most shunned religious minority of all.

In the 18th century, small Jewish communities existed in many western European cities, where some became known for their intellectual life and financial institutions. However, by the 18th century, the vast majority of European Jews lived in eastern Europe (about 3,000,000), especially in Poland, Lithuania, and the Ukraine. There were perhaps as many as 150,000 in the Habsburg lands, primarily Bohemia, by 1760. In contrast, fewer than 100,000 lived in Germany, about 40,000 in France, and fewer than 10,000 in England. Their religious beliefs, rituals, and community set them apart from others, and laws, political decrees, and social institutions enforced this separation and kept them in situations of social inferiority. For example, in 1762 Catherine the Great of Russia specifically excluded Jews from a manifesto that welcomed foreigners to settle in Russia. Jews were allowed to convert to Christianity, in which case restrictions might be lifted, but those that remained true to their faith could be expelled from the cities where they lived, and their property could be confiscated.

Religious, cultural, and social patterns that characterized 18th century Europe complemented the political consolidation of power in the hands of absolute or constitutional monarchs, and these patterns shaped and reacted to economic developments of the time. However, by the end of the century, intellectual developments with roots in the Scientific Revolution would change first the lives of the elites, and eventually many ordinary Europeans as well.

IDENTIFICATIONS AND CONCEPTS

Bach, Johann Sebastian
Carnival
classicism (in art)
Defoe, Daniel
elite culture
extended family
Fox, George
Geoffrin, Marie-Thérèse
ghettoes
Goethe, Johann von
"Grand Tour"
Handel, George Frederick
Haywood, Eliza
learned academies
masonic lodges
Methodism
Mozart, Wolfgang Amadeus
neoclassicism (in poetry)
nuclear family
pogroms
popular culture
primogeniture
Quakerism
"republic of letters"
Richardson, Samuel
Robinson Crusoe
rococo
romanticism
salons
tenant farmers
"Third Estate"
Wesley, John
Wordsworth, William

CHAPTER 11:
THE AGE OF ENLIGHTENMENT

"What is the Enlightenment?
Dare to know! Have the courage to make
use of your own understanding."

Immanuel Kant
German Philosopher
1784

Perhaps there is no better description of the **Enlightenment** than that offered by Immanuel Kant quoted above. He spoke at a time when economic expansion, the stabilization of European political systems, and the spread of common cultural interests generated much optimism about the future. These important changes supported the development of an intellectual movement called the Enlightenment that advocated the application of the principles of the Scientific Revolution to an understanding of all life. In the quote, Kant not only presented his understanding of the meaning of the movement, but he also captured the enthusiasm of its supporters, who saw their time in history as transformative. The thinkers and writers of the Enlightenment believed their role was to bring light and progress to the world through the application of reason to virtually every problem they encountered. Unlike most scientists of the 16th century, they wanted their ideas to reach the general reading public, and they urged their readers to develop their own individual abilities to apply critical thinking to their own lives. The new secular, scientific, and critical attitude first emerged in the late 17th century, as critics began to evaluate everything from the nature of absolute rule to the traditional role of women in society. During the 18th century, the movement spread across Europe and encouraged the expression of ideas that would shape the unfolding of events not only in that time period, but in later ones as well.

THE POPULARIZATION OF SCIENCE

The writers of the Enlightenment had an unfettered belief in the powers of the scientific method to solve not only the mysteries of the universe, but also the everyday problems of people on earth. They shaped the questions of science and the explanations of natural phenomena into a scientific spirit that rested in an unflagging confidence in the power of reason. They aimed to transform the values of western civilization by translating the discoveries of scientists into clear and even amusing general reading. Their work made names like Galilei Galileo and René Descartes household words, and most revered of all was **Isaac Newton**, who developed his influential theories during the late 17th and early 18th centuries.

The Importance of Newton

Earlier scientists – such as Copernicus, Kepler, and Galileo – had made fundamental breakthroughs that overturned many premises of the old astronomy and physics. However, their discoveries had not been woven together into a single system of explanations of motion both on earth and in the skies until Newton. It was his supreme achievement to show that Kepler's laws of planetary motion and Galileo's laws of terrestrial motion were two aspects of the same laws. Kepler had discovered that the planets tend to fall toward the sun, resulting in elliptical orbits around it, and scientists had also observed that the moon tended to fall toward the earth. Yet Galileo had discovered that bodies move in a straight line unless deflected by a definite force. How could these two observations – straight movement forward vs. the tendency to fall toward larger bodies – be reconciled? Early in his studies, Newton suspected that the explanation was the existence of a universal gravitation, or pull that characterized all bodies in the solar system. However, it took him many years to prove it. Finally his calculations were brought together by his invention of calculus and his use of new experiments with measurement of circular motion. In 1687, he published *Principia Mathematica,* one of the most important books in history.

In his book, Newton showed that all motion that could be timed and measured, whether on the earth or in the solar system, could be described by the same mathematical formulas. These formulas were dynamic and complex, and for two hundred years afterward scientists worked to understand all their implications, but the key feature of the **Newtonian synthesis** was the law of universal gravitation. According to this law, every body in the universe attracts every other body in an exact mathematical relationship, and the force of attraction is proportional to the quantity of matter of the objects and inversely proportional to the square of the distance between them. Newton's central argument – his "synthesis" – was that the whole universe is unified by gravitation in one majestic system. Not until the 20th century were the limitations of the law found, and its relevance has been verified over and over again.

The Impact of Science on the Enlightenment

The Scientific Revolution was the single most important factor in the creation of the new world-view of the Enlightenment. Writers submitted a rich mix of ideas

THEMATIC LEARNING OBJECTIVE: OBJECTIVE KNOWLEDGE AND SUBJECTIVE VISIONS NEWTON'S *PRINCIPIA MATHEMATICA*

In his famous ***Principia Mathematica,*** **Isaac Newton** showed that all bodies in the universe – earthly objects as well as moons, planets, and stars – obey the same laws of motion and gravitation. The book was revolutionary because medieval thinkers had always drawn a sharp distinction between the heavens and the earth, and yet Newton argued that the universe was one. Despite this important break from the past, Newton – a devout Anglican – believed that God had created this superbly organized universe. His convictions are evident in the following passage from the *Principia.*

"This most beautiful system of the sun, planets, and comets could only proceed from the counsel and dominion of an intelligent and powerful Being. And if the fixed stars are the centers of other like systems, these, being formed by the like wise counsel, must be all subject to the dominion of One, especially since the light of the fixed stars is of the same nature with the light of the sun and from every system light passes into all the other systems; and lest the systems of the fixed stars should, by their gravity, fall on each other mutually, he hath placed those systems at immense distances from one another....the true God is a living, intelligent and powerful Being....he governs all things, and knows all things that are or can be done....In him are all things contained and moved; yet neither affects the other: God suffers nothing from the motion of bodies; bodies find no resistance from the omnipresence of God...."

Reference: Sir Isaac Newton, *The Mathematical Principles of Natural Philosophy, Book III,* trans. Andrew Motte (London: H.D. Symonds, 1803), II, 310-314.

from science to a growing number of well-educated readers, with these central concepts most basic to Enlightenment thinking:

- **Reason** – A favorite word of Enlightenment thinkers was "reason," which to them referred to the application of the methods of natural science to examine and understand many aspects of life. Reason requires that nothing be accepted on faith, and that everything must be submitted to the rational scientific way of thinking. Because Enlightenment thinkers did not hesitate to question religious beliefs, they often clashed with church officials who based their beliefs on Christian theology.

- **The Birth of Social Science** – A special emphasis of Enlightenment thinking was the confidence that the laws of science also apply to human society, and that the scientific method could discover forces that govern human nature and human interactions, just as gravity governs the natural universe. This application of science to society came to be called "social science."

- **The Importance of Progress** – Enlightenment philosophers believed that discovery of the laws of human existence (or the laws of nature, as they often said) made it possible to create better societies and better people. Through the use of social science methods, then, progress could be made, and many societal problems from the past could be conquered.

Spreading Scientific Ideas and Achievements

Scientific works – like Newton's *Principia* – were not easy to understand, even for educated Europeans, so the popularization of the Scientific Revolution depended on writers who could explain them to their readers. One of the first popularizers was **Bernard de Fontenelle**, whose book, *Conversations on the Plurality of Worlds* (1686), provided a direct link between 17th century scientists and 18th century intellectuals. He used the form of an intimate conversation between an aristocratic lady and her lover to present an account of Newton's universe. The two gaze at the stars, and they begin to enthusiastically discuss astronomy. Fontenelle's lady does not regret the loss of traditional understanding, but instead rejoices in the great progress that the human mind had made. Many educated elite of Europe learned their science in this entertaining way. By 1700, mathematics and science had become fashionable pastimes in high society, and an increasing number of lecturers made the circuit across Europe, explaining scientific discoveries to newly enthusiastic listeners.

One result of the popularization of science was the development of an increasingly skeptical attitude toward attempts to enforce religious conformity. Pierre Bayle – a French Huguenot refugee living in the Netherlands – bitterly criticized Louis XIV's policies in *News from the Republic of Letters,* first published in 1684. A few years later Bayle published the *Historical and Critical Dictionary,* in which he pointed out the ways that religions had promoted irrational beliefs in the past. He went so far as to say that atheists might possess moral codes as admirable as those of the devout. Other scholars challenged the authority of the Bible by comparing its records to new data provided by science. For example, comets had long been considered evil omens, but the new thinkers urged people to think of them as natural phenomena. Others attacked beliefs in witchcraft, trying to convince the public that these beliefs were based on superstition and prejudice. Because these skeptics so willingly questioned religious and political authority, they were often seen as dangerous threats by state officials. The French government took the lead in suppressing the more outspoken works, and as a result, publishers fled to the Dutch Republic, Britain, or Switzerland, where they produced books that eventually would be smuggled back into France.

The Importance of Locke

Newton's success in physics inspired his countryman **John Locke** to explain human psychology in terms of experience. Locke's theory of knowledge had a great impact on 18th century intellectuals. In his *Essay Concerning Human Understanding,* written in 1690, Locke argued that all humans enter the world a ***tabula rasa***, or blank slate. He disagreed with Descartes by asserting that personality is the product of the environmental sensations that an individual experiences through his or her life. Locke concluded that experience, not innate biological characteristics, shapes human character. As a result, he reasoned, human nature is changeable and can be altered or molded by modifying the surrounding physical and social environment. His point of view shaped the general Enlightenment belief that progress in human society is possible. He also rejected the Christian doctrine that human beings are permanently flawed by sin, and that they need to wait for the grace of God to better their lives. Instead, he believed that people are the masters of their destiny, if only they rely on the power of reason to help better their lives.

PERSPECTIVES:
JOHN LOCKE'S *TABULA RASA*

John Locke, an English writer of the late 17th and early 18th century, influenced the development of western philosophy in many ways. One of his early contributions was to argue that every person is born with a *tabula rasa,* or a blank mind. His writing reflected the hope of most Enlightenment thinkers that humans were capable of creating a much better world if only they would rely on their ability to reason. His optimism is apparent in the passage below, excerpted from *An Essay Concerning Human Understanding,* written in 1690.

"Let us then suppose the mind to be, as we say, white paper, void of all characters, without any ideas. How comes it to be furnished? Whence comes it by that vast store which the busy and boundless fancy of man has painted on it with an almost endless variety? Whence has it all the materials of reason and knowledge? To this I answer, in one word, from experience.... Our observation, employed either about external sensible objects or about the internal operations of our minds perceived and reflected on by ourselves, is that which supplies our understanding with all the materials of thinking."

Reference: John Locke, *An Essay Concerning Human Understanding,* Vol. 1 (London: Everyman's Library, 1961), pp. 77-78.

Hobbes and Locke on Government

As the Enlightenment undermined traditional religion, political theorists began to question divine right as the basis for sovereignty and political authority. If Newton's vision of a mechanical universe operating by the law of nature was correct, then how could God intervene in the affairs of humans by designating one person as ruling with divine authority? One early attempt to address this issue was **Thomas Hobbes** in *Leviathan*, published in 1651, only a few years after the English Civil War ended. He sided with the king in the conflict, and the chaos that followed shaped his political theory. Hobbes was the first to write about a "**social contract**", or agreement between rulers and subjects, by which the subjects give power to their ruler in return for his protection. He concluded that this arrangement was desirable and inevitable since he assumed that humans by nature were quarrelsome and selfish. In his words, life in the state of nature was "solitary, poor, nasty, brutish and short." From fear of each other, humans surrendered their freedom to a ruler, who in turn agreed to protect them from one another. Only by granting the ruler unrestricted or absolute power could order be maintained, and questioning the actions of the government would reopen the way to chaos. Government, then, had to be a "Leviathan," a term used in the Bible to refer to a monster.

John Locke was heavily influenced by Hobbes, but he reached very different conclusions about the role of government in society. Like Hobbes, his writings reflected the power struggle between the king and British parliament, and he was concerned about the correct balance between order and liberty. He believed that in the **"state of nature"** people are naturally free and equal, but that freedom led inevitably to inequality, and eventually to chaos. Locke agreed with other philosophers of the day (such as Hobbes) that the state of nature changed because humans are basically self-centered. However, he differed from Hobbes when he theorized that humans could be rational and even moral. Even though people serve self-interests first, they fear violence, particularly violent death. He argued that people have **natural rights** from the state of nature that include the right to "life, liberty, and property." In his *Second Treatise of Government*, Locke stated that people form governments to protect these natural rights, giving up their freedom to govern themselves through a social contract between government and the governed. The only valid government is one based on the **consent of the governed**. This consent creates a social contract that both sides are obligated to honor. If for any reason the government breaks the contract through neglect of natural rights, the people have the right to dissolve the government.

WHY FRANCE?

Although heavily influenced by Newton, Hobbes, and Locke (all Englishmen), the Enlightenment began in Paris and spread to many other areas, including the German states, the Dutch Republic, and North America. Enlightenment ideas were central to the cosmopolitan "republic of letters" (see p. 244) that transcended national political boundaries; men and women from various countries and colonies read many of the same books and shared ideas freely. Why did the Enlightenment begin in France? Some reasons include:

- **French as an International Language** – Most educated people in Europe and North America could speak and read French, and many preferred French tutors because France was still the cultural leader, and was also the wealthiest and most populous country in Europe. Many royal courts, which often sponsored Enlightenment thinkers and readings, used French as the language of high culture to confirm the sophistication of their rulers. For example, one reporter from Potsdam revealed that at the court of Frederick the Great of Prussia "the language least spoken is German." French was not the only language of philosophic discourse, but it was a necessary one for anyone who aspired to belong to the "republic of letters."

- **The "Middling Nature" of French Absolutism** – The French monarchy was absolutist, but not as repressive as many regimes in eastern Europe. Critical books were often banned by French censors and authors were sometimes jailed or exiled, but they were not tortured or executed. On the other hand, the French had fewer constitutional guarantees of individual freedom than Great Britain and the Dutch Republic. The French government wanted to keep its position as the center of cultural thought, and so the Enlightenment thinkers were tolerated and often encouraged, but at the same time, the court wished to keep its absolute power. French elites had reason to complain, and they also had the means to make their complaints known, but they often had to strike a delicate balance between acceptable criticisms and those that would provoke a negative reaction from the censors.

- **Support for Social Reform** – The French Enlightenment thinkers took Immanuel Kant's words to heart: "Have the courage to make use of your own understanding." They were not content to just ask fundamental philosophical questions about the meaning of life; they also were determined to reach and influence as many economic and social elites as possible to sponsor true social reform. Many did not approve of absolutism, and they also wished to spread the recognition of individual freedoms and political rights. Their goals clearly challenged the traditional authority of the French monarchy, and eventually came to threaten the social structure as well.

- **Parisian salons** – The large drawing rooms of wealthy urban women became the settings for **salons**, regular social gatherings that brought the wealthy together with philosophers, writers, artists, scientists, and other great intellects to discuss ideas and enjoy artistic performances. Salons were well-organized and some of the hostesses became famous for the role they played in shaping and promoting the "republic of letters." Intellectuals across Europe vied for the honor of speaking or reading for the salon audiences, and their recognition confirmed the Enlightenment belief that talent and creativity were more important than noble lineage.

THE PHILOSOPHES

Enlightenment thinkers were known as *philosophes*, the French word for "philosopher." The French word is used in English to refer to a group of writers who were not philosophers in the true sense of the word (those who address ultimate questions of knowledge or existence). Instead, these *philosophes* approached important subjects of the day in a critical and inquiring spirit. They were social or literary critics or popularizers of Enlightenment ideas, and they shared a common desire to reform thought, society, and government for the sake of human liberty. Most *philosophes* were men, but some women also participated in the "republic of letters," some as salon hostesses and others as writers. For example, the French writer **Emilie du Châtelet** translated Newton and explained the significance of the new theories in her scientific essays. In earlier days, writers had been professors or clerics, or possibly protégés of aristocratic patrons, but during the Enlightenment many were freelancers or journalists who wrote to gain attention. They might be found in London coffee houses, the salons of Paris, the country houses of nobles, or the courts of monarchs across Europe. They delivered their message in many forms: books, pamphlets, newspapers, plays, novels, philosophical treatises, and encyclopedias. Their audience included not only the nobility, but the educated middle class as well.

The Enlightenment evolved over the course of the 18th century and involved writers from various countries. Its early exponents popularized the Scientific Revolution and argued for social reform based on rational conclusions regarding societal problems. By mid-century, *philosophes* were corresponding with one another and defending each other against the political and religious authorities. By the second half of the century, they were addressing specific abuses, and their books and articles had become more specialized and more practical. As the century progressed, more of them focused on politics rather than religion, and their ideas became the fuel for major change. Many writers considered themselves to be *philosophes*; some of the most famous and influential among them were Voltaire, Diderot, Montesquieu, Rousseau, and Smith.

Voltaire

Perhaps the most famous *philosophe* of all was **Voltaire**, a French writer, critic, and reformer whose presence was valued at salons, country houses, and royal courts all across Europe. Born François-Marie Arouet to a middle-class family, he took the pen name Voltaire after one of his early plays became a big success. His life illustrated the careful balance that *philosophes* had to maintain between the creativity and outspokenness that made them sought after, and the flaunting of authority that could arouse the censors. His mockery of the regent for the French king led to his imprisonment in 1717, and a later dispute with a leading courtier led to his exile to Britain for two years.

While Voltaire was in England, he visited the best literary circles, and was very much impressed with the tolerant intellectual and religious climate. He also admired England's moderate political atmosphere, scientific accomplishments, and economic prosperity. In 1733 he published ***Letters on the English***, which praised the virtues of the English and indirectly criticized the abuses of French society. Voltaire portrayed Britain as a more rational society than France, and he believed that the British government was more workable and its economy less crippled by the remnants of feudal privilege. In 1738 he published *Elements of the Philosophy of Newton,* which popularized the thought of the great scientist. Both works were widely read and gave Voltaire a reputation as an important writer.

After his sojourn to England, Voltaire lived part of the time in France and part near Geneva, just across the French border, safe from the government authorities. He used satire and sarcasm to target one evil after another in French and European life. In his most famous satire, ***Candide*** (1759), he attacked war and religious persecution and criticized aristocratic privilege and the power of clerics. He took special aim at the naiveté of *philosophes* who had overly optimistic views of the human condition. Voltaire believed that the centuries of abuses in European society could only be overturned by intense struggle, and he became involved in several well-publicized legal cases that pitted individuals against the authority of the Church. He also wrote many political pamphlets urging reform.

Denis Diderot's *Encyclopedia*

Many Enlightenment writers collaborated on the 28-volume *Encyclopedia: The Rational Dictionary of the Sciences, the Arts, and the Crafts,* edited by **Denis Diderot**, who, the son of an artisan, became a man of letters. The ***Encyclopedia,*** the result of 25 years of his labor, stands as the greatest single monument to the Enlightenment. It encapsulated the central message that knowledge is rational, and that it follows the laws of nature. Diderot's stated goal was "to change the general way of thinking," as well as to bring glory to France, and the *Encyclopedia* set out to educate the literate and intellectually-curious social elite.

ORIGINAL DOCUMENT:
VOLTAIRE ON THE ENGLISH MODEL

Voltaire developed a great admiration for the political system of England while in exile there from his native France from 1726 to 1729. His idealization of England did not dim over his lifetime, but his criticism of France grew bolder as he grew older. Although he does not mention France by name, his contempt is clear in this excerpt from his *Philosophical Dictionary*, first published in 1764.

"And, in truth, invaluable privileges [in England] they are in comparison with the usages of most other nations of the world! To be secure on lying down that you shall rise in possession of the same property with which you retired to rest; that you shall not be torn from the arms of your wife, and from your children, in the dead of night, to be thrown into a dungeon, or buried in exile in a desert; that, when rising from the bed of sleep, you will have the power of publishing all your thoughts, and that, if you are accused of having either acted, spoken, or written wrongly, you can be tried only according to law. These privileges attach to every one who sets his foot on English ground. A foreigner enjoys perfect liberty to dispose of his property and person; and if accused of any offence, he can demand that half the jury shall be composed of foreigners.

I will venture to assert, that, were the human race solemnly assembled for the purpose of making laws, such are the laws they would make for their security."

Reference: Voltaire, *Philosophical Dictionary,* in Voltaire, *Works,* trans. W.F. Fleming (New York: E.R. Dumont, 1901), vol. 5, pp. 293-294.

Published over a period of more than twenty years, beginning in 1751, the massive work consisted of 60,000 articles and 2,885 illustrations and was a bold attempt to organize and classify all knowledge gathered from the entire world. Its contributors included leading scientists, famous writers, skilled workers, and progressive priests. After the appearance of the first volume, which dealt with atheism, the soul, and blind people (all words that start with "a" in French), the government temporarily banned the book. The pope later placed the *Encyclopedia* on the Catholic Church's index of forbidden works and pronounced excommunication on all that read it. Not every article of the *Encyclopedia* was controversial or original, but the overall effect was extraordinary. Science and artisan crafts were exalted, religion and immortality were questioned. It was first bought by the wealthy, but as word of the publication of subsequent volumes reached more and more people, its sales multiplied, and it ended up on the shelves of many middle-class people.

EXAMINING THE EVIDENCE:
VOLTAIRE AND
EMILIE DU CHÂTELET

Many *philosophes* were in close communication with one another, but one remarkable intellectual and emotional relationship stands out among the rest: that of Voltaire and Emilie du Châtelet.

After the publication of his *Letters on the English* in 1733, Voltaire's criticism of France forced him into exile from Paris, and, at Madame Châtelet's invitation, he took refuge in her country home. Madame Châtelet studied physics and mathematics and published scientific articles and translations, the most famous of which was a translation/commentary on Newton's *Principia*. Because of her gender, she was excluded from the French Royal Academy of the Sciences, and, as a young woman, she depended on private tutors for instruction. She concentrated on spreading the ideas of others, particularly Newton, and she found in Voltaire an apt and admiring pupil. Voltaire came to greatly admire Newton, and, under Châtelet's tutelage, he became much more knowledgeable about the sciences. The two companions shared a serious belief in the need to apply scientific rationality to human affairs, and they reinforced one another's work for fifteen years, until her sudden death in 1749.

Booksellers sold it all across Europe, as they convinced potential buyers that ownership would reflect their standing as knowledgeable *philosophes*. Thomas Jefferson helped promote the *Encyclopedia* in America, finding several subscribers, including Benjamin Franklin.

Montesquieu

Like Locke, the baron de **Montesquieu** (born Charles-Louis de Secondat) had a special interest in analyzing European political systems. He was a member of an eminent judicial family and a high-ranking French judge, but his privileged life did not prevent him from criticizing the French government. His *Persian Letters*, published in 1721, was written in the form of reports sent home by two Persian visitors to Paris, and it quickly became a best seller. In the book, Rica and Usbek leave Persia – widely considered to be among the most despotic of all countries at the time – "for love of knowledge" and travel to Europe. They visit France in the last years of Louis XIV's reign, writing of the king: "He has no mines of gold like his neighbor, the king of Spain: but he is much wealthier than that prince, because his riches are drawn from a more inexhaustible source, the vanity of his subjects. He has undertaken and carried on great wars, without any other supplies than those derived from the sale of titles of honor." Other passages ridiculed the pope. Beneath the satire was a serious investigation into the true meaning of good government and morality. His Persian travelers constantly compared France to Persia, suggesting that the French monarch was just as despotic as a Persian ruler. In *Persian Letters,* Montesquieu also presented the first critical examination of the institution of slavery by a *philosophe.* He saw slavery as an extension of despotism, concluding that "slavery is against natural law, by which all men are born free and independent."

A second influential book – *The Spirit of the Laws* – was published in 1748. In it, Montesquieu applied the scientific principles of observation, experimentation, and analysis to the social and political foundations of states. He took illustrative examples from political experiences of both ancient and modern nations. From these he concluded there could be no single set of political laws that applied to all people at all times and in all places. Instead, forms of government were shaped by history, geography, and customs. However, he argued that certain conditions promote liberty and prevent tyranny, and he believed that despotism could be avoided if political power was divided and shared by a variety of classes and legal orders. Montesquieu did not argue for equality among social classes; he supported a strong, independent upper class to check the power of the monarch. He especially admired the English balance of power among the king, the houses of Parliament, and the independent courts.

These thoughts shaped his powerful model of government – one with three branches, characterized by **separation of powers** and **checks and balances**. He took Britain as an example, describing its executive power as residing in the king, legislative power in the Parliament, and judicial power in the courts. He explained that any two branches could check and balance the power of the other, an arrangement that promoted sharing of political power and avoided despotism. His analysis reflected some important misunderstandings about how the British system actually worked, and he failed to foresee the emergence of the British cabinet system, but his ideas profoundly shaped the evolution of liberal democracies that would follow over the next two centuries.

Rousseau

Whereas both Voltaire and Montesquieu praised British institutions highly, **Jean Jacques Rousseau** thought almost as ill of British as of French government. Rousseau was born into a poor family in Geneva, and moved to Paris as a young man, but he was never comfortable with the other *philosophes,* and he lived most of his life in isolation. Indeed, he not only criticized the status quo; he came to believe that the *philosophes* themselves were part of the problem. Rousseau was most concerned with the issue of moral freedom, and he found society far more

Politics

THEMATIC LEARNING OBJECTIVE: STATES AND OTHER INSTITUTIONS OF POWER: MONTESQUIEU ON "CIVIL SLAVERY"

In his highly influential book, *The Spirit of the Laws,* Montesquieu analyzed many political and social topics that were of interest to Enlightenment thinkers. One such issue was slavery, a question that he also addressed in his earlier *Persian Letters.* In the 17th century, absolutists and capitalists had accepted slavery in the course of their trade, but Montesquieu examined the institution under the light of reason, and found it unnatural and evil, especially in countries that espoused Enlightenment ideas. The following excerpt is from Book XV of *The Spirit of the Laws,* entitled "Of Civil Slavery."

"In despotic countries, where they are already in a state of political servitude, civil slavery is more tolerable than in other governments. Every one ought to be satisfied in those countries with necessaries and life. Hence the condition of a slave is hardly more burdensome than that of a subject.
But in a monarchical government, where it is of the utmost importance that human nature should not be debased or dispirited, there ought to be no slavery. In democracies, where they are all upon equality; and in aristocracies, where the laws ought to use their utmost endeavours to procure as great an equality as the nature of the government will permit, slavery is contrary to the spirit of the constitution: it only contributes to give a power and luxury to the citizens which they ought not to have."

Reference: Montesquieu, *The Spirit of the Laws,* trans. by Thomas Nugent, revised by J. V. Prichard (London: G. Bell & Sons, Ltd.), 1914.

oppressive than most *philosophes* would admit. In the essay that first won him fame, he argued that the lustrous cultural and scientific achievements of recent decades had produced pretension, conformity, and idle luxury. He believed that European society was decadent, and he advocated a return "to the simplicity which prevailed in earliest times." This simple life that he envisioned should focus on physical exercise, self-reliance, and independent thinking.

Rousseau had a strong confidence in the essential goodness of human nature. He urged a return to nature and an abandonment of the artificial world of the salon. In the novel Émile, he envisioned a system of education which would preserve the natural goodness of children by allowing relatively free expression of their natural inclinations. The book began by declaring, "Everything is good as it comes from the hands of the Author of nature, but everything degenerates in the hands of man." Émile, the main character, is gradually exposed by his tutor to nature during walks to explore the countryside, so that his education was guided by emotional, not purely rational, reactions to a world free from artifice and pretension. In all his works, Rousseau exhibited a depth of feeling that was alien to the rationalistic, skeptical, mocking tradition of Voltaire, but which won for him a wide audience and many enthusiastic followers of his **"noble savage"** who controls his own life and destiny.

Rousseau carried these same concerns to the world of politics, and addressed the political world directly in his book, *The Social Contract*, published in 1762. He advanced a democratic theory of sovereignty, and rather than propose specific reforms, he outlined the kind of political structure he believed would overcome the evils of contemporary politics and society. Rousseau's social contract was different from Locke's: Locke believed that the contract was between ruler and subject, but Rousseau saw it as the consensus of a community of citizens with equal political rights. Ideally, these communities should be small, since city life did not encourage the development of the spirit of community. The social contract, he argued, had been made among the general body of the people, who by an act of will, organized themselves into a civil society, adopted laws, and established institutions of government. Such a contract could be changed at will, and if a government failed to satisfy the people over whom it ruled, then the people had reason to change the government in any way they saw fit. One of his most controversial and difficult concepts is the "**general will**", or the notion that the best interest of the community must be every individual's best interest as well. It is more than the idea of majority rule; it is based on Rousseau's belief that an individual ultimately must do what one *ought* to do, not simply what one *wants*. Under the social contract, the individual "will be forced to be free."

Adam Smith and Economic Freedom

Whereas many *philosophes* focused on political and social problems of their day, another area of concern was economic policy. Some reacted against mercantilist legislation that protected a country's trade from external competition. These economic reformers – called *physiocrats* in France – believed that regulations by governments interfered with natural laws, and as a result, actually hampered the expansion of trade, manufacture, and agriculture. The most famous of the proponents of this "free market" approach was Scottish philosopher **Adam Smith**, the author of an immensely influential book, *The Wealth of Nations*, published in 1776. Mercantilism had always assumed that the earth's resources are limited and scarce, so that one nation could only acquire wealth at the expense of others. Smith's book challenged this assumption, arguing that the resources of nature – water, soil, minerals, air – are boundless, and that no nation need be poor. Instead, entrepreneurship should be encouraged in order to exploit nature's infinite

COMPARISON:
HOW WAS ROUSSEAU DIFFERENT FROM
MOST OTHER *PHILOSOPHES?*

Jean Jacques Rousseau is often seen as the most unique and controversial thinker among the *philosophes.* Perhaps the most obvious difference was that he did not frequent the salons of Paris or the royal courts of Europe. In contrast, Voltaire and Montesquieu thrived in those environments. Rousseau emphasized the relationship between humans and nature, and encouraged people to leave the artifice of the city behind them and embrace the primitive. Also, Rousseau interpreted freedom in a very different way. Most *philosophes* followed the lead of John Locke, who regarded human beings as individuals and society as a collection of individuals pursuing personal, individual goals. A major concern, then, of most *philosophes* was liberating individuals from the restraints of government. Instead, Rousseau proclaimed that "All men are born free, but everywhere they are in chains," and he argued that human beings living alone can achieve very little. Through their relationship to the larger community they become moral creatures capable of significant, positive action. Although Rousseau generally took the view that humans are not born as selfish, evil beings, his emphasis on primitiveness as a virtue provoked this response from Voltaire: "I have received, Monsieur, your new book against the human race, and I thank you. No one has employed so much intelligence turning men into beasts. One starts wanting to walk on all fours after reading your book. However, in more than sixty years I have lost the habit."

resources to create "the wealth of nations." Smith's analysis laid the basis for the development of capitalism, an economic system that became an important force during the 19th and 20th centuries.

Smith believed that the force behind the economy should be the **"invisible hand"** of competition, not the forceful hand of government. Under Smith's system, the laws of supply and demand should govern the marketplace. If demand increases, prices will rise, and producers will scramble to meet the demand. Once demand is met, supplies will naturally dwindle, since people won't be willing to pay for the product. To Smith, any government control is "interference" with supply and demand. He did not oppose all government activity touching the economy. For example, he argued that the state should provide schools, armies, navies, and roads, and that it should support some commercial ventures too expensive or risky for private enterprise. However, the "invisible hand" should be allowed to work freely, and government does harm when it interferes with this natural process.

THEMATIC LEARNING OBJECTIVE: POVERTY AND PROSPERITY: ADAM SMITH'S "INVISIBLE HAND"

Adam Smith's *laissez-faire* economic policy was based on the belief that individual self-interest is essential for economic progress. The excerpt below from *The Wealth of Nations* contains his famous reference to the "invisible hand."

"Every individual is continually exerting himself to find out the most advantageous employment for whatever capital he can command....But it is only for the sake of profit that any man employs a capital in the support of industry.... [In so doing] he generally neither intends to promote the public interest, nor knows how much he is promoting it....he intends only his own security; and by directing that industry in such a manner as its produce may be of the greatest value, he intends only his own gain. [But] he is in this, as in many other cases, led by an invisible hand to promote an end which was not part of his intention. By pursuing his own interest he frequently promotes that of the society more effectually than when he really intends to promote it.

What is the species of domestic industry which his capital can employ, and of which the produce is likely to be of the greatest value, every individual, it is evident, can, in his local situation, judge much better than any statesman or lawgiver can do for him...."

Reference: A. Smith, *An Inquiry into the Nature and Causes of the Wealth of Nations,* 1776, book 4, ch. 2.

Smith's theory always assumed that part of a free market is a cycle in which some times are more prosperous than others. Recessions, small market downturns, or even depressions – big downturns – will happen. And, in those times of economic decline, the government should play a role to protect people until the forces of the marketplace eventually restore economic health. Smith believed that high tariffs, guild restrictions, and mercantilist restraints on free trade all artificially obstructed the free market during his time, and only interfered with the natural cycle of prosperity, downturns, and recovery. He became a founding father of *laissez-faire* economic theory, based on the belief that governments should not interfere with individuals' pursuit of their own economic interests. In the long run, free individual enterprise would create more wealth than any artificial regulation could encourage. His arguments began to affect policy before the end of the century, with France and Britain signing a free-trade treaty that lowered protective tariffs on imported textiles in 1786. In 1791, the government of France permanently dissolved all guilds and restrictive trade associations, and in the 1790s, the British Parliament revoked laws regulating apprenticeships.

THE ENLIGHTENMENT AND RELIGION

Voltaire's cry, "Crush the Infamous Thing," expressed the attitude that many *philosophes* had toward the Catholic Church and Christianity. During this time, organized religion of any type was open to criticism; Enlightenment-inspired thinkers complained that the churches hindered the pursuit of a rational life and the scientific study of human nature and society. For example, the Scottish philosopher **David Hume** argued in *The Natural History of Religion* (1755) that belief in God rested on superstition and fear rather than on reason. Through the doctrine of **original sin**, the clergy – both Catholic and Protestant – taught that humans were depraved because of their evil nature, and could only become worthy through divine grace. In contrast, most *philosophes* believed that human beings were capable of controlling their own destinies and that individual human effort would be the basis of constructive societal reform. Also coming under fire was the Calvinist doctrine of predestination (see p. 80) that denied any relationship between virtuous individual actions in this life and the fate of the soul after death.

Criticisms of religion were bold moves because religious institutions wielded enormous power in society, and traditionally most people considered religion an essential foundation of good society. In France, the Catholic Church owned large amounts of land and collected tithes from peasants before any secular authority collected its taxes. Most clergy were exempt from taxes and made only voluntary contributions to the government. The upper clergy in most countries were relatives of aristocrats. In Britain, Anglican clergy served in the House of Lords, and on the Continent, they advised princes and kings. In Protestant countries, the leading local landowner usually appointed the parish clergy, and in most parts of Europe, those that were members of the dominant religion of the country had political and economic advantages that others did not have.

Deism

Although they were critical of organized religion, many *philosophes* were not opposed to all religion. Some did declare themselves to be **atheists**, or nonbelievers in the existence of any kind of God, but many followed **deism**, a movement based on the belief that religion and reason could be combined. What they sought was a religion that accepted the power of human reason and was tolerant of various religious views. For example, Voltaire loudly criticized the practice of monasticism and the behavior of priests in the Catholic Church, and he argued that the church promoted superstitions that led to fanaticism that bred the religious wars of the 16th and early 17th centuries. As a deist, Voltaire hoped that educated Europeans would recognize God as the benevolent, all-knowing Creator of the

PERSPECTIVES:
VOLTAIRE ON RELIGIOUS FANATICISM

An important criticism that the *philosophes* had against organized Christianity was that it bred fanaticism that led to violence in the name of religion. Perhaps the most famous attack on religious fanaticism came from Voltaire in his *Philosophical Dictionary*, published in 1764. In the following excerpt, Voltaire cited an example of the religious intolerance spawned by the Reformation, and, rather surprisingly, he praised Confucianism.

"Fanaticism is to superstition what delirium is to fever and rage to anger....
The most detestable example of fanaticism was that of the burghers of Paris who on St. Bartholomew's Night [1572] went about assassinating and butchering all their fellow citizens who did not go to mass, throwing them out of windows, cutting them in pieces.
Once fanaticism has corrupted a mind, the malady is almost incurable....
There is only one religion in the world that has never been sullied by fanaticism, that of the Chinese men of letters. The schools of philosophy were not only free from this pest, they were its remedy; for the effect of philosophy is to make the soul tranquil, and fanaticism is incompatible with tranquility. If our holy religion has so often been corrupted by this infernal delirium, it is the madness of men which is at fault."

Reference: Voltaire, *Philosophical Dictionary,* trans. by P. Gay (New York: Basic Books, 1962), pp. 267-269.

world, who once the universe was set in motion, allowed it to operate according to natural laws without divine intervention. Voltaire also argued that Christianity's threat of eternal damnation or salvation after death was a dangerous superstition that contradicted Newton's vision of the universe as an eternally existing, self-perpetuating machine. Deists believed that human beings lived on their own in an ordered universe, and that religion properly functioned on a personal level as a matter of private contemplation, not as public worship dictated by strict creeds.

Toleration

The Enlightenment value of religious toleration was first encouraged by French critic **Pierre Bayle** in his *Critical and Historical Dictionary,* published in 1697. Bayle put Christian traditions to the test of critical reason, and he concluded that many were little more than myths or fairy tales. Like Voltaire in his *Philosophi-*

cal Dictionary, published much later, Bayle condemned Christianity's record of fanaticism and persecution. He particularly targeted Christianity's attempts to impose common views and practices on all, and he advocated complete toleration that would allow anyone to practice any religion or none at all.

Bayle's influence led later *philosophes,* including Voltaire, to actively promote religious toleration. For example, in 1761, a judicial case in Toulouse, France, provoked an outcry when a local Calvinist, Jean Calas, was accused of murdering his son to prevent the son's conversion to Catholicism. The all-Catholic parlement of Toulouse tried to get Calas to confess by breaking all his bones, and then executed him even though he claimed that his son committed suicide. Voltaire launched a successful campaign to restore Calas's good name and to return his property – which had been confiscated – to his family. Voltaire's efforts helped to restore civil rights to French Protestants and spawned crusades to abolish the legal use of torture.

One important result of the 18th century movement for toleration was the Edict of Toleration issued by the Habsburg emperor Joseph II in 1781. For the first time, a Catholic Habsburg ruler recognized the religious rights of non-Catholics. In this landmark decree, Joseph granted "Lutheran and Calvinist religions, and also the non-Uniat [non-Orthodox] Greek religion, everywhere, the appropriate private practice of their faith," although he explicitly stated that only Catholics could engage in public worship. He also granted non-Catholics the right to buy property, practice as master craftsmen, and to take posts in public service.

THE ENLIGHTENMENT AND WOMEN

During the Enlightenment, women's roles in society became the subject of great debate. Despite the overall emphasis on individual rights and the tendency of traditional institutions and customs to squelch human potential, most Enlightenment thinkers did not advocate equal rights for women. Many male thinkers argued that male domination of women was based on "natural" biological differences between men and women. For example, in Rousseau's *Émile,* his female character, Sophie, was a sensitive wife-to-be without vain aristocratic pretenses, who received an education with more emphasis on virtue and much more limited in scope than that of Émile. According to Rousseau, "Sophie is educated for a domestic role as wife and mother, and she is taught to be obedient, always helpful to her husband and family, and removed from any participation in the public world." Male writers were often critical of the attempts of some women to write about intellectual issues, arguing that women by nature were intellectually inferior to men. Others resented what they saw as the growing power of women, especially in the salons.

Some Enlightenment thinkers offered more positive views of women. For example, Diderot observed that men and women were not all that different, although the *Encyclopedia* that he edited did not include the condition of women as a focus of reform. Voltaire – almost certainly influenced by Madame du Châtelet – asserted that intellectually "women are capable of all that men are." Many women agreed with Voltaire, and a few were outspoken about it. **Mary Astell,** from a wealthy English family, argued in *A Serious Proposal to the Ladies* (1697) that women needed to become better educated. She said that women are "as capable of learning as men are, and that it becomes them as well". The most famous advocate for women's rights was the English writer **Mary Wollstonecraft,** who is often viewed as the founder of modern western feminism. In her book, ***Vindication of the Rights of Woman***, published in 1792, she identified two contradictions in the views of Enlightenment thinkers toward women. First, she said that the belief that it is proper for a woman to obey a man was contrary to the Enlightenment argument that a monarch's power over a subject is arbitrary and unjust. The subjection of a woman to a man, she argued, was just as wrong as a slave owner's power over a slave. A second contradiction was based on the Enlightenment belief that reason is innate in all human beings. If women have reason, Wollstonecraft declared, then they too are entitled to the same rights that men have.

THEMATIC LEARNING OBJECTIVE: INDIVIDUAL AND SOCIETY: MARY WOLLSTONECRAFT ON THE EDUCATION OF WOMEN

In her book, *Vindication of the Rights of Women,* Mary Wollstonecraft argued that a better education for women was necessary to end their subjugation to men. In the excerpt below, she described the nature of that education, and she placed particular blame for gender inequality on *philosophes* such as Rousseau.

"The conduct and manners of women, in fact, evidently prove that their minds are not in a healthy state; for, like the flowers which are planted in too rich a soil, strength and usefulness are sacrificed to beauty....One cause of this barren blooming I attribute to a false system of education, gathered from the books written on this subject by men who, considering females rather as women than human creatures, have been more anxious to make them alluring mistresses than affectionate wives and rational mothers....

[T]he most perfect education, in my opinion, is such an exercise of the understanding as is best calculated to strengthen the body and form the heart. Or, in other words, to enable the individual to attain such habits of virtue as will render it independent. In fact, it is a farce to call any being virtuous whose virtues do not result from the exercise of its own reason. This was Rousseau's opinion respecting men: I extend it to women..."

Reference: Sandra M. Gilbert and Susan Gubar (eds.), *The Norton Anthology of Literature by women: The Tradition in English.* W.W. Norton Co, 1985.

The Enlightenment *philosophes* celebrated science and reason, and were confident that humans could reach their full potential through thought, study, education, and action. They built on the Scientific Revolution to foster a new world-view among the educated elites of western civilization, one that was critical and secular, and would eventually come to be shared by commoners as well. Political authority, they thought, is not ordained by God, but should be shaped by a rational consideration of what form of government functions best to meet the needs of its subjects. They generally spoke out against religious intolerance, torture, and slavery, although most did not extend equal rights to women. Despite the limitations of their movement, the *philosophes* greatly influenced public opinion with their commitment to individual freedom, and by the late 18th century they had inspired momentous political change that would shake the foundations of absolutism and eventually lead to new forms of government.

CONCEPTS AND IDENTIFICATIONS

Astell, Mary
atheists
Bayle, Pierre
Candide
Châtelet, Emilie du
consent of the governed
deism
Diderot, Denis
Encyclopedia
Enlightenment
Fontenelle, Bernard de
"general will"
Hobbes, Thomas
Hume, David
"invisible hand"
Letters on the English
Leviathan
Locke, John
Montesquieu
natural rights
Newtonian synthesis
Newton, Isaac
"noble savage"
original sin
Persian Letters
philosophes
Philosophical Dictionary
Principia Mathematica

Rousseau, Jean Jacques
salons
Second Treatise of Government
separation of powers / checks and balances
Smith, Adam
"social contract" (Hobbes vs. Locke)
The Social Contract (Rousseau)
The Spirit of the Laws
state of nature
tabula rosa
Vindication of the Rights of Women
Voltaire
The Wealth of Nations
Wollstonecraft, Mary

CHAPTER 12:
FROM ABSOLUTISM TO
REVOLUTIONARY UPHEAVAL:
1740-1815

By 1740, Europe had experienced economic, political, cultural, and social change that set the stage for revolutionary upheavals by the end of the century. An important force at work was Enlightenment thought, which challenged traditional political regimes that rested on aristocratic privilege and the inherited power of monarchs. Most countries – with the notable exception of Britain – were ruled by kings who did not claim to share power with anyone else. Their authority usually rested on military power, hereditary lines, and divine sanction, and even though their will was sometimes backed by law codes, rulers often had an extraordinary amount of power. Their authority was challenged when their armies failed or their ability to rule slipped, and their replacement was generally someone who could restore the respect for authority that had been lost. Almost always, the ruler was expected to act in the best interest of his subjects, but he was accountable only if his military and political skills did not withstand a direct challenge to the throne.

Throughout the time period from 1740 to 1815, the countries of Europe sparred with one another, ever mindful of keeping a balance of power among themselves under the traditional authority of hereditary monarchs. The Enlightenment stirred people to rethink basic premises about political power, and to accept the notion that "subjects" are also citizens with individual rights of life, liberty, and property, as explained by European philosophers of the 17th and 18th century. These radical thoughts came from people on both sides of the Atlantic; they inspired political revolutions first in North America, then in France, and eventually in many other parts of the network that had formed around the Atlantic Ocean in the previous era. These revolutions encouraged the development of strong national identities based on the abstract concept of a nation-state instead of the authority of a king.

"ENLIGHTENED DESPOTS"

The words in the phrase "enlightened despots" appear to contradict one another. How can a despotic, absolute ruler truly claim to be a child of the Enlightenment, with its basic belief in individual rights and freedoms? Yet the phrase illustrates the fact that the two contradictory forces – Enlightenment values and absolutism –

were at work throughout the 18th century, and the tension between the two shaped the revolutionary outcomes from 1789 to 1815.

Whether or not such a thing as enlightened despots actually existed in 18th century Europe is a matter of dispute among historians today, but most *philosophes* believed that such a rule was best for most countries. They did not envision the development of democracies, but instead advocated rule by a hereditary monarch who allowed religious toleration, freedom of speech and the press, and the rights of private property. Only strong monarchs had the authority to bring necessary reform, so enlightened despotism appeared to be the best form of government for most European countries. Three monarchs who have often been identified as this type of ruler were Frederick II of Prussia, Joseph II of Austria, and Catherine the Great of Russia.

Frederick II of Prussia

Frederick II, who ruled Prussia from 1740 to 1786, was one of the best-educated and most culturally sophisticated monarchs of the 18th century. Often called **Frederick the Great**, his rule followed that of Frederick William I (see pp. 191-192), who strengthened Prussia by building an efficient bureaucracy as well as the fourth-largest army in Europe (after France, Russia, and Austria). Frederick William had little use for intellectual pursuits, and he was appalled by his son's high regard for French culture, poetry, and flute playing. In a letter written to Frederick in 1728, Frederick William chastised him as an "effeminate fellow who has no manly tastes, who cannot ride or shoot…and wears his hair curled like a fool". Frederick conscientiously followed his father's advice by training himself to effectively direct the bureaucracy and command the army when he became king, but he kept his interest in Enlightenment thought. French was the main language of his court, and he greatly admired Voltaire, whom he invited to come to Prussia as his guest. Voltaire stayed in Prussia for three years, where he became a celebrity.

Some of Frederick's policies reflected Enlightenment values, but he still ruled with absolute power. He continued the Hohenzollern policy of religious toleration by allowing Catholics and Jews to settle in predominantly Lutheran Prussia, and he protected Catholics living in Silesia, an Austrian province he seized in 1740. However, he almost always appointed Protestants to major positions in the government and army. Frederick knew that the *philosophes* condemned serfdom, but he did not abolish it, since he did not want to disrupt the social structure of his state. He established a single code of laws for his domains that forbid torture except in treason and murder cases. His stated goal for the new codification was to rationalize the existing legal system, making it more efficient, but he saw legal reform as a means of increasing his power. Frederick granted a limited freedom of speech and the press, but he reversed his father's policy of allowing commoners to hold high positions in the civil service. Instead, Frederick favored members of the

nobility for these positions, and the burden of taxation continued to fall dispropor-
tionally on peasants and townspeople.

Like his father, Frederick took a great interest in the Prussian army, and he used
it to assert his power. His seizure of Silesia from the Austrians involved Prussia
in two major wars, the War of the Austrian Succession and the Seven Years' War.
He gained territory from Poland in 1772, and by the end of his reign, Prussia was
recognized as a great European power. In many ways, Frederick modernized the
concept of state by strengthening the institutions of the bureaucracy, the law, and
the army so that they would remain intact after his death. His reference to himself
as "the first servant of the state" reflected the changing concept of an impersonal
state – with its enduring institutions – that was no longer dependent on the power
of a single monarch.

Politics

THEMATIC LEARNING OBJECTIVE: STATES AND OTHER INSTITUTIONS OF POWER: FREDERICK THE GREAT – A NEW STYLE OF MONARCHY

Whether or not Frederick the Great of Prussia actually ruled as an "enlightened
despot" is a matter of some debate among historians, but the concept of the
proper role of the king as he described in his *Political Testament* is clearly
influenced by Enlightenment values. The excerpt below outlined his vision of a
government that is both rational and highly centralized in the hands of the
monarch.

"A well conducted government must have an underlying concept so well integrated that it could be likened to a system of philosophy. All actions taken
must be well reasoned, and all financial, political and military matters must
flow towards one goal: which is the strengthening of the state and the furthering of its power. However, such a system can flow but from a single brain,
and this must be that of the sovereign. Laziness, hedonism and imbecility,
these are the causes which restrain princes in working at the noble task of
bringing happiness to their subjects...a sovereign is not elevated to his high
position, supreme power has not been confined to him in order that he may live
in lazy luxury, enriching himself by the labor of the people, being happy while
everyone else suffers. The sovereign is the first servant of the state. He is well
paid in order that he may sustain the dignity of his office, but one demands that
he work efficiently for the good of the state, and that he, at the very least, pay
personal attention to the most important problems...."

Reference: Frederick II, *Political Testament,* in George L. Mosse et al., eds., *Europe in Review* (Chicago: Rand
McNally, 1957), pp. 110-112.

Joseph II of Austria

Despite its many different nationalities, languages, religions, and cultures, the Austrian Empire had become one of the great European states by the beginning of the 18th century. However, it faced a crisis in 1740 when Holy Roman Emperor Charles VI died without a male heir. He had designated his 23-year-old daughter, **Maria Theresa**, as his successor, but Frederick II of Prussia took advantage of the situation by invading the rich Austrian province of Silesia. France joined Prussia in an attempt to weaken its traditional rival (Austria), but the British allied with Austria to prevent the French from taking the Austrian Netherlands. The **War of the Austrian Succession** (1740-1748) eventually involved the overseas colonies of Britain and France, and colonists in North America fought on both sides. The peace that settled the war in 1748 recognized Maria Theresa as the ruler of Austria, but Prussia kept control of Silesia. Empress Maria Theresa ruled until 1780, and one lesson that she took from the early challenge to her authority was to make administrative reforms to centralize and strengthen the Austrian Empire. She enlarged and modernized the armed forces and the bureaucracy and imposed a much more efficient system of tax collection. She was concerned about the welfare of the peasants and serfs, but not for humanitarian reasons: she mainly wanted to assure a good pool from which to draw military recruits. Maria Theresa remained staunchly Catholic and conservative and was not open to the wider reforms called for by the *philosophes*. Her son and successor, **Joseph II** was.

Joseph, co-ruler with his mother from 1765 and sole ruler by 1780, boldly implemented reforms long advocated by Enlightenment thinkers, although he did not openly identify with the *philosophes,* and he remained a loyal Catholic. His reforms supported freedom of expression, religious toleration, greater state control over the Catholic Church, and legal reform. For example, he reduced royal censorship, making it possible for Vienna to become a major cultural center that was frequently visited by members of the "republic of letters." He issued the Edicts of Religious Toleration for Protestants and Jews, and he forced the clergy to modernize the rituals and services of the Catholic Church. He codified criminal laws to reduce the use of the death penalty, end torture, and apply laws evenly to all social classes.

Joseph's most ambitious reforms aimed to transform the economic and social position of the peasants. He built on Maria Theresa's reforms, but his were much more drastic, touching the very structure of Austrian society. He sought to make the landlords' authority over peasants more moderate and subject to the oversight of royal officials. In a radical move, he abolished serfdom as a legally sanctioned state of servitude. Peasants were granted many personal freedoms, including the right to marry, work as artisans, and train their children as artisans without the landlord's permission. He also encouraged landlords to change land leases so it would be easier for peasants to inherit them, and he decreed in 1789 that landlords had to pay taxes, just as peasants had always done. His goal was to make peasants more productive and industrious farmers. Unfortunately for him, these reforms resulted in chaos throughout his regime. Part of the problem was that he consulted almost no one before he issued his decrees, and as a result, he antagonized almost everyone, including the peasants whom he tried to help. Predictably, the landowning nobles were upset, but the peasants generally did not comprehend his drastic changes, and they distrusted his motives. His insistence on reforms within the Catholic Church offended the clergy as well.

In the end, Joseph resorted to suppressing dissent by crushing it. He restored censorship, and gave the police unprecedented powers to keep law and order in his increasingly autocratic state. So he died a disillusioned man, and his successors rolled back most of his reforms, going so far as to restore serfdom.

Catherine the Great of Russia

By 1740, Russia had experienced significant westernization under Tsar Peter the Great, who built a navy, improved the military, expanded to the shores of the Baltic Sea, and increased Russia's interactions with western Europe. His reforms were solidified and expanded by **Catherine the Great**, who ruled Russia from 1762 to 1796, the time when Enlightenment thought stimulated the American and French Revolutions. Like Peter, Catherine had a vision of a more powerful Russia supported by western technology and warm-water ports. Catherine also was an absolute ruler, but she was familiar with the works of the *philosophes.* She claimed that she wished to reform Russia according to Enlightenment ideas, but she understood that her success depended on the Russian nobility. Catherine was not Russian, but instead was a German princess who married Peter the Great's grandson, who eventually became Tsar Peter III. Her husband was killed in a palace coup that Catherine almost certainly supported, and she ascended the throne in 1762, following a tradition set by Peter the Great, who had named his wife as his successor.

Catherine was well-read, and she followed events in western Europe carefully, but she understood the dangers that democratic institutions – such as parliaments and constitutions – posed to her autocratic rule. She supported the economic development of Russia's towns and cities, but she was not willing to allow them to have any substantial political power. She also supported the rights of the nobility, especially in regard to control of the serfs who worked on their lands. Catherine encouraged the nobles to travel in western Europe but she was always mindful of keeping her own power and authority. Her willingness to resort to despotism was illustrated by her reaction in 1773-4 to a major rebellion led by **Emelian Pugachev**, a Cossack who lived in the steppes north of the Caspian Sea. Pugachev raised an army to support his goals of ending taxes and the military draft and securing the right for peasants to own land. The tsar's army crushed the rebellion, captured Pugachev, and displayed his quartered body publicly, just as previous tsars had reacted to rebellious subjects. After Pugachev's rebellion, Catherine's tendencies toward absolutism were more apparent than her desire to reform Russia, especially after she saw the results of the French Revolution, which occurred late in her reign.

Under Catherine, Russia continued to expand, gaining lands that gave it access to the Black Sea, as well as some of the lands of Poland, to Russia's west. Catherine coordinated plans with Frederick II of Prussia and Maria Theresa of Austria to attack Poland and "partition" the kingdom among the three great powers that surrounded it. At Catherine's death in 1796, Russia was much stronger than it had been when she took the throne, but she did little to change the tradition of the tsar's absolute rule. The cultural conflict created by Peter – westernization in order to gain power versus the Slavic tendency to protect old traditions – continued under Catherine's reign and shaped Russia's development during the 19th century.

WAR AND DIPLOMACY

Despite the fact that *philosophes* condemned war as a waste of human life and resources fueled by foolish quarrels, the rivalry among states that led to costly wars continued unabated in Europe during the 18th century. Frederick the Great, who recognized the evolution of the state beyond personal monarchy still believed that "the fundamental rule of governments is the principle of extending their territories."

States fought over territory with economic and strategic value, not only in Europe, but, increasingly, in profitable colonies abroad. Dynastic claims to lands were still major causes of war, just as they had been in earlier times. The century opened with the War of the Spanish Succession (see pp. 189-190), and later the succession of the Austrian Habsburgs provoked a widespread war (see p. 279), with the major powers of Europe lining up on both sides as they played out traditional rivalries and attempted to keep the balance of power. Since royal claims to land often inspired countries to seek isolated bits of land, the wars between European powers became extremely complex. For example, when Prussia attacked Silesia (an Austrian possession), France joined on Prussia's side in order to weaken its traditional rival (Austria), but later, when Prussia invaded Saxony to extend its territorial claims, France switched sides and allied with Austria to destroy Prussian power. Wars, then, were carried out with complex systems of alliances and were followed by border adjustments that reflected the changing control of small, scattered territories. Smaller states in Germany and Italy were pulled into the wars as well, as the great powers tried to outmaneuver one another.

Wars of the 18th century were fought with increasingly refined weapons and tactics. More reliable muskets were introduced, and a bayonet that could slip over a musket barrel without blocking the muzzle was invented. Troops were carefully drilled to coordinate the use of bayonets, and the training of artillery and cavalry forces was standardized. Even though warfare became increasingly professional, it was still uncertain, with unpredictable results. Not only were the armies of great powers often very evenly matched, but less disciplined and poorly equipped forces could paralyze great armies by cutting their supply lines. The farther away from home the armies went, the more susceptible they were to disruptions to supply lines.

Colonial Competition between France and Britain

The importance of international trade and colonial possessions grew enormously in the 18th century, resulting in a great deal of tension between France and Britain, especially concerning their interests in North America. Between 1715 and 1785 Britain's trade with North America rose from 19 to 34% of its total trade, and its trade with Asia and Africa rose from 7 to 19%. By the end of the century more than half of all British trade and more than a third of all French trade was non-European.

The British North American colonies grew rapidly, increasing from a population of about 250,000 in 1700 to about 1.7 million by 1760. Through its policy of mercantilism, Britain provided its colonies with manufactured goods, and raw materials – such as tobacco, rice and indigo (for dye) – were shipped from North America to Britain, where they were sold all across Europe. In contrast, French North America was sparsely populated, with only about 56,000 people in 1740,

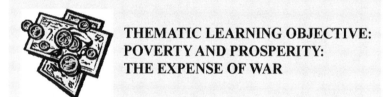

THEMATIC LEARNING OBJECTIVE: POVERTY AND PROSPERITY: THE EXPENSE OF WAR

The more sophisticated warfare became during the 18th century, the more of a burden it put on a state's resources and administration. Even for large states like France and England, huge portions of the treasury were devoted to the costs of war. Prussia – smaller and poorer – supported its army only by extraordinary effort, with an incredible 80% of its state revenue spent on sustaining the army. Almost always, commoners suffered more than the nobility, since in many states (Britain was an exception) the aristocracy paid few or no taxes. In Prussia and Russia, peasants were conscripted into the army, placing a significant burden on peasant communities who were left with fewer people to tend the crops.

but the French still had major land claims on the continent. The French extended their fur trapping west and north along the Great Lakes to make tremendous profits. The two countries inevitably came into conflict over trading rights, especially in the areas along the Ohio River Valley, the Hudson Bay, the St. Lawrence River, and the Gulf of St. Lawrence. Squabbles also broke out over fishing rights.

Even more important to both Britain and France were their holdings in the Caribbean, where the British held Jamaica, Barbados, and the Leeward Islands, and the French claimed Guadeloupe and Martinique. The Spanish and Dutch also held islands, and sugar produced on plantations by slave labor was a major source of profits for all.

The Seven Years' War

The growing importance of international trade helped to fan a European conflagration into a major world war: the **Seven Years' War**, which lasted from 1756 to 1763. In 1756, a major reversal of alliances reshaped relations among the great powers, and set off a chain of events that eventually spread from Europe to North America and India. When Prussia and Great Britain signed a defensive alliance, Austria reacted by forming an alliance with France, despite two centuries of hostility between the two countries. Russia, Sweden, and many of the smaller German states joined the Franco-Austrian alliance. Frederick II of Prussia opened hostilities by invading Saxony in a preemptive strike against what he correctly perceived as a conspiracy by Saxony, Austria, and France to destroy Prussian power. He surprised Europe with a victory in Saxony over a much larger Franco-Austrian army. His efforts to save Prussia were helped when Russia withdrew from the war at the death of Empress Elizabeth. Her successor, Peter III, greatly admired Frederick, and a peace treaty was signed between Prussia and Russia in which Frederick kept his territory, including Silesia. Otherwise, territorial claims in Europe were little changes, with Saxony regaining its independence, although much reduced in size.

The fighting continued until 1763, and in North America the French and British battled on land and sea, where the British eventually prevailed. In this North American war, known as the French and Indian War, there were two primary areas of fighting. One was along the waterways of the Gulf of St. Lawrence, protected by French forts along the way, and the other was the Ohio River Valley. Despite early French gains, the British were ably guided by **William Pitt the Elder**, who decided to make a minimal effort in Europe and concentrate British resources in North America. He sent more than 40,000 regular English and colonial troops against the French in Canada. British naval superiority, only fully realized in the 1750s, allowed Britain to defeat French fleets in major battles in 1759, making it difficult for France to protect its garrisons. Quebec fell to the British, followed by

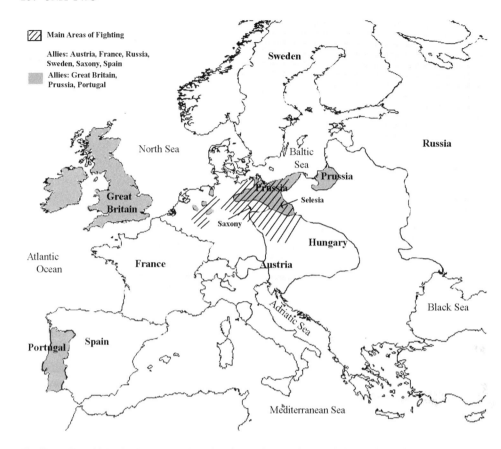

The Seven Years' War in Europe, 1756-1763. The war began when Frederick II of Prussia invaded Saxony, a territory claimed by Austria. Despite overwhelming odds, Frederick won major victories against his enemies and held on until Russia withdrew and the coalition against him fell apart. The treaty between Austria and Prussia simply restored borders to their pre-war status. However, the war spread to North America, the West Indies, and India, where Britain forced major land concessions from France, resulting in Britain becoming the dominant power of the seas.

Montreal, the Great Lakes area, and the Ohio Valley. The French were forced to make peace. In the Treaty of Paris of 1763, France gave up virtually all of Canada, and agreed to withdraw its armies from India. In exchange, France kept its rich West Indian (Caribbean) islands, but the humiliating losses to Britain eventually motivated France to support the British North American colonists in the American Revolution just 15 years later.

The Partition of Poland

Although Prussia lost many soldiers during the Seven Years' War, Frederick's ability to outlast his opponents earned him the title "the Great," and the army continued to grow in power and prestige. Meanwhile, Russia grew under the leadership of Catherine the Great, largely at the expense of the Ottoman Empire to the south. At the same time, Austria was ambitious to expand in the same direction, so the three countries continued to keep watch on one another's moves. In this atmosphere, Frederick the Great made a proposal to Russia and Austria that would give each something it wanted and would prevent further conflict among the three powers. After long, complicated, secret negotiations, the three countries agreed in 1772 that they would each take territory from Poland, a country that had long been dominated by the aristocracy. Poland paid dearly for its weak monarchy and quarrelsome nobility, and was helpless as it lost nearly one-third of its territory to strong neighbors. Prussia received land that allowed Frederick to unite two previously separate sections of his realm, Austria took Galicia (a territory with important salt mines), and Russia received a large chunk of territory to its west.

Politics

THEMATIC LEARNING OBJECTIVE: STATES AND OTHER INSTITUTIONS OF POWER: FREDERICK THE GREAT ON POLAND'S WEAKNESS

In the following excerpt from his *Political Testament,* published years before the first partition of Poland in 1792, Frederick the Great described the vulnerability of Poland and explained why he had little respect for the country.

"Poland can scarcely be counted among the European Powers. The lack of population in that kingdom, arising from the fact that the landowners treat their subjects as slaves, is one of the defects of that republic. There are many others which contribute to its low rating, such as poor financial administration, and a force of only 13,000 men instead of an army. All the faults of the old feudal forms of government have been preserved there to our own day: elections of their kings, followed by civil wars; turbulent Diets [parliaments], of which not one runs its course; no legislation, no justice. It is the reign of anarchy. Poland would long ago have been subjugated, had not her jealous neighbors restrained by armed deterrence the ambitious rulers who sought to subdue her.
....The nobility is proud and arrogant in prosperity, cowardly in misfortune, corrupt and incapable of taking vigorous measures or following them through. In a word, in my opinion, Poland is the least important nation in Europe."

Reference: Frederick II, *Political Testament,* in George L. Mosse et al., eds., *Europe in Review* (Chicago: Rand McNally, 1957).

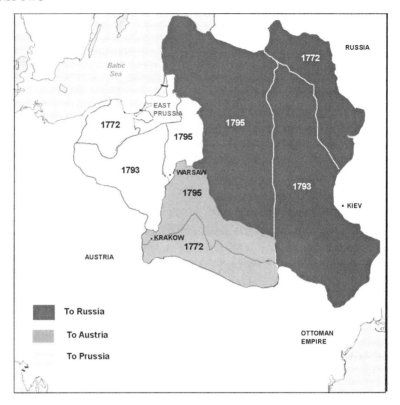

The Partition of Poland. Between 1772 and 1795, Prussia, Russia, and Austria each took chunks of Polish territory, so that by 1795, Poland disappeared from the map of Europe.

Poland responded by attempting to strengthen its government and military, but it was too late, and another partition took place in 1793. Finally, in 1795, a third partition totally removed Poland from the map of Europe for more than a century. Each time, Austria, Russia, and Prussia claimed that they were saving themselves from Poland's anarchy, a threat that was intensified by the French Revolution that began in 1789.

THE AMERICAN REVOLUTION

The first major Enlightenment-inspired revolution occurred among the British colonies in North America, far from the philosophical centers in Europe. The conflict evolved from the Seven Years' War, and even though Britain emerged from that conflict as the world's greatest colonial power, the war was expensive. To help pay for the war and the administration of the newly enlarged empire, the British Parliament levied new taxes on the colonies, an action that was quite unpopular in North America. The colonists were not only incensed by new laws, such as the Stamp Act of 1765, the Townshend Act of 1767, and the Tea Act of 1773, but by a strict enforcement of old navigation laws that had been widely ignored before. Their argument of "no taxation without representation" was testament to the power of Enlightenment thought: as British subjects, they should have had a say in the creation of policies that affected their welfare. Tensions escalated as colonists boycotted British products, dumped British tea into Boston Harbor, and skirmished with British troops charged with keeping order in the area around Boston, where resistance was most evident.

On July 2, 1776, a congress of delegates from Britain's thirteen colonies along the coast of North America signed the **Declaration of Independence** that, from its point of view, severed ties to Britain and created an independent country. Since Britain did not agree, a war followed, fought entirely in North America, that eventually resulted in victory for the colonists and a humiliating defeat for one of the most powerful empires in the world. The last battle was fought at Yorktown, Virginia in 1781, where British forces surrendered to American General **George Washington**. The peace treaty was finally signed in Paris in 1783.

Consequences in North America

Many factors shaped the success of the American Revolution, including the ability of the colonies to enlist the help of France in their struggle for independence. Other factors were the persistence of the revolutionaries, serious blunders made by the British, and French participation that threatened to escalate the conflict. In the peace treaty of 1783, the British government formally recognized American independence. In 1789 the new country, the United States, implemented a constitution based on Enlightenment principles, including separation of powers and checks and balances among the branches of government, as well as written guarantees of individual liberties. Some limited voting rights gave the government a basis in popular sovereignty (rule of the people), and a **federalist system** was created, in which political powers were divided between national and state levels in an effort to avoid concentrating control in the hands of one person.

Consequences in Britain

The loss of the North American colonies was a tremendous blow to Britain and had important consequences for the evolving relationship between the king and Parliament. Almost a century before, the Glorious Revolution of 1688 had established important powers for Parliament, including making laws, levying taxes, and passing the budget. Then, early in the 18th century, the governments of England and Scotland were officially united and became known as the United Kingdom of Great Britain. The king chose ministers to set policy and guide Parliament, and these ministers remained responsible primarily to him. A major change, however, occurred when a new dynasty – the Hanoverians – came to the throne in 1714 after the last Stuart – Queen Anne – died without an heir. The Hanovers were German, and the first ruler – George I – did not even speak English. His successor, George II, followed his father's example of allowing the king's ministers to handle

THEMATIC LEARNING OBJECTIVE: EUROPE AND THE WORLD: THE AMERICAN DECLARATION OF INDEPENDENCE

The first paragraphs of the American Declaration of Independence provide an enduring example of the influence of Enlightenment thought on the political revolutions of the late 18th and early 19th centuries. Penned by Thomas Jefferson, John Locke's ideas are evident in his references to "unalienable rights" and the "consent of the governed." Below is an excerpt:

"We hold these truths to be self-evident; that all men are created equal, that they are endowed by their Creator with certain unalienable rights, that among these are life, liberty, and the pursuit of happiness. That, to secure these rights, governments are instituted among men, deriving their just powers from the consent of the governed. That whenever any form of government becomes destructive of these ends, it is the right of the people to alter or to abolish it, and to institute new government, laying its foundation on such principles, and organizing its powers in such form, as to them shall seem most likely to effect their safety and happiness...when a long train of abuses and usurpations, pursuing invariably the same object, evinces a design to reduce them under absolute despotism, it is their right, it is their duty, to throw off such government, and to provide new guards for their future security."

parliamentary business, since he had little knowledge of the British political system. This situation gave a great deal of power to the talented **Robert Walpole**, the prime minister that shaped the development of the modern cabinet system in British government. Gradually, the king's opinion mattered less and less, and as the British trade empire grew, the prime minister gained even more importance as an international political force, even though the king theoretically remained in charge.

This trend toward more parliamentary power and less royal power was challenged by **George III**, the first Hanover to take a real interest in governing. Predictably, his efforts to regain royal prerogatives were resented by Parliament, and the loss of the American colonies gave the king's enemies the platform they needed to contain his attempts to regain royal control. A crisis was avoided when George appointed **William Pitt the Younger** as prime minister, an action that assuaged the earlier dismissal (in 1761) of William Pitt the Elder, who had great support in

**THEMATIC LEARNING OBJECTIVE:
INDIVIDUAL AND SOCIETY:
SOCIAL CHANGES IN
NORTH AMERICA**

Despite the revolutionary nature of the political changes in late18th century North America, social changes were not as radical. Although a number of representatives at the Constitutional Convention in 1787 supported the abolition of the slave trade, the decision was to extend it for 20 years, and the institution of slavery was left intact. Voting rights were established by the states, but generally only property-owning free males could vote, leaving a large number of people without the franchise. Even so, the framework of the new political system, based on Enlightenment values of freedom and equality, provided the basis for extending individual rights in later years.

Parliament. The loss of the colonies, then, did not diminish the power of the British Empire significantly, since it went on to become even larger and more influential in the 19th century. However, the American Revolution did confirm and shape parliamentary government, as this institution gained political power at the expense of the hereditary monarch.

REVOLTS AND REFORM IN THE NETHERLANDS AND POLAND

After the successful outcome of the American Revolution, revolts in the name of liberty broke out in the Dutch Republic, the Austrian Netherlands (present-day Belgium and Luxembourg), Poland, and France. These revolutions, like the American Revolution, were the product of long-term prosperity and a growing **bourgeoisie,** or middle class, who were impatient with authoritarian rule. Europeans of the 18th century were generally more prosperous than they had been in previous centuries, but the Dutch, Belgians, and French were among the wealthiest and best educated people on the continent.

The Dutch Patriot Revolt, 1787

Dutch banks were important in European trade and finance, so when political protest broke out in the Dutch Republic in 1787, other countries paid attention. The protestors called themselves **Dutch Patriots**, and their demands echoed conflicts regarding centralization of political power that had characterized the 17th century.

The House of Orange had long dominated politics, and when William and Mary became king and queen of England in 1688, the ties between the Dutch Republic and England were secured (pp. 207-208). By the late 18th century the Prince of Orange was still a stadholder with great powers, and the Dutch Patriots came to see him in the same light that the American colonists saw the British king. Building on support among middle-class bankers, merchants, and writers, the Patriots' demands for political reforms intensified, and they organized armed citizen militias of men called Free Corps to help them achieve their goals. The Free Corps forced local officials to set up new elections to replace councils that had been packed with Orange supporters, and in 1787, the protesters demanded "the true republican form of government in our commonwealth." When the Free Corps got the upper hand in its clash with the troops of the Prince of Orange, Frederick William II of Prussia, whose sister had married the stadholder, sent thousands of troops into the Dutch Republic to put down the rebellion. Chaos followed, with lower-class mobs pillaging the houses of prosperous Patriot leaders, forcing many to flee the country. The Dutch rebellion ended in failure, but the Patriots' demand for a more democratic government was a prelude to the bigger revolution that occurred in France two years later.

The Belgian Independence Movement

When Joseph II tried to introduce Enlightenment-inspired reforms to the Austrian Empire, there were some unexpected consequences in the Austrian Netherlands. In reorganizing the administrative and judicial systems, Joseph eliminated many offices that belonged to nobles, sparking a protest among the upper class, which in turn inspired supporters of a more representative government to form a counter-protest. The counter-protestors organized armed companies to prepare an

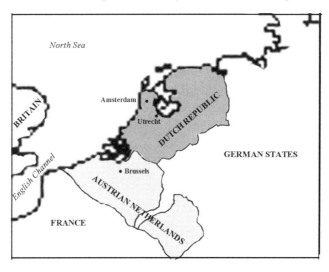

The Low Countries in 1787

uprising, and by late 1789, each province had separately declared its independence. Delegates from the provinces declared themselves the United States of Belgium, a clear reference to the new country in North America. However, social divisions prevented this new union from being successful, and soon the Catholic clergy and many peasants joined the aristocrats in demanding the downfall of the democrats. The result was the return of Austrian control under Emperor Leopold II (r. 1790-1792) who had succeeded his brother.

Reform in Poland

Even before the first partition of Poland in 1772, King **Stanislaw August Poniatowski** (r. 1764-1795) had tried to strengthen his weak country by modernizing it along western European lines. He was well versed in Enlightenment philosophy and regularly corresponded with the Parisian salon hostess Madame Geoffrin. King Stanislaw tried to end the *liberum* veto (the ability of a single noble's vote to dissolve the legislature), and to curtail the right of courts to impose death sentences. He also established a number of schools. He was supported by a reform party called the Patriots, who had enough support in parliament to enact a constitution in 1791, which established a hereditary monarchy with somewhat strengthened authority, eliminated the *liberum* veto, and granted townspeople limited political rights. However, Catherine the Great of Russia found these developments alarming since they might revive Poland's power and threaten Russian expansion. She reacted to the Polish reforms by invading the country, causing Austria and Prussia to demand territorial compensation as well. By 1795, Poland's independence was ended for more than a century through three partitions of its territories.

THE FRENCH REVOLUTION

A few years after the American Revolution, the Enlightenment spawned an important revolution in France. Whereas the American Revolution was fought in North America, with colonists challenging their mother country, the French Revolution was a civil war. No doubt, the French Revolution was inspired by the success of the American Revolution, particularly since French military personnel had fought in North America on the Americans' side. However, the roots of the French Revolution began to develop much earlier. Whereas the major goal of the American Revolution was independence (or liberty) from the mother country, the French Revolution directly challenged the country's basic political and social structure, demanding an end to absolutism and aristocratic privilege in France. The French slogan, "**liberty, equality, fraternity** [brotherhood]", reflects the multiple goals of their revolution that literally shook French society to its core.

The Three Estates

French society before the Revolution of 1789 is often called the *Ancien Régime*, which consisted of three **estates**, or social classes.

- **The First Estate** – About 130,000 members of the Catholic clergy made up the First Estate. The church controlled about 10% of the land. The clergy were exempt from the *taille,* the chief tax; however, the church agreed to pay a contribution every five years to the state. Although their numbers were relatively small, the members of the First Estate were quite socially varied, with the lower clergy often identifying with the poor and the higher clergy usually supporting the nobility.

- **The Second Estate** – About 350,000 nobles were members of the Second Estate. They continued to hold many important positions in the government, the military, the law courts, and the higher church offices. They held about 30% of the land. Like the First Estate, members of the Second Estate were divided, with one group called the nobility of the robe holding offices of the government, and a second group – the nobility of the sword – claiming to be descended from the original medieval nobility. Both groups sought to expand their privileges at the expense of the king, and they, like the First Estate, were also exempt from the *taille.*

- **The Third Estate** – About 75-80% of the population belonged to the Third Estate, and by the late 18th century, they were vastly different in terms of occupation, level of education, and wealth. As a class, they owned about 35 to 40% of the land, but more than half the peasants had little or no land. For the most part, serfdom no longer existed, but peasants still had obligations to their local landlords that they deeply resented. Some members of the Third Estate were artisans, shopkeepers, and other wage earners in the cities. Like the peasants, they were disgruntled, but their concerns were the rising costs of food and other consumer goods, with no comparable rise in wages. About 8%, or 2.3 million members, of the Third Estate were the **bourgeoisie**, or middle class, who owned about 20-25% of the land. Their occupations were varied, including merchants, bankers, industrialists, doctors, lawyers, holders of public offices, and writers. The bourgeoisie were well-educated, and many were influenced by Enlightenment ideas that led them to criticize an old regime that treated them much the same as peasants and the urban poor, with few political rights that they thought they deserved.

Financial Problems

Financially, the American Revolution directly contributed to the events that led to the French Revolution. The French government was already in serious debt when they decided to help the Americans, and the military expense involved may well have pushed the financial situation into crisis. Years of war and the extravagant maintenance of the French court had increased the national debt to epic proportions. Although the French economy had grown over the course of the 18th

PERSPECTIVES:
"WHAT IS THE THIRD ESTATE?"
BY ABBÉ SIÉYÈS

As a clergyman from Chartres, Abbe Emmanuel-Joseph Siéyés was a member of the First Estate, yet he wrote a widely-distributed pamphlet called "What Is the Third Estate?" that summed up the grievances of the Third Estate. Written in January 1789, it boldly confronted the system of privilege of the Old Regime and challenged the authority of the king...In this document the French Revolution found its rallying point. The opening argument is excerpted below.

"1st. What is the third estate? Everything.
2nd. What has it been heretofore in the political order? Nothing.
3rd. What does it demand? To become something therein....

Who, then, would dare to say that the third estate has not within itself all that is necessary to constitute a complete nation? It is the strong and robust man whose one arm remains enchained. If the privileged order were abolished, the nation would not be something less but something more. Thus, what is the third estate? Everything; but an everything shackled and oppressed. What would it be without the privileged order? Everything; but an everything free and flourishing. Nothing can progress without it; everything would proceed infinitely better without the others... it is necessary, moreover, to prove that the nobility does not belong to the social organization at all; that, indeed, it may be a burden upon the nation, but that it would not know how to constitute a part thereof."

Reference: John Hall Stewart, *A Documentary Survey of the French Revolution* (New York: The Macmillan Company, 1951), pp. 44, 45.

century, periodic economic crises still occurred. Bad harvests in 1787 and 1788 resulted in food shortages and rising prices for food that angered the urban poor.

In 1787, **Louis XVI**'s controller-general, Charles Calonne, warned the king that France was facing outright bankruptcy if something wasn't done. He proposed a new tax, called the "territorial subvention," to be imposed on the yield of all landed property, without exemptions. Hoping to get support for the controversial tax, the king called the Assembly of Notables, a group of 150 influential men who were mainly but not exclusively from the aristocracy. Not only did the Assembly refuse to endorse the new tax, it denounced the lavish spending of the court and demanded that Louis convene the **Estates General** to consider the financial crisis. For many years the French kings had resisted calling the Estates General – a medieval assembly of nobility, church officials, and bourgeoisie – because doing so would question the absolute rule of the king. However, the need for tax reform was so great that Louis called the assembly to meet in the spring of 1789. He hoped to convince the assembly to support new and increased taxes to pay the bills for multiple wars and an extravagant royal life style, but the middle-class representatives drew strength from gathering in one place, and decided to demand that the Estates General become a real parliament that shared power with the king. Their decision was voiced in the **Tennis Court Oath**, signed when they were locked out of their meeting place and forced to move to an indoor tennis court. The bourgeoisie vowed to meet until they had produced a French constitution, and after gaining support from some of the nobles and clergymen, they succeeded in outmaneuvering Louis in their demands for political power. The Estates General was transformed, then, into a parliament called the **National Assembly**.

Popular Revolts

A series of disruptions over the summer of 1789 included a mob attack on a royal armory (**the Bastille**) that involved ordinary Parisians. When the army eventually fell, the Bastille became a popular symbol of triumph over despotism. Paris was lost in chaos, and the disruptions spread to the countryside, with peasant rebellions occurring throughout France from July 19 to August 3. A vast panic called the **Great Fear** spread across the country, with citizens forming militias and permanent committees to contain the violence. Peasants who resented new taxes and feudal dues rose against their landlords, and townspeople too felt the uneasiness. By October, a large group of women marched from Paris to the King's palace at Versailles, demanding that Louis and his wife, Marie Antoinette, pay attention to the fact that their children were starving.

A New Regime

By early August of 1789, the National Assembly acted to destroy the *Ancien Régime* when they voted to abolish the old estates, including the fiscal privileges of nobles, clergy, towns, and provinces. Like the Americans, the French wrote an Enlightenment-inspired declaration, but unlike the American Declaration of Independence, the **Declaration of the Rights of Man and the Citizens** was not intended to declare political independence, but rather to proclaim freedom of thought. Both documents affirmed the "natural rights" of citizens. The French also began writing a constitution for their new republic with the intention of providing a blueprint for a new political system that limited the power of the king and gave new authority to the National Assembly. Representatives to the National Assembly were selected by an indirect system of election that preserved power in the hands of the most affluent members of society. However, the conflict did not end there for the French, but instead spawned internal disagreements about the type of government they wished to establish.

Financial problems continued. Clerics rose to protest the imposition of the **Civil Constitution of the Clergy**, which secularized the Catholic Church and confiscated church lands for the government. The urban poor got no relief from escalating food prices, and peasants were angry because they still had to pay dues to the landlords. Despite these problems, most political leaders still supported the king until June 1791, when Louis XVI and his family tried to flee France. The escape failed, and they were brought back to Paris, where they remained heavily guarded, but the event helped to turn the revolution in a more radical direction.

A part of the king's escape plan was for Austrian forces to meet him on the other side of the French border. The Austrian king, Leopold II, was the brother of **Marie Antoinette**, Louis's wife, and he was growing increasingly wary of the progress of the French Revolution. After Louis and Marie were forced to return to captivity in Paris, Leopold and Frederick William II of Prussia invited other European

ORIGINAL DOCUMENT: THE DECLARATION OF THE RIGHTS OF MAN AND CITIZEN

Like the American Declaration of Independence, the French Declaration in 1789 was based on the ideology of John Locke. Thomas Jefferson, who was the U.S. ambassador to France, advised the French as they constructed their document, as is evident from the following excerpts from the Declaration of the Rights of Man and Citizen.

"First Article: Men are born and remain free and equal in rights. Social distinctions may be based only on common utility.
Article 2. The goal of every political association is the preservation of the natural and inalienable rights of man. These rights are liberty, property, security, and resistence to oppression.
Article 3. The principle of all sovereignty resides essentially in the nation. No body and no individual can exercise authority that does not flow directly from the nation.
Article 4. Liberty consists in the freedom to do anything that does not harm another. The exercise of natural rights of each man thus has no limits except those that assure other members of society their enjoyment of the same rights. These limits may be determined only by law..."

monarchs to use force to reestablish monarchical authority in France. In reply, the National Assembly declared war on Austria in April 1792. The war went badly for France, food shortages continued, and hostility toward the king increased. Radical Parisian political groups, organizing themselves into "communes," attacked the royal palace and the National Assembly in August 1792, seized the king, and forced the assembly to suspend the monarchy and call for a national convention chosen on the basis of universal male suffrage that gave every adult man a vote. The new **Paris Commune** that staged the election was composed of people who called themselves the *sans-culottes,* literally "without short pants," indicating that they were not aristocrats who wore stockings and pants to the knee, but instead were ordinary people who wore long pants.

The Radical Revolution

In September 1792, the newly elected **National Convention** first met, and it began to draft a new constitution. Acting as the sovereign ruling body of France, the representatives were generally much more distrustful of the king than the previous government had been. On one side, the radical **Jacobins** stressed the Enlightenment value of equality, and on the other were the **Girondins** who were more interested in liberty, especially in terms of laissez-faire economics. In between were centrists committed to the revolution, but uncertain which path to follow. When the Jacobins won the debate, the decision was made to execute the king in January 1793, completing the destruction of the old regime. By this time, most of Europe – Austria, Prussia, Spain, Portugal, Britain, the Dutch Republic, and Russia – had aligned against France and were poised to attack. In reaction, the Convention gave broad powers to an executive committee of twelve called the **Committee of Public Safety,** headed by **Maximilien Robespierre**, the leader of the Jacobins.

After the king's execution, many others who were suspected of disloyalty to the new regime went to the guillotine, a device originally invented to provide more humane executions. This time of mass executions in 1793 and 1794 was known as the **Reign of Terror**, which ended only with the guillotining of Robespierre himself. Revolutionary courts were organized to protect the country from internal enemies, and in the course of less than a year, 16,000 people were officially guillotined, but the truer number was probably closer to 50,000. Many others fled the country as the Terror spread, while others were executed by cannon fire and drowning.

In its attempt to create a completely new society, the National Convention sought to remove all vestiges of religion from France, instituting a new calendar numbering from 1792 rather than the birth of Jesus, removing the word *saint* from street names, closing churches, and encouraging priests to marry. All titles were eliminated, and everyone – male and female – was addressed as "Citizen". Robespierre became obsessed with "purifying" France of all its old abuses, and he began to

COMPARISON:
EDMUND BURKE AND WILLIAM WORDSWORTH
ON THE FRENCH REVOLUTION

When the French Revolution began in 1789, people in other countries of Europe responded in different ways. Two contrasting reactions were those of Edmund Burke, an English politician, and William Wordsworth, an English poet. Wordsworth's view, however, changed over time.

Burke commented, "Can I now congratulate the same nation [France] upon its freedom? Is it because liberty in the abstract may be classed amongst the blessings of mankind, that I am seriously to felicitate a madman, who has escaped from the protecting restraint and wholesome darkness of his cell, on his restoration to the enjoyment of light and liberty? Am I to congratulate an highwayman and murderer, who has broke prison, upon the recovery of his natural rights?..."

In contrast, upon hearing about the revolution's outbreak, Wordsworth wrote,
"Bliss was it in that dawn to be alive,
But to be young was very heaven!"

A few years later, Wordsworth's view changed, reflecting the growing horror of people outside France as the events of the Terror unfolded. He wrote:
"Friends, enemies, of all parties, ages, ranks,
Head after head, and never heads enough
For those that bade them fall."

accuse other political leaders – including Danton, the leader of the Paris Commune – of disloyalty. Finally the accusations were made against Robespierre by the National Convention in a turnabout known as the **Thermidorian reaction**, and he was guillotined on July 28, 1794. The Terror then began to abate, as France tried to reorganize its government while facing the hostility of all the rest of Europe.

The Directory

As the Reign of Terror came to an end with Robespierre's death in mid-1794, France was in chaos. Thousands had been executed, and even more people had fled the country to seek refuge in Britain, other areas of Europe, or the Americas. To make matters worse, the French were at war with Austria, where Queen Marie Antoinette's brother ruled, and other monarchs in Europe were beginning to ally against the upstart republic. The extremes of the radical revolution ended, and the more moderate Thermidorians drafted a new constitution (1795) that proclaimed a general amnesty, and created a constitutional republic, known as the **Directory**, headed by a five-man executive meant to prevent the rise of a dictator. This government, though still repressive, was mild compared to the rule during the Terror, and it allowed the full range of political attitudes to be heard. Groups that emerged included:

- **Ultraroyalists** – As the name implies, this group hoped to overthrow the Republic altogether and bring back the king. Some were émigrés exiled from France, and some worked with the exiled Bourbon princes and with British secret agents.

- **Moderate Royalists** – This group supported a monarchy, but they hoped to win control of the Republic's political institutions and to create a new government lawfully. Like the Ultraroyalists, they hoped to rid France completely of Jacobinism.

- **Neo-Jacobins** – This group did not advocate a return to the Terror or the use of force to regain power, but they supported the moderate Republic of 1795 and sympathized with the egalitarian spirit behind the radical experiment. They supported free public education and progressive taxation that required the rich to pay more than the poor. Neo-Jacobins promoted grassroots activism through local organizations and activities.

- **Babeuvists** – This most radical group was named for and led by François-Noël Babeuf, who saw the radical phase of the revolution as a prelude to a final revolution in the name of the masses. The Babeuvists believed that a small revolutionary vanguard would carry out the final revolution, and they considered the Republic of 1795 to be simply a new form of oppression by the elites.

Conflicts among these groups left the government unable to find a definitive path, and the Directory increasingly relied on the military to maintain its power. This led to a coup d'état in 1799 by the military.

Women and the Revolution

Women such as Mary Wollstonecraft, a feminist writer of the day, argued that those who believed in Enlightenment values should logically recognize equal rights for women. Since the French Revolution valued equality as well as liberty, it seemed to many women that a new era had opened for them. Indeed, they were actively engaged in local conflicts over the Civil Constitution of the Clergy, and in the towns, they agitated for food prices and goaded the national guards into action. Most famously, in October 1789 Parisian women led a mass demonstration to Versailles that forcibly returned the king and queen to Paris and ensured that the king would sign the Declaration of Rights. Women often watched from the

EXAMINING THE EVIDENCE:
THE ORIGINS OF THE POLITICAL TERMS
"LEFT" AND "RIGHT"

The political terms "left" and "right" originated during the era of the French Revolution when it became the custom for deputies in the assemblies to sit according to their political beliefs. The most conservative deputies took their places to the right of the speaker's rostrum, in the horseshoe-shaped banks of seats, while the others ranged themselves according to their political inclinations in the center or to the left of the speaker. A shift in the composition of successive assemblies changed as the French Revolution progressed. From 1789 to 1794 more and more conservative deputies of one assembly failed to be reelected to the next, so those in the center moved to the right to take their places. At the same time, the leftist members of one legislative body were forced to move to the center in the next to make room for newly elected deputies of even more radical views. After the Terror ended in 1794, the trend was reversed and a movement in the opposite direction set in as more conservative deputies began to be elected again. Despite the changing meaning of "left" and "right," the terms were widely used, and today are commonly used to describe political leanings in many countries.

galleries of the Assembly and later the National Convention, and they formed auxiliaries to local Jacobin clubs, where they debated political issues and shared readings of revolutionary tracts. Some legislation advanced the civil status of women. For example, laws created a more equitable family life by restricting paternal power over children. Women's property rights were acknowledged, and an unprecedented number of universal and free primary schools were opened to girls as well as boys.

On the other hand, the Revolution did not change the status of women as much as might be expected. Although a "Declaration of the Rights of Women," penned by playwright **Olympe de Gouges**, advocated women's suffrage, women did not gain voting privileges. Rousseau's influence almost certainly was at work here, with his notion that men and women should occupy separate spheres, with women playing supporting roles. Most political leaders believed that women were too emotional to participate equally in politics, and they were barred from holding public office.

Nations and Nationalism

Despite the contrasting early outcomes of the American and French Revolutions, both played a role in the creation of a new type of political organization based on the concept of a **nation**, a group of people bound together by a common political identity. Common identities may be seen in earlier civilizations, such as the Chinese identity as "Han," or religious identities based on Islam, Christianity, or Hinduism. European rulers earlier in the 18th century had paved the way for the movement, but they had never questioned the central control of the monarchy. For example, Frederick the Great envisioned the bureaucracy and the army as institutions that would give the state continuity after a monarchical succession took place. He saw himself as the "servant of the state," but he never doubted that the state operated according to his will. What was newly created by the revolutions of the late 18th century was the separation of political identity from loyalty to a king or ruler, replacing it with constitutions and laws that provided the necessary political unity. Ideally, political boundaries were drawn around cultural identities, so that people with a common language and similar customs – such as the Americans or the French – would each be united under their own government. One result of this process of creating nations was **nationalism**, or the sense of belonging and identity that distinguishes one nation from another. Nationalism has often been translated as patriotism, or the resulting pride and loyalty that individuals feel toward their nations. This transition from "Long Live the King!" to America's "My Country 'Tis of Thee!" and the rousing French anthem, "La Marseillaise," was an important "marker event" that eventually produced a world organized into competing nation-states, each with its own sense of righteousness and destiny.

THE AGE OF NAPOLEON

From the anarchy created by the Revolution and its aftermath, a young army officer saw an opportunity he never would have had under the old regime, and he took it upon himself to save France. In promoting himself, he played a pivotal role in the creation of the new political order, the world of nation-states. This man, **Napoleon Bonaparte**, was destined to be one of the most famous men in history, partly because of the charisma of his leadership, but also because he inspired French nationalism that lived on long after he was gone. Napoleon also is one of the most controversial of all historical figures because despite his emphasis on the nation-state, he eventually became a virtual dictator of France with few checks on his power.

The Rise of Napoleon

Napoleon, who grew up in Corsica (an island off the southern coast of France), would never have been more than a middle-rank officer had the revolution not come along, because only French nobility could hold high military positions in pre-revolutionary days. Under the new egalitarian regime, he made a name for

THEMATIC LEARNING OBJECTIVE: OBJECTIVE KNOWLEDGE AND SUBJECTIVE VISIONS: "LA MARSEILLAISE"

Amour sacré de la Patrie,	Sacred patriotic love,
Conduis, soutiens nos bras vengeurs	Lead and support our avenging arms
Liberté, Liberté chérie,	Liberty, cherished liberty,
Combats avec tes défenseurs ! (bis)	Fight back with your defenders! (repeat)
Sous nos drapeaux que la victoire	Under our flags, let victory
Accoure à tes mâles accents,	Hurry to your manly tone,
Que nos ennemis expirants	So that our enemies, in their last breath,
Voient ton triomphe et notre gloire !	See your triumph and our glory!
Aux armes, citoyens !	To arms, citizens!
Formez vos bataillons !	Form your battalions!
Marchons, marchons !	March, march!
Qu'un sang impur	May tainted blood
Abreuve nos sillons !	Water our fields!
Aux armes, citoyens !	To arms, citizens!
Formons nos bataillons !	Let us form our battalions!
Marchons, marchons !	Let us march, let us march!
Qu'un sang impur	May tainted blood
Abreuve nos sillons !	Water our fields!

The French National Anthem. Above are the last verse and the chorus of the official French National Anthem, "La Marseillaise," written during the French Revolution. It reflects the spirit of nationalism that existed by the late 18th century and still thrives in France today. The complete song has many verses that have changed over time, but have shared one continuity – the necessity of bloodshed in support of one's country. A less gory version of the anthem is taught to young children.

himself by successfully leading the army against Austria, invading Egypt to gain access to the Red Sea, and threatening British control of the sea route to India. A weak five-person Directory governed France after Robespierre's death, and when Austria, Britain, and Russia formed an alliance in 1799 to attack France, Napoleon took the opportunity to stage a coup d'état, and he named himself the "consul" (as in Ancient Rome) who controlled the entire executive authority of government. He also dominated the legislature, appointed members of the bureaucracy, led the army, and conducted foreign affairs. In 1802, Napoleon was made consul for life and in 1804 returned France to monarchy when he crowned himself emperor Napoleon I. As a result, France had come full circle – from king to radical republic to emperor – all in the fifteen years between 1789 and 1804.

Napoleon's Rule

Once Napoleon gained control of France, military victories made him a popular leader, and he stabilized the country by rolling back some of the most radical measures passed during the Reign of Terror. For example, the Constitution of the Clergy had seized property from the Catholic Church, and Robespierre had even tried to eliminate the Church as an anti-egalitarian force in the republic. Napoleon retained church property for the state, but he recognized Roman Catholicism as the preferred religion of France, and he agreed to pay the clergy as employees of the state. He reduced the National Assembly to a rubber stamp, but he confirmed religious freedom, and guaranteed equal rights for men, though not for women, in new laws organized as the **Napoleonic Code**. Under this legal system, however, laws were erased that had made divorce an easy process for both husbands and wives, restricted the rights of fathers over their children, and allowed all children to inherit property equally. Thus Napoleon's Civil Code restored the control of fathers over their families, and divorce, though still allowed, was made more difficult for women to obtain. Napoleon also strengthened the French bureaucracy, and filled government and military positions with competent people, whom he rewarded by naming them nobles in his new merit-based aristocracy. He carefully chose aspects of the Revolution that he agreed with – such as advancement based on merit – but denied those that he disagreed with, such as freedom of the press and an egalitarian social structure.

Meanwhile, Napoleon remained a hero to many of his subjects because he continued to be a successful military general. He began aggressively attacking countries around him, and by 1810, he was at war with every other major power on the continent. As he conquered those around him, he tried to destroy the old order, and he stripped nobility and clergy everywhere of their special privileges. He decreed equality of opportunity, making offices open to talent, and establishing equality before the law and religious toleration. At its height, this new French Empire directly held or controlled as dependent states most of western Europe. One testament to Napoleon's power was the elimination of the Holy Roman Empire, a configuration that was never to appear again on a map of Europe. However, Napoleon's ambition was ultimately thwarted. His drive to power was halted in 1812 when he unsuccessfully attacked Russia, where most of his men died from the cold, not from Russian bullets. The tactical blunder of marching an army toward Moscow so far from his supply lines resulted in tremendous loss of military personnel. On the opposite side of Europe, he also met stiff resistance from Spanish rebels. When he attempted to destroy the British economy by establishing the **Continental System**, which forbade Britain to trade with France and its dependencies, his efforts failed. Alarmed by Napoleon's bold moves, the British led the alliance against Napoleon that captured Paris in 1814, and finally defeated him in 1815 at the Battle of **Waterloo** (present day Belgium). He was banished first to

Elba, an island in the Mediterranean Sea, and then to St. Helena, a small island in the Atlantic, where he died several years later.

Ironically, the nationalism that had allowed Napoleon to rise to power in France was also a factor in his defeat. He had been able to recruit a vast army because many believed they were fighting for the glory of France, a sentiment that he reinforced with a charismatic leadership style that inspired people to fight for him. Yet as the army grew more and more formidable, those that Napoleon conquered were awed by the power of French nationalism, arousing in them their own patriotism in opposition to France. For example, when Napoleon placed his brother on the Spanish throne, a nationalist movement grew in protest in Spain that kept French forces stymied there for years.

The Haitian Revolution, 1789-1804

In 1789 the French colony of Saint-Domingue was one of the wealthiest in the Americas, with its large plantations producing sugar, cotton, indigo, and coffee. However, the turmoil in France destabilized the established order as French

Napoleon's Empire at its Height. By 1812 France controlled Europe to the borders of Russia, either through conquest, agreement, or alliance. Napoleon's decision to attack Russia was a tactical error that stopped the expansion of France and proved to be the turning point for his decline.

colonists interpreted Enlightenment values in different ways. For the large plantation owners, revolutionary trends were an opportunity to gain home rule and greater economic freedom, or perhaps even independence, as the United States had achieved. However, another group called **gens de couleur** – mixed-race small planters and urban merchants – sought political equality with whites. They did not seek freedom for slaves because many owned slaves themselves, but they wanted to end the discrimination that they believed kept them from the prosperity that the large plantation owners enjoyed. The tension between the aristocratic planters and the gens de couleur was heightened by the message from France that all slavery was illegitimate. When a leader of the gens de coulcur returned from a mission to France, he was murdered by the planters, setting off open warfare between the two groups.

As slave owners fought among themselves, slaves saw their opportunity to rebel, and under the leadership of **Francois Dominique Toussaint L'Ouverture**, a former domestic slave, the rebellion spread throughout the colony. Plantations were destroyed, crops were burned, and slave owners were killed. Toussaint was a talented leader who organized the rebellion and built a strong, disciplined army. By 1797 his forces controlled most of Saint-Domingue, and in 1801, he produced a constitution that granted citizenship and equality to all residents of the colony, although he did not declare independence from France. These events occurred at the same time that Napoleon reached the height of his power, and he responded by sending French troops to restore order in Saint Domingue. Toussaint was arrested and sent to France where he died in prison. Despite the loss of their leader, the slave forces gained the upper hand in their struggles against the French soldiers, who died in large numbers when yellow fever swept through their ranks. In 1804, Toussaint's successors declared independence, making Haiti the first independent black republic in the Western Hemisphere. Unfortunately, independence did not restore stability: the economy was destroyed, years of disorder corrupted public administrators, and violence and economic problems continued in Haiti throughout the 19th and 20th centuries.

The Aftermath

Diplomats from major European powers met at the **Congress of Vienna** to decide what to do with France once Napoleon was exiled. The decisions made there put in place a **balance of power** in Europe that stabilized the continent for more than fifty years. France lost most of its new territories, and the countries around it were made stronger with a tactic called "the encirclement of France": the Austrian Netherlands was united with the Dutch Republic to form a single Kingdom of the Netherlands, previously disparate German states were united to form the German Confederation, and Switzerland was recognized as an independent and neutral nation. The French monarchy was also restored, with Louis XVI's brother crowned as Louis XVIII. In an effort to balance power, Britain gained new colonial territories and Russia gained substantial holdings in Poland.

If we compare the results of the two revolutions – American and French – as of 1815, the contrast appears to be stark. By 1815, America again had defended itself successfully against Britain in 1812, and had settled in with its new form of government to concentrate on a major expansion west. France had slipped into chaos, turned to a military general who became emperor, and finally returned to a monarchy. Indeed, it seemed as if the experiment had failed in France. However, the new nationalism sparked by the revolution and then by Napoleon did not die, but instead lived on as a strong movement in France to restore the republic. The republicans battled the supporters of the king, and the country teetered back and forth between republican government and monarchy, with the last king forced to flee the country in 1848. The republic that followed was taken over by Napoleon's

COMPARISON:
ALEXIS DE TOCQUEVILLE
ON DEMOCRACY IN AMERICA AND FRANCE

In the 1830s a young Frenchman named Alexis de Tocqueville became quite interested in the question of why a democratic republic took root in America much more readily than it did in France. In his classic book, *Democracy in America,* which reflected a great deal of respect for the young United States and its people, Tocqueville identified several reasons:

1) Abundant and fertile soil – America's vast, open lands created many opportunities for people to acquire property and make a living. Success was possible by just moving west. No such frontiers existed in France.
2) No feudal aristocracy – In contrast to France, no feudal aristocracy monopolized the land, or imposed taxes or legal restraints on commoners.
3) Independent agriculture – The nation was populated with small, independent farmers, unlike the traditional European arrangement of landless peasants with no control over their land.
4) Individualism – Tocqueville identified "moral and intellectual characteristics" of Americans that supported a democratic republic. He saw the value of individualism as a central characteristic – the belief that individuals are responsible for their own actions and well-being. Individualism of course was a key value of the Enlightenment, but in France it had to battle with values from the Old Regime.

nephew, Napoleon III, who restored the empire for about 20 years, until France suffered a humiliating military defeat by Prussia. A shaky republic emerged in 1871, but even by the end of this era – 1914 – the French were still suffering the effects of radical shifts back and forth between very different styles of government.

Despite the problematic effects of revolution on French political stability, the impact of the two revolutions reverberated far beyond the United States and France. In Latin America, independence movements against Spain and Portugal succeeded, and in Europe, the new political ideologies clashed with old to inspire revolutions in Greece and the Balkans. The importance of the revolutions was later summed up by Ralph Waldo Emerson when in 1837 he described the first fighting at Lexington that started the American Revolution in 1775 as the "shot heard round the world".

CONCEPTS AND IDENTIFICATIONS

Ancient Régime
balance of power
Bastille
bourgeoisie
Catherine the Great
Civil Constitution of the Clergy
Committee of Public Safety
Congress of Vienna
Continental System
Declaration of Independence (American)
Declaration of the Rights of Man and the Citizen
Directory
Dutch Patriots
Estates-General
federalist system
Frederick II (the Great)
George III
Girondins
Gouges, Olympe de
Great Fear
Jacobins
Joseph II of Austria
"left" and "right"
"liberty, equality, fraternity"
Louis XVI
Maria Theresa
Marie Antoinette
Napoleon Bonaparte

Napoleonic Code
nation, nationalism
National Assembly
National Convention
Paris Commune
Partition of Poland
Political Testament
Pugachev, Emelian
Reign of Terror
Robespierre, Maximilien
sans-culottes
Seven Years' War
Stanislaw August Poniatowski
taille
Tennis Court Oath
Thermidorian reaction
the Three Estates
Walpole, Robert
War of the Austrian Succession
Washington, George
Waterloo
William Pitt the Elder
William Pitt the Younger

UNIT TWO QUESTIONS

MULTIPLE-CHOICE QUESTIONS:

(Questions 1-3 are based on the following chart):

IMPORTS OF PRECIOUS METALS TO SPAIN FROM
THE NEW WORLD, 1591-1660

The value of precious metals in the chart below is calculated in Spanish ducats.

1591-1600	85,536,000
1611-1620	65,568,000
1631-1640	40,110,000
1651-1660	12, 785,000

Adapted from J.H. Elliott, *Imperial Spain, 1469-1716.* Edward Arnold, Hodder Neadling PLC Group, 1964, p. 175.

1. Which of the following was an important reason why imports of precious metals to Spain declined between 1591 and 1660?

   (A) Mines in the New World failed as few new supplies of silver and gold were found.
   (B) The Spanish government turned its attention to trade with Asia.
   (C) The English and French took control of New World silver mines.
   (D) Demand for silver and gold decreased significantly during the time period.

2. The decline of Spanish prosperity during the 17th century allowed the rise in power of

   (A) Austria and Russia
   (B) England and France
   (C) Portugal and the Holy Roman Empire
   (D) Sweden and Denmark

3. One consequence of the decline of imports of precious metals to Spain between 1591 and 1660 was

(A) the defeat of the Spanish Armada
(B) a decline in trade between Spain and England
(C) the unification of Spain under one monarch
(D) Spanish recognition of Dutch independence

(Questions 4-6 are based on the following quote):

I was immediately handled and tossed up to see if I were sound by some of the crew, and I was persuaded that I had gotten into a world of bad spirits and that they were going to kill me. Their complexions too differing so much from ours, their long hair and the language they spoke (which was very different from any I had every heard) united to confirm me in this belief...When I looked round the ship too and saw a large furnace of copper boiling and a multitude of black people of every description chained together, every one of their countenances expressing dejection and sorrow, I no longer doubted of my fate.

Olaudah Equiano

4. The passage describes an 18th-century journey made on the

(A) first leg of the Atlantic Circuit
(B) route from the Caribbean to the southern states of the English colonies
(C) Middle Passage
(D) route of the Spanish galleons

5. Which of the following was the most common destination for ships such as the one described in the passage?

(A) Brazil
(B) Cuba
(C) southern coastal states of pre-1776 North America
(D) Dutch West Indies

6. Most of the people on the ships were destined to work on (in)

(A) cotton plantations
(B) sugar plantations
(C) Spanish silver mines
(D) small farms in Spanish America

(Questions 7 and 8 are based on the following excerpt):

> "Being the third son of the family, and not bred to any trade, my head began to be filled very early with rambling thoughts. My father, who was very ancient, had given me a competent share of learning, as far as house-education and a country free school generally goes, and designed me for the law, but I would be satisfied with nothing but going to sea; and my inclination to this led me so strongly against the will, nay, the commands, of my father, and against all the entreaties and persuasions of my mother and other friends, that there seemed to be something fatal in that propension of nature tending directly to the life of misery which was to befall me....My father, a wise and grave man, gave me serious and excellent counsel against what he foresaw was my design...But being one day at Hull, where I went casually, and without any purpose of making an elopement that time; but I say, being there, and one of my companions being going by sea to London, in his father's ship....I consulted neither father nor mother any more, or so much as sent them word of it... and in an ill hour, God knows, on the first of September, 1651, I went on board a ship bound for London."

> *Robinson Crusoe*
> Daniel Defoe

7. Future prospects for the young man described in the excerpt were limited by the English practice of

(A) enclosure
(B) tenant farming
(C) primogeniture
(D) mercantilism

8. The excerpt is taken from a new form of literature new in the 18th century called the

(A) essay
(B) novel
(C) cantata
(D) journal

(Questions 9-11 are based on the following quote):

> "And, in truth, invaluable privileges…they are in comparison with the usages of most other nations of the world! To be secure on lying down that you   shall rise in possession of the same property with which you retired to rest; that you shall not be torn from the arms of your wife, and from your children, in the dead of night, to be thrown into a dungeon, or buried in exile in a desert; that, when rising from the bed of sleep, you will have the power of publishing all your thoughts…"

9. The quote above from Voltaire's *Philosophical Dictionary* describes rights and privileges in

(A) France
(B) the United States
(C) England
(D) the Netherlands

10. The passage most directly reflects values inspired by the

(A) Renaissance
(B) Scientific Revolution
(C) Protestant Reformation
(D) Enlightenment

11. Voltaire's praise of the country identified in #9 was by implication a direct criticism of

(A) Spain
(B) France
(C) Russia
(D) Austria

(Questions 12-14 are based on the following map):

Europe: 1754-1763

12. The map above illustrates the fighting in the

   (A) Napoleonic Wars
   (B) Seven Years' War
   (C) War of the Austrian Succession
   (D) The War of Spanish Succession

13. Which of the following was most responsible for fanning a conflagration into the major international war referred to in #11?

   (A) the ambitions of French military leaders
   (B) demands for democratic governments in western Europe
   (C) the attempts by Russia to gain territory to the east and south
   (D) the growing importance of international trade

14. The war referred to in #11 resulted in important political and economic changes in

(A) Prussia's borders
(B) Spain's style of government
(C) North America
(D) the relationship between Russia and Sweden

SHORT-ANSWER QUESTION (12 minutes):

**CHANGE OVER TIME:
ESTIMATES OF POPULATION
GROWTH DURING THE 18TH
CENTURY**

Since the first censuses were not taken until the early 19th century, all population figures are only estimates.

	Beginning of the 18th Century	End of the 18th Century
Europe Overall	100-120 million	180-190 million
Spain	7.5 million	11.5 million
England and Wales	5-6 million	9-10 million
France	19 million (1715)	26 million (1789)
Russia	19 million (1722)	29 million (1766)
Italy	11.5 million	17.5 million

The chart above shows estimates of population growth in Europe during the 18th century.

(A) Briefly explain ONE demographic pattern in 18th century Europe reflected in the chart.

(B) Identify and explain TWO causes of the pattern you identified in part (A).

FREE-RESPONSE DOCUMENT-BASED QUESTION (Suggested reading time – 15 minutes; suggested writing time – 40 minutes)

Write an essay that:

- Provides an appropriate, explicitly stated thesis that directly addresses all parts of the question.

- Supports the thesis with evidence from all or all but one of the documents and your outside knowledge of European history

- Analyzes a majority of the documents in terms of intended audience, point of view, purpose, argument strength, and/or social context

- Places the argument in broader regional, national, or global contexts.

Analyze European attitudes toward hereditary monarchs and identify changes that occurred in these attitudes during the period from 1648 to 1815.

Document 1

They that are subjects to a monarch, cannot without his leave cast off Monarchy, and return to the confusion of a disunited Multitude; nor transferre their Person from him that beareth it, to another Man, or other Assembly of men: for they…are bound, every man to every man, to [acknowledge]…that he that already is their Soveraigne, shall do, and judge fit to be done; so that [those who do not obey] break their Covenant made to that man, which is injustice.

> Thomas Hobbes,
> English philosopher
> *Levianthan*
> 1651

Document 2

The royal power is absolute....The prince need render account of his acts to no one....'I counsel thee to keep the king's commandment, and that in regard of the oath of God...Where the word of a king is, there is power; and who may say unto him, What doest thou?' [Eccles. 8:2-5]. Without this absolute authority the king could neither do good nor repress evil. It is necessary that his power be such that no one can hope to escape him, and finally, the only protection of individuals against the public authority should be their innocence. This confirms the teaching of St. Paul: 'Wilt thou then not be afraid of the power? Do that which is good.' [Rom. 13:3].

> Bishop Jacques-Benigne Bossuet,
> Court preacher and tutor to Louis XI
> Late 17th century

Document 3

The Victory which the King of Poland hath obtained over the Infidels, is so great and so compleat that past Ages can scarce parallel the fame; and perhaps future Ages will never see any thing like it.... we see the King of Poland, who goes out of his Kingdom, with part of his Army, and hastens to succour his...Allies,...to march against the enemies of the Christian religion willing to act in Person on this Occasion, as a true Buckler of Religion.

> Polish manuscript describing
> King John III Sobieski
> 1683

Document 4

That the pretended power of suspending of laws or the execution of laws by regal authority without consent of parliament is illegal.

That the pretended power of dispensing with laws or the execution of laws by regal authority as it hath been assumed and exercised of late is illegal....

That the raising or keeping a standing army within the kingdom in time of peace unless it be with consent of parliament is against the law.

English Declaration of Rights
1688

Document 5

For he that thinks absolute power purifies men's blood, and corrects the baseness of human nature, need read but the history of this or any other age, to be convinced of the contrary. He that would have been so insolent and injurious in the woods of America, would not probably be much better in a throne; where perhaps learning and religion shall be found out to justify all that he shall do to his subjects and the sword presently silence all those that dare question it...

John Locke
English philosopher
Second Treatise of Government
1689

Document 6

Political liberty is to be found only in moderate governments; and even in these it is not always found. It is there only when there is no abuse of power. But constant experience shows us that every man invested with power is apt to abuse it, and to carry his authority as far as it will go...When the legislative and executive powers are united in the same person, or in the same body of magistrates, there can be no liberty: because apprehensions may arise, lest the same monarch or senate should enact tyrannical laws, to execute them in a tyrannical manner.

Baron de Montesquieu
The Spirit of Laws
1748

Document 7

A well conducted government must have an underlying concept so well integrated that it could be likened to a system of philosophy. All actions taken must be well reasoned, and all financial, political and military matters must flow towards one goal: which is the strengthening of the state and the furthering of its power. However, such a system can flow but from a single brain, and this must be that of the sovereign. Laziness, hedonism and imbecility, these are the causes which restrain princes in working at the noble task of bringing happiness to their subjects...a sovereign is not elevated to his high position, supreme power has not been confined to him in order that he may live in lazy luxury, enriching himself by the labor of the people, being happy while everyone else suffers. The sovereign is the first servant of the state. He is well paid in order that he may sustain the dignity of his office, but one demands that he work efficiently for the good of the state, and that he, at the very least, pay personal attention to the most important problems....

Frederick the Great of Prussia
Political Testament
1768

Document 8

Upon entering the Assembly hall, I was greatly surprised to find the King, the Queen, the Prince, the King's oldest sister, Madame Elisabeth, and others [of the royal entourage] all very carefully dressed, with heads lowered like wet hens; they had all taken refuge in the Legislative Assembly to seek there the safety which could no longer be found in the palace. The cannoneers, having been ordered to do their duty if the people were to force its way into the palace, had instead simply unloaded their cannon; knowing this, the King's closest advisers had advised him to flee the palace and come amongst the nation's representatives.

Account of the attack on the Tuileries
(Louis XVI's Palace in Paris)
1792

LONG-ESSAY QUESTION (35 minutes):

Compare the roles that the Glorious Revolution and French Revolution had in the emergence of representative government as an alternative to absolutism.

UNIT 3:
A CENTURY OF CHANGE
1815-1914

The period from 1815 to 1914 began and ended with two important "marker events" – the Congress of Vienna in 1815 and World War I in 1914. During the century in between, Europe experienced important political, economic, social, demographic, and cultural changes, sometimes by upheaval, but more often by gradual or incremental reform.

From 1789 to 1815, Europe was disrupted by revolution and war, and so the peace that came after the settlement at the Congress of Vienna in 1815 was a welcome change for most people. However, the tensions that produced the upheavals continued to shape the unfolding events of the 19th century, as monarchs struggled to maintain control of their regimes and aristocrats tried to preserve traditional privileges. The questions that had been raised about how power should be organized, what institutions should direct society, and who should participate in policymaking did not go away. Different ideologies suggested different solutions to these questions, and the threat of revolution always remained.

Despite the difficulty of maintaining international stability in this age of nationalism and revolution, European countries managed to stay out of all-consuming war throughout the 19th century. The Crimean War did occur at mid-century, and many countries experienced internal revolutions that, for the most part, were unsuccessful. Throughout Europe, the memory of the Napoleonic Wars supported the principle of the balance of power among nations until late in the century, when imperialistic ambitions stirred up old rivalries and led to the formation of alliances that clashed in the buildup to World War I in 1914.

Economic changes were also important in the 19th century, as the Industrial Revolution spread through many parts of Europe, greatly impacting everyday life and social structures already challenged during the previous century. Populations grew, and people moved to the cities to work in new industries, putting urban areas under pressure and creating new social problems. Industrialization increased inequalities in the distribution of wealth, and great divisions grew between rich and poor people, as well as between industrialized and non-industrialized nations.

The varying reactions to the problems of industrialization fed the rich mix of ideologies that were already reacting to political questions. Even the Enlightenment-inspired respect for reason and order was questioned, as new movements that emphasized romanticism and cultural relativity vied for acceptance among educated Europeans.

THE BIG PICTURE:
1815-1914

The "chunk" of European history from 1815 to 1914 may be distinguished from other periods in these ways:

1) The Industrial Revolution spread from Britain to the Continent, and its path was determined by factors that either encouraged or discouraged it. The growth of industry was fostered by assistance from states, solidifying a political and economic partnership.
2) Everyday life changed as populations grew, and many people moved to urban areas where the nature of work changed significantly.
3) European countries struggled to maintain international stability in an age of nationalism and revolution, and by the second half of the century, a new type of conservative ruler emerged to lead the nation states.
4) A range of ideologies emerged to address economic and political change, including liberalism, conservatism, and socialism. Intensification of nationalism led to Pan-Slavism, Pan-Germanism, and Hellenism, as well as to a sharp competitiveness among nation-states.
5) European global interests spread as technological innovatons and industrial demands grew, and a new imperialism became an extension of earlier European colonization patterns. These global interests interacted with nationalistic rivalries to create the tension that eventually led to World War I.
6) The worldview of educated Europeans changed, as the objectivity prized by Enlightenment thinkers was challenged by more subjective intellectual and cultural movements, such as romanticism. Romanticism encouraged cultural experimentation that resulted in new aesthetic movements, such as realism, impressionism, and cubism. In science, acceptance of Newton's view of an ordered universe was challenged by Einstein's theory of relativity, and Darwin's new analysis of the nature of humans stirred \ controversy.

CHAPTER 13:
THE SPREAD OF THE
INDUSTRIAL REVOLUTION
AND ITS IMPACT ON SOCIETY

The spread of the Industrial Revolution during the 19th century transformed many parts of Europe from a traditional, labor-intensive economy based on farming and handicrafts to a more capital-intensive economy based on manufacturing by machines, specialized labor, and industrial factories. Although the Industrial Revolution took decades to spread, it fundamentally changed Europeans, their society, and their relationships to other people. As people moved to cities to work for factories, the traditional bonds of rural community life were broken and replaced by impersonal coexistence with others in tightly compressed spaces. By the late 19th century, higher levels of productivity led to a worldwide search for new consumers and sources of raw materials. This in turn encouraged a revolution in transportation that made international travel much easier. The growth of an urban middle class and a huge industrial working class substantially changed traditional social relationships.

During the late 1700s and early 1800s, industrialization took place primarily in Britain, but by the mid-1800s, it had spread to France, Germany, Belgium, and the United States. By then, the continent had settled down after the disruptions of the French Revolution and the Napoleonic wars, which had done away with many previous trade barriers between countries. Industrialization on the continent first appeared in Belgium, which had rich coal deposits to fuel machinery for new glass, iron, and textile factories. From Belgium, an industrial belt developed that followed coalfields that stretched from northern France and the Netherlands, through Germany and reaching Poland by the 1870s. By 1830, French businesses were adopting the new mechanized production methods, and industry continued to grow during the 19th century as railroads were built across the country. Germany developed industry later, partly because of political instability caused by competing German states. Once Germany united as a country in 1871, rapid industrialization followed.

THE SPREAD OF THE INDUSTRIAL REVOLUTION BY 1850

By the early 1800s, the Industrial Revolution was well established in Britain, where natural resources, good supplies of capital, a growing food supply and population, and a strong middle class supported it. British factories supplied high quality goods for lower prices than those in continental Europe, and their goods were in demand in the Americas and southern Asia, where Britain controlled almost all trade with India. The British textile industry was one of the first to develop, and before the mid-19th century, it was part of a vast worldwide economic network. Much of the raw cotton that fed the new British textile mills came from the southern United States, where it was cultivated by black American slaves, though Britain itself had been trying to end the slave trade since 1807. The finished products were shipped from British mills all over the world along sea lanes protected by the British navy. Other industries – such as iron making, shipbuilding, and china production – also prospered, and profits were invested all over the world, but especially in the Americas. The enormous wealth generated by this activity gave Britain economic influence that allowed it to dominate the globe by the end of the 19th century.

The Revolution in Transportation

James Watt's invention of the steam engine in 1764 inspired the development of a higher quality of iron for making machines. Consequently, the use of machinery spread to many industries, including transportation. During the early 19th century inventors produced steam engines that powered locomotives and ships, which revolutionized transportation because railroads and steamships dramatically lowered transportation costs. Much larger cargoes could be carried, and the amount of time required for travel was cut dramatically. Thousands of miles of railroad tracks were built, first in Britain, and eventually all over Europe, the United States, and other parts of the world. Railroads triggered industrialization in new areas because they provided efficient transportation of goods to market. Steamboats greatly facilitated travel on rivers in the United States, and in 1838 two steamers crossed the Atlantic on steam power alone. Sailing ships remained important means of water transportation throughout the 19th century, but new steamships helped to support the rapid growth of world trade.

Railroads and Steam

In 1804, Richard Trevithick developed the first steam-powered locomotive in southern Wales. It pulled 10 tons of ore and 70 people at 5 miles per hour. The first public railway line – called *Rocket* – opened in 1830 between Liverpool and Manchester, a distance of 32 miles. With its improved locomotive (invented by George Stephenson), *Rocket* traveled at 16 miles per hour, and within twenty years, locomotives could go as fast as 50 miles per hour. In the 1840s alone,

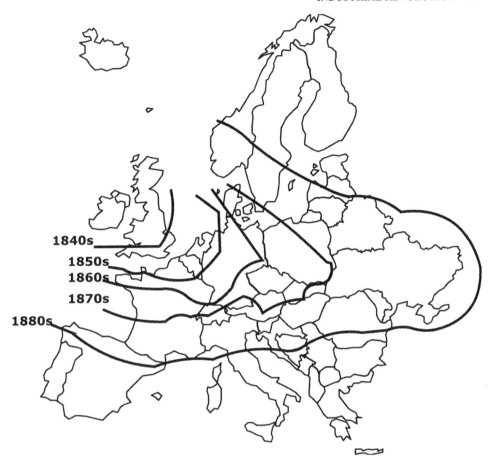

The diffusion of the Industrial Revolution across Europe. The Industrial Revolution began in England in the late 18th century, and diffused across Europe, following belts of coalfields and iron ore.

railroad track mileage more than doubled in Great Britain, and British investment in railways jumped dramatically. The British also began to build railroads in India, and inspired the development of rail transportation in the United States and Belgium in the 1830s and 1840s. By 1850, France had 2,000 miles of railroad, and other countries began to sponsor development of more rail lines, so that the world had 23,500 miles of track by midcentury.

Railroad building not only stimulated industrial development; it also encouraged state power to grow. Governments participated in the construction of railroads by helping private companies to pay for the massive amounts of iron, coal, heavy machinery, and human labor necessary to build and run them.

Railroads, then, caused other industries to grow to keep up with their needs. For example, Britain produced 17,000 tons of iron in 1740; by the 1840s, over 2 million tons; and by 1852, almost 3 million tons. The iron industry grew in other countries too, but Britain produced more than the rest of the world combined. The availability of a cheaper and faster means of transportation caused market to grow, increasing demand which in turn stimulated the growth of factories and provided more job opportunities. Steam-powered engines made Britain the world leader in manufacturing, so that by 1850 more than half of Britain's national income came from manufacturing and trade.

Industrialization in North America

British trade stimulated the spread of industrialization across the Atlantic to North America, where natural resources and available land space encouraged economic development. The first U.S. textile mill was built in Rhode Island in 1791 by Samuel Slater, a former worker in an English factory. The U.S. government protected the industry through embargoes on European trade, and the industry grew accordingly. Before 1860, North America's industry concentrated on processing abundant food and lumber resources. Iron and steel industries rapidly developed during the late 19th century. Most early industry flourished along the coast of the

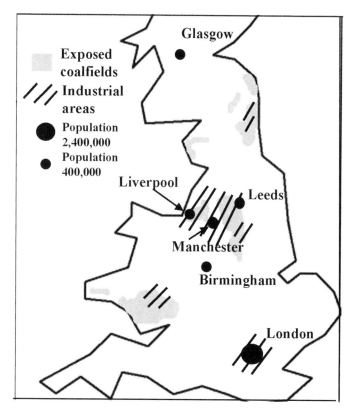

Industrial Britain by 1850. The first industries arose in northern and western England around abundant coal and iron-ore deposits. Railroads connected the major cities to one another and to the coast for shipping.

northeastern United States, where despite a lack of abundant natural resources, the large populations from Boston in the north to Washington D.C. in the south provided markets for consumption of industrial products. New York City became one of the world's great ports, with a huge skilled and semiskilled labor force, and a fine natural harbor for **break-of-bulk** (transfer of cargo from one type of carrier to another) from ships to trains and barges and vice versa.

Industrialization in Continental Europe

A major hurdle for industrialization as it spread to continental Europe was the lack of technical knowledge outside Britain. The British tried to prevent the borrowing of their techniques and practices by prohibiting their artisans from leaving the country and forbidding the export of important machinery and machine parts. Inevitably, however, Britain was not able to control the spread of industrialization by legislation, and by 1825 at least 2,000 skilled British mechanics were working in continental Europe, and British equipment was being sold abroad. As local people learned the necessary skills, a new generation of skilled workers in France and Belgium spread their knowledge east and south. New technical schools were established to train even more workers, making it possible for more countries to industrialize. Belgium, rich in iron and coal, became the fastest-growing industrial power on the continent by mid-century, with the number of steam engines there quadrupling between 1830 and 1844.

Even more than in Britain, the governments of countries on the continent played an important role in the development of industrialization. Since political and economic power had long been held by central governments, they often picked up the costs of technical education, financed factories, awarded grants to inventors and foreign entrepreneurs, and exempted foreign industrial equipment from import duties. Governments also paid for the construction of new roads, canals, and railroads. By 1850, a network of iron rails spread across the Continent, although most were still in Belgium and the German states. Governments also protected new industry by imposing tariffs on imports. For example, after the Napoleonic wars ended in 1815, France was flooded with superior goods produced cheaply in British factories. The French government responded by imposing high tariffs on many English imports in order to protect the French economy. Even so, by mid-century continental Europe still lagged almost twenty years behind Great Britain in industrial development.

THE SECOND INDUSTRIAL REVOLUTION

In the second half of the 19th century, a significant increase in production spurred by new products and methods of manufacture created what is sometimes called the **Second Industrial Revolution**. In 1856, **Henry Bessemer** discovered a method that greatly decreased the time necessary for producing steel, and later advances made steel production even more efficient by the 1870s. As steel production increased, its price fell because of greater efficiency, and as a result, the rail system expanded, steamship fleets appeared, and new buildings proliferated. This time period is sometimes called the "age of steel," as the alloy became the material that spurred new growth. After 1870, chemical industries also grew with the production of synthetic substances for dyes for textiles, fertilizers for agriculture, and explosives for construction. Plastics became available in the late 19th century. Inventors were also experimenting with electricity, most notably **Thomas Edison**, whose laboratory in New Jersey produced incandescent light bulbs, fuses, sockets, and switches.

Between 1850 and 1870, the economies of Belgium, the German states, and France grew at unprecedented rates because of industrial development. One factor in this growth was the development of **corporate banks** – first pioneered in Belgium – that were owned by many shareholders, large and small. These banks usually worked in collaboration with governments, and they mobilized impressive resources for investment in big industrial companies. In contrast, the advance of industrialization in eastern Europe was slow, mainly because serfdom was still in place there, hindering the necessary mobility of labor. Landlords had few incentives for investing in new enterprises, and peasants could not migrate to factory towns because they were legally tied to the land as serfs.

Sea-based Transportation and New Communications

Industrialization made it possible for Europeans to penetrate beyond the seacoasts in many lands. Whereas in the previous era sea-based powers were often confined to sea-lanes (except in the Americas), steamboats and railroads allowed them to explore internal rivers and lands far away from the coasts. Along with new speed, advances in refrigeration changed food transport. Formerly, foods could only be cooled with natural ice cut from frozen ponds and lakes, but this changed in the 1870s with the introduction of ice-making machines. By the 1880s, dairy products and meat could be transported long distances by both rail and sea, making it possible for the United States and Australia to export these products to Europe and other areas of the world. Another invention that linked people across the seas was the telegraph, with telegraph wire laid in both Europe and North America in the 1860s, followed by the transatlantic cable. By the 1870s, telegraph lines extended 650,000 miles, connecting 20,000 towns and villages around the world. As a result, information could be sent and received within a time period of a few minutes, instead of the days, weeks, or months such communications took only a few years earlier.

An important consequence of industrialization for world commerce was the construction of the **Suez Canal** (1859-1869) and the **Panama Canal** (1904-1914). These canals were incredible engineering accomplishments that were made possible by new industrial technologies. They greatly facilitated the travel of ships

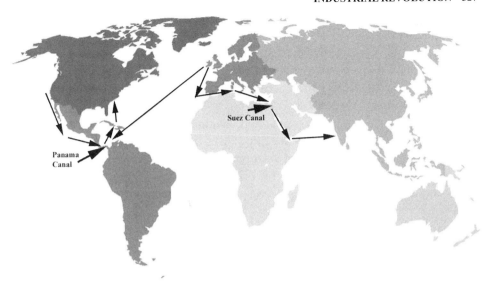

The Canals and World Transportation. The completion of the Suez Canal in 1869 and the Panama Canal in 1914 greatly decreased many travel distances from one place in the world to the next. The Suez Canal was financed by both England and France, and it allowed both countries to more quickly reach their colonial possessions in Asia. The Panama Canal gave Europeans another route to reach East Asia, and it also allowed the new American navy to travel between the east and west coasts of the United States.

between the world's seas and oceans, and lowered the costs of trade between imperial powers and the territories they controlled. The canals also made communications much easier. For example, in the 1830s, it often took as long as two years for someone in Britain to receive a reply to a letter sent to India by sailing ship. Once steamships came along in the 1850s the time was cut to about four months. However, after the construction of the Suez Canal, it took less than two weeks for a steamship to get from Britain to India.

Spread of Industrialization to Russia and Japan

After 1870, industrialization spread to two other important areas of the world: Russia and Japan. Even by the 1840s, factories were being built in Russia, and by the late 19th century, the tsarist government promoted industrialization by encouraging the construction of railroads to link the far-flung parts of the empire. The most ambitious was the **Trans-Siberian Railroad** line, which spanned the distance from Moscow east to the Pacific Ocean. The line made it possible to access the coal and iron resources in Siberia and also provided a transportation link between western Europe and eastern Asia. By 1900, Russia had well developed coal, iron, oil, and steel industries. In Japan, the government pushed industrialization by modernizing iron foundries and dockyards, and also built railroads, opened mines, organized a banking system, and became much more involved in international trade. By 1900, Japan was the most industrialized area in Asia and had laid the foundation for becoming a world power in the 20th century.

SOCIAL EFFECTS OF INDUSTRIALIZATION

During the 19th century, the reorganization of work impacted human lives far beyond the technological innovations that people learned to work with. One important change was the migration of many people in industrializing countries from rural to urban areas. Large landowners who experimented with new crops adopted farm machinery that increased production, making small farms less viable. Families were disrupted as young people from farms flocked to cities, where everyday life was not always an improvement over rural living, as they had hoped. As workers moved to be close to the factories, many neighborhoods became overcrowded, and sanitation and crime became huge problems that the city governments were not prepared to cope with. Middle-class families tried to escape the crowdedness and pollution of the cities by moving farther away, forming the basis for a new style of suburban living.

Population Growth

Population increases that began in the 18th century became much more dramatic during the 19th century. The total European population almost doubled from an estimated 140 million in 1750 to about 266 million in 1850. The death rate continued to decline, and nutrition levels continued to increase, as the Agricultural Revolution in Britain spread to more areas. Famine largely disappeared from western Europe, although Ireland was a major exception.

Irish peasants led difficult lives of poverty until they began to cultivate the potato, a crop that reached Europe from the Americas as a result of the Columbian Exchange (pp. 137-138). Potatoes were nutritious and relatively easy to grow, and they produced three times as much food per acre as grain, enabling Irish peasants to expand their numbers. Between 1781 and 1845, the Irish population doubled from four to eight million, with probably half depending on the potato for survival. However, everything changed in the summer of 1845, when potatoes in Ireland were hit by a fungus that made them inedible. The problem endured until 1851, and the resulting famine decimated the Irish population. More than one million people died of starvation and disease, and almost two million more emigrated to the United States and Britain. Of all the countries of Europe, Ireland was the only one in which population declined during the 19th century. Despite the fact that an average of 110,000 people per year emigrated from Europe between 1821 and 1850, populations continued to increase overall.

The New Rural and Urban Environments

Long before the Industrial Revolution began, very few wilderness areas were left in western Europe because almost all land had been altered by agriculture. The most serious problem of the period from about 1450 to 1750 had been deforestation, especially as people cut timber to build ships and construct merchant areas for the growing trade that characterized the era. In the 19th century, deforestation pressures were relieved in Europe because coal and iron ore replaced wood as major energy sources. However, mining caused environmental problems of its own. Miners dug deep tunnels to extract the minerals, and the earth and rock removed in this process was heaped up in mounds that at times covered acres of land. Industrial wastes from the cities polluted lakes, rivers, and air. In the United States, the environment changed rapidly as populations increased and moved west. East of the Appalachian Mountains, pioneers cut down and burned trees to build houses, and then a few years later, moved further west to start the whole process again. In the American South, forests were cut down to plant cotton, a crop that rapidly drained nutrients from the soil, and farmers deserted the depleted land to plant more cotton on new soil.

PERSPECTIVES: THOMAS MALTHUS ON POPULATION INCREASE

In 1798, a British economist named **Thomas Malthus** became the first critic to note that the world's population was increasing faster than the food supplies needed to sustain it. In *An Essay on the Principle of Population as It Affects the Future Improvement of Society,* Malthus used the principles of exponential growth v. linear growth to make his point. Population increases exponentially, or at what he called a "geometric rate," whereas food supplies grow at an arithmetic rate. Exponential growth is illustrated by the series of numbers 2,4,8,16,32 (geometric rate) because once children are born, they grow up to have children of their own. So once the population base gets so large, population will not immediately stabilize even if people begin having fewer children. Meanwhile, the linear growth of food is represented by the series 2,3,4,5, 6 (arithmetic rate) because even with new agricultural technology, farmland is limited.

Malthus, a clergyman, recognized that population growth could be stopped by birth control and/or abstinence, but he morally objected to the former and considered the latter to be highly unlikely. Therefore, the "gloomy parson" saw a future in which famine would surely prevail, accompanied by disease and wars fought for space on earth. These "negative checks" would be the forces that keep population growth contained.

Industrialization caused cities and towns in western Europe and the United States to grow rapidly. In 1700, London had a population of about 500,000; by 1850, its numbers had grown to about 2,400,000 – the largest city the world had ever known. Other large cities were Manchester and Liverpool in England, and New York City in the United States. Census figures show that by 1851, Britain was a predominantly urban society, the first country to have as many people living in cities as in the countryside. Germany reached that milestone in 1891, but France did not until 1931. Although the proportion of people who lived in urban areas varied from one country to the next, this urbanization trend continued throughout the 1800s and throughout the 20th century as well.

Cities attracted people not only from the countryside, but also sometimes from long distances away. Large cities like Paris drew from almost all areas of France, and many industrial centers even attracted people from beyond a nation's borders. For example, the Irish arrived in large numbers to work in the factories of northern and western England, and Poles sought employment in the Ruhr Valley of western Germany. Many large cities had increasingly heterogeneous populations, which included people with different native languages, religions, and national origins. Some port cities – such as Amsterdam, Marseille, and Liverpool – also had significant populations of Africans and Asians.

Urban Problems

In most cases, local officials were at first unable to cope with the rapid growth of cities. For example, in Manchester, England, the population grew from 25,000 in 1772 to 455,000 in 1851, but there were few provisions for urban organization, and the city had few municipal officials, tax-raising structures, and lawmaking powers. As a result, it was difficult for Manchester and the other new factory towns to deal with problems of rapid urbanization, and they were slow to provide for police protection, water supply and sewage removal, and the disposal of garbage.

The inequality caused by industrialization was evident as the wealthy built fine homes and patronized museums, theaters and churches. On the other hand, as people migrated to cities to labor in the factories, developers often built inexpensive, shoddy row houses for them, and these tenements became overcrowded. In these neighborhoods, sanitation and safety became big problems, and air and water pollution plagued the areas around the factories. Soot spewed from factory chimneys, and everything was covered with dirt and grime. In 1858, the stench from sewage and other garbage was so strong that the British House of Commons was forced to suspend its sessions. Not surprisingly, diseases – such as small pox, dysentery, and tuberculosis – often became epidemic. Death rates soared in many cities, especially among the poor. For example among upper-class families in Liverpool, the average life span was 35, but for the working poor it was 15. In

THEMATIC LEARNING OBJECTIVE: INDIVIDUAL AND SOCIETY: LIVING CONDITIONS IN URBAN SLUMS

Class differences were apparent in 19th century European cities, and many found living conditions in urban slums to be appalling. Physician James Philips Kay, a physician in Manchester, England, provided the following description in 1832.

"A whole family is often accommodated on a single bed, and sometimes a heap of filthy straw and a covering of old sacking hide them in one undistinguished heap, debased alike by penury, want of economy and dissolute habits. Frequently the inspectors found [that]...more than one family lived in a damp cellar, containing only one room, in whose pestilential atmosphere from twelve to sixteen persons were crowded. To these fertile sources of disease were added the keeping of pigs and other animals in the house, with other nuisances of the most revolting character."

Reference: J.P. Kay, *The Moral and Physical Condition of the Working Classes Employed in the Cotton Manufacture in Manchester* (London: James Ridgway, 1832), pp. 6, 14-15, 19.

1800, boys living in urban slums were 8 inches shorter than the sons of the urban wealthy.

A problem of particular concern to well-to-do urbanites was a rising crime rate, especially for crimes against property, such as theft and arson. 19th-century crime statistics were generally incomplete and unreliable, so it is difficult to know how much the crime rate increased, but the concern for keeping cities safe led to the formation of police forces. Another problem was public drunkenness, as beer halls and pubs proliferated in cities. In London, for example, twenty-three pubs lined one street within a distance of three hundred yards. Professional police forces that were charged specifically with domestic security – in contrast to armies that protected countries from organized attack – did not really exist until the early 19th century, and their creation supported the emergence of orderly European societies. Professional police appeared in Paris and London in 1828, and they were charged with maintaining order in public places, keeping traffic moving, and arresting those that broke the law. Berlin established a police force after the Revolution of 1848, and other cities soon followed with their own forces. All wore easily recognized uniforms, but police on the Continent were armed, while those in Britain were not.

Social Class Distinctions

In rural societies, wealth was based primarily on land, so the primary division of social classes was almost always drawn between those who owned land and those who did not. In the new industrial order, the wealthiest people were the captains of industry who headed big businesses. This new elite came to challenge the traditional aristocrats, such as those who held titles of nobility. The middle class, or **bourgeoisie**, composed of the owners of small businesses, factory managers, accountants, and service professionals, like doctors and lawyers, grew substantially with industrialization. Those who were industrial entrepreneurs constructed the factories, purchased the machines, and determined where the markets were for their products. The opportunities for making money were great, but the risks were considerable, since they often had to raise a great deal of capital to start their business ventures. Their comfortable lifestyles were made possible by the wealth generated from industry.

By 1850, in Britain at least, a new business aristocracy emerged, as sons inherited successful businesses and came to amass much wealth. Others were bankers who prospered as business grew. As members of the newly wealthy bourgeoisie bought great estates, they gained social respectability and political power. As a result, the composition of the elite classes changed, as those from entrepreneurial families merged with the traditional landed elites, who eventually accepted them as social equals.

The lower classes in urban areas were the laborers who worked in the factories, and a substantial number also worked in mines owned by the elite. Most had fewer skills than artisans of earlier periods, and they generally worked for low wages and lived in crowded urban housing or in company towns in mining areas. Most factory work was dirty and tedious, and few factory owners protected their workers against dangerous substances or circumstances. With no safety provisions, the workers were prone to accidents. Incomes were so low that workers normally spent between two-thirds and three-fourths of their budget on food. The work hours were long, and usually all able-bodied family members worked outside the home, including women and children.

The urban factory workers came to be called the **proletariat**, a term that originally applied to the poorest urban dwellers in Ancient Rome, but now described the growing class of people who lived around the factories where they worked. The proletarians were largely unskilled workers who were totally dependent on the factory owners for their livelihood. The guild system that had once protected urban workers was long gone, and there was no assurance of regular employment.

Layoffs and job losses occurred with any downturn in the economy, and machines often replaced skilled workers, especially those who specialized in hand-crafted products.

Family Life

Families from all social classes had to adjust to a major change: the separation of the work place from family life. Farm families generally worked together, all on the same land, so that work and family life blended together and everyone understood the work that all family members did. In industrialized society, people had to leave home to go to work, were often gone all day, and then came home to another world at night. This new arrangement profoundly affected the ways that family members interacted, often causing them to lead separate lives. Reports that described children toiling long hours in British textile factories alarmed the British Parliament so that by the 1840s laws were passed to regulate child labor and eventually outlaw it.

Social class greatly affected family lifestyles and the roles that men and women played in society. Among the working classes, both men and women often worked outside the home for wages so meager that the family could not survive without two incomes. In a sense, this situation gave men and women "equality," except that women's wages were generally lower than men's. Many lower-class women also became domestic servants for the growing middle classes and elites, so that they were still doing "women's work," but just in someone else's home. Others became factory workers who usually lived in supervised dormitories run by factory owners. Despite this effort to protect young girls, the growth of factories and mines brought unheard-of opportunities for girls and boys to mix on the job, free of supervision by their families, and those associations often continued after work. The rate of illegitimate births increased as fewer women who became pregnant before marriage found the newly mobile fathers willing to marry them.

Gender roles in middle-class and elite families were quite different. Successful businessmen generally enjoyed elevated status, since their responsibilities gave them a great deal of economic power. One source of pride for such a man was the fact that his wife did not have to work and that his income alone was enough to keep the family comfortable. Middle-class men in particular were interested in self improvement, and so reading books, attending lectures, and supporting churches became some of their leisure-time activities. They sometimes tried to instill these values in their workers who often did not see the point, especially if their jobs were composed of tedious chores created by the new division of labor at factories and businesses. From their perspective, leisure time was better spent in escapist activities, like attending sporting events and spending evenings in bars and pubs. These developing differences in social values tended to deepen the social class distinctions that were already clearly delineated at work.

For the middle classes.x the gender distinction between work and family was complete, and more than any other group, middle-class women were limited to the roles of wife and mother. They enjoyed considerable luxuries, with homes full of manufactured items and staffed with servants, and a chief goal was for women to provide for men private refuge at home from the rough and tumble world of business. Middle-class women were often responsible for handling spending accounts and family correspondence, but their positions as keepers of the hearth led to idealized concepts of women as paragons of virtue, and all that is good and pure in the world. This separation of women from the world outside the home and the creation of an insulated world of home, servants, children, and management of the family's social life is sometimes called the "**cult of domesticity**".

THEMATIC LEARNING OBJECTIVE: INDIVIDUAL AND SOCIETY: THE CULT OF DOMESTICITY

Industrialization increased the wealth of middle-class Europeans during the 19th century and, as a result, reordered their social lives. Women slipped into roles defined by the "cult of domesticity," as explained in the excerpt below from *Woman in Her Social and Domestic Character:*

"Domestic life is the chief source of her influence; and the greatest debt society can owe to her is domestic comfort: for happiness is almost an element of virtue; and nothing conduces more to improve the character of men than domestic peace. A woman may make a man's home delightful, and may thus increase his motives for virtuous exertion. She may refine and tranquillize his mind, – may turn away his anger or allay his grief. Her smile may be the happy influence to gladden his heart, and to disperse the cloud that gathers on his brow. And in proportion to her endeavors to make those around her happy, she will be esteemed and loved. She will secure by her excellence that interest and regard which she might formerly claim as the privilege of her sex, and will really merit the deference which was then conceded to her as a matter of course....

Nothing is so likely to conciliate the affections of the other sex as a feeling that woman looks to them for support and guidance....There is, indeed, something unfeminine in independence. It is contrary to nature, and therefore it offends...A really sensible woman...is conscious of inferiority, and therefore grateful for support."

Reference: Mrs. John Sandford, *Woman in Her Social Domestic Character* (Boston: Otis, Broaders and Co., 1842), pp. 5-7, 15-16.

The Demographic Transition

An important demographic change came about in the industrialized west as families adjusted to industrialization. Birth rates began to fall as children lost their economic value as workers on the farm, and instead became family members who had to be supported by adult workers. In the middle classes, the value of self-improvement was instilled at an early age, and mothers became most responsible for the emotional and social development of the children. Instead of working, middle-class children spent their time being educated, making them dependent on their parents for a longer period of time. The expenses of this lifestyle encouraged husbands and wives to limit the number of children that they had, creating a **demographic transition** during the second half of the 19th century. Low birth rates combined with low death rates that resulted from improved hygiene and health to create a fairly stable population level in most western countries. By the end of the century, many people in western countries – even those in the working class – enjoyed a lifestyle above the subsistence level. Diets and housing improved, and deaths of infants and children declined significantly, partly because of better hygiene during childbirth and better care at home. Medical advancements – such as Louis Pasteur's discovery of germs – allowed doctors and nurses to develop more sanitary health care.

REACTIONS TO INDUSTRIAL SOCIETY: REFORM AND RADICALISM

The vast social changes brought about by industrialization generated a number of ideological reaction. One was **laissez-faire**, a policy most famously espoused by **Adam Smith** in *The Wealth of Nations*, written in 1776. Smith believed that the force behind the economy should be the "invisible hand" of competition, not the forceful hand of government. Under Smith's system, the laws of supply and demand should govern the marketplace. If demand increased, prices would rise, and producers would scramble to meet the demand. Once demand was met, supplies snaturally dwindled, since people weren't willing to pay high prices for the product. To Smith, government control was "interference" with supply and demand. This theory led governments to dismantle previous regulations, and the booming population meant that the supply of labor went up, so wages were low, and the gap between the rich and poor grew.

Socialism

In opposition to practices inspired by laissez-faire, an ideology called **socialism** grew, and its advocates worked to combat the economic inequalities that industrialization brought. The term "socialism" first appeared around 1830 in the form of **utopian socialism**, which sought to set up ideal communities based on political, social, and economic equality. Early socialists, such as Charles Fourier and Robert Owen, planned model communities based on cooperation, not competition, where no one was rich or poor, but basic needs were met for all. Experimental communities grew up in many countries during the 19th century, but most ultimately failed, so reformers turned to other means to address the problems of the day.

The most radical of the socialists was **Karl Marx,** a German theorist who believed that revolution – not reform – was the only solution to the misery and unfairness that resulted from industrialization. Often known as the father of communism, he addressed the issues in a sweeping interpretation of history and vision for the future, ***The Communist Manifesto,*** written in 1848. He believed capitalism – or the free market – to be an economic system that exploited workers and increased the gap between the rich and the poor. He also believed that conditions in capitalist countries would eventually become so bad that the proletariat

**THEMATIC LEARNING OBJECTIVE:
OBJECTIVE KNOWLEDGE AND
SUBJECTIVE VISIONS:**
THE COMMUNIST MANIFESTO
BY KARL MARX

Karl Marx is one of the most influential theorists in modern history, and his socialist views, often referred to as "communism," have shaped the development of many nation-states and the direction of world politics. One of his basic ideas was that the private ownership of property is the root of all inequality, and to create a just society, it should be eliminated in favor of communal sharing. Below are the closing statements to his famous 1848 work, *The Communist Manifesto.*

"In short, the Communists everywhere support every revolutionary movement against the existing social and political order of things. In all these movements, they bring to the front, as the leading question in each, the property question, no matter what its degree of development at the time. Finally, they labor everywhere for the union and agreement of the democratic parties of all countries.
The Communists disdain to conceal their views and aims. They openly declare that their ends can be attained only by the forcible overthrow of all existing social conditions. Let the ruling classes tremble at a communist revolution. The proletarians have nothing to lose but their chains. They have a world to win.
Proletarians of all countries, unite! "

Reference: The Communist Manifesto, Karl Marx and Frederick Engels, 1848. Trans. by Samuel Moore, 1888

(workers) would join together in revolution, and overcome the **bourgeoisie**, or owners of factories and other means of production. Marx envisioned a new world after the revolution, one in which social class would disappear because ownership of private property would be banned. According to Marx, communism encourages equality and cooperation, and without property to encourage greed and strife, governments would be unnecessary and would wither away. He developed his views fully in a much longer work called *Das Capital.*

Labor Unions

A less radical, yet still controversial, reaction to industrialization was the formation of labor unions. The old guilds from medieval times had been dismantled during the 17th and 18th centuries, leaving no organizations for workers in place during the early years of industrialization. Starting in the 19th century, labor unions formed to protect the rights of workers within the new work arrangements that industrialization had brought. Through most of the 19th century, both employers and governments considered labor unions to be illegal on the grounds that they restrained trade. One of the most controversial union tactics was the strike, in which union members refused to work until their demands for better wages and/or working conditions were met. Employers tried to hire replacements, who often got into violent confrontations with strikers, and governments enjoined union members to go back to work. Gradually, unions gained power and respectability, and were instrumental in gaining better working conditions and pay for workers by the early 20th century.

Luddites and Chartists

Trade unionism was not the only type of collective action by 19th century workers. The **Luddites** were skilled craftsmen in the Midlands (central) and northern England who in 1812 physically attacked the machines that they believed threatened their livelihoods. Under the leadership of the mythical General Ned Ludd, they enjoyed so much local support that British troops were never able to track them down for punishment. German weavers went on machine-destroying campaigns in the 1830s and 1840s.

Another group of people with widespread support in England were the **Chartists**, so called because they created a People's Charter, drawn up in 1838, that demanded six specific reforms: universal manhood suffrage, annual election of the House of Commons, the secret ballot, electoral districts of equal size, abolition of property qualifications for members of the House of Commons, and payment of salaries to members of the House of Commons. For more than ten years the Chartists agitated for their reforms, and the Charter was presented to Parliament on three occasions, each time signed by millions of supporters. Although their petitions were rejected, the Chartists created a working-class consciousness that eventually led to the acceptance of their goals.

Like the political revolutions of the late 18th century, the Industrial Revolution of the 19th century brought changes that impacted Europe greatly in almost all realms of life. Because of ties to Europeans that started as early as the 16th century, the Americas were tightly bound to influences from Europe, and during the 1815 to 1914 era, events in the Americas – such as technological inventions in the United States – reverberated in Europe. By 1914, industrialization had clearly transformed the western world, and the innovations in the ways that economic life was organized in the west also had far-reaching implications for virtually every corner of the globe.

CONCEPTS AND IDENTIFICATIONS

Bessemer, Henry
bourgeoisie
break-of-bulk
Chartists
Communist Manifesto
corporate banks
cult of domesticity
demographic transition
Edison, Thomas
laissez-faire
Luddites
Marx, Karl
Panama Canal
proletariat
Second Industrial Revolution
Smith, Adam
socialism
Suez Canal
Trans-Siberian Railroad
utopian socialism
The Wealth of Nations

**CHAPTER 14:
RESTORATION, IDEOLOGIES,
AND UPHEAVALS
1815-1850**

Until about 1815, the economic and political revolutions of the late 18th century evolved separately, with the Industrial Revolution in England having little impact on continental Europe, and the French Revolution having limited influence on the operation of the English government. As the factory system and capital growth progressed in England, the almost continual warfare on the Continent kept these changes from spreading. Meanwhile, the aristocracy kept firm control of the British Parliament, and they suppressed all forms of political radicalism at home. British troops eventually joined the forces that gathered against Napoleon's armies, reflecting their support of monarchical government, even if their king's powers were checked by Parliament. After peace returned in 1815, the situation changed, and economic and political developments tended to reinforce one another, as industrialization and political ideologies interacted to shape the course of European history for the rest of the 19th century.

THE CONGRESS OF VIENNA, 1814-1815

The eventual triumph of revolutionary economic and political forces was not readily apparent at the end of the Napoleonic wars. The coalition of nations that rose against Napoleon forced him to abdicate his crown in 1814, and after restoring the monarchy by naming Louis XVI's brother as the king of France, it assembled as a diplomatic congress at Vienna. There they began to squabble about what to do with Poland and Saxony, but they promptly buried their differences when Napoleon escaped his prison on the island of Elba and returned to France to rally a new army. In June 1815, an allied army under the Duke of Wellington met Napoleon at Waterloo in Belgium, and routed him once and for all. After Napoleon's exile to St. Helena in the South Atlantic, the **Congress of Vienna** resumed its meetings with new resolve to settle the future of Europe.

A principal goal of those assembled was a restoration of monarchical power, and to do that, they redrew the map of Europe that had been so affected by Napoleon's conquests. France was given generous terms, partly to help the French public accept the restoration of the Bourbons to the throne, and partly as a result of the skillful diplomacy of **Charles Talleyrand,** the French representative at the Congress. Talleyrand's talents were apparent as he successfully argued that the restored French monarch could succeed only if the country retained its great-power status and participated fully in the negotiations. Since France was a defeated power, Talleyrand's participation was highly unusual in a situation where the victors could have easily taken their spoils. As it turned out, France remained as one of the major European powers.

The map created at the Congress of Vienna balanced France's great-power status with the desire to check further French aggression, which had threatened the European **balance of power** since the days of Louis XIV. Austria's chief negotiator was Foreign Minister **Prince Klemens von Metternich**, who worked closely with the British Prime Minister **Robert Castlereagh** to ensure an agreement that would prevent further outbursts of revolutionary disturbance. Some important changes included:

- **Creation of the German Confederation** – Based on Napoleon's Confederation of the Rhine (which Napoleon formed in 1806 after he dismantled the Holy Roman Empire), the new **German Confederation** consolidated 38 separate German states under one loosely organized government. However, the Congress ignored the wishes of German nationalists for a strong unified Germany, since all the member states remained virtually sovereign. Still, the Confederation became part of the ring of powers that surrounded France.

- **Consolidation of the Dutch Republic and the Austrian Netherlands** – The new Kingdom of the Netherlands was created with the merger of the Dutch Republic and the Austrian Netherlands, forming a stronger state along the northern French border.

- **Prussian Control of the Rhine** – Almost all the German left bank of the Rhine River was ceded to Prussia, which was to be, in Castlereagh's words, a kind of "bridge" spanning central Europe, a powerful state that checked both France in the west and Russia in the East.

- **Austrian Control of Italian States** – The Austrian Habsburg family was given control of several Italian states, with the exception of the Papal States and Sardinia, which itself was enlarged by the addition of Genoa. These Italian lands were given to Austria not only to contain French power, but also to compensate for the loss of the Austrian Netherlands and Polish territory.

- **Russian and British Gains** – Most of Poland was awarded to Russia, while as compensation Prussia gained most of Saxony, and Austria was given control of Italian lands. Great Britain picked up more overseas possessions by annexing Malta, South Africa, part of Guiana and some other colonial territories.

The problem of maintaining the future peace received much attention at the Congress of Vienna. On the initiative of **Tsar Alexander I** of Russia, a **Holy Alliance** was forged among the rulers of Russia, Prussia, and Austria that bound them to conduct their governments according to Christian principles. They pledged to "remain united by the bonds of a true and indissoluble fraternity" in order "on all occasions and in all places to lend each other aid and assistance." The British king was invited to join the Holy Alliance but declined to do so on the ground that he lacked the constitutional powers to fulfill its provisions. Except by the highly religious tsar of Russia, the Holy Alliance was not taken very seriously by the rulers and ministers of Europe whose visions of the future were shaped by a secular, practical approach to international politics.

However, all four great victorious powers – Austria, Russia, Prussia, and Great Britain – did take the **Quadruple Alliance** that they formed seriously, with the

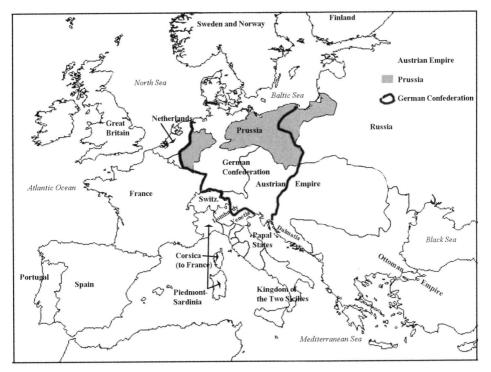

Europe after the Congress of Vienna, 1815. The Congress of Vienna redrew the map of Europe to ensure a balance of power among the nations of Europe. France returned to its 1789 borders, and the new kingdom of the Netherlands was created by combining the Austrian Netherlands and the Dutch Republic. Most of Poland was given to Russia, and Austria received the Italian states of Lombardy, Venetia, and the Dalmatian Coast. Prussia gained territory in Saxony and on the left bank of the Rhine.

agreement that periodic congresses were to be called to discuss outstanding problems. The arrangement was called the **Concert of Europe.** In a few years, France was invited to join, and the nations vowed to preserve peace and to take steps to maintain the status quo should it be threatened by revolutionary disturbances in any part of Europe.

19ᵀᴴ-CENTURY IDEOLOGICAL INFLUENCES

The restoration of monarchical power and the redrawing of the map of Europe to maintain a balance of power among nations were efforts to reverse the effects of the French Revolution and the Napoleonic wars. However, those important events were not forgotten, but instead continued to shape the developments of the 19th century. As a result, the ideologies of **conservatism**, **liberalism**, and **radicalism** each found supporters with different visions for the organization of European societies.

- **Conservatives** wanted to roll back the clock to the days before the French Revolution to restore the monarchies in all countries, including France. These voices prevailed at the Congress of Vienna and remained strong, especially in Russia, Prussia, and Austria. Conservatives benefitted from the disillusionment that many Europeans felt after 1815. They viewed Napoleon as a tyrant who ruled for his own benefit, and they also feared the chaos that the Reign of Terror had brought to France. They favored monarchies over republics, tradition over revolution, and established religion over Enlightenment philosophy. An influential spokesperson for conservatism was **Edmund Burke**, a British politician who argued that revolutionaries were wrong to believe they could construct an entirely new government based on reason. Instead, he believed that stable, strong governments evolve over long periods of time and are grounded in tradition. Church, state, and traditional family could not just be tossed aside for a new society based on nature and reason. Not surprisingly, conservatism was favored by royal families, and at the Congress of Vienna, both Alexander I of Russia and Metternich of Austria were strong conservatives. Their vision led to the restoration of Bourbon rule of France and defended monarchical government throughout the century.

- **Liberals** were interested in checking the power of monarchs and increasing parliamentary authority. They supported the original goals of the French Revolution, including a government defined by constitutional law and the guarantee of personal freedoms of religion, press, and assembly. Although Napoleon called his own system liberalism, the term was first used in Spain among opponents of Napoleonic occupation. The word began to be used in France, where it became associated with opposition to royalism after the restoration of the Bourbons in 1814. Liberal political theorists also had influence in England, and a new Liberal Party became an important force in British politics during the 1850s. The meaning of liberalism (the word itself derived from the Latin word *liber,* meaning free) varied from country to country, but it usually included an emphasis on the rights and liberties that individuals should possess as citizens. Most liberals were **bourgeoisie** – middle class professionals or businessmen – who wanted their views to be represented in government and their economic goals to be unhampered by government interference. Liberals clearly emphasized the right of private property-ownership, and they advocated free trade with low or no tariffs so as to allow individual economic opportunities to blossom. They generally thought of churches and landed aristocracies as obstacles to advancement. They wanted orderly change through legislation, and they disapproved of the instability that revolution brought.

THEMATIC LEARNING OBJECTIVE: OBJECTIVE KNOWLEDGE AND SUBJECTIVE VISIONS: JOHN STUART MILL ON LIBERTY

John Stuart Mill was one of Britain's most famous voices for liberalism, and his essay, *On Liberty,* excerpted below is a classic statement of the liberal belief in individual freedom.

"....There is a sphere of action in which society, as distinguished from the individual has, if any, only an indirect interest; comprehending all that portion of a person's life and conduct which affects only himself, or if it also affects others, only with their free, voluntary and undeceived consent and participation....This then is the appropriate region of human liberty. It comprises, first, the inward domain of consciousness; demanding liberty of conscience in the most comprehensive sense; liberty of thought and feeling; absolute freedom of opinion and sentiment on all subjects, practical or speculative, scientific, moral, or theological....
....The peculiar evil of silencing the expression of an opinion is, that it is robbing the human race; posterity as well as the existing generation; those who dissent from the opinion, still more than those who hold it. If the opinion is right, they are deprived of the opportunity of exchanging error for truth; if wrong, they lose, what is almost as great a benefit, the clearer perception and livelier impression of truth, produced by its collision with error."

Reference: John Stuart Mill, *Utilitarianism, On Liberty, and Representative Government.* (New York: Viking Press, 1914).

- **Radicals** emphasized equality more than liberty, with most advocating wider voting rights and more direct government participation by ordinary people. The term "radicalism" originated in England about 1820 with a group called the Philosophical Radicals, composed of both working-class leaders and new industrial capitalists who were still unrepresented in Parliament. These English radicals had much in common with the rationalist French *philosophes* before the Revolution because they wanted a total reconstruction of laws, courts, prisons, and municipal organization. Many promoted social reforms to help the poor gain some measure of economic security. On the Continent, radicalism was represented by militant **republicanism**, which first was voiced during the Reign of Terror; its supporters valued equality and justice above all. Most republicans were drawn from intelligentsia, such as students and writers, and from working-class leaders, and they generally supported revolution as a valid method for achieving their goals. Most were also bitterly anticlerical, and they regarded the Catholic Church as the enemy of reason and liberty. They were opposed to monarchy of any kind, even to constitutional monarchy, and they often organized in international secret societies to plot the overthrow of existing regimes by force.

A small branch of radicals attacked private property as the source of inequality and urged the government to actively work to increase equality. They called themselves **socialists,** and they regarded the existing economic system as profoundly unjust, since it created great inequalities between the workers and their employers. They generally favored some kind of communal ownership of banks, factories, machines, land, and transportation. Socialists flatly rejected the laissez-faire beliefs of liberals, and they believed that the French Revolution only promoted civil and legal equality, and that a further step toward social and economic equality was necessary. This branch of radicalism gave inspiration to **Karl Marx**, sometimes known as the father of communism, by the mid-19th century.

NATIONALISM

Nationalism was a theme that both liberals and radicals often supported, and political protests against the traditional monarchies were common, even in the more conservative states. Nationalism first rose as a force for change during the French Revolution, and Napoleon forwarded his own agenda for France by appealing to the growing sense of French unity based on common institutions, traditions, language, and customs. After Napoleon's defeat, nationalism grew to be an even more powerful ideology as it spread to people outside France. Many people came to believe that each nationality should have its own government. For example, German nationalists wanted national unity with one central government for Germany, and they pushed to make the German Confederation a true nation-state. Many people in eastern Europe who were subjects to the monarchs also advocated

self determination, or the right to establish their own autonomy. For example, the Hungarian nationalist movement wanted to be free from domination by the Austrian Habsburgs.

Nationalism was an important tool for almost all states, and even the conservative rulers often called upon their subjects' devotion to their nations to strengthen the power of the governments. For example, the Russian tsars encouraged all Russians to be devoted to their "fatherland" under their enlightened autocracy. However, nationalism often threatened to upset the existing political order, both internationally and nationally, so it was sometimes seen as a form of radicalism. A united Germany or Italy would upset the balance of power established in 1815, and independence for subject people would mean the breakup of great empires, such as Austria and Russia. Because many European states were multinational, conservatives tried very hard to repress nationalism. At the same time, in the first half of the 19th century, nationalism was supported by many liberals who believed that freedom could be realized only by people who ruled themselves. To them, the boundaries of government should coincide with those of nationalities.

ROMANTICISM

An important artistic movement called **romanticism** intertwined with nationalism to further alter the influences of the Enlightenment during the 19th century. Whereas the Enlightenment often went hand in hand with **classicism** in the arts to emphasize reason, symmetry, and cool geometric spaces, romanticism glorified nature, emotion, and imagination. Classicism had idealized models from Greek and Roman history, while romanticism sought inspiration from folklore and medieval legends. Romantics often expressed their emotions through poetry, music, and painting, and they supported many different ideologies, but they were most politically influential when they expressed nationalist feelings.

Romantics hoped to discover truth not through preoccupation with reason, but through a balance of reason with feeling, emotion, and imagination. Characteristics that romantics shared include:

- **An emphasis on the sentimental** – Many romantic heroes and heroines were tragic figures brought down despite their inherent goodness. An important model was Werther in *The Sorrows of the Young Werther,* a novel by **Johan Wolfgang von Goethe.** Werther was a Romantic figure who sought freedom but was misunderstood by society, most specifically by a young woman who by rejecting his love inspired his suicide.

- **Individualism** – Whereas individualism was also an Enlightenment value, romantics emphasized rebellion against middle-class conventions. They often expressed their inner drives through unusual clothing, hairstyles, and jewelry.

- **Interest in the past** – Romantics were particularly interested in medi-eval history, and they inspired a revival of Gothic architecture in public buildings and pseudo-medieval castles. Fairy tales – previously passed on mainly by word of mouth – were collected and published by the Grimm brothers in Germany and Hans Christian Anderson in Denmark.

- **Attraction to the unusual** – Related to their emphasis on individualism, romantics often enjoyed the bizarre and horrifying. One manifestation was called "**Gothic literature**," which focused on horror stories such as "The Fall of the House of Usher" by Edgar Allan Poe, and *Frankenstein* by Mary Wollstonecraft Shelley. This obsession with pursuing the ex-traordinary led some romantics to experiment with cocaine and opium to achieve altered states of consciousness.

Romantic Literature

Poetry was a favored literary form for Romantic writers, since many believed that it was the most perfect vehicle for expression of one's soul. One of the most famous masters of Gothic poetry was **Samuel Taylor Coleridge,** whose best

EXAMINING THE EVIDENCE: ROMANTICISM IN SIR WALTER SCOTT'S *IVANHOE*

One of the most popular romantic novelists was **Sir Walter Scott**, a prolific writer from Edinburgh, Scotland. In the excerpt below from Chapter 1 of *Ivanhoe* (1819), Scott reflected the romantics' tendency to glorify nature and the medieval past.

"In that pleasant district of merry England which is watered by the river Don, there extended in ancient times a large forest, covering the greater part of the beautiful hills and valleys which lie between Sheffield and the pleasant town of Doncaster. The remains of this extensive wood are still to be seen at the noble seats of Wentworth, of Wharncliffe Park, and around Rotherham. Here haunted of yore the fabulous Dragon of Wantley; here were fought many of the most desperate battles during the Civil Wars of the Roses; and here also flourished in ancient times those bands of gallant outlaws whose deeds have been rendered so popular in English song."

Reference: Walter Scott, *Ivanhoe*. *http://www.online-literature.com/walter_scott/ivanhoe/*

known work was probably *The Rime of the Ancient Mariner.* In this poem, Coleridge related the story of a sailor cursed for killing an albatross (a large sea-bird). This act was depicted as a crime against nature and God that caused the sailor to feel such a sense of guilt that he eventually discovered the true beauty of nature and humanity. After his repentance, the sailor was delivered from his curse (a dead albatross around his neck), as described at the end of the poem:

> O happy living things! No tongue
> Their beauty might declare:
> A spring of love gushed from my heart,
> And I blessed them unaware…
> The self-same moment I could pray;
> And from my neck so free
> The Albatross fell off, and sank
> Like lead into the sea.

Other famous poets were William Blake and William Wordsworth, both of whom emphasized the importance of seeing the beauty of the natural world. Two romantic writers lived particularly passionate, unorthodox lives that reflected their poetry: **Percy Bysshe Shelley**, author of *Prometheus Unbound* (a portrait of rebellion against oppressive laws and customs), who was expelled from school for advocating atheism and drowned in a storm in the Mediterranean while trying to reform the world; and **Lord Byron,** who championed the cause of personal liberty in *Childe Harold's Pilgrimage,* and died in Greece fighting the Turks for Greek independence.

Romanticism in Music and Painting

Another important artistic expression for romantics was music. Whereas the 18th century had been the age of classical music, 19th century music was heavily influenced by romanticism. One of the greatest composers of all times, **Ludwig van Beethoven** served as a bridge between the two eras. Beethoven studied under Mozart in Vienna, and his early works were very much in the classical style. However, his Third Symphony, *Eroica,* composed for Napoleon in 1804, was a truly romantic creation with music that evoked the fear, terror, and pain that romantics so celebrated. Critics proclaimed his symphonies and string quartets to be philosophically profound, and audiences listened in reverential silence. Beethoven composed many moving pieces of music, including his famous Ninth Symphony, written later in life when he was totally deaf.

Romantic painters were most concerned with natural landscapes, especially as they were threatened by industrialization. For example, the German romantic painter **Caspar David Friedrich** depicted scenes far from cities – often in the mountains – with melancholy human figures who were overpowered by the vastness of nature. Many of his landscapes had religious meaning as well, such as *The Cross in the Mountains,* which showed a Christian cross in a mountain scene, controversially detached from any formal church building. The French painter **Eugène Delacroix** preferred unconventional scenes of great turbulence to emphasize light and color. One of his most famous works was *Death of Sardanapalus,* based on Lord Byron's verse account of the decadent Assyrian king who ordered that his harem women and valued horses go to their death with him.

Romanticism and Ideology

Romanticism appealed to people of virtually every political ideology. Conservatives saw the romantic values as a powerful rejection of Enlightenment rationalism that had led to the disastrous consequences of the French Revolution and Napoleon's conquests. They also appreciated the romantic attachment to the Middle Ages, a time when custom and religion were still highly respected. On the other hand, radicals admired the unconventional impulses of the romantics, which were necessary for anyone who wanted to help create a new society free from the shackles of the past. In Germany and England many romantics had, like Wordsworth, initially welcomed the French Revolution only to change their minds as the Reign of Terror began. On the other hand, the French writer **Victor Hugo** became a lifelong advocate of radical change. Though extremely conservative in his youth, Hugo moved to radicalism as the decades passed; he became a passionate supporter of republicanism, and his work touched upon most of the political and social issues and artistic trends of his time. He was known in France for his poetry, but his best known works outside France were two novels: *Les Misérables* and *the Hunchback of Notre Dame.*

THE PILLARS OF CONSERVATISM

The guardians of the European restoration put in place at the Congress of Vienna were Russia, Austria, and Prussia. They were all absolutist states quite alarmed by the French Revolution and Napoleon's conquests, and they reacted by centralizing political power, building larger armies, and increasing control over their subjects.

Russia

After the death of Catherine the Great in 1796, conservatism was reinforced in Russia by the excesses of the French Revolution, and her successors of the early 19th century responded to the Napoleonic Wars with the same cautious protection of the rights of monarchs. Tsar Alexander I successfully led Russia to resist Napoleon's 1812 invasion, which quelled his early leanings toward liberal philosophy, and he responded by supporting conservative forces at the Congress of Vienna. He formed a **Holy Alliance** with Austria and Prussia as a defense of the established order, which included both monarchs and religious officials. Despite Alexander I's efforts, he was not able to stop the filtering of liberal ideas into Russia, which inspired some intellectuals to question the status quo. Nationalist problems erupted in Poland, where the tsar reigned as a limited monarch, having granted a constitution that provided for an elected Polish parliament and guarantees of free speech and press. By 1818, Alexander began retracting these concessions, and Polish students and military officers responded by forming secret nationalist societies to plot for change by illegal means. The government then cracked down, arresting student leaders and dismissing professors who promoted reforms.

Shortly after Alexander's death, his successor, **Nicholas I**, faced the **Decembrist Revolt,** a major uprising in 1825 led by western-oriented army officers who sought political reform. As most tsars before him had done, Nicholas responded with repression, and after crushing the rebellion, paid little attention to reform during the rest of his reign. Newspapers and schools were strictly supervised, political opponents were arrested, and the secret police was expanded – all in an effort to protect Russia from western influences that threatened its Slavic roots. Russian tsars continued their efforts to maintain political authority, but at the same time, they kept their ambitions to expand Russian territories, which meant that they became embroiled in international politics. For example, Russia supported many nationalist movements in the Ottoman-controlled Balkans, even though the movements reflected liberalism. The Russian desire to weaken the Ottoman Empire by stirring up trouble among its subjects was greater than the Russian commitment to conservatism, especially since Russia stood to gain territory at the expense of the Ottomans.

Russia's resistance to westernization during the early 19th century extended to industrialization. In response to Western demand for Russian grain, the government tightened the labor obligations of serfs rather than look to technology to increase production. In Russia, as well as most other areas of eastern Europe, the labor system remained feudalistic, although some western machinery was imported and a few factories opened to imitate those in western Europe. This pattern continued until Russia's territorial ambitions were stopped by the Crimean War in 1856, in which the superior technology and war tactics of France and Britain clearly showed how far behind Russia had fallen. This humiliating defeat robbed Russia of the opportunity to encroach on the periphery of the weakening Ottoman Empire and served as a wakeup call that its power could no longer be promoted by conservatism alone.

Austria

The Habsburgs ruled over many nationalities, so to no other country were the programs of liberalism and nationalism more potentially dangerous. Germans, Czechs, Slovaks, Slovenes, Italians, Hungarians, and Poles populated the empire, and the Austrian government stood firm in its resolution to maintain control over them. So far as Metternich and other Austrian officials were concerned, the

ORIGINAL DOCUMENT: RUSSIA'S POLICY OF "OFFICIAL NATIONALITY"

Tsar Nicholas I (r. 1825-1855) resisted all attempts to reform Russia, largely because he wanted to protect the empire from the political turmoil that had occurred in western Europe during the Napoleonic era. In the document excerpted below, Nicholas' minister of education, S.S. Uvarov, explains the basic principles behind the tsar's policy of "official nationality."

"In the midst of rapid collapse in Europe of religious and civil institutions, at the time of a general spread of destructive ideas...it was necessary to establish our fatherland on firm foundations upon which is based the well-being, strength, and life of a people; it was necessary to find the principles which form the distinctive character of Russia, and which belong only to Russia....Sincerely and deeply attached to the church of his fathers, the Russian has of old considered it the guarantee of social and family happiness...A Russian devoted to his fatherland, will agree as little to the loss of a single dogma of our Orthodoxy as to the theft of a single pearl from the tsar's crown. Autocracy constitutes the main condition of the political existence of Russia...An innumerable majority of the subjects of Your Majesty feel this truth...The saving conviction that Russia lives and is protected by the spirit of a strong, humane, and enlightened autocracy must permeate popular education...Together with these two national principles there is a third, no less important, no less powerful: nationality."

Reference: cited in *Nicholas I and Official Nationality in Russia, 1825-1855,* by Nicholas Riasanovsky (Berkeley: University of California Press, 1959), pp. 74, 75.

recognition of political rights of any of these groups would mean the probable demise of the empire. If Austria permitted representative government, Metternich feared that the national groups would create internal disruptions that would weaken Austria's international power.

About one quarter of Austria's population was German, and so Metternich worked hard to prevent the formation of a national state that would unite German people both within Austria's borders and without. He dominated the newly formed German Confederation, and many political leaders in Austria were German, so their loyalty to the Habsburgs was reinforced. The main sign of German resistance came from university students, who formed nationalist student societies, or *Burschenschaften,* but Metternich convinced the leaders of the biggest German states to issue decrees – most famously, the **Carlsbad Decrees** – to censure and dissolve the groups.   Secret societies also formed in Austria's Italian provinces, but even though they attracted tens of thousands of members, they had no common program across Italy and no central organization.   The Austrian domestic policies that were aimed at restraining nationalist impulses largely succeeded until the 1840s through heavy censorship and the use of a secret police that opened letters of even the highest officials.

Prussia

Like Austria, Prussia exerted its influence over the states of the German Confederation and worked to control the formation of a German national state.   In 1815, **Frederick William III** recognized German enthusiasm for victory in the "War of Liberation" by promising some mode of constitutional government for those under Prussian control.   However, he stalled on his pledge, and in 1817, he rescinded it, and instead created a new Council of State.   This Council increased administrative efficiency, but it was not based on constitutionalism.   In 1819, Frederick moved even further away from reform when he replaced his most liberal-leaning ministers with staunch conservatives.   By 1823, he had established eight provincial estates, or advisory councils, that were dominated by the landholding Junker class, and had solidified the old bonds linking monarchy, army, and aristocracy that had long characterized the social and political order in Prussia.

Meanwhile, Prussian influence increased.   Its national educational system included the new but prestigious University of Berlin, the army was more efficiently organized than ever, and its policies included measures that stimulated economic growth.   In 1818, Prussia lowered tariffs, encouraging raw materials to enter Prussia, and its tariff system was adopted by many of the smaller surrounding states.   The Prussian customs union came to be called the **Zollverein,** and by 1833, most German governments except Austria had joined it.   These successful Prussian policies supported **economic liberalism** based on free-market principles, but the Prussian conservative state denied **political liberalism,** which would have required individual rights of freedom of speech, press, and assembly.

CONSERVATISM IN BRITAIN AND FRANCE

In both Britain and France, conservative governments worked to maintain the old order reflected in the agreements forged by the Congress of Vienna.   Although the British Parliament shared power with the king, both the House of Commons and the House of Lords were dominated by the aristocratic landowning classes.   Within Parliament, both political factions – the Tories and the Whigs – were composed of aristocrats, although the Whigs were beginning to receive support from the new industrial middle class.   Most ministers before 1830 were Tories, and demands for electoral reforms were repressed.

In France, **Louis XVIII,** the restored Bourbon king, understood the need to accept some of the changes brought to France by the Revolution and Napoleon. For example, he accepted Napoleon's Civil Code, which recognized the principle of equality before the law. The property rights of those who had bought confiscated lands during the revolution were also preserved. France was permitted a constitution called the Charter, presented as a gift from the king and not as a right. It granted the legislature more authority than Napoleon had allowed but left the government largely in the hands of the king. Generally Louis pursued a course of administrative efficiency and political restraint. However, when Louis died in 1824, he was succeeded by his brother, **Charles X,** who attempted to restore the old regime as completely as possible. His government gave the Church fuller control of education and granted a cash indemnity to those who had lost land in the Revolution. In 1829 he filled his cabinet with **ultraroyalists** who supported an unrestrained monarchy. When the Chamber of Deputies (the French Parliament) rejected his ministers, the situation led quickly to another revolution in France in 1830.

REFORMS AND REVOLUTIONS

For a few years after the Congress of Vienna, the conservatives generally held sway over Europe, but liberalism and radicalism remained strong ideologies, and they successfully challenged conservatism in the years between 1830 and 1850, especially in western Europe. In some countries, change occurred gradually and peacefully, but in others it took the form of violent upheavals.

Uprisings in Spain and Italy

When Ferdinand VII regained the Spanish crown in 1814 after Napoleon's control collapsed, he restored the old institutions of the nobility, church, and monarchy. He allowed the publication of only two newspapers, and he forbid foreign books and newspapers to enter the country. Many middle-class Spaniards, especially those exposed to liberal French ideas, responded by joining secret societies. When the revolt spread to army officers, Ferdinand was forced to convene the *cortes* (parliament), but no agreements could be reached. In 1823, Ferdinand won the upper hand when a French army invaded and restored him to absolute power. The other members of the Concert of Europe backed the French invasion, and the restored Spanish government tortured and executed hundreds of rebels and imprisoned and exiled many others.

Shortly after the Spanish uprising began, rebellious soldiers in the Italian kingdom of Naples joined forces with the **carbonari** ("charcoal burners," or secret societies that marked each new member's forehead with a charcoal mark) to demand a constitution. When they succeeded in getting a new parliament to assemble, the

THEMATIC LEARNING OBJECTIVE: OBJECTIVE KNOWLEDGE AND SUBJECTIVE VISIONS: THE REVIVAL OF RELIGION

The restoration of monarchical government was not the only conservative reaction to the revolutionary upheavals of the late 18th and early 19th centuries. Another strong impulse was the revival of religious groups to reinforce the status quo. In France the Catholic Church sent missionaries to hold public ceremonies where people could express repentance for the outrages of revolution. The pope reestablished the Jesuit order, which had been disbanded during the Enlightenment, and other religious societies were sponsored by conservative governments to combat reformers.

The religious revival, however, did not always support the status quo. For example, the English Methodists – who first appeared during the 18th century – continued to challenge the practices and beliefs of the Anglican Church. Protestants also sponsored religious movements in Germany and the United States, where a second "Great Awakening" (the original one had occurred in the early 18th century) emphasized emotional religious ceremonies that included dancing, falling into trances, and speaking in tongues. These practices reflected a rejection of the Enlightenment reverence for reason, and instead rallied people to openly express and spread their religious beliefs and feelings.

promise of reform spread the rebellion into Piedmont-Sardinia. Austria signaled an alarm to the other great powers since its sway over northern Italian states was threatened, and with the backing of Prussia and Russia, the Austrians defeated the rebels in Naples and Piedmont in 1821. Even though Britain opposed the suppression of the Italian states, Metternich convinced the other powers to agree to Austria's actions.

Revolutions in the Americas

Enlightenment values appealed to many people throughout Europe and the Americas, especially after the successes of the American and French Revolutions. The earliest response was in Haiti, when slaves in the French colony of Saint-Domingue rebelled against their masters, and later revolutions broke out all across Latin America, so that by 1830, most Spanish colonies and the Portuguese colony of Brazil had gained their independence.

By 1800, the creoles (Europeans born in Latin America) far outnumbered the pen-insulares (Europeans born on the Iberian Peninsula), who still ruled the Spanish and Portuguese colonies. Many creoles were wealthy and powerful owners of plantations and ranches, and others were well-to-do urbanites involved in trade or business. Like their counterparts in the British North American colonies, the creoles resented control by representatives from their mother countries. Many were well read in Enlightenment philosophy, and like the bourgeoisie in France, wanted political rights that were equivalent to their economic accomplishments. As a result, creoles were attracted to the idea of political independence as the British colonies in North America had achieved, but they were not particularly interested in social egalitarian reform, such as the revolution in Haiti had aimed for. Between 1810 and 1825, creoles led revolutionary movements all over Latin America that secured their political control of the newly independent countries.

The precipitating event for most of the revolutions was Napoleon's invasion of Spain and Portugal in 1807, and the rebel groups that resisted his control created instability on the Iberian Peninsula, especially since Napoleon named his brother Maximillian as the king of Spain. In Latin America **juntas**, or organizations of military leaders, were set up to rule in the name of the deposed King Ferdinand of Spain, but soon the juntas – which were mainly staffed with creoles – had their own pro-independence agendas to follow.

Spanish South America

Independence movements in Spanish South America started in two places: north-ern South America near Caracas and southern South America near Buenos Aires. The first one began in 1810 under the leadership of **Simón Bolívar**, a wealthy Creole military officer who raised enough support between 1817 and 1822 to win a series of victories against the Spanish in Venezuela, Colombia, and Ecuador. His junta spurred large numbers of loyalists to rally free blacks and slaves to defend the Spanish Empire. Bolívar was able to eventually defeat the Spanish, partly through military skill, and partly through the force of his personal ability to hold the loyalty of his troops, attract new allies, and build coalitions. Until 1830, the area that he controlled was called Gran Colombia, and Bolívar dreamed of some-day uniting all South Americans under one government. However, political and regional interests led to the breakup of Gran Colombia, and to his south, another junta leader, **José de San Martín** rose to power in Argentina. Buenos Aires was a growing trade city whose residents resented Spanish restrictions, and San Martín, like Bolívar, hoped to unite many people under him. His army united Chileans and Argentines who crossed the Andes Mountains to attack Spanish strongholds in Chile and Peru. However, just as Bolívar could not keep regional factions from forming, San Martín was not able to stop splits among Argentina, Uruguay, Paraguay, and Bolivia. By 1825, all of Spanish South America had gained its po-litical independence, and all the new states founded republics with representative governments.

Brazil

The movement for independence took a different path in Brazil, partly because of the large number of slaves that worked the sugar, cotton, and cacao plantations. Although the planters sometimes resented Portuguese control of trade and political decisions, they were more afraid of a general slave uprising such as had occurred in Haiti. As a result, potential movements inspired by Enlightenment ideas were unsuccessful until Napoleon's troops invaded Portugal in 1807, causing the entire Portuguese royal family to flee the country to find a haven in Brazil. The family ruled in exile from Rio de Janeiro, and all government business was conducted from this new capital city of the Portuguese Empire. Seeing the rising tide of independence movements in Spanish America, **King Pedro I** took the initiative in declaring Brazil an independent empire in 1822. Of course, the empire was a monarchy, but Pedro was willing to concede many liberal principles, including a written constitution in 1824 that provided for an elected parliament and granted personal liberties. However, he made some enemies when he openly opposed slavery. After he ratified a treaty with Britain in 1831 to end Brazilian participation in the slave trade, slave owners cried out against him, and military losses from his effort to control neighboring Uruguay made his rule more difficult still. He was forced to abdicate to his five-year old son, Pedro II, who became emperor after a nine-year regency and ruled until he was overthrown by republicans in 1889.

Mexico

Napoleon's invasion of Spain in 1807 also caused unrest in Mexico, the largest and richest of the Spanish colonies in the Americas. The Mexican Revolution began in 1810 when a priest, **Miguel Hidalgo y Costilla**, called upon his parishioners to rise against Spanish officials. In the tradition of priests as champions for the rights of natives, Father Hidalgo was particularly charismatic, and tens of thousands of poor Amerindians joined his movement. Their targets were not only Spanish officials but also many wealthy creoles who owned mines and ranches that exploited their workers. As a result, the creoles supported Spanish authorities and turned on Hidalgo's masses, capturing and executing Hidalgo in 1811. Despite the death of their leader, the popular rebellion continued for another few years under the guidance of another priest, Jose Maria Morelos, who was caught and executed in 1815. At that point, events from Europe again intervened when a military revolt in Spain weakened the king and the central government. Not wanting to be cast with Spanish officials, a creole military officer, Augustín de Iturbide, struck an agreement with the rebellious peasants, and with combined forces declared Mexico's independence in 1821. However, Iturbide was proclaimed emperor of Mexico, a conservative solution that greatly offended liberals, and he was overthrown by the military and executed. This rapid turnover of leadership in the first few years of Mexico's independence created an atmosphere of instability and military coups d'état that characterized Mexico's political system well into the 20th century.

By 1830 most of the American colonies were independent nations. Exceptions were British North America (now Canada); British Guiana, Dutch Guiana, and French Guiana in northern South America; Cuba, the Bahamas, Jamaica, Puerto Rico and Trinidad in the Caribbean; and Patagonia in southern South America, which was disputed by Argentina and Chile.

Revolutionary Ideals and the Abolitionist Movement

Enlightenment-inspired revolutions generally resulted in some measure of liberty and/or equality for middle-class and elite males, but applying the concept of "natural rights" to slaves was another challenge – one that called for even more serious breaks with past traditions. Solutions did not come immediately during or after the revolutions, but as a result of reform movements that achieved their goals gradually over time.

The movement to end slavery in Europe and its colonies began in the late 1780s, as **abolitionists** who blended Enlightenment thought with principles of Christianity sought to end the slave trade. The earliest push came from members of the British Parliament who succeeded in passing legislation in 1807 to end the slave trade.

COMPARISON:
MOTIVES FOR REVOLUTION IN
THE AMERICAS AND FRANCE

Almost all the revolutions of the late 1700s and early 1800s in the Atlantic world were rooted in Enlightenment philosophy. However, each revolution emphasized different aspects of the ideology, resulting in some complex, contrasting motivations to both lead and support the insurgencies. For example, the main motivation of colonists in the American Revolution was independence from Britain, and its leaders emphasized the Enlightenment value of liberty. French leaders valued liberty, but the radicals that took over the French government during the Reign of Terror pushed for equality among male citizens and sought to rid the country of all vestiges of the old unequal social order, including the nobility and the Catholic Church. In Latin America, the creole leaders generally were attracted to the same goals that appealed to the colonists in North America – freedom to conduct their own affairs, free of Spanish or Portuguese control. In contrast, Toussaint L'Overture led a slave rebellion in Haiti, emphasizing the inequality of that social system and reflecting another aspect of Enlightenment thought. Mexico's complex sequence of events that led to its independence in 1821 weaves several Enlightenment themes: oppression of Amerindian people, creole desires for independence, and the motivation to establish a republican government. In contrast to France, where the Catholic Church was seen as a cause for unequal stations in life, in Mexico the cry for equality first came from a Catholic priest, Father Hidalgo.

Other countries soon followed with anti-slave trade legislation: the United States in 1808, France in 1814, the Netherlands in 1817, and eventually Spain in 1845. The British even sent their navy to patrol African ports to enforce their law, although illegal slave trade continued for a number of years until governments took action to outlaw the practice of slavery as well. In Haiti, slavery itself ended with the success of the slave rebellion in 1804, and many newly independent countries in Latin America passed laws forbidding slavery. Eventually slavery was ended by all the Atlantic states by the end of the 19th century, with Britain banning slavery throughout its empire in 1833. The United States ended slavery in 1865, and Brazil was the last major American state to ban slavery in 1888.

Once slavery was abolished, political equality did not follow immediately. Property requirements kept most former slaves from voting, and even though constitutions were changed – as in the United States – economic, political, and social inequality continued to be issues for minorities of African background for years to come. Although the slave trade and the slave system were banned in many areas, they were not totally abolished and are still practiced in some places today. However, the abolitionist movements of the 19th century did put an end to the extreme reliance on slave labor that characterized the era from about 1500 to 1800 and set the stage for later equality movements of the 20th century.

National Liberation in Greece

Whereas the early revolutions in Spain and Italy failed, Greece succeeded in its attempt to gain independence from the Ottoman Turks in a revolution that began in 1821 and continued until 1830. Since the 15th century, the Greeks had lived under Ottoman rule, but their sense of nationality had remained strong through common customs, the Greek language, and the Greek Orthodox religion. As nationalist movements spread across Europe during the early 19th century, secret societies formed in Greece, and in 1821, a revolt erupted, led by Alexander Ypsilanti, a Greek Patriot and a general in the Russian army. Many Russians supported the Greeks, since they shared the Orthodox faith, as well as a common enmity against the Ottoman Turks. However, other great powers, particularly Austria under Metternich, opposed any revolution, even if it was against the Ottoman Empire.

Despite Austria's opposition, many Europeans sympathized with the Greeks. Educated Europeans came to see the Greek struggle as an attempt to revive the culture of classical Greece, long suppressed by a foreign power. Romantic writers and artists, including Lord Byron, thought of Greek freedom as basic to that of all western societies, and their works inspired others to support the cause. In 1827, Great Britain, France, and Russia responded to popular demands at home and sent military forces to convince the Turks to allow Greek freedom. The Turkish fleet was destroyed at Navarino, and Russia attacked and occupied Rumania, which had also been under Turkish rule. The Turks were unable to stop the three powers, and they declared Greece independent in 1830, creating the first fissure in Metternich's conservative order.

Liberal Reform in Britain

By the early 19th century, Britain had practiced constitutionalism for many years, and the growing influence of liberalism was reflected by the country's withdrawal in the 1820s from Metternich's Concert of Europe. Even so, the government's economic policies still favored the rich, and demands for reform swept the country. An early warning sign occurred with a mass meeting for reform at St. Peter's field, Manchester, in 1819. The local government responded by calling out troops to attack, and hundreds of demonstrators – including women and children – were wounded, and several were killed. Reformers nicknamed the incident the **Peterloo Massacre**, and their protests rose to new heights after Parliament passed laws that restricted public meetings, facilitated the prosecution of radicals, and imposed a tax on the radical press. Protestant dissenters and Roman Catholics openly criticized the special privileges accorded the Church of England.

CHANGE OVER TIME:
MAJOR REFORM LEGISLATION
IN BRITAIN

In Britain, change after 1815 took place in a series of reforms that helped to avoid revolution, even though they still caused serious conflict. Major milestones in British reform before 1850 included these pieces of legislation passed by Parliament.

1828 – Restrictions of non-Anglican Protestants lifted

1829 – Restrictions on Catholics lifted; Catholics allowed in Parliament

1832 – The Reform Bill of 1832 changed the British electoral system; suffrage increased and representation redistributed

1833 – Slavery abolished in British Empire; child labor in factories restricted

1834 – Poor Law further restricted child labor in factories

1846 – Corn Laws repealed

1847 – Ten Hours Act limited the workday for women and young people in factories to ten hours

Tories and Whigs disagreed over how to respond to demands for reform, but even the conservative Tories recognized the need to lift newspaper censorship and allow Catholics and religious dissenters to vote and hold public office. In 1828, the government put domestic order in the hands of civil authority by creating a police force. After the more reform-minded Whigs gained power, Parliament passed the important **Reform Bill of 1832**, which marked a fundamental change in Britain's electoral system. Though rejected by the House of Lords, the bill had the support of the House of Commons and the king, and it greatly increased suffrage, allowing some 800,000 well-to-do, property-owning men to vote for the first time. The bill also redistributed representation in Parliament to better reflect population shifts caused by industrialization. As a result, industrial cities – such as Birmingham and Manchester – that had been underrepresented now had voices in the House of Commons. Other reforms of the 1830s abolished slavery in Britain's colonies and restricted the hours that children could work in factories. Another law extended suffrage even more by allowing all resident taxpayers to vote in municipal elections.

During the 1840s Britain's **Corn Laws**, which benefitted the landowning classes, came under attack. These laws placed tariffs on imported grain in order to protect British landowners, but they negatively impacted middle and working-class people because they increased the price of bread. The Anti-Corn Law League spread across the country from its origins in Manchester, appealing to supporters through parades, rallies, songs, speeches, and pamphlets. The government responded by twice lowering duties on a wide range of items, including grain, but the League pressed for more, and finally, the Corn Laws were repealed in 1846. The prime minister – Robert Peel – was ultimately swayed by the potato famine in Ireland, since he believed that repealing the laws would free up more food there. He convinced both the Commons and the Lords to support the repeals, although his actions brought great criticism from conservatives, and ultimately ended his ministry.

The Revolutions of 1830

In 1830, a new wave of liberal and nationalistic movements broke out to challenge the conservative order. The first one took place in France in reaction to the ultraroyalists' attempt to restore the old regime under Charles X. As resistance increased in the Chamber of Deputies, Charles repudiated the Constitutional Charter, issued decrees stripping much of the wealthy middle class of its voting rights, and censored the press. Spontaneous demonstrations in Paris led to fighting on July 26, beginning what became known as the **July Revolution**, and after three days of fighting, the government collapsed. Charles X went into exile in England, and in order to stabilize the country, a group of moderate liberal leaders agreed to give the crown to Charles X's cousin, **Louis Philippe**, duke of Orléans.

Louis Philippe accepted the Constitutional Charter of 1814, and adopted the flag of the French Revolution. He even dressed like a member of the middle class, in business suits and hats. Constitutional changes that favored the interest of the prosperous bourgeoisie were instituted, and financial qualifications for voting were reduced, increasing the number of voters from 100,000 to almost 200,000. However, many supporters of liberalism were bitterly disappointed in these results, since few beyond those in the upper middle class benefitted from the revolution.

Whereas the 1830 revolution in France was primarily motivated by liberal demands, the revolution in the Netherlands was based on nationalism. The area in the south known as the Austrian Netherlands had been merged with the Dutch Republic by the Congress of Vienna, but the people there identified themselves as Belgians, not Dutch. The Belgians – inspired by the July Revolution in France – rose against the Dutch, and King William of the Netherlands appealed to the great powers to intervene. The powers disagreed among themselves, but finally reached an agreement that Belgium could gain its independence in exchange for its neutrality in international affairs. Belgium became a constitutional monarchy in 1831 when the crown of the new kingdom was offered to Leopold of Saxe-Coburg, who abided by the neutrality provision, and set the pattern for Belgian diplomacy for many years to come.

Revolts based on nationalism also took place in 1830 in Italy and Poland. One reason that Russia and Austria did not intervene in the Netherlands was that they were both preoccupied with their own revolts – Russia with the Poles and Austria with Italian provinces. Anti-Austrian uprisings in Italy were unsuccessful when the French refused to support them, but the Polish revolt was more difficult. It began with students in the streets of Warsaw, and then spread to Polish aristocrats – who had long resisted royal control of government. They formed a provisional government, but despite some initial Polish victories on the battlefield, Russian forces crushed the rebels when no other European powers came to aid the Poles. Russia reacted by abolishing the Polish constitution that Tsar Alexander I had initially granted them, and thousands of Poles were executed or exiled.

The Revolutions of 1848

In 1848, liberal and nationalistic revolutions broke out across Europe and were even more widespread than in 1830. Like most of the previous revolutions, these were led by political liberals, who were generally drawn from the middle classes. Throughout the Continent, liberals were pushing for their programs of more representative government, civil liberty, and unregulated economic life. In Britain, revolution was avoided through a series of reform laws: most importantly the Reform Bill of 1832 and the repeal of the Corn Laws in 1846. However, on the Continent, peaceful tactics were less successful, so political liberals gained the support of the urban working classes, who wanted improved working and economic conditions rather than a liberal framework of government. Their discontent was intensified by crop failures across Europe beginning in 1845, with the Irish potato famine only the worst of many.

Outside France, nationalism was an important common factor in the uprisings that ensued. Germans, Hungarians, Italians, Czechs, and many other groups in eastern Europe wanted their own national states. The Austrian Empire was most profoundly endangered by nationalism, but in the end the nationalities failed to unite against the old empire. Despite the outbreak of so many major uprisings, the revolutions failed to establish genuinely liberal or national states, partly because the rebels had such different goals for their reforms.

Revolution in France

A severe economic depression beginning in 1846 convinced many working class urbanites and peasants to support the middle-class disgruntlement with Louis Philippe's government. The middle class wanted to extend suffrage, but the government resisted, and so with growing support from others, a group of moderate and radical republicans overthrew the monarchy and established a provisional government and declared France to be a republic once again in February 1848. The new government issued liberal reforms – an end to the death penalty for political crimes, the abolition of slavery in the colonies, and freedom of the press – and agreed to support universal manhood suffrage.

The provisional government established national workshops, which provided the unemployed with jobs, but the cost of the program led to a new surtax on property taxes, alienating peasants and landowners. Women, too, demanded workshops, but the government was able to provide only a few for women workers. Soon a split developed between the moderate republicans, who had the support of most of France, and the radical republicans, whose main supporters were from the Parisian working class. Voters elected a largely moderate National Assembly in April 1848, which – frightened by the growing deficits – closed the workshops on June 23, but the workers rose in protest. In the **June Days** – as the following period

THEMATIC LEARNING OBJECTIVE: INDIVIDUAL AND SOCIETY: RADICAL AND MODERATE WOMEN'S GROUPS IN 1848

The February Revolution of 1848 in France inspired many feminists to demand equal rights for women. Many joined a wide variety of political clubs that emerged, and some women even tried unsuccessfully to vote in the various elections of 1848. The most radical group of women called themselves the *Vesuvians,* after the volcano in Italy. They demanded full equality for women in the home, the right for women to serve in the military, and similarility in dress for men and women. A more conservative group of women – the *Voix des Femmes* (Voice of women) – organized a daily newspaper that addressed women's issues. They supported traditional gender roles, but tried to elevate the importance of family and motherhood. They argued that women must receive better educations, the right to work, equal civil rights, property rights, and the right to vote.
By the end of the year, the *Vesuvians* and the *Voix des Femmes* suffered the same fate as that of the radical workers. Their workshops were shut down, and women were forbidden to participate in political clubs. A few years later, two leaders associated with the *Voix des Femmes* were arrested, tried, and imprisoned for attempting to organize groups to improve the economic situation for working-class women. The efforts of both women's groups were totally erased, just as earlier French feminists had been defeated in 1793.

came to be called – tens of thousands took to the streets of Paris, and the government summoned the army to fight the workers. The republic's army crushed the protest, with more than 10,000 killed, 12,000 arrested, and 4,000 deported to the French colony of Algeria in northern Africa.

With the defeat of the Parisian workers, the moderates prevailed, confirming that middle-class desires for political representation and protection of private property would dominate the French government. The victor in the presidential election in December 1848 was **Louis Napoleon Bonaparte**, a nephew of the great emperor. Within four years, President Napoleon would follow the pattern set by his famous uncle to become the emperor of France.

Prussia and the Frankfurt Assembly

The February revolution in Paris sparked revolutions in many other parts of Europe, including the German states. Many German rulers promised constitutions, a free press, and other liberal reforms, and even Prussia made concessions. Prussian liberals hoped to transform absolutist Prussia into a liberal constitutional monarchy, which would in turn take the lead in merging all other German states into a unified nation. After the Prussian army failed to push back a major demonstration in front of Berlin's royal palace on March 18, 1848, **King Frederick William IV** agreed to abolish censorship and work for a united Germany. An important result was the election – by universal manhood suffrage – of the **Frankfurt Assembly**, an all-German parliament called to prepare a constitution for a new united Germany. However, the 800 delegates to the assembly had little practical political experience, and they had no real means of compelling the German rulers to accept the constitution that they drew up. As in France, the delegates were mainly moderates from the middle class, and their desire for political unity clashed with the demands from the working class, and so the rebels were divided. The advantage lay with the princes, who controlled the armed forces, and by the fall of 1848, Frederick William IV had a change of heart, and sent his army to crush the revolution in Berlin. By 1849, the leadership of the German unification effort passed from the liberals at Frankfurt to the Prussian military monarchy.

Ethnic Fighting in Austria

The revolts among nationalities in the Austrian Empire began in Hungary, which had long been a region of discontent. The Hungarian liberals under **Louis Kossuth** demanded "commonwealth" status, which would allow them to have their own legislature while keeping the Habsburg monarch. In March 1848, demonstrations in Buda, Prague, and Vienna led to Metternich's dismissal, and he fled to England in disguise. Emperor Ferdinand promised a constitution, an elected parliament, and the end of censorship. Hungary was granted its own legislature, a separate national army, and control over foreign policy and budget. In Bohemia, the Czechs demanded their own government as well and convened a Slav congress similar to the Frankfurt Assembly for Germans. This action provoked Germans in areas with Slav majorities to protest, and so the nationalities began to argue among themselves. As in France and Germany, divisions between radical and moderate revolutionaries weakened their movement as well.

Sensing these divisions among the rebels, the Austrian government took action in June by sending military forces to suppress the Czech rebels in Prague. By October, the Austrian forces had crushed the rebels in Vienna, and by December Ferdinand was forced to abdicate to his nephew, Francis Joseph I, who turned his attention to Hungary. He gained support from Tsar Nicholas I of Russia, who sent troops to help suppress the Hungarians. Hungary was put under martial law, and Kossuth fled to the United States. Autocratic government was restored, and no liberal or radical reforms remained in place by 1849.

The Revolutionary Movement in Italy

The reestablishment of Austrian control over the Hungarians and Czechs led to the defeat of the revolutionary movement in Italy also. At first, most Italian states rallied behind Sardinian leaders, but there were serious differences among the insurgent Italians. The question of the future status of the Papal States was a particular problem, since the pope protected the age-old independence of his domain. Divisions made the Italian states vulnerable to defeat by Austrian armies that challenged them. The revolutionary forces were defeated, and the king of Sardinia was required to abdicate as punishment for leading the movement. Despite this setback, the kingdom of Sardinia emerged after 1849 as the one source of hope for the national unification of Italy. Republican schemes were discredited by the failures of 1848-49, but more and more, nationalistic Italians turned toward Sardinia in much the same fashion as Germans began to look to Prussia to unify them. In both countries, Austria had become the arch-enemy of all liberal and nationalistic reform.

Throughout Europe in 1848, popular revolts forcefully demanded the formation of liberal constitutions and governments, and many nationalities also revolted in pursuit of self-government. However, these revolutions failed, since divisions – between moderates and radicals, middle and working classes, and among various ethnic groups – diffused and ultimately undermined their goals. However, liberalism and nationalism would eventually prevail in the second half of the 19th century, and radicalism would survive to provide strong challenges for traditional regimes.

CONCEPTS AND IDENTIFICATIONS

Alexander I
balance of power
Beethoven, Ludwig van

Bolívar, Simón
Bonaparte, Louis Napoleon
bourgeoisie
Burke, Edmund
burschenschaften
Byron, Lord
carbonari
Carlsbad Decrees
Castlereagh, Rubert
Charles X
classicism
Coleridge, Samuel Taylor
Concert of Europe
Congress of Vienna
conservatism
Corn Laws
Decembrist Revolt
Delacroix, Eugène
economic liberalism, political liberalism
Frankfurt Assembly
Frederick William III
Frederick William IV
Friedrich, Charles Caspar
German Confederation
Goethe, Johan Wolfgang von
Gothic literature
Hidalgo y Costilla, Miguel
Holy Alliance
Hugo, Victor
Ivanhoe
July Revolution
June Days
juntas
liberalism
Kossuth, Louis
Louis XVIII
Louis Philippe
Marx, Karl
Metternich, Prince Klemens von
Mill, John Stuart
nationalism
Nicholas I
On Liberty

Pedro I
Peterloo Massacre
Quadruple Alliance
radicalism
Reform Bill of 1832
republicanism
romanticism
San Martín, José de
Scott, Sir Walter
self determination
Shelley, Percy Bysshe
socialism
Talleyrand, Charles
ultraroyalists
zollverein

CHAPTER 15:
THE AGE OF NATIONALISM,
REALISM, AND MASS POLITICS
1850-1914

The revolutions of 1848 failed largely because those that agitated for change could not agree on common goals. Particularly, the tensions between middle and working classes were manifestations of ideological differences that crystallized in 1848 with the publication of Karl Marx's *Communist Manifesto* on the eve of the revolution in France. As Marx and his colleague Friedrich Engels agitated on behalf of an international socialist revolutionary movement, the latent antagonism between liberal and socialist ideals became clear and definite. Forces in European politics realigned as the middle classes became increasingly uncomfortable with more radical social revolutionary doctrines, and liberals all over Europe shifted emphasis to the goal of national unification. The era that followed, then, from 1850 to 1914, may be characterized above all as an "age of nationalism."

The era was also characterized by a new kind of intellectual and political realism. After the failure of the 1848 revolutions, idealism and romanticism were discredited in European culture and politics. Revolutionaries became less optimistic, and conservatives more resigned to the use of repression. Imaginings of what ought to be were replaced by acceptance of what was real, but the trend did not halt the changes set in place by the mixture of conservative, liberal, and radical ideologies. By the end of the century, Europe had moved into the age of mass politics, accelerated by mass-circulation newspapers, increasing levels of education, and rapid economic growth. Universal manhood suffrage was a reality in many countries, and political parties grew in numbers and diversity of political beliefs, including socialism. Mass politics reinforced the growing nationalism as communications improved and access to government improved, and more governments organized around the concept of nationality.

FRANCE UNDER NAPOLEON III

After the Revolution of 1848, **Louis Napoleon**, nephew of Napoleon Bonaparte, was elected president of the new Second Republic. The Bonaparte name reassured voters during this time of turbulence, and Louis cooperated with the legislature and did his duties as president while gaining personal popularity among the French people. During the short life of the Second Republic – from 1848 to 1852 – republicans and socialists, who had cooperated to overthrow King Louis Philippe in 1848, soon quarreled, and after some months the socialists were repressed by force. After Louis's request to stand for reelection was turned down by the National Assembly in 1851, he used the military to seize control of the government. In 1852, he first restored universal manhood suffrage, and then used a device invented for France by his uncle – the **plebiscite,** or a national referendum – to get support for restoring the empire. The French people voted overwhelmingly to support their new emperor, who was crowned on December 2, 1852, as **Napoleon III** (Napoleon's son had briefly held the title of Napoleon II in 1814), and the Second Republic was replaced by the Second Empire. The collapse of the French Second Republic ushered in an age of conservative leadership in France.

More than any other political leader of the era, Napoleon III symbolized a new combination of economic liberalism, nationalism, and authoritarian rule. He kept an extravagant court with royal ceremony, and as chief of state, he controlled the armed forces, police, and civil service. Only he could introduce legislation and declare war. Yet he maintained universal manhood suffrage, he did not pretend to reign by divine right, and he repeatedly called for plebiscites to reinforce the legitimacy of his rule. Napoleon III also supported economic liberalism by promoting a strong economy, public works programs, and jobs, and so kept the support of many middle and working-class people. These policies and practices successfully undermined the appeal of radical politics.

Economic prosperity and political success characterized Napoleon III's first years in office. He believed that the government should actively promote the economy, and he took many steps that stimulated economic growth. He initiated slum clearance projects that provided healthier living conditions, and he sponsored other public works projects, such as ports, roads, railroads, and grand new public buildings. Railroad connections grew tremendously under Napoleon III, and iron production boomed. One of his most famous projects was the reconstruction of the city of Paris, in which many narrow medieval streets and city walls were destroyed and replaced by broad boulevards and large public squares. Additionally, an underground sewage system was constructed. The projects not only made the new Paris look more modern, but the broad streets also made it almost impossible for rebels to throw up barricades to protest the regime. The new configuration also allowed military troops to move easily around the city should revolts occur. Since these projects provided jobs for urban workers, and the new rail lines allowed peasants to get their produce to market more efficiently, most French people enjoyed better living standards as a result of economic growth during the 1850s and 1860s.

In international affairs, Napoleon III's main goal was to reinvigorate French power after the constraints imposed by the Congress of Vienna. He unabashedly desired to restore international glory for France, and in the true Bonaparte style, he also sought to exert his own personal power. He challenged Russia in the Crimean War, and then confronted Austria in the War of Italian Unification. Louis Napoleon also asserted French rule in Algeria and Southeast Asia and maneuvered (unsuccessfully) to restore monarchical power in Mexico. In the 1860s, when his authoritarian methods began to be questioned more seriously, he liberalized his regime by legalizing trade unions and granting workers the right to strike. He also allowed the Legislative Corps (an elected body with little previous power) more say in policymaking, including debate over the budget. These tactics caused him to remain immensely popular, so that when a plebiscite was held in May 1870 on whether to accept a new constitution that might restore a parliamentary government, the people again supported their emperor.

THE CRIMEAN WAR

The growing nationalism in Europe was promoted at mid-century by the **Crimean War,** fought in 1853-4. The war encouraged the nations of Europe to realign and become more suspicious of one another, leading them to ignore the concerns of other major powers and focus on their own national interests.

The Crimean War had many causes, and once it started, it revealed to all the major powers how weak the Ottoman Empire had grown. The war was sparked as Russia's armies attacked southward, threatening Ottoman lands that Russia had wanted for many years. Fearing that the Ottomans would fall under Russian pressure, France and Britain sent troops to the area. France feared that a successful war against the Ottomans would provide European powers the opportunity to redraw the continent's borders, which might decrease French power and influence. Britain had long worried that the collapse of the Ottoman Empire would lead Russia to seek territorial gains in the Mediterranean, which would challenge Britain's naval supremacy in that region. Austria and Prussia remained neutral, since Austria had its own ambitions in the Balkans, and, for the moment, Prussia followed Austrian leadership. Much of the fighting took place on the Crimean Peninsula on the north shore of the Black Sea. It resulted in a sound, humiliating defeat of Russia, but it also cast the Ottomans in the role of a lesser power that had to be protected by others.

The Crimean War was significant beyond its effects on the individual countries that fought in it, partly because it marked a transition from traditional to modern warfare. The high casualty rate was largely due to varying levels of technology that were used by different sides at different times. For example, highly trained cavalry traditionally had been used to break through the front lines of the infantry while the infantry reloaded their guns. The cavalry did not carry guns because they were too heavy. During the Crimean War, however, this situation made them vulnerable to the new technologies of the percussion cap and the breech-loading rifle. Both inventions, which had been adopted throughout Europe in the years preceding the war, made firing rapid and more accurate. The result was widespread slaughter of cavalry. Warfare methods had to change, since a line of marching soldiers could be decimated by the new technology.

The war changed the balance of power among European countries in many ways. First, it shattered the image of an invincible Russia that had influenced the Continent's international politics since the close of the Napoleonic wars. Just as importantly, the Concert of Europe was dismantled as a means of dealing with international relations among European powers. This occurred because, following the successful repression of the 1848 revolutions, the powers feared uprisings less than they had earlier in the century, and they moved away from the bonds created by the Congress of Vienna. France, of course, was glad to be distanced from the agreements that had thwarted its ambitions (especially since its new leader was a Bonaparte), Prussia became increasingly impatient with Austria's domination of German politics, and Russia was motivated to overcome the humiliation of

MARKER EVENT: HYGIENE ON THE BATTLEFIELD

Throughout history, a soldier who escaped death on the battlefield did not always survive the war. Often people died from diseases, such as septicemia and dyssentery, or from wounds that bled excessively or became infected. An important turning point for hygiene for battlefield wounds came in the mid-1800s when a young Englishwoman named **Florence Nightingale** applied techniques she learned in France and Prussia to bring about significant improvements in British healthcare. Nightingale went to the Crimea to tend to wounded soldiers in the war there in 1853-1854, and she found the need to improve the sanitation of the hospitals. Her influence led the British government to flush out the sewer systems and improve ventilation, measures that greatly reduced death rates. When she returned to London she established institutes for nursing that were widely imitated in other countries.

One reason that Florence Nightingale became so well known is that she lived in a time when another technological marker event – the telegraph – made it possible for news from the battlefield to get back home quickly. To sell their papers, journalists looked for heroic actions, and Florence Nightingale became a "star" with the folks back home.

revealing its weakness by losing the Crimean War. The breakup of old patterns of international relations, then, set the stage for each country to shift emphasis to its own military power and diplomatic influence, which could be strengthened through nationalism. It opened the opportunity for two nations – Italy and Germany – to at last become unified under their own governments.

ITALIAN UNIFICATION

Italy had never been a united nation prior to 1860, but had been divided into competing city-states since the Middle Ages. After the power of the city-states waned during post-Renaissance days, the Italian peninsula became a battleground for great powers, and was ultimately reorganized in 1815 at the Congress of Vienna. The northern provinces of Lombardy and Venetia were given to Austria, Sardinia and Piedmont had been united, central Italy and Rome were ruled by the papacy, and Naples and Sicily were ruled by a branch of the Bourbon family.

Attempts to Unify during the Early 19th Century

Between 1815 and 1845, two charismatic leaders – **Giuseppe Mazzini** and **Vincenzo Gioberti** – led unsuccessful movements to unite Italy. Mazzini sought a centralized democratic republic based on universal suffrage and the will of the people, and Gioberti – a Catholic priest – called for a federation of existing states under the leadership of the pope. When Mazzini's republicanism was snuffed out by Austria in 1848, another option for unification became more viable – consolidation of states under Sardinia's monarch, **Victor Emmanuel**, who granted a liberal constitution to his country in the same year. Sardinia had a parliamentary government, with elected representatives who had real power over taxes. To many middle-class liberals, this option seemed much more reliable than Mazzini's radical republicanism. The pope, too, became reconciled to unification under a constitutional monarch after he was temporarily driven from Rome during the upheavals of 1848, a situation that caused him to fear republicanism.

Cavour and Garibaldi in Italy

Victor Emmanuel's able chief minister, **Camillo Benso di Cavour**, emerged as an important architect for the unification of Italy during the 1850s. Cavour – an aristocrat – embraced the economic doctrine and business activities associated with the prosperous middle class, and so he led the way for the alliance between the aristocracy and the middle class under the banner of the strong nation-state. He joined the Crimean War on the side of France and Britain, and impressed the diplomats at the peace conference with his intelligence and political ability. His national goals were limited and realistic; until 1859 he sought unity only for the states of northern and perhaps central Italy in a greatly enlarged Sardinia. His program of highway and railroad building, civil liberties, and opposition to clerical privilege appealed to moderates throughout northern Italy. In order to drive

Austria from the northern Italian states, Cavour enlisted the aid of Napoleon III to goad Austria into attacking Sardinia. Napoleon came to Sardinia's defense, but once victorious, he turned on Sardinia and made a compromise peace with the Austrians. Cavour felt betrayed, but the war had driven Austria from most of northern Italy. Dedicated nationalists in central Italy supported his cause, so the people in several central Italian states voted in early 1860 to join with Sardinia under Victor Emmanuel's rule.

By 1860, Napoleon was quite concerned about the rising power of Sardinia, but Cavour expanded his dream of a united Italy by calling on superpatriot **Giuseppe Garibaldi** for support. Garibaldi had fought in the revolution of 1848 for the cause of republicanism, but he set aside his ideological differences with Cavour in order to achieve unification. He seized the momentum gained from the unification of northern Italy to support Sicilian rebels who rose against the Bourbon-controlled government of the kingdom of Naples. In May 1860, Garibaldi set sail from Genoa with a thousand poorly trained but dedicate red-shirted volunteers to Palermo, where his forces defeated the better-equipped government army, and within two months he had occupied almost all of Sicily. Volunteers from all over Italy joined Garibaldi, and with this support, he sailed to the Italian mainland, where he won the entire kingdom of Naples.

Cavour shared Garibaldi's goal of unification, but he feared that Garibaldi's charisma would unleash support for republicanism, so he sent his army to occupy the Papal States to ensure that Garibaldi did not overthrow the pope, who was reluctant to give up his lands to a unified Italy. Although Garibaldi supported republicanism over constitutional monarchy, he accepted the leadership of Sardinia, and he willingly submitted the southern part of Italy – which he controlled – to King **Victor Emmanuel II**. Garibaldi and the king met in Naples to seal the union of north and south, and their historic ride through the streets together symbolically created the country of Italy. Venice became part of the kingdom in 1866, and Rome joined in 1870. The new kingdom was neither radical nor democratic, but Cavour had succeeded in turning popular nationalism in a conservative direction.

THE UNIFICATION OF GERMANY

After the Frankfurt Assembly failed to achieve German unification in 1848-1849, German nationalists looked to Austria and Prussia as the only two states powerful enough to lead the unification movement. However, these two traditional rivals constantly sought to check one another's influence, so little progress toward a united Germany was made during the 1850s. However, Austria's fear that nationalism would tear its empire apart eventually tilted the leadership toward Prussia. Another factor that supported Prussian leadership was the rapid growth of industry in the north, which – along with the German customs union (Zollverein) – greatly enriched Prussia. Austria tried to destroy the Zollverein, but without success, so that the exclusion of Austria from the new Germany became an economic reality.

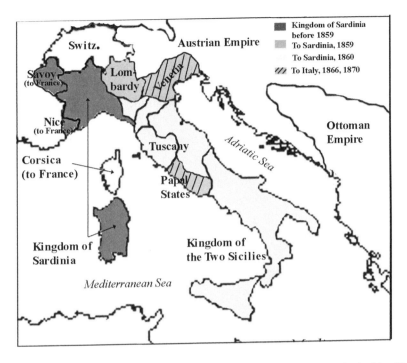

The Unification of Italy. The Italian peninsula united between 1859 and 1870 under the leadership of Sardinia.

The Rise of Bismarck

Italy's Sardinian-led national uprising greatly encouraged Prussia to do likewise in Germany. The Prussian king, **Wilhelm I**, who came to power in 1861, had great ambitions to strengthen the country further through military reform. However, Prussia had emerged from 1848 with a parliament populated by the landed aristocracy and the wealthy middle class whose goal it was to make Prussia less, not more, militaristic. Above all, these representatives wanted to establish the principle that parliament, not the king, had the ultimate political power. In 1862, the king appointed Count **Otto von Bismarck** as prime minister, hoping that together they could enlarge and strengthen the military. Bismarck ignored parliament's opposition to the reforms, and he collected the necessary taxes and reorganized the government anyway. From 1862 to 1866, Bismarck governed Prussia with little input from the legislature, and he promoted an active foreign policy, which led to war and German unification. In 1863, elections sustained the liberal majority in parliament, so Bismarck found a way to attract popular support away from parliament and toward the monarchy and the army. Playing on German nationalism to support the military in its conquests, he, like Cavour in Italy, brought about unification through conservative institutions, and held populist republican impulses at bay.

Bismarck's approach to Germany unification is often termed ***realpolitik,*** or the politics of reality. Rather than following an ideal dream of natural brotherhood, he strategized from a practical perspective, meeting facts and situations as they arose. The wars that he waged were chosen when all other diplomatic alternatives had been exhausted and after he was reasonably confident that he could win. *Realpolitik* is a German term, and Bismarck was its most famous proponent, but many others – including Louis Napoleon and Camillo di Cavour – also used it to their advantage.

Wars with Denmark and Austria

Bismarck's first war was with Denmark over the duchies of Schleswig and Holstein, after the Danish king tried again in 1864, as in 1848, to claim them for a centralized Danish state. Their populations were a mixture of Germans and Danes, but Holstein belonged to the German Confederation, and Bismarck convinced

**ORIGINAL DOCUMENT:
BISMARCK'S "BLOOD AND
IRON" SPEECH**

In September 1862 there was a crisis in Prussia where the Prussian Landtag, or lower parliamentary house, refused to approve increased military spending in defiance of the king's wishes. On September 17th, the crisis had reached such a pitch that Wilhelm I seriously considered abdicating his throne. His royal authority was saved by the appointment as prime minister of Otto von Bismarck, who asserted authoritarian control over the unruly legislators with these famous words:

"The position of Prussia in Germany will not be determined by its liberalism but by its power...Prussia must concentrate its strength and hold it for the favourable moment, which has already come and gone several times. Since the treaties of Vienna, our frontiers have been ill-designed for a healthy body politic. Not through speeches and majority decisions will the great questions of the day be decided – that was the great mistake of 1848 and 1849 – but by iron and blood."

Over time, the last phrase of the speech has been reversed, so that it is known in history as the "blood and iron" speech, a tribute to military might and the Industrial Revolution.

Reference: Louis L. Snyder, ed., *Documents of German History* (New Brunswick, N.J., 1958), p. 202.

Austria to join him in attacking Denmark. Together the two large states easily defeated Denmark, and they agreed to divide the supervision of the two duchies, with Prussia taking Schleswig and Austria administering Holstein. However, Bismarck used this joint supervision to create friction with the Austrians and provoke them into a war in the summer of 1866.

Austria went to war with the support of most small states in the German Confederation. Within a few weeks the modernized Prussian army, using railroads and breech-loading rifles against the more traditional Austrian military, won a decisive victory. Bismarck then was in a position to exclude Austria from German affairs, and he organized a North German Confederation controlled by Prussia. He coerced the south German states to sign a military treaty with Prussia, and he also established a customs parliament for all the members of the Zollverein, including the southern German states. The southern states, though, were Catholic and sympathetic to Austria, so further measures were needed to convince them to unify under Prussian control.

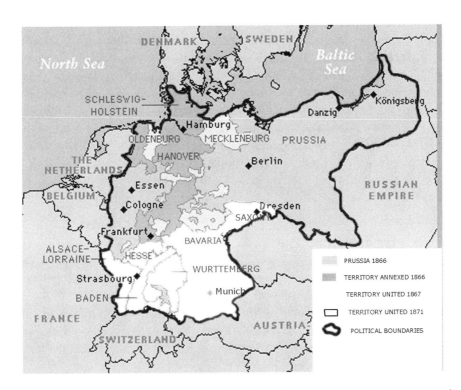

The Unification of Germany. Otto von Bismarck, chief minister of Prussia, maneuvered the German states into three wars that dramatically increased the size of the territory under his control. In 1871, all the territory enclosed by the dark boundary on the map above was included in the German Empire.

The Franco-Prussian War

Bismarck realized that a patriotic war with France would convince the south German states to accept Prussian leadership of a unified Germany, and he understood the territorial ambitions of the French emperor, Napoleon III. The pretext for the dispute was whether a distant relative of Prussia's Wilhelm I might become king of Spain, but the French needed little prodding to declare war in 1870, since Napoleon III wanted to bolster his star power with the French people. He also reacted with alarm to Bismarck's growing power. With the motivation of teaching Prussia a lesson, France declared war on Prussia on July 15, 1870. The south German states reacted as Bismarck had calculated they would, and gave the Prussians their wholehearted support. The war was short; it ended on September 1, 1870, with Prussia's decisive, humiliating defeat of the French army at a battle at Sedan, where Napoleon III himself was captured. Three days later, republicans in Paris vowed to continue fighting in an effort to restore the French Republic, but they surrendered in January 1871 to Bismarck's siege.

The victorious Wilhelm I was proclaimed emperor ("kaiser," a derivative of the word "Caesar") of Germany in the Hall of Mirrors in Versailles Palace in the splendid surroundings that had once graced the court of Louis XIV. There the **Second German Empire** was proclaimed as a follow-up to the Holy Roman Empire that Napoleon I had destroyed. The terms of the peace treaty signed in May 1871 required France to cede the rich industrial provinces of Alsace and Lorraine to Germany and to pay a multibillion-franc indemnity. As a result of this great victory, Germany became the most powerful state on the Continent in less than a decade. At last, Germany was united and liberals rejoiced, although the deed had been accomplished by an authoritarian monarchy using military might, an illustration of the adaptability of the concept of nationalism. All ideologies embraced nationalism as it became a powerful force in reshaping virtually every corner of Europe.

NATION BUILDING: 1850-1914

Although the unifications of Italy and Germany greatly changed the balance of power in Europe, other countries were also focused on nationalism, and sought to strengthen their governments as they kept a watchful eye on developments in the two new countries. Like Italy and Germany, most were based on conservative principles, but all were affected by demands to liberalize, and radical movements gained followers in many areas.

France: 1870-1914

The loss of the Franco-Prussian War and the overthrow of Napoleon III left the French more divided than ever on the question of whether France should be a

Politics

THEMATIC LEARNING OBJECTIVE: STATES AND OTHER INSTITUTIONS OF POWER: THE FORESIGHT OF ALEXIS DE TOCQUEVILLE

In early 1852, shortly after Louis Napoleon had seized the French government through a coup d'état, Alexis de Tocqueville – a shrewd political observer and writer – communicated his concern in this excerpt from a letter he wrote to his friend, Henry Reeve:

"We know this only too well in France; governments never escape the law of their origins. This one, which arrives by means of the army, which can only endure by means of the army, which minds its popularity and even its reason for existing only in the memories of military glory, this government will be dragged fatally into wanting territorial expansion, spheres of influence, in other words, into war. This is, at least, what I fear, and what all sensible people dread with me. In war, it will surely find death, but perhaps then its death will cost us very dearly."

Although his concerns were not validated until 1870, his description is chillingly accurate, as he foretold the impending doom of Napoleon III's brave new empire at the hands of the Prussian army in the Franco-Prussian War.

Reference: Quoted in Alexis de Tocqueville, *Selected Letters on Politics and Society,* ed. by Robert Boesche, trans. by James Toupin and Roger Boesche (Berkeley: University of California Press, 1985), pp. 283-284.

monarchy or a republic. As had been true since the French Revolution, political radicals still had powerful voices, and Karl Marx's vision of a socialist society had great appeal among many, especially in Paris. Monarchists dominated the National Assembly, who gave executive power to Adolphe Thiers, an experienced politician, to negotiate the peace treaty with Prussia in May 1871. Even before the peace treaty was signed, Parisians elected a new municipal government, called the **Paris Commune**, in protest to the conservative government. Political radicals and socialists participated in the Commune, and the National Assembly – meeting at Versailles – sent an army to bombard the city. During seven days in May the troops restored order to Paris and reclaimed political control of the city at the cost of about 20,000 lives.

The Paris Commune became a legend all across Europe. Marxists proclaimed that it was a true proletarian government that had been suppressed by the bourgeoisie. However, the Commune was supported by many middle-class Parisians, and its goal was not a worker's republic according to Marx's vision, but rather the creation of small, democratic self-governing communities. The National Assembly's army managed to keep France from literally splintering apart, but its actions set Paris against the provinces, just as had happened in 1848.

The Third Republic

Despite the chaos of 1870-1871, France managed to establish a new republic that stabilized the country until 1914. One reason that the National Assembly decided on a republican form of government was that the monarchists, with loyalties divided between the Bourbon and Orléans families, could not agree about who should be king,. The quarrel was exacerbated by the Bourbon claimant's insistence that the white flag of the Bourbons be restored as the official flag of France. While the monarchists argued, the republicans gained strength. They benefitted from Thiers's destruction of the radical Commune, showing the fearful middle-class provincials that a republic could also be moderate and socially conservative. In 1875, the National Assembly, still monarchist in sentiment but unable to find a king, created the structure for the **Third Republic**, with a Chamber of Deputies elected by universal manhood suffrage, a Senate chosen indirectly, and a president elected by the two legislative bodies. In contrast to the divided monarchists, the republicans had strong leaders, most notably Léon Gambetta, who was an eloquent politician who appealed to both middle and working-class people. He brought stability after the first president – the autocratic Marshall MacMahon – was forced to resign by the National Assembly, and by 1879, the majority of the National Assembly were republicans.

The republican government brought stability to France, but its effectiveness was limited by the lack of a strong executive. The parliamentary government was meant to check the ambitions of potential dictators, but the two-house legislature often governed inefficiently. The government's ability to rule was further weakened by the multiparty system. Parties represented the many divided ideologies that had emerged since the French Revolution, and since no one party could command a majority in parliament, coalition cabinets were formed. These coalitions were fragile and apt to fail as parties argued among themselves. However, despite its inadequacies, the Third Republic was the longest in all of French history, lasting until 1940, and as a result of its longevity, France never returned to its monarchical past.

The Dreyfus Affair

The greatest challenge to the Third Republic came in 1894, when France was torn apart by the **Dreyfus Affair**. In many ways, the arguments represented the conflict between traditional monarchists and the fragile alliance of republicans that had disrupted France as the Third Republic was beginning. The Roman Catholic Church had generally supported the monarchist cause, and republican leaders promoted an anticlerical campaign, designed to reduce the church's influence in national life. Anti-Semitism was another important factor in creating the crisis, with some clergy and monarchists believing that the republic was backed by a conspiracy of Jews. In this atmosphere, a Jewish captain in the French army, **Alfred Dreyfus**, was charged with spying for Germany, and in December 1894, he was sentenced to imprisonment in the penal colony of Devil's Island in French Guiana.

Many doubts remained about Dreyfus's guilt, and in early 1898, Colonel Georges Picquart, the new head of the French intelligence service, provided evidence indicating that Major Ferdinand Esterhazy was guilty and Dreyfus was innocent. Although Esterhazy was acquitted by a court-martial, it came to light that key documents used by the prosecution against Dreyfus had been forged. In 1898, a French novelist, Émile **Zola,** published an article titled "*J'accuse*" (I Accuse), on the front page of a Paris daily newspaper, in which he argued that the army had deliberately denied due process to Dreyfus and had suppressed or forged evidence. Zola was convicted of libel and received a one-year prison sentence, but he escaped to England. The Zola article led to public riots and numerous quarrels in many households, and it eroded public confidence in the Republic and in French institutions. The government finally pardoned Dreyfus in 1899, and in 1906, a civilian court set aside the results of both military trials.

The Habsburg Empire

Following the revolutions of 1848, Austria sought to create a modern, united state under **Franz Joseph I**. For the first time, the empire imposed uniform laws and taxes, and most internal customs barriers were abolished. The capital city of Vienna was modernized, and some industrialization took place as railways were built and foreign capital financed construction projects. Yet Franz Joseph still ruled as an absolute monarch, and liberals and many ethnic minorities saw him as a roadblock to change. Caught in the changing times, Franz Joseph announced a new federal constitution in 1860, one that gave considerable authority to regional assemblies. Yet the plan only provoked arguments among liberals, bureaucrats, and ethnic groups, and so the following year the emperor reversed his position, and instead established a centralized bicameral parliament in Vienna. The arguments increased, and Hungary in particular objected, since a centralized parliament would be dominated by the German-speaking middle class.

The Dual Monarchy

By 1866, Franz Joseph was in a position of weakness after his defeat by Prussia, and yet the Hungarians were not strong enough to break the emperor's power. A compromise was reached, and the Hungarian elites forced the emperor to accept a **Dual Monarchy**, in which the Magyars (the dominant Hungarian ethnic group) had home rule over the Hungarian kingdom. Hungary became an autonomous state joined to Austria only through the emperor, and Franz Joseph became king of Hungary. The emperor kept his authority in foreign policy, but the Hungarians mostly ruled themselves after 1867, and common policies – such as tariffs – were negotiated in Vienna. The unusual arrangement lasted for fifty years, and it served as a roadblock to strengthening the empire from the center.

Pan-Slavism

Although the Dual Monarchy addressed Hungarian demands for self rule, it also strengthened the demands of other ethnic groups to have self-determination, too. In giving authority to the Magyars in Hungary, it suppressed the voices of the Romanians, Croatians, and Serbs. For dissatisfied ethnic groups all over Austria, a nationalistic movement called **Pan-Slavism** took hold that bound the loyalty of all ethnic Slavs together, linked through a common heritage across national boundaries. Since Russia was the largest Slavic country, Slavic people in Austria often felt nationalistic bonds with Russian Slavs, a situation that weakened their loyalties to the Habsburg dynasty.

Russia: the Reform Era

Alexander II, the tsar that followed the very conservative Nicholas I, reacted to Russia's disastrous defeat in the Crimean War by focusing on the economy, particularly the need to industrialize. He saw the serf labor system as the biggest obstacle to crafting an industrial economy, and as a result, he emancipated serfs in 1861, a few years before slaves were freed in the United States. Serfdom had been abolished in western Europe after 1789 and in Prussia and Hungary after they had experienced revolutions in 1848. Alexander did not wish to turn away from Russian traditions completely; he was trying to keep the balance between westernization and preservation of Slavic traditions. The decision to eliminate serfdom was a practical one that he hoped would pave the way for a more productive economy that would restore Russia's place in a world where balance of power among nations was increasingly important. Although serfs received land (in contrast to slaves in the U.S.), they gained no new political rights, and they were still tied to their villages until they could pay for the land they were given. Since these payments were difficult for most peasants to make, they came to resent the nobles who collected their money. As a result, in many ways discontent worsened rather than improved after emancipation.

Another reform implemented by Alexander II was the creation of local political councils, called **zemstvos**, to replace the nobility's traditional authority over the serfs. The zemstvos set local policies, such as road building and educating children, and they gave a voice to some middle-class professionals, such as doctors

ORIGINAL DOCUMENT:
THE DUAL MONARCHY EXPLAINED
BY THE AUSTRIAN PRIME MINISTER

In his memoirs, the Austrian Prime Minister, Friedrich Ferdinand Count von Beust, explained why the government recognized Hungary as a separate kingdom while other groups were not. His view of Hungary as a special case – based on the Magyar kingdom from ancient times – is reflected in the excerpt below.

"Now my object is...to show the various elements of this great empire that it is to the benefit of each of them to act in harmony with its neighbor....But to this I have made one exception. Hungary is an ancient monarchy, more ancient as such than Austria proper....I have endeavoured to give Hungary not a new position with regard to the Austrian empire, but to secure her in the one which she has occupied. The Emperor of Austria is King of Hungary; my idea was that he should revive in his person the Constitution of which he and his ancestors have been the heads....It is no plan of separation that I have carried out: on the contrary, it is one of close union, not by the creation of a new power, but by the recognition of an old one...."

Reference: Memories of Friedrich Ferdinand Count von Beust, Vol. I, ed. by Baron Henry de Worms (London: Remington, 1887), pp. xx-xxvi.

and lawyers, in the political process. However, they did not limit the tsar's power, nor did they restrict national policies set by the tsar's extensive bureaucracy. Alexander II also strengthened the army by extending recruitment and providing education for soldiers. Improved education meant that literacy rates climbed considerably during the late 19th century, but the tsar made no moves to increase political rights for commoners.

Since the middle class was very small in Russia, initiatives for industrialization had to come from the central government, a process that was similar to the model for westernization set up by Peter the Great 200 years before. A major achievement was the building of the **Trans-Siberian Railroad**, which connected the bulk of the population in the east to the Pacific Coast by the end of the 19th century. The railroad not only stimulated the iron and coal industry, but it made the export of Russian grain to the west easier, bringing more capital for further industrial development. Siberia's many natural resources became much more accessible as a result of the railroad, and Russia was able to turn some attention toward protecting and promoting its Asian lands. By the 1880s, modern factories appeared in Moscow and St. Petersburg, attracting rural peasants to the cities to become urban workers. There they produced textiles and fashioned metals into sellable items. Western investment was encouraged, and by 1900, about half of Russian factories were foreign owned, especially by British, German, and French entrepreneurs.

Political Unrest and Protest

Despite – or perhaps because of – Alexander's attempts to moderate the effects of his policies by balancing westernization with traditional Slavic society, Russia became increasingly unstable during his rule. One problem was that his reforms encouraged people to make even more demands, including minority nationalities that Russia had encompassed as it expanded. The emphasis on Russian nationalism encouraged people to assert their own identities, and many educated Russians listened to those expressions of concerns through the lens of Enlightenment ideals that they had read about and discussed. A group of radical **intelligentsia** emerged – people who were encouraged to voice their political opinions through the expansion of universities and access to the printed word. Some were so alienated from the political elite that they formed groups that endorsed terrorism as a way to bring about change. The groups had diverse goals and philosophies, but most considered westerners to be materialistic and morally inferior to Russians, and they saw the tsar and his government as stumbling blocks to achieving Russian greatness. Many became **anarchists** opposed to any formal government, and they sought to attack the existing order through assassinations and bombings. In 1881, one of the groups managed to assassinate the tsar, and his successor, Alexander III, saw the event as a sign that reform had gone too far. He returned to conservatism and repression, but his actions only spurred the protest groups to intensify their attempts to overthrow the regime.

One current of philosophy that had begun in the west a few decades earlier was particularly powerful in promoting the crisis that occurred in Russia at the beginning of the 20th century. Marxism – with its message of proletariat revolution – appealed to some Russian intelligentsia, most notably to **Vladimir Ilyich Ulyanov**, known as **Lenin**. However, according to Marxism, socialist revolutions would take first place not in Russia, but in more developed capitalist countries like Germany, France, and England. At the turn of the century, Russia was still primarily an agricultural society in the early stages of industrial development. Nevertheless, Lenin believed that the situation in Russia was so bad that the revolution could occur even though it was still primarily an agricultural society. In his 1905 pamphlet, *What Is To Be Done?*, Lenin changed the meaning of Marxism when he argued for **democratic centralism**, or a "vanguard" leadership group that would lead the revolution in the name of the people. His followers, known as **Bolsheviks**, grew in numbers as Russian workers – far more radical than their Western counterparts – were attracted to Lenin's political ideas.

THEMATIC LEARNING OBJECTIVE: OBJECTIVE KNOWLEDGE AND SUBJECTIVE VISIONS: *WHAT IS TO BE DONE?* BY V.I. LENIN

Vladimir Ulyanov, better known as Lenin, wrote an important pamphlet called *What is to be Done?* that circulated around radical intellectual circles in early 20th-century Russia. His doctrine argued that the proletariat revolution could occur in a pre-industrial society such as Russia if stimulated by a small but dedicated group of visionaries. His ideas came to be known as **Marxism-Leninism,** which altered Marxism to fit the situation in Russia. The following excerpt explains his radical concept of the "**vanguard of the revolution.**"

"Class political consciousness can be brought to the workers only from without, that is, only from outside the economic struggle, from outside the sphere of relations between workers and employers. The sphere from which alone it is possible to obtain this knowledge is the sphere of relationships of all classes and strata to the state and the government, the sphere of the interrelations between all classes...To bring political knowledge to the workers the Social Democrats [Bolsheviks] must go among all classes of the population; they must dispatch units of their army in all directions...For it is not enough to call ourselves the 'vanguard', the advanced contingent; we must act in such a way that all the other contingents recognise and are obliged to admit that we are marching in the vanguard."

Reference: V. I. Lenin, *Collected Works, Vol. 5* (London: Lawrence and Wishart, 1973).

Russia's loss in the Russo-Japanese War in 1904-05 sparked the **Revolution of 1905**. The fighting took place in Manchuria, a long distance away from most Russians, who lived in the western part of the Empire. The Russian army received its supplies by means of the Trans-Siberian Railroad, and even though the railroad represented Russian progress, the distances were too great to make for a smooth flow of supplies. Perhaps no one was more surprised by the Japanese victory than the Japanese themselves, but their army and navy were better trained and better equipped than the Russians. The shock of the defeat led to a popular uprising, the Revolution of 1905, that forced Tsar Nicholas II to concede a constitution and an elected parliament, called the **Duma**. However, the reforms were too little too late to meet the growing anger of the radical intellectuals, who inspired ordinary Russians to follow them as they supported Marx's vision of an egalitarian society that contrasted so starkly with the unequal lifestyles of the rich and the poor in Russia at that time.

Britain: Toward Democracy

In contrast to most states on the Continent, Britain's political development during the second half of the 19th century went fairly smoothly, as economic prosperity increased and Parliament continued to initiate gradual reform that built on legislation from the earlier part of the century.

The Evolution of the Monarchy

By the 1850s, the monarchy symbolized the stability of the age, with **Queen Victoria** ruling from 1837 to 1901. In contrast to many of her predecessors, she and her husband Albert were models of morality and propriety who lived frugally by royal standards. Their lifestyle appealed to the growing middle class of the second half of the 19th century, and the queen cultivated the image of being a symbol of national unity who was above politics. Although Victoria had less power than many monarchs on the Continent, many of those were toppled, while the constitutional monarchy endured in Britain. So great was Victoria's influence that the entire era was known as the **Victorian Age,** partly because the growing middle classes in Britain saw in her a reflection of their own values. Within Victorian morality public drunkenness was frowned upon, anti-alcohol movements flourished, and public festivals were regulated to make them less rowdy.

Parliamentary Reforms

Voting rights continued to expand during the late 19th century, building on the Reform Bill of 1832, as the political party system was flexible enough to allow for a relatively smooth policymaking process. The Tory Party evolved into the **Conservative Party**, which generally favored the status quo while still supporting liberal reform that aided economic development and strengthened representative government. The Whig Party changed its name to the **Liberal Party**, which – as its name implies – promoted economic and political liberalism. In 1867, the Conservatives, led by **Benjamin Disraeli**, passed the **Second Reform Bill**, which made a million more men – mostly from the middle class and the more highly-paid segments of the working class – eligible to vote. Parliament passed this reform, as well as many others, partly because interest groups had gradually increased in power and in numbers, and they actively promoted their particular causes. Liberal reform was supported very strongly by **William Gladstone**, the Liberal Party Prime Minister four times between the 1860s and 1890s. Gladstone's ministry passed education reforms that provided state support for elementary education, and his government instituted competitive examinations for the civil service. Later in the century, Parliament became convinced that all working class men were worthy of the vote, and so the **Third Reform Bill of 1884** provided suffrage for almost every adult male in Britain. Under Liberal leadership, several social welfare measures were passed between 1906 and 1914, including national health insurance, unemployment benefits, and old-age pensions.

Irish Home Rule

The most serious challenge to British nation-building during this time period was the "Irish question." As political rights were extended for most British citizens, Irish nationalists sought to achieve **home rule**, or local rule by an Irish Parliament, for their homeland. During his first ministry, Gladstone had sponsored two pieces of legislation: one that freed Irish Roman Catholics from paying taxes to support the Anglican Church, and one that provided compensation to Irish land tenants who were evicted by their absentee English landlords. However, the Irish question festered, as the resentment of Irish tenants toward their profit-oriented land ords grew. The Irish members of Parliament – led by **Charles Stewart Parnell** – demanded British support for home rule in exchange for Irish votes for programs

PERSPECTIVES:
WILLIAM GLADSTONE
ON IRISH HOME RULE

By the 1880s, agitation for Irish home rule reached a peak, and Liberal Prime Minister William Gladstone, announced his support for it in a speech to Parliament in 1886. The issue split Gladstone's Liberal party, and those that opposed home rule sided with the Conservatives to defeat Gladstone's bill. The following excerpt from the speech reflects Gladstone's respect for Irish nationalism and shame for Britain's past treatment of Ireland.

" ...Can anything stop a nation's demand, except its being proved to be immoderate and unsafe? But here are multitudes...who feel this demand to be neither immoderate nor unsafe....Ireland stands at your bar expectant, hopeful, almost suppliant. Her words are the words of truth and soberness...Go into the length and breadth of the world, ransack the literature of all countries, find, if you can, a single voice, a single book, find, I would almost say, as much as a single newspaper article, unless the product of the [present] day, in which the conduct of England towards Ireland is anywhere treated except with profound and bitter condemnation. Are these the traditions by which we are exhorted to stand? No; they are a sad exception to the glory of our country. They are a broad and black spot upon the pages of its history..."

Reference: Quoted in Hans Kohn, ed., *The Modern World: 1848 to the Present, 2ⁿᵈ ed.* (New York: The MacMillan Company: London: Collier-Macmillan Limited, 1968), pp. 116, 118.

supported by the major political parties.   Gladstone accommodated Parnell with bills on home rule, but Conservatives refused to go along, and when the Conservative Party was in power, it refused to recognize Irish demands.   The government used forgeries and other questionable means to destroy Parnell, who was eventually brought down by scandal in his personal life.   His affair with a married woman offended Victorian morality, and he died in disgrace in 1891, without accomplishing his goal of Irish home rule.

REALISM IN SCIENCE AND THE ARTS

Just as political leaders of the last half of the 19th century turned away from strict ideologies toward the *realpolitik* of practical nation-building, scientists and artists also reflected the realism of the age.   Scientific knowledge grew rapidly, as did its impact on the western world view, and romanticism in literature and art shifted to realism, with its focus on the outer, material world.

New Scientific Developments

The Scientific Revolution of the 16th and 17th centuries emphasized a modern, rational approach to the study of the natural world, and during the 18th century, the Enlightenment had extended that view to society and politics.   During the 19th century – as the Industrial Revolution progressed – science came to be valued for its ability to improve technology, and so new scientific research was promoted and appreciated for its practical application to industrial technology.   Many fields were affected.   For example, the study of thermodynamics – the relationship between heat and mechanical energy – helped to improve the steam engine.   The laws of thermodynamics, in turn, led to the development of modern physics.   In the area of medicine, germ theory disease, as explored by **Louis Pasteur**, had a great impact on the development of modern medical practices.   Michael Faraday explored electromagnetic induction and laid the foundations for the efficient generation of electricity by the 1870s.

As these examples illustrate, science became increasingly specialized during the 19th century.   In the 18th century, the scientist had been a well-educated amateur practicing a hobby.   In the 19th century, the state and industry became more involved in promoting scientific research, and so scientists became professional employees of universities, hospitals, and the government.   Scientific journals appeared, and specialists attended international meetings where they learned about the latest research.   In chemistry, new elements were discovered almost every year, and in 1869, Russian chemist **Dmitri Mendeleev** developed the periodic table, in which the elements were arranged by their atomic weight.   Many breakthroughs occurred in medicine, too, with the development of anesthesia and disinfectant, as well as with Pasteur's discovery of disease-carrying germs that could be killed by heat.

The New Physics

From the 17th century through most of the 19th century, most westerners' view of the universe was shaped by the mechanical conception provided by Isaac Newton. Newton described the universe as a giant machine in which matter, space, and time existed independently of the individuals observing them. Scientists had discovered that atoms make up matter, but they believed that they were indivisible and solid.

By the end of the 19th century, these traditional views were questioned. Through their studies of rays of radiation that came from within the atom, the French scientist **Marie Curie** and her husband Pierre first discovered that atoms were composed of subatomic particles, such as electrons and protons. In Berlin, **Max Planck** discovered that a heated body radiates energy discontinuously, in irregular streams that he called "quanta." Most notably, in the early 20th century, German-born **Albert Einstein** came up with new theories that replaced Newton's concept of the universe. He published his **theory of relativity** in 1905, which explained that space and time are not absolute – as Newton had said – but relative to the observer, and that neither had an existence independent of human experience. He also theorized that matter and energy reflected the relativity of time and space, and his famous formula $E = mc^2$ explained that each particle of matter is equal to its mass times the square of the velocity of light. Matter, then, contained huge amounts of energy that could be used for many purposes, including the building of an atomic bomb.

Charles Darwin and the Impact of Evolution

Of all the natural sciences, biology and the life sciences had the greatest impact upon general thinking during the 19th century. The most famous naturalist of the day was **Charles Darwin**, whose 1859 publication of ***The Origin of Species*** was a landmark that had profound influence far beyond the field of biology. Darwin argued that each new species of plants and animals evolved as a result of natural selection and survival of the fittest, with some small variations being more useful than others. Those with variations that promoted survival passed them down to their offspring, and over time the whole species gradually changed. This theory stirred great controversy first in Great Britain but eventually in many parts of the world because it seemed to contradict the account of creation in Genesis, the first book of the Bible of Christianity and Judaism. Many people also found Darwin's theory disturbing because they believed it implied a world in which aggression, violence, and destruction of rivals were the only means to assure survival. Darwin himself was concerned only with the origin and interrelation of species, and did not draw any general philosophical conclusions from his theories. Another book, the *Descent of Man,* fanned even more controversy by tracing human ancestry to the great apes, a theory that many thought to be contradictory to the creation of man in the image of God. Others supported Darwin's theory as supportive of the new practical realism: adaptation to nature simply brought about the success of survival, and no norms of good or bad should be attached to the facts of evolution.

Although Darwin's arguments had to do strictly with biological evolution, **Social Darwinists** applied survival of the fittest to social situations as well. The best known Social Darwinist was **Herbert Spencer**, who argued that successful individuals and races emerged to dominate others as a result of "survival of the fittest". His ideas were used to justify both the wealth of entrepreneurs in opposition to their laborers, as well as the domination of European imperialists over subject peoples. Spencer's theory was one of many that shaped newly-developing fields in the social sciences.

Birth of the Social Sciences

Growing feelings of nationalism led many people to study their own national histories, encouraging the development of a modern view of history – one that emphasized the objective and dispassionate (scientific) study of the past. The term "social sciences" came to describe not only history, but also new, specialized fields of study, such as anthropology, psychology, and sociology. Anthropology – the comparative study of people in different societies – became popular as more Europeans came into contact with people from other continents; a favorite topic was race, with anthropologists theorizing about the causes of differences among races. Psychologist Ivan Pavlov "conditioned" dogs to salivate automatically at the ringing of a bell, implying that a great part of animal behavior – and presumably human behavior – could be explained by conditioned response. Auguste Comte – often called the "father of sociology" – inspired social scientists to study their societies objectively. By the end of the century, professional historians, anthropologists, psychologists, and sociologists were teaching at universities and engaged in social research.

One of the most significant of all the developments in the study of human behavior was the work of **Sigmund Freud**, a Viennese physician that founded psychoanalysis at the turn of the 20th century. He came to believe that an individual's emotional disturbances could be traced to earlier episodes of his or her life, and if the source could be identified, the patient could be cured or at least helped. After first trying various techniques – including hypnosis – he developed a method called "free association," or free recall, in which the patient brought disturbing unconscious memories to the conscious level as a starting point for recovery from the illness. Freud's work led him to believe that the unconscious plays an important role in all human behavior, and he particularly stressed the sexual drive. In *The Interpretation of Dreams,* he identified dreams as key to understanding the unconscious. Freudian concepts greatly shaped developing fields of human behavior, not only among professional social scientists, but also in popular culture.

Although Freud identified with the scientific traditions of the Enlightenment, his theories revealed wide areas of human behavior outside conscious control, calling into question just how rational human behavior actually is.

Realism in Literature

The literary realists rejected the importance that romantics attached to heroes in unusual settings. Instead, they focused on ordinary characters from real life, often with the intent of examining important social issues. The influence of science is apparent in their concern with careful observation and accurate description, and their avoidance of the elaborate, sentimental language used by the romantics. As the development of schooling spread literacy, all types of readers responded to novels and biographies of political leaders, past and present. Realism in literature,

EXAMINING THE EVIDENCE: REALISM IN CHARLES DICKENS' *HARD TIMES*

British novelist Charles Dickens wrote about 19th century English society with a realist's eye, describing everyday people and events. His novel *Hard Times* was a stinging indictment of the squalor of English industrial cities, and his writing stimulated social reform. In the excerpt below, Dickens described the need for one of his characters, Stephen Blackpool, to escape the industrial city where he lived.

"As Coketown cast ashes not only on its own head, but on the neighbourhood's too – after the manner of those pious persons who do penance for their own sins by putting other people into sackcloth – it was customary for those who now and then thirsted for a draught of pure air, which is not absolutely the most wicked among the vanities of life, to get a few miles away by the railroad, and then begin their walk, or their lounge in the fields....

Though the green landscape was blotted here and there with heaps of coal, it was green elsewhere, and there were trees to see, and there were larks singing (although it was Sunday), and there were pleasant scents in the air, and all was over-arched by a bright blue sky. In the distance one way, Coketown showed as a black mist; in another distance hills began to rise; in a third, there was a faint change in the light of the horizon where it shone upon the far-off sea."

Reference: Sources of the Western Tradition, ed. by Marvin Perry, et. al. (New York: Houghton Mifflin, 2003), p. 174.

then, fed the nationalism of the age, avoiding the drama of heroes and revolutions, but reinforcing the concern for practical reform.

One leading novelist was **Gustave Flaubert**, whose *Madame Bovary* was set in provincial France. It examined the sterile blandness of bourgeois society through the eyes of Emma Bovary, who was a free spirit trapped in a dull life as a doctor's wife. Flaubert's straightforward description of Emma's life was characteristic of the realist novelists even if his frank picture of women's sexuality was considered to be somewhat scandalous. **William Thackeray**'s *Vanity Fair* deliberately flaunted Romantic conventions with its subtitle: *A Novel Without a Hero*. Perhaps the best known novelist of the age was **Charles Dickens**, whose books first appeared in serial form in magazines and periodicals. His characters included starving orphans, intrusive judges, and ruthless opportunists, whose lives provided evidence for the need for serious social reform. In Russia, writers – including **Fyodor Dostoevsky** – explored the meaning of Russian culture and the sources of Russian nationalism. In Dostoevsky's famous *Crime and Punishment*, highly intelligent characters who were forced to lead absurd lives allowed the author to emphasize traditional Russian values, especially as they influenced the lives of ordinary people.

Art: Realism and Impressionism

The late 19th century was a period of enormous change in the visual arts as well. The development of photography had a direct impact on painting, since the new technology allowed a scene to be depicted in a very realistic fashion. Various experiments in the late 18th century, as well as the inventions of Louis Daguerre, made the camera usable by the 1830s. Its widespread use began in the 1890s with the introduction of celluloid film and George Eastman's invention of the Kodak camera, which made photography affordable for the general public. Photographic services became more and more available as more people began to make a living as photographers.

Photography encouraged some painters to be true to reality, to reproduce on canvas something similar to a photograph. Others reacted by rejecting realism, believing that since photography was capturing reality, the mission of a painter was to produce something that the new technology could not. Two French painters – Gustave Courbet and Jean-François Millet – favored peasants and manual laborers as subjects, but did not romanticize them as earlier artists had. Instead they depicted the bleak reality of harsh working conditions and tedious work. In England painters who called themselves "pre-Raphaelites" concentrated on the realistic simplicity of nature, as painters had done in the days prior to Raphael during the Renaissance.

A group that rebelled against realism came to be called **impressionists**, after the title of a painting – *Impression: Sunrise* – by **Claude Monet**, one of the leaders of the movement. The impressionists were influenced by new theories of physics that claimed images were transmitted to the brain as small light particles that the brain then reconstituted. Their aims were to capture scenes as they appear before the brain distorts them and to capture a single moment by focusing on ever-changing light and color. This style called for spontaneity because painters were looking for just the right moment to capture light from just the right angle. Using splotches and dots, impressionists moved away from precise realism, and their unique style drew many critics. The new style was encouraged, however, by the manufacture of a broader range of pigments, allowing artists to use a wider, more intense spectrum of colors than ever before. Besides Monet, famous impressionist artists included Edgar Degas, Camille Pissarro, and Auguste Renoir.

By the 1880s, a new movement known as **post-impressionism** started in France and spread to other countries. Post-impressionism emphasized light and color, just as impressionism did, but it strayed even further from realism. Post-impressionists focused on expressing inner feelings to make their own personal statements, and their paintings withdrew from the artist's traditional task of depicting the external world. As such, these painters were the forerunners of modern art. The most famous post-impressionist was probably **Vincent van Gogh**, whose originality and power of expression made a strong impact on later artists. Whereas he often painted objects – such as buildings or plants – as they look in reality, the focus of his art was usually color used to convey a spiritual experience.

By the beginning of the 20th century, many painters had deserted the reproduction of reality almost completely, marking the earliest forms of modern art. An important modern artist was **Pablo Picasso**, perhaps one of the most flexible painters of all times. He developed a style called **cubism** that used geometric designs to re-create reality in the viewer's mind. By 1910, abstract painting had evolved, in which no reference to visual reality is made, but like the impressionists and post-impressionists, the emphasis was on color.

THE AGE OF MASS POLITICS

By the early 1870s, most of Europe was organized into strong nation-states, although many ethnic groups in Ireland, Russia, Austria-Hungary, and the Balkans still were not recognized as self-determined independent nationalities. However, most countries had developed common frameworks, anchored by the nation-state concept, that allowed their citizens to feel patriotic pride despite ethnic differences within political boundaries. Between 1871 and 1914, nationalism continued to grow, and Europe increasingly became a continent of competing nation-states.

Universal Manhood Suffrage

One reason for the increasingly nationalistic sentiments of the era was the expansion of voter rights to more and more citizens. By 1914 universal male suffrage had become the rule rather than the exception. The right to vote recognized an individual's worth as a citizen and also gave him a greater stake in politics, especially since voting was no longer attached to wealth or education. Even in the most authoritarian states, expanding voting rights created "**mass politics**", or a system that valued the opinions of ordinary people, and not just the elite, as had been true in previous times. Some important changes were that national parliaments became more responsive to the public, and most parliaments had representatives from several competing political parties. The multiparty system existed in most countries, so parliamentary majorities were built on shifting coalitions that usually prevented one party from dominating politics for a long period of time. As governments passed reform measures that benefitted the masses, their legitimacy usually increased, so their political authority was enhanced as well.

THEMATIC LEARNING OBJECTIVE:
OBJECTIVE KNOWLEDGE AND
SUBJECTIVE VISION:
GIUSEPPE MAZZINI'S NATIONALISM

Giuseppe Mazzini was a revolutionary in the romantic tradition, and his attempts to unify Italy in the 1830s and 1840s failed, only to be accomplished under Cavour's more pragmatic, conservative leadership later in the century. Nevertheless, Mazzini remained an influential exponent of nationalism, as is indicated by his most famous essay, "The Duties of Man," which is excerpted below.

"But you tell me...The individual is too insignificant, and Humanity too vast. The mariner of Brittany prays to God as he puts to sea: *Help me, my God! my boat is so small and thy ocean so wide!* And this prayer is the true expression of the condition of each one of you, until you find the means of infinitely multiplying your forces and powers of action.
This means was provided for you by God when he gave you a country; when, even as a wise overseer of labour distributes the various branches of employment according to the different capacities of the workmen, he divided Humanity into distinct groups or nuclei upon the face of the earth, thus creating the germ of Nationalities. Evil governments have disfigured the divine design.... But the Divine design will infallibly be realized. Natural divisions, and the spontaneous innate tendencies of the peoples, will take the place of the arbitrary divisions sanctioned by evil governments....
O my brothers, love your Country! Our country is our Home, the house that God has given us, placing therein a numerous family that loves us, and whom we love...."

Reference: Emilie Ashurst Venturi, *Joseph Mazzini: A Memoir* (London: Alexander & Shepheard, 1875), pp. 312-315.

A less positive side to mass politics was the potential for manipulation of nationalistic sympathies, especially by governments headed by authoritarian leaders who ruled by charisma or by their ability to divert attention away from underlying class conflicts. Appeals to nationalism could lead to blind patriotism that could be mobilized against people perceived by leaders as threats, such as workers who voted socialist. By 1914, intensified nationalism also led to increased international tensions as citizens thought in terms of "us" and "them", and other nations became objects of hostility because they threatened one's own dearly cherished nation.

Women's Suffrage

By 1914, despite the expansion of suffrage to almost all adult men, women still did not have the right to vote in any European country except Norway, which granted it in 1907. Some anticlerical male liberals feared that women's votes would benefit political conservatives because they believed that women were unduly controlled by the clergy. Many women too were reluctant to support feminist causes, since they, like men, were usually sensitive to their own class and economic interests. It was often difficult for middle and working-class women to cooperate with one another since their points of view and lifestyles were so different, and others – from all class levels – feared that feminist agitation might upset nationalistic patriotism. With all of these objections in place, feminist goals – including the right to vote – were widely viewed as unorthodox and quite out of the mainstream. As a result, the obstacles to women's rights movements were numerous and strong.

Europe's most advanced women's movement was in Great Britain, where feminists often cooperated with their contemporaries in North America. In both places, the movement was split between moderates – who believed women would gain the vote only when legislatures became convinced they were responsible enough for political activity – and radicals – who believed that their goals could only be accomplished through disruptive political tactics. In Britain, the moderate view was represented by the National Union of Women's Suffrage Societies, while the radicals supported the Women's Social and Political Union, founded by **Emmeline Pankhurst** in 1903. By 1910, neither approach had moved Parliament to action, so the radicals resorted to the violent tactics of arson, window breaking, and sabotage of mailboxes. Some were imprisoned and force-fed when they went on hunger strikes in jail.

Women's movements in Continental Europe found even less support than those in Britain. In France, almost no other women joined Hubertine Auclert when she began campaigning for the vote in the 1880s. By the turn of the 20th century, women's organizations had formed, but did not always support the franchise. Even though the French revolutionary tradition included plenty of violence, French feminists

THEMATIC LEARNING OBJECTIVE:
INDIVIDUAL AND SOCIETY:
AMERICAN FEMINISTS IN LONDON

Elizabeth Cady Stanton and Lucretia Mott were two Americans who took
Enlightenment ideals seriously in their support for the international
abolitionist movement of the early 19th century. Both women attended
the International Anti-Slavery Convention in London, England in 1840,
Stanton with her delegate husband and Mott selected as a delegate in her
own right. However, the convention refused to allow them to participate in
the meetings, and instead, required them to sit in a roped-off section away
from the men's view. One prominent male abolitionist, William Lloyd
Garrison, was so offended by the convention's decision that he refused to
take his seat, and instead sat with the women.

Stanton and Mott were impressed by the irony of this situation and
decided to focus their attention on the fledgling women's rights movement
instead. As a result of their efforts, a conference of feminists was called
in 1848 at Seneca Falls, New York (Stanton's hometown) that produced the
famous Declaration of Sentiments, a document for women's rights based
on the Declaration of Independence.

rejected any form of violence, in contrast to women in Britain. No mass rallies
were organized, and French women did not receive the right to vote until after
World War II. In Germany, women were forbidden by law to engage in political
activity. Since few German men enjoyed extensive political rights either, women
were not encouraged to agitate for the vote, especially since it almost certainly
would be seen as subversive to the state. In 1894, the Union of German Women's
Organizations was formed to improve women's social conditions, and the group
called for women's suffrage in 1902. The German Social Democratic Party supported this effort, but the socialist party was so disdained that its endorsement only
weakened the cause.

Jewish Rights

European Jews had long been denied equal citizenship, but during the late 19th
century, they successfully won more rights. After the revolutions of 1848, Jews
attained full rights of citizenship in Germany, Italy, the Low Countries, and Scandinavia. After 1858, Jews in Great Britain could sit in Parliament, and they gained

PERSPECTIVES: ANTI-SEMITIC VIEWS IN LATE 19TH CENTURY GERMANY

Despite many new liberal guarantees of equal rights that were put in place during the second half of the 19th century, anti-Semitism was still relatively common in Europe. The following excerpts are from a speech to the German Reichstag (parliament) by Hermann Ahlwardt, a Reichstag member, on March 6, 1895.

"My political friends do not hold the view that we fight the Jews because of their religion....We would not dream of waging a political struggle against anyone because of his religion....We hold the view that the Jews are a different race, a different people with entirely different character traits....when countless specimens prove the existence of certain racial characteristics and when those characteristics are such as to make impossible a common life, well, then I believe that we who are natives here....have a duty to take a stand against the Jews who are of a quite different nature....Wherever there are opportunities to make money, the Jews have established themselves, but not in order to work – no, they let others work for them and take what the others have produced by their labor....it is imperative that we realize that Jewish racial characteristics differ so greatly from ours that a common life of Jews and Germans under the same laws is quite impossible because the Germans will perish....I beg you from the bottom of my heart not to take this matter [prohibition of Jewish immigration] lightly but as a very serious thing..."

Reference: Paul W. Massing, *Anti-Semitism in Imperial Germany* (New York: Harper Collins Publishers, 1949), p. 232.

full legal rights in Austria-Hungary in 1867. One clear exception was Russia, where prejudice and discrimination continued. Jews in Russia were treated as aliens, and restrictions on where they could live continued. The police conducted *pogroms* – organized riots – against Jewish neighborhoods and villages.

Outside Russia, Jews became quite active in the literary and cultural life of their nations, and they intermarried freely with non-Jews as laws changed to lift earlier restrictions. Jews also served in the highest offices of government in many countries, and politically they often aligned with liberal parties that championed equal rights. Freedoms were generally more widespread in western Europe, so many Jews migrated from Russia and other parts of eastern Europe to western Europe and the United States. However, during the last two decades of the 19th century, some of this newfound security began to erode in western Europe as well, as anti-

Semitic voices blamed Jews for the economic woes that beset Europe during that time. In France, anti-Semitism was apparent in the Dreyfus Affair (see pp. 378-379), and organized groups in Germany spoke out against Jewish influence. Still, most Jewish leaders believed that these attitudes were contained by the liberal legal protections that they had gained, and Jews – especially in western Europe – generally believed that their communities would remain safe.

Labor Movements

European workers, like most other people during the 19th century, stopped rioting in the streets to air their grievances after 1850. Instead they turned to new institutions and ideologies, including trade unions, democratic political parties, and socialism.

Governments began to extend legal protections to trade unions during the second half of the 19th century, and Britain fully legalized them in 1875 and France in 1884. In Germany, unions were allowed to function with little government interference after 1890. While earlier unions organized skilled workers, by the close of the century, industrial unions for unskilled workers had organized. As union power increased, opposition from employers intensified, and numerous strikes occurred in the early 20th century as unions sought to promote better working conditions and higher wages. Despite the gains in union membership, by 1914 most workers in Europe still did not belong to unions.

As governments around Europe passed laws for universal manhood suffrage, new political parties emerged to represent workers and other new voters. Socialist parties courted them most strongly, since the older, more established parties were generally controlled by people of property who had long had the right to vote. However, working class people of this era were often also strongly nationalistic, and so the socialist ideology that was supposed to unite the working classes across national borders often lacked appeal.

One form of socialism that had some success was Marxism, first introduced in 1848 by Karl Marx and Friedrich Engels. Marx was able to put aside his theoretical arguments that predicted the disintegration of capitalism, and he supported practical, public political activity to promote the rights of the proletariat. In 1864, a group of British and French trade unionists founded the International Working Men's Association, which promoted efforts to reform the condition of labor within the existing political and economic processes. This first international workers organization was fully supported by Marx, but internal dissension soon damaged the organization, and it failed in 1872. In its place, separate Marxist-inspired parties appeared in many countries, but the most successful was the **German Social Democratic Party**, which received a great deal of support from urban workers. In 1890, it received 1.5 million votes and 35 seats in the Reichstag. When it received 4 million votes in the 1912 elections, it became the largest single political party in Germany. As the socialist parties gained supporters, their leaders formed the **Second International** in 1889, as an attempt to coordinate their individual efforts. However, not only nationalism hampered their efforts. New splits occurred as Marxists disagreed about what their true goals should be. Some believed in pure Marxism that accepted the imminent collapse of capitalism and the vision of a classless society of the proletariat. Others argued that workers should organize within the established economic and political structures and should work through national political parties instead. By 1914, with most workers having voting rights, the latter vision of Marxism prevailed in most countries, where workers counted on trade unions and workers' political parties to advance their causes.

The most clearly defined characteristic of European countries in the second half of the 19th century was a strengthening and enduring nationalism. Nationalism was the main force behind the unifications of Italy and of Germany, and it played an important role in strengthening other nation-states as they balanced the contrasting ideologies of conservatism, liberalism, and radicalism. The politics of this era were decidedly practical in nature, as countries valued stability above all after the tumultuous upheavals of the early part of the century. This realism was also reflected in scientific developments, literature, and art. However, as the 20th century began, and memories of war and revolution subsided, the nationalistic impulses stirring within different nation-states were often at odds, and these feelings intensified as their competitive spirits gained a world stage.

CONCEPTS AND IDENTIFICATIONS

Alexander II
anarchists
Bismarck, Otto von
Bolsheviks
"blood and iron"
Cavour, Camillo Benso di
Conservative Party (Britain)
Crime and Punishment
Crimean War
Curie, Marie
democratic centralism
Dickens, Charles
Disraeli, Benjamin
Dostoevsky, Fyodor
Dreyfus Affair, Alfred Dreyfus
Dual Monarchy
Duma
Einstein, Albert
Flaubert, Gustave

Franco-Prussian War
Franz Joseph I
Freud, Sigmund
Garibaldi, Giuseppe
German Socialist Democratic Party
Gioberti, Vincenzo
Gladstone, William
impressionism
intelligentsia
Irish home rule
Lenin, V.I.
Liberal Party (Britain)
Marxism-Leninism
mass politics
Mazzini, Giuseppe
Mendeleev, Dmitri
Monet, Claude
Napoleon III (Louis Bonaparte)
Nightingale, Florence
The Origin of Species
Pankhurst, Emmeline
Pan-Slavism
Paris Commune
Parnell, Charles Stewart
Pasteur, Louis
Picasso, Pablo
Planck, Max
plebiscite
pogroms
post-impressionism
realpolitik
Revolution of 1905 (Russia)
Second German Empire
Second International
Second Reform Bill (Britain)
Social Darwinism
Spencer, Herbert
Thackeray, William
theory of relativity
Third Reform Bill (Britain)
Third Republic (France)
Trans-Siberian Railroad
universal manhood suffrage

CHAPTER 16
IMPERIALISM AND
INTERNATIONAL
RIVALRIES

In earlier times, European rulers who wanted to expand their territory faced many challenges. During the Middle Ages they faced land-owning nobles and clergy who often resisted royal authority. As power became more centralized, kings had to deal with one another, and land gains by one were often taken away from another. Then, as early as the 16ᵗʰ century, European countries began to look across the Atlantic Ocean for land to claim, but there they also fell into disputes with one another. By the early 19ᵗʰ century, kingdoms had grown into nation-states, and nationalistic pride led to boundary disputes, but rulers found very little land for expansion that had not been claimed by someone else. By the second half of the 19ᵗʰ century, new types of **imperialism** – or empire building – appeared that differed substantially from earlier versions of territorial expansion.

During the 19ᵗʰ century the forces of nationalism and industrialization made it possible for European nations to build global empires that stretched across the continents. The famous statement that "the sun never sets on the British Empire" describes the huge network of control that Britain was able to establish by the end of the century, making it among the most powerful empires in all of world history. Nationalism enabled governments to rally their citizens' support for overseas expansion. Industrialization allowed them to produce goods to sell in foreign markets, and it encouraged them to look for raw materials not available at home. The European countries that became great imperialist powers during the 19ᵗʰ century – Britain, France, Germany, the Netherlands, and Russia – were mostly small countries in land space (with Russia as the exception). Claiming lands far away increased their ability to create wealth and assert power. Industrialization also made communications and transportation so much more efficient that it became possible to link lands together across the globe under one imperial banner. By the early 20ᵗʰ century, the United States and Japan had joined Europeans in forming overseas empires, giving the West – and increasingly Japan – hegemony over virtually every corner of the globe.

TYPES OF IMPERIALISM

The term "imperialism" was coined to describe the new type of empire-building that began in the 19th century by European nations and eventually the United States and Japan. These countries did not always take over territories completely as in previous days, but limited control in ways that served their motives. Several types of imperialism could be combined in different ways to gain the power that the imperialistic country wanted:

1) **Colonial imperialism** – This type of imperialism is the most complete, with a territory or colony actually occupied and ruled by a foreign nation. This "old style" imperialism was illustrated by the conquest of the Americas during the 16th and 17th centuries, where the areas were completely taken over, with European countries setting up governments, controlling the economy, exporting citizens to populate colonies, and imposing their lifestyles on the people they defeated.

2) **Political imperialism** – In this form of imperialism, the dominant country uses diplomacy or military force to influence the internal affairs of a weaker nation. For example, as we will see in this chapter, European countries tried to break down tribal affiliations and ruling councils in order to establish more "modern" governments in Africa, and the United States took over the government of the Dominican Republic to manage its affairs so that it would not be taken over by a European country.

3) **Economic imperialism** – This type of imperialism was inspired by the desire to control global trade and commerce, especially as industrialization of western countries increased their production and transportation capacities. A good example of economic imperialism during the 19th century was the creation of spheres of influence in China. The main motivation for the British declaration of war in the Opium Wars was economic; they had no desire to occupy China and take over the government, and the spheres of influence were created to establish trade zones. Similarly, the United States had no desire to occupy and rule Japan; Matthew Perry's motivations in Japan in 1853 were economic, even though the demands were backed by the powerful presence of his "black ships."

4) **Social-cultural imperialism** – Empire-building may be based on a desire to influence the people in a territory to adopt the cultural values and social customs of the imperialist country. For example, the controlling country might expect the people to speak its language and prefer the foods that its own citizens enjoy. Social-cultural imperialism may be seen in some actions of Christian missionaries as they tried to convert people in other lands to western religions. Although imperialism implies force, and

PERSPECTIVES: RUDYARD KIPLING'S *"THE WHITE MAN'S BURDEN"*

The British writer and journalist Rudyard Kipling lived a great deal of his life in India, a place that he deeply loved, and yet his famous poem, *"The White Man's Burden"* reflects his belief that British customs and values should be instilled, a form of social-cultural imperialism. Notice it in the excerpts below.

"Take up the White Man's burden –
　Send forth the best ye breed –
Go bind your sons to exile
　To serve your captives' needs;
To wait in heavy harness,
　On fluttered folk and wild –
Your new-caught, sullen peoples,
　Half-devil and half-child...

Take up the White Man's burden –
　And reap his old reward;
The blame of those ye better,
　The hate of those ye guard –
The cry of hosts ye humor
　(Ah, slowly!) toward the light;

Why brought ye us from bondage,
　"Our loved Egyptian night?"

Take up the White Man's burden –
　Ye dare not stoop to less –
Nor call too loud on Freedom
　To cloak your weariness;
By all ye cry or whisper,
　By all ye leave or do,
The silent, sullen peoples
　Shall weigh your Gods and you."

Reference: "The White Man's Burden," by Rudyard Kipling. *McClure's Magazine* 12:4 (1899): 290-291.

missionaries were not known for the use of force, in many cases their attempts were unwanted (as in Japan), and their actions reflected the point of view that their religion was superior to that of the natives

In any one situation, more than one type of imperialism could be practiced. Colonial imperialism by its very nature encompasses the other three types because taking over an area completely means that political, economic, and socio-cultural imperialism takes place.

FORMS OF IMPERIALISM

By the end of the 19th century, imperialist countries had set up two forms of colonies: **tropical dependencies** in Africa, Asia, and the South Pacific; and **settlement**

colonies, such as Canada, Australia, New Zealand, South Africa, Algeria, Kenya, and Hawaii. In tropical dependencies, a small number of Europeans ruled non-western people, who came under European rule during the late 19th and early 20th centuries. Settlement colonies were destinations for European settlers, so their populations had large percentages of people of European ancestry. In some – such as Canada, New Zealand, and Australia (and the United States before its independence), the majority of the population were European, since the relatively small number of indigenous people had been killed or pushed out of the way or had died of disease. In others – such as South Africa, Algeria, Kenya, and Hawaii – large numbers of indigenous people continued to live in the area, and as a result, European land claims were often contested, with frequent clashes over land rights, control of natural resources, and cultural and social differences.

COMPARISON: TROPICAL DEPENDENCIES VS. SETTLEMENT COLONIES

During the 19th century, European countries – and eventually the U.S. and Japan – practiced many types of imperialism, but when they chose to set up colonies, they used two different models, as compared in the chart below.

Tropical Dependencies	Settlement Colonies
Areas generally less appealing to European settlers	Areas generally more appealing to European settlers
Main goal usually exploitation of natural resources	Dual goals of settlement and exploitation of natural resources
Few European settlers, many natives	Many European settlers; some had few natives, others had equal or larger numbers of natives
Problems included control of natives, potential uprisings, native elite resentment, control of governments	In colonies with few natives, fewer conflicts occurred; in those with many natives, problems were similar to those in tropical dependencies
Most colonies located in Africa, Asia, and the South Pacific	Colonies located in many areas, including Canada, New Zealand, Australia, Hawaii, and South Africa

INDUSTRIALIZATION AND IMPERIALISM

Industrialization fundamentally changed the nature of empire building among European nations. Instead of seeking gold and silver and land for growing crops as empire builders did in the Americas before the 19th century, they looked for raw materials for factories – cotton, hemp, metals, and dyes. As European nations became the global center for manufacturing goods, they also looked for overseas markets for machine-made goods that were so rapidly being produced. Production was spurred on by the competitiveness among European nations, as each tried to capture raw materials and markets before the others could reach them. A second wave of technological advances that began around 1860 made it possible to spread the influence of industrialized nations to many more parts of the globe. One important innovation was the **Bessemer steel converter** that allowed iron ore to be converted to steel very efficiently. Steel is stronger and more durable than iron, and its use greatly accelerated the effectiveness of machinery and other manufactured products, such as rails for railroads. Advances also occurred in chemical industries, which grew after 1870 with the production of synthetic substances for dyes for textiles, fertilizers for agriculture, and explosives for construction. Plastics became available in the late 19th century. Inventors were also experimenting with electricity, most notably **Thomas Edison**, whose laboratory produced incandescent light bulbs, fuses, sockets, and switches.

Industrialization made it possible for Europeans to penetrate beyond the sea coasts in many lands. Whereas in earlier times, sea-based powers were often confined to sea-lanes (except in the Americas), steamboats and railroads allowed them to explore rivers and lands far away from the coasts. Since industrialization most directly impacted the economy, it promoted economic imperialism above all other types, and if economic goals could be accomplished without controlling a territory's government, social customs, and cultural beliefs, the imperialist countries often would be content with simply controlling economic policies and actions. The construction of the Suez Canal in 1869 and the Panama Canal in 1914 shortened sea voyages – as did the new, faster steam-powered ships – so that sustained contact between the imperialist country and dependent lands was much easier.

THE BRITISH EMPIRE IN INDIA

One of the first of the great land-based empires to feel the impact of European imperialism was India. As Mughal power weakened in the 18th century, Muslim princes – called **nawabs** – asserted regional control at the expense of the empire, and they often made independent agreements with British, Dutch, and French companies that were eager to establish trading posts along the long shorelines of India. By 1750, these European outposts were staffed by **company men**, whose job it was to organize trade and protect warehouses and offices. To assist in the protection, the company men often hired and trained Indian troops known as **se-**

poys. An early center for Britain's East India Company was Calcutta. After the widely publicized death of some company men who had been arrested and imprisoned in a small cell by the local nawab, company forces overthrew the nawab to avenge the treatment of their men in what they referred to as the "Black Hole of Calcutta". As a result of their actions, the East India Company gained permission from the weak Mughal emperor to allow the company to rule Calcutta and the region (Bengal) around it by 1765. Other areas were secured in the south and on the western coast at Bombay, and as Britain gained the upper hand in the Seven Years War (1756-1763) with France, the East India Company often secured trading posts at the expense of the French.

Rule by the East India Company

By 1818, the East India Company had secured so many footholds in India that it controlled vast areas of the subcontinent, establishing the **British raj** (reign). Since the company's motives were economic, this early control is a good example of economic imperialism, even though the British government was not directly involved. However, a desire to protect their property and trading rights led to political imperialism as they came to rule the regions in place of the nawabs. To keep order, the company expanded the number of sepoy regiments, and they also disarmed Indian warriors who had formerly fought for the nawabs. The company also encouraged Christian missionaries to come to India to convert its people, and although they had limited success with conversions, this social-cultural imperialism encouraged British-style social reforms. On the other hand, just as the company had to rely on Indians to fill the ranks of their armies, they also felt it necessary to allow Indian princes to rule under the supervision of British overlords. This arrangement gave Indian princes – both Muslim and Hindu – more power than they had ever had before in India's history of political fragmentation.   As a result, a dual message was sent to Indians: preserve your cultural heritage but also conform to British customs and beliefs. As the Industrial Revolution progressed, economic demands changed as well, in some cases helping the Indian economy, but in other cases hurting it. The British raj created new jobs for Indians in trade and the military, but the Indian handicraft textile industry was seriously weakened by competition from British factories. India had once been the leading exporter of cotton finished goods, but by the mid-19th century, British manufacturing centers were demanding that India export raw cotton, not finished goods, to them.

The Sepoy Rebellion

By the 1850s the East India Company was much more than a business enterprise, but still the British government was not directly involved in ruling India. That situation changed with the massive **Sepoy Rebellion** in 1857 that convinced the British government that only colonial imperialism would work in India. The rebellion was sparked by a classic conflict of cultures when new procedures for firing rifles were implemented. The bullet cartridges used in the new shipment of Enfield rifles were protected by paper waxed with animal fat, and the British officers instructed the sepoys to tear the paper off with their teeth. Hindu sepoys refused because the fat might be from cows, which they considered to be sacred, and Muslim sepoys refused because the fat might be from pigs, which they believed to be unclean. Even though the British officers changed the procedures as soon as they understood the problem, the incident sparked a rebellion that almost certainly was already festering. The Hindu sepoys staged a mutiny and proclaimed their allegiance to the Mughals, and they were soon joined by elites and peasants alike, so that the rebellion became widespread enough that it threatened British rule in India. As a result, the British government sent forces to India to contain the trouble, and by 1858, order had been restored and direct imperial rule had been imposed.

British Imperial Rule

Queen Victoria established a cabinet position within her government that was responsible for India, and a viceroy representing British royal authority was sent to India. The viceroy's elite **Indian Civil Service** was staffed almost completely by Englishmen, although some Indians served in low-level bureaucratic positions. The British formulated and executed virtually all domestic and foreign policy in India from 1858 on, resulting in significant lasting changes for almost everyone that lived on the subcontinent. The last traces of Mughal and company rule were eliminated, but British rule continued to emphasize both Indian tradition and modern reform. Queen Victoria proclaimed that all Indians had equal protection of the law and the freedom to practice their religions and social customs. The rights of Indian princes to rule their territories were also guaranteed, as long as they served as her loyal subjects. However, their power was compromised by the powerful and efficient bureaucracy set up by the British to establish a strong central government for India.

To establish the legitimacy of the viceroys, the British government set them up in luxurious palaces with many servants, in order to simulate the pomp that had surrounded the Mughal rulers. Elaborate ceremonies honored the Indian princes, and great pageants called "durbars" were staged to celebrate British events, such as the proclamation of Queen Victoria as the "Empress of India" in 1877 and the coronation of King Edward VII in 1902-1903. The Indian Civil Service held the senior administrative and judicial positions, and British-style courts were set up throughout the empire. Theoretically, these highly desirable positions were open to everyone, but the examinations for entrance into service were given in England, making it almost impossible for Indians to take them, and as a result, excluding them almost entirely from the top posts.

Economic imperialism transformed India through massive British investment in the Indian infrastructure, committing money to cities, harbors, canals, and other public works. Railroad building received priority and by 1870, India had the largest railroad system in Asia and the fifth grandest in the world. The companies that owned the railroads were British, as were the top officials, although the vast majority of the employees were Indian. Steamboats travelled Indian rivers, as well as the canals that the British built to connect them. Indian products, exchanged for centuries in long-distance trade, began to be shaped by the needs of industrial England as it expanded its international trade. Most of the exports were agricultural commodities for processing in England, including cotton, opium, tea, silk, and sugar.

Another impact of British economic reorganization in India was the growth of cities and easier movement in and out of them. During the 19th century, disease traveled as people moved about the country, increasing deaths from cholera. The epidemic spread to Europe, and the deaths were mounting when officials connected the rise of cholera to the Hindu practice of bathing and drinking from sacred rivers and pools. A new sewage system was installed in Calcutta in 1865 and a filtered water supply in 1869, significantly reducing cholera deaths there. Other sanitary measures eventually lowered death rates in other areas, but by 1914, cholera was still a serious health threat in India.

THEMATIC LEARNING OBJECTIVE: INDIVIDUAL AND SOCIETY: BRITISH REFORM AND TRADITION IN INDIA

Even thought the main motives of the British East India Company in India were economic, the company was pressured by social reformers in Britain to actively promote changes in Indian social customs and beliefs. The reformers, many of whom were evangelical Christians, believed that the decadent Indian civilization would benefit from a western-style education, so they pushed for schools that taught the English language and customs. The reforms were supported by non-evangelicals who also believed in the superiority of British culture.

The reformers were most vocal in their opposition to the practice of sati, the Indian ritual in which widows threw themselves onto the burning funerals pyres of their dead husbands. Sati was most usually practiced by upper caste Hindus, but by the 19th century, it had spread to other castes as well. In the 1830s, the British raj outlawed sati, and those that protested what they considered to be a violation of Indian customs were punished according to British custom: hanging and confiscation of property.

Indian Nationalism

During the early 19th century the British decided to emphasize western-style schools for the children of the Indian elite. Part of the reason was practical: the raj needed people to fill administrative posts who understood the English language and customs, and in addition they envisioned that such Indians would help keep order among their fellow citizens. These schools transmitted technical and scientific knowledge necessary to keep the new economy running, and they also taught western literature and manners, and instilled western values and beliefs. By the late 19th century, a sizeable group of Indians had received western educations, and some had studied in England or in other British colonies. Their fluency in English united these Indians, who previously had been separated in fragmented parts of the subcontinent, and some unintended consequences followed. They soon found out that they had some common grievances: although they had developed into "Englishmen" in almost every sense of the word except for race, they were still excluded from the top jobs and they were socially segregated from the Europeans. On the other hand, western-educated Indians no longer had much in common with traditional Indians, including many of their own family members.

In their western studies, this new class of Indians encountered liberal values that had been spawned by the Enlightenment and honed through the revolutions that promoted them. Ideas such as "equality," "justice," and "freedom" did not escape the notice of these new western recruits, and they could not help but apply these values to their own situations. Why were they excluded? If people could fight for the right to identify as a French nation, why couldn't they fight to preserve an Indian identity? Weren't their rights being abused? Such thoughts led to serious political discussions in their common language of English, and thus the Indian nationalist movement was born.

The first of the prominent Indian nationalists was **Rammohun Roy**, who promoted Pan-Indian nationalism in the early 19th century. He founded a society called Brahmo Samaj, whose goal was to reconcile western values with the ancient religious traditions of India, and he joined the British in their campaign to ban sati, or the burning of widows at their husbands' funeral pyres. By the late 19th century other leaders were emerging from the growing Indian middle class, which had prospered from India's industrialization. In 1885, a group of educated and ambitious Indians convened the first **Indian National Congress**, which aimed to create a larger role for Indians in the Civil Service. However, in the years before World War I, they were unable to develop a broad appeal among ordinary Indians, and so their movement did not bring about much change in British India until well into the 20th century.

PERSPECTIVES:
ROMESH DUTT ON
INDIAN NATIONALISM

By the turn of the 20th century, Indian nationalism was beginning to turn its focus from just getting better jobs for Indians within the British system to asserting the need to get rid of the British entirely. In the following excerpt, Indian Nationalist Romesh Dutt expresses the growing discontent with British rule.

"The British manufacturer [strangled Indian competition and] millions of Indian artisans lost their earnings; the population of India lost one great source of their wealth. It is a painful episode in the history of British rule in India; but it is a story which has to be told to explain the economic condition of Indian people...The invention of the power-loom in Europe completed the decline of the Indian industries; and when in recent years the power-loom was set up in India, England once more acted towards India with unfair jealousy. An excise duty has been imposed on the production of cotton fabrics in India which disables the Indian manufacturer from competing with the manufacturer of Japan and China, and which stifles the new steam-mills of India...

The dawn of a new century finds India deeper in distress and discontent than any preceding period of history...and every Englishman and every Indian, experienced in administration and faithful to the British empire, feel it their duty to suggest methods for the removal of the gravest danger which has ever threatened the Empire of India."

Reference: *The Economic History of India under Early British Rule,* Vol. I, by Romesh Dutt (London: Kegan Paul, Trench, Trubner, 1902; reprint edition, New York: Augustus M. Kelly, 1960), pp. ix-xi, xxiii-xxiv.

IMPERIALISM IN SOUTHEAST ASIA

Competition among European powers led them to Southeast Asia, with its advantageous location for trade, as early as the 16th century when Spain claimed the Philippines as a foothold for controlling trade between China and Spanish America. In the 16th century, many islands in Southeast Asia were captured by the Dutch, and as European rivalries intensified during the 19th century, Dutch officials tightened their control and claimed most of the islands that today make up Indonesia, calling their land the Dutch East Indies. The islands were important sources of sugar, tea, coffee, tobacco, rubber, and tin, and so were important colonies for the Dutch to hold on to.

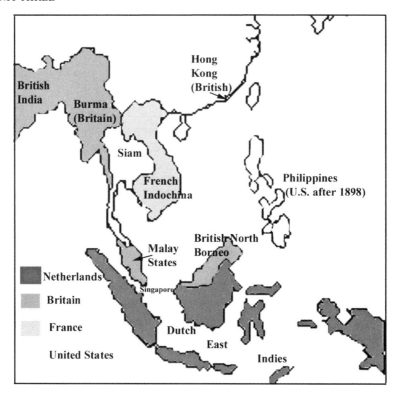

Imperialism in Southeast Asia. By the turn of the 20th century, virtually all of Southeast Asia, except for Siam, was controlled by four western countries: the Netherlands, Britain, France, and the United States. Siam was left as a buffer zone between Britain and France to ward off conflicts.

Once the British took possession of India, they turned toward Southeast Asia in order to stimulate more trade between India, Southeast Asia, and China. By the 1880s, they had gained control of Burma, which was a valuable source of teak, rubies, jade, and ivory. The port of Singapore had been established by the British in the 1820s, and during the 1870s and 1880s, they used it as a base to conquer Malaya (now Malaysia), which not only had many lucrative ports, but also had abundant supplies of tin and rubber. After the French lost their claims in India to the English, they too turned toward Southeast Asia, to establish French Indochina (now Vietnam, Cambodia, and Laos). In order to avoid border disputes, Britain and France agreed that neither would claim Siam as a colony, although the king of Siam could hardly act independently in a region dominated by Europeans. In 1898, after the defeat of Spain in the Spanish American War, the United States took the Philippines as a territory, so by the turn of the 20th century the only independent kingdom in Southeast Asia was Siam (now Thailand).

IMPERIALISM IN CHINA

early indication that the Europeans and Chinese would clash came in 1792
he **Macartney mission**, a delegation (headed by George Macartney) sent

by the British government to open more trade between China and Britain. The government was worried about a massive trade deficit with China brought about by the huge demand for Chinese luxury goods in England that was not balanced by Chinese demand for British goods. British silver went to China to pay for the imported tea, silk, and decorative items, but Britain was offended by the Qing restrictions on trade, called the **Canton system,** because British goods had to come into only one Chinese port – Canton. The failure of the Macartney mission is a classic study in ethnocentrism on both sides, with each considering itself to be superior to the other, and neither willing to bend. Macartney expected the Qing bureaucracy to accept his credentials from the British government, but they refused to acknowledge them. The Qing officials insisted that Macartney perform the kowtow (a submissive bow), which he refused, and he in turn asked Qing officials to bow before a portrait of the king of England, and they refused. Macartney went home frustrated and empty-handed, and British attitudes toward China began to change from admiration to criticism of the regime as authoritarian, self-satisfied, and out-of-date.

The Opium Wars

Following the death of Emperor Qianlong in 1795, the era of strong leadership that had begun with Kangxi in the mid-17th century ended. The 19th century emperors were conservative, government officials were often corrupt, and the empire did not keep up with technological innovations that were changing the world around them. Although the Chinese regarded the Europeans as "barbarians" similar to those who had incurred on Chinese territory throughout history, the scientific revolution and industrialization had transformed the European countries into formidable foes. England was much smaller in population than China, but its technology was superior, and its government and military were well organized. However, the issue that sparked the dispute between Britain and China reflects something about the desperation the British felt over their inability to solidify beneficial trade between the two countries. The trade imbalance was so serious that the British looked carefully to find a product to sell to the Chinese, and they found it in India. By the early 19th century the East India Company had monopolized trade in India and had discovered that the Chinese would trade their porcelain, tea, and silk for Indian opium, allowing the company to avoid paying with precious gold and silver. The British had the crop grown cheaply in India, and their ships carried it from Indian ports to Canton. There the trade was so brisk by the 1820s that China was not only exporting luxury goods but was paying large amounts of silver for the drug.

Most people in China had never used opium before, but once its addictive effects became apparent, the Chinese government began to protest the trade in the name of public health. From the early 18th century, Qing emperors had forbidden the opium traffic, but little had been done to enforce their demands. First, Chinese government officials filed protests with the East India Company and then with the British government, with no results. Next, the government began to enforce the ban on the opium trade and drove opium dealers from Canton to nearby islands and other areas along the coast. Still the illegal trade continued, so the emperor sent a high official, Lin Zexu, to Canton to blockade European trading areas, search their warehouses, and confiscate and destroy any opium they found. The British reacted by proclaiming that Lin's actions had violated the principle of "free trade," and that the property rights of British merchants in Canton had been abused. In 1839, the British declared war on China, and the conflict that followed reflected how badly the Chinese had fallen behind western nations in war technologies. The Chinese war junks were routed by the British gunboats, and on land the Chinese fought with swords, knives, spears, and outdated muskets against well-trained British infantrymen with the latest, most accurate rifles. The Chinese government surrendered after the British sent their steam-powered gunboats up the Yangtze River and the Grand Canal, where they took over virtually all territory along the way. A second conflict broke out in the late 1850s, after which the British government was able to control trade with China with little resistance from Chinese government officials.

The Unequal Treaties

After the Opium War of 1839-42, the Chinese and British signed the **Treaty of Nanking**, which dismantled the old Canton System, increased the number of ports open to foreigners from one (Canton) to five (Canton, Xiamen, Fuzhou, Ningbo, and Shanghai), and made the island of Hong Kong a long-term British colony. British residents in China gained extraterritorial rights, which meant that they could live and conduct business under British laws rather than Chinese laws. The Chinese government had to accept a low tariff of 5 percent on imports and had to pay a stiff penalty for "starting" the war. The following year a treaty forced the Chinese to guarantee most-favored-nation status to Britain, giving it trading advantages over all other nations. After the second set of wars of 1856-60, Beijing was occupied by British and French soldiers, and more treaty ports were opened, including inland centers along the Yangtze River, now patrolled by British gunboats. Through this series of treaties known as the **unequal treaties**, the Chinese government lost control of foreign trade, and the opium trade continued to expand. The treaties applied not only to Britain, but to many other European countries, the United States, and Japan. By 1900, most Chinese ports were controlled by foreign powers as **spheres of influence**, with each port controlled by a designated foreign nation.

IMPERIALISM IN AFRICA

The Industrial Revolution in western nations brought dramatic change to Africa. To most Europeans, the continent was mysterious and strange, often described as

THEMATIC LEARNING OBJECTIVE: EUROPE AND THE WORLD: LIN ZEXU ON THE OPIUM TRADE

In 1838 the Chinese official Lin Zexu was sent to Canton to enforce the government's ban on the opium trade. His aggressive attempts to stop the trade triggered the Opium Wars between China and Britain, with Britain claiming that he abused British citizens' rights to free trade and private property. When the Chinese lost the war, Lin was exiled to a remote province of the empire. However, his reasons for the stern measures he took are revealed in a letter to Queen Victoria of England, written in 1839 to convince her to halt the flow of opium. The letter was never sent, but the excerpts below reflect his strong opinions.

"...this poison has spread far and wide in all the provinces. You, I hope, will certainly agree that people who pursue material gains to the great detriment of the welfare of others can be neither tolerated by Heaven nor endured by men.. Heaven is furious with anger, and all the gods are moaning with pain! It is hereby suggested that you destroy and plow under all of these opium plants and grow food crops instead, while issuing an order to punish severely anyone who dares to plant opium poppies again...

Since a Chinese could not peddle or smoke opium if foreigners had not brought it to China, it is clear that the true culprits of a Chinese's death as a result of an opium conviction are the opium traders from foreign countries. Being the cause of other people's death, why should they themselves be spared from capital punishment?"

Reference: China in Transition by Dun J. Li (New York: Van Nostrand, 1969), pp. 64-67.

"deepest, darkest Africa." Before the 19th century, European explorers and traders were consigned to the peripheries of Africa, to establish their trading posts but never to go far into the interior. Once the technological capacity to go inland was possible, the abundance of diamonds, gold, and copper in central and southern Africa stimulated western explorations. The "**Scramble for Africa**" – European nations competing for land claims – was further promoted by modern journalism that provided stories about the mysterious continent to its readers. Among the early adventurers were Christian missionaries such as **David Livingstone**, whose whereabouts became a subject of great interest to Europeans and Americans alike.

Northern Africa

Egypt under **Muhammad Ali** (1769-1849) was one of the first kingdoms to come under European sway. Technically subservient to the Ottoman sultan, he envisioned Egypt as a beneficiary of western technology, introducing new irrigation projects to boost the productivity of Egyptian cotton farmers. The cotton fed European textile mills, but Ali also established mills in Egypt, modernized the army, built a system of secular state schools, and increased the efficiency of the government. Unfortunately, too much money was borrowed for internal improvements, and the debt became crushing just about the time the American Civil War ended, allowing American cotton to return to the world marketplace and decrease the demand for Egyptian cotton. These hardships led European creditors to lean heavily on the Egyptian government, first insisting that European advisors be installed in political positions, and eventually leading to Britain sending its forces into Egypt to protect the Suez Canal. By the 1880s, Egypt had become one of Britain's subject countries.

The French first asserted control in Africa by invading Algeria in 1830 to suppress piracy and to collect debts owed them by the Algerian government. They occupied Algiers and two other ports. When they showed no signs of leaving, resistance to their presence erupted under Abed al-Qadir, who raised an army to defend the government that he had set up to establish Algerian independence. Warfare broke out, and even though the French won, hostility toward their occupation continued to fester. New revolts broke out. By the 1870s, the French occupied even the rural areas, and had opened Algeria to French settlers.

South Africa

The Dutch established Cape Colony at the southern tip of Africa in 1652 as a stopping point for their ships going back and forth between Europe and South Asia. Other Europeans settled there as well, and it grew slowly over the years. During the early 19th century, the expansion of the colony contributed to political and social unrest among the surrounding African states. In 1816, a leader named **Shaka** seized control of his small **Zulu** kingdom, organized an army, and attacked neighboring African states to acquire more grazing land. Although the fighting was traditional, with spears, shields, and knives, Shaka devised a short, stabbing spear that gave his men a tremendous advantage over their adversaries. The state grew to be one of the most powerful in Africa by the time Shaka was killed by his relatives in 1828. Despite the fact that his reign only lasted ten years, his armies displaced other groups – such as the Soshagane, Nguni, and Sotho people – and many fled to the Cape Colony. Meanwhile, the British had gained control of the Cape Colony as a result of their victories in the Napoleonic Wars, and in reaction, many Dutch settlers moved inland away from British-controlled port cities. This Great Trek of people of Dutch descent (called "Boers") inland to claim land for farming added to the turmoil of Africans newly displaced by the Zulus, with the Boers fighting the natives, enslaving some of them, and restricting others to reservations while claiming the best lands for themselves. The Boers established two republics in the interior, the Orange Free State and the Transvaal, where they sought freedom from British control, and the British paid little attention to them until diamonds were discovered in the Orange Free State in 1867.

When the Suez Canal was completed in 1869, it seemed as if the Cape Colony had lost its usefulness, but the discovery of diamonds and gold deposits in the 1870s and 80s revitalized the colony, and brought a whole new round of Europeans to seek their fortunes there. British entrepreneurs, such as **Cecil Rhodes**, and prospectors moved into the Orange Free State, increasing hostilities between British and Dutch settlers as both competed to control the diamond and gold mines. Rhodes, an aggressive imperialist, once said he would "annex the stars" if he could. He founded De Beers Consolidated, a company that began in the Orange Free State diamond fields and came to dominate the world's diamond

Africa in 1870. By 1870, evidence of western overseas expansion can be seen along the coastal areas where Britain, France, and Portugal set up trading posts and port cities. By 1900, only Liberia and Ethiopia were left as independent states; all other land space on the continent had been claimed by European countries.

trade. Rhodes was not content with economic success, but also wished to establish British political domination as well, and at his encouragement, the British South Africa Company pushed into Central Africa. There two new colonies were named after Rhodes: Southern Rhodesia (now Zimbabwe) and Northern Rhodesia (now Zambia). When the British tried to annex the Boer republics, Transvaal and Orange Free State, it sparked a war between the British and the Boers which lasted from 1899 to 1902. This South African War was called the "Boer War" by the British. Although the British won the war decisively, they left the settlers to govern themselves, and the Afrikaners eventually came to dominate the government of the country created in 1910 – the Union of South Africa.

Explorers and Missionaries

Before the middle of the 19th century European missionaries were heading to Africa, with the most famous one, **David Livingstone**, arriving in 1841 at his post at the edge of the Kalahari Desert in southern Africa. A Scottish Protestant, he was clearly influenced by the reform movements of his day in his desire to not only convert Africans to Christianity but also to free them from slavery. He xwas one of the greatest European explorers of Africa, whose journeys inland were inspired not only by the desire to find new converts, but also to explore and map areas previously unknown to Europeans. He made several expeditions throughout southern and central Africa and made detailed maps of the areas he explored. He also sent descriptive journals home that appeared in magazines and newspapers, enough to develop a great interest in his travels in Europe and the United States. His most extensive early travels were along the Zambezi River that flowed from the interior of Africa to the Indian Ocean. On a return trip to Britain he made a round of speaking tours and published his best-selling "Missionary Travels and Researches in South Africa," which filled huge gaps in western knowledge of central and southern Africa. Returning to central Africa, he began a search for the source of the Nile River, and it was this journey that secured his fame throughout the western world. After nothing was heard from him for several months, an American journalist, **Henry Stanley**, set off amidst great publicity to find him. He finally met Dr. Livingston near Lake Tanganyika in October 1871, and legend has it that Stanley greeted him with the famous phrase: "Dr. Livingstone I presume?" Although he received new supplies from Stanley, Dr. Livingstone died a few months later without accomplishing his goal of locating the Nile's source. Stanley returned home by way of the Congo River, where he established trading stations for King Leopold II of Belgium. He profited personally from both the publicity of his expedition and the trading arrangement with King Leopold, and he – as well as Dr. Livingstone – stimulated the "Scramble for Africa" that followed.

The Scramble for Africa

Between 1875 and 1900, European imperial powers set off to claim lands in Africa, inspired by the information and maps compiled by adventurers and explorers such as Livingstone and Stanley. The knowledge gained about the great African rivers – the Nile, Niger, Congo, and Zambezi – allowed others to reach inland regions, following Henry Stanley's example of developing commercial ventures. King Leopold II declared the basin of the Congo River to be a free-trade zone, but he filled it with rubber plantations run by forced African labor that increased his personal wealth. Meanwhile, the British laid claim to Egypt, and other European statesmen feared that their countries would be left behind unless they too claimed territories. Using the principle of balance of power, as established by the Congress of Vienna in 1815, Otto von Bismarck, chancellor of the newly created German Empire, called a meeting of fourteen states to convene in Berlin in 1884. **The**

**THEMATIC LEARNING OBJECTIVE:
EUROPE AND THE WORLD:
DR. LIVINGSTONE'S JOURNAL**

One of the most impressive "discoveries" that David Livingstone made on his journey down the Zambezi River was a huge waterfall that the natives called *Mosi-oa-Tunya*, or "smoke that thunders." He named the falls after the queen of England, Victoria, and described in his journal his reactions upon seeing them for the first time:

"After twenty minutes' sail from Kalai we came in sight, for the first time, of the columns of vapor appropriately called 'smoke'; rising at a distance of five or six miles, exactly as when large tracts of grass are burned in Africa. Five columns now arose, and, bending in the direction of the wind, they seemed placed against a low ridge covered with trees; the tops of the columns at this distance appeared to mingle with the clouds. They were white below, and higher up became dark, so as to simulate smoke very closely. The whole scene was extremely beautiful; the banks and islands dotted over the river are adorned with sylvan vegetation of great variety of color and form...no one can imagine the beauty of the view from any thing witnessed in England. It had never been seen before by European eyes; but scenes so lovely must have been gazed upon by angels in their flight. The only want felt is that of mountains in the background. The falls are bounded on three sides by ridges 300 or 400 feet in height, which are covered with forest, with the red soil appearing among the trees."

Reference: "Livingstone Discovers Victoria Falls, 1885", Eyewitness of History, http://www.eyewitnesstohistory.com/livingstone.htm

Berlin Conference was meant to calm rivalries and to avoid war, and it produced an agreement that any European state could establish colonies in unclaimed land in Africa, but must first notify the other states of its intentions. Representatives then sat down with a map of Africa and literally carved its territories up among them. Then each country sent armies to validate their claims, and the Africans' spears and outdated muskets were no match for European cannons and machine guns. By 1900, all areas of Africa were colonized, except for Ethiopia, which successfully kept the Italians at bay until the 1930s, and Liberia, a small republic in west Africa founded by freed slaves from the United States.

IMPERIALISM IN THE PACIFIC

In the Pacific Ocean basin, European powers established settler colonies in Australia and New Zealand, but most of the smaller Pacific islands became tropical dependencies with largely native populations left in place. In 1770, **Captain James Cook** anchored on Australia's southeast shore, close to modern day Sydney, and declared that the area would be suitable for British settlement. A few years later about 1000 settlers arrived – most of them convicted criminals – to establish the colony of New South Wales. Most became sheepherders, and soon non-convict colonists arrived, followed by a great increase in immigration after gold was discovered in Australia in 1851. Soon the nearby islands of New Zealand became destinations for British settlers, who settled into agriculture and trade.

In both Australia and New Zealand, the arrival of European settlers was disastrous for the native people, partly because diseases such as smallpox and measles killed large numbers of them. In Australia, the aborigines were primarily hunters and gatherers, so the British did not consider them true inhabitants of the land. Land was seized, and the more British settlers who came, the farther into the desert the aborigines were pushed. When they fought back, they were evicted by military force from most of the land that was suitable for agriculture or herding. In New Zealand, the native people – the Maori – signed a treaty that put them under British protection, and British settlers soon took the best lands, provoking a series of wars between settlers and natives from 1860 to 1864. Like the aborigines in Australia, the conflict resulted in most Maoris being placed on reservations.

Until the late 19th century, Europeans had little interest in colonizing the small islands of the Pacific. Most visitors to the islands were whalers, missionaries, and merchants, each with their own goals, which did not include colonization. However, as competition among European nations increased with the Scramble for Africa and the takeover of Southeast Asia, the imperialist countries began to stake their claims in the Pacific as well. France claimed Tahiti, the Marquesas, and New Caledonia; the British colonized Fiji; and Germany took over the Marshall Islands. The Berlin Conference that partitioned Africa also struck agreements regarding Oceania.

Hawaii – far away from the islands of the South Pacific – did not become a colony until the United States annexed the islands in 1898, although, like Australia, Hawaii was visited by Captain James Cook in the late 18th century. Cook found a people untouched by modern technology. On his second trip there, he was killed by warriors who tried to take his ship for its metal nails. The British soon convinced a Hawaiian prince to unify the islands under him, and with western tutelage he won a series of wars that resulted in a friendly environment for western merchants and businessmen. Protestant missionaries from New England were inspired to come to Hawaii after two powerful queens banned female subordination, and large numbers of conversions to Christianity followed. The missionaries established western-style schools, and Hawaiian customs, dress, and languages were discouraged. As in many other places of colonization, disease struck the native population, and by 1850, only about 80,000 Hawaiians remained, in contrast to the 500,000 or so who lived there when the Europeans first arrived. Western investors began buying up land for sugar plantations, and increasing numbers of settlers came to the islands, especially from the United States. Asian workers were brought in to work on the plantations, further diversifying the population. With a series of weak Hawaiian kings after 1872, disorder threatened the plantations, so the planters turned to the United States to protect them. An American naval base was established at Pearl Harbor, and eventually American troops were posted all around Honolulu, the main city. An annexation movement led by settlers in the American west convinced the U.S., fresh from victory in its "Splendid Little War" with Spain in 1898, to officially take over Hawaii in order to protect American lives and property, as the planters had successfully argued. Hawaiians were not enslaved, and soon they ceased to threaten the planters at all, and so the colony settled in as a diverse population of Americans, native Hawaiians, Chinese, and Japanese.

GLOBAL CHANGES IN THE AGE OF IMPERIALISM

Just as industrialization widened the gap between the rich and the poor within industrial nations, imperialism widened the gap between rich and poor nations. The global economy that developed consisted of countries that controlled and countries that were controlled, or the "haves" and the "have nots." Almost all areas of the world were affected by industrialization, even if they remained agricultural, because by 1914, many of those areas were under the sway of imperialism, either as direct colonies, or as subordinates fashioned by unequal treaties for trade and business. The forces of industrialization became more powerful as the 19th century progressed, and western nations explored the ends of the earth for natural resources and markets to keep their burgeoning prosperity going. By 1914, western European nations were joined by Russia, the United States, and Japan, and the competition that resulted from their quest for expansion affected more and more people around the world.

- **Economic Changes** – The global economy was reorganized so that imperialist countries controlled natural resources in their subject societies around the world. Many of these resources served as raw materials destined for the factories of Europe, North America, and Japan. Global trade in diamonds, rubber, petroleum, and timber increased as new natural resources were discovered, and transportation improved as larger, faster ships and rail lines were built across many lands. As in the previous era, trade in cotton, tea, coffee, gold, silver, and cacao continued, but at a more rapid pace. Sometimes the subject lands continued to produce what they had long produced, such as cotton in India, but in this era India sent raw cotton to Europe for manufacture, instead of making textiles by hand at home. In other cases, crops that had never been produced in an area were introduced, so that much of the land was taken up by crops for export, often at the expense of raising food necessary for the subject people. For example, rubber plantations came to dominate agriculture in the Malay Peninsula and Sumatra, and also along the Congo River in Africa.

- **Labor Migrations** – In order to more efficiently make use of the natural resources they found all over the globe, imperialist countries encouraged people to migrate to areas where their labor was most needed. As a result, massive worldwide migrations took place to areas where job opportunities abounded. Many of these migrants – especially those from Asia, Africa, and the Pacific islands – became **indentured servants**, who worked in return for payment of their passage. As slave labor systems declined, the plantations made use of contract laborers recruited from lands where poverty levels were high and populations were dense. Some common patterns included Indian migrants to work on rubber plantations in Southeast Asia, South Africa, and the Pacific Islands; Chinese laborers to work on sugar plantations in the Caribbean, gold mines in South Africa and Australia, and railroad construction sites in the United States, Canada, and Peru; Japanese and Chinese to sugar plantations in Hawaii; and African laborers to sugar plantations in the Caribbean islands. A large-scale migration of Europeans also occurred during this era, but most were not indentured servants; instead they sought cheap land to cultivate as independent farmers or paid laborers in factories. Most of these migrants headed to the colonies controlled by their homeland, such as British to Australia and New Zealand, while people from many countries headed to the United States, where expansion west provided cheap land and the industrializing cities offered plentiful factory jobs.

- **Social Consequences** – As people from different lands came into contact with one another, conflicts often emerged, especially between colonizers and colonized. As Europeans went to the colonies, they tended to segregate themselves from the natives, living in enclaves of all whites and socializing only with one another. In most areas, mixed marriages or living arrangements were frowned upon, a taboo reinforced by the large number of missionaries that travelled to the colonies. Particularly for women and children, who did not have the work-related contacts that the men had, their European world was highly insulated from its surroundings, so that the only natives they knew were servants or nannies. Upper and middle-class natives seldom socialized with Europeans, and their exclusion from the imperialists' world bred resentments that eventually developed into support for independence movements. One important consequence of colonization for some women in traditional societies was the creation of educational opportunities they had not had before. Missionary girls' schools were first established to provide literacy skills to deprived social groups, but by the end of the 19th century women from the growing middle class were also attending schools sponsored by European colonizers. As men in these societies became increasingly westernized, some began to wish the same for their wives, so educational opportunities were opened for women. However, most schools with European curricula were male-centered, and education for women tended to focus on improvement of their domestic skills. Some European women who went to the colonies – either as settlers, missionaries, or nurses – found liberation in their new roles from social constraints back home, although others that made the journey found a recreated European social system already in place in their destinations.

- **Scientific Racism** – The new imperialist world order benefitted European countries, the United States, and Japan much more than the lands that were colonized, and alongside the economic changes came an academic pursuit known as **scientific racism**. This "science" was based on the assumption that the world is divided into four main racial groups, each with its own distinct traits. One early theorist, Joseph Arthur de Gobineau, characterized Africans as lazy and unintelligent, Europeans as intelligent and morally superior, Asians as smart but nonassertive, and American natives as arrogant yet dull. Other scientists who agreed with him supported the notion that Europeans were an inherently superior race, and by implication, the natural masters of the world. Scientific racists used **Charles Darwin**'s theories in *The Origin of Species* **(1859)** to devise their theories of **Social Darwinism**. According to Darwin, an English biologist, all species developed over time through a process of survival of the fittest, so that species that didn't adapt to changing conditions died out and those that did adapt survived. Whereas Darwin's arguments had to do strictly with biological evolution, Social Darwinists applied survival of the fittest to social situations as well. The best known Social Darwinist was **Herbert Spencer**, who argued that successful individuals and races emerged to dominate others as a result of "survival of the fittest". His ideas were used to justify both the wealth of entrepreneurs in opposition to their laborers, as well as the domination of European imperialists over subject peoples.

INTERNATIONAL RIVALRIES

Before 1914, the major European powers had not been involved in a major war with one another for almost fifty years. However, a series of crises had occurred, but did not lead to general war, primarily because Otto von Bismarck of Germany orchestrated the balance of power. One action he took in 1879 was to form an alliance with Austria to ward off a possible anti-German alliance between France and Russia. In 1882, Italy joined with Germany and Austria-Hungary to form the Triple Alliance. The three countries vowed to support the existing political order. At the same time, Bismarck signed a separate treaty with Russia, hoping to prevent a French-Russian alliance against him. This delicate balancing act was designed to preserve peace and the status quo, but all was upset when Emperor

THEMATIC LEARNING OBJECTIVE: OBJECTIVE KNOWLEDGE AND SUBJECTIVE VISIONS: SOCIAL DARWINISM AND IMPERIALISM

Social Darwinism gained popularity during the late 19th century as an application of Darwin's new ideas about biology to nations and races. In the following excerpt, Englishman Karl Pearson tried to connect concepts from Darwin's evolutionary theory to the development of human societies.

"History shows me one way, and one way only, in which a state of civilisation has been produced, namely, the struggle of race with race, and the survival of the physically and mentally fitter race.
This dependence of progress on the survival of the fitter race, terribly black as it may seem to some of you, gives the struggle for existence its redeeming features; it is the fiery crucible out of which comes the finer metal...
The path of progress is strewn with the wreck of nations; traces are everywhere to be seen of the hecatombs of inferior races, and of victims who found not the narrow way to the greater perfection. Yet these dead peoples are, in very truth, the stepping stones on which mankind has arisen to the higher intellectual and deeper emotional life of today."

Reference: Karl Pearson, *National Life from the Standpoint of Science, 2nd ed.* (Cambridge, England: Cambridge University Press, 1907), pp. 21, 64.

Wilhelm II dismissed Bismarck and began to direct Germany's foreign policy himself.

Bismarck's Demise

Until 1890, Bismarck continued to guide German policy. His actions generally supported his assertion that Germany wanted no further territorial gains, and was satisfied with the position in European politics that it held after German unification. He certainly wanted to avoid a new war that might undo his achievement, as was reflected in his attempt to settle the "Scramble for Africa" at the Berlin Conference in 1884. The alliances and other treaties that he signed with other nations resulted from his use of the full range of diplomatic weapons: appeasement and deterrence, threats and promise, secrecy and openness. When he was forced into retirement by Wilhelm II in 1890, relationships among the great powers became increasingly tense.

Wilhelm II came to the German throne in 1888 at the age of 29, a young man with a very different perspective of Germany's role in international affairs. Like many Germans of his generation, he believed that Germany was destined to be the leading power of Europe, and he saw Britain as the greatest threat to his ambition. His grandmother was Queen Victoria, and some historians believe that part of his motivation was based on family rivalries. Whatever the reason, he argued for a navy as a defense against a British landing in North Germany, and so began to build what he hoped would be a navy superior to Britain's.

Once Bismarck resigned, Wilhelm took control of policymaking in Germany, and one of his changes was to drop Bismarck's treaty with Russia. From Wilhelm's view, this treaty was contradictory to Germany's alliance with Austria, but once the treaty ended, Russia turned to France for support, just as Bismarck had feared. In 1894, Russia and France formed a military alliance. Britain was ever wary of German aggression – especially in building its navy – and drifted closer to France as a result. Soon two opposing camps were formed: the Triple Alliance (Germany, Austria-Hungary, and Italy) and the Triple Entente (France, Russia, and England).

Crises in the Balkans, 1908-1913

As tensions among the great powers increased, European politics grew more unsettled, as was evidenced in disputes that erupted in the Balkans between 1908 and 1913. Since the late 1870s Bosnia and Herzegovina had been protectorates of Austria, but in 1908, Austria tried to annex them. Both territories were heavily populated with Slavs, and feelings of Pan-Slavism sparked neighboring Serbia to protest. Part of Austria's motivation in seizing these lands was to prevent their possible union with Serbia, and so Serbia called on Russia for aid. Russia was not only a fellow-Slavic nation, but it also had its own ambitions to seize territories in the Balkans. Serbia then – with Russia's backing – prepared to go to war with

Austria. At this point, Germany intervened and insisted that Russia recognize Austria's annexation of Bosnia and Herzegovina. Russia, fresh from its humiliating defeat in the Russo-Japanese War, backed down, but resentments still simmered.

The area again erupted in 1912 when Greece, Serbia, Bulgaria, and Montenegro organized the **Balkan League** to defeat the Ottomans and drive them out of their lands. However, the countries could not agree about how to split up the lands they had won, and so went to war with one another in the Second Balkan War in 1913. As a result, Bulgaria lost most of its claims, and Greece, and Serbia gained land. Still, Serbia had ambitions that were left unfilled by these wars. One Serbian goal was to gain territory from Albania so the country could have access to the Adriatic Sea, an ambition blocked by the creation of an independent Albania at the London Conference, with the support of Austria and Germany. As a result of all this conflict, Austria-Hungary and Serbia greatly mistrusted one another, and France and Russia did not want to back down from their alliances.

The crisis in the Balkans almost certainly would have been contained to that region in an earlier era. However, the massive political and economic changes in Europe that first transformed societies there increasingly impacted other areas of the world as the 19th century progressed. Political ideas, such as liberalism and nationalism, spread throughout the world as Europeans came to dominate other

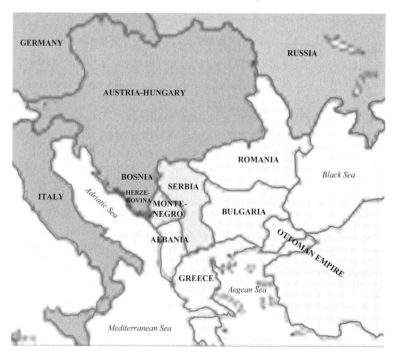

The Balkans in 1913

areas as a result of their new industrial might; at the same time, the economic world order changed as non-European people and lands came to supply the labor and natural resources needed by industrialized countries. The United States and Japan emerged as new industrial powers, but as the era drew to a close, competition among European powers was increasing, and their conflicts would draw others into a world war that impacted virtually all areas of the world in 1914.

CONCEPTS AND IDENTIFICATIONS

Ali, Muhammad
Balkan League
Berlin Conference
Bessemer steel converter
British raj
Canton system
company men
Cook, Captain James
Darwin, Charles, *The Origin of Species*
Edison, Thomas
imperialism (colonial, political, economic, social-cultural)
indentured servants
Indian Civil Service
Indian National Congress
Livingstone, David
nawabs
Opium Wars
Panama Canal
Rhodes, Cecil
Roy, Rammohun
scientific racism
Scramble for Africa
sepoys, Sepoy Rebellion
settlement colonies
Social Darwinism
Spencer, Herbert
spheres of influence
Shaka
Stanley, Henry
Suez Canal
Treaty of Nanking
tropical dependencies
unequal treaties
Wilhelm II

QUESTIONS - UNIT THREE

Multiple-Choice Questions:

(Questions 1-3 are based on the following quote):

"Domestic life is the chief source of her influence; and the greatest debt society can owe to her is domestic comfort: for happiness is almost an element of virtue; and nothing conduces more to improve the character of men than domestic peace. A woman may make a man's home delightful, and may thus increase his motives for virtuous exertion. She may refine and tranquillize his mind, – may turn away his anger or allay his grief. Her smile may be the happy influence to gladden his heart, and to disperse the cloud that gathers on his brow. And in proportion to her endeavors to make those around her happy, she will be esteemed and loved. She will secure by her excellence that interest and regard which she might formerly claim as the privilege of her sex, and will really merit the deference which was then conceded to her as a matter of course...."

> Mrs. John Sandford
> *Woman in Her Social*
> *Domestic Character,*
> 1842

1. The lifestyle described in the excerpt above is often called

   (A) the cult of domesticity
   (B) utopian socialism
   (C) the demographic transition
   (D) romanticism

2. Which of the following economic changes most directly contributed to the development of the lifestyle described in the excerpt above?

   (A) imperialism
   (B) industrialization
   (C) enclosure
   (D) mercantilism

3. Which of the following would most likely read and be influenced by Mrs. Sandford's book?

(A) an upper-class woman, living in a great house in the English countryside
(B) the wife of a noble, living in eastern Europe
(C) a working-class woman, living in a city in western Europe
(D) a middle-class woman, living in a city in western Europe or England

(Questions 4-6 are based on the following excerpt):

"....There is a sphere of action in which society, as distinguished from the individual has, if any, only an indirect interest; comprehending all that portion of a person's life and conduct which affects only himself, or if it also affects others, only with their free, voluntary and undeceived consent and participation....This then is the appropriate region of human liberty. It comprises, first, the inward domain of consciousness; demanding liberty of conscience in the most comprehensive sense; liberty of thought and feeling; absolute freedom of opinion and sentiment on all subjects, practical or speculative, scientific, moral, or theological....

....The peculiar evil of silencing the expression of an opinion is, that it is robbing the human race; posterity as well as the existing generation; those who dissent from the opinion, still more than those who hold it. If the opinion is right, they are deprived of the opportunity of exchanging error for truth; if wrong, they lose, what is almost as great a benefit, the clearer perception and livelier impression of truth, produced by its collision with error."

John Stuart Mill
1914

4. Which of the following ideologies is most directly reflected in the excerpt above?

(A) conservatism
(B) liberalism
(C) radicalism
(D) nationalism

5. The phrase, "The peculiar evil of silencing the expression of an opinion is, that it is robbing the human race," is a direct criticism of the power of

(A) parliaments
(B) proponents of radicalism
(C) hereditary monarchs
(D) military leaders

6. Supporters of Mill's point of view would most likely support

(A) government promotion of economic security for the poor
(B) stable, strong governments grounded in tradition
(C) the right of religious leaders to participation in the political process
(D) the right of private ownership of property

(Questions 7-9 are based on the following map):

7. The dark boundary on the map above delineates the territory named in 1871

    (A) Prussia
    (B) the Holy Roman Empire
    (C) the German Confederation
    (D) the German Empire

8. The man primarily responsible for the unification of the country identified in #7 was

(A) Kaiser Wilhelm II
(B) Franz Joseph I
(C) Alexander II
(D) Otto von Bismarck

9. Which of the following was the most important result of the creation of the political entity illustrated in the map?

    (A) It upset the balance of power established by the Congress of Vienna.
    (B) It enforced the growing importance of parliamentary rule.
    (C) It unified ethnically homogeneous people within its boundaries.
    (D) It represented the triumph of mass politics as a pathway to democracy.

(Questions 10 and 11 are based on the following painting):

Nightingale receiving the Wounded at Scutari, by Jerry Barrett

10. The soldiers in the painting were wounded during the

(A) French Revolution of 1848
(B) Crimean War
(C) American Civil War
(D) Prussian war with Austria

11. The central figure in the painting is Florence Nightingale, best known for her success in

(A) reducing the number of soldiers who died while in battle
(B) getting supplies through enemy lines to British soldiers
(C) improving sanitation in nursing practices that greatly reduced death rates
(D) negotiating peace between warring nations in Europe

(Questions 12-14 are based on the following quote):

"History shows me one way, and one way only, in which a state of civilisation has been produced, namely, the struggle of race with race, and the survival of the physically and mentally fitter race.

This dependence of progress on the survival of the fitter race, terribly black as it may seem to some of you, gives the struggle for existence its redeeming features; it is the fiery crucible out of which comes the finer metal...

The path of progress is strewn with the wreck of nations; traces are everywhere to be seen of the hecatombs of inferior races, and of victims who found not the narrow way to the greater perfection. Yet these dead peoples are, in very truth, the stepping stones on which mankind has arisen to the higher intellectual and deeper emotional life of today."

Karl Pearson
1907

12. The quote above reflects Mr. Pearson's support of the academic pursuit known as

(A) scientific racism
(B) impressionism
(C) realism
(D) democratic centralism

13. The argument in the quote above was based on the scientific theories of

(A) Albert Einstein
(B) Max Planck
(C) Charles Darwin
(D) Dmitri Mendeleev

14. The argument in the quote above was meant to justify

(A) economic aid from wealthy countries to poor countries
(B) the domination of European imperialists over subject peoples
(C) limitations on the rights of property owners in underdeveloped countries
(D) the drawing of national boundaries based on ethnic identities

Short-Answer Question:

Using your knowledge of European history, answer parts (A), (B) and (C) below:

(A) Briefly explain ONE impact that political developments of the late 19th century had on science.

(B) Briefly explain ONE impact that political developments of the late 19th century had on literature.

(C) Briefly explain ONE impact that political developments of the late 19th century had on art.

Free-Response Document-Based Question (Suggested reading time – 15 minutes; suggested writing time – 40 minutes)

Write an essay that:

- **Provides an appropriate, explicitly stated thesis that directly addresses all parts of the question.**

- **Supports the thesis with evidence from all or all but one of the documents and your outside knowledge of European history**

- **Analyzes a majority of the documents in terms of intended audience, point of view, purpose, argument strength, and/or social context**

- **Places the argument in broader regional, national, or global contexts.**

Using the following documents, analyze the impacts of imperialism on subject states during the 19th century. Identify one additional type of document and explain briefly how it would help your analysis.

DOCUMENT 1

...this poison has spread far and wide in all the provinces. You, I hope, will certainly agree that people who pursue material gains to the great detriment of the welfare of others can be neither tolerated by Heaven nor endured by men... Heaven is furious with anger, and all the gods are moaning with pain! It is hereby suggested that you destroy and plow under all of these opium plants and grow food crops instead, while issuing an order to punish severely anyone who dares to plant opium poppies again...Since a Chinese could not peddle or smoke opium if foreigners had not brought it to China, it is clear that the true culprits of a Chinese's death as a result of an opium conviction are the opium traders from foreign countries. Being the cause of other people's death, why should they themselves be spared from capital punishment?

Letter from Lin Zexu to Queen Victoria on the opium trade, 1839

DOCUMENT 2

It is well known to all, that in this age the people of Hindoostan, both Hindoos and Mohammedans, are being ruined under the tyranny and oppression of the infidel and treacherous English. It is therefore the bounden duty of all the wealthy people of India...to stake their lives and property for the well being of the public.

[Grievances]

Section 1: *Regarding Zemindars* [land holders]. It is evident, that the British Government in making zemindary settlements have imposed exorbitant *Jumas* [taxes], and have disgraced and ruined several zemindars, by putting up their estates to public auction...

Section 2: *Regarding Merchants.* It is plain that the infidel and treacherous British Government have monopolized the trade of all the fine and valuable merchandise, such as indigo, cloth...

Section 3: *Regarding Public Servants.* It is not a secret thing that under the British Government, natives employed in the civil and military services, have little respect, low pay, and no manner of influence...

Proclamation by Indian rebels, the 1857 "Mutiny" against the British East India Company

DOCUMENT 3

To sum up the whole, the British rule has been – morally, a great blessing; politically peace and order on one hand, blunders on the other, materially, impoverish-
ment (relieved as far as the railway and other loans go).   The natives call the
British system, "Sakar ki Churi," the knife of sugar.   That is to say there is no oppression, it is all smooth and sweet, but it is the knife, notwithstanding.   I mention
this that you should know these feelings.

> Dadabhai Naoroji
> first Indian to be elected to the
> British Parliament
> speech in London, 1871

DOCUMENT 4

Men are like turtles; they are classified and valued according to their shells.
In this, and indeed in other respects, the inhabitants of the Philippines at
that time were turtles, so that a description of Captain Tiago's house is of
some importance….the paintings crowded on the walls, depicting such religious themes as *Purgatory, Hell, The Last Judgment*….[and] in the place
of honour, set off by an elegant and splendid frame carved in the Renaissance style…a strange canvas…The sight of these paintings…might have
led the visitor to think that his cynical host [disguised] his judgment [of
European guests and] he had hung the room about with charming Chinese
lanterns, empty bird-cages…stuffed fishes, and other such decorations,
the whole coming to a point in fanciful wooden arches, half Chinese, half
European…

> Jose Rizal,
> *Noli Me Tangere,* a novel
> published in 1887
> description of a wealthy Filipino's house

DOCUMENT 5

Would I like to have the old days back?   Well, the white men have brought
some good things.   For a start, they brought us European implements –
plows; we can buy European clothes, which are an advance.   The Government has arranged for education and through that, when our children grow
up, they may rise in status.   We want them to be educated and civilized
and make better citizens….But under the white people, we still have our
troubles…In our own time we could pick our own country, but now all
the best land has been taken by the white people.   We get hardly any price
for our cattle; we find it hard to meet our money obligations…When we

have plenty of grain the prices are very low, but the moment we are short of grain and we have to buy from Europeans at once the price is high… As it is, if we do raise anything, it is never our own: all, or most of it, goes back in taxation.

Ndansi Kumalo
a Ndebele warrior,
defeated by the British in
uprisings in South Africa
1890s

DOCUMENT 6

The Rhodes Colossus: Caricature of Cecil John Rhodes, after he announced plans for a telegraph line and railroad from Cape Town to Cairo, 1892.

DOCUMENT 7

"Take up the White Man's burden –
      Send forth the best ye breed –
Go bind your sons to exile
      To serve your captives' needs;
To wait in heavy harness,
      On fluttered folk and wild –
Your new-caught, sullen peoples,
      Half-devil and half-child...

Take up the White Man's burden –
      And reap his old reward;
The blame of those ye better,
      The hate of those ye guard –
The cry of hosts ye humor
      (Ah, slowly!) toward the light;
Why brought ye us from bondage,
      "Our loved Egyptian night?"

Long-Essay Questions (35 minutes):

3. Compare the impacts that nationalist ideology had on western Europe with the impacts that it had on Russia in the time period between 1815 and 1914.

**UNIT FOUR:
FROM THE GREAT WAR
TO THE NEW GLOBALISM
1914 – PRESENT**

Most historians agree that analyzing the "marker events" and important patterns of recent events is more difficult than assessing those of earlier periods, largely because we don't know yet what the full consequences of the present and recent past will be. It is clear that major changes did occur during the 20th century, and that the Europe of 1914 was very different from today's Europe, but the process of identifying the most important events and trends is by its very nature a tentative one. As we have seen throughout history, each era builds on the developments of the previous one; the era of 1914 to the present began with the important "marker event" of World War I, whose roots lay in events and developments of the century before it.

The world in the early days of the 20th century before 1914 was very much dominated by western powers, who exercised political, economic, and social-cultural control over lands in Africa, Latin America, Asia, and the Pacific Islands. This global power resulted from three interrelated changes that occurred during the era from about 1815 to 1914:

1) **The formation of nation-states** – Political organizations were transformed from those based on the traditional power of kings to ones based on the concept of nation-states – people bound together by a common identity and rule of law. As a result, governments were better able to mobilize popular support for their ambitious economic and political endeavors.

2) **The Industrial Revolution** – The economic power of western states was greatly enhanced by the Industrial Revolution, which dramatically increased production and technological capacity and provided a market incentive to control other areas of the world.

3) **Imperialism** – The new world order created by industrialization divided countries into "have" and "have not" categories, and increased inequalities between rich and poor nations, allowing western powers to exercise political, economic, and social-cultural control.

At the turn of the 20th century the British Empire was very much in its heyday, and other European powers – such as France, the Netherlands, and Germany – were also strong imperialist states. However, tensions were building among them as had happened in Europe so many times before. The quarreling states had clashed in the post-Napoleonic era of the 19th century – for example, in the Crimean War – but they had also succeeded in avoiding conflicts by agreeing on the balance of power principle established at the Congress of Vienna in 1815. By the early 20th century European dominance of the globe increased competiveness among the continent's nations, leading to two great wars that ended the imperialist world order of the 19th century.

The pace of change quickened significantly after 1914, so even though this era has run just over 100 years so far, dynamics of interactions between societies are radically different today than they were in the early 20th century. As a result, we can periodize this era into four phases that correspond to unit chapters:

- **Chapter 17** – 1914 to 1929 – World War I lasted until 1918. The Versailles Treaty tried to reestablish order and stability, but despite the fact that the 1920s were relatively prosperous years, the peace was uneasy and the balance of power uncertain. The revolution and the resulting major regime change in Russia added to the instability of the time.

- **Chapter 18** – 1929 to 1945 – A worldwide economic depression and political uneasiness created ideological clashes that increased tensions among European powers. World War II – a far more global war than World War I – put Europe at the epicenter of a struggle that left most of its countries economically devastated and its international power in decline.

- **Chapter 19** – 1945 to 1989 – The economic and political challenges faced by Europe in the aftermath of World War II were accompanied by cultural and social changes as reconstruction efforts took place in a world dominated by the United States and the Soviet Union. This new world order put western Europe on the fringes of international influence, and as the continent struggled to find a new relationship to the rest of the world, eastern Europe fell under Soviet control.

- **Chapter 20** – 1989 to the Present – The new world order is still taking shape, but Cold War politics clearly have been replaced by new interactions and patterns, including both globalization and fragmentation based on established allegiances and divisions. Europe has taken bold new steps toward regional cooperation that is reconfiguring the old nation-state system.

Although we cannot know the future consequences of events during this period of Europe's history, clearly some important developing patterns are shaping the continent's continuing story. The relative influence of major areas of civilization is rebalancing, contacts between them are intensifying, and patterns of interactions are evolving. No matter what the eventual outcomes are, they will be heavily influenced by the people, events, and processes that preceded them, since the threads of the past are inextricably woven with those of the present and future.

THE BIG PICTURE:
1914 – PRESENT

These four themes run through the era from 1914 to the present that make it distinct from other eras:

1) Two world wars, revolutions, and the Cold War reconfigured the system of nation-states in Europe. Two revolutions in Russia – in 1917 and 1991 – greatly altered relations among European countries, and cooperation among them created supranationalism, or a new political order that has challenged the traditional organization of nation-states.

2) Wars, revolutions, and economic disaster and recovery clearly changed Europe's place in the world, causing Europeans to re-evaluate their values and priorities. The 20th century brought genocide, terror, environmental disasters, and youth rebellions that challenged old values and cultural norms.

3) Important social movements – such as rights for women and minorities, and environmentalism – succeeded in at least some of their goals with the development of a post-industrial consciousness of equalty and quality-of-life issues. At the same time, the optimism brought to people in previous eras by science and technology was replaced by mixed attitudes, as both positive and negative outcomes of "progress" were weighed.

4) The everyday life of Europeans was altered by demographic shifts, urban migration, wide-scale warfare, and challenges to traditional social patterns. Mass culture expanded, and opportunities for education increased for many. Family life was impacted by changing gender roles, and birth rates declined further. Individuals were influenced by culture and technology from the United States, and ethnic and racial compositions of many countries, cities, and neighborhoods changed significantly.

CHAPTER 17:
WAR, REVOLUTION, AND
THE SEARCH FOR STABILITY
1914-1929

By the early 20th century the world order was clearly based on imperialism and the ability of western countries to dominate all others. However, the competition that imperialist ambitions provoked among European nations led to World War I in 1914, a deadly conflict that did not resolve underlying issues. The peace treaties that ended the war did little to solve the underlying problems, and the decade that followed was one of uncertainty and anxiety, as people tried to repair not only the physical destruction of the war, but also to rebuild some semblance of order to their lives that had also been challenged by the cataclysmic series of events.

WORLD WAR I (1914-1918)

The Great War, as it was called before World War II began, lasted from August 1914 to November 1918 and involved more countries than any previous war in history. It was the first **total war** in which the governments mobilized virtually every person and natural resource available to support the war effort. Nationalism bound civilians to the war much more than in the past, as winning the war became a matter of national pride. Technologies brought about by industrialization allowed the war to take place on a vast scale, and the number of human casualties – both military and civilian – was enormous. The number of military casualties alone was far greater than those of any previous war, with about 9,000,000 soldiers dead, and 21,000,000 injured from combat. This total war not only killed and maimed; it seriously damaged the national economies of European nations on both the winning and losing sides, as most were left with huge public debts and rising inflation. World War I was the first step toward the loss of western European hegemony, and it opened the way for the United States and the Soviet Union to emerge as world powers later in the century.

Underlying Causes of the War

European countries have had a long history of conflict, dating back to the days when they were competing kingdoms and principalities with feudal loyalties that were often at cross-purposes. In more recent times, the continent was engulfed by the Napoleonic Wars, which were intensified by fierce feelings of nationalism. Although the Congress of Vienna of 1814-15 struck a balance of power among nations that achieved decades of peace, that balance was upset during the late 19th century by the creation of new empires, particularly Germany. Otto von Bismarck's armies humiliated older powers such as France, and a united Germany challenged even Britain, despite the latter's control of a vast worldwide empire. The economic and military competition extended to the world stage, as Germany joined the quest for new colonies in Africa and Asia.

Some factors that contributed to the outbreak of the war include:

1) **Rivalries intensified by nationalism** – By the late 19th century, all the industrialized nations of Europe were aggressively competing for foreign markets and raw materials, but the rivalry between Britain and Germany had become the most intense by 1914. The rapid industrialization of Germany brought its share of the world's total industrial output to about 14%, roughly equal to Britain's. In 1870, Britain's share had been about 32% and Germany 13%, a comfortably wide margin. Whereas the increase in production in the United States was largely responsible for the drop in Britain's share, British production was beginning to slow, increasing Germany's threat. An expensive naval race increased tensions between the two nations, and Germany was playing catch-up to Britain's lead in sea power. Their intense competition led both countries to develop huge navies.

2) **Colonial disputes** – The scramble for empire was spurred by nationalist rivalries among European countries, and it spread their historic rivalries to virtually every corner of the globe. In their haste to grab land, they often came into conflict with one another. For example, Britain and Russia disputed land claims in Persia and Afghanistan, and Britain and Germany argued over east and southwest Africa. Since Germany had only been a unified country since 1871, its leaders had a late start, but they aggressively challenged the French and English in many parts of the globe. England and France argued so intensely in Southeast Asia that, to prevent a war that neither wanted, they allowed Siam to remain independent as a buffer zone between British-owned Burma and French Indochina. In 1905, France and Germany almost went to war over Morocco in northern Africa, and war among the Balkan states in 1912-1913 created hostilities among European states who wished to exploit the unrest.

3) **Self determination** – The spirit of nationalism that spread throughout Europe and many other parts of the world during the 19th century supported the notion that people with common national identities have the right to form their own sovereign states. This belief was formalized into the

PERSPECTIVES:
KAISER WILHELM II
AND THE GERMAN NAVY

An important component of Kaiser Wilhelm II's plan to build German power was his decision to construct a massive navy, and he was particularly determined to match England's development of a revolutionary battleship type, the **Dreadnought**. As the German navy grew, the British responded by building more ships, leading to a dangerous military buildup that eventually led to war. Wilhelm's political motivations were mixed with personal ones that reflected his mixed heritage: his father was Prussian, but his mother was the daughter of the English Queen Victoria, and as a boy Wilhelm spent a great deal of time in England. The kaiser explained his reasons for building the German fleet at a dinner aboard one of his proudest ships, the *Hohenzollern*, in 1904:

"When, as a little boy, I was allowed to visit Portsmouth and Plymouth hand in hand with kind aunts and friendly admirals, I admired the proud English ships in those two superb harbors. Then there awoke in me the wish to build ships of my own like these someday, and when I was grown up to possess as fine a navy as the English."

The kaiser's chancellor, Bernhard von Bulow, censored the speech for the press because he feared that the Reichstag (parliament) would not fund naval construction based on the kaiser's "personal inclinations and juvenile memories."

Reference: Quoted in *Dreadnought,* by Robert K. Massie (New York: Random House, 1991), p. 151.

doctrine of **self determination** that inspired many people in eastern Europe to fight for their independence. Many of them were encompassed by the multinational empires of the Ottoman, Habsburg, and Russian dynasties, and they hoped to follow the examples of Greece, Romania, and Bulgaria which had gained independence from the weakening Ottoman Empire. In Austria-Hungary, many Slavic people – such as Czechs, Slovaks, Serbs, Croats, and Slovenes – had nationalist aspirations that spawned resistance to Habsburg rule. Russia, always hoping to gain lands that accessed the Black Sea, encouraged **Pan-Slavism**, a feeling of cultural and ethnic kinship among the Slavic people that the empire hoped would weaken Austria-Hungary's hold in the Balkans.

4) **Entangling alliances** – The Great War was sparked in 1914 by the assassination of Archduke Ferdinand of Austria-Hungary by a Serb nationalist, an incident that would never have led to widespread war had it not been for the system of alliances that had been building up in Europe over the previous decades. As countries competed, they looked for backing from others in order to challenge their enemies. For example, as Germany moved to become stronger than Britain and France, it formed an alliance with Austria-Hungary and Italy in 1902 called the Triple Alliance. France and England responded with an Entente ("understanding") in 1904, with Russia joining in 1907. These alliances combined with a build-up of each country's military to divide Europe into two hostile armed camps, poised for war.

A Serbian nationalist group called "The Black Hand" claimed responsibility for the assassination of Archduke Ferdinand in Sarajevo, a city in Austria-Hungary with a large population of Serbs who believed it should become a part of Serbia. Austria-Hungary declared war on Serbia, touching off agreements made within the alliances to provide military aid for those attacked. Germany supported Austria-Hungary and Russia backed Serbia's position; one by one, the countries of Europe took sides, and within days, most of them had declared war on one another. Ties of empire drew millions of colonists into the war to serve as soldiers and laborers, and the Great War began.

The Course of the War

The war began with France, Britain, and Russia on one side (**The Triple Entente**) against Germany, Austria-Hungary, and the Ottoman Empire (**The Central Powers**). Even though Italy had allied with Germany and Austria-Hungary before the war, the Triple Alliance broke up when Italy ultimately joined the Allies after a secret agreement that guaranteed it control of land in its north, which had long been disputed with Austria-Hungary. Most other European countries took one side or the other, but a few – such as Spain, Switzerland, and the Scandinavian nations – remained neutral. As the Triple Entente gained allies, they came to be known as the "**Allied Powers**". The United States and Japan joined later in the war, contributing to the worldwide nature of the conflict.

Most people felt that the war would be a short one, basing their prediction on the precedents in Prussia's rapid victories in the 1860s and 1870 and the relatively quick defeat of Russia in the Russo-Japanese War of 1904-05. The four years of **total war** that followed, which mobilized entire societies behind their armies, was unforeseen and produced unprecedented horror.

The war was fought along two major fronts: the **Western Front** where German troops faced French and British troops, and the **Eastern Front,** where Germany and Austria-Hungary faced Russia. Once Italy joined the war in 1915, a third

(Italian) front developed between the Italians and the Austrians. The Germans were guided by the **Schlieffen Plan**, named after its author, former General Alfred von Schlieffen. The plan determined a sequence for Germany to combat its foes on both the eastern and western fronts. It called for a rapid, concentrated attack on France to the west, which – it was predicted – would cause France to fall within six weeks. The armies would march across Belgium, whose neutrality was guaranteed by treaty, to get to France quickly. The Germans believed the Russians would be slow to mobilize, so would not create a threat while the armies were busy with France. The German armies would then turn their attention to Russia in the east, which without the aid of France, would fall relatively easily. The German plans went awry early when they encountered resistance from Belgium and were tricked by diversionary tactics of the French. The result was that the armies were slowed down, giving the Russians time to mobilize, even though the Germans launched many successful attacks against them. All and all, though, the Schlieffen Plan did not work and the war continued, with neither side able to defeat the other.

The style of fighting on the Western Front was called **trench warfare**, in which, in an effort to protect themselves, opposing armies dug vast systems of trenches facing each other. However, modern technologies made it impossible to avoid high casualty rates. Both sides made use of machine guns that were responsible for a great deal of the slaughter, and poison gas made warfare deadly even when the artillery was silent. The war quickly bogged down into a stalemate, with one side launching an offensive that gained a few of the other side's trenches, only to lose them again when a counteroffensive was launched. By 1916, the Germans had lost 850,000 men, and the French and English combined lost 1,100,000, all with no real progress on either side. The countryside – mostly in northeastern France – was pock-marked by miles of trenches divided by areas called "no man's land" strewn with shell craters and body parts.

Most of the fighting on the Eastern Front took place in western Russia, but fighting also spread to the Balkans, where Austria defeated Serbia and the other small states joined one side or the other. Because the front was much longer, fighting was more fluid than on the Western Front, but Germany had the challenge of fighting on both fronts, and the forces of Austria-Hungary were relatively weak, providing too little support for the strong German forces. However, the Russian armies fought badly, first driven out of East Prussia and Poland in 1915, and then their counterattacks failed in 1916 and 1917. The heavy casualties and lack of leadership increased hostilities toward Tsar Nicholas II and brought chaos and civil war to Russia, leading to the overthrow of the tsar, the takeover by V. I. Lenin and the Bolsheviks, and the eventual withdrawal of Russia from the war in 1917. When the U.S. joined the war in 1917, most of its soldiers went to the Western Front where fresh troops – called "doughboys" – helped to break the stalemate.

World War I. Europe was divided into two camps: the Triple Entente Powers (and allies) and the Central Powers, with several neutral states, including Switzerland, Denmark, Norway, Sweden, and the Netherlands. Fighting on the Western Front was stalemated in trench warfare between Germany on one side and France and Britain on the other, with the United States sending troops there in 1917. Germany and Austria-Hungary fought Russia on a much more fluid Eastern Front. The British unsuccessfully tried to take the Dardanelles from the Ottomans, before turning to subvert the Empire from within.

The war also took place at sea, where German submarines blocked British ports and attacked sea lanes that brought people and supplies to Britain. In May 1915, German submarines sank the British passenger ship *Lusitania* and killed 1198 people, including 124 Americans. Although the United States officially remained neutral after the *Lusitania* incident, the German submarine attacks on U.S. ships were largely responsible for U.S. entry into the war in 1917. The war at sea, like the war on land, remained indecisive, especially after the battle of Jutland in May 1916, when the German fleet could not defeat the British navy, and the battle ended with no clear winner.

The War Outside Europe

The United States at first remained neutral in the conflict, with many Americans believing it to be a European war. American businesses sold goods to both sides, but on balance, the American leadership was pro-British, and German submarine warfare against U.S. ships eventually convinced the country to officially side with Britain and France. The United States was only involved in the war for eighteen months, and none of the fighting took place there, and as a result, the country did not suffer nearly as many ill effects as European nations did from the war. British dominions of Canada, Australia, and New Zealand also sent forces to several fronts throughout most of the war.

Minor skirmishes were fought around the German colonies in Africa, involving Africans as colonial troops, and France also sent many of its African colonists to fight on the Western Front. Large numbers of troops from India fought for the British in Europe, and many Indian nationalists hoped that their support would promote India's independence once the war was over. Japan and China both entered the war on the side of Britain and France, and Japan advanced its own imperialist designs by taking over German holdings in China's Shandong Province. In the Middle East, the British successfully weakened the Ottoman Empire by sponsoring an internal rebellion by Arab nationalists against the sultan's forces. The British also gained support from Jewish settlers in Israel by promising to help them carve a homeland out of the Ottoman Empire. Allied actions set in motion a drive for independence among the various Ottoman subjects, bringing on the final collapse of the Empire when the Central Powers lost the war.

The Home Front

World War I was a total war that involved not just military might but civilian support as well, creating a **home front** that ran parallel to the actual war fronts where the fighting took place. In most cases, the war strengthened the central governments, which took control of coordinating the countries' resources with the needs of the armies. This control included **conscription** – or mandatory military service – of recruits and government supervision of private businesses to turn their enterprises to war production. Laissez-faire capitalist notions could not be tolerated, and civilians had to give up their personal needs and wants to the common cause. To ensure that civilian support was constant, the governments churned out war propaganda – information campaigns that inspired nationalism as well as hostility toward the enemy. For example, Germans were depicted in cartoon-like English and French posters as primitive, war-mongering monsters, and German propaganda pictured Russians as semi-Asiatic barbarians. Governments also established wage and price controls, and sometimes determined workers' hours. Freedom of speech and the press were curtailed in the name of national security, and bad news from the war front was censored.

**THEMATIC LEARNING OBJECTIVE:
INTERACTION OF EUROPE AND
THE WORLD:
THE BALFOUR DECLARATION**

After the fighting on the Western Front settled into stalemate, the British tried to defeat the Central Powers by subverting internal support for the weakest member of the alliance, the Ottoman Empire. They gained cooperation from Arab nationalists within the empire, and the British Foreign Secretary, Sir Arthur Balfour, responded positively to Jewish nationalists – called **Zionists** – who wanted to carve a Jewish homeland out of the Ottoman Empire in Palestine. Below is the statement from the Foreign Secretary, called the **Balfour Declaration:**

"His Majesty's Government view with favor the establishment in Palestine of a national home for the Jewish people and will use their best endeavors to facilitate the achievement of that object, it being clearly understood that nothing shall be done which may prejudice the civil and religious rights of existing non-Jewish communities in Palestine."

The British were concerned with the immediate need to win the war, and did not foresee that the statement would contribute later to conflicts between Palestinian and Jewish settlers.

An important consequence of the war effort was the large-scale filling of jobs in the labor force by women. Since most able-bodied men volunteered or were drafted into the army, women worked in traditional male jobs, such as managing their husbands' farms and businesses, working in factories, and serving as postal employees and police officers. Especially crucial to the war effort were the several million women who worked in munitions plants, making shells and working with explosives. Many middle- and upper-class women, who had long been confined to their homes in Victorian polite society, reported that the experience of directly supporting the war effort was liberating. Women who had seldom ventured into the business world sometimes found themselves relying on themselves rather than their husbands or fathers, and these feelings almost certainly pressured legislatures to pass women's suffrage measures after the war was over. For working class women, the war brought fewer changes, since many were working outside their homes before the war began. Their wages did rise, and most of the governments promised equal pay for equal work, but the wage gap between men and women never closed. When the war was over and the men returned, traditional roles resumed, but some important changes were put in motion, with voting rights were extended to women in Britain in 1918, Germany in 1919, Austria in 1919, and the United States in 1920.

THE RUSSIAN REVOLUTION OF 1917 AND THE CREATION OF THE UNION OF SOVIET SOCIALIST REPUBLICS

World War I precipitated a political crisis in Russia that had been building during the late 19th and early 20th centuries. The last Romanov tsars clung to absolutism despite the growing number of dissidents in the country, and for many, the inability of Tsar Nicholas II to manage the war was the last straw. As the Germans threatened, the Russian army lacked food and essential equipment, and officers were unable to stop the large-scale mutiny of troops. Of all the countries involved in the war, Russia sustained the greatest number of casualties – 7.5 million by 1917. Fighting on the Eastern Front drove peasants into the Russian interior, where they remained as hungry, homeless, and diseased reminders of the catastrophic war efforts.

The Revolutions of 1917

In March 1917 (February in the rest of Europe), crowds of working women marched in the streets of Petrograd (St. Petersburg) protesting harsh living conditions. Looting began, and factory workers and other civilians joined them. Chaos descended as street riots broke out under pressure from a council of workers called a **soviet.** The tsar abdicated his throne when his army deserted him, leaving the government up for grabs. A provisional government briefly took control under revolutionary leaders eager to institute parliamentary rule based on western liberalism. The most prominent of these leaders was **Alexander Kerensky**, who supported religious and other freedoms, but he resisted the major land redistribution expected by the peasants, and serious popular unrest continued even as the war effort faltered badly. Conflict emerged between the aristocratic and middle-class government officials and the workers councils (soviets) over just how conservative, liberal, or radical the government should be. Kerensky used his considerable oratory skills to arouse patriotism, but his wartime government faltered as he – like Tsar Nicholas II before him – lost control of the army, whose soldiers were some of the biggest agitators for radical change.

In April, **V. I. Lenin** arrived from exile in Switzerland to lead his Bolsheviks in a second revolution that toppled the provisional government. His transportation home was provided by the Germans, who hoped to further destabilize Russia, their war enemy. Upon his return to Petrograd, Lenin issued the April Theses, a radical document that called for Russia to withdraw from the war and for the soviets to seize power on behalf of the proletariat. His aim was to topple the provisional government and replace it with Bolshevik rule. Using his interpretation of Marxism, the **"vanguard of the revolution"** forced its way to the top by dismantling other parties and declaring the victory of the proletariat. In November (October) 1917 he seized power, but in January 1918, elections for a legislative assembly failed to give the Bolsheviks a plurality. Lenin used troops to disrupt the assembly and take over the central government, and then he seized town and city administrations and closed local councils (zemstvos). True to Marxist doctrine, Lenin's government abolished private property and relocated the capital to Moscow.

The Creation of the Union of Soviet Socialist Republics

Lenin's assertion of power resulted in a newly named "**Union of Soviet Socialist Republics**", but many elements inside and outside of Russia did not support his rule. Britain, France, the United States, and Japan all sent troops and supplies to defeat the communist threat, but their efforts to reinstate the provisional government failed. Internal resistance was even more serious, with aristocrats, army generals, faithful Russian Orthodox peasants, and many minority nationalities united in their efforts to unseat the new government. Lenin's decree to redistribute land to peasants and the **nationalization** (state takeover) of industry sparked major protests from land-owning peasants, creating even more opposition to the government. Civil war raged throughout the country from 1918 to 1921 before Lenin finally regained stability through the effective use of the **Red Army**, led by his second-in-command, **Leon Trotsky**. Lenin's willingness to promote army officers from humble backgrounds and his ability to make recruits believe in the brave new regime of communism helped him to control the dissidents. He also put in place a **New Economic Policy**, which promised small business owners and land-owning peasants the retention of their rights and freedoms, while the state set basic economic policies. The economy responded, and food production recovered from its precipitous fall during the civil war period. By 1923, Lenin's **democratic centralism** – a system of one-party rule in which the actions of all levels of government must follow the direction of the central leadership – was firmly in place, yet each of the "soviet socialist republics" was set up in recognition of different ethnic minorities within the country's borders. The central government was controlled by ethnic Russians, and despite a new constitution and the promise to respect human rights, competitive elections were prohibited, and the Communist Party established an authoritarian system under central party bureaucracy.

The End of the War

After the Russian Revolution took the tsar from power in late 1917, the new government led by V. I. Lenin had little interest in carrying on what they considered to be the "tsar's war". Instead the new country – the Union of Soviet Socialist

EXAMINING THE EVIDENCE: THE OUTBREAK OF THE RUSSIAN REVOLUTION

The tsarist government of Russia collapsed after a revolution in March 1917, when a soviet of workers joined with a Duma committee to seek a provisional government. An important key to the tsar's abdication was the failure of his army to oppose the dissidents, as documented in the accounts below.

The French ambassador to Russia, Maurice Paléologue, described the dramatic scene when the army confronted the mob on the morning of March 12, 1917. "I heard a strange and prolonged din which seemed to come from the Alexander Bridge. I looked out; there was no one on the bridge which usually presents a busy scene. But almost immediately, a disorderly mob carrying red flags appeared at the end...on the right bank of the Neva [River] and a regiment came towards them from the opposite side. It looked as if there would be a violent collision, but on the contrary, the two bodies coalesced. The army was fraternizing with the revolution."
Later in the morning, Alfred Knox, a British general, heard "that the troops of the garrison had mutinied and were coming down the street. We went to the window...Craning our necks, we first saw two soldiers – a sort of advance guard – who strode along the middle of the street, pointing their rifles at loiterers to clear the road....Then came a great disorderly mass of soldiery...led by a diminutive but immensely dignified student. All were armed and many had red flags fastened to their bayonets..."

Reference: Quoted in *Nicholas and Alexandra* by Robert K. Massie. (New York: Dell Publishing Group, 1967), p. 401.

Republics – turned its attention to restructuring Russian society and to addressing the civil war that the revolution provoked. As a result, the Soviet government signed the **Brest-Litovsk Treaty** with the Germans in March 1918, giving up substantial territories in western Russia as a concession. However, Germany had to dedicate considerable manpower to occupying the new territory, taking away from their ability to address the issues on the Western Front, where the Entente powers now had the advantage of an infusion of fresh soldiers from the United States. The French, English, and Americans launched a counteroffensive in response to a failed German surge, and Germany simply could not provide the troops to keep the war effort going. After the failure of Habsburg forces in Italy and the Balkans and the abdication of the German Kaiser, the Central Powers surrendered in November 1918, bringing the war to an end.

POST-WAR DIPLOMACY

In 1919, diplomats of the victorious nations gathered at Versailles Palace in France to fashion a peace settlement. None of the Central Powers were represented nor was Russia, so those countries had no say in the agreements that resulted from the compromises reached by the twenty-seven nations that were present. The most influential leaders at the conference were those from Britain, France, and the United States, and the three countries had very different views about what the terms of the peace settlement should be. President Woodrow Wilson of the United States approached the conference with a vision of making the world "safe for democracy", and a dream that this war would be a "war to end all wars". He expressed his point of view in a document called the **Fourteen Points** that he presented to the other Allied powers as his plan for peace. Britain and France had more practical approaches, shaped by the history of conflict among European nations, and they both looked to punish Germany. France particularly wanted revenge, and both countries sought **reparations** (payment of war expenses) from Germany, as well as the permanent weakening of German power. Most of the fighting on the Western Front had occurred in France, and almost 1,400,000 French soldiers had died, with more than 3,000,000 wounded. In contrast, the U.S. casualties were 115,000 dead and 206,000 wounded. While the conference was going on, the British continued to blockade Germany, and the Allies threatened to renew the war if the Central Powers did not accept their terms. In the end a compromise was reached, but overall, the agreement heavily penalized Germany, creating resentments and economic hardships that erupted twenty years later in a far larger war, a second and more deadly installment of 20th century global warfare.

The Versailles Treaties (the Peace of Paris)

Several treaties were signed at Versailles – collectively known as the **Peace of Paris** – with the central treaty laying down the terms for Germany, including these:

- **War guilt** – Article 231 was the "war-guilt" clause that placed sole blame for World War I on German aggression. As a result, the treaty dictated that Germany had to pay reparations to the Allies to compensate for the enormous costs of the war. The final reparations bill came to $31 billion which Germany was to pay in installments over the next 30 years. This acceptance of war guilt was not only expensive, but also psychologically difficult for Germans because they thought it was unfair for one country to be blamed for starting the war.

- **Territorial losses** – Germany lost about 13% of its land where nearly 10% of its people lived. France, Poland, Belgium, and Denmark all received parts of this land. France regained Alsace-Lorraine, which Germany had taken in the Franco-Prussian War in 1871. Poland, which had disappeared

THEMATIC LEARNING OBJECTIVE: OBJECTIVE KNOWLEDGE AND SUBJECTIVE VISIONS: THE PRINCIPLE OF SELF DETERMINATION IN WOODROW WILSON'S FOURTEEN POINTS

U.S. President Woodrow Wilson had thought through his aspirations for peace long before he departed for the Versailles Conference in 1919. In fact, he presented his Fourteen Points for peace to Congress on January 8, 1918, several months before the war actually ended. His speech strongly supported the principle of self determination, or the idea that people should have the right to determine for themselves who governs them and how. Wilson explained his support for self determination in these words:

"What we demand in this war, therefore, is nothing peculiar to ourselves. It is that the world be made fit and safe to live in; and particularly that it be made safe for every peace-loving nation, which, like our own, wishes to live its own life, determine its own institutions, be assured of justice and fair dealing by the other peoples of the world as against force and selfish aggression. All the peoples of the world are in effect partners in this interest, and for our own part we see very clearly that unless justice be done to others it will not be done to us."

from the map of Europe in the 1790s, once again became an independent nation, with land carved from Russia and Germany. All of Germany's territories in Africa and the Pacific were given as **mandates** to Britain, France, and Japan, which meant that they were administered on behalf of the **League of Nations**, the new international peace organization created by the treaty. The Allies were to govern these lands until they determined their readiness for independence.

- **Military restrictions** – The size of the German army was strictly limited, and Germany could place no troops at all in the Rhineland, a strip of land in western Germany between the Rhine River and the French border. Germany was also forbidden to manufacture war materials, including airplanes and submarines. The intent of these restrictions was to keep Germany from ever again waging war against other European nations.

- **The creation of the League of Nations** – The Allies agreed to create an international peace organization charged with keeping another war from occurring, but also, in the event of aggression by any nation, a collective effort to stop the aggression. The League of Nations was one of Wilson's Fourteen Points, and he saw it as a forum where differences among nations could be worked out peaceably rather than by resorting to war. The League's Executive Council was to consist of the United States, Britain, France, Italy, and Japan (the winners of the war), and a General Assembly would represent 42 Allied and neutral nations. Germany and Russia were not given representation in the new organization.

The treaty clearly reflected the revenge that France and Britain desired, and its intentions to check German power are clear. The treaty with Germany was just one of five signed in France during 1919 and 1920; the other Central Powers were penalized in the other ones. For example, Bulgaria had to give up land to countries that had supported the Allies – Romania, Greece, and Yugoslavia (a new country). Bulgaria also had to pay almost half a billion dollars in reparations. Austria-Hungary and the Ottoman Empire were totally dismantled, and their lands were distributed among newly-created countries and mandates. Russia, too, was severely punished in the agreements because, even though the country had fought on the Allied side, the tsar had been overthrown, and the Versailles powers did not trust the new government led by V. I. Lenin. First, Germany had to cancel the Treaty of Brest-Litovsk in which it had taken large amounts of Russia's territory in the west, but that land was not returned to Russia. In fact, Russia lost even more land space as a result of the treaties signed at Versailles than it had in the earlier treaty with Germany.

Despite the punitive nature of these agreements, the Allies did not simply seize all of the land for themselves. Instead, the principle of national **self determination** that rose from 19th-century liberal traditions played some role in the redrawing of much of the map of Europe at Versailles. Austria-Hungary was carved into new countries based on ethnic identity: Poland was recreated for the Poles, since it had been seized by Prussia, Austria, and Russia more than 100 years earlier; Czechoslovakia was created for two different Slavic peoples – the Czechs and the Slovaks; and the borders of the new Yugoslavia encompassed Serbs, Croats, and Slovenes. Out of Russia came Finland, Estonia, Latvia, and Lithuania, which had all declared their independence in 1918, but were now officially recognized by the Allied Powers. Despite the application of the principle of self determination, there were inconsistencies that stirred up problems and resentments. For example, one third of the people in Poland did not speak Polish, and Czechoslovakia also had large populations of Germans, Ruthenes, and Hungarians. Part of the problem was that drawing political boundaries was difficult because populations were often intermixed or unevenly divided among ethnic groups within a given area.

THEMATIC LEARNING OBJECTIVE: INTERACTION OF EUROPE AND THE WORLD: POST-WORLD WAR I TREATIES AND EUROPEAN BIASES

At the Versailles Conference, U.S. President Woodrow Wilson protested the idea of Allies taking lands controlled by the Central Powers as colonies, and he insisted that the principle of self determination be applied. The other Allied powers agreed, but the differences they made among possessions reflected their belief in the superiority of people of European ancestry. Eastern Europe was divided into new ethnically-based countries, acknowledging their rights to self determination. However, the Turks – a non-European people – had to fight and negotiate to be recognized as an independent nation, as did Iran and Saudi Arabia. Other Arab people – in Lebanon, Syria, Palestine, and Iraq – did not win independence at all; their lands were put under the protection of France and Britain, causing them to deeply resent their treatment. Germany's African and Asian colonies also did not receive their independence. Whether these actions are interpreted as kindly gestures that resulted from the "White Man's Burden," as Rudyard Kipling explained, or as simple disguises for imperialistic greed, the comparative treatment of European and non-European people at Versailles left a bitter legacy of conflict that continued to destabilize world politics during the 20th and early 21st centuries.

The Mandate System

One of the most controversial decisions made at Versailles had to do with the creation of the **mandate system**, which set up territories as "trusteeships" under the care of the newly created League of Nations. Whereas eastern European people were organized into independent states, however imperfectly, many of the Arab territories of the Ottoman Empire and Germany's former colonies in the Pacific and in Africa were designated as mandates. According to Article 22 of the Covenant of the League of Nations, these areas were "inhabited by peoples not yet able to stand by themselves under the strenuous conditions of the modern world... the tutelage of such peoples should be entrusted to the advanced nations who... can best undertake this responsibility."

The establishment of mandates among the Arab states of the former Ottoman Empire violated promises made to Arabs by both France and Britain during the war, and Jewish nationalists in Europe saw the system as a violation of the Balfour Declaration. As soon as the war was over, Italy and Greece tried to take lands

Europe after the Peace Settlements of 1919-1920. The political boundaries in central, east, and east-central Europe changed significantly as a result of the Russian Revolution and the Peace of Paris. The Ottoman Empire and Austria-Hungary were broken up into multiple small states, and Germany and Russia lost significant amounts of territory. The Russian Empire was renamed the Union of Soviet Socialist Republics (U.S.S.R.).

around Istanbul that were inhabited primarily by Turks. These efforts were met with fierce resistance by the Turkish leader, **Mustafa Kemal**, or **Ataturk**, who managed to negotiate a new Turkish republic in 1923. However, the rest of the Ottoman holdings were divided up as mandates of the League of Nations, with Britain controlling Palestine and Iraq, and France taking Syria and Lebanon. In response, other kingdoms – such as Iran and Saudi Arabia – organized to assert control over their own lands. The results were a fragmented Middle East and a legacy of resentment toward western nations.

Problems with the League of Nations

The acceptance of the League of Nations as an integral part of the peace treaties was in many ways a "marker event" in world history because it signaled a new type of international organization whose purposes went beyond those of nation-states. According to Woodrow Wilson's 14th point, "a general association of nations must be formed under specific covenants for the purpose of affording mutual guarantees of political independence and territorial integrity to great and small states alike." He clearly did not see the League as a substitute for the nation-state, but as a power that could help countries avoid war in the future. Unfortunately, the organization was doomed almost from the start, even though 26 of the original 42 members were non-European, signaling a truly international organization.

One problem was that the League had no power to enforce its decisions, and so even though international disputes were arbitrated, countries that did not want to comply did not have to. Another issue was the principle of **collective security**, or the agreement that if any of the member nations of the League were attacked, the others were bound to give it military aid. This clause was strongly opposed by Senate leaders in the United States because in their view it violated the traditional isolationist foreign policy of the United States. In his bid to gain public support for the League, Wilson embarked on a speaking tour across the country, but he tragically suffered a debilitating stroke that left him unable to defend his efforts, and the United States refused to sign the Versailles Treaty and did not join the League of Nations. Germany and Japan believed that the League served Allied needs only, and both withdrew their membership in 1933. The Soviet Union joined the organization in 1934, but it was expelled in 1940.

With all of these problems, the League was unable to stop the onset of World War II, and it collapsed as the new war began. However, the League of Nations set the precedent for a new type of international organization, and plans for its successor – the United Nations – were being made even before the older organization collapsed.

THE AGE OF ANXIETY

After the Versailles Treaties were signed, most Europeans were relieved to greet peaceful times once more, and they hoped that the prosperity and progress of pre-war days would return. However, the war had changed too many areas of life for people to go back to the way things were before. The economic devastation of the war combined with the total dismantlement of the old balance of power meant that economic and political stability remained elusive goals. Perhaps less predictably, the war had also changed cultural and social norms and values, so that the 1920s and 1930s have often been called the **Age of Anxiety**, a time when people realized that the old days were truly gone, but no one knew for sure what the new age would bring.

Economic Issues of the 1920s

France was the hardest-hit of the Allied countries not only in terms of wartime destruction along the Western Front, but also in terms of dollar debts to the United States. As a result, France was determined to extract reparations from Germany.

WORLD WAR I:
A CULTURAL MARKER EVENT

World War I was clearly a political and economic marker event, in that it so seriously wounded the economies of European countries that it resulted in their decline as imperialist powers. Although less apparent on first glance, the cultural changes brought about by the war were equally important, so that we can see distinctly different lifestyles and values after the war than before. Social restrictions loosened in Europe and the United States so that pleasure-seeking behavior unimaginable before the war – such as drinking, racy dancing, and looser sexual morality – characterized urban life styles during the 1920s. The changes for women were particularly notable in less modest dress styles, unescorted attendance in public places, and less deference to fathers and husbands. Secular values replaced the religious in many cities, and the rift between urban and rural life styles widened as the decade progressed. The reasons for these changes are complex, but the war clearly sparked them. One explanation is that the horrors of war caused many to react by seeking escape through pleasurable, immediately gratifying behaviors. Another explanation is that the war interrupted normal social patterns, separating men and women from their traditional roles, sending women into the work place and suspending breadwinner roles for men.

Britain and other Allies also expected economic relief from the reparations, and as a result, the reparations bill for Germany was enormous. Another source of economic strain for Germany was its own staggering war debt, made more burdensome because the Kaiser had refused to raise taxes, especially on the rich, during the war. In an effort to gain the trust of its citizens, the new German government – called the **Weimar Republic** – also refused to raise taxes.

Caught without a way to pay its bills, the government tried to stretch out its reparation payments, but France responded by occupying several cities in the Ruhr (an important industrial area) until Germany agreed to an acceptable schedule. The German government printed more money to pay its debts, making its currency – the mark – almost worthless. To make matters worse, workers in the Ruhr had gone on strike to protest French occupation, and the resulting decline in production (the Ruhr usually produced 80% of Germany's steel and coal) made it more difficult to bring badly needed income to the country. Runaway inflation caused by the trillions of marks printed by the government meant that people had to carry money in bags to do their normal shopping. The accumulated savings of many retired and middle-class people were wiped out, creating intense resentment among German citizens. Looking for someone to blame, they criticized France and Britain, but they also turned on their own government.

Eventually in 1924 the **Dawes Plan** – an agreement by an international committee headed by American banker Charles G. Dawes – reduced Germany's reparation payments, an action that promoted economic recovery. Essentially, Germany received private loans from the United States to pay reparations to France and Britain, and in turn France and Britain repaid their debts to the United States. The system worked as long as American prosperity lasted, and in 1929 – just before the bottom fell out of the world economy – the Young Plan (also named after an American businessman) reduced German reparations even further.

During the 1920s the cycles of boom and bust that had characterized the late 19th century returned, adding to the economic uncertainty. A short postwar economic boom encouraged post-war rebuilding, but it was followed by an economic downturn that was most severe between 1920 and 1922. Despite the return of economic prosperity later in the decade and Germany's economic recovery by 1929, the seesaw economy of the 1920s left Europeans in the malaise of the decade – the Age of Anxiety.

Political Developments of the 1920s

Although the 1920s are often called "The Roaring Twenties", the image of a carefree decade masks the serious problems of restoring social stability and implementing democracy. Four autocratic governments had collapsed as a result of the war, leaving the new governments to fend for themselves.

Eastern and Central Europe

In eastern Europe, most of the new republics were unprepared for independent participation in the world markets, and nationalist forces continued to be problematic, since the new borders still did not coincide with national sentiments. For example, a large number of Ukrainians, Belorussians, and Germans lived within the borders of the reunified Poland, and the Poles themselves were divided based on cultural preferences for Austrian, German, or Russian customs. Poland's new constitution guaranteed equal rights for all ethnicities and religions, but the new democratic government was weakened by strikes and violence brought by the economic downturn in 1922-1923.

In Germany, the Weimar Republic faced the task of establishing political loyalty from its citizens, many of whom felt nostalgia for the pre-war heyday of the German Empire. The government's stability was also hampered by extremist political parties, including right-wingers who favored violence rather than consensus building, and often directed their protests toward democratic leaders and Jews. Support for the far right came from wealthy landowners, businessmen, and members of the lower-middle and middle classes whose standard of living had dropped because of inflation. One group – called the "Brown Shirts" – was led by a charismatic newcomer, **Adolf Hitler**. In 1923, Hitler led a coup d'état – or *putsch* – to protest the French occupation of the Ruhr. Called the "Beer Hall Putsch" because it began in a beer hall, the coup was suppressed by government troops, and Hitler spent a year in jail. Despite his absence from the political scene while he was imprisoned, he emerged as a hero to many right wingers.

France and Britain

In France and Britain, right-leaning parties had less political impact, mainly because parliamentary institutions were well established. In France, coalitions among moderate leftists, moderates, and moderate rightists formed to address the reconstruction of war-torn areas, and hoped to replenish the population by making the distribution of birth-control information illegal and severely punishing abortions. In Britain, the first prime minister from the Labour Party took office in 1924, but despite the victory of the relatively new party, the government still had to deal with labor unrest caused by boom and bust economics. In 1926, workers launched a nine-day general strike against wage cuts and dangerous working conditions in the mines. The country would have been paralyzed except for the fact that many middle-class people temporarily filled vital jobs, such as driving trains and working on docks.

The question of Irish home rule returned, with Irish republicans attacking government buildings in Dublin even while the war was going on. Once the war ended, republican leaders announced Ireland's independence from Britain and created their own Irish Parliament. The British government responded by sending troops – called the Black and Tans, after the colors of their uniforms – to recapture control. The situation deteriorated into **guerilla warfare** (fighting in small groups that specialize in surprise and terrorist tactics) and resulted in bombing of buildings and shooting into crowds. In 1922, a treaty was negotiated that created the **Irish Free State**, a self-governing dominion owing allegiance to the British crown, but also separated the six northern countries of Ulster from the rest of Ireland. As Northern Ireland, these counties remained a part of Britain with representation in the British Parliament. Although the fighting ended for the time being, the agreement provided the basis for further tension and conflict that continued throughout the century.

CULTURAL UNCERTAINTY

After the wild economic swings of the early-to-mid 1920s, Europe generally enjoyed renewed prosperity by the latter part of the decade. Common involvement

The British Settlement with Ireland, 1922. In December 1922, after intense guerilla warfare in Ireland, the Irish parliament sitting in Dublin proclaimed the existence of the Irish Free State, a self-governing dominion which included all of Ireland except the six northern counties of Ulster, where Protestants outnumbered Catholics by about 60% to 40%. These counties formed Northern Ireland, which still sent representatives to the British Parliament.

in the war had blurred class lines and accelerated the trend toward a **mass society**, or one in which ordinary people increasingly defined culture, partly through new mass media such as film and radio. Mass production of consumer goods also shaped society, especially the growing affordability of the automobile made possible by American automaker Henry Ford's use of the assembly line that mass produced autos and parts quickly and efficiently. Other products – such as radios, phonographs, and clothing of the new synthetic fiber called rayon – became widely available as mass production drove prices down. The eight-hour workday advocated by Henry Ford became a reality for some workers, and led to decreased hours spent at work for others. As a result, leisure time grew, allowing people to attend movies, listen to the radio, and take vacations.

Despite this growth of popular culture, the decade of the 1920s generally was not an optimistic one. Before the war, most Europeans had accepted the inevitability of progress, believing that life was getting better with each generation. That belief was framed by Newton's comforting concept of an ordered universe, and by practical scientific discoveries that improved health. Although Einstein devised his theory of relativity before the war, by the 1920s other scientists had confirmed his discovery that time and space are relative, reinforcing the feelings of uncertainty that the war brought. The war itself was so destructive that it literally tore away the belief in progress, since it left in its wake not only horribly disfigured landscapes, but also severely traumatized soldiers who had endured the grueling trench warfare that had killed so many of their comrades. The disillusionment that set in echoed especially strongly among intellectuals, who even before the war had questioned the general assumption of progress, and now felt a despair that infused their works in an attempt to find some new framework to define the meaning of life.

Philosophy

Before the war, German philosopher **Friedrich Nietzsche** laid the groundwork for the gloomy philosophers of the 1920s. He argued that westerners had overemphasized rationality since the time of the ancient Greeks, and had stifled passion and true creativity. Nothing escaped his critical voice, including Christianity, which he believed supported weakness, envy, and mediocrity. He foresaw a dark future for the west, one of decline brought about by false values.

The war made Nietzsche's words more appealing to later philosophers, and it was in this critical spirit that **logical empiricism** developed, or the belief that any issues that cannot be objectively proved are not the proper domain of philosophy. Whereas philosophers before the 1920s – including Nietzsche – had grappled with concerns such as the nature of God, freedom, and morality, logical empiricists proclaimed that scientific evidence could not be presented to prove or disprove any statement about these topics. Therefore, they concluded, these issues lie outside the realm of philosophy. The best known logical empiricist was **Ludwig Wittgenstein**, who argued in *Tractatus Logico-Philosophicus* (1922) that philosophy is only the logical clarification of thoughts, and therefore it became the study of language, which expresses thoughts. Other philosophers took their pessimism in a completely different direction – toward **existentialism** – which concentrated on finding a new morality in the wake of the death of the old one. Existentialists saw themselves as the true carriers of Nietzsche's tradition, and their movement grew in importance later in the century.

Art and Literature

The search for new meaning was evident in the art and literature of the era. Both were influenced by Sigmund Freud's emphasis on the influence of the unconscious mind on human behavior. An artistic movement called **surrealism** sought a reality beyond the material sensible world and found it in the world of the unconscious. The most famous was **Salvador Dalí**, a Spaniard who sought to reveal the world of the unconscious – or the "greater reality" – by portraying recognizable objects separated from their normal context. One of his most famous works was *The Persistence of Memory,* in which he portrayed familiar but contorted objects – clock watches – against an unexpected desert-like environment. Other paintings were designed to challenge the senses by presenting contradictory images that drew from the viewer's imagination – for example, an image that appeared from one angle to be a young woman looking at the sea, but from another perspective, the image appeared to be Abraham Lincoln. **Abstract expressionism** – an earlier artistic movement that had deserted any attempt to recreate reality – became more important during the 1920s.

Writers of literature were also interested in exploring human irrationality. An early example was **Marcel Proust**, who died in 1922, but whose novels were widely read in the 1920s. *Remembrance of Things Past* had very little action, but instead focused on one man's inner thoughts that presented a picture of life among upper-class Parisians. The German writer **Franz Kafka** described fantasies that conveyed the inner agony of anxiety. In *The Trial* he explored the psychology of guilt as the narrator told of his trial, conviction, and execution on charges that

PERSPECTIVES:
THE DECLINE OF THE WEST

Oswald Spengler's ***The Decline of the West***, one of the most widely read books of the 1920s, gave a gloomy prognosis for the future of western societies, a sentiment in keeping with the culture of the era. The author compared civilizations to biological organisms with predictable life cycles that end in death. He believed that World War I was the beginning of the end of Western civilization, as it marched toward its end, as predetermined by history. The last paragraph of the book reflected this inevitable march toward decline.

"For us, however, whom a Destiny has placed in this Culture and at this
   moment of its development – the moment when money is celebrating its last
   victories, and the Caesarism that is to succeed approaches with quiet, firm
   step – our direction, willed and obligatory at once, is set for us within narrow
   limits, and on any other terms life is not worth the living. We have not the
   freedom to reach to this or to that, but the freedom to do the necessary or to do
   nothing. And a task that historic necessity has set *will* be accomplished with
   the individual or against him.
      '*Ducunt Fata volentem, nolentem trabun*' [The Fates guide the willing and
      drag the unwilling]."

Reference: Oswald Spengler, *The Decline of the West*, Charles Frances Atkinson (tr.) (Alfred A. Knopf, 1970).

the author never revealed. **James Joyce**, an Irish exile, used a "stream of consciousness" technique to reveal the innermost thoughts of his characters. *Ulysses,* published in 1922, told of one day in the life of ordinary people in Dublin and made parallels to the adventures of Homer's hero Ulysses on his way home from ancient Troy. Another writer, **Virginia Woolf**, became more popular with later generations, but even during the 1920s she was influential in England's intellectual circles. She, like her male counterparts, emphasized the interior states of mind, but she also focused on the unappreciated importance of female thought and emotions. Her *A Room of One's Own* (1929) argued that women too need the time and space to develop creativity, as reflected in the book's title.

As the 1920s drew to a close, even more upheavals were on the horizon. The anxiety and uncertainty of the era were capped by the devastating crash of the U.S. stock market in October 1929, and the economic disaster that characterized the 1930s was followed by a war even more catastrophic than the Great War. The drama of the 20th century unfolded with little relief for those who sought order and peace, but instead confirmed that Europe was once again experiencing a major transformation.

CONCEPTS AND IDENTIFICATIONS

abstract impressionism
Age of Anxiety
Allied Powers (World War I)
Ataturk (Mustafa Kemal)
Balfour Declaration
Brest-Litovsk Treaty
Central Powers
collective security
conscription
Dalí, Salvador
Dawes Plan
The Decline of the West
democratic centralism
Dreadnought
Eastern Front
existentialism
Fourteen Points
The Great War
guerilla warfare
Hitler, Adolf
home front
Irish Free State
Joyce, James

Kafka, Franz
Kerensky, Alexander
League of Nations
Lenin, V.I.
logical empiricism
mandates
mass society
nationalization
New Economic Policy
Nietzsche, Friedrich
Pan-Slavism
Proust, Marcel
putsch
Red Army
reparations
Schlieffen Plan
self determination
soviet
surrealism
total war
trench warfare
Triple Entente
Trotsky, Leon
Union of Soviet Socialist Republics
vanguard of the revolution
Versailles Treaties (the Peace of Paris)
Weimar Republic
Western Front
Wittgenstein, Ludwig
Woolf, Virginia
Zionists

CHAPTER 18
ECONOMIC DEPRESSION
AND WORLD WAR II

The New York stock market crash in October 1929 was followed by a disastrous economic depression and then a second world war fought on a much grander scale than the first. By the end of World War II, the countries of western Europe were seriously weakened, and the foundations of European imperialism had crumbled. Although most colonies were not officially lost until a decade or two after 1945, the overall impact of the two wars and the depression was so devastating to traditional European powers that the United States and the Soviet Union emerged as the world's superpowers even before World War II ended.

ECONOMIC INSTABILITY AND THE GREAT DEPRESSION

Whereas the 1920s are often seen as a time of prosperity in industrialized countries, a great deal of economic instability characterized the era. It is true that industrial productivity returned to prewar levels by the mid-1920s, but the recovery was fragile, and in 1929, stock market crashes in major western cities sparked a deep economic depression that reflected the total collapse of the old capitalist system. During the 1930s, industrial production shrank, world trade dropped dramatically, and unemployment rose to unprecedented levels. Known as the **Great Depression**, the worldwide economic patterns did not change for the better until after World War II began, when demand for war production was pivotal in bringing a return to prosperity by the 1950s.

Economic Problems of the 1920s

After World War II, the economies of European countries and the United States were grounded in war debts among the Allies and the flow of money from the United States to Europe. Because Germany was saddled with a huge reparations debt, the U.S. loaned Germany money and invested funds in rebuilding the German economy. Germany had to have this money to pay reparations to Britain and France, who in turn needed that money to repay money that the U.S. loaned them during the war. When the U.S. began pulling back on their investments in Europe in mid-1928, the lack of capital caused the whole repayment structure to collapse.

Although they had won the war, France and Britain were not immune to serious economic problems. France generally had a well-balanced national economy, and German reparations and the return of Alsace and Lorraine to French control helped feed post-war prosperity. However, France had lost 1.5 million people in the war, and German reparations could only gradually make up for the $23 billion in war damage to French property. Britain's economic problems were more apparent during the 1920s, partly because British economic health had actually slipped before the war began. English mines and factories out-produced consumption even within the extended British Empire, and unemployment levels became quite high as demand for workers decreased. Britain's merchant marine had suffered great losses during the war, and could no longer hold the links of empire together. In addition, the United States had taken over as the financial center of the world. As the British economy declined, capital that had once been invested by Britain around the world came to be supplied by the United States, causing British production to fall further and unemployment rates to stay high. In contrast, the United States had suffered little damage and relatively few casualties in World War I, and its industrial power and pool of capital grew, so that it became the prime creditor nation in world trade by the early 1920s. By 1929, economies around the world were dependent on the prosperity of the United States, and when the New York Stock Exchange faltered, the depression it triggered set off a chain reaction of economic collapse that affected almost all other areas of the world.

Colonies around the world suffered as the imperialist nations experienced economic setbacks. For example, in Africa and Latin America, plantations that raised coffee, sugar, and rubber expanded their production to make up for a fall in prices, leading to overproduction and further reductions in prices and wages. As colonial people lost the ability to buy manufactured goods, the economies of industrialized countries suffered as well; global interdependence reinforced global economic problems, which generally were ignored by the nations' leaders. Instead, western nations turned to **protectionism,** characterized by high tariff barriers that were meant to protect each country's industries and nationalistic concerns at the expense of world economic growth.

The New York Stock Market Crash and the "Great Depression"

The events that led to the economic collapse of capitalist countries were rooted in the depressed state of agriculture resulting from the war. While Europe was unable to produce crops during the war, farmers in the United States, Canada, Argentina, and Australia expanded their production. When European farmers went back to work after the war ended, it caused worldwide food surpluses and triggered falling prices. Farm families suffered and were unable to buy manufactured goods, causing factories to be left with large surplus inventories by 1929. The impact was less serious in the United States, where many urban workers and middle-class businessmen continued to earn enough income to invest in speculative ventures on the stock market. One particularly damaging behavior was buying stock on the **margin** – putting up only a small fraction of a stock's price in cash and borrowing the remainder from stock brokers. As long as stock prices climbed, the speculators made money. However, by 1929, so many people had borrowed heavily that when prices stumbled, a panic swept the financial markets as brokers called for their loans to be repaid. When the New York stock market crashed, United States banks collapsed because they depended heavily on their stock investments. When banks failed, depositors lost their money, and the economic impact spread far beyond the financial markets.

The economic collapse became international when Americans began to call back earlier loans to Europe, resulting in key bank failures in Austria and Germany. The whole infrastructure built on repayment of war debts caved in as investment funds vanished and creditors went bankrupt or tried to call in their loans. The downward spiral continued as lack of investments caused industrial production to fall, leading to massive layoffs of workers, who in turn could not buy anything since they were unemployed. With farmers already in serious economic trouble, the crisis expanded to affect almost every sector of industrial societies and their colonies around the world. The situation in Europe worsened when businesses were unable to export goods to the United States because in 1930 the U.S. government placed high tariffs on foreign products to protect their own industries. Also greatly affected was the Japanese economy, which was very dependent on the U.S. market. Between 1929 and 1931, the value of Japanese exports dropped by 50 percent, and workers were left with decreased incomes or without jobs.

In **primary producing economies**, such as Latin America, export of raw materials and agricultural goods plummeted as demand from industrialized countries decreased. These economies were often dependent on the export of one primary product (such as coffee, sugar, cotton, minerals, ores, or rubber), and when the market for that product disappeared, they had little to fall back on. Latin American countries tried to raise prices by holding supplies off the market, but these efforts failed, and unemployment rates increased rapidly. Although most imperialist countries suffered from the depression, their colonies could provide at least some of the products they needed, and as a result, some colonies – such as many in Africa – were protected from the international downturn as they continued to trade according to the dictates of their mother countries. Countries with economies that were not dependent on foreign trade felt the effects of the worldwide depression less than others. For example, Russian leader Joseph Stalin emphasized the development of **"socialism in one country"** – his own – so no serious unemployment occurred there, and industrial production increase steadily. Also, China's large agriculture-based economy was protected, since the largest share of Chinese markets was domestic.

EXAMINING THE EVIDENCE: SOCIAL EFFECTS OF THE DEPRESSION

Although the Great Depression was an economic catastrophe, it did not impact all Europeans equally. The majority held on to their jobs throughout the 1930s, and they benefitted from a drastic drop in prices of consumer goods. However, those with jobs feared the threat of becoming unemployed, especially in industrial cities, where large numbers of people were out of work.

The economy upset family life for many. If a man lost his job, his wife could often find a low-paying job doing housework for others. Although the family's livelihood might be saved by such an arrangement, it often upended traditional gender roles, with women becoming breadwinners and men staying home to look after the family. Unemployed young men often loitered in public areas, and their discontent led them to listen to public speakers who railed against the government. The climate was such that many people were inspired by Nazi and fascist politicians who promised to restore both national and personal dignity.

Discontented people were often looking for someone to blame for their economic woes, and right-wing politicians found their targets in ethnic minorities, particularly Jews in central and eastern Europe. For example, throughout eastern Europe, peasant political parties blamed Jewish bankers for farm foreclosures and Jewish civil servants for new taxes and inadequate government assistance. So prejudices that had long been present in Europe festered under the weight of economic depression.

Despite the unevenness of the global effects of the Great Depression, the international financial and commercial network of capitalist economies was destroyed. Governments reacted by practicing economic nationalism through high tariffs as well as import quotas and prohibitions, which provoked retaliation from others. As a result, international trade dropped sharply, decreasing by more than 66% between 1929 and 1932, and world production declined 38%.

Political Reactions to Economic Woes

According to Adam Smith's free enterprise theory described in his influential book, *The Wealth of Nations*, the force behind the economy should be the "invisible hand" of competition, not the forceful hand of government. According to this "laissez-faire" approach, governments should stand by while normal business cycles took place. Recessions (small market downturns) and depressions (big downturns) will happen, and if the government doesn't interfere, a natural recovery will take place. However, this theory was seriously challenged by the Great Depression that began after the stock market crash of 1929.

In the United States, President Herbert Hoover waited for the natural upturn, but instead conditions worsened, and he was voted out of office in 1932. The new president, **Franklin Roosevelt**, searched for a new philosophy. He found it in the writings of English economist **John Maynard Keynes**, who warned that if people do not consume enough or invest enough, national income will fall. Keynes argued that the best way to increase national income is for the government to do the spending and investing if private enterprise can't or won't. Roosevelt reasoned that people and businesses in the United States had been so burned by terrifying experiences during the early days of the Great Depression that they were afraid to consume or invest. Roosevelt began a great number of **New Deal** programs, which involved massive government spending aimed to prevent the collapse of the banking system, provide jobs and farm subsidies, give workers the right to organize and bargain collectively, guarantee minimum wages, and provide social security in old age.

The British Prime Minister Ramsay MacDonald reacted to failing government revenues by reducing payments to the unemployed, and Parliament did not allowed women to collect unemployment insurance, even though they had contributed to the unemployment fund. To protect jobs, the government placed huge protective tariffs on imports, an action that discouraged a revival of international trade. Until 1933, the British government did little to relieve economic misery, and only resorted to New Deal-type programs (called "pump-priming") to stimulate the economy when all else failed.

Depression hit France later, but the country still suffered serious popular disruptions from people unhappy with the government. As had often been true since the days of the French Revolution, people with opposing political points of view clashed, and right-wing paramilitary groups increased the tension among groups. In February 1934, paramilitary groups joined Communists and other angry people in riots that disrupted the area around the parliament building in Paris. Hundreds of demonstrators were wounded and killed, but French democracy generally was strong enough to resist the attractions of military dictatorship.

In Japan the government first was passive, but after widespread unrest and violence, Japan's leaders intervened forcefully in the economy with programs to build public works, incentives and subsidies for selected industries, devaluation of the currency, and wage control. These measures stimulated economic recovery by 1931. In Germany, Adolf Hitler's government also intervened aggressively in the economy after 1933 with large public works projects to stimulate employment and deficit spending directed toward military preparation, bringing about economic recovery by the mid-1930s.

Despite the fact that the Soviet Union did not suffer many of the ill effects of the Great Depression, the Soviet people had to endure the repressive, terrorist tactics of Stalin's government in the modernization of Russia. Besides industrialization, the government collectivized agriculture by consolidating small private farms into vast commonly owned fields. Each collective was expected to supply the government with a fixed amount of food to be consumed by industrial workers and distribute what was left among its members. Collectivization met resistance, especially among **kulaks**, or prosperous peasants, who stood to lose their farms to the government. Kulaks slaughtered their own livestock rather than give it to the government, and Stalin ruthlessly ordered the "liquidation of kulaks as a class". Millions were arrested or sent to labor camps, and many were executed. To prevent any further resistance or rebellion, the NKVD, Stalin's secret police force, scoured the countryside, and even members of the Communist Party elite were arrested and expelled from the party. Millions of people were sentenced to death without trials, and many were sent to gulags (labor camps) far away from their homes.

THE RISE OF FASCISM

The changes in Russia frightened people all over Europe and North America, and led to a fear that communist elements would take over other countries. The Great Depression made people uncertain of their future, and the two factors together – communism and the apparent collapse of free-market capitalism – made many turn to the radical political solution of **fascism**. The name was derived from the *fasces,* an ancient Roman symbol of power consisting of a bundle of rods wrapped together around an axe. Fascism emphasized an extreme form of nationalism, and encouraged individuals to subordinate their will to the state and to its leaders. Fascist leaders promised to bring back full employment, stop communism, and conquer new territories. They condemned the communist model for abolishing private property, but they used Stalin's tactics to accomplish their goals: one-party rule of a totalitarian state with a powerful secret police that terrorized and intimidated the people.

Fascism in Italy

The term fascism was first used by **Benito Mussolini**, who gained control of Italy in 1922 and established a one-party dictatorship. The Fascist Party took over all positions in government, the press, and public education, and it gave employers control over their workers. Known as "Il Duce" (the leader), Mussolini applied the techniques of modern mass communications to rule his people through his oratory talents. By the 1930s fascist movements had appeared in most European countries, as well as in Latin America, China, and Japan. Fascism appealed to people who were frightened by rapid changes and economic insecurity, and placed their hopes in charismatic leaders who promised to lead their countries to glory.

Fascism in Germany

The most notorious version of fascism grew in Germany under the **Nazi Party** led by **Adolf Hitler**. Nazi leaders advocated an aggressive foreign policy to reverse Germany's humiliating defeat in World War I and the terrible aftermath that plunged the country into the depths of economic depression. Hitler abolished the Weimar Republic and built a totalitarian state under his control. In flagrant violation of the terms of the Versailles Treaty, he deliberately reconstructed the German war machine under the premise that war is the main function of the state. Hitler expanded arms production, created new jobs, and rebuilt the German economy. He advocated the doctrine that Germans were racially superior to all others, particularly to the Jewish minority who lived in the country. He referred to "**Aryans**" as a superior people who came from Europe's original racial stock, tracing its ancestry to the Indo-Europeans who began migrating from western Asia around 2000 B.C.E. He believed that all others were inferior, and had no legitimate place in German society. Nazism appealed to members of the lower-middle classes, many of whom had lost almost everything they had as Germany's economy had collapsed.

Hitler's new order required all to submit to the government in order to achieve greatness, and the rigid hierarchy that emerged included the reinforcement of traditional roles for women. Whereas communism usually had the effect of elevating the status of women through its emphasis on equality, fascist regimes generally limited women's rights. Nazis were alarmed by the declining birth rate spurred by the demographic transition in Germany, and they launched a campaign to increase births to strengthen the country. Abortions were outlawed, birth control centers were closed, and information about family planning became nonexistent. Women with large numbers of children were given special awards, and propaganda extolled the virtues of motherhood. Despite these efforts, birth rates remained low, since the demands of urban life made large numbers of children impractical for most families.

Nazism also drew on theories of scientific racism from the 19th century to establish its plan to suppress Germany's Jewish population. According to Hitler's theories, Jews were not from Aryan stock because their language was Semitic and not derived from Indo-European languages, such as Greek, Latin, Celtic, Persian, Sanskrit, or Balto-Slavonic. Starting in the early 1930s, discriminatory laws deprived German Jews of their citizenship and prohibited marriage between Jews and other Germans. Jewish civil servants lost their jobs, Jewish professionals lost their non-Jewish clients, and Jewish-owned businesses were seized by the Nazi Party. In 1938, many Jews left Germany after *Kristallnacht,* the notorious night of November 9-10, when Nazis destroyed thousands of Jewish stores, burned synagogues, and murdered more than 100 Jews.

THEMATIC LEARNING OBJECTIVE: OBJECTIVE KNOWLEDGE AND SUBJECTIVE VISIONS: *MEIN KAMPF* BY ADOLF HITLER

After becoming the leader of the National Socialist German Workers' Party (the Nazis), Adolf Hitler was imprisoned by the German government for staging an attempted coup d'état. During the nine months that he spent in prison he wrote the first volume of his major work, **Mein Kampf** (My Struggle.) The book, excerpted below, explained his racist doctrines that eventually guided his policies and actions as the German *Fuehrer* (dictator).

"All the great civilizations of the past died out because contamination of their blood caused them to become decadent...In other words, in order to protect a certain culture, the type of human who created the culture must be preserved. But such preservation is tied to the inalterable law of the necessity and the right of victory of the best and the strongest...

What we see before us today as human culture, all the yields of art, science, and technology, are almost exclusively the creative product of the Aryans. Indeed this fact alone leads to the not unfounded conclusion that the Aryan alone is the founder of the higher type of humanity, and further that he represents the proto-type of what we understand by the word: MAN...[whose spirit] has permitted humans to ascend the path of mastery over the other beings of the earth. Elimi-nate him and deep darkness will again descend on the earth after a few thousand years; human civilization will die out and the earth will become a desert...

The Jew provides the greatest contrast to the Aryan...the Jews lack the most basic characteristic of a truly cultured people, namely an idealistic spirit."

Reference: Adolf Hitler, *Mein Kampf* (Munich: F. Eher Nachfolger, 1927), trans. by J. Overfield.

In Japan, the regime turned more authoritarian and expansionist as it sought to stave off the ill effects of the Great Depression. Whereas most Japanese pre-ferred moderate political parties, the country's leadership fell into the hands of a military group that advocated a "defense state" under its control. The Japanese army marched into Manchuria in 1931, proclaiming the region to be independent from China. In 1932, the military leadership was responsible for killing the prime minister, and by 1937, Japan's military rulers began aggressively attacking other areas of Asia.

THE RISE OF STALINISM

By 1918, a civil war had broken out in Russia between the **White Army**, led by Russian military leaders and funded by the Allied Powers, and the **Red Army** led by Lenin. The Reds won, and in 1920 Lenin instituted his **New Economic**

COMPARISON:
FASCISM AND COMMUNISM

The discontent fed by World War I and the Great Depression created a fertile atmosphere for the rise of philosophies that competed with the liberalism widely favored by western Europeans during the 19th and early 20th centuries. Two such movements that gained followers during the 1930s were fascism and communism. Although they both challenged liberalism, they are very different philosophies, and they both still exist today.

Communism, in contrast to liberalism, generally values equality over freedom Whereas liberal democracies value the ideal of equal opportunity, they usually tolerate a great deal of inequality, especially within the economy. Communism rejects the idea that personal freedom will ensure prosperity for the majority. Instead, it holds that an inevitable result of the competition for scarce resources is that a small group will eventually come to control both the government and the economy. For communists, liberal democracies are created by the rich to protect the rights and property of the rich. To eliminate the inequalities and exploitation, communists advocate the takeover of all resources by the state that in turn will insure that true economic equality exists for the community as a whole. As a result, private ownership of property is abolished. Individual liberties must give way to the needs of society as a whole, creating what communists believe to be a true democracy.

Fascism is often confused with communism because they both devalue the idea of individual freedom. However, the similarity between the two ideologies ends there. Fascism also rejects the value of equality, and accepts the idea that people and groups exist in degrees of inferiority and superiority. Fascists believe that the state has the right and the responsibility to mold the society and economy and to eliminate obstacles (including people) that might weaken them. The powerful authoritarian state is the engine that makes superiority possible. The classic example is of course Nazi Germany. No strictly fascist regimes currently exist, but fascism still is an influential ideology in many parts of the world.

Policy, which allowed a great deal of private ownership to exist under a centralized leadership. The plan brought relative prosperity to farmers, but it did not promote industrialization. Would Lenin have moved on to a more socialist approach? No one knows, because he died in 1924 before his plans unfolded and before he could name a successor. A power struggle followed, and Josef Stalin, the "Man of Steel," won control and led the country to the heights of totalitarianism.

Stalin vastly changed Lenin's democratic centralism (also known as **Marxism-Leninism)**. Stalin placed the Communist Party at the center of control, and allowed no other political parties to compete with it. Party members were carefully selected, with only about 7% of the population actually joining it. Communists ran local, regional, and national governments, and leaders were identified through *nomenklatura*, or the process of party members selecting promising recruits from the lower levels. Most top government officials also belonged to the Central Committee, a group of 300 party leaders that met twice a year. Above the Central Committee was the **Politburo**, the heart and soul of the Communist Party. This group of about twelve men ran the country, and their decisions were carried out by government agencies and departments. The head of the Politburo was the general secretary, who assumed full power as dictator of the country. Joseph Stalin was the general secretary of the Communist Party from 1927 until his death in 1953.

Collectivization and Industrialization

Stalin's plan for the U.S.S.R. had two parts: **collectivization** and industrialization. Stalin replaced the New Economic Policy with "**collective farms**" that were state run and supposedly more efficient. Private land ownership was done away with, and the farms were intended to feed workers in the cities who contributed to the industrialization of the nation. Some peasants resisted, particularly those who owned larger farms. These kulaks were forced to move to cities or to labor camps, and untold numbers died at the hands of government officials.

Stalin established his first **Five Year Plan**, which set and surpassed ambitious goals for production of heavy industry, such as oil, steel, and electricity. Other economic plans followed, and all were carried out for individual factories by **Gosplan,** the Central State Planning Commission. Gosplan became the nerve center for the economy, determining production and distribution of virtually all goods in the Soviet Union.

Stalinism, then, was this two-pronged program of collectivization and industrialization, carried out through central planning, and executed with force and brutality.

Stalin's Foreign Policy

During the 1930s Stalin's primary focus was internal development, so his foreign policy was intended to support that goal. He advocated "**socialism in one country**" to emphasize his split with traditional Marxism, and he tried to ignore the fascist threat from nearby Germany and Italy. Stalin signed a non-aggression pact with Nazi Germany in 1939, only to be attacked by Germany the following year. Russia then joined sides with the Allies for the duration of World War II, but tensions between east and west were often apparent at conferences among allied

THEMATIC LEARNING OBJECTIVE: PROSPERITY AND POVERTY: JOSEPH STALIN'S FIVE YEAR PLANS

The worldwide depression of the 1930s generally did not affect the U.S.S.R. because Joseph Stalin, the Russian leader, instituted economic policies that emphasized internal development and self-sufficiency. These policies took the shape of **Five Year Plans** in which development goals were set at the beginning of a five-year period to be met by the end. Stalin's first Five Year Plan began in 1928, and in 1933, he reported the country's progress in a report to the Central Committee of the Communist Party of the Soviet Union. The excerpts below cite some of the plan's achievements.

"We did not have an iron and steel industry, the foundation for the industrialization of the country. Now we have this industry.

We did not have a tractor industry. Now we have one.

We did not have an automobile industry. Now we have one.

We did not have a machine-tool industry. Now we have one.

We did not have a big and up-to-date chemical industry. Now we have one...

We did not have an aircraft industry. Now we have one...

In the output of oil products and coal we were last on the list. Now we rank among the first...

As a result of all this the capitalist elements have been completely and irrevocably eliminated from industry, and socialist industry has become the sole form of industry in the U.S.S.R. "

Reference: Joseph Stalin, "The Task of Business Executives" in *Problems of Leninism* (Moscow, 1940), pp. 359-360.

leaders, and as soon as the war ended, the situation escalated into the Cold War. These significant shifts in foreign policy all accommodated his main goal: the industrial development of the U.S.S.R.

WORLD WAR II

World War II formally began in 1939, but in many ways it resulted from a renewal of tensions from World War I that had never been resolved. The causes of the war were global, with Japanese expansion sparking conflicts in Asia, and fascist movements in Europe encouraging military aggression in the name of nationalism. Germany withdrew from the League of Nations as Hitler rebuilt the military. In 1935, Mussolini attacked Ethiopia in a nationalistic attempt to make up for Italy's failure to claim the area in the imperialist aggression of the 1890s. Fascism

THEMATIC LEARNING OBJECTIVE: INTERACTIONS OF EUROPE AND THE WORLD: THE NANKING MASSACRE

On December 13, 1937, the Nationalist Chinese capital of Nanking fell to an invading Japanese army, beginning a notorious occupation in which Chinese civilians experienced mass killings, systematic arson, torture, and rape. Hundreds of thousands of people were affected, but the horror may well have been worse except for the intercession of a handful of American and European residents who created the "Nanking Safety Zone," a neutral area in the center of the city that served as a refuge of those escaping the Japanese army. Below are some excerpts from the diary of John Rabe, a German businessman who witnessed the horror and headed the effort to save lives.

"The Japanese march through the city in groups of ten to twenty soldiers and loot the shops. If I had not seen it with my own eyes I would not have believed it. They smash open windows and doors and take whatever they like...Of the perhaps one thousand disarmed soldiers that we had quartered at the Ministry of Justice, between 400 and 500 were driven from it with their hands tied. We assume they were shot since we later heard several salvos of machine-gun fire ...these events have left us frozen with horror...We manage quickly to find lodging in some vacant buildings for a group of 125 Chinese refugees, before they fall into the hands of the Japanese military. Mr. Han says that three young girls of about 14 or 15 have been dragged from a house in our neighborhood.."

Reference: Edwin Wickart, ed., and John Woods, trans., *The Good Man of Nanking: The Diaries of John Rabe* (New York: Alfred A. Knopf, Inc., 1998), p. 67.

gained enough support in Spain to trigger a civil war between liberals and authoritarians, resulting in a fascist takeover in 1939.

The Road to War

During the 1930s, the economic depression increased the tension worldwide as Hitler, Mussolini, and Japan's military leaders sought to boost their prestige and avoid economic catastrophe. These leaders all wanted to expand their empires, and they were undeterred by efforts by the League of Nations to stop them. Many political leaders in France and Britain sought to avoid war through negotiation, since they believed that the powers had rushed too quickly into World War I.

Inspired by its defeat of Russia in the Russo-Japanese War, Japan occupied German lands in East Asia after World War I ended in 1918, and invaded Manchuria in 1931. Since China claimed Manchuria as theirs, China appealed to the League of Nations to help control Japanese aggression. The League condemned the Japanese attack, but the powers refused to impose sanctions. Japan reacted by withdrawing from the League and keeping control of Manchuria. In 1937, Japan attacked China south of Manchuria, justifying its attack as an attempt to liberate the region from Western imperialism. U.S. President Franklin Roosevelt embargoed U.S. exports of airplane parts to Japan, and later put stringent economic sanctions on crucial raw materials for Japanese industry. However, the western powers did not effectively resist Japan's territorial expansion in Asia.

Like Japanese leaders, Mussolini and Hitler rode the waves of nationalism, playing on their citizens' beliefs that their countries suffered at the hands of the old imperialist powers – Britain and France. Hitler demanded **Lebensraum**, or living space for the Aryan race to be taken from Slavs and Bolsheviks, whom he viewed as inferior people. In 1933, Germany withdrew from the League of Nations, and in 1935, Hitler denounced the clauses of the Versailles Treaty that limited German military strength and began to publicly rearm the country. In defiance of the Versailles Treaty, Hitler sent his troops in 1936 to the Rhineland. In 1935, Mussolini invaded Ethiopia, one of only two African states that remained independent after imperialist takeovers of the continent during the late 19th century. The attack was intended to establish Italy as an imperialist power, and although the Ethiopians put up strong resistance, their capital, Addis Ababa, fell in 1936. The League of Nations imposed an embargo on Italy, but France and Britain would not support any strict sanctions, so Italy remained in control of Ethiopia.

The Spanish Civil War, 1936-1939

The Spanish monarchy was overthrown by republicans in 1931, and for the first part of the decade they debated among themselves as to what type of government should replace it. Communists, socialists, anarchists, and constitutionalists all held different views, and their debates kept them from focusing on building wide support in the countryside. In 1936, pro-republican forces formed a **Popular Front** coalition in an attempt to hold the country together, but they were not strong enough to fend off a coup organized by army officers in 1936. Led by General **Francisco Franco**, Spanish military forces launched a brutal three-year-long civil war against the democratic government. Franco had the support of monarchists, landowners, the clergy, and the fascist Falange Party, and he soon had the help of fascists in other parts of Europe. Arms, money, and men flowed from Italy and Germany to support the rightist rebels, while the government was assisted by 40,000 foreign volunteers and trucks, planes, tanks, and military advisers from the Soviet Union. Finally, the capital city, Madrid, fell in March of 1939, and Franco established a dictatorship that favored large landowners, businessmen, and the Catholic clergy. Tens of thousands of republicans fled the country, and Franco's critics often were imprisoned, while others disappeared.

EXAMINING THE EVIDENCE: SPAIN'S LOST CHILDREN

In November 2008 Judge Baltasar Garzón ordered provincial judges in Spain to investigate the "disappearance" of children taken during the Spanish Civil War from left-wing families as part of an effort to purge Spain of Marxist influence. Historians and associations that represent Franco's victims say hundreds of children were taken from families who had supported Franco's Republican opponents during the war or who were suspected of ties to left-wing groups. The children were adopted or sent to religious schools and state-run homes. Some were baptized with new names, their birth records destroyed, they say. Others were sent into exile and brought back after the war was over and given new identities.

Franco's top military psychologist, Antonio Vallejo Nágera, claimed that Spain could be saved from Marxism by isolating children from Republican parents. A 1940 decree allowed the state to take children into custody if their "moral formation" was at risk. According to Ricard Vinyes, a professor of modern history at the University of Barcelona, "Their logic was that the solution lay in separatating children from their mothers."

In his 152-page court order, Judge Garzón wrote, "There was a 'legalized' disappearance of minors, who lost their identity, and whose number remains uncertain." He suggested that there could be thousands of "lost children," alhtough some historians say that figure may be inflated.

Reference: "Families Search for Truth of Spain's 'Lost Children,'" by Victoria Burnett, *The New York Times,* March 1, 2009, p. 12.

The Onset of War

In 1938, Hitler invaded the Sudetenland, a German-speaking part of Czechoslovakia, and European powers called the **Munich Conference** to address Czechoslovakia's protests. The response from Britain and France was weak, as they agreed on British Prime Minister Neville Chamberlain's **appeasement policy**, which allowed Germany to keep the Sudetenland in return for Hitler's promise to cease his aggressions. However, Hitler did not keep his word, and went on to capture all of Czechoslovakia in March 1939. In August, Germany and the U.S.S.R. signed a nonaggression agreement that provided that if one country became embroiled in war, the other country would remain neutral. Additionally, Stalin and Hitler secretly agreed to divide Poland and the Baltic States – Latvia, Estonia, and Lithuania – at some future date. The **Nazi-Soviet Pact** ensured that Germany would not have to fight a two-front war as it had in World War I. Since he had met no resistance up till then, Hitler attacked Poland on September 1, 1939, hoping that Britain and perhaps even France would not fight. However, this action was so provocative that it resulted in a formal declaration of war by Britain and France on Germany. Germany and Italy joined together in an alliance called the **Rome-Berlin Axis** as Mussolini declared that the rest of Europe would revolve around this central pact between the two countries.

By the time the war began in Europe in 1939, fighting was already underway in Asia between Japan and China. Skirmishes broke out in 1937 in the Beijing area as Japanese forces occupied cities and railroads in eastern China. Although the conflict drifted into a long-lasting stalemate in China, Japan used the outbreak of war in Europe as a reason to attack other areas in Asia, seizing Indochina from French troops and attacking British Malaya and Burma. In 1940, the two main areas of fighting – central Europe and eastern Asia – came together when Germany, Italy, and Japan signed the **Tripartite Pact** that united the three countries as the leaders of the **Axis Powers**. Even though Japan never cooperated closely with Germany and Italy, the alliance clearly spread the war into two major theatres: the Pacific and Europe. Whereas much of World War I was fought along fairly well-defined fronts, the areas of fighting were much broader in World War II, spreading from Hawaii to the South Pacific to East Asia, and from North Africa across the Mediterranean over most of Europe.

As war broke out between 1937 and 1939, Britain and France did little to prepare for war since both countries were still feeling the debilitating effects of World War I and had little appetite for another conflict. Only in late 1938 did Britain begin an expansion of its army and aircraft production that proved to be important in defending their island, but it took until 1942 and 1943 for the Allies to stop early German and Japanese successes.

The Nature of the War

Like World War I, World War II was a **total war** in which vast resources and emotional commitments of civilians supported massive military efforts. Mobilization for war was extensive and required government control of natural and labor resources. The steadily more destructive technologies of World War I – battleships, tanks, poison gas, machine guns, and long-range artillery – were used in World War II, along with airplanes, aircraft carriers, new bombing technology, rocketry, and ultimately the atomic bomb. Since the areas of fighting were so much greater in World War II, the increasingly sophisticated technology insured that this war would be far more destructive than any other in history. World War II also saw the blurring of the distinction between military personnel and civilians, so that whole civilian populations not only supported the war, but were also subject to

THEMATIC LEARNING OBJECTIVE: INDIVIDUAL AND SOCIETY: THE SS PLAN FOR EXTERMINATION

When Hitler's armies invaded the Soviet Union, specially trained "SS units" accompanied them. Their assigned task was to find and get rid of Communist Party officials and adult male Jews. However, along the way, some began murdering Jewish woman and children as well, so that by late November 1941, the Nazis had killed 136,000 Jews, mostly by shooting them in the invaded Soviet territories. Almost certainly, these duties took a psychological toll on even the most devoted Aryan.

During the early part of the war, the Germans also faced the fact that with the conquest of Poland, they controlled a much larger Jewish population than before. The Polish situation, along with the inefficiency of the SS efforts in the Soviet Union, led the German government to devise a more systematic and impersonal method of mass extermination by late summer 1941. Reinhard Heydrich of the SS developed a detailed plan, and by fall, German and Austrian Jews were sent to the ghettos in Poland and efforts to prevent Jewish emigration were stepped up. By March 1942 several extermination camps had been constructed for full-scale mass killing, targeting first the Polish Jews who had already been confined to ghettos. The camps were equipped with gas chambers and crematoria that allowed large numbers of people to be killed and their bodies disposed of as efficiently as possible. These camps operated for the remainder of the war.

its destruction. Bombing raids were launched on cities, killing large numbers of civilians, and the final actions of the war – dropping atomic bombs on Nagasaki and Hiroshima – targeted civilian populations.

A catastrophic aspect of total war during World War II was the **Holocaust**, a mass extermination of European Jews and many others by Nazi Germany. The primary victims were Jews who, after years of social, economic, and political exclusion, were sent in huge numbers to extermination camps in southern Germany and eastern Europe in what Hitler called the "final solution to the Jewish problem." This **genocide** – the murder of an entire people – took place mostly in the camps, where modern industrial methods were used to execute people by asphyxiation with poison gas and dispose of their bodies by cremation in large ovens. Some became victims of "medical experiments" in which they were tortured or killed, and others worked in the camps until they starved to death. By the end of the war, about 6 million Jews had been exterminated, as well as many others judged to threaten the purity of the Aryan race – such as gypsies, homosexuals, Polish Catholics, and the mentally and physically disabled.

War in Europe and North Africa

In World War I, defensive fighting had characterized the Western Front, so in World War II the Germans took advantage of new motorized technology to benefit from offensive movements. Their warfare, called *blitzkrieg* ("lightning war"), involved three carefully synchronized steps. First, fighter planes scattered enemy troops and disrupted communications; secondly, tanks rolled over enemy defense lines; and third, the infantry invaded and actually occupied the targeted land. *Blitzkrieg* forced the surrender of Poland, Austria, Norway, Denmark, and Belgium within the early days of the war, and France quickly collapsed to German attack in mid-1940. Until 1944, northern France was occupied by German forces who ruled from Paris, while a puppet government, controlled by Germany, ruled the south from Vichy. French Resistance troops staged guerilla attacks in the southern half of the country where German troops were less entrenched. However, the quick defeat of France in 1940 left Britain essentially alone in resisting Germany until Russia and the United States joined the war in 1941.

Britain was protected from Germany's lightning war tactics because it was an island, and under the leadership of **Winston Churchill**, Britain withstood a massive air attack from the German *Luftwaffe* (air force) that lasted from June through

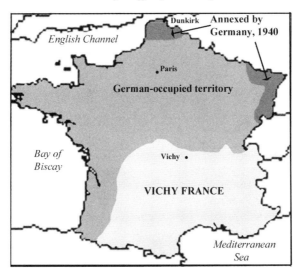

The Division of France, 1940. Hitler launched his *blitzkrieg* on France in May 1940, while Mussolini attacked from the southeast in June. The French army could not withstand the attack, and British and French soldiers trapped on the beaches of Dunkirk in northern France only narrowly escaped through a heroic evacuation effort across the English Channel. The French government surrendered on June 22, 1940, leaving Germany to rule the northern half of the country, including Paris. In the south, a puppet French government ruled from the city of Vichy, where Henri Pétain – a World War I hero – was nominally the governor.

September of 1940. In this **Battle of Britain**, the British Royal Air Force successfully counterattacked the German planes, using the new technology of radar to detect the enemy's approach. Unable to defeat Britain, Hitler turned eastward to Russia in 1941, even though he had signed a non-aggression pact with Stalin in 1939. In reaction to his invasion – the largest in history – Russia hastily joined the war on the side of the Allies, but within five months, the German army conquered the Baltic states, Ukraine, and half of European Russia. However, Hitler suffered the same fate that Napoleon had experienced more than 100 years earlier: the weather turned cold, supply lines were overextended, and his army was so seriously diminished that his summer of 1942 attack on Stalingrad (now Volgograd) failed. Since Russia had joined on the side of the Allies after Hitler's invasion, the victory at Stalingrad was the first major Allied victory of the war. After the United States joined the war in late 1941, the U.S. and Britain planned a strategy of striking the Axis from northern Africa, at the "soft underbelly" of Europe in Italy, clearly the weaker of the two European Axis powers. The British victory at El Alamein in northern Egypt was achieved partly because of the Allies' ability to break German codes, and the German army was finally expelled from Africa in May 1943. From there Allied armies captured Sicily and invaded Italy.

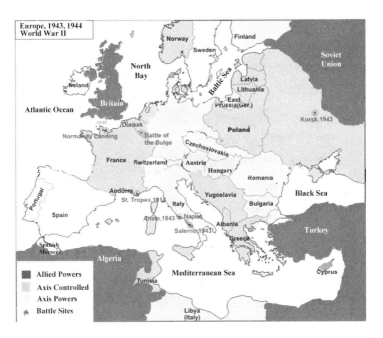

War-torn Europe in the Middle of World War II. By 1942 the Axis powers controlled much of Europe, but the Allied powers began to regain lost territory in 1943 by stopping the German advance into Russia, attacking Italy from Northern Africa, and invading occupied France across the English Channel. By 1945, Germany was surrounded and then dissected, as Russian armies came from the east and western armies from the west, forcing Germany's surrender in May 1945.

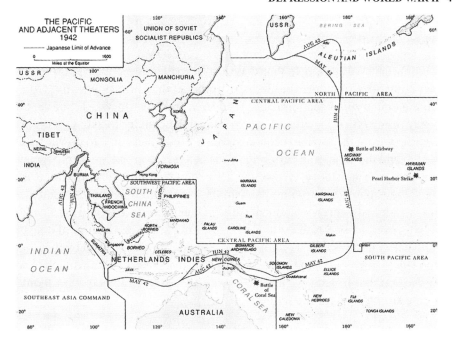

The War in the Pacific in 1942. By mid-1942 the Japanese had advanced southward across the Pacific Ocean almost to Australia in the south, but their attack was thwarted by U.S. forces at the Battle of Coral Sea. The Japanese advance to the east was stopped at the Battle of Midway in June, 1942, and from there U.S. troops began their "island hopping" campaign that eventually led them to Japan.

The War in Asia and the Pacific

Once France fell to Hitler's invasion in 1940 and Britain was busy defending its territory from German air attack, the Japanese saw their opportunity to seize European colonies in Southeast Asia. Britain and the United States responded by stopping shipments of steel and oil to Japan. Because the Americans insisted that Japan give up its newly acquired territories, the Japanese war cabinet made plans to attack the U.S. Navy in Hawaii, even though the United States was still officially neutral in the war. The December 7, 1941 attack on the American naval base at **Pearl Harbor** in Hawaii prompted the U.S. to declare war on Japan the following day, and the mobilization of the American war effort began. However, the American fleet of warships was decimated by the losses at Pearl Harbor, and the Japanese were able to capture Hong Kong, Singapore, Thailand, the Philippines, and Malaya by March 1942. However, in May 1942, the Americans were able to stop the Japanese at a great sea/air battle in the Coral Sea northeast of Australia, protecting Australia from Japanese invasion. The next month the Japanese lost four of its six large aircraft carriers at the **Battle of Midway**, west of Hawaii, and the U.S. navy and air forces began an **"island-hopping"** campaign of capturing key islands in the Pacific while making their way slowly toward Japan.

The Home Front

Even more than World War I, World War II depended on industrial productivity to keep both sides fighting. In Germany, production capacity was limited even though the country had economically recovered from World War I, but the quick efficiency of the *blitzkrieg* attacks at first helped the country to avoid diverting resources away from the civilian economy. Since Hitler had come to power with the promise to end the economic suffering of the between-war era, he wanted to avoid imposing wartime austerity. However, after the German defeats on the Russian front and the American entry into the war, the economic situation changed. Early in 1942, Hitler had to massively increase armaments production and the size of the army. However, he still refused any dramatic cuts in the production of consumer goods. The economy was not totally mobilized until July 1944, and by that time, it was too late to prevent German defeat. Hitler also resisted calling women to work during the war, but instead emphasized their role as good mothers who should be producing strong sons for the fatherland.

In contrast, Allied governments were quite successful in generating civilian participation, especially among women. In the Soviet Union women made up more than half the workforce by war's end, and about 800,000 volunteered for the military. As the Germans invaded, Soviet citizens moved communities and factories eastward, and more than half of Soviet national income went for war materials. In the United States, more than one million black Americans migrated from the rural South to the industrial cities of the North and West to fill jobs in war production. Many women also relocated in order to produce the tanks, airplanes, guns, and other necessary war materials. Britain developed the most thoroughly coordinated war economy of all, producing more tanks, aircraft, and machine guns than Germany did between 1940 and 1942. By law, men ages 18 to 50 and women ages 20 to 30 were subject to military or civilian war service, and the upper age limits were raised as the war progressed. Almost 70% of the three million people added to the British work force during the war were women.

The End of the War

The Battle of Stalingrad in 1942 was a major turning point of the war in Europe, and by 1943, the Russian army began pushing the Germans westward. In western and southern Europe, the United States, Britain, and other Allies staged two invasions: one across the Mediterranean Sea to Italy in 1943, and the other across the English Channel to the coast of Normandy in June 1944. Italy signed an armistice in 1943, and the invasion of France was successful as Allied troops landed in Normandy on **D-Day** – June 6, 1944 – and made their way to Paris by August. From there, the Allies advanced into Belgium where they decisively defeated the Germans at the **Battle of the Bulge**. As Britain and the United States – now joined by

French forces – marched east across Germany, the Russians marched west, and the two armies met at the Elbe River, signifying the conquest of Germany. On May 7, 1945, a week after Hitler committed suicide, German military leaders surrendered to the Allies.

The war in the Pacific continued until August, with a formal surrender signed in early September. By early 1945, U.S. forces had "island-hopped" (or "leap-frogged") their way to Iwo Jima and Okinawa, two islands south of Japan. After bitter fighting, the U.S. took the islands and prepared for an invasion of Japan. Then on August 6, 1945, the United States dropped an atomic bomb on Hiroshima, killing about 80,000 people immediately and leaving another 120,000 to die from the after-effects of burns and radiation. Three days later, a second bomb was dropped on Nagasaki, and Emperor Hirohito of Japan ordered surrender on August 14.

MARKER EVENT:
THE ATOMIC BOMB CONTROVERSY

Should the United States have dropped the atomic bomb? The decision to drop atomic bombs on the Japanese cities of Hiroshima and Nagasaki is one of the most controversial "marker events" of the 20th century, perhaps of all times. Summarized below are arguments on both sides.

PROS	CONS
The events brought about the surrender of Japan, winning the war for the Allies.	The bombs killed civilians indiscriminantly, the ultimate cruelty of "total war."
Aggressive nations must be dealt with aggressively.	Many died slow, agonizing deaths due to radiation poisoning and burns that would not heal.
The events saved lives in the long run, since it shortened the war.	
Technological advantages win wars, and must be used to secure victory.	The United States opened a "Pandora's Box" of weapons that could destroy the world, making it a more dangerous place for all.
The bombs paved the way for a secure peace, allowing no opportunity for a revival of hostilities, as happened after World War I.	The U.S. should have warned Japan more clearly before they used the horrible new weapon; if they had, perhaps Japan would have surren-
If Germany had developed the bomb first, they would have used it against the Allies.	dered without using the bomb.

World War II marked the end of an important era in world history: the age of European domination. The war also was the most widespread, deadliest war in history, illustrating the powers unleashed by technologies of the industrial era. By the mid-20th century, the interdependence of the nations of the world was greater than it had ever been before, as two superpowers – the United States and the Soviet Union – emerged to compete for control of technological knowledge and assert their hegemonic power over most of the world.

CONCEPTS AND IDENTIFICATIONS

appeasement policy
Aryans
Axis Powers
Battle of Britain
Battle of the Bulge
blitzkrieg
Churchill, Winston
collectivization, collective farms
D-Day
Five Year Plans
fascism
Franco, Francisco
genocide
Gosplan
Great Depression
Hitler, Adolf
Holocaust
"island hopping"
Keynes, John Maynard
kulaks
Lebensraum
margin
Marxism-Leninism
Mein Kampf
Midway, Battle of
Munich Conference
Mussolini, Benito
Nazi Party
Nazi-Soviet Pact
New Deal
New Economic Policy
nomenklatura
Pearl Harbor
Politburo

Popular Front
primary producing economies
protectionism
Red Army
Rome-Berlin Axis
Roosevelt, Franklin
"socialism in one country"
Stalinism
total war
Tripartite Pact
White Army

CHAPTER 19
RECONSTRUCTION AND
POST-INDUSTRIAL GROWTH
IN THE THREE-WORLDS ERA:
1945-1989

World War II was an important marker event of the 20th century because it changed not only Europe, but the entire world order, although in many cases it cemented changes that began much earlier in the century. The two superpowers – the United States and the Soviet Union – that emerged had been building their power for some time, but in the era between 1945 and 1989, they dominated the globe. The old imperialist order collapsed as European powers granted their colonies independence, so that by 1970, very few colonies remained officially tied to their old masters. Even though colonial imperialism virtually disappeared, political, economic, and social-cultural imperialism continued, with the world clearly divided into "have" and "have not" countries. Politically, the global struggle for power and influence between the United States and the Soviet Union divided the world into three categories: friends of the United States (The First World), friends of the Soviet Union (The Second World), and those whose support both superpowers sought (The Third World). Internationalism had failed in the early part of the century, but new international organizations formed and strengthened during this period, continuing a trend away from organizing the world exclusively into nation-states, although nation-states remained strong. Economically, more countries continued to industrialize, but those that had industrialized earlier went into a post-industrial phase characterized by new goals and values, including an emphasis on enhancement of the quality of life, the realization of individual rights for minorities and women, and improvement of the environment.

COLD WAR POLITICS

The rivalry between the United States and the Soviet Union began before World War II was over. Wartime cooperation between Britain and the United States was close, anchored by the regular contacts between Winston Churchill – the British prime minister – and Franklin Roosevelt – the president of the United States. Neither leader trusted Joseph Stalin nor approved of the Soviet Union's communist system. Likewise, Stalin saw the United States and Britain as essential, but not trusted, allies in the war effort. As the defeat of Germany and Japan drew near, this divisiveness became clear, as each side vied to contain the power of the other. Tensions were apparent at three Allied conferences held during the war.

Allied Conferences during World War II

Improved transportation and communications made it possible for the leaders of the Allied Powers to hold meetings and conferences during the war, with some more formal than others. Three conferences – one in 1943 and two in 1945 – clearly illustrated the growing tension between the United States and Britain on one side and the Soviet Union on the other. At the **Tehran Conference** in 1943, the Soviet government encouraged the western powers to open a new front in France, which they did with the D-Day invasion of Normandy in 1944. With the United States and Britain focused on France, the Soviet Union was free to occupy eastern Europe as its forces pushed the German armies back. Britain negotiated with the Soviets to maintain western dominance in Greece and influence in Yugoslavia and Hungary, but the United States asserted its support of self determination of these small nations, as Woodrow Wilson had done at Versailles after World War I. At the **Yalta Conference** in 1945, the countries could not agree on a cooperative approach to handling post-war Germany, so they divided Germany into four occupation zones: the British, American, French, and Russian sectors. The Soviet Union wanted to eliminate German industrial power, but Britain and the United States did not agree, since they believed that Germany might ally with them against Russia. Strong arguments erupted over the status of the eastern European countries, with Stalin wishing to control their governments, and Britain and the United States wanting them to become liberal democracies.

By the time of the **Potsdam Conference** in July 1945, the war in Europe was over, but was still going on in the Pacific. Since Yalta, the Soviet Union had installed communist regimes in Romania, Bulgaria, Poland, Hungary, and Yugoslavia, and had dismantled German, Austrian, and Hungarian industrial equipment for shipment to the Soviet Union. In response to these moves, Winston Churchill and the new U.S. President, Harry Truman, met with Stalin to protest these actions, and Stalin let them know that he had no intention of keeping promises made at Yalta regarding the freedom of eastern European countries. The conference arranged further details of occupation of and terms of future Japanese surrender, but did not resolve the question of eastern Europe. In a further sign of growing tension between the U.S. and the Soviet Union, Truman disclosed to Churchill his plans to use the atomic bomb in Japan, but did not share the news with Stalin. Now that Hitler's threat to Europe had passed, the differences among the Allies – with capitalist, democratic Britain and the United States on one side and communist Soviet Union on the other – became increasingly apparent, setting the stage for post-War political divisions.

Because of the rising hostility between the Soviet Union and the United States, no peace treaty was signed with Germany, and by the late 1940s a divided Germany had solidified into two countries, with West Germany supported by the United States and western Europe, and East Germany supported by the Soviet Union. A similar division occurred in Asia, with the United States alone occupying Japan (since the surrender had occurred because of U.S.-developed technology – the atomic bomb) and Korea occupied half by the Soviets and half by the Americans. When no agreement could be reached between the United States and the Soviet Union on holding countrywide elections, communist North Korea and noncommunist South Korea became independent states in 1948, officially divided at the 38th parallel.

The Emergence of the "Superpowers"

While tension was building between the United States and the Soviet Union, Britain gradually lost its pre-eminent role in determining world politics. When Franklin Roosevelt died in 1945, the famous Churchill/Roosevelt partnership was broken, and then, shortly after the war ended, Churchill's Conservative Party lost its majority control of Parliament. As a result, Churchill lost his position as prime minister. Although he later regained the position, the winning Labour Party turned toward domestic affairs, leaving the United States as the pre-eminent foe of the

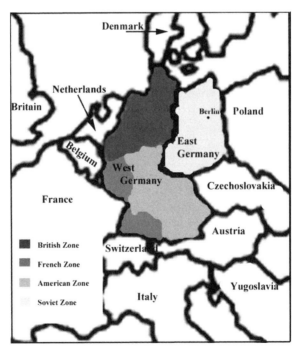

Post-World War II Germany. At the Yalta Conference in 1945, the Allies divided Germany into four occupation zones: British, French, American, and Soviet sectors. Since the capital city of Berlin was in the Soviet zone, they agreed to split the city into four zones of control as well. Once the war was over and the Cold War began, the country split into two parts: West Germany (a democratic country) and East Germany (a communist country). Berlin was divided in a similar way, with West Berlin controlled by the western nations and East Berlin by the Soviet Union.

EXAMINING THE EVIDENCE: DISCUSSIONS OF THE ATOMIC BOMB AT POTSDAM

When Winston Churchill, Harry Truman, and Joseph Stalin met in July 1945 at Potsdam, Germany, Truman knew that the United States was ready to use the atomic bomb. He discussed the news with Churchill, who strongly supported the bomb's use, but he was unsure how to handle the news with Stalin, whom he did not trust. He resolved the dilemma as to whether to treat Stalin as an ally or an enemy by vaguely mentioning it to him toward the end of the conference. According to Truman's recollection,

"I casually mentioned to Stalin that we had a new weapon of unusual destructive force. All he said was that he was glad to hear it and hoped we would make 'good use of it against the Japanese.'"

Truman did not share any specifics about the weapon, and he noted that Stalin seemed neither surprised nor the least bit curious. Stalin, however, did not need to ask because he had a spy, Klaus Fuchs (a naturalized British citizen), at the U.S. "top secret" research site in Los Alamos, New Mexico, who had been supplying the Russians with atomic secrets for some time. As a result of this intelligence, Stalin understood perfectly what Truman had said, although Truman did not know it at the time.

Reference: David McCulloch, *Truman* (New York: Simon and Schuster, 1992), pp. 442-3.

Soviet Union. In 1947, President Harry Truman asserted the new superpower's position with a statement known as the **Truman Doctrine**. In Truman's own words, "I believe that it must be the policy of the United States to support free peoples who are resisting attempted subjugation by armed minorities or by outside pressures." When the British government informed the United States that it could no longer support the Greeks in their fight against a communist insurrection supported from the outside, President Truman asked Congress for legislation in support of both Greece and Turkey. This statement clearly reflected the change in Western leadership; the United States had replaced Britain as the protector of western values and authority.

The United States responded to Russia's power plays in eastern Europe not only by supporting regimes in Iran, Turkey, and Greece that were under Soviet pressure, but by proclaiming the **Marshall Plan**, a program that would provide loans to aid the nations of western Europe to rebuild war-torn lands. From the Soviet point of view, the United States was trying to dominate Europe economically, and the lines between western and eastern Europe began to be drawn firmly in the sand. The Soviet drive to control eastern Europe was based partly on the belief that it was recovering lands that had been taken away at Versailles in 1919. However, the roots of Russian desires were much deeper. With all of their ambitions to westernize Russia, Peter the Great and Catherine the Great could never have dreamed that their "backward" country would ever hold a base so close to the heart of Europe or that Russia would eventually become a "superpower," as celebrated nations of western Europe faded from the world scene.

Germany was the focus of the Cold War in the early years. The Soviets took the point of view that seizing German goods and factories served as reparation for

**THEMATIC LEARNING OBJECTIVE:
INTERACTION OF EUROPE AND
THE WORLD:
THE "IRON CURTAIN" SPEECH**

British Prime Minister Winston Churchill was known for his rhetorical skills, and even though his country's power was fading at the end of World War II, he helped to shape the advent of the Cold War in a famous speech delivered in Fulton, Missouri in 1946. He defined the existence of what came to be known as the Cold War by identifying an "**iron curtain**" that divided Europe.

"From Stettin in the Baltic to Trieste in the Adriatic, an iron curtain has descended across the Continent. Behind that line lie all the capitals of the ancient states of central and eastern Europe. Warsaw, Berlin, Prague, Vienna, Budapest, Belgrade, Bucharest and Sofia; all these famous cities and the populations around them lie in the Soviet sphere and all are subject in one form or another, not only to Soviet influence but to a very high and increasing measure of control from Moscow...
...If the western democracies stand together in strict adherence to the principles of the United Nations Charter, their influence for furthering these principles will be immense and no one is likely to molest them. If however, they become divided or falter in their duty, and if these all-important years are allowed to slip away, then indeed catastrophe may overwhelm us all."

Reference: "Winston Churchill's Speech at Fulton," in *Vital Speeches of the Day*, Vol. 12 (New York: City News Publishing), March 15, 1946, pp. 331-332.

the war. The western Allies prevented Russia from intervening in their zones and gave West Germany economic support – such as in the Marshall Plan – to rebuild. In 1947, the Soviet Union blockaded the city of Berlin, so that no supplies could reach the areas under control of western countries. The United States responded with a massive airlift to keep the city supplied, and by 1948, the two Germanies were separated by heavy fortifications along their mutual borders. Cold War divisions spread to more countries with the formation of two military alliances: **The North Atlantic Treaty Organization (NATO)**, created in 1949, which grouped western European countries, Canada and the United States; and **The Warsaw Pact** (1955), in which the Soviet Union organized eastern European countries to counter NATO. In 1949, tensions escalated even further when the Soviet Union developed its own atomic bomb, starting an arms race that lasted into the 1980s. Both sides built more and more sophisticated nuclear arsenals of weapons and missile systems to deliver them. More conventional forces also expanded, with large amounts of each country's national budget allocated to military buildup.

The United Nations and Cold War Politics

Even before the United States officially entered World War II, President Roosevelt and Prime Minister Churchill signed the **Atlantic Charter**, which supported the establishment of a world peacekeeping organization after the war. Although the League of Nations had failed, Allied leaders continued to believe that such an organization could succeed if they corrected earlier structural and administrative mistakes and expanded their vision of what could be accomplished. In 1944, representatives from the United States, Britain, Russia, and China drafted proposals that eventually resulted in the **United Nations Charter**, ratified on October 24, 1945, only a few weeks after World War II officially ended. The formation of this new organization was an important step toward internationalism, or the bonding of nation-states into larger international political and economic blocs.

The Charter created two main bodies: the **General Assembly**, with representatives from all member-states, and the smaller **Security Council** dominated by the major Allied powers. The Security Council was charged with keeping world peace by dealing with situations that threatened the national security of United Nations member-states. It was composed of five permanent members – Britain, China, France, the Soviet Union, and the United States – who all had to approve any action that the United Nations took in world crises. Decisions of the Council also had to have majority consent from seven rotating members. The General Assembly voted on non-security issues, and only majority consent was necessary to pass measures there. A full-time bureaucracy headed by a Secretary General carried out the day-to-day business of the United Nations, and various agencies – such as the Food and Agriculture Organization (FAO) and United Nations Educational, Scientific and Cultural Organization (UNESCO) – were set up to address important international issues.

The United Nations was more flexible than the League of Nations had been because it did not require unanimous approval for decisions, as the League's charter had specified. However, Cold War politics often rendered the Security Council helpless, because so often the United States and the Soviet Union were on opposite sides of the issues. Other times Britain and France were at odds as they lost control of their colonies around the world. A further complication occurred when a communist government took over China in 1949, only to have the United Nations reject its legitimacy until 1972.

One crisis in the U.N.'s early years was decisively addressed by the Security Council, but only because the Soviet delegation was absent when the Council voted to condemn North Korea's invasion of South Korea in 1950. United Nations troops were sent to defend South Korea, although most soldiers were either South Korean or American. The **Korean War** lasted until 1953, and even though the United Nations was directly involved, the situation reflected the fact that the real forces at work were nation-states, not this new international organization. The United States was the primary ally of South Korea, and the People's Republic of China (the new communist regime) and Russia gave substantial support to North Korea. Since the PRC was not recognized as a nation by the United Nations, the actions of the international organization were subsidiary to those of powerful nation-states.

"Limited War"

The Korean War represented a new style of fighting that emerged during the post-World War II era: **"limited war"**. Even though the superpowers had the ability to launch global warfare, they instead faced one another in clashes that were limited to the regions where they initially broke out. Hanging over all was the threat of a "World War III" in which atomic weaponry could be used to annihilate both sides and even bring about the destruction of all civilization on earth. As a result, every regional crisis contained the seeds of nuclear war, with each side "rattling their sabers" at the other, sometimes stepping to the brink of total war, and then retreating before absolute disaster could occur. In Korea, the United States feared that launching attacks into China might bring retaliation from China's ally, the Soviet Union, and so even though both sides played it very dangerously, the war soon bogged down at the border between North and South Korea. The fighting settled into a war with troops on either side of the 38th parallel that separated the two countries, and even though a truce was signed in 1953, both sides have continued to arm the border, and the possibility of renewed warfare remains a threat today.

A long-lasting "limited war" shaped by Cold War politics was fought in Vietnam, a part of French Indochina until 1954. The conflict began as a nationalist rebellion against the French, led by **Ho Chi Minh**, a Marxist trained in Moscow, who defeated the French on the battlefield and installed a communist regime in the northern half of the country in 1954. When the French left Vietnam, U.S. President

Dwight Eisenhower decided to fund the government in the south, and agreed to hold free elections for a national Vietnamese government. Elections were never held because the U.S. feared that Ho would manipulate them, and in 1961, President John Kennedy sent U.S. ground and air power to counter increasing guerrilla activity in the south. Then in the mid-1960s President Lyndon B. Johnson, who inherited a small-scale war, escalated it in order to bring it to a successful conclusion. By the end of 1966, 365,000 U.S. troops were engaged in the **Vietnam War**, but they were unable to defeat the Viet Cong, as Ho's supporters were called. Although China supplied the Viet Cong, Chinese soldiers never became actively involved, so the U.S. losses came at the hands of the North Vietnamese. With expenses of the war and military deaths mounting, a significant antiwar movement grew in the United States, finally bringing about a treaty between North Vietnam and the United States in 1973. In 1975, the treaty was violated when Viet Cong and North Vietnamese troops overran the South Vietnamese army and captured the southern capital of Saigon, reuniting the two parts of Vietnam into a single communist state ruled from the north.

The Nuclear Arms Race

Although "limited war" grew from a fear of nuclear warfare, both the United States and the Soviet Union continued to develop more and more powerful nuclear weapons. After the Soviet Union exploded its first atomic bomb in 1949, the U.S. developed a far more powerful weapon, the hydrogen bomb, which was exploded in 1952, only to have the Soviets reveal their own version a year later. One of the most dangerous conflicts occurred in 1962 when the Soviet Union deployed nuclear missiles in Cuba, an action it took in response to U.S. efforts to overthrow Fidel Castro's government. When United States reconnaissance planes discovered the missiles, President John Kennedy prepared to invade or blockade Cuba, and for a few tense days it looked as if the U.S. and the U.S.S.R. would at last go to war. Catastrophe was avoided at the last minute, however, when the Soviet leader, Nikita Khrushchev, stopped Russian ships from breaking the U.S. quarantine that surrounded the island. Khrushchev eventually withdrew the missiles from Cuba, and the U.S. removed its missiles from Turkey. As frightening as the **Cuban missile crisis** was, ultimately both countries acted to avoid using nuclear weapons that could have sparked all-out total war.

The commitment of both sides to contain the tensions of the Cold War was reflected in a series of arms limitation treaties. In 1963, Britain, the United States, and the Soviet Union agreed to ban the testing of nuclear weapons in the atmosphere, in space, and underwater in the interest of reducing the danger of radioactive fallout. The Nuclear Non-Proliferation Treaty that limited further development of nuclear weapons was signed by 137 countries in 1968, and talks between the U.S. and the Soviet Union continued for several years as they painstakingly negotiated weapons limits. By 1975, attention turned from arms limitation to an attempt to ease tensions in general. In the Helsinki Accords, western nations agreed to recognize the Soviet-dictated boundaries of eastern European nations in return for more liberal exchanges of people and information between East and West.

One highly competitive offshoot of the nuclear arms race was space exploration, with the two superpowers competing to build larger and more accurate missiles for launching space satellites. The U.S.S.R. successfully placed a satellite called *Sputnik* in space in 1957, and the U.S. responded with its own (less successful) satellite a few months later. The **space race** continued during the 1960s as both countries strived to reach the moon first, an accomplishment claimed by the United States in 1969.

POLITICAL AND ECONOMIC RECOVERY IN EUROPE

In contrast to World War I, when physical destruction was limited to the front lines around the trenches, the nature of warfare during World War II brought much more

**PERSPECTIVES:
A RUSSIAN VIEW OF THE
SPACE RACE**

When the Soviet Union managed to successfully launch the first satellite into space in 1957, the event shook American pride and confidence to its core. In contrast, many people in the U.S.S.R. were overjoyed that their country had made this important leap ahead in the space race. In the excerpt below, Semyon Reznik, a Soviet journalist and author who later moved to the United States, recalled the joyous event.

"The day our satellite *Sputnik* was launched, a special voice came over the radio to announce it to us. Traditionally, in the Soviet Union a few of the radio announcers were hired to read only the most urgent news on the radio... On an October morning in 1957, we heard one of those voices announce, 'Attention. All radio stations of the Soviet Union are broadcasting...Our satellite *Sputnik* is in space.' I felt so proud. Who did it? We did it! The Soviet Union is first in space! I was in my second year of college and just couldn't imagine that this could happen in my lifetime. In my mind, space travel only existed in science fiction. We didn't even know that the project was in the works..."

Reference: Peter Jennings and Todd Brewster, *The Century.* (New York: Doubleday, 1998), p. 357.

widespread damage to Europe. Cities had been bombed so that streets were full of rubble and many people were homeless. Roads and bridges no longer connected towns and cities, and basic commodities for living were in short supply everywhere. Amid the despair, tens of millions of refugees wandered the continent. Many had been released from prisons and death camps, but the world they knew before the war had been destroyed, so they had to find a way to rebuild their lives completely. Others fled westward to escape the Russian army as it occupied eastern Europe; their destinations were often to countries that experienced the least war damage, such as Denmark, Sweden, Canada, and Australia.

Recovery in Western Europe

Thanks to the economic aid of the Marshall Plan, the countries of western Europe recovered relatively rapidly. Between 1947 and 1950, European countries received $9.4 billion to be used for rebuilding their damaged infrastructure. By 1950, industrial output in Europe was 30% above prewar levels, with the prosperity continuing well into the 1960s. During these decades, the economies of western Europe transitioned to **post-industrialism**, in which the majority of people were employed in the service sector, including such industries as technology, health care, business and legal services, finance, and education. These contrasted to the most common type of jobs created earlier by industrialization, the industry sector, which employed people to create tangible goods, such as cars, clothing, or machinery. The agricultural sector shrank even more than it had during industrialization, since mechanized farming (first developed during the industrial era) meant that only a few farmers could produce enough food to feed all the workers in the industry and service sectors.

As post-industrialization developed, the countries of western Europe continued to evolve into **advanced democracies**, characterized not only by regular and competitive elections, but also by civil liberties, the rule of law, open societies that allow citizens to lead private lives, and neutrality of the judiciary. Political party systems – with parties on the left, middle, and right – provided competitive alternatives for citizens that ranged from the Communist Party on the left to extreme nationalist parties on the right. During this era, the "Iron Curtain" separated western and eastern Europe, but the urge to integrate, first economically and eventually politically, continued, and the basis was laid by agreements among the countries of western Europe for the European Union that was formally created in 1991.

Economic Cooperation

The nations of western Europe formed NATO in military union after World War II; they also took some important steps toward economic cooperation in order to rebuild war-damaged areas and restore trade. In 1951, France, West Germany, Belgium, the Netherlands, Luxembourg, and Italy formed the **European Coal and Steel Community (ECSC)** with the purpose of creating a common market for coal and steel products. In 1957, the same six countries formed the **European Economic Community (EEC)**, also known as the Common Market, to eliminate customs barriers and create a large free-trade area. The Common Market was protected from the rest of the world by an external tariff, and the free trade among the countries encouraged cooperation and standardization of economic practices. All the member nations benefited economically, and the EEC became the second largest steel producing area of the world, surpassed only by the United States. Also in 1957, these countries took further cooperative steps by creating the European Atomic Energy Community to further peaceful uses of nuclear energy.

West Germany

In 1949, the unification of the three western zones into the Federal Republic of Germany became official, and the first chancellor was **Konrad Adenauer**, who was the founding father of West Germany. Adenauer oriented his policies toward the west, and made special efforts to reconcile with France. In 1961, Berlin's division became clearly visible when the East German government built the Berlin Wall that separated East Berlin from West Berlin, intended to prevent its citizens from fleeing to the noncommunist areas of the city. Adenauer remained chancellor until 1963; during his time in office, the West German economy revived, so that even though the country had only 75% of the population and 52% of the territory of prewar Germany, by 1955, the West German gross national product exceeded that of prewar Germany.

During the early 1960s, the economy of West Germany experienced such enormous growth that the era is often called the "economic miracle." There was more work than could be done by Germans alone, prompting the government to enter into labor recruitment agreements with Spain, Italy, Greece, Yugoslavia, and Turkey. As a result, the ethnic composition of West Germany changed significantly, so that by 1970, 4.3% of the population was non-German. After an economic recession in 1973 triggered widespread unemployment, Germany stopped recruiting foreign labor, but the foreign-born who were already there were sometimes resented for taking jobs from Germans. The 1970s also saw a change in policy as **Willy Brandt** – a socialist – came to the chancellorship and took a more independent stance in relation to the western bloc. He sought to improve relations between West Germany and the Soviet bloc while still keeping his ties to the west. Under Brandt relations with East Germany also improved in a policy called *Ostpolitik*, and he managed to bridge the gap between east and west and deepen the postwar consensus in West Germany.

Britain

During World War II, Prime Minister Winston Churchill emphasized the importance of putting class conflicts aside for the duration of the war. Although he gained the Prime Minister's post as leader of the Conservative Party, he headed

EXAMINING THE EVIDENCE: "DENAZIFICATION" IN POST-WAR GERMANY

After World War II ended, Europeans – especially Germans – faced the challenge of recovering from their Nazi past. The crimes committed in ghettoes and death camps were particularly disturbing. The surviving major Nazi leaders were tried and almost all were condemned as war criminals at the Nuremberg trials in 1945 and 1946. As part of a continuing effort to "denazify" Germany, the Allied Powers extended war crimes trials to lesser officials, and the efforts continued as the West German government took over prosecuting the cases. Beginning in 1953, the West German government also began to make payments to Israel and to Holocaust survivors and their relatives in order to make some restitution for Nazi crimes.

However, even before the 1940s decade closed, the focus of westerners began to shift away from Nazis toward Communists. As hostility between the west and the U.S.S.R. rose, some accused westerners of forgetting the atrocities too easily. On the other hand, some Germans complained that the trials of Nazis merely reflected the retribution of the victors rather than a well-deserved punishment of the guilty. The West German government pointed out that the German prisoners of war held in Soviet camps were also real casualties of war. Denazification, then, has never been completed, and the Nazi past still haunts European culture and politics today.

an all-party coalition government with ministers from both major parties. The primary objective was to win the war. After the war was over, the spirit of collective consensus continued until well into the 1960s, with both Labour and Conservative parties supporting the development of a modern welfare system. Before the war was over, both parties accepted the **Beveridge Report**, which provided for a social insurance program that made all citizens eligible for health, unemployment, pension, and other benefits. One goal of the Beveridge Report was to guarantee a subsistence income to every British citizen. In 1948, the **National Health Service** was created under the leadership of the Labour Party. Even when Conservatives regained control in 1950, the reforms were not repealed. Although the electorate was divided largely by social class, with 70% of working class voting Labour and even larger percentages of middle class voting Conservative, both parties shared a broad consensus on the necessity of the welfare state. As a result, the foundations were laid for a **mixed economy**, with the government directing the economy and nationalizing major industries without giving up basic principles of capitalism, such as private ownership of property.

The collective consensus began to break apart with social and economic problems beginning in the late 1960s. Britain's economic problems included declining industrial production and a decline in international influence, both exaggerated by the loss of colonies and the shrinking of the old empire. The impact of oil price increases and embargoes by OPEC (Organization for Petroleum Exporting Countries) was devastating, causing recession, high unemployment rates, a drop in the GNP, and inflation.

The serious decline in the economy was followed by a growing divide between the Labour and Conservative parties. Labour took a sharp turn to the left, endorsing a socialist economy and serving as a mouthpiece for labor union demands. The economic problems led labor unions to demand higher wages, and crippling strikes, such as the coal strike of 1972-73, plagued the nation. The Labour Party lost membership, and many voters turned to the Liberals, the Conservatives, or the various nationalist parties. Many middle class voters reacted against Labour, and the Conservatives selected **Margaret Thatcher** as their leader. Her very conservative stance on political issues was appealing enough to sweep the conservatives to power in 1979.

Margaret Thatcher blamed the weakened British economy on the socialist policies set in place by the government after World War II. Her policies were further influenced by a distinct shift to the left by the Labour Party that gave a great deal of power to labor unions. In response, she privatized business and industry, cut back on social welfare programs, strengthened national defense, got tough with the labor unions, and returned to market force controls on the economy. She was a controversial prime minister for eleven years. Her supporters believed her to be the capable and firm "Iron Lady", but her critics felt that her policies made economic problems worse and that her personality further divided the country. Thatcher resigned office in 1990 when other Conservative Party leaders challenged her leadership.

France

France was liberated by the Allied armies in 1944, and the hero of the French Liberation forces, **Charles De Gaulle**, headed the provisional government that replaced the Nazis. However, the Fourth Republic, founded in 1944, proved disappointing to De Gaulle, with its emphasis on parliamentary government and its lack of a strong executive. De Gaulle resigned as head of the provisional government in 1946,x and retired to his country house while the Fourth Republic languished. The National Assembly was deadlocked with splits among several antagonistic political parties, and a parliamentary majority was impossible. Cabinets had to include coalitions of several parties, and virtually any issue could split the cabinet apart. A pattern emerged in which governments were constantly forced to resign.

The government proved inadequate in postwar France, and the **Algerian crisis** of 1958 proved the need for a strong executive. The Algerian Revolution of that year came after several other colonial struggles that the French lost. Algerian nationalist forces had been resisting French rule since 1954, and in 1958, a French army bombing in Algeria caused a dispute that brought down the government of Prime Minister Felix Gaillard. Politicians turned to their old hero, De Gaulle, who was given sweeping new powers to address the Algerian crisis and reshape French politics. In 1958, De Gaulle created the **Fifth Republic**. Once again, France had turned to a strong man to save it from chaos, and citizens and other government officials gave De Gaulle almost complete authority to craft a government to his liking. From 1958 to 1981, De Gaulle's political party dominated French politics, even though he left office in 1969.

After World War II, the French economy grew rapidly as De Gaulle encouraged industrial growth that France had resisted before the war. Formerly, French industry was dominated by family-run, small, inefficient businesses. Under DeGaulle, the government helped forge mergers that created larger, more competitive firms. This approach to the economy was known as ***dirigisme***, or state management of a capitalist economy. Although nationalized industry did exist, the government guided mergers of private companies into larger firms. As a result of *dirigisme*, France became an international industrial power by the early 1970s. However, starting in the mid-1970s, the growth of the French economy slowed substantially, and in 1981, the French voters chose socialist François Mitterrand as president, but no government, either rightist or socialist, was able to reinvigorate the economy during the 1980s.

Eastern Europe during the Cold War

At the end of World War II, Soviet military forces occupied almost all of eastern Europe and the Balkans, except for Greece, Albania, and Yugoslavia. These occupied states became **"satellite states"** in the Soviet sphere of influence, and their governments and economies were controlled by the Soviet government. Between 1945 and 1948, Communist governments were installed in East Germany, Bulgaria, Romania, Poland, Hungary, and Czechoslovakia. Albania and Yugoslavia both had strong resistance movements to Communist takeover during the war, and although a Stalinist regime was established in Albania after the war, the country grew increasingly independent of the Soviet Union over the years. Yugoslavia remained under the control of a Communist leader called **Tito**, whose real name was Josip Broz. During the war, Tito had led a strong Nazi resistance movement, and after the war he gained support from Serbs, Muslims, and Croats to mount a Communist revolution to establish a government that was free from Soviet control. Yugoslavia was held together by Tito's forceful personality and strong organization, but the country's borders enclosed culturally diverse groups that formed six

Yugoslavia under Tito. After World War II, Tito led a revolution that established Yugoslavia as a Communist country free from Soviet domination. Its six republics and two independent provinces within Serbia reflected the different ethnic groups that made up the country.

republics and two independent provinces. Holding these diverse groups together became much more difficult after Tito's death in 1980.

Between 1948 and Stalin's death in 1953, the eastern European satellites followed Stalin's policies of industrialization and collectivization of agriculture. However, after Stalin died, the new Soviet leaders, including Nikita Khrushchev, interfered less in the domestic affairs of their satellites, and since communism was not deeply rooted in these states, some signs of reform began before 1960. All remained communist, but some – particularly Poland and Hungary – demanded an independent socialist path. In 1956, worker protests erupted in Poland, and the Hungarian leader – Imre Nagy – declared Hungary a free nation. The Soviet Union responded by sending troops into Hungary to reclaim control. In 1968, the Czechoslovakian leader, Alexander Dubcek introduced freedom of speech and press, freedom to travel abroad, and a relaxation of secret police activities, a period called the **"Prague Spring"** by reform-minded supporters. However, that reform movement was also crushed by the Soviet army, and Dubcek was replaced by a Soviet puppet.

DECOLONIZATION AND NEW NATIONAL IDENTITIES

National identities changed in many important ways during the period from 1945 to 1989. Whereas China had been transformed from an ancient empire to a new communist state, other areas of the world that had been colonized by imperialist powers asserted their identities in successful independence movements that resulted in dozens of new countries. Political scientist **Samuel Huntington** has linked this **decolonization** (former colonies becoming independent countries) to the second of what he called **"three waves" of democratization**. Historically, democratic governments have been based on rule of law, selection of leaders by popular election, and the guarantee of individual liberties and rights. The first wave came with the revolutions in America and France during the late 18th century, developed slowly, and then hit obstacles of totalitarianism in the early 20th century that caused the number of democracies to fall from 29 to 12 in the era between the two world wars. The "second wave" started with the Allied victory in World War II and continued until about 1962, and included the formation of new countries in Africa, South Asia, and Southeast Asia. Huntington's "third wave" started in the mid-1970's when three dictatorships in southern Europe came to an end (in Greece, Portugal, and Spain), followed by countries in eastern Europe that escaped Soviet control, and finally with the dissolution of the Soviet Union itself in 1991.

Why did these last two rapid "waves" of democracy occur in the mid-to-late 20th century, when the first wave had taken so many years to develop? According to Huntington, some factors are:

- the loss of legitimacy by both right and left wing authoritarian regimes, as illustrated by the defeat of Hitler's Germany and Mussolini's Italy;

- the expansion of an urban middle class in developing countries as the old imperialist system collapsed and industrialization took place in other parts of the world;

- a new emphasis on "human rights" by the United States and western Europe, as an alternative foreign policy to Cold War containment of communism;

- the "snowball" effect, or the fact that when one country in a region becomes democratic, it influences others to do so. An example is Poland's influence on other nations of eastern Europe during the 1980s.

As we have seen in the era from 1815 to 1914, stirrings for independence movements in India and Egypt started long before World War I began, as native elites struggled to protect their lands from European domination. World War I encouraged these movements as the imperialist powers turned on one another, with each looking to its colonies for soldiers, laborers, food, and raw materials. For example, in India, the British encouraged expansion of industrial production – contrary to long-standing colonial policy – to supplement the efforts of British factories to keep up with war demands. Administrative personnel in the colonies were called to fill wartime posts, requiring that the colonial jobs be filled by African and Asian administrators.

The Indian Independence Struggle

During World War I, British leaders had promised Indians that if they continued to support the war effort, they would move toward self-government within the empire once the conflict was over. The Government of India Act, passed in 1919, pleased both the Indian National Congress and the Muslim League (independence organizations founded before World War I). It transferred powers over agriculture, public works, local self-government, and education to Indian elected legislators at the provincial level. However, the British waffled between treating India as a budding democratic home-ruled nation and a colony, and their mixed messages frustrated many Indians, who had heard Woodrow Wilson's advocacy of self determination in his Fourteen Points and expected the principle to be applied to them. Yet The British government did not support freedom of the press and assembly, and independence rallies were met with repressive control. Voices for independence became much louder as they organized under the direction of **Mohandas K. Gandhi**, known to many of his followers as "Mahatma" or "great soul."

Gandhi was an English-educated Hindu who practiced law in South Africa before he returned to his native India during World War I to join the Indian National Congress. Although from a well-to-do family himself, Gandhi showed his sympathy for the poor by wearing simple peasant garb: a length of homespun cloth below his waist and a shawl to cover his torso. He attracted large numbers of admirers, and he transformed the cause of Indian independence from an elite movement of the educated into a mass movement that centered on his charismatic presence. Gandhi's ideals came to be symbolized by a spinning wheel – the traditional mechanism used by Indians to spin cotton yarn before the British began sending Indian cotton to factories in England. He sparked nationalistic feelings among his followers by advocating a return to Indian self-sufficiency and the shedding of British control. In 1929, he led a few followers on an 80-mile walk to gather salt from the sea in an act of civil disregard for the government's monopoly on salt. This famous action illustrated his belief that **civil disobedience** – peacefully breaking unjust laws – and non-violence were the best practices for bringing about change.

One conflict that Gandhi could not heal was the rift between Muslims and Hindus in India. Even though he fasted for twenty-one days in 1924 to promote Hindu-Muslim unity and walked through violence-torn areas in 1947 to advocate peace, Muslims associated the independence movement with Hinduism. **Muhammad Ali Jinnah**, the leader of the Muslim League, who eventually led the movement for a separate Pakistan after World War II, did not trust Gandhi's Indian National Congress to deal equitably with Muslims. Gandhi also disagreed with his succes-

THEMATIC LEARNING OBJECTIVE:
INDIVIDUAL AND SOCIETY:
GANDHI ON PASSIVE RESISTANCE

Mohandas Gandi advocated passive resistance – a combination of civil disobedience and non-violence – for his followers in their efforts to bring about Indian independence from Britain. In the passage below, he explains why these methods are superior to armed resistance.

"Passive resistance is a method of securing rights by personal suffering; it is the reverse of resistance by arms. When I refuse to do a thing that is repugnant to my conscience, I use soul-force. For instance, the government of the day has passed a law which is applicable to me: I do not like it, if, by using violence, I force the government to repeal the law, I am employing what may be termed body-force. If I do not obey the law and accept the penalty for its breach, I use soul-force. It involves sacrifice of self....

...Wherein is courage required – in blowing others to pieces from behind a cannon or with a smiling face to approach a cannon and to be blown to pieces? Who is the true warrior – he who keeps death always as a bosom-friend or he who controls the death of others? Believe me that a man devoid of courage can never be a passive resister...

Passive resistance is an all-sided sword; it can be used anyhow; it blesses him who uses it and him against whom it is used. Without drawing a drop of blood, it produces far-reaching results."

Reference: Mohandas Gandhi, *Indian Home Rule* (Madras, India: Ganesh & Co., 1922), pp. 90-91.

sor, **Jawaharlal Nehru**, who supported the creation of a modern industrial India. By the time that World War II began, Indian entrepreneurs had built plants to manufacture iron and steel, cement, paper, cotton and jute textiles, and sugar – all protected by high tariff barriers with British approval.

When World War II ended, Britain's new Labour Party government agreed to Indian independence, but the process was complicated by disagreements between Hindus, as represented by Nehru's Indian National Congress, and Muslims, as represented by Jinnah's Muslim League. Violent rioting between Hindus and Muslims broke out, even though Gandhi begged for tolerance and cooperation. Finally, in 1947, the agreement was made to partition India into two states – one secular but dominated by Hindus and the other Muslim – and the new India and Pakistan became independent countries. The Indian National Congress, led by

Nehru, formed the first government of India; Jinnah and the Muslim League established a government for Pakistan.

Despite the fact that India was at last independent, the transition was chaotic, with Muslim and Hindu neighbors turning on one another in violence. For centuries Hindus and Muslims had intermingled, but now Hindus in Pakistan had to move to India to avoid attack by Muslims, and Muslims in India became refugees as they sought to escape massacre by Hindus. Within a few months some 12 million people had left their ancestral homes, and 500,000 lay dead, including Gandhi, who was killed in January 1948 by a Hindu refugee. When the violence finally settled down, one state with a Muslim majority – Kashmir – remained in India because the local maharajah was Hindu, and the state held the headwaters of rivers that irrigated many Indian farms in the northwestern part of the subcontinent. This situation contributed to continued unrest, since many Muslims in Kashmir would have preferred to join Pakistan.

Decolonization in Southeast Asia

Britain gave independence to Burma – a colony east of India – in 1947, Ceylon (now Sri Lanka) in 1948, and Malaysia in 1963. The French, too, pulled forces out of parts of Southeast Asia even before the battle of Dien Bien Phu in Vietnam in 1954, when Ho Chi Minh's supporters decisively defeated the French army. Like the British, the French had been so devastated by World War II that holding onto its colonies became economically impossible. French Indo-China was carved into separate nations, and the countries of Laos and Cambodia were created in 1949 and 1954 respectively. Because of continuous war between Ho Chi Minh's communist forces in the north and the French and U.S. supported government in the south, North and South Vietnam remained separate countries until the Vietnam War ended in 1973. The independence wave in Southeast Asia extended to Indonesia, where the Dutch decolonized in 1949, and to the Philippines, finally released in 1946 from the United States, which had controlled it since 1898.

Decolonization in Sub-Saharan Africa

As happened in India, the African independence movements were led by men newly educated in European ideals, mainly in universities in Europe and the United States, who came to dream of democracy and nationalistic independence for colonies in Africa. During the 1930s newspapers began appearing in some British colonies, although only a small percentage of Africans were literate by 1960. Just as Indians did, Africans served in the world wars in support of their mother countries, giving soldiers exposure to lands far from home, and they too became disillusioned with the brutality of Europeans fighting Europeans. Seeds of African discontent lay in the treatment of Africans working in the mines, plantations, railroads, and docks for Europeans who controlled the economy and often projected an air of racial superiority that made Africans long for independence.

New African Countries

Britain and France came to understand that the wars had weakened their economies so severely that they could no longer afford to keep their colonies, so both
countries devised plans for granting independence but also keeping the good will
of the new countries. They wanted to keep profitable trade going, and so they
invested in projects to support the African infrastructure, such as hydroelectric
schemes on major river systems, and agricultural, veterinary, and fishing technology. Educational facilities were increased, with four university colleges established by the British between 1945 and 1949. Even so, African economies
remained weak.

The first black African country to win independence was the Gold Coast, choosing a name – Ghana – that linked the new country to an earlier African empire.
Kwame Nkrumah, educated in the United States, led the movement in Ghana,
and after independence was won in 1957, he convened the All African People's
Conference at Accra (the capital of Ghana), the first time that the conference ever
met in Africa. Three years later, Britain granted independence to Nigeria, which
became the most populous country in Africa. Like many other African nations,
the borders were drawn arbitrarily, grouping many unrelated, often hostile, groups
within the same country and separating groups that were related. Nigeria was
composed of three regions based on ethnicity: the Hausa majority in the north,
the Yoruba in the southwest, and the Ibo in the southeast. Not only were tribal
affiliations different, but the people in the north – influenced by the slow cultural
diffusion of Islam across the Sahara to Sub-Saharan Africa – were mainly Muslim;
those in the south – influenced by missionaries coming from Britain – were mainly
Christian. These differences made nationalism a serious problem for Nigerians,
a common pattern experienced by many other newly-created African countries.

In 1956, France turned over local self-government to its colonies in West and
Equatorial Africa, but still kept them within the French Empire. Two years later, it
offered each of its colonies the choice between complete independence and more
limited self-government under French protection. By 1960 Guinea and French
Somaliland (Djibouti) chose independence, but in all others, strong ties continued
between France and its former African colonies. For example, in those countries,
many currencies remained tied to the French franc, some African governmental
positions were filled by French expatriates, the French military maintained a presence in some colonies, and former colonies received preferential trading rights
with France.

The freeing of the Belgian colonies was accompanied by violence, with Belgium,
unlike Britain and France, doing little preparation for independence. In 1959, in
response to rioting and looting of Belgian shops in Leopoldsville, the capital of
the Belgian Congo, Belgium suddenly decided to pull out of the country within the

year, leaving it in chaos that soon turned into civil war. The colonial government had been one of the most cruel and exploitative, and the new government's prime minister, Patrice Lumumba, expressed his bitterness at the independence ceremony, only to be deposed in a coup and assassinated a few months later. In nearby Ruanda-Urundi (present-day Rwanda and Burundi), the Belgians had allowed the Tutsi minority (about 15 percent of the population) to dominate the government, and when independence came in 1962, the majority Hutus challenged the Tutsis for control. Tensions broke out into warfare and massacres by 1972, escalated in the 1990s, and continues today.

South Africa

After 1980, South Africa was the only white-ruled country in Sub-Saharan Africa. About 1/5 of the population was white, some with Dutch ancestry called

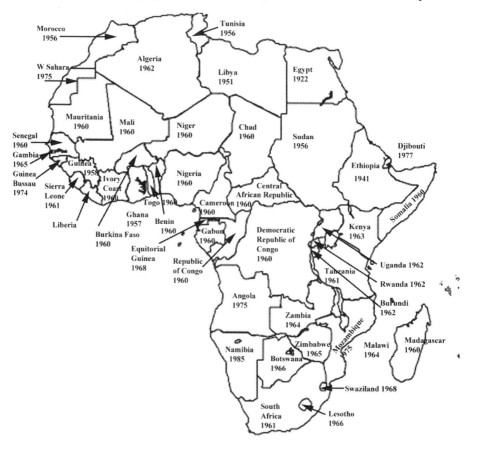

The Decolonization of Africa. Ethiopia was only colonized by Italy under Mussolini for a few years, Liberia had been established as an independent state, and Egypt was granted independence in 1922, but most African states gained their independence after World War II. Each colonial power had its own pattern for granting independence, and although many experienced violence, the British and French hoped to establish friendly relations, whereas the Portuguese and Belgians left their colonies less willingly.

"Boers" or "Afrikaners," and some of British descent. The British and Dutch had fought the Boer War of 1899-1902, but had come together to form the Union of South Africa in 1910. The majority black and "colored" (mixed) populations were ruled harshly, with no political rights, few economic opportunities, and the right to purchase land only in specified areas. In 1913, the **African National Congress (ANC)** formed as a party of protest, but it was unable to convince the white government to liberalize its racial policies. In 1948, **apartheid** – segregation of the races – was established. Under apartheid, black who worked in the cities could not live near their work, but were forced to live in black residential areas far away or in dormitories apart from their families.

As most colonies in Africa declared their independence and set up governments run by natives, international pressure built against the South African government to dismantle the apartheid system, but they resisted any change. The ANC then shifted to more aggressive methods, including strikes and sabotage of white property, and its leader, **Nelson Mandela**, who was already incarcerated, was sentenced to life imprisonment in 1964. These actions first brought support from surrounding countries to the ANC, and in 1976, the United Nations unanimously condemned the elevation of one of the black "homelands", Transkei, into an independent state because it remained dependent on South Africa. Not one country in the world recognized the new state, but in 1982, almost one million black South Africans were transferred to another country – Swaziland – without their having any say in the matter. Through the United Nations as well as through unilateral actions, many nations adopted sanctions against South Africa, restricting trade, or withdrawing economic investments. Enforcing the sanctions proved difficult because South Africa had a wealth of natural resources, including diamonds and gold, which provided incentives for trade. Additionally, the South African military was very strong.

Ultimately, many blacks demonstrated, held strikes, and rioted over the government's discriminatory practices. As a result, the sanctions gradually worked and diplomatic pressure mounted abroad for change. In 1990, Nelson Mandela finally was released from prison, and he was elected president of the African National Congress the following year. In 1993, he received the Nobel Peace Prize, and on May 10, 1994, he was elected South Africa's first black president in that country's first truly democratic election, with all races able to vote.

Decolonization and Change in North Africa and the Middle East

Whereas most Sub-Saharan African countries were colonized during the late 19th century, areas in North Africa and the Middle East experienced many different patterns within many time frames as nation-states were formed. The entire Arab world is included in this region, but all the inhabitants are not Arabs. Iran's heritage is more Persian than Arab, but it shares a Muslim heritage with Arab countries, as does Turkcy, which inherited the mantle of the Ottoman Turks. In 1947, the founding of Israel meant that the number of Jews in the Middle East increased rapidly. The fact that this area is one of the oldest centers of civilization lends it a complexity that is reflected in different patterns of nationalism and varied responses to decolonization and the declining influence of the west.

Turkey

After **Mustafa Kemal (Ataturk)** unified Turkey as an independent country in 1923, he set about creating a secular nationalist state. To do so, he curbed the power of Islam by abolishing shari'a law, the practice of polygamy, and the office of caliph in the government. He replaced Arabic script with the Roman alphabet, encouraged all Turks to wear western clothes and women to discontinue wearing veils. His goals were similar to those of the Ottoman Empire in earlier days – to adopt western technology and customs in order to have a respected place in the world. However, his quest for modernity included the acceptance of a loan from the Soviet Union to buy Soviet equipment to use in the country's sugar and textile industries. By the time that World War II broke out, Turkey had made some amazing economic and educational strides, and true to nationalist impulses, it remained neutral for most of World War II, siding with the Allies only toward the end of the war.

Despite these accomplishments, Ataturk's secular nationalism was highly controversial, especially among Muslim clerics, and his actions created a rift in Turkish society between those who wished to keep the state secular and those who wanted to return to a Muslim state. The presence of a large Kurdish population complicated Turkey's statehood, since the Kurds advocated a separate state composed of people spread out into six Middle Eastern countries. To add to the tensions, the armed forces have intervened periodically in politics so that the government has alternated between democratic elections and military dictatorships. As in times past, Turkey's geographic location split its orientation between Europe and western Asia.

States in Northern Africa

Egypt had operated as an independent state since the days of Muhammad Ali in the early 19th century, even though it remained technically a part of the Ottoman Empire until World War I. However, the British held a great deal of economic control, even though independence was officially granted in 1922. During World War II, the British put the government in the hands of the *Wafd*, an Egyptian nationalist party, and the new government took the leadership in establishing the **League of Arab States**, a regional organization designed to strengthen and unite countries with Arab majorities. In 1952, the army drove out the Egyptian king and cut many ties with the British, paving the way for the emergence of **Gamel Abdel Nasser** as the new nationalist leader. Nasser took advantage of Cold War

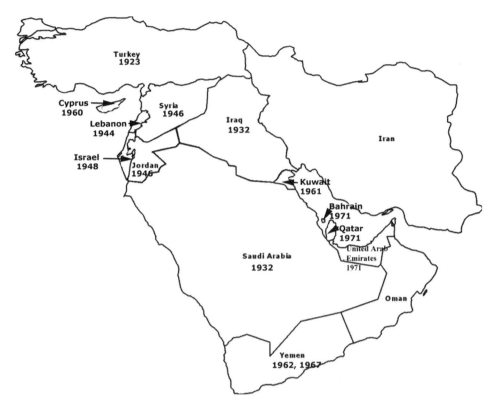

The Middle East and Independence. Independence dates for countries in the Middle East vary more than those for most of Sub-Saharan Africa. Some were never colonized – such as Iran and Oman, although Oman was a British protectorate. Others formed into nation-states after World War I – such as Turkey, Iraq, and Saudi Arabia. Most others were part of the decolonization that occurred around the world after World War II, although the dates in this category range from 1944 to 1971.

politics to seek and gain aid from both the United States and the Soviet Union, but joined meetings with states that aligned with neither superpower. In 1956, he declared that the Suez Canal belonged to Egypt, and despite the protests of Britain and France in the United Nations Security Council, the United States sided with Nasser and pressured its allies to support Egypt's nationalization of the canal. Nasser's move was successful, and his bold challenge to the imperialist order was one more example of the transition from western European global hegemony to the Cold War era of "Third World" countries balancing the competition between the U.S. and U.S.S.R. in order to curry benefits.

Even before World War II, an Arab-Islamic nationalist movement had developed in Algeria, which was a French colony in northern Africa. After the war was over and France was having trouble controlling its world empire, the movement in Algeria intensified into a revolution in the mid-1950s. The Arab nationalists were united as the National Liberation Front, and they fought against those who wished to keep ties to France intact. The violence spread throughout Algeria and eventually to France, triggering the fall of the Fourth French Republic. The situation was contained by **Charles De Gaulle**, the leader of the French Resistance during World War II, who ushered in a new government in France – the Fifth Republic – and negotiated Algerian independence in 1962. The new state was limited by the exodus of virtually all of Algeria's one million European residents, some of whom had filled the most important positions in the government. The new leaders encouraged industrialization, and oil revenues financed government programs to build roads, infrastructure for industries, and the education system. Despite these efforts, many Algerians immigrated to France, and control of the country remained fragile as the military and Islamic fundamentalists struggled for power.

SOCIAL AND CULTURAL TRENDS

By the end of the 1960s, a new generation of western Europeans had grown to adulthood in post-industrial societies unmarred by global economic depressions and all-encompassing war. A spirit of activism characterized the era that encouraged young people to question the Cold War order, and to address issues of equality that emerged from their experiences as citizens of maturing democracies and post-industrial economies. In the United States, a civil rights movement succeeded in gaining political, social, and economic rights for black Americans, and student activism grew on both sides of the Atlantic. American students protested the Vietnam War, and European youth all over the Continent demanded reform. In 1966, Prague students held public celebrations to commemorate the 10th anniversary of the "Prague Spring," and in 1968, students in Paris began demonstrations that threatened the legitimacy of the French Fifth Republic.

In a series of events that culminated in the **Events of May**, protests began in suburban Paris when students staged a rally at a branch of the University of Paris to protest campus facilities and dormitory rules. Students around Paris supported the protests with a series of nightly demonstrations in March 1968 that led to violent clashes with the police. By May, students had erected barricades in the streets, and students took over buildings on the Sorbonne campus. The discontent spread to workers, who began occupying factories all over the country, and by the middle of May about 8 million people were on strike. The Events of May came to represent a large number of people and groups that objected to the centralization of political power under Charles De Gaulle, and even though the conservative government retained power, the movement did force De Gaulle to call for new elections to confirm the government's legitimacy.

The Women's Movement

Although women in most western countries had gained the right to vote during the post-World War I era, other rights for women remained unchallenged for decades. Once the goal of suffrage was reached, women's movements dissipated during the

1920s, and the economic depression of the 1930s created such a shortage of jobs that women who sought work were often seen as unfairly grabbing work from men who were the traditional breadwinners for families. The all-out mobilization of World War II, however, brought women back to the workforce in Britain and the United States, though not in Germany. American and British women took jobs previously done by men, and once the war was over, some were reluctant to give up their independence. In most cases, however, they returned to their homes to allow men to once again fill the workforce. During the post-war period, many couples that had delayed starting families during the war years began having children, and economic prosperity made it less necessary for women to work.

Starting in the late 1960s, a new women's movement began – inspired by the success of the black civil rights movement in the United States – that emphasized cultural, sexual, and economic rights that went well beyond the right to vote. Two important sexual issues were abortion and contraception rights. During the 1960s and 1970s, hundreds of thousands of European women worked to repeal laws that prohibited abortion and the use of contraceptives, and met with some success. In 1968, a law was passed in France that permitted the sale of contraceptive devices, and in 1979, a new French law legalized abortion. Although the Catholic Church remained strongly opposed to abortion, legislation allowing contraception and abortion was passed in many other European countries, even those that were devoutly Catholic.

Other women's movements emphasized women's need to venture into the world outside the home. In the United States, journalist Betty Friedan helped organize the National Organization for Women (NOW) in 1966 to "bring women into full participation in the mainstream of American society now." NOW advocated equal pay for women and sought many legal reforms as well. In Sweden, women lobbied to lower the gender-based division of labor that separated "men's work" from "women's work." A few Soviet women even protested low and no pay for work done by women. One result of this activism was an increase in the number of women in the workforce. In Britain, for example, the percentage of women in the workforce increased from 32% in 1970 to 44% in 1990. Women also began to enter new areas of employment, partly because new educational opportunities allowed women to take jobs as lawyers, doctors, and business professionals.

Trends in Philosophy, Literature, and Art

The values that formed the democracies of post-World War II Europe may be described as reflecting **post-modernism**. **Modernism** is a set of values that came along with industrialization. Values of modernism included secularism (an emphasis on non-religious aspects of life), an emphasis on reasoning (rationalism), materialism (valuing concrete objects and possessions), technology, bureaucracy, and an emphasis on freedom rather than collective equality. In other words,

THEMATIC LEARNING OBJECTIVE:
INDIVIDUAL AND SOCIETY:
SIMONE DE BEAUVOIR'S *THE SECOND SEX*

French author Simone de Beauvoir voiced her criticism of traditional gender roles long before the women's movement of the 1960s and 1970s began. Her very important book, *The Second Sex,* was first published in 1949 at a time when few others were questioning tradition, but her concept of woman as the "Other" was a powerful image that shaped the later protests. In the excerpt below, she explored why women's movements had so often had limited success.

"The couple is a fundamental unity with its two halves riveted together, and the cleavage of society along the line of sex is impossible. Here is to be found the basic trait of woman: she is the Other in a totality of which the two components are necessary to one another....

Now, woman has always been man's dependent, if not his slave; the two sexes have never shared the world in equality. And even today woman is heavily handicapped, though her situation is beginning to change. Almost nowhere is her legal status the same as man's, and frequently it is much to her disadvantage....it is still a world that belongs to men – they have no doubt of it at all and women have scarcely any. To decline to be the Other, to refuse to be a party to a deal – this would be for women to renounce all the advantages that have been conferred on them by their alliance with the superior caste. Man-the-sovereign will provide woman-the-liege with material protection and will undertake the moral justification of her existence; thus she can evade at once both economoic risk and the metaphysical risk of a liberty in which ends and aims must be contrived without assistance..."

Reference: Simone de Beauvoir, *The Second Sex,* J.M. Parshley, trans. (Alfred A. Knopf, Inc, 1952).

industrialization encouraged making money and gaining economic success. By the mid-20th century, the countries of the west experienced post-modernism, a set of values that emphasizes quality of life over concern for material gain. Some examples of post-modern values are the preservation of the environment and the promotion of health care and education. These values accompanied the economic changes of **post-industrialism**, in which the majority of people were and still are employed in the service sector, including such industries as technology, health care, business and legal services, finance, and education. Both modernist and post-modernist values are reflected in the philosophy, literature, and art of the era from 1945 to 1989.

One of the most influential early post-modern philosophers was **Jean-François Lyotard**, a French writer who was largely concerned with how human culture changed in the post-industrial world. Drawing his inspiration from Nietzsche, he argued that modern philosophies were based on the grounds of accepted stories or "metanarratives" about the world. He argued that because the world had changed, these stories were no longer valid as a philosophical base. Instead he believed that people were developing a new "language game" – not based on absolute truths, but on ever-changing relationships.

The questioning of old values was apparent in the work of the Irish-born writer **Samuel Beckett**, especially in his plays *Waiting for Godot* (1952) and *Endgame* (1957). Through Beckett's characters, the audience saw themselves going through the motions, with nothing worth saying or doing, as their lives were molded by conventions of a worn-out culture. The same sense of anxiety and despair shaped the growing popularity of **existentialism**, a philosophy that first sprang from early 20th century writers who were influenced by the works of Nietzsche in the late 19th century. The post-World War II existentialists explored what it meant to be human in a world without cultural moorings, without clear guideposts, standards, or values. The two most influential existentialists were **Albert Camus** and **Jean-Paul Sartre**. For both, God no longer existed in the universe, which meant that humans were utterly alone with no preordained destiny. For Beckett, the horrors of World War II created an absurd world with no meaning, but for Camus and Sartre, humans had to make some sense of this new world. Camus suggested that traditional values like friendship and tolerance were not dead, but could be used to reshape life's meaning. At the very least, he said, we might learn to stop killing one another. Camus and Sartre disagreed about the viability of Marxism, with Sartre believing that existentialism could be used to revitalize Marxism, whereas Camus believed that communism was part of the problem.

By the mid-1970s, communism came under renewed attack because of the writings of the exiled **Alexander Solzhenitsyn**, who wrote disturbing descriptions of the Soviet gulag, or forced-labor camps. Some intellectuals asked whether or not Marxism necessarily implied Stalinist repression, while others criticized the west for the horrors of the 20th century and insisted that older traditions must be reinstated. For the French Catholic thinker Jacques Maritain, for example, this meant that a return to religious traditions was the only answer, but to others – such as British writer T.S. Eliot – family and a return to localism were important keys to shaping the new world.

In art, modernism emphasized the importance of "cutting edge" work, and was expressed in **abstract expressionism**, or the creation of works that were completely abstract with no attempt to recreate visual reality. One of the best-known abstract artists was **Jackson Pollack**, an American who specialized in drip paintings. Paint swirled across his canvases, creating chaotic patterns that broke all previous artistic conventions. By the 1960s **Pop Art** emerged, an art form that transformed images of popular culture. **Andy Warhol** – once a New York advertising illustrator – was best known for his adaptation of images from commercial art to the artist's canvas. One of his most famous works featured a Campbell's soup can. By the 1980s, post-modernist thought re-emphasized traditional values that improve the quality of life, and were reflected in works that elevated traditional craftsmanship – such as weaving and furniture-making – to the level of fine art.

Between 1945 and 1989, European history was shaped by the aftermath of World War II, with all the destruction that it brought, both to the physical infrastructure and to the human soul. The power plays of the United States and the Soviet Union in the Cold War also cast a shadow of fear and anxiety across the world, especially with the threat of nuclear arms. The "Three Worlds" that emerged and persisted during the period split Europe in two, along lines between east and west that had long been there, but now came to be played out on the world stage. However, as the last decade of the 20th century approached, this entire pattern changed again, and Europe emerged with the hope of reunion and cooperation, a promise that had long eluded the diverse peoples of the continent.

CONCEPTS AND IDENTIFICATIONS

abstract expressionism
Adenauer, Konrad
advanced democracies
African National Congress
Algerian crisis
apartheid
Atlantic Charter
Beckett, Samuel
Beveridge Report
Brandt, Willy
Camus, Albert
civil disobedience
Cuban Missile crisis
decolonization
De Gaulle, Charles
denazification
dirigisme
European Coal and Steel Community
European Economic Community (Common Market)
Events of May
existentialism
Fifth Republic (France)
Gandhi, Mohandas

General Assembly
Ho Chi Minh
Huntington, Samuel
"iron curtain"
Jinnah, Muhammad Ali
Kemal, Mustafa (Ataturk)
Korean War
League of Arab States
limited war
Lyotard, Jean-François
Mandela, Nelson
Marshall Plan
mixed economy
modernism, post-modernism
Nasser, Gamel Abdel
NATO
National Health Service
Nehru, Jawaharlal
Nkrumah, Kwame
Pollack, Jackson
Pop Art
post-industrialism
Potsdam Conference
Prague Spring
Sartre, Jean-Paul
"satellite states"
Security Council
Solzhenitsyn, Alexander
space race
Sputnik
Tehran Conference
Thatcher, Margaret
"three waves of democratization"
Tito (Josip Broz)
Truman Doctrine
United Nations, UN Charter
Vietnam War
Yalta Conference
Warhol, Andy
Warsaw Pact

CHAPTER 20
THE NEW EUROPE:
1989 TO THE PRESENT

As the last decade of the 20th century began, almost everyone – experts and ordinary people alike – assumed that Cold War politics would continue indefinitely, so the break-away of satellite states and the collapse of the Soviet Union were astonishing, unanticipated events. Although the repercussions of this abrupt end to the Cold War are far from complete, it is clear that 1989 marks a new era in European history. No one knows how important the change actually was because, after all, the Cold War itself lasted less than fifty years – a microcosm of time in the ongoing history of Europe. Even the longer trend of the decline of European power may be changing, as the European Union has become a major international force since 1991. It is too early to know which trends will last and which will prove to be only brief intervals that have little impact on the future. However, this chapter analyzes various current economic, political, social, and cultural trends, and only the passage of time will reveal which are the true harbingers of the future.

THE BREAK-UP OF THE SOVIET UNION

After Stalin died in 1953, a power struggle among top Communist Party leaders resulted in **Nikita Khrushchev** being chosen as party secretary and premier of the USSR. In 1956, he gave his famous "secret speech," in which he revealed the existence of a letter written by Lenin before he died. The letter was critical of Stalin, and Khrushchev used it to denounce Stalin's rules and practices, particularly the purges that he sponsored. This denouncement led to **deStalinization**, a process that included reforms, such as loosening government censorship of the press, decentralization of economic decision-making, and restructuring of the collective farms. In foreign policy, Khrushchev advocated "peaceful coexistence," or relaxation of tensions between the United States and the Soviet Union. Other members of the Politburo (the governing body of the Soviet Union) criticized him from the beginning for the suggested reforms, and his diplomatic and military failure in the Cuban Missile Crisis led to his removal from power. Furthermore, by the early 1960s most of his reforms did not appear to be working. He was replaced by the much more conservative Leonid Brezhnev, who ended the reforms and tried to cope with the increasing economic problems that were just under the surface of Soviet power.

The Gorbachev Reforms

After Brezhnev died in 1982, he was succeeded briefly by aged party leaders, but in 1985, the Politburo selected **Mikhail Gorbachev**, a reformer from a younger generation. Gorbachev was unlike any previous Soviet leader in that he not only looked and acted more "western," but he also was more open to western-style reforms than any other, including Khrushchev. Gorbachev inherited far more problems than any outsider realized at the time, and many of his reforms were motivated by shear necessity to save the country from economic disaster. His program was three-pronged:

- *Glasnost* – This term translates from the Russian as "openness." The policy allowed more open discussion of political, social, and economic issues as well as criticism of the government. Although this reform was applauded by western nations, it caused many problems for Gorbachev. After so many years of repression, people vented hostility toward the government that encouraged open revolt, particularly among some of the republics that wanted independence from Soviet control.

- **Democratization** – Gorbachev believed that he could keep the old Soviet structure, including Communist Party control, but at the same time insert a little democracy into the system. Three such moves included the creation of 1) a new Congress of People's Deputies with directly elected representatives; 2) a new position of "President" that was selected by the Congress; and 3) competitive elections for positions in the government of the Soviet republics, regions, and cities. The reforms did bring a bit of democracy. However, many of the new deputies were critical of Gorbachev, increasing the level of discord within the government.

- *Perestroika* – This economic reform was Gorbachev's most radical, and also his least successful. Again, he tried to keep the old Soviet structure, and modernize from within. Most significantly, *perestroika* transferred many economic powers held by the central government to private hands and the workings of the market economy. Specific reforms included authorization of some privately owned companies, penalties for under-performing state factories, leases of farm land to private individuals, price reforms, and encouragement of joint ventures with foreign companies.

None of Gorbachev's reforms were ever fully carried out because the Revolution of 1991 swept him out of office.

Rebellions in Eastern Europe

Before the Gorbachev reforms, central and eastern Europe remained under the tight control of Communist Party bosses who clung to old Stalinist principles and resisted virtually all pressures to change. However, as *glasnost*, democratization, and *perestroika* began to take effect, eastern Europeans began to openly discuss the shortcomings of their centrally-planned economies, which had stagnated since the 1970s. In Poland, the dissidence began as early as 1980, when workers went on strike to protest government-increased food prices. A charismatic **Lech Walesa** – an electrician – and Anna Walentynowicz – a crane operator – started an independent labor movement called **Solidarity**. Soon others joined the movement, and when Solidarity workers occupied factories to protest deteriorating living conditions in Poland, they did so with wide support from other Poles and worldwide sympathy created through media coverage. As protests spilled into the streets, the Communist Party – with Soviet support – outlawed Solidarity, but the movement stayed alive through underground activities.

In 1989, a series of revolutions broke out throughout central and eastern Europe. In June 1989, the Polish government, on the verge of economic collapse and without Soviet support to suppress rebellion, relented to the pressure to hold free parliamentary elections. Solidarity candidates overwhelmingly defeated the Communists, and in early 1990, Lech Walesa became president. Gorbachev reversed the policy of his predecessor, Leonid Brezhnev, and refused to interfere in Poland's internal political processes. Gorbachev's respect for Polish sovereignty inspired other satellite nations to assert their independence from Soviet rule.

Like Poland, Hungary had experimented with free-market principles since the 1960s, so it was the next country to successfully assert its independence in 1989. The strong ethnic identity of Hungarians also supported political reform, and popular demands of liberalization led the parliament to dismiss the Communist Party as the official ruling institution. East Germany – where dissidents had been active since the early 1980s – also rebelled, as citizens flooded the borders to escape to the west. After Gorbachev visited the country and signaled that force should not be used to prevent reform, the government issued an ambiguous statement that encouraged guards to allow free passage across the Berlin Wall that separated East Berlin from West Berlin. Excited Berliners on both sides reacted by tearing down the wall in the midst of a great celebration widely captured by international media. Shortly after this dramatic event, the Communist Party structure dissolved and government leaders were arrested on charges of corruption and embezzlement. Reunification of the two Germanies moved swiftly, with their economies merging first, and finally on October 3, 1990, the two states formally united to become a liberal democracy called the Federal Republic of Germany, and its capital was reestablished within a few years in Berlin.

In Czechoslovakia, dissidents had continued to speak out after the Soviet invasion in 1968, and in 1977 playwright **Vaclav Havel**, along with other intellectuals and workers, signed Charter 77, which was a public protest against the regime that resulted in his arrest. In response to Gorbachev's televised endorsement of free speech in the mid-1980s, demonstrators protested in the streets for democracy. The government responded by turning the police on them. At the same time that Poland, Hungary, and East Germany successfully threw off Communist dictators in 1989, Czech leader **Alexander Dubcek** addressed the crowds in Wenceslas Square in Prague, encouraging them to rebel. The Communist leadership resigned in a **"velvet revolution"** noted by its smooth, bloodless success.

Politics

THEMATIC LEARNING OBJECTIVE: STATES AND OTHER INSTITUTIONS OF POWER: VACLAV HAVEL ON THE FAILURE OF COMMUNISM

After Czechoslovakia's successful revolution in 1989, Vaclav Havel, a playwright who embodied the dissident movement, gave a 1990 New Year's Day address to the Czech people. In the excerpt below, he described how the communist regime had abused its power by morally tainting its citizens.

"The previous regime, armed with a proud and intolerant ideology, reduced people into the means of production, and nature into its tools. So it attacked their very essence, and their mutual relations....Out of talented and responsible people, ingeniously husbanding their land, it made cogs of some sort of great, monstrous, thudding, smelly machine, with an unclear purpose. All it can do is slowly but irresistibly, wear itself out, with all its cogs.

If I speak about a spoiled moral atmosphere I don't refer only to our masters.... I'm speaking about all of us. For all of us have grown used to the totalitarian system and accepted it as an immutable fact, and thereby actually helped keep it going. None of us are only its victims; we are all responsible for it....

Freedom and democracy, after all, mean joint participation and shared responsibility. If we realize this, then all the horrors that the new Czechoslovak democracy inherited cease to be so horrific. If we realize this, then hope will return to our hearts....

Now it depends only on us whether this hope will be fulfilled....Your Government, my people, has returned to you."

Reference: New York Times, January 2, 1990.

Another major successful coup of 1989 took place in Romania, which had been ruled since the mid-1960s by **Nicolae Ceauşescu**, perhaps the most repressive Communist dictator in all of eastern Europe. An opposition movement began in early December, and workers demonstrated against the government. The tide turned when the army rose against the dictator as well, and on Christmas Day, Ceauşescu was tried by a military court and then executed. The fall of so many satellite states left the Soviet Union vulnerable, and its demise followed in quick succession.

A Failed Coup and the Russian Revolution of 1991

In August 1991, "conservatives" (those that wanted to abandon Gorbachev's reforms) from within the Soviet Politburo led a coup d'état that tried to remove Gorbachev from office. The leaders included the vice-president, the head of the KGB (Russian secret police), and top military advisers. The coup failed when popular protests broke out, and soldiers from the military defected rather than support their leaders. The protesters were led by **Boris Yeltsin**, the elected president of the Russian Republic and former Politburo member, who had been removed from the Politburo a few years earlier because his radical views offended the conservatives. Yeltsin advocated more extreme reform measures than Gorbachev did, and he won his position as president of the Russian Republic as a result of the new more democratic electoral system put in place by Gorbachev. Gorbachev was restored to power, but the U.S.S.R. only had a few months to live. By December 1991, eleven republics had declared their independence, and eventually Gorbachev was forced to announce the end of the union, which put him out of a job. The fifteen republics went their separate ways, but Boris Yeltsin emerged as the president of the largest and most powerful republic, now renamed the Russian Federation. A weak **Confederation of Independent States** was formed, consisting today of nine of the fifteen former republics of the Soviet Union, but the organization has had little formal power over its members.

A NEW WORLD ORDER

The Soviet Union held hegemony over huge portions of the world for much of the 20th century, and when it fell apart in 1991, that dominance was broken. The 1990s were a time of chaos and humiliation for Russia, as Yeltsin had to rely on loans from its old nemesis, the United States, to help shake the economic doldrums. As the 21st century began, the new president, **Vladimir Putin**, set out to redefine Russia's place in the world, a two-dimensional task that required a new interpretation of the country's relationship with the west, as well as its role among the former Soviet States. The biggest adjustment for Russia was the loss of its superpower status from the Cold War era. The United States emerged as the lone superpower in 1991, and the two old enemies – Russia and the United States – had to readjust their attitudes toward one another. U.S. Presidents George H. Bush and

The Former Soviet Union. The solid black line divides the former republics from neighboring states. When the Soviet Union broke apart in 1991, it split into fifteen separate countries – the former Soviet Republics that made up the U.S.S.R. The fifteen former republics are Estonia, Latvia, Lithuania, Belarus, Ukraine, Moldava, Armenia, Georgia, Azerbaijan, Turkmenistan, Uzbekistan, Kazakhstan, Tajikistan, Kyrgyzstan, and Russia.

Bill Clinton both believed that it was important to maintain a good working relationship with Russia, and they also knew that the economic collapse of Russia would have disastrous results for the world economy. Both presidents sponsored aid packages for Russia, and they also encouraged foreign investment in the country's fledgling market economy.

The United States: A Lone Superpower?

With the sudden fall of the Soviet Union in 1991, the United States unexpectedly found itself the winner of the Cold War. U.S. foreign policy had been guided first by **containment** (keeping communism from spreading) and then by **detente** (coexisting peaceably with the Soviet Union), but without the Soviet Union, foreign policy had to change. The attacks on the World Trade Towers and the Pentagon on September 11, 2001, shaped the country's direction significantly, as the government under President George W. Bush spearheaded an international "war on terrorism." The "war" was directed first at finding **Osama bin Laden**, the head of **Al-Qaeda**, the international terrorist organization that claimed responsibility for the attacks. In 2003, the United States government decided to invade Iraq to remove **Saddam Hussein** from power based on the premise that he was harboring

CHANGE OVER TIME:
RUSSIA IN THE 20TH CENTURY

During the 20th century, Russia experienced some dramatic changes reflected in the marker events listed below.

1905 – Russian dissidents challenged the tsar's authority in the Revolution of 1905. Though their goals were unmet, the incident foreshadowed the upheaval that was to come.

1917 – Two revolutions – one in March and one in November – overthrew the tsar and replaced him with V.I. Lenin and his Bolshevik followers. A civil war began that Lenin eventually won in 1921, and in 1922 the country was renamed the Union of Soviet Socialist Republics..

1927 – After Lenin's death, Joseph Stalin replaced him as the Russian leader, beginning the era of Stalinism – "socialism in one country" – that lasted until 1953.

1945 – Although Russia suffered heavy losses during World War II, the decline of western Europe left it as one of two superpowers that dominated the world stage until the early 1990s.

1989 – Revolutions in eastern Europe stripped Russia of control over most of its satellite states.

1991 – The Soviet Union fell apart as its republics declared independence. The Russian Republic was renamed "The Russian Federation."

1993 – The Russian Constitution created a structural democracy headed by a directly-elected president.

During the 20th century, the Russian state changed from an absolute monarchy to a communist state to a structural democracy. In the early 21st century, it has become increasingly authoritarian, even though the democratic political structure is still in place.

Al-Qaeda operatives and constructing **Weapons of Mass Destruction (WMDs)** to use against the United States. To justify the war in Iraq, President Bush used a foreign policy of **preemption**, or the principle of attacking before being attacked. No WMDs were found, and the United States was widely criticized for its actions, and its credibility as a "superpower" was questioned because of its inability to bring stability to Iraq in the post-Hussein era.

GLOBALIZATION AND SUPRANATIONALISM

The new world order since 1991 is still taking shape, and the roles that Russia, the United States, European countries, and China play in international affairs are very much in flux. All countries exist within an interactional environment with other governments, but more and more they are affected by international organizations whose influence and authority go beyond national boundaries. In the 20th century, many national governments established relationships with regional organizations – such as NATO, the European Union, NAFTA, and OPEC – and with international organizations, such as the United Nations.

These international organizations reflect the phenomenon of **globalization** – an integration of social, environmental, economic, and cultural activities of nations that has resulted from increasing international contacts. Globalization has changed the nature of world politics, largely because it breaks down the distinction between international relations and domestic politics, making many aspects of domestic politics subject to global forces. Likewise, it also internationalizes domestic issues and events. Because globalization deepens and widens international connections, local events, even small ones, can have ripple effects throughout the world. Perhaps most apparent is the effect of technology and its ability to ignore national boundaries. For example, the Internet allows news from every corner of the globe to rapidly spread to other areas, so that what happens in one place affects others around the world. On the other hand, many political scientists point out a counter trend – **fragmentation** – a tendency for people to base their loyalty on ethnicity, language, religion, or cultural identity. Although globalization and fragmentation appear to be opposite concepts, they both transcend political boundaries between individual countries.

World-Wide Organizations

The United Nations continues to function as a major peacekeeping organization, although its authority is limited and its challenges are many. The organization's goals have broadened over the years, so that many international organizations are sponsored and funded under its umbrella. Two other important international organizations of the late 20th and early 21st centuries include:

- **The World Trade Organization** – Established in 1995, the WTO is an organization of member states who have agreed to rules of world trade among nations. It is responsible for negotiating and implementing new trade agreements, it serves as a forum for settling trade disputes, and it supervises members to be sure that they follow the rules that the organization sets. Most of the world's trading nations belong to the WTO, with Russia belatedly joining in 2012. The WTO oversees about 60 different agreements that have the status of international legal texts that bind its members. The process of becoming a WTO member is unique to each applicant country, and the terms of membership are dependent upon the country's stage of economic development and current trade network. The process takes about five years, but it can take more time if the country's economic status is questionable or if political issues make it objectionable. For example, China was denied WTO status for many years because of questions about human rights abuses, but its growing economic prowess finally influenced member states to approve it.

- **The World Bank** – Although the World Bank was created in 1944 to aid countries in rebuilding after World War II, its focus today is on loaning money to low and middle-income countries at modest interest rates. The Bank's goals are to eliminate poverty in these countries and to support economic development through investment in projects that build businesses, improve transportation and communications, provide jobs, and eliminate corruption in government. The Bank has also supported health initiatives – such as vaccination programs for disease and research to combat AIDs – and efforts to reduce greenhouse gases that contribute to global warming.

Regional Organizations

During the Cold War era, regional military alliances appeared, and countries joined them based on their affiliation either with the United States or Russia. **The North Atlantic Treaty Organization** (NATO) was formed in the late 1940s with fourteen European members, the United States, and Canada, for the purpose of providing mutual defense in case of attack. An opposing alliance – the **Warsaw Pact** – was composed of the Soviet Union and six Eastern European countries. Together the two organizations were designed to maintain a bipolar balance of power in Europe. The Warsaw Pact disbanded with the breakup of the Soviet Union, and many of its former members joined NATO. Other regional organizations include the Organization of American States (OAS) to promote social, cultural, political, and economic links among member states in the Western Hemisphere, and the African Union, which has promoted the elimination of minority white-ruled governments in southern Africa.

The European Union

By the late 20th century, all the countries of Europe were affected by **integration**, a trend that ran counter to their many years as separate, competing nation-states. Integration is a process that encourages states to pool their sovereignty in order to gain political, economic, and social clout. Integration binds states together with common policies and shared rules. The **supranational organization** that currently integrates the states of Europe is called the European Union.

Europe's history is one of diverse national identities. Its wars have encompassed the continent as first its kingdoms, and then its countries, fought over religion, power, land, and trade. Perhaps most dramatically, its conflicts erupted in two devastating world wars during the 20th century. Shortly after World War II ended, European leaders decided on a new direction – cooperation among nations – that led to the creation of the European Union, a supranational organization that has not supplanted nationalism, but has altered its members' policymaking practices substantially, since many sovereignty rights are integrated.

A Brief History

The organization began in an effort to revitalize a war-torn Europe after World War II ended. The most immediate need was to repair the nations' broken economies, so the initial goals were almost completely economic in intent. In 1949, the Council of Europe was formed, and although it had little power, it provided an opportunity for national leaders to meet. The following year an international authority was formed to coordinate the coal and steel industries, both damaged heavily during the war. Later evolutions of the new organization included:

- **The EEC (European Economic Community)** – The Treaty of Rome established the EEC – informally named the "Common Market" – in 1957. Its most important provisions called for the elimination of all tariffs between European nations and the creation of new ones that applied to all.

- **The EC (European Community)** – Established in 1965, the EC expanded the organization's functions beyond economics. One major concern other than tariffs and customs was a unified approach to the peaceful use of atomic energy. However, the development of the EC was limited by disagreements as to how much power it should be given, with many nations concerned that their national sovereignty would be weakened. The urge toward integration was given a boost by the collapse of Soviet dominance in eastern Europe in the late 1980s. With new democracies emerging, their transitions from communism to capitalism demanded guidance from a supranational regional power.

- **The EU (European Union)** – The 1991 Maastricht Treaty created the modern organization, and gave it authority in new areas, including monetary policy, foreign affairs, national security, transportation, the environment, justice, and tourism. An important goal was to coordinate economic policies, particularly through a common currency (the euro) to replace the national currencies of the member-states, such as the French franc and the German mark; and a common European Central Bank, with enormous supranational authority to influence the economic policies of the member-states. The treaty established the three pillars, or spheres of authority:

- Trade and other economic matters, including economic and monetary union into a single currency, and the creation of the European Central Bank
- Justice and home affairs, including policy governing asylum, border crossing, immigration, and judicial cooperation on crime and terrorism
- Common foreign and security policy, including joint positions and actions, and common defense policy

Membership

Ongoing expansion is a major characteristic of the European Union, with a total membership of 28 countries as of 2015. The organization began with six members in 1957: Belgium, France, Germany, Italy, Luxembourg, and the Netherlands. Denmark, Great Britain, and Ireland joined in the early 1970s; Greece in 1981; Portugal and Spain in 1986; and Austria, Finland, and Sweden in 1995. Ten countries joined on May 2, 2004: Cyprus (Greek part), the Czech Republic, Estonia, Hungary, Latvia, Lithuania, Malta, Poland, Slovakia, and Slovenia. Bulgaria and Romania joined on January 1, 2007. Enthusiasm for further growth has waned in recent years, as questions of economic and political stability of newer members has threatened to break the union apart. Even so, Croatia was admitted for membership in June 2013.

EU 15

NEW
COUNTRIES
2004-13

The European Union. Ongoing expansion is a major characteristic of the European Union, with a total membership of 28 countries as of 2015.

Several countries are currently under consideration as candidates for membership, including Macedonia and Turkey. Turkey is controversial for many reasons, including its relatively low Gross Domestic Product per capita of about 12,000 euro, considerably less than the EU average. Turkey has been questioned because of its history of authoritarian governments. Turkey's candidacy also brings up the question of whether or not it is actually a European country since most of the country is technically in Asia. A deeper issue is the largely Muslim population of Turkey. If the EU is mainly an economic organization, then it shouldn't matter that Turkey's religious leanings are quite different from those of current members, whose populations are overwhelmingly Christian. However, if the EU fulfills its other pillars (justice and home affairs, and common foreign and security policy), some fear that religious differences could hinder the integration process.

Even though the political and economic muscle of so many countries united is considerable, rapid integration presents many difficult issues for the EU. First, organizational issues abound. Structures that work for six countries do not necessarily operate smoothly for 28. Second, the expansion brings in many former communist countries whose economies were relatively weak by the end of the 20th century. In addition, older member-states worry that immigrants from the east will flood their labor markets and strain their economies. EU supporters believe that these problems will be overshadowed by the benefits of common markets, currencies, political policies, and defense.

In order to be accepted for membership, candidate nations must provide evidence to meet three important criteria:

- a stable and functioning democratic regime
- a market-oriented economy
- willingness to accept all EU laws and regulations

The rapid growth of the EU has brought about what some have called **enlargement fatigue**. Polls show a decline in support for enlargement among EU voters, and many believe that the French and Dutch rejections of the European Constitution partly reflected dissatisfaction over the 2004 enlargement. Many EU governments have lost their enthusiasm for further growth, particularly France, Germany, and Austria. The economic benefits of the recent expansions are still questionable, and the concerns surrounding Turkey have cooled some support. Of course, there is a limited amount of growth potential remaining because only a few countries of the continent are non-members, including Norway, Russia, Switzerland, the Balkan states, Belarus, Moldova, and Ukraine.

Organization

The European Union is composed of four major bodies: The Commission, the Council of Ministers, the European Court of Justice, and the European Parliament.

- **The Commission** – This body currently has 28 members, one from each member state of the EU, supported by a bureaucracy of several thousand European civil servants. Each Commissioner takes responsibility for a particular area of policy, and heads a department called a Directorate General. The Commission is headed by a president. Although their home governments nominate them, commissioners swear an oath of allegiance to the EU and are not supposed to take directions from their national governments. The Commission's main responsibility is to initiate and implement new programs, and it forms a permanent executive that supervises the work of the EU, much in the way that a national cabinet operates.

- **The Council of Ministers** – Whereas the Commission acts cooperatively in directing EU activities, the Council demonstrates the continuing power of the states. The Council consists of foreign ministers, finance ministers, the president of France, and the prime ministers of all the other members. They hold frequent meetings – some for only one type of minister – and the heads of state meet every six months as the **European Council**. The Council is central to the EU's legislative process. Until 2009, the president of the Council rotated every six months, but the Lisbon Treaty made the position permanent and full-time, with a 2½ year term of office, renewable once. The first president appointed under these conditions was Herman Van Rompuy of Belgium, who was reappointed in 2012. The Commission may initiate legislation, but its proposals don't become law until they have been passed by the Council. Each country is assigned a number of votes in proportion to its share of population.

- **The European Parliament** – Contrary to the implications of its name, the European Parliament historically has not had a great deal of legislative power. However, since 1979, its members (MEPs) have been directly elected by the people of their respective countries, so they do have some independence from their national governments. Parliament may propose amendments to legislation, and it may reject proposals from the Council outright. However, the Council may override a rejection by a unanimous vote. Elections for representatives to the EP take place every five years. Apportionment of representatives is not strictly based on population, and smaller member-states have disproportionately greater representation than larger ones. The meetings of the EP are held in Strasbourg, although committees meet in Brussels. The Lisbon Treaty enhanced the power of the EP significantly, since new rules govern its relationship with the European Council.

- **The European Court of Justice** – The ECJ is the supreme court of the European Union, and it has the power of judicial review. It meets in Luxembourg, where it interprets European law, and its decisions may limit national sovereignty. For example, the ECJ ruled against Italy's policy of jailing illegal migrants who do not obey expulsion orders. In 2011, it decided that insurance companies in Britain were not allowed to charge women drivers (less of an accident risk) a lower premium than men. As such, the ECJ is more powerful than most national judicial systems of the EU's member-states. It has a broad jurisdiction, and hears cases that rule on disagreements among the Commissioners, the Council of Ministers, and the members of parliament. It also may settle disputes among member nations, private companies, and individuals. The ECJ consists of 28 judges, with each one nominated by a different member state. Cases are decided by a simple majority.

Policymaking Power

Although the European Union has made only rudimentary policy in many areas – such as defense and social policy – it clearly sets strong policies in other areas that previously were controlled by the individual countries. Three areas of active policymaking are:

- **Creating and maintaining a single internal market** – By and large, the EU has removed most of the old tariffs and other barriers to trade among its members. For example, trucking goods across national borders is much easier today than it was before the EU was created. Also, most professional licenses, such as those for doctors and beauticians, are accepted in all member states. The exception is that lawyers' licenses are only good in the country that issues them. So, policy differences still exist among the nations, but the single market has greatly affected both European governments and their citizens. More options are available to shoppers and consumers now that goods are freely transported across national borders.

- **Union of monetary policy** – The EU has made remarkable strides in its ability to set European **monetary policy**, or control of the money supply. Today the euro has replaced many of the old national currencies, which are mostly phased out. Also, the power to set basic interest rates and other fiscal policies is being passed from national banks and governments to the **European Monetary Union** and its new central bank. Today, in most of the member countries, the euro is accepted as a common currency both in banking and for everyday business transactions. Most of the newer members are in the process of changing their currencies to the euro, but two exceptions to the rule are Britain and Sweden, which still refuse to give up their national currencies in favor of a common European currency. The economic recession that began in late 2007 has been a challenge for the viability of the euro, but so far there has been no strong movement to abandon it. For most of the newer members, the recession has made

conversion to the euro even more important, since their national currencies are generally not as stable as the euro. The recession has also put
pressure on the economic coordination capabilities of the EU. Most of the
stimulus money generated in Europe after the worldwide monetary crisis
in September 2008, came from individual member-states. In November
2008 the European Commission set out proposals for a Europe-wide fiscal
stimulus, but it had no authority to compel member-states to contribute,
so it had to serve mainly a coordinating role. What followed was disagreement among member-states over how or whether to use the stimulus
money, illustrating the reluctance that governments have in ceding control
over their own revenues and expenditures.

- **Common agricultural policy** – Implementation of policy in this area has
  generally been less successful than others, but the EU has put in place significant new agricultural programs, with almost half of the organization's
  budget going to this policy. One goal has been to modernize inefficient
  farms so that they might compete in the common market. In order to meet
  this goal, the EU established **farm subsidies**, guarantees of selling goods
  at high prices. The subsidies have proved very expensive and have yet to
  improve farm efficiency in any measurable way. Recent reforms of the
  system have transferred subsidies away from price supports for specific
  crops and toward direct payments to farmers. A growing chunk of the
  money goes to rural-development projects, not farming as such.

By the late 1990s, the European Union began to lay the groundwork for future
policies in these areas:

- **Common defense** – European integration began with economic policy, so
  EU defense policy is much less well developed than those for trade and
  common currency. However, the Maastricht Treaty made foreign and defense policy one of the three "pillars" of the EU, so some defense policies
  have been put in place. In 1999, the European Council placed **crisis management** tasks at the core of the development of common security and defense of EU members. Crises were defined as humanitarian, rescue, and
  peacemaking tasks. The Council set as a goal that the EU should be able
  to deploy up to 60,000 troops within sixty days that could be sustained for
  at least one year. The agreement left troop commitment and deployment
  up to the member-states, and, as a result, did not create a European army.

- **Justice and Home Affairs** – The 1997 **Treaty of Amsterdam** set major
  policy initiatives for judicial affairs. The aim was to establish within a
  few years the **free movement** of European Union citizens and non-EU
  nationals throughout the Union. Free movement has involved setting
  policy regarding visas, asylum, and immigration. Additionally, the Treaty

of Amsterdam helped to define cooperation among national police forces and judicial authorities in combating crime. Although member nations may support an EU structure in areas of justice, freedom, and security, they are not compelled to participate. In these areas, Britain, Ireland, and Denmark restrict their participation to only a few select provisions.

- **Terrorism** – The EU has become very concerned about terrorism since the September 11, 2001 attacks on the World Trade Towers and the Pentagon in the United States. More recent bombings have rocked transportation systems in Spain (2004) and Britain (2005), reminding Europeans that terrorists have almost certainly taken advantage of the increasing ease of travel across country borders created by integration of nations. Beginning in April 2004, United States and European Union officials held a series of policy dialogues on border and transportation security that have focused on better addressing common security concerns and identifying areas where U.S.-EU cooperation and coordination might be enhanced.

The European Constitution and the Lisbon Treaty

On October 29, 2004, European heads of government signed a treaty establishing a **European Constitution**. The intention of the Constitution was to replace the overlapping sets of treaties that govern member-states' interactions, and to streamline decision-making as the organization has grown to its current 28 states. The Constitution was scheduled to go into effect on November 1, 2006. However, in mid-2005, French and Dutch voters rejected the treaty in separate referenda, prompting other countries, including Britain, to postpone their ratification procedures. In an effort to salvage the goals of the Constitution, the heads of state or government of the then 27 member-states signed the **Lisbon Treaty** in December 2007, a document that attempted to consolidate previous treaties that were still in force. Some important provisions of the treaty are:

- **A strengthening role for the European Parliament** – The treaty gives the Parliament new powers over EU legislation that place it on an equal footing with the European Council, gaining new rights in farm subsidy policies, border controls, asylum, and integration. Members of the European Parliament (MEPs) also have more say over the EU Budget, bowing to national government in only a handful of areas like tax and foreign policy.

- **A greater involvement of national parliaments** – National parliaments have more opportunities to be involved in the work of the EU, particularly through a new mechanism that ensures that the Union only acts where results can be better achieved at EU level. The aim is to enhance democracy and increase legitimacy in the functioning of the Union.

- **Clarification of the relationship between member-states and the EU** – The treaty created a system called "categorization of competences" that more clearly delineates the realms of responsibility of the EU in contrast to the initiatives best left up to the national governments.

- **Withdrawal from the Union** – For the first time, the possibility for a member-state to withdraw from the EU is recognized.

- **The creation of a permanent president of the EU** – Before the treaty was signed, the presidency of the European Council rotated every six months and it was usually filled by the top executive of one of the member-states, and so the position has a limited amount of power. The Lisbon Treaty made that position permanent and full-time, and provides for a 2 ½ year term of office, renewable once.

- **Introduction of a Charter of Fundamental Rights** – The Charter promotes individual civil, political, economic, and social rights for European citizens.

The negative reactions in France and the Netherlands to the European Constitution reflect a growing resistance to integration, especially as the European Union membership continues to grow. Many fear that the power shift from national to supranational institutions will result in a **democratic deficit**, or the loss of direct control of political decisions by the people. The European Parliament is the only directly elected body, and it is the weakest of the major EU bodies. The EU, then, is perceived by many as lacking accountability to citizens in member-states. The provisions of the Lisbon Treaty were meant to address these concerns, but it too was rejected by a popular referendum, this time in Ireland in June 2008. However, the treaty was eventually ratified by all the member-states, and it went into effect in December 2009.

The post-World War II visionaries that first conceived of a European Union saw not only an economically united Europe, but one with close political cooperation as well. So far, the European Union has shown little movement toward political integration, although the Maastricht Treaty of 1991 did include it within the "three pillars", or spheres of authority. More cooperation in foreign and national security policy is still on the EU's agenda, but economic integration remains the focus today.

Economic Issues

The European Union has long been defined by a tension between economic liberalism that favors open, free markets and an economic nationalism that seeks to protect national economic interests from the uncertainty of free markets. The older, more established EU members tend to reflect the latter policy orientation,

COMPARATIVE CAPITALISM:
THE EUROPEAN AND U.S. MODELS

Whereas capitalism is the accepted economic philosophy in the United States and Europe today, two competing models had developed by the late 20th century. The U.S. model, largely shared by Britain since Thatcherism took hold in the 1980s, places greater emphasis on free enterprise and the market, whereas continental western Europe has evolved a **social market economy** that is team-oriented and emphasizes cooperation between management and organized labor. The European model provides a stronger economic safety net – such as universal health care, day care for children, and generous pensions for government workers. Government-subsidized transportation systems are also characteristic of the social market economy.

The two systems are based on two different attitudes toward equality, with the U.S. culture emphasizing the individual's right to compete in the marketplace and accepting any inequality that results from that competition. Many Europeans tend to view unrestricted competition more as a threat than an opportunity, since it can lead to vast inequalities. One explanation for these different views is that Europeans are more accustomed to a strong government role in society, and Americans tend to distrust their government more. Another explanation is that Americans see more possibilities for upward mobility, with each individual believing that (s)he will someday be rich, too.

while the newer, less economically-stable members often favor economic liberalism. Supranationalism encourages economic integration but the proper balance with national interests is often a controversial topic. The sovereign debt crisis that began with the near-collapse of the Greek economy in 2010 illustrates this tough issue, and the arguments that have erupted since then strike at the heart of this old tension.

It was no surprise that the debt crisis began in Greece, which failed to join the euro area when it was set up in 1999 because it did not meet the economic or fiscal criteria for membership. Revisions to its budget figures showed that it probably shouldn't have been allowed in when it did join in 2001. After the international banking crisis of 2008, concern for "sovereign debts" (debts of individual EU countries) increased, especially for those with high debt-to-GNP ratios. Attention focused first on Greece, and in May 2010, the eurozone countries and International Monetary Fund agreed to a large loan to Greece, conditional on the implementation of harsh austerity measures. The Greek bailout was followed by a rescue package for Ireland in November and another for Portugal in May 2011. Despite several cash injections, the Greek economy remains fragile, with a shrinking GNP and unemployment rates almost 26% in late 2014.

These bailouts have been controversial, with some arguing that they are essential for keeping the economic health of the entire EU region, while others complain that it is unfair to expect taxpayers in healthier countries to pay for the economic woes of less stable members. The bailouts are particularly unpopular in Germany, where one poll in 2011 showed that a majority of the public thought that the rescue of Greece was a mistake. As talk of a second bailout for Greece materialized in mid-2011, there was strong resistance in Germany to further assistance to the Greek economy. At summit meetings in 2011, European political leaders discussed the possibility of "restructuring" the economies of Greece, Ireland, and Portugal. Economic structural adjustment would mean that at least part of the debt would be forgiven. Supporters of restructuring claim that it is the only way to allow the weakened countries to recover; critics believe that restructuring makes the stronger countries pay for the weaker ones, a process that they claim weakens the entire continent. The crisis calls into question the economic stability of the euro and the European banking system, and so the solutions that European leaders find will almost certainly influence the future development of the EU.

The sovereign debt crisis has impacted the economies of almost all European countries, not just those with the most fragile economies. The countries that adopted the euro were supposed to adhere to strict spending standards to prevent their debt from getting too big. They agreed to a debt target of 60% of their economic output. Some did, but others only could finance their deficit spending at relatively low interest rates as long as Europe's economy remained healthy. However, when the financial crisis erupted, the economies shrank and their debts ballooned. Investors began to lose faith in the ability of those countries to repay their debts. In 2012, according to estimates by the *New York Times,* not even the strongest economies in Europe met the target. Germany's ratio of gross government debt to gross domestic product is 79%, but other countries have much higher ratios, such as Greece, with a ratio of 153%.

ETHNIC TENSIONS IN MODERN EUROPE

Many of the ethnic tensions that exist in modern-day Europe have very deep historical roots. For example, conflicts between the Irish and the English have been going on for centuries. The many ethnic groups in eastern and central Europe that sparked the debate over self determination during the 20th century continue to shape political boundaries today. Other issues – such as the increasing number of non-European immigrants in many countries – are of more recent origin, but all form a countertrend to the integration encouraged by the European Union.

Irish-English Conflicts

English claims to Irish lands were settled shortly after World War I ended, when Ireland was granted home rule, with the exception of its northeast corner, where Protestants outnumbered Catholics by about 60% to 40%. Home rule came largely because of pressure from the Irish Republican Army (the IRA), which used guerilla warfare tactics to convince the British to allow Irish independence. Finally, in 1949, the bulk of Ireland became a totally independent country, and Northern Ireland has remained under British rule, but not without a great deal of conflict between Protestants and Catholics. The issues surrounding British claims to Northern Ireland intensified during the early 1970s after British troops killed thirteen Catholics in a "bloody Sunday" incident in January 1972. The IRA and Protestant paramilitaries stepped up their campaigns of violence. British Prime Minister

ORIGINAL DOCUMENT: THE GOOD FRIDAY AGREEMENT

Also called the Belfast Agreement, the Good Friday Agreement was signed in Belfast on April 10, 1998 (Good Friday) by the British and Irish governments and endorsed by most Northern Ireland political parties. The goals of the agreement are excerpted below:

"...We are committed to partnership, equality and mutual respect on the basis of relationships within Northern Ireland, between North and South, and between these islands.

...We reaffirm our total and absolute commitment to exclusively democratic and peaceful means of resolving differences on political issues, and our opposition to any use or threat of force by others for any political purpose, whether in regard to this agreement or otherwise.

...We acknowledge the substantial differences between our continuing, and equally legitimate, political aspirations. However, we will endeavor to strive in every practical way towards reconciliation and rapprochement within the framework of democratic and agreed arrangements. We pledge that we will, in good faith, work to ensure the success of each and every one of the arrangements to be established under this agreement."

Tony Blair, who headed the government between 1997 and 2007, made it a priority to work out a political settlement that both sides could accept. In the 1998 **Good Friday Agreement**, Britain agreed to devolve some power to a parliament that was set up for Northern Ireland, although London shut down its activities after violence broke out in 2002. The Northern Ireland Assembly remained suspended for almost five years, not reopening until May 2007. Although in recent years the groups have consented to negotiate with the government, the threat of violent eruptions remains strong today.

The Break-up of Yugoslavia

After the downfall of communist regimes in eastern Europe in 1989, ethnic nationalism again came to the forefront as a major political and social issue after years of suppression. Czechoslovakia divided peacefully in 1993 into the Czech Republic and Slovakia in response to Slovak pressures. However, in Yugoslavia – the large, ethnically-diverse federation that had been created at Versailles in 1919 – national and religious tensions tore the state apart violently. Under Tito, Yugoslavia broke with the Soviet Union, but remained communist. Tito himself was a Croat who suppressed all separatist movements with an iron hand, but he allowed each of the ethnically-based republics a degree of autonomy. As long as Tito lived, Yugoslavia retained its national unity, but after his death in 1980, separatist movements reemerged. When in 1989 communism lost control of most of eastern Europe, Yugoslavia collapsed. Only Serbia and Montenegro voted to maintain the federal republic. All others – Croatia, Slovenia, Macedonia, and Bosnia – voted for parties committed to independence.

Tensions erupted in 1990, when a Serb Communist, **Slobodan Milosevic**, became president of Serbia and asserted Serbian nationalism by rallying Serbs in Bosnia, Croatia, and Slovenia to fight to remain under Serb control whenever their states seceded. In reaction, Croatia and Slovenia each held a referendum and in 1991 proclaimed independence, hoping for a confederation of independent republics. Instead, the Serb-dominated Yugoslav army invaded Croatia and took almost a quarter of its territory. In Bosnia-Herzegovina, where a Muslim majority tried to create a multiethnic state, Bosnian Serbs formed a guerrilla army backed by the covert military support of Milosevic's government. Civil war broke out by mid-1991, and Serb paramilitary forces, reinforced by army units from Belgrade, carved out enclaves in the secessionist states in an effort to drive out non-Serbs. The war raged on for a decade, and tens of thousands died as Serbs under Milosevic's leadership pursued a policy called **ethnic cleansing**, in which they attempted to wipe out all other nationalities through genocide. Croatian forces also murdered people of other ethnicities, and military forces on all sides destroyed anything that represented the cultural heritage of its opponents, including libraries, museums, and bridges.

The Former Yugoslavia, 2000. By 2000, Yugoslavia had broken into ethnically-based republics as a result of a decade of civil war. In 2003, Serbia and Montenegro created a new federation, but Montenegro declared its independence in 2006.

None of the international organizations of the day – the United Nations, NATO, or the newly created European Union – was able to stop the bloodshed. Even though a cease-fire was mediated in 1994 and agreements were reached, the fighting went on. In 1995, the Croatian army repulsed the Serb military and recovered most of the territory it had lost to the Serbs four years earlier. In 1996, the United States mediated an agreement on new boundaries, with UN peacekeepers supervising the settlement in Bosnia. However, fighting resumed when Serb forces attacked Muslims of Albanian ethnicity living in the Yugoslav province of Kosovo. From 1997 to 1999, thousands of Albanian Kosovars were slaughtered, and many more fled their homes. Finally, the international community acted assertively by sending NATO pilots to bomb the region and by enforcing an interethnic truce with UN peacekeeping forces. A new regime emerged in Serbia, and Milosevic was turned over to the **World Court** (International Court of Justice) in the Netherlands to be tried for crimes against humanity. In 2006, however, Milosevic died while in prison. Serbia and Montenegro created a new federation in 2003, and the name,

Yugoslavia, was no longer used. Tensions continued in Kosovo, which remained under UN administration.

Ethnicity Issues in Russia

The most important single societal cleavage in the Russian Federation today is nationality. Although about 80% are Russians, the country includes sizeable numbers of Tatars, Ukrainians, Armenians, Chuvashes, Bashkis, Byelorussians, and Moldavians. These cleavages determine the organization of the country into a "federation," with "autonomous regions," republics, and provinces whose borders are based on ethnicity. Like the breakaway republics of 1991, many would like to have their independence, although most receive trade benefits from the Russian government that induce them to stay within the Federation. A notable exception is **Chechnya**, a primarily Muslim region that fought for years for freedom. In the 1990s, the Russian government had considerable difficulty keeping Chechnya a part of Russia, and the independence movement there is still very strong. A few years ago, Chechens were involved in terrorist acts, including the 2004 seizure of a school in southern Russia that resulted in gunfire and explosions that killed more than 350 people, many of them children. Almost certainly, other regions within Russia's borders have been watching, and the government knows that if Chechnya or any other part of the federation is successful, other independence movements may break out in the country. In an effort to gain legitimacy for the Russian government in Chechnya, a referendum was held to vote on a new constitution for the region. The constitution was approved by the Chechen voters, even though it declared that their region was an "inseparable part" of Russia.

Crisis in Ukraine

The breakup of the Soviet Union in 1991 into fifteen separate countries resulted in sovereignty issues, especially in regard to Russia's ongoing dominance of the region. The relationship between Russia and Ukraine has been particularly problematic, with conflicts erupting – often along ethnic lines – between Ukrainians who favor stronger ties to the West and those with allegiances to Russia. During the 2004 presidential election campaign in Ukraine, challenger Viktor Yushchenko accused Russian President Putin of providing financing and political advisors for Prime Minister Viktor Yanukovich's campaign for the presidency. Putin himself went to Ukraine twice to campaign for Yanukovich. Popular protests broke out after Yanukovich won, with claims that the election was fraudulent. The elections were held again, and Yushchenko's victory in this round increased ethnic tensions within Ukraine.

Yanukovich eventually was elected president in 2010, but Ukraine's internal and external tensions eventually led to his ouster in 2014. In late 2013, Yanukovych rejected an agreement with the European Union that would bolster integration and trade between the EU and Ukraine. Instead, he agreed to take a $15 billion loan from Russia that would move the country toward a "Eurasian Union" with Belarus, Kazakhstan, and Russia. The decision sparked protests in Kiev by EU supporters, and clashes grew so violent, that Yanukovych fled to Russia, and a coalition government formed that supported EU agreements. This turn of events led to opposition in Crimea, a region of Ukraine with a large number of ethnic Russians. Armed men, presumably Russian soliders, in unmarked uniforms and masks seized airports and regional government buildings, and a new government of pro-Russian leaders decided to hold a referendum on Crimea's future in March 2014. The Russian parliament authorized deploying troops in Ukraine, and 97% of the voters in the extremely controversial referendum supported joining Russia. Putin signed a treaty formally annexing Crimea, and the U.S. and the E.U. ordered sanctions imposed on Russia. Fighting between government forces and pro-Russian separatists has continued despite domestic and international efforts to de-escalate the crisis.

Non-European Immigration Issues

Increased numbers of immigrants from eastern Europe, Turkey, the Middle East, and Africa have fed anti-foreign feelings in many countries, including Italy, Germany, Britain, and France. In Italy, a new party, the Northern League, gained political support – particularly in the prosperous north – by its opposition to immigration. In Germany, immigrants from struggling eastern European countries inspired incidents in which gangs of **neo-Nazis**, who reiterated Adolf Hitler's racist doctrines, burned immigrant housing, and demonstrated against foreigners. Since reunification in 1990, dozens of foreigners – almost all of them Turks, Africans, or Asians – have been killed by neo-Nazis in fire bombings, beatings, or stabbings. These movements have been denounced by many figures of authority throughout Europe. When the anti-immigrant Freedom Party gained a share in the ruling coalition in Austria in 2000, the other EU nations refused to formally cooperate with the Austrian government.

In France, the division between natives and immigrants from northern and equatorial Africa is a major source of discord within the society and the political system. After Algeria received independence from the French in the 1950s, many Algerians associated with the colonial system immigrated to France to escape the new Algerian government's wrath. Today, there are some 9 million foreigners living in France, about 16% of the entire population. Between 4 and 5 million are Muslims from northern and equatorial Africa, and this group's arrival in France has caused racial tensions. Many have not assimilated into French society, partly because of prejudice toward them, and partly because they don't want to abandon their customs. For example, some French people have been horrified by the polygamous practices of some Muslim families. Many French schools have required students to wear uniforms, and some Muslim girls have refused to abandon their head coverings as signs of their religion. The result has been the creation of immigrant

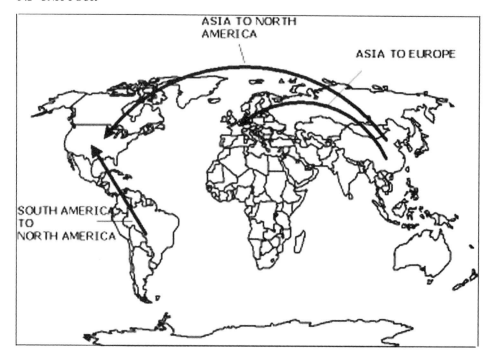

Major Global Migrations. The non-European immigration issues in modern Europe are part of a worldwide pattern. The largest flows of people in the modern world are from Asia to North America, Asia to Europe, and South America to North America. In many cases people are leaving areas where jobs are less plentiful and lower paying, and migrating to areas where the job market is more promising.

ghettoes with high crime rates and accusations that the police harass Muslim men. Politically, the National Front – a political party on the far right – has focused on a policy of deporting Muslims, and not integrating them into French society.

In January 2015, tensions in France erupted after two masked gunmen attacked the office of Charlie Hebdo, a newspaper that published satirical cartoons of the Prophet Muhammad, thus offending many Muslims. Twelve people were killed in the attack, including the newspaper's top editor, prominent cartoonists, and police officers. After an enormous manhunt across the Paris region, the gunmen were captured and killed, as was a third gunman who took hostages at a kosher supermarket in Paris the day after the attacks on the newspaper occurred. The twin incidents highlighted not only ethnic tensions in France but also questions of freedom of the press internationally.

Although far right parties have had less success in Britain, anti-immigrant feelings have concerned the government, especially after two minority men were arrested in connection with attacks on Glasgow Airport in 2007. According to a 2010 esti-mate, only about 7.7% of the British population was of non-EU origin, with most coming from countries that were formerly British colonies However, the minority ethnic population has grown from 3 million in 1991 to 7.5 million in 2011. The main groups were Indian, Pakistani, Afro-Caribbean, and Black African. Because of tight immigration restrictions in the past, most ethnic minorities in Britain today are young, with about half of the population under the age of 25. The growth in percentages of minorities has grown despite the restrictions that were placed on further immigration during the Thatcher administration of the 1980s. Immigration restrictions are currently under debate, but the government has allowed the restrictions to remain in place.

Britain has often been accused of adjusting poorly to their new ethnic population. Reports abound of unequal treatment by the police and physical and verbal harassment by citizens. The May 2001 race riots in several cities increased tensions, and new fears of strife have been stoked by post 9/11 world politics. Today there is some evidence that whites are leaving London to settle in surrounding suburban

PERSPECTIVES:
THE "AUSTRIA FIRST" PLATFORM
OF THE FREEDOM PARTY

One of the most successful right-wing political leaders in Europe is Jörg Haider of the Freedom Party, whose anti-immigrant stance caused the EU to impose sanctions on Austria for one year in 1999. Haider stepped down as party leader in order to improve the Freedom Party's international reputation. The party's controversial philosophy is reflected in the 12 points of Haider's "Austria first" initiative:

1. A constitutional provision: "Austria is no country of immigration"
2. An end to immigration until accommodation and unemployment issues are solved
3. An ID requirement for foreign employees at the work place
4. An expanded police-force to trace illegal foreigners and combat crime
5. The creation of permanent border controls
6. Limitation of foreign school children to a maximum of 30%
7. Regular education only for those with adequate knowledge of German
8. No right to vote for foreigners in general elections
9. No premature granting of Austrian citizenship
10. Rigorous measures against illegal business activities of foreigners and the abuse of social benefits.
11. Immediate deportation and residence ban for foreign offenders of the law
12. The establishment of an Eastern Europe Foundation to prevent migration

Reference: "Multiculturalism and Love of One's Country" by Jörg Haider in *The Free I Mean* (Pine Plains, NY: Swan Books), 1995.

areas, resulting in a higher percentage of minority population living in London. Despite this segregation, the mixed race population appears to be increasing, with the census of 2001 offering for the first time in British history a category for mixed race people.

Europe in the early 21st century faces many challenges. Economically, the continent has experienced a significant recovery since World War II, and the European Union has expanded to include most countries on the continent. However, significant economic, political, and social differences still exist between east and west, north and south. Despite the newfound supranationalism, diverse cultural groups still inhabit Europe, as they always have, and ethnic tensions abound. Does the European Union represent the larger trend toward globalization in the world? Or is it a better example of fragmentation and regionalism? Perhaps the EU is forging the way toward global connections, particularly in terms of trade and economic cooperation. On the other hand, it may be forming a bloc that invites other parts of the world to create blocs of their own, setting the stage for fragmentation and conflict among cultural areas. Only time will tell.

CONCEPTS AND IDENTIFICATIONS

Al-Qaeda
bin Laden, Osama
Ceaușescu, Nicolae
Chechnya
The Commission
Commonwealth of Independent States
containment
Council of Ministers
deStalinization
détente
Dubcek, Alexander
enlargement fatigue
ethnic cleansing
European Council
European Court of Justice
European Monetary Union
European Parliament
fragmentation
glasnost
globalization
Good Friday Agreement
Gorbachev, Mikhail
Havel, Vaclav
Hussein, Sadam

integration
Khrushchev, Nikita
Maastricht Treaty
Milosevic, Slobodan
monetary policy
NATO
neo-Nazis
perestroika
preemption
social market economy
Solidarity
supranationalism, supranational organizations
three pillars
"velvet revolution"
Walesa, Lech
Warsaw Pact
weapons of mass destruction
World Bank
World Trade Organization
Yeltsin, Boris

UNIT FOUR QUESTIONS

Multiple-Choice Questions:

(Questions 1-3 are based on the following excerpt):

"His Majesty's Government view with favor the establishment in Palestine of a national home for the Jewish people and will use their best endeavors to facilitate the achievement of that object, it being clearly understood that nothing shall be done which may prejudice the civil and religious rights of existing non-Jewish communities in Palestine."

1. The Balfour Declaration quoted above was a statement that was inspired primarily by Britain's need to

   (A) contain instability caused by Zionist protests
   (B) win World War I
   (C) combat Arab unrest in the Middle East
   (D) undermine the political influence of Austria-Hungary

2. Which of the following would have been most likely to support the sentiments of the declaration?

   (A) the Ottoman ruler
   (B) Mustafa Kemal (Ataturk)
   (C) Konrad Adenauer
   (D) Zionists

3. The Balfour Declaration contributed directly to later conflict between

   (A) British prime ministers and French presidents
   (B) Jewish nationalists and German leaders
   (C) Palestinian and Jewish settlers
   (D) leaders of the Allied Powers and leaders of the Central Powers

(Questions 4 and 5 are based on the following quote):

"For us, however, whom a Destiny has placed in this Culture and at this moment of its development – the moment when money is celebrating its last victories, and the Caesarism that is to succeed approaches with quiet, firm step – our direction, willed and obligatory at once, is set for us within narrow limits, and on any other terms life is not worth the living. We have not the freedom to reach to this or to that, but the freedom to do the necessary or to do nothing. And a task that historic necessity has set will be accomplished with the individual or against him.

'Ducunt Fata volentem, nolentem trabun' [The Fates guide the willing and drag the unwilling]."

> Oswald Spengler,
> widely-read author of the 1920s
> *The Decline of the West*

4. The sentiments in the quote support Spengler's argument that

(A) World War I was the beginning of the end of western civilization
(B) the decline of the West was not inevitable
(C) the decline of the West would inevitably mean that China would come to dominate the world
(D) the United States would eventually replace Britain and France as the most important world power

5. Spengler based his arguments on a comparison of

(A) the life cycles of civilizations and biological organisms
(B) European nations and older civilizations in Asia
(C) ancient Rome and ancient Greece
(D) art and politics

(Questions 6-8 are based on the following excerpt):

> "We did not have an iron and steel industry, the foundation for the indus
> trialization of the country. Now we have this industry.
> We did not have a tractor industry. Now we have one.
> We did not have an automobile industry. Now we have one.
> We did not have a machine-tool industry. Now we have one.
> We did not have a big and up-to-date chemical industry. Now we have
> one...
> We did not have an aircraft industry. Now we have one...
> In the output of oil products and coal we were last on the list. Now we
> rank among the first..."
>
> > > Joseph Stalin
> > > Report to the Central
> > > Committee
> > > 1933

6. In the excerpt, Stalin is reporting the success of

   (A) the New Economic Policy (NEP)
   (B) his first Five Year Plan
   (C) his collectivization policies
   (D) international Marxism

7. Stalin's philosophy that shaped the program identified in #6 as well as his foreign policy until 1940 was

   (A) Marxism-Leninism
   (B) fascism
   (C) "socialism in one country"
   (D) self determination

8. Partly as a result of Stalin's philosophy, the U.S.S.R. was not seriously affected by

   (A) the worldwide depression
   (B) internal power struggles
   (C) Adolph Hitler's territorial expansions
   (D) World War II

(Questions 9-11 are based on the following map):

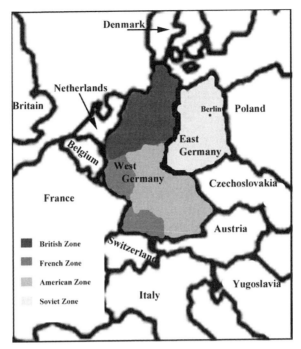

9. Germany, as illustrated on the map above became a major focus of conflict during the early years   of

   (A) World War I
   (B) World War II
   (C) the Cold War
   (D) the war on terrorism

10. Which of the following statements best compares West Germany and East Germany within 20 years after the creation of the divisions illustrated in the map?

   (A) Travel between east and west became much less difficult.
   (B) West Germany became much more prosperous and populous than East Germany.
   (C) Disputes among Britain, France, and the U.S. broke out in West Germany, but East Germany remained much more politically and economically stable.
   (D) West Germany and East Germany had nearly equal populations, and their gross national products were very similar.

11. The eventual reunification of West and East Germany most directly contributed to the

    (A) break-up of the Soviet Union
    (B) formation of the United Nations
    (C) intensification of Cold War hostilities
    (D) formation of the European Union

(Questions 12-14 are based on the following excerpt):

"...We are committed to partnership, equality and mutual respect on the basis of relationships within Northern Ireland, between North and South, and between these islands.

...We reaffirm our total and absolute commitment to exclusively democratic and peaceful means of resolving differences on political issues, and our opposition to any use or threat of force by others for any political purpose, whether in regard to this agreement or otherwise.

...We acknowledge the substantial differences between our continuing, and equally legitimate, political aspirations. However, we will endeavor to strive in every practical way towards reconciliation and rapprochement within the framework of democratic and agreed arrangements. We pledge that we will,

 in good faith, work to ensure the success of each and every one of the arrangements to be established under this agreement."

Good Friday Agreement
April 10, 1998

12. In the Good Friday Agreement, excerpted above, Britain agreed to

    (A) grant Ireland home rule
    (B) allow Ireland to become a totally independent country
    (C) dissolve the Irish Republican Army
    (D) devolve some power to a parliament for Northern Ireland

13. The dispute between Ireland and Britain that led to the agreement was based largely on

    (A) Irish attempts to gain land in Wales and western England
    (B) longstanding English claims to Irish lands
    (C) conflicts between authoritarian and democratic governments
    (D) the migration of large numbers of Irish to English lands

14. Which of the following is the most important factor that promoted twentieth-century tensions between Ireland and Britain?

(A) differences based on religion
(B) socialism vs. capitalism
(C) immigration issues
(D) control of smaller islands offshore from Ireland

Short-answer question (12 minutes):

The map above shows Europe after the Versailles peace settlements of 1919-1920.

Using the map and your knowledge of European history, answer both parts (A and B) of the question below.

(A) Describe TWO changes in the map that were drawn up at Versailles.

(B) Briefly explain ONE reason for one of the changes that you identified in (A).

Free-Response Document-Based Question (Suggested reading time – 15 minutes; suggested writing time – 40 minutes)

Write an essay that:

- **Provides an appropriate, explicitly stated thesis that directly addresses all parts of the question.**
- **Supports the thesis with evidence from all or all but one of the documents and your outside knowledge of European history**
- **Analyzes a majority of the documents in terms of intended audience, point of view, purpose, argument strength, and/or social context**
- **Places the argument in broader regional, national, or global contexts.**

Analyze the forces that both promoted and hindered the growth of internationalism in Europe during the 20th century.

Document 1

War and peace, with their strong contrast, alternate against a common background. For the catastrophe of 1914 the Germans are responsible. Only a professional liar would deny this....

I have sometimes penetrated into the sacred cave of the Germanic cult, which is, as every one knows, the *Bierhaus* [beer hall]. A great aisle of massive humanity were there accumulate...the popular rumblings of a nationalism upheld by the sonorous basses blaring to the heavens the supreme voice of Germany, *Deutschland über alles! Germany above everything!* Men, women, and children...brows furrowed with irrepressible power...mouths twisted by the intensity of willpower...There you have the ultimate framework of an old but childish race.

> George Clemenceau
> Prime Minister of France, 1917

Document 2

The authorized representatives of the Serbs, Croats, and Slovenes, in declaring that it is the desire of our people to free itself from every foreign yoke and to constitute itself a free, national, and independent State, a desire based on the principle that every nation has the right to decide upon its own destiny, are agree in judging that this state should be founded on the following modern and democratic principles...

> The Corfu Pact that created
> Yugoslavia, 1917

Document 3

It shall be the aim of the Community, by establishing a Common Market and progressively approximating the economic policies of Member States, to promote throughout the Community a harmonious development of economic activities, a continuous and balanced expansion, an increased stability, an accelerated raising of the standard of living and closer relations between its Member States.

> Article II of the Treaty of Rome
> Establishing the Common
> Market
> 1957

Document 4

To try to suppress nationhood and concentrate power at the center of a European union would be highly damaging and would jeopardize the objectives we seek to achieve. Europe will be stronger precisely because it has France as France, Spain as Spain, Britain as Britain, each with its own customs, traditions, and identity. It would be folly to try to fit them into some sort of standardized European personality. Certainly we want to see Europe more united and with a greater sense of common purpose, but it must be in a way which preserves the different traditions, parliamentary powers, and sense of pride in one's own country.

> Margaret Thatcher,
> British Prime Minister
> September 1988

Document 5

[A testing ground] consists in how we deal with the temptation to open the back gate to the demons of nationalist collectivism with an apparently innocent emphasis on minority rights and on the right of minorities to self determination. At first sight, this emphasis would seem harmless and beyond reproach. But one real consequence could be new unrest and tension, because demands for self determination inevitably lead to questioning the integrity of the individual states and the inviolability of their present borders, and even the validity of all postwar treaties.

> Vaclav Havel,
> President of the Czech Republic
> 1993

Document 6

1. A constitutional provision: "Austria is no country of immigration"
2. An end to immigration until accommodation and unemployment issues are solved
3. An ID requirement for foreign employees at the work place
4. An expanded police-force to trace illegal foreigners and combat crime
5. The creation of permanent border controls
6. Limitation of foreign school children to a maximum of 30%
7. Regular education only for those with adequate knowledge of German
8. No right to vote for foreigners in general elections
9. No premature granting of Austrian citizenship
10. Rigorous measures against illegal business activities of foreigners and the abuse of social benefits.
11. Immediate deportation and residence ban for foreign offenders of the law
12. The establishment of an Eastern Europe Foundation to prevent migration

12 Points of Jóng Hader's
"Austria first" Program, 1995

Document 7

Guided by treaties that scarcely anybody can understand, towards a destination on which nobody can agree, the European Union has survived, and often thrived, for almost half a century. The need for a lasting peace in western Europe gave it early momentum. It offered devastated countries the vision of a supranational order intrinsically more peaceful than the nationalism which had fed Hitler's war. The attractions of this order diminished for nation-states as the memories of war receded. But the collapse of the Soviet empire, and the opportunity to restore and rebuild the eastern half of Europe, gave the EU a new leading role. It offered a vision of freedom and prosperity for which countries hungered after decades under communist rule. This enlargement is the happy outcome of that offer.

The Economist Magazine
2003, on the eve of a major
enlargement of the European
Union

Document 8

Percent favorable of EU

	2012	2013	2014	'13-'14 Change	
UK	45%	43%	52%	+9	
Poland	69	68	72	+4	
Germany	68	60	66	+6	
France	60	41	54	+13	
Greece	37	33	34	+1	
Spain	60	46	50	+4	
Italy	59	58	46	-12	
Median	**60**	**46**	**52**		

Source: Spring 2014 Global Attitudes survey. Q15f.

PEW RESEARCH CENTER

Long-Essay Question (35 minutes):

Analyze whether or not World War I can be seen as a turning point in European political and social history.

PRACTICE EXAM

Multiple-Choice Questions (55 minutes)

(Questions 1 and 2 refer to the following quote):

> "We are taught by the words of the Gospel that in this church and in power there are two swords, a spiritual one and a temporal one...Certainly anyone who denies that the temporal sword is in the power of Peter [the disciple of Jesus] has not paid heed to the words of the Lord when he said, 'Put up thy sword into its sheath' (Matthew 26:52)."

1. The quote above from *Unam Sanctam* in 1302 supports the belief that

(A) separation of church and state is necessary
(B) religious power is greater than the power of kings
(C) the king's power is greater than that of the pope
(D) religious leaders should take no interest in political power

2. The document quoted above created tensions that directly led to the

(A) Great Schism
(B) discontinuance of the sale of indulgences
(C) establishment of the Anglican Church
(D) Catholic Reformation

(Questions 3-5 are based on the following map):

Italy in 1494

3. The Republic of Florence and the Republic of Venice illustrated on the map
   above had governments best described as

   (A) democracies
   (B) oligarchies
   (C) absolute monarchies
   (D) limited monarchies

4. In the late 15th century, in contrast to cities in Italy, cities in northern Europe
   were usually

   (A) more independent
   (B) richer
   (C) subject to the rule of kings or princes
   (D) more competitive with nearby cities

5. Which of the following historical movements most directly supported the eventual unification of the Italian peninsula during the 19th century?

(A) the trend toward internationalism
(B) the development of mass politics
(C) the growing influence of nationalism
(D) the growing influence of romanticism

(Questions 6-8 refer to the following excerpt):

They [the Spanish] forced their way into native settlements, slaughtering everyone they found there, including small children, old men, pregnant women, and even women who had just given birth. They hacked them to pieces, slicing open their bellies with their swords as though they were so many sheep herded into a pen. They even laid wagers on whether they could manage to slice a man in two at a stroke, or cut an individual's head from his body, or disembowel him with a single blow of their axes...They spared no one, erecting especially wide gibbets [gallows] on which they could string their victims up with their feet just off the ground and then burn them alive thirteen at a time, in honor of our Savior and the twelve Apostles...

6. The quote above from Bartholomé de Las Casas describes the Spanish treatment of

(A) Amerindians
(B) African slaves in the New World
(C) Africans along the Slave Coast
(D) Aboriginal Australians

7. De Las Casas belonged to a religious order formed as part of a movement known as the

(A) Protestant Reformation
(B) Catholic Reformation
(C) Great Awakening
(D) Inquisition

8. In which area of the world did De Las Casas's religion become dominant by the end of the 16th century?

(A) North America
(B) Africa
(C) Middle and South America
(D) China

(Questions 9-11 refer to the following quote):

"Among other vices I cruelly hate cruelty, both by nature and by judgment, as the extreme of all vices…I live in a time when we abound in incredible examples of this vice, through the license of our civil wars; and we see in the ancient histories nothing more extreme than what we experiece of this every day. But that has not reconciled me to it at all."

Michel de Montaigne,
"On Cruelty",
mid-16th century

9. Montaigne's comments were shaped by his reactions to French civil wars between

(A) nobles and peasants
(B) farmers and urban workers
(C) Catholics and Protestants
(D) the king and the nobility

10. "On Cruelty" is an example of Montaigne's development of a new literary genre,

(A) the novel
(B) the essay
(C) historical fiction
(D) the epic poem

11. Montaigne's philosophy anticipated those of many 18th-century thinkers who emphasized

    (A) secularism and skepticism
    (B) faith and religious certainty
    (C) emotion and passion
    (D) disillusionment and pessimism

(Questions 12-14 refer to the following quote):

> "There are four classes of Idols which beset men's minds...the Idols of the Tribe...The Idols of the Cave...Idols of the Market Place...Idols of the Theater..."

12. The quote above from Francis Bacon's *New Organon* was written to replace the *Organon* written by

    (A) Thomas Aquinas
    (B) Erasmus
    (C) Nasir al-Din
    (D) Aristotle

13. Bacon identified the four classes of Idols as

    (A) sinful habits that must be overcome
    (B) distractions that discourage serious study
    (C) false notions that hamper human understanding
    (D) principles that guide scientific investigation

14. Bacon's new worldview, reflected in the excerpt, encouraged seeking knowledge through

    (A) deductive reasoning
    (B) sensory reactions
    (C) empirical calculations
    (D) inductive reasoning

(Questions 15-17 refer to the following quote):

> Political liberty is to be found only in moderate governments; and even in
> these it is not always found. It is there only when there is no abuse of pow-
> er. But constant experience shows us that every man invested with power
> is apt to abuse it, and to carry his authority as far as it will go...When the
> legislative and executive powers are united in the same person, or in the
> same body of magistrates, there can be no liberty: because apprehensions
> may arise, lest the same monarch or senate should enact tyrannical laws,
> to execute them in a tyrannical manner.
>
> Baron de Montesquieu
> *The Spirit of Laws,* 1748

15. In the quote above, Montesquieu argued in support of which of the following types of government?

    (A) an absolute monarchy
    (B) a republic
    (C) a direct democracy
    (D) a limited monarchy

16. Montesquieu's point of view was most directly influenced by his admiration for the government of

    (A) Britain
    (B) France
    (C) the United States
    (D) Austria

17. Montesquieu's point of view reflected growing support in 18ᵗʰ-century western Europe that participation in government should be

    (A) limited to monarchs and nobles
    (B) expanded to the bourgeoisie
    (C) opened to all citizens
    (D) guided by religious and political leaders

(Questions 18-20 refer to the following two quotes):

In 1789, reacting to an international event, English poet William Wordsworth wrote,

> "Bliss was it in that dawn to be alive,
> But to be young was very heaven!"

A few years later, Wordsworth's view of the event changed. He wrote:

> "Friends, enemies, of all parties, ages, ranks,
> Head after head, and never heads enough
> For those that bade them fall."

18. The excerpt from Wordsworth's poetry reflects his changing attitudes toward the

(A) American Revolution
(B) rise of Napoleon
(C) Glorious Revolution
(D) French Revolution

19. Which of the following was directly responsible for Wordsworth's changing attitudes?

(A) the storming of the Bastille
(B) the battle of Waterloo
(C) the Reign of Terror
(D) the beheading of the English king

20. Which of the following would have been least likely to agree with Wordsworth's view expressed in the second excerpt?

(A) Louis XVI
(B) Maximilien Robespierre
(C) William of Orange
(D) Edmund Burke

(Questions 21-24 refer to the following quote):

"[In pin-making] one man draws out the wire, another straightens it, a third cuts it, a fourth points it, a fifth grinds it at the top for receiving the head; to make the head requires two or three distinct operations; to put it on is a peculiar business, to whiten the pins is another; it is even a trade by itself to put them into the paper; and the important business of making a pin is, in this manner, divided into about eighteen distinct operations... ten persons, therefore, could make among them upwards of forty-eight thousand pins in a day. Each person, therefore, making a tenth part of forty-eight thousand pins might be considered as making four thousand eight hundred pins in a day...But if they had wrought separately and independently, and without any of them having been educated to this peculiar business, they certainly could not each of them have made twenty, perhaps not one pin in a day..."

> Adam Smith
> *The Wealth of Nations*
> 1776

21. In the excerpt above, Adam Smith explained the advantages of

  (A) industrialization
  (B) the putting-out system
  (C) social class distinctions
  (D) division of labor

22. From Smith's point of view, the process described in the excerpt supports the virtues of

  (A) a free-market economy
  (B) mercantilism
  (C) economic control exercised by the government
  (D) higher wages for working-class men

23. One consequence of industries adopting the process described in the excerpt was a devaluing of

(A) individual craftsmanship
(B) international trade
(C) factory-based work
(D) urban development

24. Another famous economic principle explained by Adam Smith was

(A) *tabula rasa*
(B) the invisible hand
(C) the social contract
(D) the general will

(Questions 25-27 refer to the following quote):

A well conducted government must have an underlying concept so well integrated that it could be likened to a system of philosophy. All actions taken must be well reasoned, and all financial, political and military matters must flow towards one goal: which is the strengthening of the state and the furthering of its power. However, such a system can flow but from a single brain, and this must be that of the sovereign. Laziness, hedonism and imbecility, these are the causes which restrain princes in working at the noble task of bringing happiness to their subjects...a sovereign is not elevated to his high position, supreme power has not been confined to him in order that he may live in lazy luxury, enriching himself by the labor of the people, being happy while everyone else suffers. The sovereign is the first servant of the state. He is well paid in order that he may sustain the dignity of his office, but one demands that he work efficiently for the good of the state, and that he, at the very least, pay personal attention to the most important problems....

> Frederick the Great of Prussia
> *Political Testament*
> 1768

25. In the excerpt above, Frederick the Great argued the advantages of a government ruled by

(A) both a chief executive and a legislature
(B) a single monarch
(C) a military leader
(D) an oligarchy

26. By arguing that "all actions taken must be well reasoned," Frederick's description of a well conducted government reflects the influence of

(A) the divine right of kings
(B) nationalism
(C) the Enlightenment
(D) the principle of the balance of power

27. Which of the following political leaders most likely would have agreed with Frederick's statement?

(A) Napoleon Bonaparte
(B) Robert Walpole
(C) Nicholas I
(D) Catherine the Great

(Questions 28-30 refer to the following quote):

The Governments, having lost their balance, are frightened, intimidated, and thrown into confusion by the cries of the intermediary class of society, which, placed between the Kings and their subjects, breaks the scepter of the monarch, and usurps the cry of the people – the class so often disowned by the people...We see this intermediary class...applying itself to the task of persuading Kings that their rights are confined to sitting upon a throne, while those of the people are to govern, and to attack all that centuries have bequeathed as holy and worthy of man's respect...

> Prince Klemens von Metternich
> Austrian minister
> 1820

28. In his reference to the "intermediary class of society," Metternich's observations were most directly shaped by the actions of

(A) the bourgeoisie in late 18th and early 19th-century France
(B) Hungarian peasants who threatened the unity of Austria
(C) factory workers in industrialized Britain
(D) elites who based their status on military conquests

29. Metternich's description of governments "having lost their balance" provided evidence for his argument that the countries of early 19th-century Europe were best ruled by

(A) monarchs and parliaments who shared power
(B) traditional monarchs
(C) elected executives and legislatures
(D) a merit-based elite

30. Metternich was influential in defining and shaping the 19th century ideology of

(A) radicalism
(B) liberalism
(C) nationalism
(D) conservatism

(Questions 31 and 32 refer to the following quote):

"In short, the _____ everywhere support every revolutionary movement against the existing social and political order of things. In all these movements, they bring to the front, as the leading question in each, the property question, no matter what its degree of development at the time. Finally, they labor everywhere for the union and agreement of the democratic parties of all countries."

31. The movements that the author described were united by the common ideology of

(A) liberalism
(B) communism
(C) utopian socialism
(D) laissez-faire capitalism

32. A basic premise of the movements described in the quote is that the root of all inequality is

(A) religion
(B) absolute governments
(C) private property
(D) biology

(Questions 33-35 refer to the following quote):

> The position of Prussia in Germany will not be determined by its liberalism but by its power...Prussia must concentrate its strength and hold it for the favourable moment, which has already come and gone several times. Since the treaties of Vienna, our frontiers have been ill-designed for a healthy body politic. Not through speeches and majority decisions will the great questions of the day be decided – that was the great mistake of 1848 and 1849 – but by iron and blood.

> Otto von Bismarck
> Prussian prime minister
> Speech to the Reichstag
> 1862

33. Bismarck's "great mistake of 1848 and 1849" was a reference to the

(A) failure of the Frankfurt Assembly to achieve German unification
(B) loss of territory to France after military defeat
(C) rise to power of Wilhelm I, Prussian king
(D) wars with Denmark and Austria

34. The excerpt from Bismarck's 1862 speech reflects his approach to governing known as

(A) mass politics
(B) democratic centralism
(C) realpolitik
(D) zemstvos

35. In the excerpt, Bismarck argued that Prussia could be successful if its leadership emphasized

(A) parliamentary decision-making
(B) industrialization and military strength
(C) centralized control of government through the balance of power
(D) careful diplomatic negotiation with other European countries

(Questions 36-38 refer to the following quote):

"History shows me one way, and one way only, in which a state of civili-sation has been produced, namely, the struggle of race with race, and the survival of the physically and mentally fitter race. This dependence of progress on the survival of the fitter race, terribly black as it may seem to some of you, gives the struggle for existence its redeeming features; it is the fiery crucible out of which comes the finer metal...

The path of progress is strewn with the wreck of nations; traces are every-where to be seen of the hecatombs of inferior races, and of victims who found not the narrow way to the greater perfection. Yet these dead peo-ples are, in very truth, the stepping stones on which mankind has arisen to the higher intellectual and deeper emotional life of today."

Karl Pearson
1907

36. Pearson's argument supports the doctrine of

   (A) self determination
   (B) republicanism
   (C) the vanguard of the revolution
   (D) Social Darwinism

37. Pearson's argument is meant to directly justify

   (A) the wealth of entrepreneurs over their laborers
   (B) human suffering in industrial cities
   (C) the domination of European imperialists over subject people
   (D) militant republicanism

38. Which of the following would have been most likely to agree with Pearson's statement?

   (A) Charles Darwin
   (B) Herbert Spencer
   (C) Charles Dickens
   (D) Giuseppe Garibaldi

(Questions 39-41 refer to the following excerpt):

> O happy living things! No tongue
> Their beauty might declare:
> A spring of love gushed from my heart,
> And I blessed them unaware...
> The self-same moment I could pray;
> And from my neck so free
> The Albatross fell off, and sank
> Like lead into the sea.

Samuel Taylor Coleridge

39. The verse above from *The Rime of the Ancient Mariner* is a good example of the artistic movement called

(A) realism
(B) impressionism
(C) classicism
(D) romanticism

40. Supporters of the artistic movement identified in #39 generally rejected a strong emphasis on

(A) reason
(B) sentimentalism
(C) individualism
(D) the extraordinary

41. Which of the following works of literature directly flaunted the conventions of the artistic movement identified in #39?

(A) Johan Wolfgang von Goethe's *The Sorrows of Young Werther*
(B) William Thackeray's *Vanity Fair: A Novel without a Hero*
(C) Percy Bysshe Shelley's *Prometheus Unbound*
(D) Lord Byron's *Childe Harold's Pilgrimage*

(Questions 42-44 refer to the following British war poster):

British War Poster, 1915

42. The poster was intended to

    (A) convince men to enlist as soldiers
    (B) encourage civilians to support the war effort
    (C) persuade the United States to enter the war
    (D) support the training of men who had enlisted as soldiers

43. The poster provides evidence that World War I was an early example of

    (A) total war
    (B) limited war
    (C) the balance of power
    (D) trench warfare

44. The poster most directly reflects the

(A) willingness of young men to enlist for military service
(B) importance of the United States in winning the war for the Allies
(C) British government's struggle to pay war expenses
(D) British government's efforts to mobilize the country for war

Questions 45-47 refer to the following excerpt):

"What we demand in this war, therefore, is nothing peculiar to ourselves. It is that the world be made fit and safe to live in; and particularly that it be made safe for every peace-loving nation, which, like our own, wishes to live its own life, determine its own institutions, be assured of justice and fair dealing by the other peoples of the world as against force and selfish aggression. All the peoples of the world are in effect partners in this interest, and for our own part we see very clearly that unless justice be done to others it will not be done to us."

> Woodrow Wilson
> Speech to U.S. Congress
> January 8, 1918

45. This excerpt from Wilson's speech describes his deep commitment to the principle of

(A) collective security
(B) containment
(C) self determination
(D) limited war

46. Which of the following regions was MOST affected by the redrawing of national boundaries based on this principle at the Versailles Conference in 1919-1920?

(A) western Europe
(B) eastern Europe
(C) the Middle East
(D) northern Africa

47. Which of the following actions at Versailles best support Wilson's argument for the viability of the principle in the excerpt?

(A) Mandates were established among the Arab states of the former Ottoman Empire.
(B) The new borders of Yugoslavia encompassed Serbs, Croats, and Slovenes.
(C) Czechoslovakia was created for two different Slavic people – the Czechs and the Slovaks.
(D) Austria-Hungary was carved into new countries based on ethnic identity.

(Questions 48-51 refer to the following quote):

"All the great civilizations of the past died out because contamination of their blood caused them to become decadent...In other words, in order to protect a certain culture, the type of human who created the culture must be preserved. But such preservation is tied to the inalterable law of the necessity and the right of victory of the best and the strongest...

What we see before us today as human culture, all the yields of art, science, and technology, are almost exclusively the creative product of the Aryans. Indeed this fact alone leads to the not unfounded conclusion that the Aryan alone is the founder of the higher type of humanity, and further that he represents the prototype of what we understand by the word: MAN...[whose spirit] has permitted   humans to ascend the path of mastery over the other beings of the earth. Eliminate him and deep darkness will again descend on the earth after a few thousand years; human civilization will die out and the earth will become a desert...

 The Jew provides the greatest contrast to the Aryan...the Jews lack the most basic characteristic of a truly cultured people, namely an idealistic spirit."

Adolf Hitler
Mein Kampf
1927

48. In the above excerpt, Hitler draws directly on 19th-century theories of

(A) scientific racism
(B) militant republicanism
(C) political liberalism
(D) political realism

49. Hitler's argument about the "creative product of the Aryans" took hold in Germany during the 1930s largely because it represented hope for

(A) a democratic representative government to emerge
(B) a successful challenge to the growing global power of the United States
(C) the country to recover from hardships after its humiliating defeat in
    World War I
(D) new diplomatic ties to be established with France and Britain

50. In which of the following ways was Hitler's fascism in Germany similar to Stalin's communism in Russia?

(A) Both emphasized the elimination of private property.
(B) Both devalued the idea of individual freedom.
(C) Both rejected the value of equality.
(D) Both emphasize the negative effects of industrialization.

51. The ideas in the excerpt later provided Hitler with justification for

(A) abolishing private property and challenging landholders' rights
(B) overturning the Weimar Republic
(C) paying war reparations to Britain and France
(D) forcing Jews into extermination camps

(Questions 52-55 refer to the following excerpt):

"From Stettin in the Baltic to Trieste in the Adriatic, an iron curtain has descended across the Continent. Behind that line lie all the capitals of the ancient states of central and eastern Europe. Warsaw, Berlin, Prague, Vienna, Budapest, Belgrade, Bucharest and Sofia.....

...If the western democracies stand together in strict adherence to the principles of the United Nations Charter, their influence for furthering these principles will be immense and no one is likely to molest them. If however, they become divided or falter in their duty, and if these all-important years are allowed to slip away, then indeed catastrophe may overwhelm us all."

Winston Churchill
Speech at Fulton, Missouri
1946

52. Although Britain's power was fading by 1946, in the above excerpt from this famous speech, Winston Churchill nevertheless helped to shape the

(A) decolonization of Africa
(B) beginning of the Cold War
(C) emergence of the United States as the only superpower
(D) denazification of Germany

53. Which of the following organizations was formed as an example of "western democracies [standing] together" in 1949?

(A) the United Nations
(B) the Warsaw Pact
(C) the European Union
(D) the North Atlantic Treaty Organization

54. The response from western democracies that Churchill called for in the excerpt is an example of which of the following developments of the 20th century?

(A) the growing acceptance of international cooperation
(B) the lingering influence of isolationism
(C) the waning power of western Europe
(D) a new emphasis on the balance of power among European nations

55. Which of the following would most likely disagree with Churchill's description of the "iron curtain"?

(A) Charles DeGaulle
(B) Harry Truman
(C) Joseph Stalin
(D) Lech Walesa

Short-answer Questions (50 minutes): You must answer all four question, using complete sentences throughout.

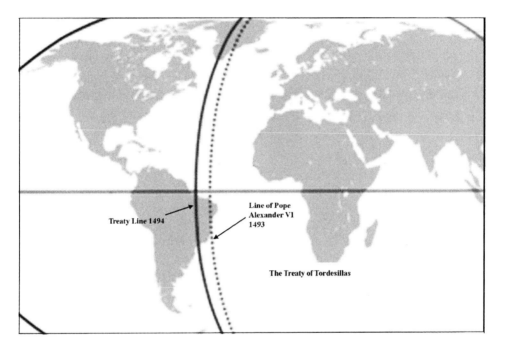

1. The map above shows the lines drawn by the Treaty of Tordesillas. Using your knowledge of European history, answer parts (A) and (B) below.

(A) Briefly explain the purpose of the Treaty of Tordesillas.

(B) Briefly explain TWO consequences of the redrawing of the line in 1494.

"We hold these truths to be self-evident; that all men are created equal, that they are endowed by their Creator with certain unalienable rights, that among these are life, liberty, and the pursuit of happiness. That, to secure these rights, governments are instituted among men, deriving their just powers from the consent of the governed. That whenever any form of government becomes destructive of these ends, it is the right of the people to alter or to abolish it, and to institute new government, laying its foundation on such principles, and organizing its powers in such form, as to them shall seem most likely to effect their safety and happiness...when a long train of abuses and usurpations, pursuing invariably the same object, evinces a design to reduce them under absolute despotism, it is their right, it is their duty, to throw off such government, and to provide new guards for their future security."

American Declaration of Independence
1776

"First Article: Men are born and remain free and equal in rights. Social distinctions may be based only on common utility.

Article 2. The goal of every political association is the preservation of the natural and inalienable rights of man. These rights are liberty, property, security, and resistance to oppression.

Article 3. The principle of all sovereignty resides essentially in the nation. No body and no individual can exercise authority that does not flow directly from the nation.

Article 4. Liberty consists in the freedom to do anything that does not harm another. The exercise of natural rights of each man thus has no limits except those that assure other members of society their enjoyment of the same rights. These limits may be determined only by law..."

French Declaration of the Rights of
Man and Citizen,
1789

2. Referring to the excerpts on the opposite page, answer parts (A) and (B) below.

Like the American Declaration of Independence, the French Declaration of Rights of Man and Citizen was based on the ideology of English philosopher John Locke.

(A) Explain TWO similarities between the American Declaration and the French Declaration.

(B) Explain ONE difference between the American declaration and the French declaration.

3. Using your knowledge of European history, answer parts (A) and (B) below.

Historians have proposed various events as key to changing the balance of power among European nations during the second half of the 19th century, including:

- The Crimean War

- The unification of Italy

- The unification of Germany

(A) Briefly explain why ONE of the above events on the list above was the most important key event in changing the balance of power in Europe. Provide at least ONE piece of evident to support your argument.

(B) Briefly explain why ONE of the other events was a less important factor in changing the balance of power than the one you identified in (A).

4. The sovereign debt crisis that began in 2010 has increased tensions among member-states of the European Union.

(A) Describe the sovereign debt crisis.

(B) Explain one argument in favor of EU-supported emergency loans to individual countries.

(C) Explain one argument against EU-supported emergency loans to individual countries.

Free-Response Document-Based Question (Suggested reading time – 15 minutes; suggested writing time – 40 minutes)

Write an essay that:

- Provides an appropriate, explicitly stated thesis that directly addresses all parts of the question.

- Supports the thesis with evidence from all or all but one of the documents and your outside knowledge of European history

- Analyzes a majority of the documents in terms of intended audience, point of view, purpose, argument strength, and/or social context

- Places the argument in broader regional, national, or global contexts.

Analyze changes and continuities in attitudes toward Europeans in early modern times through the mid-18th century.

Document 1

"When one comes to recount cases regarding the Franks [Europeans], he cannot but glorify Allah, exalted is he!, and sanctify him, for he sees them as animals possessing the virtues of courage and fighting but nothing else; just as animals have only the virtues of strength and carrying loads... everyone who is a fresh emigrant from the Frankish lands is ruder that those who have become acclimatized and have held long association with the Moslems...The Franks are void of all zeal and jealousy. One of them may be walking along with his wife. He meets another man who takes the wife by the hand and steps aside to converse with her while the husband is standing on one side waiting for his wife to conclude the conversations. If she lingers too long for him, he leaves her alone with the conversant and goes away."

Usamah ibn Munqidh
Arab adversary of the
European Crusaders,
12th century

Document 2

"The Feringis [Europeans] are most cruel and crafty. Their arms are superior to those of other foreigners. Some years ago they came suddenly to the city of Canton, and the noise of their cannon shook the earth. Those who remained [in Canton] disobeyed the law…Those who came to the Capital were proud and struggled to be heard. Now if we allow them to come and go and to carry on their trade, it will inevitably lead to fighting and bloodshed, and the misfortune of our South may be boundless."

He Ao
Bureaucrat, Ming China
1540

Document 3

"He [a servant of the court] had been sent to the port of Goa [Portuguese stronghold in India]…to bring to his country the excellent arts and rarities of that place…He came to do homage, attended by a large number of persons dressed up as Christians and playing European drums and clarions. He produced before his Majesty [Akbar, Mughal ruler] the choice articles of that territory. Craftsmen who had gone to acquire skill displayed the arts which they had learned…The musicians of that territory breathed fascination with the instruments of their country [Portugal], especially with the organ. Ear and eye were delighted and so was the mind."

Abu'l Fazi
Historian for the Mughal court
(India)
Late 16th century

Document 4

"We consider ourselves...much happier than thou, in this that we are very content with the little that we have...[We] find all our riches and all our conveniences among ourselves, without trouble, without exposing our lives to the dangers in which you find yourselves constantly through your long voyages."

> An anonymous
> Quebec Amerindian leader
> Addressing French settlers
> late 17th century

Document 5

"7. If there are any Southern Barbarians [Westerners] who propagate the teachings of padres [Catholic priests], or otherwise commit crimes, they may be incarcerated in the prison...

8. All incoming ships must be carefully searched for the followers of padres."

> Tokugawa Iemitsu, Japanese leader
> Close Country Edict of 1635

Document 6

"In order to obtain greater improvement in this respect [military forces], and to encourage foreigners, who are able to assist us in this way, as well as artisans profitable to the State, to come in numbers to our country, we have issued this manifesto, and have ordered printed copies of it to be sent throughout Europe...

Western dress shall be worn by all the boyars, members of our councils and of our court...The upper dress shall be of French or Saxon cut, and the lower dress... – waistcoat, trousers, boots, shoes, and hats – shall be of the German type."

> Peter the Great
> Russian tsar
> Decrees, 1701-1702

Document 7

"At last we came in sight of the island of Barbados, at which the whites on board gave a great shout and made many signs of joy to us. We did not know what to think of this, bust as the vessel drew nearer we plainly saw the harbor and other ships of different kinds and sizes, and we soon anchored amongst them off Bridgetown. Many merchants and planters now came on board, though it was in the evening. They put us in separate parcels and examine us attentively. They also made us jump, and pointed to the land, signifying we were to go there. We thought by this we should be eaten by these ugly men, as they appeared to us; and when soon after we were all put down under the deck again, there was much dread and trembling among us…"

Olaudah Equiano
Captive African,
New World arrival
Mid-18th century

Free-Response Question (Suggested writing time – 35 minutes)

Answer ONE question from the two questions below, choosing the question that you are best prepared to answer thoroughly in the time permitted. You should spend 5 minutes organizing or outlining your answer.

Write an essay that:

- **Has a relevant thesis.**
- **Addresses all parts of the question.**
- **Supports thesis with specific evidence.**
- **Is well organized.**
- **Applies historical thinking skills.**

Analyze the economic and political consequences of 19th century colonization for western European countries.

OR

Compare the goals and outcomes of the women's movement of the early 20th century with those of the women's movement of the late 20th century.

Books by Ethel Wood

American Government: A Complete Coursebook. Boston: Great Source, a Division of Houghton-Mifflin Company, 2000, 2002.

AP Comparative Government and Politics: A Study Guide (editions 1-6) Germantown, NY: WoodYard Publications, 2003, 2005, 2007, 2009, 2001, 2013.

AP European History: An Essential Coursebook, (editions 1 and 2) Germantown, NY: WoodYard Publications, 2009, 2015.

AP Human Geography: A Study Guide, editions 1, 2, and 3. Germantown, NY: WoodYard Publications, 2007, 2009, 2012.

AP United States History: An Essential Coursebook, editions 1 and 2. Germantown, NY: WoodYard Publications, 2011, 2014.

AP World HIstory: An Essential Coursebook (editions 1 and 2) Germantown, NY: WoodYard Publications, 2008, 2011.

The Immigrants: A Historical Reader (editor) Boston: McDougal Littell, 2003.

Introduction to Sociology: A Nextext Coursebook, Boston: McDougal Littell, 2004.

Multiple-Choice and Free-Response Questions in Preparation for the UP United States Government and Politics Examination (editions 1-6), New York: D&S Marketing Systems, 1990, 1994, 1998, 2002, 2005, 2009.

Multiple-Choice and Free-Response Questions in Preparation for the AP World History Examination (editions 1 and 2), New York: D&S Marketing Systems, 2004, 2011.

The Presidency: A Historical Reader (editor), a Nextext Reader, Boston: McDougal Littell, 2001.

Teacher's Guide: AP Comparative Government and Politics . New York: The College Board, 1998.

ORDER INFORMATION

Six ways to order:

1) Fill out and send this form to:

WoodYard Publications
285 Main Street
Germantown, NY 12526
Full payment must accompany the order. Make checks payable to
WoodYard Publications.

2) Purchase Orders (for schools only) - Send purchase order to the
above address or Fax to 610-372-8401.

3) Order from Amazon. Go to www.amazon.com for order information.

4) Pay for one student book through Pay Pal. Go to the website
(http://woodyardpublications.com, click on "Order Form," and
order.

5) Use your credit card by phoning 610-207-1366. Visa, Mastercard,
American Express, and Discover cards accepted.

6) To pay for multiple orders online, go to the website or send an email
to ejw@woodyardpublications.com and instructions will be sent
to order through PayPal.

Questions? Call 610-207-1366 or e-mail at ejw@woodyardpublications.
com.

Please use order form on the reverse side.

Order Form

Please send _____copies of AP European History: An Essential Course-book, 2nd edition, to:

Name_____

Mailing Address_____

City, State, Zip_____

Phone_____

E-mail Address_____

School_____

School Address_____
City, State, Zip_____

Please check one: Please send book(s) to
_____Home Address
            or
_____School Address

Prices:

1 book - $24.95 + $5.05 Priority Mail shipping = $30.00

2-4 books - $19.95 each + 8% shipping (minimum shipping charge of $5.05)
5-49 books - $16.95 each + 8% shipping
50+ books - $14.95 each + 8% shipping

Mail this form with check payable to WoodYard Publications, 285 Main Street, Germantown, NY 12526. School purchase orders also accepted.
.